BOSCO
BOSCO
BOSCO

Bartolomeo Bosco
His Career   His Family
His Impostors

Rowan Gibbs

Wellington
2021

Copyright © Rowan Gibbs 2021
Published by Smiths Bookshop Ltd
ISBN: 978-0-9876684-5-5

To
G. A. B.

who liked this Bosco anecdote

Among Bosco's many excellent tricks was exchanging the heads of two doves,
putting the head of a living white dove on the body of a living black dove.
After one performance he was approached by a farmer asking
if he could do the same on his wife and his sister-in-law?
He would gladly pay whatever the fee was.

CONTENTS

Introduction		9
Abbreviations		12

Boscos
Europe

B1.	Bartolomeo Bosco (1793-1863)	13
B2.	Eugenio Bosco (1830?-189-?)	156
B3.	Italo Bosco (1868?-?)	206
Excursus on Bartolomeo's family (his marriages and children)		207
B4.	Giovanni Melchiorre Bosco (Don Bosco, priest, 1815-1888)	218
B5.	Carlo Bosco (mythical)	220
B6.	Karla Bosko (said to have toured Russia in 1840s)	221
B7.	Bosco der Zweite (Aachen 1838)	221
B8.	Hermann Bosco(1) (Nantes 1846)	222
B9.	Mignard-Bosco (France 1846-50)	222
B10.	Petit-Bosco (Victor Houdmon, active 1847-60)	223
B11.	Bosco (Marseille 1857)	224
B12.	Signor Bosco (Alfred Bosco(1); Marcus Epstein; Sigmund Epstein)	224
B12a	Adam Epstein (H.A. Epstein; Henry Adams; Adam Brøndum)	249
B12b.	Professor Sigismund Epstein (Finland 1875)	260
B12c.	Dr A. Epstein (Finland 1880; England 1881)	260
B12d.	Professor Epstein (Heksch; Holland 1870)	262
B12e.	Professor Epstein (Holland 1883)	262
B13.	Charlemagne Bosco (France 1861)	263
B14.	Bosco (Holland, *ca.*1860)	263
B15.	Bosco (France, 1868)	263
B16.	Herr Bosco (Wolf Wilhelm Blumenfeld, 1849-1906)	263
B17.	A. Bosko (Klagenfurt 1875)	264
B18.	Herr Ritter von Bosco (Herr Bosco Jun.; 1878-9)	264
B19.	H. Bosko (Rumburg 1874)	265
B20.	Bosco (Rome 1880, age 9)	265
B21.	Bosco fils (Crémy *et al.*; France *ca.*1880-83)	265
B22.	Hofschwarzkünstler Bosko (Linz 1879)	266
B23.	Le Fils Bosco (Paris 1879)	266
B24.	Bosco (Znaim 1880)	266
B25.	Le Bosco Moderne (1) (M. Auguste L.; Toulouse 1846)	267
B26.	Le Bosco Moderne (2) (Antoine Viarizio, active 1843-68)	267
B27.	Le Bosco Moderne (3) (Enghien-les-Bains 1878)	267
B28.	Le Bosco Moderne (4) (Émile Alphonse Duval; Paris 1896)	267
B29.	Le Bosco Moderne (5) (Professeur Félix; Algeria 1903)	268
B30.	Gacou, Le Bosco helvétique (Nîmes 1880)	268
B31.	Bosco II (Salzburg 1879)	268

B32.	Josef Bosco (Bosco der Jüngste; Josef Racskay-Bosko)	268
B33.	Oscar Boulay, dit Bosco (Oran 1884)	269
B34.	Bosco (Forbach 1887)	270
B35.	Leonardo Bosco (Nîmes 1891)	270
B36.	Professor Theodor Bosco (Holland 1883)	270
B37.	J. R. Borkini Bosco (Holland 1884-6)	270
B38.	Professor Bosco (Leiden 1888)	271
B39.	Professor Bosco Jr. (Holland 1887-8)	271
B40.	Robertus Bosco (Amsterdam 1893)	271
B41.	J. Bosco Jr. (Holland 1887)	272
B42.	Professor J.G. Bosco Jr. (Holland 1888)	272
B43.	Professor Bosco (Dutch East Indies 1890)	272
B44.	Professor Don Giovanni Bosco (Holland 1886-1924)	272
B45.	Professor Bosco (Schoonhoven 1891)	273
B46.	La Troupe Bosco (Switzerland 1896)	273
B47.	Bosko (Rosenheim, 1897)	273
B48.	Faustinus Petersen as Bosco (Denmark 1900)	274
B49.	Mikhail Pavlovich Trachtenberg (1873-1943)	274
B50.	Gennady Mikhailovich Trakhtenberg (1917-2000)	274
B51.	Ludwig Krieger (Pop Krieger, Louis Krieger; 1851-1934)	274
B52.	Olivero Bosco (Switzerland 1906)	274
B53.	Bosco (Avignon 1921)	274
B54.	Józef Pokrywka-Brzeziński (1877-1951)	275
B55.	Stuller-Bosco (Joseph Stuller; 1885-1962)	275
B56.	John Olms (Richard Lisch, 1888-1955)	275
B57.	Jean Bosco (Belgian conjuror in England in 1915)	275
B58.	Fritz Bosko (Vienna 1915)	275
B59.	Bosco (Berlin 1948)	275
B60.	Theodor von Schledorn (1896-1975)	275
B61.	Bernard Bosco (Bernard Voinson)	276

Britain

B62.	Professor W.J.L. Millar (1825-1910)	276
B63.	Saul (Solomon) Abram Warschawski (1833?-1906)	284
B64.	Alfred Herbert Jacob Warschawski (Alfred Bosco(2); 1864-1932)	284
B63a.	Saul Warschawski's unidentified partner (Scotland 1863)	294
B65.	Louis Susser (1836-1908)	295
B66.	David Hyam (1843-1914)	306
B67.	Hermann Bosco (active London 1863)	313
B68.	Brothers Bosco of Poland (Glasgow 1863)	313
B69.	Morton Bosco (*ca.*1840-1887)	313
B70.	Leopold Bosco (1864-1901)	313
B71.	Mastrilio Bosco (1868-1946)	313
B72.	Sig. I. Bosco (Wakefield 1866)	316
B73.	Signor Bosco Junior (Hartlepool 1866)	316
B74.	Alfred Bosco, Jun. (England 1867)	316

B75.	Lawrence Bosco (London 1867-70)	316
B76.	Henri Bosco (Newbiggin 1874)	317
B77.	Leotard Bosco (James Frederick Greathead, 1851?-1895)	317
B78.	Nelson Bosco (died Coventry 1880)	321
B79.	Bosco Wylde (active Birmingham 1876-93)	321
B80.	Professor Bosco (Richard Reynolds; England 1881)	321
B81.	Bosco (England 1881)	321
B82.	Herr Bosco (England 1877)	322
B83.	Bosco Brothers (Daniel Fisher *et al.*; England 1890s)	322
B84.	Lyndale Bosco (active England 1894-7)	323
B85.	Professor Sinclair Bosco (Yorkshire 1899)	323
B86.	William Mortimer Bosco (England 1901)	324
B87.	Leon Bosco (Alexander Van Gelder, 1863-1923) and successors	324
B88.	Allan Bosco (snake handler and conjuror, England 1926)	324
B89.	The Original Bosco (England 1916)	325

North America

B90.	Professor Bosco (Milwaukee 1862)	325
B91.	Prof. Otto Bosco (Indiana 1862)	325
B92.	Herr Bosco (Missouri 1863)	326
B93.	Signor Bosco with Kate Weston (1864)	326
B94.	Bosco (Troy, N.Y., 1864)	327
B95.	Bosco with the "Cyclopean Gift Show" (1865)	327
B96.	Signor Bosco (Long Branch, N.J., 1865)	327
B97.	Prof. Bosco, Prestidigitator (1868-9)	328
B98.	Carl Bosco (1845-1878)	328
B99.	Carl Bosco (2) — impersonator (1879)	332
B100.	John Bosco, fils (New York 1869)	332
B101.	Prof. Bosco (Chicago 1869)	333
B102.	Prof. Otto Bosco (Salt Lake City 1870)	333
B103.	Bosco (Wisconsin 1871)	333
B104.	Dr. Bosco (Brooklyn 1874)	333
B105.	Bosco (died 1877)	333
B106.	Paul and Nellie Bosco (Montana 1879)	334
B107.	P. Bosco (California 1883)	334
B108.	Mons. Bosco (Arizona 1882)	334
B109.	Fiasco Bosco (St Louis 1889)	334
B110.	Professor Bosco (Kansas 1889)	335
B111.	Professor Bosco and his versatile wife Louise (1891)	335
B112.	Bernardo Bosco (1) (active 1911-13)	335
B113.	Bernardo Bosco (2) (active 1915-20)	335
B114.	De Bosco Hughes (active 1877-9)	336

Central and South America

B115.	Bosco (?José Curvello D'Avila; Brazil, active 1876-95)	337
B116.	Bosco (Argentina 1888)	338
B117.	Bosco (Mexico 1896)	338

B118.	Julio F. Bosco (Jules F. Bosco; active 1863-1893)	339
B119.	Bosco Ruchwaldy (Bernhard Ruchwald, 1844-1909)	343

Asia

B120.	Professor Bosco (Darjeeling 1892)	349

Australasia

B121.	Bosco (Philip Dent, Dinte, Schpinesky; active 1874-82)	349
B122.	Bosco, unidentified impostor Brisbane 1874	349
B123.	Signor Bosco (active 1891-3)	350
B124.	Prof. Bosco (New Zealand 1884)	350
B125,	Prof. Bosco (New Zealand 1893)	350

Female Boscos

BF1.	Madame Bosco (1) (Mrs Millar)	351
BF2.	Madame Bosco (2) (Marian Ball)	352
BF3.	Madame Bosco (3) (Madame de Lonno)	354
BF4.	Signora Bosco (Albina di Rhona)	354
BF5.	Unidentified female Bosco in France 1868	354
BF6.	Mme Bosco (Dijon 1881)	354
BF7.	Frau Nina Bosco (Estonia 1883)	355
BF8.	Emma Bosco (Holland 1884)	355
BF9.	Lina Bosco (with Max Rossner 1881-92)	355
BF10.	Giovanna Bosco (Holland 1885)	355
BF11.	Mlle Sellina Bosco (Holland 1887)	355
BF12.	Hedwig Bosco (Hedwig Stuller)	356

Self proclaimed Pupils and Relatives

C1.	M. Abadie-Gasparin (pupil of Bosco, 1884)	356
C2.	Giovanni Barbarigo-Clementini (pupil of Bosco, 1885-6)	357
C3.	Ferdinand Friedrich Becker, 1813-1835 (associate of Bosco)	357
C4.	MM. Belval, père et fils (father pupil of Bosco; active from 1846)	357
C5.	Francesco Benevolo, 1865-1939 (pupil of Bosco)	359
C6.	E. Bentheim (Prague 1995, pupil of Bosco)	359
C7.	Karoline Bernhardt (Caroline Bernhard); colleague of Bosco, 1838)	359
C8.	August Broëta (pupil of Bosco, active 1864-70)	359
C9.	Matteo Bassi (companion of Bosco; active 1833-7)	362
C10.	Valentin Burzinski (pupil of Bosco, active 1839-55)	362
C11.	Callet (pupil of Eugenio 1891)	363
C12.	Maximilian Ritter von Caspary (pupil of Bosco, active 1849-54)	363
C13.	Bernard Cazeneuve, 1839-1913 (pupil of Bosco, Toulouse 1882?)	364
C14.	Charlesco (pupil of Bosco, France 1894)	365
C15.	L.M. Cohn (follower of Bosco, Holland 1850)	365
C16.	Professor Debraine (performing "as Bosco", Germany 1858)	365
C17.	Philippe Demeure (pupil of Bosco, Namur 1852)	365
C18.	Mdlle Élisabeth (pupil of Bosco, France 1862)	365
C19.	Faure-Nicolay, 1831-1903 (pupil of Bosco)	366
C20.	Emil Gottlieb (Georg Gottlieb), 1851-1934 (pupil of Bosco)	366

C21.	August Günther (active 1848-53, brother-in-law of Bosco)	366
C22.	Heer Heijneman (pupil of Bosco, Holland 1868)	367
C23.	K. Hofmann (pupil of Bosco; active 1860-66)	367
C24.	Eduard Jentzsch (pupil and supporter of Bosco; active 1861-2)	367
C25.	Franz Kehry (pupil of Bosco; active 1866-71)	368
C26.	Sakarinie Kinsbergen (pupil of Bosco; born 1824)	368
C27.	Johann Krämer (pupil of Bosco; born 1833)	370
C28.	Julius Laschott (pupil of Bosco, 1846)	371
C29.	Signora Laurenzia (pupil of Bosco, France 1861-3)	371
C30.	Hermann Lindmüller (pupil of Bosco; active 1853-67)	372
C31.	Manuel Lopez ("Donato"; pupil of Bosco, active 1871-77)	373
C32.	Loramus (Alexandre-Charles Dabain, 1834-1895, pupil)	379
C33.	Herr Lorch (pupil of Bosco, Germany 1860?)	380
C34.	Bartolomeo Marchelli, 1834-1903 (pupil of Bosco)	380
C35.	Mares (pupil of Bosco, Spain 1886)	380
C36.	Joh. Mesjetz (pupil of Bosco, 1857)	380
C37.	Victor Mihoy (pupil of Bosco, 1860)	380
C38.	Charles Mirano (pupil of Carlo Bosco [!] 1868)	381
C39.	G. Moreni (pupil of Bosco; active 1865-77)	381
C40.	Adolphe P.*** (pupil of Bosco, France 1837)	382
C41.	Henryk Rapelewski (pupil of Bosco, active 1864-78)	383
C42.	Giovanni Rossi (pupil of Bosco, Alessandria 1844)	385
C43.	Le sieur Royné (pupil of Bosco, Bourges 1833)	385
C44.	Sarrade (pupil of Bosco, Aix 1860)	385
C45.	Professeur Sartini (pupil of Bosco, active France 1880-2)	385
C46.	Madame Schulz (Bosco's daughter; France 1868)	386
C47.	Ferdinand Stärff (pupil & former associate of Bosco)	386
C48.	Bernhard Steffen (pupil of Bosco, active 1857-8)	387
C49.	Professor St. Roman, *ca.*1830-1916 (Bosco's nephew)	387
C50.	Karl Töpfer (pupil of Bosco, 1836)	387
C51.	Unidentified pupil in Oloron-Sainte-Marie 1845	388
C52.	Unidentified pupil (Herr François?), Hamburg 1846	388
C53.	Herr Winter (pupil of Bosco, Munich 1846)	388
C54.	Carlo Zenetti ("pupil" in his book *Das Zauber-Theater*)	388

Bosco sound-alikes
Prof. Alexander Boskos (New Orleans 1868) — 389
Signor Boz (Arthur William Weston, 1848-80, Britain) — 389

Magicians with tricks named after Bosco — 389

"Bosco" as a Generic Term — 391

Snake Boscos — 392

Mechanical Boscos	393
Bosco in Fiction	394
Prose	394
Plays	404
Poems	405
Music	407
Films	407
Bosco Books	409
Czech (LCz1-15)	409
Danish and Norwegian (LDaN1-6)	413
Dutch (LDu1-18)	414
English (LEn1-3)	418
Estonian (LEs1-2)	419
French (LFr1-12)	419
German (LGe1-195)	422
Hungarian (LHu1-9)	467
Italian (LIt1-54)	469
Latvian (LLat1-6)	478
Polish (LPol1-23)	479
Russian (LRu1-19)	483
Swedish (LSw1-16)	488
Bosco Games and Toys	491
Appendices	
Z1 Mathilde Bannholzer	493
Z2 Bill Matter and the Boscos in Britain	495
Z3 "Emil Franzisco" — Francesco Cetti	500
Z4 Ephraim Hambujer	507
Z5 Herr Dobler	509
Z6 Kratky-Baschik	510
Z7 Plate Spinning	511
Z8 Physician—*Fisico*—*Physicien*	517
Z9 Rubini	518
Z10 The Sandframe	519
Z11 Annie Vernone (stage name Veroni)	520
Z12 Who performed at Balmoral September 24th 1855?	526
URLs	527
INDEX	546

INTRODUCTION

This is an attempt to list and where possible identify the bewildering array of Boscos on stage as magicians in Europe, Britain, America, Asia, and Australasia in the 19th and early 20th century,[1] all capitalising on the name and fame of the original Bartolomeo Bosco and none born with the name Bosco.[2]

The most comprehensive attempt to record these impostors is offered by the *Lexikon der Zauberkünstler*;[3] some are discussed by Rusconi in his biography of Bartolomeo,[4] a few have entries in Whaley,[5] 'ZauberPedia',[6] 'Magicpedia'[7] or 'Magier der Welt',[8] and on a very small number of them there are separate books or articles (those I am aware of are noted in their individual entries). I have drawn on all these with gratitude and have expanded the list considerably, mainly from online newspapers in a wide range of countries and languages.

Some of these *Boscos* are, and will remain, merely names to us, and false names at that; a few are well-known and with those I have merely summarised their life and career and given references to sources, in some cases adding additional information. The length of my biography of each is not necessarily intended as a reflection of the subject's importance — except in the case of Bartolomeo and Eugenio.

My original intention was merely to summarise the lives and careers of Bartolomeo and his son but I continued to find so much new information on them, thanks to the vastly increased number of newspapers and genealogical records made available online in recent years, that I have added extensive biographies of them both. There is considerable additional material here on their families, with new children for both, and a lot more on their careers, including Bartolomeo between 1819 and 1821.

I have disentangled as best I could the various Dutch and American Boscos, and especially the interesting and significant *Signor Boscos* in Great Britain who came to the fore when Epstein left in 1857 (effectively impostors of Epstein not of Bartolomeo himself), some previously wrongly identified or largely or even completely unrecorded, such as Louis Susser, his brother-in-law David Hyam, Saul Warszawski, Leotard Bosco, Morton Bosco, and the intriguing Professor Millar who managed Epstein, briefly took over his Bosco role when Epstein broke his leg, then turned his wife into the first "Madame Bosco", finally taking her to America where she became the first conjuror to perform there under the name "Bosco".

There are also notes of various lengths on several magicians who crossed Bosco's path or who are otherwise relevant to the story: if I had nothing new to say about them I have merely referred to standard works; on a number I have written quite detailed biographies offering new information. There are biographies here of over 150 magicians, and for ease in cross-referencing I have given each a number. The *Contents* lists them individually, with further references given in the *Index*.

The initial summary listing of Boscos is arranged by the broad area where they most performed (Europe, Britain, the Americas…), then by date, but keeping family members together; next come female "Bosco" magicians; then notes on some performers who claimed to be Bosco's pupil or even his relative; and on some who adopted stage-names deceptively similar to "Bosco"; some who named a trick after Bosco; and a few examples of "Snake Boscos", Mechanical Boscos, and of "Bosco" used generically.

Each entry opens with a list of the variant names the person was known by and all include footnoted source references. I have sometimes listed rather detailed itineraries tracing their travels from town to town… to town… to stress the vast distances many of them covered (B66, whom many people will never have heard of, once toured for 125 consecutive weeks, covering 27,000 miles…: p.309).

Also included is a summary list of books on conjuring which claim to have a Bosco connexion, and notes on some of the fiction written about Bosco (and Boscos).

Because several of the performers described here had intersecting careers or connected family relationships there is some deliberate duplication in their entries to allow each to stand on its own, on the assumption that few people will read this book from cover to cover. Some overgrown footnotes have been made into Appendices, partly to allow the inclusion of source footnotes.

The sources here are in a dozen languages. Some short pieces are quoted in the original language (retaining the original contemporary spelling), most are translated with the text in inverted commas but preceded by "[tr.]". Some longer extracts, especially in reviews, are given in an *abridged paraphrase* rather than a translation — these are in italics. With some languages that I am less familiar with, such as Polish (especially hand-written genealogical records), I have included the original text in full for the benefit of those more competent.

People and places are for consistency referred to by their usual names in English, and place-names are given as they were known in the 19th century (with the modern name added for clarity); similarly terms and phrases reproduce what was current at the time, so I trust that 'actress' and 'trick' will not cause offence.

There are a number of web page references in the text which can be a problem unless you are reading this online. I have numbered each *url* and listed these all together in a separate section which I would be happy to email to any owner of the book to give them live links. But note that some of the websites are accessible only to subscribers (though in some cases also through libraries and universities).

Rowan Gibbs, Wellington, New Zealand
rowan.gibbs.nz@gmail.com

NOTES TO INTRODUCTION

[1] Many of the celebrated 19th century magicians had impostors who stole their name, but "Bosco" was rivalled as an appropriated stage-name for aspiring magicians of the period probably only by "Blitz", imitated from Antonio Blitz, 1810-1877, and his father, brother, and nephew: they, and their host of impostors, are discussed at length in my forthcoming *Signor Blitz: The Blitz Family of Magicians and their Namesakes*.

[2] Except the priest Giovanni Bosco (B4), and, of course, Bartolomeo's son Eugenio (B2) and grandson Italo (B3).

[3] Stephan Oettermann / Sibylle Spiegel, *Bio-bibliographisches Lexikon der Zauberkünstler: 4500 Becherspieler, Eskamoteure, Manipulatoren, Falschspieler, Illusionisten und Experimentatoren, Entfesselungs- und Verwandlungskünstler, Papierzerreißkünstler und Handschattenspieler, Fakire, Schwertschlucker, Feuer- und Hungerkünstler, Rechenkünstler und Mnemotechniker, Bauchredner und Stimmen-Imitatoren, Laternisten und Phantasmagoren, Mental-Magier, Muskelleser, Hypnotiseure und Telepathen*. Offenbach am Main: Edition Volker Huber, 2004. ISBN: 9783921785867.

[4] Alex Rusconi, *Bartolomeo Bosco, Vita e meraviglie del mago che conquistò l'Europa.* Florence: Florence Art Edizioni, 2017. ISBN: 9788899112455. This wonderful evocation of Bartolomeo I have read with great care and admiration, and I regret that I usually refer to it here only when I very occasionally venture to disagree with it.

[5] Barton Whaley, *Who's Who in Magic, An International Biographical Guide from Past to Present.* Oakland, Ca.: Jeff Busby Magic, Inc., 1990; 2nd printing ("additional 6 pages of corrections"), 1991.

[6] http://www.zauber-pedia.de/index.php?title=Kategorie:Biografien

[7] http://geniimagazine.com/wiki/index.php?title=Category:Biographies

[8] http://www.mzleipzig.de/hokus-art/magier%20der%20welt.htm

"Le nom seul de Bosco est une recommandation puissante auprès du public…"
L'Écho rochelais 8 Feb.1850.

"Der Herr, der sich für einen Sohn des berühmten Bosco ausgiebt, würde ein Pseudo-Bosco sein… Der gegenwärtig in Berlin anwesende Bosco kann daher nur ein Homonyme, wenn nicht, ein falscher Bosco sein. Der name Bosco wurde übrigens schon von vielen mißbraucht, um sich dadurch ein Publikum zu verschaffen, welches sie sich keineswegs durch Talente oder Geschicklichkeit zu verschaffen gewußt hätten"
Eugenio in *Vossische Zeitung* 16 June 1858

"One of the last problems of the year 1870 will probably be, which is the veritable Signor Bosco?"
Bristol Mercury 1 Dec.1870

"What a family of 'Boscos' there appears to be; it is nearly as large as that of Smith or Jones!"
Ulverston Mirror 20 Jan.1872

"James Bosco is not my real name, but is the name I have used for years"
"Is it not the name of a celebrated actor in the necromantic line that you have seized on."
"It is."
"Now, for the benefit of posterity, let us know what your name is."
"Ball"
Irish Times 18 May 1860

"If Bosco isn't Bosco who the devil is Bosco?"
The Smelter (Pittsburg, Kansas) 17 May 1889

ABBREVIATIONS

B1 to B125 refer to the numbered list of male performing Boscos
BF1 to BF12 are the female performing Boscos
C1 to C54 refer to the numbered list of *Self proclaimed Pupils and Relatives*
F1 to F69 refer to the entries in the *Bosco in Fiction* section
L entries are for "Bosco Books" —
    Czech (LCz1-15); Danish and Norwegian (LDaN1-6); Dutch (LDu1-18);
    English (LEn1-3); Estonian (LEs1-2); French (LFr1-12); German (LGe1-195);
    Hungarian (LHu1-9); Italian (LIt1-54); Latvian (LLat1-6); Polish (LPol1-23);
    Russian (LRu1-19); Swedish (LSw1-16)
url refers to the list of numbered hyperlink references

Lexikon   *Bio-bibliographisches Lexikon der Zauberkünstler* (Introduction note 3)
Rusconi   Alex Rusconi, *Bartolomeo Bosco, Vita e meraviglie* (Introduction note 4)
Whaley   Barton Whaley, *Who's Who in Magic* (Introduction note 5)

Newspaper titles are given in full except for
ATZ   used for all the manifestations of *Allgemeine Theaterzeitung, Bäuerles Theaterzeitung, Wiener Theaterzeitung, Wiener allgemeine Theaterzeitung*
DAZ   *Deutsche Allgemeine Zeitung*
KPBZ   *Königlich privilegirte Berlinische Zeitung von Staats- und gelehrten Sachen*
"(etc.)" after newspaper references indicates that the information was widely reprinted and appeared in several other papers.

Books Section:

BL	British Library
BNF	Bibliothèque nationale de France (French National Library)
DNB	Deutsche Nationalbibliothek (German National Library)
GV	*Gesamtverzeichnis des deutschsprachigen Schrifttums, 1700-1910*
LC	Library of Congress
Libris	Swedish Union Catalogue
NUC	*The National Union Catalog Pre-1956 Imprints.* 754 vols.
NUKAT	Union Catalog of Polish Research Library Collections
NYPL	New York Public Library
OPAC SBN	Catalogo del Servizio Bibliotecario Nazionale (Italian Union Catalogue)
RNL	Russian National Library (St Petersburg): http://nlr.ru
RSL	Russian State Library (Moscow): https://www.rsl.ru
ULSH	University of London Senate House Library

I would like to thank Marco Pusterla for assistance in preparing my manuscript for publication.

B1. Bartolomeo Bosco

Name:

Spelt *Gioanni Bartolommeo Bosco* on his birth registration;[1] he himself signed his name as *Bartolomeo Bosco*. His surname was sometimes given as **Bosko** in German-language publications, and is so spelt in some Polish genealogical records. His first name was sometimes localised as *Bartłomiej* in Poland; *Bartholomeo* in France; *Bartolomé* in Spain; *Bertalan* in Hungary; and in Holland and Germany as *Bartholomaeus* or *Bartholomäus;* he is also found as *Bartolo Bosko* in German; Heinrich Heine spelt his name phonetically as *Bartholomäo Bosko*. The usual Russian form is Джованни Бартоломео Боско (Dzhovanny Bartolomeo Bosko). Early in his career, in Germany in 1821, he is several times referred to as **Basco** or **Pasco**, frequently enough to imply he was trialing this as a stage name (see below).

Chevalier

He was sometimes billed as *Chevalier, Cavaliere* (and occasionally *Ritter*) Bosco, but from which country this title originated — and indeed if he had any entitlement to it — is unknown.[2]

His birth registration records him as born on January 3rd 1793 in Turin (then capital of the Kingdom of Sardinia, but soon under the rule of France until 1815). His parents were Matteo Manifacio Bosco, owner of the *Caffé Internazionale,* and his wife Cecilia Caterina, née Cuore (earlier misread as Cerore). It is said that he had a younger sister, Norina, and that his father died in 1800 and the café was then run by Cecilia.[3]

We have no reliable information on his early life before 1819. The wonderful stories of his school days, his leaving Piedmont around 1809, and his military service in the 111th Piedmontese Regiment in Napoleon's army, with his wounding at Borodino and imprisonment until 1814, rest only on the colourful but unsubstantiated anecdotes presented in his later publicity material, published in newspapers and in several pamphlets, the earliest in 1837.[4] There is no evidence to either prove or disprove these accounts,[5] but it is worth considering that he never learnt to speak fluent French despite reputedly spending time in France in 1811 and 1815, and that when he performed in Paris in 1832 and 1851 and 1853 (before Louis Napoleon himself) there is never any mention in French newspapers of early performances by him there or of his service with the *Grande Armée;* and for that service he would have been entitled to the *Médaille de Sainte-Hélène*, created by the Emperor in 1857 as an award for those who had served France 1792-1815.

1819

In November 1819 we are finally on firm ground, with the first confirmed sighting of Bartolomeo performing professionally. He is in Augsburg, in Bavaria, and he has a "Kunsttheater", a portable theatre usually for marionettes and automata, and he signs his advertisement as "B. Bosco, Mechanikus aus Turin *et Comp.*".[6] He may well have included conjuring in his performances, as some others did who described themselves as a *Mechanikus*, but he makes no references to conjuring, legerdemain, or cartomancy in his Augsburg newspaper advertisements.[7] In the *Augsburgische Ordinari Postzeitung* of November 4th 1819 he advertises "Vorstellungen in neuen mechanischen Künsten"[8] to be given in "unser Kunsttheater" in the Hochfürstlich

Fuggerischen Saale that night (Thursday) and on the following Saturday and Sunday. This first advertisement refers (prematurely) to "the universal applause which we received at our first performance" and the same phrase is used in his second advertisement on November 10th, anouncing that "Herr B. Bosco, aus Turin gebürtig" will give his final performance on November 11th. The prices are 24 fr., 12 fr., and 6 fr. in the gallery. He then states (addressing himself to *Kunstliebhaber*, gentleman amateurs) that his Kunsttheater is for sale: it is "*das Dentlersche mechanische Kunsttheater*", and it may be viewed at the café of Traiteur Schmid, where it is set up. Dentler, also as Dendler, was the famous Matthias Tendler, 1753-1823, who began as a wood carver and created wooden automata figures which he toured in his Kunsttheater. His own theatre was later owned by Johann Steinl (shown on a playbill sold in 2021).[9]

. Bosco clearly now remained in Augsburg: on November 17th an advertisement by the head of the "Harmonie-gesellschaft", a cultural society, announced that "Herr Mechanikus Bosco aus Turin" will give a performance for the members that evening, and on November 23rd Bosco advertises that he is still there "for a few days" and offers to give private performances to interested societies.

Where was he before Augsburg? If he had travelled north from Turin,[10] performing en route, it is very surprising there is not a single mention of any shows by him in the north Italian and Austrian newspapers on the *Anno* site. Bosco himself makes no claims in his Augsburg advertisements to have performed earlier anywhere else… We simply do not know.

1820

By the start of 1820 he is in Munich, and still has a *Kunsttheater,* and in his advertisements this is emphasised with a line to itself in the largest type. He announces that on January 10th and 12th "Bartolomeo Bosco, Mechanikus aus Turin" will open "ein mechanisch-physisches Kunst-Theater" in the large room of the "Gasthofes zum goldenen Storchen" (the '*Golden Stork Inn*'). He now states that he has "[tr.] displayed his experiments and the dexterity of his tricks in various large cities … to universal applause". His prices here are 24 Kreuzer and 12 Kreuzer.[11]

In early March he is in Regensburg, performing on March 9th and 11th, billed as "the renowned Bosco", offering "[tr.] the rarest mechanical, physical and magical tricks, received with total approval in the first cities of Europe, never seen here…".[12]

We next see him arriving in Passau in April,[13] but then we lose sight of him for a few months — or do we?

Performing in early July in Erlangen (just where on his way north we might expect Bosco to be) is "Herr Bath. **Pasco**"— "[tr.] a pupil of the famous Pinetti and Olivier" giving "his mechanical and physical tricks".[14] "Pasco" looks at first like a misreading of hand-written copy by the typesetter, but the following week we find "Herr Pasco" again, 40 km north in Bamberg.[15] And in August in Bayreuth he is consistently referred to as "Herr Barthol. Pasco" in the newspaper and he signs an advertisement "Bartholomeo Pasco, aus Turin". He again proclaims himself "pupil of Pinetti and Olivier" and is performing his "mechanical and physical tricks".[16]

That is the last we see of this "Herr Pasco" (though for the next year or so his name is sometimes given in newspapers, not in his own advertisements, as "Basco":

see below). It is hard to believe this was an early — his first — impostor, so either these are misreadings of handwritten advertisements (perhaps sent in advance), or Bosco decided to briefly adopt this stage name…

1821

We next see him in Dresden in January 1821, now again signing himself "Mechanikus B. Bosco, aus Turin" and "Schüler des Chev. Pinetti de Mercy". He announces that after giving several more shows there he will then perform in Leipzig, and "[tr.] flatters himself that he will be received there with the same applause as in Dresden".[17]

His shows in Dresden were very successful,[18] but in Leipzig he was not allowed to perform publicly until the Easter fair began.[19] He advertised private shows and offered tuition and to supply apparatus to interested amateurs during his intended three week stay,[20] finally opening to the Leipzig public on May 6th in the "large and brightly lit room of the Klassigsche Kaffeehaus (2nd floor)"[21] When he left in early June he saluted the public of Leipzig, thanking them for their appreciation of his shows and especially for their good will towards him.[22]

On June 29th he was in Magdeburg, where he seems to have done well — "his money bag was certainly not displeased", said a reviewer.[23]

He was also in nearby Altenburg during this period, either now or in late 1820: when he returned in 1827 he mentions "the gracious reception that his performances enjoyed" there six years earlier.[24]

On October 9th he opened in Hannover at the Salle der Harmonie, still billing himself as "*Mechanikus*" and "a pupil of Pinetti". A splendid large poster for the first night lists selected tricks in detail (a clock made to read a certain time; boxes with hemp and mustard seeds swap their contents; and card tricks) and for a small fee he offers tuition in any trick. Admission prices here are 18, 12, and (gallery) 6 mgr (*Mariengroschen*). This poster features the earliest surviving illustration of Bosco.[25]

On October 21st he performed before the King of Hannover, George IV.[26] The Hannover correspondent of the *Abend-Zeitung* reported that the presence of the King had attracted a large number of performers to the city, but Bosco was excellent, his tricks extraordinary, and his dexterity beyond belief, and "the pale magus with the little moustache, talking in his broken German and mish-mash of Italian and French, himself gives a wonderful colouring to the performance".[27] A review in a Hamburg paper (calling him "Herr Mechanikus Bartholomeo Basco [!] aus Turin") stressed the universal acclaim he received and praised his modesty as well as his dexterity,[28] and a Berlin paper (also calling him "Herr Basco aus Turin") stated that he had received from the King a written testimonial of rich rewards awaiting him in London.[29]

Bosco was not to perform in London for thirty years (and his rewards there were not rich) but when in November he arrived in Hamburg he was described as on his way to London and to be giving only one Hamburg performance, on November 14th at the *Salon d'Apollon*.[30]

Any plans for London did not come to pass and on November 20th a notice appeared, signed "Some Friends of his Art", requesting Bosco to give several further performances in Hamburg if time allowed, and encouraged all "friends of his art" not to miss the opportunity of seeing his splendid talents — "[tr.] he fully maintains the reputation that preceded him from the principal cities of Germany *and Italy...*" [my italics]: this is the only newspaper reference found to him performing in Italy before Augsburg.[31]

1822

On January 25th 1822 he opened in Berlin at the *Jagorschen Saal*, moving to *Das Englische Haus* on March 10th; he also performed for Prince Wittgenstein in the *Saal des königlichen Schauspielhauses* and for King Friedrich Wilhelm III of Prussia in the *Konzertsaal* in *Sanssouci* in Potsdam.[32]

Also in town was a rival, Carl Schumann, with a very successful beheading act — "[tr.] Two extremely skilled magicians, Schumann and Bosca [!] are contributing to the public's entertainment. The first cuts off the heads of people and animals, but puts them back on again, and the second throws watches from the audience out the window for all to see, then at their bidding has to find them again somewhere in the room".[33]

One reviewer was not impressed by Bosco — "[tr.] A Herr Basco [!] from Turin, a pupil of Pinetti's, is entertaining the public here with his mechanical-physical tricks. Thanks to so-called friends and worshippers of the art (which art?) he has received high praise in the newspapers here, but anyone who has already seen this sort of thing many times before soon finds that all these artists (*Künstler*) remain on a certain level, and none rises higher, and as a rule their tricks (*Kunststücke*) all stay the same...", and personally he preferred the panorama of Etna.[34]

Others were more appreciative, notably Heinrich Heine, who raved over Bosco — "[tr.] Bosco you must see, a true pupil of Pinetti, who can fix broken watches quicker than the watchmaker Labinski, can shuffle the cards, and make puppets dance. A pity that the chap hasn't studied theology. He is a former Italian officer, still very young, manly, strong, wears a tight-fitting jacket and trousers made of silk, and, the main thing, when he does his act his arms are almost completely bare. Women's eyes should find that even more edifying than his tricks. He certainly is a handsome fellow, you must realise, seeing his nimble figure in the light of about fifty tall wax candles set like a twinkling forest of light in front of his long table covered with mysterious magical apparatus".[35]

Another appreciative reviewer announced: "[tr.] a second Philadelphia (or a third, since Pinetti was the second) has appeared amongst us, named Bartolomäo Bosco...", praising his skill, speed, and dexterity, then launching into what he admits is a "humorous little anecdote" — the story of Bosco buying eggs in a market and "finding" coins inside. This coins-in-eggs story is the earliest Bosco anecdote found and surely signals the birth of his celebrity status.[36]

We next sight him in Posen (then in Prussia; modern Poznań), performing at the Hotel Saski in June and July, closing on July 7th,[37] followed by Königsberg (modern Kaliningrad) in September. Here he announced he would be giving 14 performances between September 10th and 25th, but extended his run as audiences remained so good. A review admired "[tr.] his dexterity and speed, his pleasing naturalness and still more his unassuming modesty ... Many of his tricks have already been seen here often, but they were successful either because of the way he performed them or, with others that depended on greater speed, or apparatus, or probably also collusion (*Verabredungen*), he himself said if he noticed something amiss that it was not magic, just sheer speed".

Another reviewer was less well disposed. The Königsberg correspondent of the *Abend-Zeitung* reported Bosco's performances there on the 10th of September, "on his way to St. Petersburg", going to the first night "[tr.] with great expectation but, while generally agreeing with the great reputation that preceded Bosco, he could not help saying that, on his first night before a large and distinguished gathering, he was to blame for crude mistakes that spoilt the illusion — surprising enough in general and especially so with such a magician — which not even an amateur would be guilty of. That aside, Herr B.B. drags out a lot of tricks to an intolerable length, and it would certainly benefit his shows if he discontinued that. His apparatus laid out on a table hung with red and lit by fifty symmetrically arranged wax candles, all in front of a black curtain, this reviewer found exceptionally attractive — but even here, and considering the yard and a half long poster listing the programme, rather less charlantry would be desirable. Many of the tricks which the reviewer has observed so far from Herr B.B. he has already seen done with more speed and more deception by a local amateur who has been engaged in such things for thirty years, and even if Bosco's extraordinary quickness with his fingers cannot be denied, he has adopted a mannerism in performing many of his tricks that is far from appealing. Herr B.B. is furnished with glowing recommendations for Russia — where he is thinking of taking himself at the start of the coming month — and there is no doubt that he will reap there a rich golden harvest".[38]

In October Bosco began a long stay in Poland, travelling to Russia the following year, and returning through the Baltic in late 1824. It was probably at this time, 1823 or 1824, that he married.[39]

His arrival in Warsaw was announced on October 14th, and a long write up the next day stressed that he was a pupil of "the famous Chevalier Pinetti ... his physical and mechanical experiments not the ordinary tricks that have been seen here so many times. He is not of the number of Charlatans, who would want us to believe that they have made a covenant with Beelzebub ... You have to see him performing to judge what he promises…".

He opened at the *Teatr Narodowy* on Monday, October 21st, and a long review on the 26th hailed his skill and dexterity, the audience "completely satisfied, every trick warmly applauded", and his play with watches was especially enjoyed, the owners putting their "crushed" returned watches to their ear to convince themselves they still worked; there are card tricks; canaries in guns; rings in boxes that turn into nuts; watches that turn into flowers; pigeons swapping heads at the firing of a gun; and more pigeons shot, plucked and fried — then flying away… "I must admit that Warsaw has not seen such a watchmaker and chef for a long time".

The gun trick, with twelve soldiers firing at him, he held back until the start of December. He also gave private shows, and closed his run with a charity benefit performance in the *Sala Redutowa* on December 3rd.[40] He next gave three performances in Płock, well attended,[41] then headed to Russia.

1823

We know almost nothing of his performances in Russia. He is said to have been honoured by Czar Alexander I in St Petersburg some time in 1823,[42] and a surviving poster, in Russian and French, announces a performance by him on December 21st 1823 at the *Maly Teatre* (на Малом театре) — not the village *Maly Umys* in Mordovia, but the "Small Theatre" (as opposed to the *Bolshoi*, the "Large Theatre") — and the French version of the text gives this as "AU PETIT THEATRE", suggesting this is the theatre in Moscow of that name, *but* the poster states that he has "recently arrived here from Moscow".[43]

One newspaper report, sent from St Petersburg to a Berlin newspaper, says that at the time of writing Bosco was in Moscow, but "reports from there are nothing out of the ordinary, with no mention of the great reputation that preceded him" — but does say that "he made 50,000 roubles". The writer then suggests that he (and two musicians also mentioned) will move on to the Makaryev Fair (then held in Nizhny Novgorod) to profit from the large gathering of merchants and travellers.[44]

1824

In early September 1824 we find him in Riga, "on his journey from St Petersburg to London". A newspaper notice, which he signs as "[tr.] A Lover of Genuine Talent",[45] announces he has arrived from a long stay in St Petersburg, and is willing to give a few performances in Riga, "not the usual magician's tricks but a series of transformations, each one more remarkable…".

He opened on September 6th, and a very enthusiastic review of his first show had not a word of criticism, the "[tr.] very agreeable young black magician … won universal admiration … showing his dexterity with a delicacy, a candour, a propriety — I would almost like to say, a dignity… one could hardly take deception to a higher level… everything he did was a success, and to the highest degree … such a master of his art will not soon be seen here again".[46]

Further shows followed, but on September 22nd he announced that he could not continue performing until he found a more suitable venue. He offers to give private shows, and adds that he is prepared to sell all or part of his apparatus ("sein mechanisches Kabinet"), with instructions on its use.[47] However, he was performing again on September 27th, his fourth show, with a fifth on 30th; the admission prices are given as 75 and 50 kopeks — there was now a rival in town, "Carl Kauffert, Mechanikus", who was charging only 50 and 30 kopeks.[48]

In October he gave five shows in Mitau (modern Jelgava), 40 km south, the last on October 23rd, with a special performance on October 17th following a banquet for the visiting *Erbprinz* of Weimar and his family.[49] Bosco then returned to Riga, giving a benefit performance on November 8th that featured the Gun trick ("den großen Schuß").[50]

He then performed in Goldingen (modern Kuldīga), and on December 10th arrived in Libau (Liepāja) on the west coast, where he opened on December 12th; he closed there on 26th with an "extraordinary show" which included the Gun trick, and on leaving was the recipient of an effusive eulogistic poem.[51]

1825

He was still in the Baltic in March and April 1825, performing in Vilnius until April 26th.[52]

This makes it unlikely he was in Marseille in January 1825, as suggested by Rusconi, pp.24-5. There is no mention of Bosco in French newspapers at this time, and the only "source" given for this is the anecdote attributed to a Marseille paper *"Giornale della Guardia Naz. di Iuglio 1834 in Marsiglia"*: but no paper of that title (*Journal de la Garde Nationale*) existed until 1848 and this is a mistaken — or mythical — reference by the author of *Curiose Avventure e Brevi Cenni sulla vita di Bartolomeo Bosco da Torino...* (1837). In fact this same anecdote of Bosco in Marseille and the missing watches had earlier appeared in a Dutch paper in 1824 — "A few days ago the famous magician Bosco came to Marseille…".[53]

1826

From Vilnius Bosco headed again to Russia: when we next sight him, arriving back in Lemberg (modern Lviv) in March 1826, he announces he has just come from St Petersburg. Soon after their arrival in Lemberg Bartolomeo and his wife had a son, whom they named Eugenio (Eugeniusz Bosko di toryno).[54]

Bosco opened in Lemberg on March 29th, with further shows on April 2nd and April 9th. A long review of his performances, published on April 10th, signed *"Ein Verehrer und Kenner der mechanischen Kunst"* ("A Worshipper and Connoisseur of the Mechanical Art"), is very adulatory — and also very familiar: it repeats exact phrases from previous reviews in previous years in distant cities, and no doubt draws on copies of those reviews in Bosco's album.[55]

Bosco announced a "final show" for April 26th, but then "a final extraordinary show" for May 7th, with the Gun trick, "to crown his artistic efforts … with no expense spared".[56] We then hear that he is postponing his departure and will continue performing.[57] The first show was on June 6th, combining with Joseph Bienes, who imitated birds, animals and musical instruments, then further shows on his own until June 25th, when he left Lemberg after a three-month stay.[58]

He then travelled as far as Jassy, the capital of Moldavia (now Iași in Romania), and performed again in Lemberg in October on his return journey, assuring the locals that during his absence he had taken the opportunity to invent many splendid new tricks...[59]

By late 1826 he was in Warsaw, where he had not performed for several years,[60]

1827

but he did not open there until April 1827, appearing first in Kraków. He arrived there in late February and opened on March 5th.[61]

At the start of April he was in Warsaw, but on April 16th their son Eugeniusz died. Bosco opened as announced on April 18th, his first performance warmly reviewed by an anonymous Mr. "A", signing himself "A Friend of and Partial Expert in the Mechanical Arts".[62]

This praise was largely echoed by a review two days later of the second night's show (signed only "Z."), admiring Bosco's "astonishing dexterity … none so skilled in this art since the days of Philadelphia and Pinetti…": birds fried then flying away at his command, gloves turned into a squirrel, a clock into a guinea-pig, and money mysteriously moved and multiplied; but he felt that a smaller venue than the theatre would be more suitable, and suggested that, "in these hard times", he lower his admission prices "by a third, or even by a half".[63] Before closing he gave a charity performance for fire victims on April 27th in the Music Conservatorium, attracting 307 spectators.[64]

A final review (unsigned) opened with some philosophical considerations— "The tricks of Pinetti and Cagliostro do not contribute to the perfection of aesthetic art, and in this respect their representation does not bring any benefit to the audience. They do not appeal to the heart, they do not move, but they can engage the senses and amaze with a skill that is often difficult to comprehend. Of such a kind is the performance of Bosco. The illusion which his skilfulness brings about is complete...", going on to admire his tricks — several with cards and coins, rings and watches, handkerchiefs shredded and restored intact, birds beheaded then flying away, and a figure of a young girl cut from paper then dancing to the sound of his guitar.[65]

In late June Bosco is mentioned as involved in a court case in Riga, making a demand for payment against a lawyer named Johann Wilpert. This presumably relates to an occurrence when Bosco was in Riga in 1824 but the details and outcome of the case remain obscure.[66]

It is very unlikely that Bosco was present in Riga for the hearing as in early July he was more than 900 km away in Kalisz, in central Poland, performing "outdoors and in daylight, and received with universal satisfaction".[67]

Bosco then headed south to Breslau (modern Wrocław), performing in the *großer Redouten-Saal* of the *Hôtel de Pologne* in Bischofs-Straße, as we know from two surviving posters.[68] The prices are given as 15, 10 and 5 Sgr (*Silber-groschen*) and four shows are announced, but he was so successful there that (as he trumpets in a later advertisement)[69] he gave "thirty four performances in Breslau, all equally well attended". The Gun trick there with twelve soldiers firing at him made a considerable impression, sparking an amusing anecdote widely reprinted in several German papers that he planned to be shot at by a twelve-pounder artillery piece: "how valuable if the country had an army of such bullet-proof people".[70]

He then began a publicity campaign to advertise a planned series of performances in the area round Dresden and Leipzig where he had so successfully opened his German career six years earlier. A long advertisement in the *Leipziger Zeitung* in early October (in the third person, this one unsigned) is dated Dresden, September 30th, and announces that Bartholmäus Bosco, so warmly received six years ago, has just completed thirty four packed shows in Breslau and plans to arrive in mid-October. His next advertisement, at the end of October, signed "Dresden, 25th October 1827, Au. K — n." tells us that the "long and widely awaited magician, Bartholmäus Bosco, is now in our midst ... it is only to be wished that he will soon give us the opportunity to see his great achievements".[71]

But he did not perform in either Dresden or Leipzig at this stage, and we next sight him in nearby Altenburg, where he gave three shows, on November 30th and December 2nd and 4th: another long advertisement, this one signed by a surely mythical "Graf v. W . . . . . f", proclaims Bosco's great success in Altenburg, performing before royalty, hailing him as the one master magician, all the rest mere pupils.[72]

He finally opened in Leipzig on December 17th. For details of his five performances there we have further advertisements in the *Leipziger Zeitung,* several reviews, and two interesting surviving posters. In a series of five advertisements, all signed with his own name, he recalls his splendid reception there six years ago, and announces shows for December 17th, 20th and 22nd, "his circumstances allow him only a short period here".[73]

Then comes a notice praising all aspects of Bosco's skills, signed apparently with the initials of a number of admirers, "W. G. C. G. H. L. B. A. D. B. R. u. m." ("u.m." = *et al.*), followed by further advertisements announcing two more shows, on 28th and 31st, with the final show to include the Gun trick (now termed "Die große Füsillade").[74]

A last notice from admirers (signed W. A. G. S. L. A. W. G. C. G. H. Z. H. S. u. A. m.) again lauds his performances, above all the speed with which he moved from one trick to the next, and especially commending one with a woman's hat, which he crumpled up, threw in a kettel, put the lid on, loaded a pistol (all done at high speed), fired it, and the hat was hanging on the roof of the proscenium 20 or 30 yards above the audience; a second shot and it floated down and was returned.[75]

There are surviving posters for his shows on December 20th and 28th. The former, his second show, promises 16 tricks not seen in his first show, naming only "die berühmte Zauberpfanne", where the cooked birds fly away. Prices ranged from 4 to 16 Groschen (or 1 Thaler for the *Fremdenloge*). The second poster, for his penultimate show, lists 16 tricks in all, including the lady's hat, "Prices as usual".[76]

Other reports of his Leipzig shows are found in *Erlanger Zeitung* (his magic like "the old Black Art brought back by a legion of devils"); in *Zeitung für die elegante Welt* ("perhaps the leading magician of his kind in Europe ... the sheer diversity and difficulty of his tricks ... no one matching him in variety and gracefulness..."); and in *Abend-Zeitung* ("...a magician *sans pareil*... indisputably the first in his field in Germany and perhaps in Europe... he has showed us only things we have not seen before, and it is all made more interesting by his spontaneous humour, his wit, his scattered Italian jokes (*Lazzis*), and even the comic way he speaks German...".[77]

1828

He opened in Dresden on January 11th. The weather was extremely cold and his first advertisement stresses that the venue, "the newly built theatre in the *Demolirungsplatz*", is "heated and warmly carpeted, with wide aisles and an excellent view from all seats". The public were invited to inspect the theatre the day before, and to look at Bosco's apparatus which had already been set up. He then advertised further shows on the 16th, and on every Wednesday, Friday and Sunday.[78]

In the audience on January 20th was the critic and classical scholar Karl August Böttiger, who published an article warmly praising Bosco's performance, though really using this as the basis for a discussion of conjuring, and especially the 'cup and balls' act, in the ancient world. He quotes the well-known passage from Alciphron, and suggests that when Bosco retires he should write an autobiography ... *How many adventures would he have to tell us, how much would he have to reveal with some harmless betrayal! ...* But, however many laurel wreaths he is crowned with, he'll find it hard to match the "pebble-practitioner" Theodorus who, according to Athenaeus, so delighted the people of Histaea (on Euboea) with his tricks that they erected a bronze statute of him in the theatre, holding a pebble in his hand — *but then our clever countryman from Italy would rather have his image not in bronze, but in g o l d.*[79]

It was on January 27th that his second daughter Adelaide was born in Warsaw.[80] A warm review of his shows, this one signed "D.v.H . . . I. A. G. W. D. *u. A. m.*", declared that, hard as it was to believe that Bosco could live up to the fame of his reputation, now that we have seen five performances he has vastly exceeded it... Why else in this bitterly cold and stormy weather would the public crowd into his shows and also enjoy so many private performances... the more one sees of him and the more one admires him, the more one is overwhelmed by admiration...[81]

He advertised the Gun trick for his show on February 8th,[82] and a final notice farewelled him at the end of the month, this one signed "C. W. G. v. M. *u. a. m.*", admiring his fortune in attracting full audiences to his shows despite "these inclement conditions and the public mourning, the lack of a venue adequate to protect against the hostile winter, and the many attractions of the carnival... we have never seen a magician take the art to this level ... astounding in his public performances and at close quarters in his private shows — *o those unforgettable blessed hours* — we say goodbye with the greatest regret...".[83]

A note in the *Abend-Zeitung* by Ludwig Ottwald writing from Leipzig on March 17th lists "the great delights awaiting us for the fair — the Osage Indians in guest roles; the debut of a famous stone-eater; the Casortis dancing pantomimes; a magician (Bosco); and perhaps the decapitator from previous years and the giraffe..." — but this is all tongue-in-cheek, perhaps a wish-list, and Bosco did not return to Leipzig that year.[84]

On April 10th he opened in Berlin, at the Jagorschen Saal (where he had opened in 1822), and had already been busy in town doing his usual self-promotion. One "victim" was the writer Ludwig Börne, who wrote to his mother —

"...at least there are plenty of shows here in Berlin — three plays every day... plus the Bach circus riders, juggler, diorama, concerts, and a splendid magician Bosco. And as regards this last I was recently made to look a fool. Sitting by myself at a small table in a restaurant, a Frenchman sat down opposite me. He cut open his bread roll and a whole plate-full of coins fell out. He looked surprised, and asked the waiter for another roll. and coins fell out of that one too. I was beside myself with astonishment and called out quite loudly to the waiter shouting 'What's going on here?'. It only occurred to me later that I was dealing with a magician. Isn't that a shame and disgrace to the whole nation? Tricksters like that always pick the biggest fools to play their tricks on...".[85]

Bosco closed at the Jagorschen Saal on May 1st, and immediately reopened at the Königstädtschen Theater in the Alexanderplatz (with the King in the audience),[86] then, at the end of June, he gave his final shows in the open area in front of the Brandenburg Gate.[87] He ended in Berlin on June 29th, having given a total of 35 shows there.[88]

This long run in Berlin was marked by an ongoing controversy with a rival, Joseph Habitt, who billed himself as an "Egyptian magician".[89] Bosco's success provoked Habitt into publishing a series of offensive and derogatory newspaper announcements against him.[90] These Bartolomeo ignored, and also pamphlets directed against him, but supporters on both sides, notably the satirist and journalist

Moritz Gottlieb Saphir in Bosco's corner, soon entered the fray, making for a lively exchange.[91]

From Berlin Bartolomeo headed to the spa towns of Teplice and Carlsbad (Karlovy Vary),[92] then opened in Prague in September, attracting great crowds despite the high prices charged. The reviews praised his skill, his amiable demeanour, and the sheer variety of his tricks which he seldom repeated from show to show (only the cup and balls in both the first and second show), especially admiring in the second show the transformations of flowers, rings and lemons; the endless bouquets; and the birds frying then flying; and in the fifth a series of card tricks, one with the two middle fingers of his right hand tied together, and the decapitated doves brought back to life.[93] His final show, on October 8th, promised a selection of his most popular tricks plus "by popular demand a fantasy on the *Luftharmonica*, with guitar accompaniment": presumably this was the same guitar and harmonica he had in Hamburg in 1830, *viz.* purely "ventriloquial" (see note 131).

Bosco then headed to Vienna, the first of what were to be three visits there during his career, all of which were to end unhappily. His arrival in Vienna was greeted with great acclaim, "Bosco the *matador* of all magicians has arrived...".[94] He performed before the Emperor and the nobility, then opened at the Theater an der Wien on October 28th,[95] with a second show the following night, and a third on November 7th which featured the Gun trick.[96] Again the reviews were excellent, praising his skill, presentation, and the splendid setting with elaborate apparatus ("*400 Maschinen*") and over 200 candles.[97]

This praise in the Viennese papers was echoed in the Italian journal *Teatri, arti e letteratura* 23 Dec.1828, which saluted Bosco as "il più famoso fra i *prestidigiatarj* di questo mondo" — "The most famous magician in the world ...We hope he will soon visit Italy"; this is the earliest mention traced of Bosco in an Italian paper.[98]

However, what had begun so well for Bartolomeo in Vienna ended badly. The third show was his last. The Director of the Theater an der Wien was the famous comic actor Karl Andreas von Bernbrunn (1787-1854), known by his stage name "Carl". He and Bosco set high entrance prices, and the first show was crowded. But Ludwig Döbler was also in town performing at the Leopold-Theater and at lower prices,[99] and Bosco's second show was less well attended than his first. For the third show the prices were lowered and again the crowds returned, but Carl now decided to cut short Bosco's run, and on November 12th appeared himself at the theatre as the stock humorous character Staberl in a show which parodied Bosco, imitating both his mannerisms and his tricks (learnt by watching Bosco; he also had some quick lessons from Hofzinser), and even revealing the secrets behind some of Bosco's deceptions.[100]

Bosco, held up to ridicule, laid a charge with the police over Carl's "perfidy"; they were unsympathetic to his complaint, but on January 14th 1829 the Chief of Police, Count Sedlintzky, instructed that Carl be issued with a reprimand.[101]

By then Bosco was long gone. He had remained in Vienna for some time giving private performances, and is said to have performed for the Emperor on December 3rd or 5th. He stated in a farewell notice dated December 9th that he was prevented from resuming his shows due to illness and the lack of a suitable venue; he would, however, be returning to Vienna, and with completely new tricks, which would be shown not by deceptive candlelight but in the full light of day.[102]

Bosco later said that he had planned to go now to Italy after Vienna,[103] but instead he opened in Preßburg (Bratislava) on December 17th, billed as the first of five shows, the last on December 28th. All were well attended and well received, and a sixth, benefit, show was (predictably) announced for January 4th, featuring tricks held back so far, including, of course, the Gun trick.[104]

1829

Bosco then spent an extended period touring Hungary. He gave three shows in Raab (Győr) with great success,[105] then arrived in Pest on January 28th. The Buda-Pest journal *Der Spiegel* welcomed him in the first of three very flattering articles with what was largely a reprint of Böttiger's 'cup and balls' piece.[106]

He performed first in Ofen (Buda) on February 24th, 27th, and March 6th, drawing good audiences, high prices notwithstanding. A review after the third show praised his skills and his demeanour ("so gefällig, so frappant und so unterhaltend…") and his geniality — "though we have seen others do similar tricks with almost equal dexterity, they lacked the certain *savoir vivre* in the art, which we admire so much in Bosco".[107] On March 5th he was invited to perform for the Palatine of Hungary, Archduke Joseph of Austria ('József nádor'), and his family at his residence, Buda castle.[108]

He gave a final benefit show on March 8th for the theatrical painter Martinelli, then opened in Pest on March 9th. *Der Spiegel* hailed him as "not merely a magician and a performer but also a poet, a master of time and space, making impossible things possible…".[109]

By mid-April Bosco was back in Vienna, receiving a glowing welcome — "[tr.] Bosco, the unsurpassed magician, whose incomparable cup and balls, whose never before seen transformations, whose inexhaustible magic tricks have rightly won him the name of Philadelphia II, is back from his *Kunstreise* to Hungary, where he won admiration and gold in abundance…". However, he did not reopen in Vienna, and it was reported that he was off to Brno, then would travel via Hamburg to London where the owner of Astley's Theatre had invited him to give twelve shows.[110]

The London shows, for whatever reason, did not go ahead. On April 30th Bosco is said to have performed for Cardinal-Archduke Rudolph Rainier, presumably in his diocese of Olomouc, near Brno.[111]

He was heading again towards Poland, opening in Breslau (Wrocław) on May 31st and closing on June 8th. He performed in a large tent — on May 30th, we are told, a splendid tent, coloured white and blue, with flags fluttering at the tips magically appeared overnight in the parade ground … the inside both comfortable and elegant, with all the seats, over 200, upholstered and fabric covered. Each show was so crowded that many people had to be turned away, even at the high entry price of 1 Thaler.[112]

He was next in Posen (Poznán), where he was fondly remembered from his 1822 visit. He performed here on June 25th, 26th, and 27th, not in a tent but at the City Theatre, making a contract with "Herr Vogt of the German Dramatic Society" for three nights.[113]

The paper then published a long article with the title 'Dziwoląg Językowy' — 'Linguistic Monstrosity', ending "[tr.] …Bosco delighted everyone yesterday", but otherwise completely devoted to the fact that his poster, originally in German, had been "so hideously translated into Polish". It was quick to point out that it was not his fault — "Bosco is neither Polish nor German — as an Italian he is not able to judge any of these languages, and is completely innocent", but, it continued, "he outrages every Pole who loves his own language … he could have found a better translator in any school…".[114]

At the end of July he arrived in Warsaw, remaining there until early October. He began by erecting his tent — "[tr.] Bosco is setting up a huge tent in Nalewki Street just outside the Krasińskich Gardens, and will open there next week", announced the papers.[115] He had a break in September to perform at a fair in Lowicz,[116] and closed in Warsaw on October 3rd.[117]

It was at this time that the first book naming Bosco in the title was published, *Scharfblicke in das Gebieth der natürlichen Magie, oder, Bosco's aufgeschlossenes Zauberkabinet*, by "Jukundus Hilarius Possenreich", first advertised in August 1829 (see *Books* LGe149).

Bosco now moved south to Königsberg (Kaliningrad), giving seven performances with great success — opening with the cup and balls, "[tr.] the very touchstone of his art, which he has brought to perfection, and with the balls disappearing into the air like soap bubbles, then reappearing, the natural appeared to become the supernatural…".[118]

In Königsberg Bosco apparently came head-to-head with the Russian magician Moritz Molduano. When performing in Riga in 1838 Molduano stated in his advertising that he had "[tr.] achieved a victory over Bosco when they performed 'in concert' in Königsberg on 15th November 1829".[119]

1830

In January 1830 Eduard Maria Oettinger in his satirical journal *Das Schwarze Gespenst*[120] reported that "Bosco is at present performing in Madrid" — but this was in his regular 'Allgemeine Lügenzeitung' (*Fake News*) section and just making fun of the playwright Carl Meisl.[121]

Bosco was in fact in Pomerania. He is listed as arriving in Cöslin (modern Koszalin) at the start of February, and the newspaper duly printed a Bosco anecdote the same day.[122] Whether Bosco performed there is uncertain, but he remained in the area for some time. In early March he was in Stettin (Szczecin), giving three well-attended shows in the *Casino* and, from March 9th, two in the Theatre.[123] At the end of the month he was in Stralsund, performing there on March 26th and 28th.[124] The newspaper commented on Bosco's strong resemblance to Napoleon. He then gave three shows in Rostock, closing on April 18th.[125]

On April 21st we find him travelling through Mecklenburg-Vorpommern and on the 25th giving a performance in the famous Golden Room of Ludwigslust Castle for the Grosherzog (Friedrich Franz I) and his court, followed by a public performance in Schwerin on April 28th.[126]

In mid-May he was in Lübeck, giving two crowded shows by May 17th, with a third promised, and by May 22nd he had arrived in Hamburg.[127]

These dates are of some interest, as his son Eugenio stated at his marriage on June 14th 1829 that his age was 35, meaning (if correct) that he was born *between 15 June 1829 and 14 June 1830*, either in Lübeck (by one account) or (by his own statement) in Hamburg.[128]

Bosco opened in Hamburg at the Apollo-Theater on June 9th.[129] A long review admired not only his tricks (especially the shredded women's hats, and — *how does he get that big umbrella into the small box?*) but equally his good qualities —wit, humour, animation, grace, charm, nimbleness, flexibility, tact, good taste... It also agreed with the Berlin and Vienna papers in trumpeting Bosco as "a Paganini of the Art of Conjuring", a happy comparison as Paganini was also in town and performing at the same time.[130]

The second show on June 13th was no less successful, as was the third on the 18th, which promised 20 tricks so far unseen. A review hailed Bosco as the master of his art, praising a performance given at a private *soirée*, with no apparatus and the spectators very close by but still mystified. The reviewer had seen Pinetti, who "stands far below Bosco", and commended Bosco for not displaying the self-satisfied smirk of triumph which Pinetti would show at having fooled his audience. He also praises Bosco's talent as a musical ventriloquist, amazing the audience when some ladies were singing at the piano by performing a guitar accompaniment *mit seinem Munde flötend* —so, the guitar was purely "ventriloquial" — and *er weiß seinen Lippen wahre Harmonika-Töne zu entlocken* — he can entice true harmonica notes from his lips.[131]

His fifth show, which included an interlude by "Herr Armonist" on his wood-harmonica (*Holz-Harmonica*), was on June 25th (postponed so as not to clash with the benefit performance of the visiting singer Pauline von Schätzel),[132] his sixth on 27th, another on 30th (a charity show for the poor), and his "final" show on July 3rd,[133] only to be followed "by public demand" by a further show on July 11th, in which he farewelled the public by firing into the air a cloud of poems of thanks printed on multi-coloured paper which floated down into the audience.[134]

Meanwhile, what should open on June 25th at the Tivoli Gardens but 'Staberl als Tausendkünstler'! The advertisements for this in the *Hamburger Nachrichten* immediately follow Bosco's own advertisements and are strikingly larger. The farce was repeated on June 27th, and again on July 15th and 22nd (with the first act rewritten) after Bosco's departure, and then revived on September 29th when Bosco returned to Hamburg.[135] One advertisement mentions "Carl", but only as the author. The performer here was the local comic Karl Hechner.[136]

While he was in Hamburg Bosco was the object of some humorous philosophical observations from the editor and poet Gotthilf August von Maltitz: At a time such as this, we are told, when the art of magic has reached its pinnacle and embraced every aspect of the human mind, so that we have Court magicians, State magicians, Medical magicians [*etc., etc.*], and soon world wide Papal and Rationalist magicians [*etc., etc.*], and the art of magic has become a field of study for the gentle sex who do tricks with the upper part of their dainty persons... and more and more each day everything, Belief, Love, Marriage, is dependent on the art of magic... at such a time we must thank Herr Bosco for making us aware of this useful art... for everything in life depends on Deception, and the Deceptions of the talented Herr Bosco can make us forget all others…[137]

Bosco next gave two shows in Altona, on June 17th and 18th, two in Oldesloe while the horse races were on, and also performed in Kiel.[138] From there he arrived in Copenhagen on August 12th, accompanied by a Secretary and three assistants.[139]

The Danish papers, which had barely mentioned Bosco in earlier years apart from reprinting an occasional anecdote, were soon devoting long articles to him. These clearly draw on previous reports in German papers, praising his skills and recalling his shows in Vienna, Berlin, Warsaw and Hamburg. The only biographical information is "born in Turin", with none of the later accretion of anecdotes of his early life or service in the army.[140]

He opened at the Morskabstheatret in Vesterbro on August 19th, with a second show on 22nd,[141] a third on 26th (promising twenty new tricks), and a "final" show on 29th,[142] prior to which he performed for the Royal family at Frederiksberg Castle on 25th.[143] He then took part in a benefit show for the Misses Lewin on September 1st,[144] and ended with a benefit show of his own on September 5th.[145] The Gun trick is not mentioned in any advertisements or reviews of his performances in Denmark.

He closed his last show, as he had in Hamburg, with a pistol shot that sent a cloud of thank-you verses on coloured paper floating down from the ceiling. It was announced that he was to give three shows in Helsingør and it was hoped that on his return he may be able to perform in the Kongelige Hoftheater.[146]

In fact only two of the three shows planned for Helsingør took place. The third, together with any return to Copenhagen and a possible show in Gothenburg, were cancelled and Bosco rushed back to Hamburg, "where his family were living during his stay in Denmark". The reason given was "familieomstændigheder" — *family circumstances*.[147]

We never hear what the "family circumstances" were that made him rush back to Hamburg, perhaps to do with baby Eugenio. He was there by September 24th and further shows were announced at the Apollo-Theater for September 26th and 27th "before his departure to London".[148] A third show followed on 29th, promising all new tricks, then others on October 2nd and 3rd.[149] Meanwhile 'Staberl als Tausendkünstler' had been revived at the Tivoli-Theater, advertised in the newspaper directly below Bosco's show, and in the same issue an enterprising publisher was advertising a book which promised: "[tr.] B. BOSCO'S TRICKS, for the most part, as well as many other magical illusions … clearly explained and taught … to be had bound in all Hamburg bookshops". The book was the third edition of Kerndörffer's *Der kleine Taschenspieler und Magiker*, which had appeared several years earlier: it opens with a section on cup and ball tricks but makes no specific mention of Bosco.[150]

We then find that Bosco is still in Hamburg on October 16th, and announces his regrets at being unable to comply with requests for further shows there as "his commitments elsewhere do not allow him to remain longer, and the settlement of matters which were preventing his departure, is now complete"; he hopes the public will extend their ongoing goodwill… This does seem deliberately vague, making no reference to why his planned visit to London was (again) cancelled and where he was going instead.[151]

He headed to Bremen, performing in the *Krameramthaus* from November 3rd,[152] then toured Germany for several months.

1831

He was in Braunschweig in late January,[153] then opened in Kassel on February 24th,[154] and in April was in Cologne.[155] On May 6th he is said to have performed for the Duke of Hesse. At the end of August he was in Darmstadt, giving two performances at the *Hoftheater* on August 30th and September 1st.[156] These were not hugely successful, said the *Abend-Zeitung* Darmstadt correspondent: the announcements inserted in the newspaper describing him as the Paganini of his art did not bring in the crowds — the large house was empty. But those present knew him as the most skilful magician of his kind and no doubt the reputation of his magic-making would have attracted everyone if his art included how to end cholera and how to make gold…[157] By October he was in Mainz,[158] and in December he was reported to be in Aachen and about to travel to Paris via Belgium.[159]

1832

His long and very successful tour of Belgium began in Liège on January 15th 1832, with further shows announced for the 16th, 20th and 22nd. His performances, held in the rooms of the *Société d'Émulation,* were all sold out, and he remained in Liège until the start of March.[160]

He was probably next in Antwerp,[161] and then opened to great anticipation in Brussels on March 13th, at the *Salle des Beaux-Arts* in the rue de Bavière, a rather small venue, tickets priced from 1 *fl.* in the pit to 2,50 *fl.* for a box and the balcony.[162]

Some reviewers were almost lost for words, so great was the quality and range of his tricks, "[tr.] each is proof of the vast gulf separating M. Bosco from ordinary conjurors and magicians, and proof that he is a true artist".[163]

Despite two other major attractions running concurrently, the play *L'homme au masque de fer* by Arnould & Fournier and the famous eccentric dancer Klishnig, his shows were crowded to overflowing, enthusiasm perhaps spurred by the spectre of cholera soon expected. The response to his second show on 16th was no less great, the audience admiring not merely his skill as he dissected shawls, broke watches, and cooked birds, but the *speed* with which it was all executed.[164] And the same with his third show on the 20th: surprise after surprise, said the reviews, with Bosco artfully keeping the best trick to the end.[165] *Turandot* was repeated on 27th and 29th, then on April 1st came what was billed as a new show "La Marchande de modes de Paris", which was equally successful.[166]

There was then a hiatus. On April 14th Bosco published a letter complaining that the mayor, Nicolas-Jean Rouppe, who on March 8th had set a fee of 5 florins per show on behalf of the poor, had after the fifth show increased the fee to 25 florins. When Bosco protested, he was told he would be charged a ten per cent levy at the door on his gross takings (including tickets given free to the newspapers). Bosco responded by citing his high expenses and his requests for a larger venue or the chance to give a special charity performance, so successful in Liège: when this was ignored, he announced he would give two final shows, on April 13th and 16th, promising (surely tongue-in-cheek) to "redouble his efforts", making this his most brilliant performance yet, combining the best of his former tricks with some yet unseen; and with that he took his leave of Brussels.[167]

He was in Naumur in early May,[168] then in Mons, and at the end of May apparently back in Brussells, "The Napoleon of conjuring", though there is no mention of his performing there again.[169]

On July 1st he opened at the Grand-Théatre in Ghent, welcomed as the "physicien prestidigitateur" who "would briefly make us forget the two great scourges of our day, the Belgian revolution and the cholera...". But the audiences was small, and after his second and third shows on 5th and 8th he left the city, heading for France, his first stop Lille.[170]

He was in Lille by early August, and next in Amiens ("...I know of no one who could rival M. Bosco, whose success here is complete", said one reviewer), then on October 7th opened to great acclaim in Paris, at the *Théatre de la Porte Saint-Martin*. Here he gave four afternoon shows (with the theatre playing its usual melodramas in the evenings).[171]

The Paris papers eagerly paraded his fame, his skills (so extraordinary, said *Le Figaro*, as to be unfamiliar to Parisians, compared to the magicians they had seen before), and his former successes, but only in Germany and Belgium — there is never a mention of Bosco ever having lived in Paris or having served under Napoleon.[172]

His shows being *matinées* pleased the *Figaro* reviewer as he did not have to write his review after midnight, nor struggle to describe some terrible play: this performance, he said, had one act, one scene, and one actor only, Bosco ... *I have only miracles to tell you: the Bible has its miracles, we have Bosco; the dead are brought back to life, so are Bosco's pigeons ... the Prophets are merely his apprentices ... If you believe in God, do not go and see Bosco...*[173]

The *Gazette des théâtres* admired not only his skill but his *originality*, describing several tricks in detail, especially *cuisine diabolique,* the cooked pigeons, and the Paris correspondent of the *Wiener Zeitschrift* was overwhelmed, paying Bosco perhaps the ultimate compliment: *He does tricks which border on (real) magic,* telling us *the audience are enraptured, transported, full of wonder at what they can see but not understand,* and admiring above all the act is which a plank is placed between the stage and the edge of a box and this Bosco climbs holding a plate with three borrowed watches he is returning; the plank sways, overturns, Bosco falls! All rush to help. The plate and watches are all broken; he is deathly pale, offering to pay for the watches and give everyone refunds, wrapping a towel round his bleeding hand... *But suddenly* there is no blood, he is not limping now, not hurt at all: he fires a pistol shot and the plates and watches are found intact hanging at the back of the theatre, to great applause...[174]

The *Gazette de France* reviewer in praising his performance (while preferring fewer pistol shots) noted how Paris had been missing such shows since Olivier and Comte.[175] Bosco is said to have sent Comte a ticket to his first show after moving to the *salle Taitbout* on October 28th, who attended and sent a letter in reply expressing his thanks and admiration of the performance, "[tr.] which I had great pleasure in attending. My compliments and praises are small compared to the universal applause you so justly deserved".[176]

The change of venue had come after difficulties arose with M. Harel of the *Théatre de la Porte Saint-Martin* following a very successful evening show given there by Bosco on October 16th. The new hall at the *salle Taitbout*, while smaller, was better suited, with the audience closer, and his shows were now all in the evenings. There he performed every Thursday and Sunday, and offered private shows on other days.[177]

Reviews were as enthusiastic as before — the *Gazette des théâtres* called the show "Merveilleux!"; *Le Constitutionnel* hailed him as "the Paganini of his art". Announcing that he would continue through the winter, he offered long-term subscription prices at a discount (the dearest a private box seating four for three shows at 48 fr. instead of 72 fr.).[178]

Bosco was the talk of Paris and very much *the fashion.* Among a swarm of anecdotes, caricatures, and political allusions was a long imaginary interview in *Le Revenant* pretending to quiz Bosco on constitutional monarchy and the Charter of 1830.[179]

From December 12th he again changed venues, performing at the *Théâtre du Palais-Royal,* his show preceded by two short plays. Originally engaged to give fifteen shows there, he proved so popular that two further shows were added on January 4th and 6th.[180] It was reported that during December the theatre's takings amounted to more than 50,000 francs.[181]

1833

Bosco remained in Paris and nearby. On January 29th we find him advertised, "not having appeared in public for some time", as to perform "for variety" prior to one of the musical concerts given by the Italian tenor Giambattista Scavarda in the *salle Chantereine.*[182] He also gave three performances in the theatre at Versailles, then was in Saint-Germain-en-Laye,[183] and in early March was back at the *salle Chantereine,* announcing two final shows on 10th and 11th "before his departure for London". His *soirées* were described as "extrèmement brillantes", Bosco as at the height of his "brillante réputation", with "le plus brillante société" there to see him, some having paid double the already high ticket price to obtain a seat.[184] Before leaving Paris he was invited to perform for King Louis Philippe and the Royal family at the Tuilleries Palace on March 13th, with the delighted audience finding themselves his "compères obligés".[185]

In March he was offered a large sum to give fifty shows in London, but would perform first in Rouen and Le Havre.[186]

All his apparatus was loaded in Paris on the steamship *Le Commerce de Rouen,* but sailing down the Seine the ship got only as far as Mantes where it collided wth a bridge pier. Much of the cargo was salvaged but badly water-damaged, and Bosco's apparatus was largely ruined. He cancelled his engagements and returned to Paris, announcing plans to replace his apparatus with something even grander.[187]

He sued the shipping company in Rouen for 10,000 fr. compensation, staying with his family in the city for several weeks. The Tribunal awarded him 2,821 fr. for his damaged apparatus plus 1,000 fr. for his expenses in Rouen and another 1,000 fr. for lost revenue. The company appealed, denying liability except for the damaged apparatus and argued that Bosco had originally said nothing of the great importance of his cases, giving the value as 12 fr. and not wanting to insure them; he had paid 40 fr. extra for a coach as cargo and 12 fr. for a servant; en route another servant had emerged from the coach!

Bosco handed a written address to the court pleading *the enormous loss, which was daily growing worse; seeking its indulgence, his only hope to avoid the misfortune stemming entirely from the fault of the Company...* and flourished his splendid album bound in green morocco (which it seems had fortunately not been on the boat) to prove he was no ordinary *escamoteur*. Thanks more to his lawyer the awards for the damage and his expenses were confirmed, though apparently not the claim for potential lost revenue. He gave several private performances in Rouen then opened at the Théâtre-Français on July 4th.[188] As an indication of the value of amounts he received in compensation, when he finally opened in Rouen his ticket prices ranged from 1 fr. 50 c to 7 fr.

His advertisements indicate that for his shows with his new apparatus the titles (and presumably the acts) were largely unchanged from his former repertoire. For the first "séance de Magie égyptienne" on July 4th (and repeated on July 6th) we have *Turando* [sic], in two parts, comprising 24 *pièces*, part 1 closing with *Les Spectateurs éblouis, ou les Montres en prison et mises en Liberté,* and the whole show closing with the cooked pigeons, *Le Repas interrompu, ou la Cuisine enchantée par les Bohémiens.* The third show on July 8th was *Le Diable déchaîné*, in two parts of 24 *pièces* (only the *Boules invisibles,* the cup and balls, shared with his earlier shows), part one ending with *Les Montres volantes retrouvées au milieu du tonnerre et des éclairs,* and part two with *Les Morts ressuscités.* The contents of his fourth show on July 11th may be new — again 24 *pièces* (kept secret!) ending with *L'Ours et le Pacha.* The next show on 14th, his benefit, was again 24 *pièces* (again secret!), part one ending with *L'Horloger du Lucifer* and the whole show ending with *Une grande Manœuvre militaire, ou le Courage de Napoléon.*

He then moved to a larger venue, the *Théâtre des Arts,* repeating *Le Repas interrompu* on 16th, and the *Grande Manœuvre* on 18th (both preceded by short plays), followed by a final show on 21st, comprising acts not in the two previous shows, ending with *Les Morts sont Rappellés à la Vie.*[189]

His high prices left a few seats unfilled, but the reviews were excellent, one nicely putting it: "[tr.] possesses in the highest degree the talent of moving money from the public's pocket to his own, and to send everyone away happy"; but again suggesting fewer pistol shots would please the audience more.[190]

In early August he performed in Elbeuf (shows on 1st and 4th August) and opened in Dieppe on August 10th.[191]

He then gave five shows in Le Havre, on September 13, 16, 19, 21, and 23.[192] Having closed at the theatre he remained for some time in Le Havre, not hiring a large house but setting up his own temporary theatre on the bare ground of the Place Louis-Philippe.[193]

By late October he was in Rennes, attracting great interest on his arrival with two of his promotional demonstrations: in a café pouring his companion a glass of Madeira, then saying it was of poor quality and refilling the glass while the person's hand was covering it; and tormenting a barber who shaved him — yet one side of his face always remained unshaved... His two shows, on October 25th and 27th, saw him described as "a whole new genre; he is not Olivier, he is not Comte, he is himself... striding the stage bare-armed amid the flames of the eau de Cologne which he pours by the flask full and the sound of gun shots… and the cup and balls, the most difficult part of the magician's art, he has taken to a level which is unbelievable…".[194]

He was next in Nantes, opening at the *Grand Théâtre* on November 5th, prices ranging from 5 fr. down to 50 cent., with further shows on 7th and 8th.[195] He then advertised private lessons, promising that all the tricks were new and of his own creation, and in three lessons pupils would be able to perform 12 to 15 tricks as well as he did them himself.[196] On November 14th he gave a fourth show, "by public demand", and on 14th a benefit for the poor on behalf of the *Bureau de Charité*.[197]

1834

He was soon reported to be heading to Marseille and possibly Algeria,[198] but in January 1834 we find him successful in Niort and then opening in La Rochelle on January 12th.[199]

In February he was in Bordeaux. Pierre Bernadau, chronicler of events in Bordeaux, describes in his *Tablettes manuscrites*[200] Bosco's performance there on February 27th 1834. After noting how much the spectators enjoyed the show, he continues: "[tr.] …*No money was taken at the door of this show. M. Bosco had distributed entrance tickets through his associates who accepted payment in secret. This was to avoid paying the charities and the management of the theatres of Bordeaux the dues they levy on fairground shows. Despite this deception, these bodies have brought a lawsuit against the conjuror to claim their rights and we will see how he fares in the courts…*". Unfortunately we do not hear the outcome of the case. *Satanas* describes a charity performance by Bosco in Bordeaux on March 29th 1834 (Rusconi p.48) but there is good evidence that on that date he was almost 600 km north in Vincennes, giving a charity performance there.[201]

In mid-April Bosco was invited to return to Bordeaux by Robillon *frères* of the Grand-Théâtre to give a further six shows.[202] In the end Bosco did not open there until the start of May, delayed by illness and barely recovered, but just as popular as he had been on his earlier visit.[203]

He then headed to Toulouse,[204] opening in early June, signed up for ten shows and also offering private lessons.[205]

By the end of June he was in Nîmes,[206] announcing his opening at the *Grand Théâtre de Nismes* on July 4th, with two further shows on 6th and 8th. However, illness meant the first show had to be cancelled;[207] the July 6th show went ahead, though drew only a small crowd, largely due to the high summer temperatures. However before leaving he gave three shows in all — and excited some disagreement between the reporters of the *Gazette du Bas Languedoc* and the *Courrier du Gard*.[208]

On July 18th he arrived in Marseille,[209] received with great acclaim and anticipation, but he advertised in late July that no performances would take place, blaming this on "the length of the shows and the excessively hot weather". He was unwell, and further distracted by having to lay charges against his *"homme d'affaires"* named Chiora for stealing 500 francs.[210]

But the real problem was that he could not find a suitable venue. Both here, and soon in Lyon, he was to encounter major problems dealing with the local theatre owners.[211] He gave lessons and private shows, and made appearances in cafés, markets and other public places, but soon announced that he would be leaving Marseille early. In a letter to the newspaper published on August 15th he stated that he had failed over six weeks to come to terms with the management of the *Grand-Théâtre* where he had planned to give 20 or 25 performances, but had now agreed with the *Théâtre Français,* about to become the *Gymnase Marseillais,* to give four shows there when it reopened on September 1st after redecoration. His show would occupy the whole programme and be given on nights when there were no plays or vaudeville. The management of the *Grand-Théâtre* indignantly replied that they had offered Bosco the same terms as to other artists, but he had refused these, unwilling to allow subscribers in free and demanding a guarantee of 700 fr. per show.[212]

He duly performed at the *Théâtre Français*, now renamed the *Gymnase Marseillais*, on September 3rd, 6th, and 7th, all well attended and well reviewed, Bosco, we are told, holding the audience of almost 1500 enthralled for three hours, and impressing with the incredible variety of his repertoire, each successive trick quite different from what came before. The show announced for the 9th was cancelled due to illness, and it was not until the 15th that he resumed, this billed as his final show. The audience was not only large but fashionable, all the boxes were occupied, which had not been the case for some years at this theatre, said the reviewer, who got rather carried away in his praises of the performance — Bosco was performing "miracles" ... *At the wedding at Cana J.C. turned water into wine. M. Bosco, more skilful than the son of God, separates purely by the force of his will a glass of beer and a glass of wine mixed in the same bottle...* Predictably a further "definitive" final show was advertised for 22nd, a great success, and so yet more shows were announced (these opening with vaudeville acts so the theatre could share the takings). His final show was on October 3rd.

On October 14th he was reported as about to leave Marseille for Grenoble and Lyon, but his next stop was Aix.[213] Following a successful visit "despite the holidays and the high seat prices", Bosco then returned to Marseille to pick up his family; while there he gave two further shows, this time, interestingly, at the *Grand-Théâtre,* on November 3rd and 6th. He now gave two shows in Avignon before travelling to Lyon.[214]

A classic Bosco anecdote is first found at this time, of Bosco in a restaurant playing havoc with the watches of his fellow guests, his own watch finally being found in the pocket of the summoned police commissioner, at which point he reveals his identity. The story appears in French papers in December, set in Marseille, and was soon widely reprinted and translated, with elaborations...[216]

He was engaged by M. Provence of the Grand Théâtre in Lyon to give three shows, on December 22nd, 23rd and 24th. The reviewers loved them — *his hands perform more miracles in one hour than there are in all the holy books, and his mighty wand would outdo that of Moses,* but again: fewer pistol shots please — they alarm the ladies and *such a man does not need that to throw "powder" in the eyes of his audience.* The three shows brought in takings of 7,800 fr., and this rose to 13,000 francs after his sixth show (see below).[216]

The public wanted more, and he gave three further shows, now at the *Théâtre du Gymnase.* The third show there (his sixth in all), despite being on New Year's Eve, drew a very large audience (unlike the *Grand Théâtre* which attracted barely 15 or 20 people that night),[217] and he ended it with one of his poems on coloured sheets of paper fired from a pistol and floating down among the audience —

> *Messieurs, je ne suis pas poète,*
>   *J'écorche le français et parle de travers,*
> *Mais la vertu de ma baguette,*
>   *En dépit d'Apollon, m'inspire quelque vers...* [etc.][218]

1835

From Marseille Bosco headed to St-Étienne, giving four shows there, then two in Vienne (in Isère)[219] before returning to Lyon.

As he explained in a letter dated January 28th, he had intended to remain in Lyon some time and had requested from the municipal authorities the right to give a further series of shows at the *Salle de la Galerie de l'Argue*. Under legislation granting privilege to established theatres this was refused unless M. Provence of the *Grand-Théâtre* gave his permission, and he demanded 40% of Bosco's takings as it would affect his business. Bosco then applied to give a *subscription* series of shows at the *Salle de la Loterie*, but this was again refused by the Mayor's office, citing several statutes, as being recreational not instructive and so also requiring the permission of M. Provence. Bosco announced he was leaving Lyon to perform in neighbouring towns less inhospitable to art...[220]

An intriguing Bosco item may date from this period: a printed 8 page poem in German, a dialogue between Bosco, Faust and Mephistopheles, together with an autograph signature by Bosco dated January 30th 1835. This was sold at a French auction in 1858; buyer and current whereabouts unknown.[221]

Bosco left Lyon on February 1st, heading to his native Italy, where he had never (unless when very young) performed professionally.[222] He was soon in Piedmont,[223] and announced in Turin on February 28th that "[tr.] having returned from his long travels in all the capitals and major cities of Europe, and lastly in Lyon" he was now in Turin and during Lent would be performing at the *Teatro D'Angennes*, the day and hour to be stated on placards. Meanwhile he was advertising private instruction, offering to teach 12 or 15 tricks in a course of three lessons, and was contactable at his residence, "contrada di Po, N°. 29, corte della Beccaccia, piano nobile".[224] He gave a command performance for Queen Maria Teresa and the court on March 1st,[225] then opened at the Theatre on Sunday March 8th — "Prima rappresentazione di Magia Egiziaca... Turandò l'Incantatore", ticket prices ranging from 3 to 25 L.[226]

A fulsome review, signed "R." (Felice Romani), listed highlights from his show — "[tr.] All things, some will say, that have been seen a thousand and a thousand more times. — Maybe yes, and maybe no; but certainly never so well done, so well prepared; with so much grace, and never with so much ease...".[227]

His second show, "L'Orso ed il Bascià", was on the following Sunday, March 15th, with Bosco now offering subscription prices to that show and the two to follow, "La Mercantessa da Moda di Parigi" on 19th and "Turandò l'Incantatore" on 22nd. Further shows were advertised for March 29th and April 2nd but Bosco became unwell and these were delayed until April 5th and 9th.[228]

For his final show on April 9th Bosco announced an innovation, the cups he used in his cup and balls act would be *transparent,* made of cut glass ("una nuova forma di Bussolotti di cristallo intagliata a punta di diamante"), which he had had specially made in Paris.[229] Unfortunately we do not hear how the performance went. It is possible that he delayed their introduction as he advertised in Milan on July 9th that that was their first use (as he did on several later occasions!).

In a final note from Turin on April 11th Bosco announced he would be performing in Alessandria later in April on his way to Genoa.[230] The poster reproduced by Rusconi on p.63 for a penultimate performance by Bosco on May 1st 1835 in an unnamed theatre in an unnamed city ["*nel Teatro del Illma Città*" — meaning that the date and place could be inserted as he travelled from place to place] is almost certainly from Alessandria: the date fits and tickets are available at the *Caffè dell' Universo* — a sig. Franza ran a café of that name in Alessandria until 1841.

He was in Genoa by May 13th and opened at the *Teatro S. Agostino* on 18th, with further shows on 22nd and on 24th, these three shows only. The reviews were excellent ("prolonged and universal applause...") but seem a little muted, as if his performances may have been overshadowed by rival shows at the other theatres in the city.[231]

In Milan Bosco opened at *Teatro Re* on June 12th to great expectation, but was immediately met with reviews that were critical and even hostile.

The reviewer in *L'Eco* launched a salvo — *watches, shawls, birds, cards... tricks we often see in Milan, and at little cost... we found nothing extraordinary, except the raised prices, a lot of gun shots (alarming the ladies), and Bosco's "mosaic" commentary — he speaks French like an Italian, and Italian like a Frenchman...* offering to reveal the deceptions himself, and criticising Bosco's outfit and the term 'Egyptian'...

The *Telegrafo* reviewer took a similar tack — *for all the praise the newspapers give him, he will be a charlatan like all the rest! Why pay a high price to see his show, to see pretty much what I've seen a thousand times — what the juggler with his cups and balls does in the public square... Dexterity and spirit he may have, but he is no Conus or Brazzaletti or Pinetti... He does thirty different tricks, and all of them with skill, but tricks seen so many times before... Speaks neither French or Italian... is it worth spending money to see this new conjuror? Well, go and see him and then decide... But are we expecting the impossible — he is after all a man not a sorcerer... Some might say that it is not clear whether I'm offering praise or criticism here — we will reply that that is what was intended...*

Il Censore Universale dei teatri, also published in Milan, was much more complimentary, praising Bosco's *"rare talent"... the tricks may be common enough but with Bosco they are more difficult and done with greater speed and skill,* and it specifically criticised *L'Eco*— *we don't belittle Paganini and Malibran simply because everyone can play the violin and sing ...* it defends his language – *any Italian would be proud to speak as good a French as he does* — and it demands above all that criticism be fair.

Most enthusiastic was the *Corriere delle Dame* — Bosco *won the admiration of a select audience ... hurry to the Teatro Re, gentle ladies, and enjoy a few hours of genuine delight...*

Il Figaro, reviewing that first show and his second on June 14th, summed up — *the judgments given so far by our newspapers on the "magical merits" of Signor Bosco are contradictory. Some have praised him to the sky, others have placed him rather too low. But all agree in praising the splendid and imposing apparatus ... and that he performs with great dexterity a number of tricks which if not new are certainly brilliant and well chosen... As for the ticket prices we do not know what to say. Bosco is entitled to value his skills at what he believes them to be worth, and equally the public can decide to attend his shows or not. We will soon see who has done their accounts better. However only half as many people attended his second show as the first, and a reduction in future prices is left to the arithmetical talent of the artist...* It hoped he would keep back some good new tricks, asked him to improve his spoken language, and demanded better, less "barbaric", music — *the orchestra should take pity, the ears of civilised people are not made of leather.*[232]

As *Il Figaro* noted, his second show on June 14th attracted only half the audience of his first, but this the *Corriere delle Dame* blamed not on the price of the tickets ("high prices have never frightened the Milanese") but on the "insufferable heat" and the smallness of the theatre, which, it said, had never done well in summer, especially with good competition playing at the other theatres in town. There was, however, "general applause".[233]

A third show followed on June 22nd. In this, *Il Figaro* tells us, he spoke only in French, but that, it said, *did not help — he does not seem born to be a good speaker... But this time he proved himself, executing with an uncommon mastery various graceful tricks which amazed a select and large audience... Where his skill was shown as truly prodigious was in making the most visible objects vanish from his own hands — with just one breath these seem to be destroyed and disappear into the air... and all done with such grace and calmness that the trick is made more beautiful, more delightful... Despite all this, there are still discontents who do not stop saying that Bosco's skill is not worth the price he places on the ticket. To win the praises of these too, it would be necessary for the talented magician to be able to send home the ill-tempered with more money in their pocket than they came in with...* And for the *Corriere delle Dame* this show "*began well and ended better*", he had kept back some new tricks, and the theatre was full.[234]

Bosco was then engaged to give two shows, on July 5th and 9th, at the *Teatro Carcarno*, which had suspended its usual dramatic fare to prepare for an upcoming opera.[235] At the second he advertised that he would be using for the first time the transparent cups, previously announced in Turin, but again they attracted no mention in any of the reviews. Both shows were very well received, despite the crowding and the hot weather,[236] and a further show was announced for July 23rd, but Bosco became unwell and that was delayed indefinitely.[237]

It was August 4th before he was well enough to perform again. The show was again a great success, but at four hours long more than one paper suggested it be broken up with musical intervals.[238] There were four more shows, on 8th, 13th, 15th, and the last, a benefit for Bosco, on 20th, all well attended.[239]

Next was Brescia, where he gave three successful shows at the *Teatro Grande* on September 15th, 17th and 20th ("una vera delizia", said the reviewer), then a fourth show for charity, with tickets half-price, on September 24th.[240]

By October 1st he was in Verona, and opened at the *Teatro Morando* on October 4th, winning "the admiration and applause of a select and large audience", with further shows following on October 7th and 11th.[241]

He is next sighted in Venice, performing at the *Teatro Apollo* on November 5th, 8th, 12th and 15th. All met with excellent reviews. While there he offered lessons as he had often done previously, contactable at his lodgings at "Casa Tassini Merceria dell' Orologio No.745".[242]

He then headed to Trieste, opening on December 2nd. The *Wanderer* correspondent reported that he gave three performances there while the theatre was preparing for the carnival, with "only modest attendance and applause"; in contrast, a very flattering review of the first show by regular *Allgemeine Theater-Zeitung* contributor Jacob Loewenthal, journalist and later economist, said that the audience numbered nearly 900, filling the hall, and filling it with applause.[243]

Passing through Venice he gave a single performance there on December 27th, this time in the *Antica Sala del Ridotto a S. Moisé*;[244] we then lose sight of him for a period.

1836

On March 3rd, 5th and 6th 1836 he gave three shows in Modena to large and enthusiastic crowds — despite the high ticket prices.[245] He is also said to have performed privately for the Duke of Parma on March 8th.

Four shows followed in Bologna at the *Teatro del Corso* on March 12th, 13th, 15th and 19th, all very successful.[246]

He then performed in Reggio Emilia on April 13th and 14th,[247] and on April 20th, 21st and 22nd in the *Ducale Teatro* in Parma.[248]

In Piacenza on April 27th in the *Teatro comunitativo* the audience included the Queen, and he performed there again on May 2nd to assist the Zocchi Comedy Company which had been having a bad run.[249]

Did he next go to Sicily? I believe not, and that his visit there took place the following year. It is improbable he had time in May 1836 to travel to Sicily and give four shows, as he was still in Piacenza on May 2nd and in Florence by May 10th.[251]

He opened in Florence at the *Teatro Goldoni* on May 31st with his usual 'Turandò l'Incantore', 30 separate tricks performed over three hours, with a ten minute interval. This received enthusiastic and prolonged applause from the "very select and large" audience, which included the Sovereign, the Royal family, and "his guest and relative, the King of Naples".[251]

Bosco, as usual, offered lessons in conjuring and had for sale magical apparatus "large and small". Shows followed on June 2nd, 4th, 9th, 11th, then more on 18th and 22nd, these all very successful.[252]

A review of June 18th announced he was soon leaving for Livorno, but it was probably September when he performed there. Bosco's letter of application to the *Governatore civile* of Livorno, Barone Giovanni Spannocchi Piccolomini, which survives in the Livorno Archives, is dated July 5th 1836,[253] but it seems clear that he was in Bagni di Lucca and Lucca prior to Livorno. A report from Lucca dated August 29th states that he recently gave three shows in the town of Bagni di Lucca, drawing poor crowds due to the high prices, and then advertised three shows at the *Teatro Nota in Lucca* for August 26th, 27th and 28th — with even worse results: "…The tickets were an extraordinary price for Lucca … hence the attendance was very small on the first night, even less on the second, and no one at all on the third, because —

because sig. Bosco had left for Livorno ... he will have reason to complain, but he had no reason to deceive the public in this way...".[254]

It would appear that Bosco travelled direct from Livorno to Naples, as according to *Curiose avventure* (p.16), when on his arrival he was suddenly invited by Maria Cristina, widow of Charles Felix, King of Sardinia, to perform at the *Real Villa della Favorita* in Ercolano, his apparatus had not yet arrived from Livorno. Nevertheless, we are told, he gave full satisfaction to Maria Cristina and to Ferdinand II, King of the Two Sicilies, and all the Royal family, and was well rewarded.

Curiose avventure then describes (p.17) what was apparently a second performance to the same audience at the same place, now with his apparatus duly arrived.

1837

His performance (but which one, if there were in fact two?) before Ferdinand II is dated by *Satanas* (claiming plausibly to be quoting Bosco's own album) to January 20th 1837.[255]

Because of the cholera outbreak Bosco had not been able to open immediately as planned at the *Teatro del Fondo*. He gave a charity show there for cholera victims,[256] then at least twelve further shows at the *Teatro del Fondo* in January and February 1837.[257] These won great acclaim, Bosco's superabundant flowers especially popular, said one review, but "Italian, his native language, did he learn to speak it? And his French still cripples him as before?".[258]

Bosco's next child, a son named Matteo Fortunato, was born in Naples on April 30th at Bosco's place of residence in the Largo del Castello and baptised on May 12th (see *Excursus on the Family*).

Did Bosco while in Naples reproduce the miracle of the liquefaction of the blood of St. Januarius (San Gennaro)? This is highly unlikely: considering what happened when Eugenio did this many years later we would have expected a lot of fuss in the contemporary newspapers, but there is nothing.[259]

It was probably at this time, in August or September 1837, that Bosco travelled to Sicily. We know that he gave four shows in Palermo: this is recorded in a contemporary note in *Annali di medicina omiopatica* [sic] *per la Sicilia*, Volume I, 1837 (url:033), pp.360-1, presumably by the editor Antonino de Blasi. This note is at the end of the 1837 volume, and p.359 refers to October ("in questo mese do ottobre") — the journal was published every two months in fascicles of at least 16 pages (p.366).

A date late in 1837 for Bosco in Sicily is confirmed by another reference, an enthusiastic review of his performance at the *Real Teatro di Santa Cecilia* written by the radical journalist and writer Salvatore Costanza. This was not published until 1839,[260] but a footnote at the end of the article states that Bosco first landed in Sicily more than a year before this (n.3: "or volge meglio di un anno") and — the significant point — that articles on Bosco appeared in issues 5, 6 and 9 of Costanza's own journal *Il Siciliano, Giornale di scienze, amena letterature, e belle arti*: this journal lasted from 20 June 1837 to 1 February 1838, published every fifteen days,[261] meaning issues 5, 6 and 9 date between August 26th and October 25th 1837, so Bosco's visit was about those dates.

1838

The evidence suggests that Bosco remained in Sicily and then in southern Italy for some months. On February 9th and 11th 1838 he performed in Reggio at the *Real*

Teatro Borbonio, and reporting this the local newspaper states he has recently appeared successfully in the leading cities of Sicily.[262]

By April he was back in Naples. On April 23rd he gave one performance at the newly reopened *Teatro San Carlo*, a two hour show 'Turandò l'Incantatore', which was preceded by a musical farce 'Valeria, ossia la cieca'.[263]

Meanwhile at the *Teatro San Carlino* a comedy by Orazio Schiano had opened on April 20th, 'Chieppe lo Smargiasso, ossia I ridicoli giuochi di Pulcinella e Pangrazio Biscegliese, sciocchi professori di Magia Egiziana', clearly making fun of Bosco, the description soon altered to leave no doubt: "I ridicoli giochi del Cavalier Bosco". The play ran (with some breaks) until at least June.[264]

A report in some distant papers[265] states that Bosco performed for the Royal court in Naples on April 30th, and "suddenly produced flowers by magic from the floor round where the Queen was sitting", adding that Bosco's shows were so crowded that "even the theatres envy him his rich takings".

In late April the *Diario di Roma* announced that Bosco would soon be in "questa Capitale" from Naples and intended to perform there once he received official permission.[266] He had arrived by May 17th but at the end of month it was reported that he had been unable to come to terms with the *impresarij* of the *Teatro Argentina* or the *Teatro Valle*,[267] and finally on June 4th he opened in a ground floor room of the *Palazzo Ruspoli,* stressing in his advertisement that the room had been reduced in size "like an amphitheatre" to allow better communication with and viewing by the spectators. He announced that his repertoire consisted of 100 tricks, of which 25 would be shown on each night, and, since the venue could hold only a moderate number of spectators, he would continue to repeat the same tricks for as many shows as were needed for everyone to enjoy them, then would announce on posters when the programme was being changed.[268]

This first show was repeated on June 6th and on two further nights, then on June 12th came "part two of his repertoire", billed as 25 tricks all different from those "in the first four shows", except the crystal cup and balls (the "*palli invisibile*"); and the second show was repeated on June 15th and 17th. A review praised his dexterity, as did the audience, especially liking the resurrected birds, plates and watches, and the disappearing large calibre cannon ball, later found in a vase where a suckling pig had been placed, the pig mysteriously disappearing from the vase and found alive in a loaf of bread.[269]

Further shows there presumably followed, then at the end of the month we hear that he is to open at the large *Teatro di Torre Argentina*, three shows on June 30th and July 3rd and 6th, each now with 30 tricks not 25, none repeated except the "palle invisibili". The third show, *Il coraggio di Napoleone al campo,* was advertised as ending with a "military manoeuvre" under Bosco's orders, and (once again) also as featuring the *first* use of the crystal cups. He was also offering lessons in conjuring and could be contacted at "vicolo de' Barbieri num.21".[270]

We then hear that in a few days Bosco will be leaving for Senigallia to perform there during the fair. But before leaving he gave probably two shows, the last on July 13th, at the *Mausoleo di Augusto*.[271] This was in fact *L'Anfiteatro Corea*, the large unroofed theatre built on the ruins of the Mausoleum, and Bosco's appearance here was not a success. We know this from references in several letters by the poet

Giuseppe Gioachino Belli. Writing to Giacomo Ferretti on July 12th he described Bosco's show as "turning out very badly" with "whistling (*fischietto*) running round the theatre". Bosco was, as Belli had written to Ferretti on July 5th, *very busy and tired ... his health is limping along ... and he has a cough*, and saying on the 7th that at his show the previous night Bosco *promised all new material, even promised it aloud on stage, but it was all old stuff, ending with his shooting act, which is very weak* (sciapa - *bland*), and the audience *grumbled a lot*; and more of the same on 13th: *as I write this Turando the wizard opens his last show at the Corea, billed as all new but all old tricks, people are grumbling about outrageous conduct and bungles...*

Belli also writes earlier of Bosco visiting his house (he was out) and *made the women's heads spin (doesn't take much) — Giovanni Battista is engraving his portrait —* on Monday at the Caffé nuovo *he made the seats and chandeliers disappear —* Bosco's problem with venues: he is *concerned about "Impresario Iacoacci"* (Vincenzo Jacovacci of the Teatro Valle), *Bosco may come back and perform when the Argentina is empty; the Alibert is too far; and the Tardinona, well... on Sunday he was arguing at the pallone game with Iacovacci and Mitterpoch and Tassinari — Bosco has made plenty of money —* then visiting Bosco, finding him unwell — *he is struggling a lot in the Argentina theatre: at least ten times more than in that room on the ground floor of Ruspoli...* and later he says he is finishing his Bosco poem, *not to be published either in print or in pen, but only passable for a recitation in the Tiberine Academy on the 23rd... God save us from tomatoes!* [272]

Belli's was not the only poem on Bosco to appear while Bosco was in Rome. In the *Diario di Roma* 21 June 1838 was published a Latin poem in his honour by the botanist Michelangelo Poggioli, accompanied by an Italian paraphrase by Giuseppe Cocchi, di Todi.[273]

Presumably Bosco did perform in Senigallia, and possibly with Alessandro Lanari, "il napoleone degli impresari".[274] There is nothing to suggest that Bosco then left Italy: *Satanas* wrongly has him in Algeria in 1838 and Robert-Houdin wrongly has him in Paris that year.[275]

In September Bosco was in Perugia, where he gave three successful shows at the *Teatro del Pavone* on September 29th and 30th and October 1st.[276]

One report puts Bosco in Naples in early November, but there is no listing for him there at this period in *Programma giornaliero degli spettacoli...*[277]

At the end of November he was back in Rome, where he gave two shows at the *Teatro Alibert* on December 2nd and 5th.[278] These were very well attended, said the Rome correspondent of a German newspaper writing on December 8th, noting that the theatres were all closed and Rome was full of foreigners who crowded into his shows — so many English tourists there that, especially when a cloud of fog came down, it seemed like one was in London.[279]

This means that Bosco could well still have been in Rome on Wednesday, January 9th (see Rusconi p.105), when he is said to have performed at the great reception and ball given by Prince Alessandro Torlonia for the heir to the Russian throne, Tsesarevich Alexander Nikolaevich (later Alexander II). But is there a contemporary source that places Bosco there? He is not mentioned in the detailed account in *Diario di Roma* of this "festa splendidissima", which names even some of the singers in the musical performances (given in a "teatrina" inside a "galleria").[280]

Which does not, of course, mean that Bosco was not present, but two days later, on Friday 11th, he was performing in Naples, more than 200 km away.[281]

1839

In Naples he performed at the *Teatro del Fondo* on January 11th, 13th and 14th, billed as "after a silence of about eight months" — it was indeed eight months since he last performed in Naples.[282]

Bosco remained in Naples until at least mid-February, performing at various theatres, first at the *Teatro Nuovo* with shows on January 25th and February 1st, then a final show there on February 9th; this lasted only one and a half hours and was preceded by a melodrama.[283]

He then gave three (possibly more) shows at the *Teatro S. Ferdinando* on February 10th, 11th and 17th, the first two of which (and probably all) also included an opera.[284]

He may have soon returned to Rome, but the only source is the brief note in *Satanas* that he performed before the "Cardinals of the Conclave" in April and May 1839. There are no references in *Diario di Roma* to Bosco being in town at this time.[285]

In late June Bosco was in the south of Sicily. His presence there was recorded in police surveillance reports: on June 22nd he was noted as having arrived in Terranova (now Gela) from Licata, and on July 1st as having left Terranova, accompanied by three other foreigners, Giuseppe Casciola from Foligno, Giacomo Rosselli from Paschiaro, and Salvatore Suttana from Malta. These may have been his staff, or simply fellow travellers.[286]

Bosco boarded the French steamer *Tancrède,* which had sailed from Marseille via Malta. He planned to sail to Athens, but got only as far as Syra in the Cyclades, then a major port. There on July 20th he met the orientalist Comte Eusèbe de Salle, sailing from Piraeus on the *Dante*, who describes[287] Bosco entertaining his fellow passengers with his vivacity and his curious Italian ("de son verve et de son jargon italien"). They told Bosco that Athens was currently sated with the tricks of the young French magician Rodolphe[288] and suggested he go instead to Alexandria, then in jubilation following the Viceroy's successes over the Sultan. So the *Tancrède* with de Salle on board sailed on to Smyrna, but Bosco headed to Alexandria.

The earliest we hear of him there is on July 27th: Bosco has arrived on a French steamship and is planning to give shows at the theatre.[289] Then a long account sent on August 12th titled 'Bosco à la Cour du Pharaon Moderne' by the Alexandria correspondent of the Marseille paper *Le Sémaphore*, after an opening essay on Egyptian magicians ancient and modern, reports Bosco's arrival and his performance in the Palace of the Viceroy before Muhammad Ali himself, numerous palace attendants of all ranks, and invited leading citizens and businessmen — but no women allowed.[290]

A rich and philanthropic local businessman, M. d'A.- -, soon had Bosco give a performance in a huge room in his "magnificent mansion" to which many guests, male and female, were invited. Bosco then gave three shows at the Théâtre Français, reopened for the occasion after a long break.[291]

On September 6th the same correspondent sent a further report of a "brilliant *soirée*" given on August 23rd by the British Consul-General, Major-General Patrick

Campbell, with Bosco among those performing for the large and wide circle of guests, male and female, which included the Egyptian Admiral and the Turkish Vice-Admiral. The evening concluded with a ball, the music provided by pupils of Donizetti's brother, Giuseppe ("Donizetti Pasha").[292]

A glimpse, apparently authentic, of Muhammad Ali's reaction to Bosco's wizardry is found in Scipion Marin's account of his time in Egypt:[293]

> Night fell; there was a gathering at the palace for Bosco's magical performance. The pasha maintained a sublime serenity, except for the whole time that the wizard's devilries filled the room with lightning flashes, ghostly glows, sudden darkness, and baleful lights. For one must tell the truth and say that Mohammad Ali, this great and intelligent man, believed in all this wizardry, these pyrotechnic tricks. No one could have convinced him that the devil wasn't behind it. He kept his distance when Bosco moved round the room. Out of politeness the magician offered to teach him some of the tricks that had most impressed the gathering: Mashallah! God forbid, he cried.

And how much, *if any*, credibility are we to place in the romance of Bosco's time in Alexandria found in 'Der Dämon der Magie: Memoiren aus B. Bosco's Leben, mitgetheilt von Kleroth' (tr.'The Demon of Magic: Memories of Bosco's Life, imparted by Kleroth'; *Fiction* F11), published in the 25th annual volume of the literary miscellany of curiosities, *Erinnerungen an merkwürdige Gegenstände und Begebenheiten,* published in Prague in 1845?

This is nothing but an amusing epistolary novella. Significantly it opens with an eerie midnight encounter between the author and Bosco, who gives him a bouquet of flowers — which, when he gets home, has turned into a packet of scented papers containing this story, a sure pointer as to how we are to regard it. And in the Contents of the book it is listed under 'Erzählungen und Novellen' — in a word: *fiction*. The author, "Kleroth", was the Prague-born *littérateur* Clemens von Wey(h)rother, 1809-76, who left the law out of a desire to tell stories ("die Lust zum 'Fabuliren'", as the *Allgemeine Deutsche Biographie* account of him puts it). He was a frequent contributor to *Ost und West* and *Erinnerungen* in Prague and to Saphir's *Der Humorist* in Vienna. I have not yet been able to confirm whether the Bosco stories were included in his *Licht und Schatten* (1845) or *Bilder und Skizzen* (1846), both collections of "Novellen und Erzählungen". The story, entertaining enough, tells (via what purports to be a series of letters written variously by Bosco to his wife in Bologna, by an Austrian countess in Alexandria, by a certain Abdul in Alexandria and his beloved Zoraide, and by Muhammad Ali no less) how Bosco entranced Ali into sparing Zoraide, whom he had chosen for his harem, and into renouncing his wicked ways and retiring to Mecca.

All delightful nonsense. Whether there are any genuine nuggets of truth regarding Bosco's daughters is discussed — and dismissed — in the *Excursus on Family*.

From Alexandria Bosco was summoned to Cairo by Abbas Pasha, grandson of Muhammad Ali and his eventual successor, who rewarded him well.

Bosco now headed to Smyrna, arriving there by October 24th,[294] then by November 27th he was in Constantinople. And so was Rodolphe.[295]

As there were no suitable venues for public performances, Bosco gave several successful private shows, including one for Mustafa Reşid Pasha, recently returned from his post as Ottoman Ambassador to France and then London.[296] He also performed twice for the Sultan, 16 year old Abdulmejid I, and the court "on two successive nights". The date of this is uncertain, but probably in late December.[297]

It appears that Bosco remained in Constantinople, or at least in Turkey, for several months, though the accounts are inconsistent (and confused by sensational anecdotes in *Satanas*). On June 2nd he is said to have performed for the Sultan in his palace, with his harem enjoying it from inside latticed boxes,[298] and on September 29th to have given a third performance in the Sultan's new palace for him and the whole of the harem.[299]

Several European papers quote the new Turkish newspaper *Ceride-i Havadis* ("Journal of News") published in Constantinople from July 30 1840 by Englishman William Nosworthy Churchill (both his name and the newspaper's variously spelt at the time). The second issue of August 9th reported that Bosco had been allowed by the Sultan to build a theatre opposite the new medical school in Galata (Pera, modern Karaköy, then the largely European section of Constantinople). The theatre is described as wooden, circular, seating 500 to 600, and decorated in the latest style. Bosco, we are told, performed there on August 12th, 16th, 18th, 19th, 23rd, 26th and 30th, while continuing to give private shows and lessons, and also performing for the Sultan in his palace.[300]

At the end of October one report announced he had by then left Constantinople, to travel to Pest and then to Vienna;[301] however, there is no mention of his being there in the Austrian newspapers, and for the rest of this year, and for 1841, we lose sight of him almost entirely.

1841

As the newspapers say nothing of him for so long, an extended period with his wife and children seems likely, then, since he was in Russia by early 1842, perhaps a long slow trip north via Odessa or Kiev, but there is no evidence for that — apart from one reference to him having performed for the Grand Duchess Helena in the Ukraine prior to performing for her in St. Petersburg (see note 306).

1842

By early 1842 at the latest Bosco was in Moscow, and by April 1842 at the earliest he was in St. Petersburg.

We are given a detailed but suspiciously self-congratulatory account of Bosco's time in St Petersburg in an article titled 'Souvenirs de Russie',[302] written by our friend Scipion Marin (note 293), who had seen Bosco in Egypt in 1839, and now takes credit for Bosco's success in St. Petersburg. Marin, after describing Bosco's performance before the Viceroy in Alexandria, tells us he had met Bosco again in Moscow the previous winter — early 1842 — and it was there that Bosco had assisted in the masked ball with tombola for the benefit of the poor organised by the *Association Française de Bienfaisance,* described in *Satanas* and its transaltions.[303] Marin then travelled with Bosco from Moscow to St. Petersburg. But Bosco, says Marin, was soon in despair. He had arrived in the shadow of Liszt,[304] whose concerts had enraptured the royal family and the aristocracy (*Lisztomanie* as Heine called it), and they were now leaving the city for their country estates: for Bosco St Petersburg was spoiled. This dates Bosco's arrival in St Petersburg to late April 1842 at the earliest.[305] Worse, summoned by General Kleinmichel, Bosco not only arrived late (as Marin tells it) but the Czar who had also happened to be there had left, greatly displeased. Marin offered to secure him a performance before the Czar, who had retired to his summer palace at Tsarskoye Selo. Through his contacts he learnt what papers the Czar read and seeded them with articles on Bosco's successes in Egypt, thus piquing the Czar's interest and winning him an invitation to the court. The Royal family were enchanted with his performance, particularly when he "read the Czar's thoughts". Soon there were invitations from Grand Duchess Helena, wife of the Czar's youngest brother,[306] and other members of the aristocracy, and he was allowed to perform for the public at the Alexandra Theatre.

All, says Scipion, thanks to me. The chronology, if not every detail, of this account seems to be correct. We know from reports in Latvian papers that Bosco opened at the Alexandra Theatre on May 17th and closed there on June 3rd,[307] and in July he was still in St Petersburg, giving a final show on July 5th at the *Anstalt für künstliche Mineralwasser*.[308]

He then headed to Stockholm, via Finland, performing in Helsinki on August 19th, 21st and 23rd,[309] and was then expected in Turku (Åbo).[310] He arrived there on August 28th on the steamer *Fürst Menschikoff* from Helsinki, accompanied by his wife; also travelling with them was a young dancer, Adele Delaune, and her mother.[311] But he proceeded straight to Stockholm, having promised to perform in Turku on his return journey to St Petersburg later in the year.[312]

He opened in Stockholm at *Kirsteinska huset* on September 10th, and "[tr.] To further increase the interest of his *soirée*, M. Bosco has engaged Mamsell Adèle, 12 years old, pupil of the renowned Taglioni, and *danseuse* at the Imperial Opera House in St Petersburg, who will have the honour of performing for the audience at the end of each representation".[313] Similar shows followed on 15th, 18th, and he then headed back towards St Petersburg.[314]

He arrived in Turku on September 24th with his wife and Delaune and her mother, and gave shows there with her on September 29th and October 2nd and 6th.[315]

Bosco, now without Delaune, gave one show in Helsinki on October 12th,[316] and also performed in Porvoo[317] and in Vyborg, closing there on November 6th.[318]

He then returned to St Petersburg and was said to be planning to spend the whole winter there, but in December it was reported that he was instead leaving for Riga, Warsaw, and then Paris.[319]

1843

At the end of January he was in Dorpat (now Tartu in Estonia),[320] in February in Riga, and possibly also in Pleskow (Pskow), then on February 21st he gave one show in Werro (Võru) during the fair, but we are told that despite "doing the best business at the fair", filling the large hall despite the high prices, he left most of the audience unsatisfied — the same old tricks… "and he hastened his departure".[321]

In early March he arrived from Riga in Mitau (Jelgava), giving shows on March 11th and 14th; a long review praised his skill and his affability, recalling his successful earlier visit there in 1824.[322] He then returned to Riga, performing in the *Blaugardschen Haus*, in Marstallstraße, to a wider public.[323] On April 6th he is passing through Mitau,[324] and we next hear of him in Wilna (Vilnius) in early May, where he gave three shows in the *Rathhaussaal*, earning him 1500 Roubles, and then a fourth show at the theatre on behalf of a needy singer, whom the paper refrains from naming. From there Bosco made his way to Poland.[325]

By June he was in Warsaw. He opened on June 17th in the concert hall at Pac Palace (*Pałac Paca*), the seating re-arranged like an amphitheatre to ensure a good view for all. There was a full house — and even Bosco, joked a reviewer, could not multiply the number of tickets to let everyone attend who wished to.[326] Further shows followed on June 20th, 24th, 27th, always with new tricks ("his repertoire is inexhaustible") and still attracting large audiences.[327] Yet more followed on July 1st, 4th, 8th,[328] and what was announced to be his final show on July 15th, which he promised would include 125 tricks, 12 completely new and specially kept to the end.[329]

Bosco evidently then remained in Warsaw, as he gave three further shows in August (13th, 20th, 27th) at the Heca Amphitheatre.[330]

He then headed to Lublin, announcing three shows — "though the magician may double the number (as in Warsaw)…",[331] and in October he gave three shows in Kalisz, on 15th, 16th and 17th, all very well attended.[332]

In November he was in Breslau (Wrocław) at the "New Theatre" — "unprecedented enthusiasm", said one review, "… all the men are infatuated with him, all the women have fallen in love with him".[333] He was there until early December, advertisements announcing that Bosco would give two final performances in the "Old Theatre" on December 7th and 10th between an orchestral concert and songs by Nina Morra, Bosco's tricks being entirely new, "never given here before".[334] All his shows sold out, high prices notwithstanding.[335]

According to a long promotional piece in the Poznań paper, where he was next expected, he gave twelve shows in all in Breslau.[336] One account has Bosco's Breslau audience fighting over the bouquets of flowers he handed out, so that the little *Sträußchen* (bouquets) ended up as one big *Strauß* (a bunch, but also a scuffle, *a bunch of fives* perhaps), with blood spilt — "Now there are two opposing parties in Breslau — the Bouquetists and the Anti-Bouquetists: what effect these parties will have on the European balance of power remains to be seen".[337] And the same paper reprinted from the *Breslauer Zeitung* a version of the old story of Bosco finding money in butter being sold at a market, here told in Silesian dialect ("…doas wär da Pusko…") by the farmer himself in nearby Trachenberg (now Żmigród) but set in "Brassel" (Breslau).[338]

Also about this time we first encounter what is surely the most bizarre Bosco anecdote of all, 'How Bosco Became Famous'. It is not terribly complimentary to him and does not extol his skills in any way, and did not make its way into *Satanas* or any of the other booklets about him. We are told that early in his career he went under the names Michalief, Lutzaris, Boghos, Wormser, or Herodes (these variously spelt) and claimed to be Chinese, Hindu or Persian, and had no success at all — until he took the name of Bosco in London making a poor living by performing in the streets and on the Thames in a cork vehicle drawn by four geese, but fame and prosperity came only when he was taken up by an unnamed aristocrat and lionised. As the geese had saved the Capitol, so they saved Bosco. Now successful, he had a large property built in Italy, with marble statues of geese outside, and is said to keep a flock of geese, never killed or eaten.

The earliest sighting of this odd story is in French, in *La Presse* 3 Oct.1843. It soon appeared in German, in the Supplement to the *Mitauische Zeitung* of 25 Oct.1843; then in *ATZ* 2 Nov.1843; *Der Adler* 9 Nov.1843, *Zuschauer* [Riga] 13 Nov.1843, *Österreichisches Bürgerblatt* 17 Nov.1843, and in other German papers. It appeared in Polish in *Kurjer Warszawski* 13 Nov.1843 (crediting the *Gazeta Wiedenska* — the *Wiener Zeitung*), and in Italian under the title 'Le oche del Gicoliere' in the annual anthology *Il Mietitore o sia raccolta di racconti, novelle, storie aneddote ecc.,* Volume 3, published in Venice in 1843: the exact date in 1843 this was published is unknown but I do not believe it was the earliest publication of the story as it states "disposte e tradotte [edited and *translated*] da Giannantonio Piucco" (a well-known translator of French works into Italian). The anecdote appeared again in French in *Messager de Gand* 25 Feb.1855 and in German in the long anecdotal obituary of Bosco in *Fremden Blatt* 18 Apr.1866 (the only version which gives a name to the English aristocrat who helped Bosco: Beau Brumell, *i.e.* Brummell); again in *Thorner Zeitung* (published in Toruń) 17 Nov.1906 (under the title 'Vom Zauberkünstler Bosco') and last found in the Luxembourg *Obermosel-Zeitung* 7 Mar.1907.

1844

Bosco opened in Posen (Poznań) on January 26th, performing again on 28th and 30th. There were the usual comments on the high prices but all the shows drew good audiences.[339] Before leaving he gave a final extra show on February 2nd, just of "12 entirely new tricks", preceding the exhibition by Louis Wlach, highly-regarded for his performances as a "living statue", imitating classical works.[340]

In late February he arrived in Berlin, and opened at the Jagorschen Saale on March 7th.[341] This was not a great success, blamed on the small venue and high prices, and when Döbler also arrived and began performing Bosco left the city to Döbler, as various newspaper suggested he should, and performed in the surrounding area.[342]

He returned to Berlin the following month and opened on April 11th at the larger Königsstädtischen Theater (where Döbler had been — he had given eighteen shows there), and here Bosco was a great success, attracting large crowds.[343]

One incident at the Königsstädtischen Theater did not go down well: he did his pretending to trip act, falling off the stage into the orchestra pit, and when he eventually emerged with his arm covered in blood, announced that he could not continue. Later when it all proved to be an act the reaction was: "He should have been hissed off the stage, he can play with cards and rabbits, but not with the good feelings of people".[344]

The resident comic actor at the Königsstadt Theatre since it opened in 1824 was the very popular Friedrich ("Fritz") Beckmann, and in May, towards the end of Bosco's run at the theatre, Beckmann had his benefit, in which Bosco played a part. There are various accounts of this but unfortunately the contemporary Berlin papers are not accessible online. The earliest reference found is in *Der Humorist* of 23 May 1844, not as a satirical piece but in its regular Berlin theatre report, 'Einsiedler's

Bericht aus Berlin'. This merely tells us that the benefit was a great success and that taking part were Bosco, some dancers from the Königliche Bühne, and Beckmann's wife, soubrette Adele Muzzarelli. The Stralsund paper, *Sundine,* quoting a report from Berlin, soon gave a longer account (29 May 1844): the curtain rose and up stepped a man in a mask dressed just like Bosco but when he opened his mouth to speak everyone shouted "It's Beckmann"; it was announced that Bosco had agreed to perform but was out of town, so the beneficiary had decided to do a few tricks himself. He began with the cup and balls but the audience were soon laughing at him, and the tricks got worse and worse. Then he noticed Bosco's magic wand, lost all his awkwardness, and conjured up Bosco himself; he fell into Bosco's arms, and the real Bosco in his black coat began his usual consummate performance.[345]

The Germanisches Nationalmuseum (Nürnberg) has a letter from Bosco dated May 8th 1844 from Berlin to "Edinger".[346] The recipient is unidentified but could well have been Burchard Edinger, the lithographer, who at this time was in Hamburg where Bosco was heading. But there is no evidence that he produced a portrait of Bosco.

Bosco arrived in Hamburg in late May.[347] He was travelling from Potsdam (so may have performed there briefly) and we know he was accompanied by one of his daughters.[348]

He opened at the Stadttheater on June 1st, his performance preceded by a farce, 'Der Corporal'. Despite the summer heat he drew large audiences, and was also to be seen performing in markets, restaurants and coffee-houses.[349] In Hamburg Bosco made a very strong impression on young and old alike, and in his sixth show he fired small souvenirs at the audience, bon bons and cigars, and small pieces of paper with an invitation to his final benefit-performance on July 22nd —"Avant qu' ick Ihnen sag' Adieu, / Je veux tous Vous remercier!".[350]

In July he moved on to Lüneburg, where he gave two shows, then five in Hannover, and intending also to perform in Braunschweig.[351]

Der Humorist announced on September 5th, in its 'Bunterlei' section, "quoting" No.274 of the *Allgemeiner Mondezeitung,* edited by *Count Saint-Germain,* that on August 23rd, Bartolomeo Bosco, great grandson of Merlin, had given, at prices increased five-fold, a performance of Egyptian magic on the moon, the first magician to do so...

He was in fact in Leipzig, his arrival hailed in the papers in glowing terms, "[tr.] ... Bosco is here, the arch sorcerer, whose imitators find honour in merely advertising themselves as Bosco's pupil ... yet merely a reflection of Bosco's glory. But now Bosco himself is here, the unreachable original, and not a bland copy...[*etc., etc.*]". The *Leipziger Tageblatt* went on at length: "...Some call him the Napoleon of magicians, others the Shakespeare of sorcerers, others again the Sirius of wizards. Others say he is a new Zoroaster, or a second Philadelphia, or Pinetti and Döbler combined... Many years ago we saw him here as a *Tausendkünstler,* now he is a *Billionenkünstler*...". And it has a long account of Bosco sitting dining with Oettinger at the Hotel de Pologne when who should come walking towards them but Bosco himself... impossible to believe, but true — read it in the *Charivari*...[352]

He remained in Leipzig from September to November, giving twenty two performances during the Fair, first to booksellers and students in the *Buchhändler-*

Börse then in his own theatre, "an amphitheatrical *salon*" which he "conjured forth" on the Königsplatz, and which was much more spacious; this was so popular that the tickets sold out within half an hour.[353]

The reviews were good but the *Zeitung für die elegante Welt* (18 Sep.1844) felt after his first show that his tricks fell "below his reputation … well executed, but of the usual sort, and in his act he fires off a lot of gun powder which was not good manners for an elegant magician even twenty years ago. Perhaps he wanted to start off modestly and then build up. He will have to do so or he will not stand up against Philippe who made such an impression here in earlier fairs…".

Also in town during the Fair was the Cuzent & Lejars Circus and a nice illustrated article in the *Illustrirte Zeitung* of 16 Nov.1844 compares their skilful lady *equestrienne* with the by now well-endowed friendly Italian who describes his wonders in four different broken languages, he with grace in his fingers, she with grace in her feet.

Bosco then performed in Altenburg and in Halle[354] before reaching Dresden in November.[355]

He had attracted huge crowds in Leipzig and did well enough in Dresden, but the reviewers were not always as enthusiastic as the public. One review of his Leipzig shows had said that, despite the large and appreciative audiences, Bosco had little new to offer, and while he was expert in vanishing tricks, everything else Döbler and Philippe did better — "his reputation is greater than his art".[356] And there were similar comments in Dresden — "he certainly offers little that is new, and for all his skill restricts himself mainly to the lower reaches — double bottoms and gunshot effects… Conjuring, like masquerades, is going more and more out of fashion…".[357]

"We were very pleased with him here", said one Dresden reviewer, "but not infatuated as in Leipzig",[358] and he went on to comment on Bosco's war of words ("Federduell") with Robert Schmieder of the *Dresdner Abendzeitung,* whose harsh reviews were an attack on Bosco's reputation. Bosco promptly reprinted the offensive passages in the rival *Dresdner Tageblatt* with a note saying that he was making them available to a wider public because fewer people were now reading the *Abendzeitung* because of Schmieder's severe critiques.

In the end Bosco had to close earlier in Dresden than he, and the public, hoped, because the area where he had pitched his tent was required for the mustering of conscripts.

One product of his time in Dresden was a polka, the 'Bosco-Galopp' for piano by Gustav Kunze.[359]

The Universitätsbibliothek Leipzig has a 2 leaf manuscript in French written by Bosco in Dresden on November 30th, titled 'Pour moi tous les pays'.[360]

1845

By January 4th Bosco was in Prague, but unwell, and delayed opening until 9th when he gave a show for the pupils of the Piarist Hostel.[361] There were also problems with the cold weather and the lack of suitable venues during the *Carneval* (solved by "magically" — and expensively — converting the Cuzent & Lejars Circus into a comfortable "Conversations-Salon" with footwarmers). He opened there on January 19th, with further shows on 21st and 26th, all well attended and warmly reviewed ("amazing … incredible … and his speed and dexterity give a new interest even to familiar tricks...").³⁶² He also gave a number of private shows, notably before Archduke Stephan, Governor of Bohemia, on February 6th.³⁶³

It was then announced he would give a Grand Farewell Show ("große außerordentliche Abschiedsvorstellung") at midday on Sunday February 23rd in the concert room on Sophieninsel (Žofínský ostrov, now Slovanský ostrov). This went off very well, and he was engaged to give three further daytime shows there on February 25th, 27th and March 2nd, each preceded by a farce or a concert. For these Bosco wore not his *Sammtcostume* but a black dress coat. These all had a full house, and were followed by a final benefit performance on March 5th.³⁶⁴

The Prague papers were full of Bosco news, reviews and anecdotes, with an explosion of Bosco fiction and fantasy published there while or soon after he was in town.

Ost und West and its supplement *Prag* made much of his performances being billed as "Egyptian Magic", their reviews of his shows saying more about Bosco in Egypt or Constantinople than about the actual shows, and it farewelled him (and his spirits) with a humorous story '[tr.] A Visit to Bosco'.³⁶⁵

The entertaining series of sketches, purely fictitious, by "Kleroth" (the Prague writer Clemens Weyroth), 'Der Dämon der Magie: Memoiren aus B. Bosco's Leben', published in the 25th annual volume of the miscellany *Erinnerungen an merkwürdige Gegenstände und Begebenheiten* (*Fiction* F11) is discussed above under Bosco's time in Egypt and below in detail in *Excursus on Family* (pp.42, 49, 211).

Moritz Saphir, who had been writing Bosco pieces since 1828, published 'Der ewige Bosco' ('Bosco the eternal') in *Wiener Bazar* no.12 (a weekly supplement to his *Der Humorist* of 15 Mar.1845). This has Bosco as 'the eternal magician' ("Ahasver, der ewige Jude, ist eine wahre Fabel gegen Bosco, den ewigen Zauberer!") putting black heads on Noah's white doves and performing Moses' magic for the Pharaoh, and much else...

Another Bosco fantasy appeared in *Bohemia* in seven instalments in February, 'Bartolomeo Bosco: Ein Capriccio in Callot-Hoffmann'scher Manier', written by J. P. Lyser. Lyser, actually Ludwig Peter August Burmeister, 1804-1870, born in Flensburg, was both a painter and a writer and here alludes to both E.T.A. Hoffmann and Jacques Callot. Bosco arrives from Leipzig in an unnamed German town where he plays some tricks on the philosopher, editor and lawyer Staarpuntzel who disbelieves in magic, finally sending him as an ink blob (*Dintenklex*) on a letter to a Brahmin on the Ganges in Dschinnistan (Wieland's fairy land) where he is turned instead into a poet and humorist, which he hates. He is returned by the same method to Saphir in Vienna but he goes mad...

Also originating from Prague at this time is the intriguing book, *Reise-Bilder aus dem Leben Boscos in zwölf Sprachen...* by Felix Francesconi (a Professor of Languages at the Karl-Ferdinands-Universität in Prague), published in German in Vienna and Prague (with editions in Czech, English, French, Greek, Italian, Hungarian, Polish, Portuguese, Russian, Spanish and Turkish promised, to be translated by his pupils).

The book gives a colourful account of Bosco's arrival in Alexandria, and, after a discourse on Isis and early Egyptian magic, his meeting with Muhammad Ali, his retinue, and European dignitaries. Bosco then visits the Great Pyramid, climbing it (and writing his name) then penetrating deep into an inner chamber not entered for thousands of years, where a Spirit hands him the Golden key to the Book of Secrets...

And this was only part one, Bosco in Egypt; part two was to be Bosco in Turkey. The book was widely noticed in the newspapers, first mentioned in *ATZ* 15 Feb. 1845, and then referred to in that paper on 26 March 1845 as now published. It was sold (both in bookshops and at Bosco's performances) for *20 fr. G. M.*, or *30 fr. G. M.* with a portrait of him. One surviving copy is known, a second edition (probably an unchanged reprint of the first), at the National Library of the Czech Republic, and this is available online.[366]

The journal *Passavia,* issued in Passau (*Pasavia* in Italian, *Pasov* in Czech) in Bavaria, where Bosco had not performed (as far as we know) since 1820, also published a series of Bosco anecdotes and stories in early 1845.

The first, 'Die Champagner-Gäste' (*Passavia* 13 Jan.1845, pp.1-2) is set in Hamburg; the second 'Bosco unter den Räubern' (*Passavia* 15 Jan.1845 pp.1-3; 16 Jan.1845 pp.1-2; 17 Jan.1845 pp.1-2) is set in Italy.

The next story, 'Wer kann daraus klug werden?' attributed to Oettinger (*Passavia* 21 Jan.1845), is followed by a shorter story, 'Der Teufel im Gasthofe'.

The last two in this sequence are 'Die Sängerin und der kleine Sänger' (*Passavia* 26 Jan.1845 pp.1-2), and 'Bei der Königlichen *Soirée* in Versailles' (*Passavia* 29 Jan.1845, pp.1-2), the latter an extended anecdote about Bosco performing for Louis Philippe.

The author of 'Die Sängerin und der kleine Sänger' (here anonymous) was Hermann Kothe, 1822-1859, who made a career of lecturing and writing on the technique of memory, calling himself variously a *Mnemoniker, Gedächtnißlehrer*, or *Gedächtnißkünstler*. In his 1848 book *Lehrbuch der Mnemonik oder Gedächtnißkunst* he quotes passages from various books with the consonants turned into numbers for easy(?) memorising, including, pp.113-5, 'Die Sängerin und der kleine Sänger', which he states is taken from his own book *Teufeleien des neunzehnten Jahrhunderts.* He probably also wrote 'Bei der Königlichen Soirée in Versailles', and he certainly wrote 'Ein Visite des Teufels, Ein sehr harmlose Bagatelle', published anonymously (*Passavia* 13, 14 June 1845; the second instalment ends with "continuation follows" but may be complete).

His book *Bosco, Teufeleien des neunzehnten Jahrhunderts,* appeared in two parts in 1844 and 1845, published on commission by Theodor Thomas in Leipzig. The *Allgemeines Bücher-Lexikon* gives Part 1 as 'Bosco hier, Bosco da, Bosco dort' (with a portrait of Bosco), Part 2 as 'Krieg den Schnurrbärten. Ein Visite des Teufels'. Part 1 is listed in the November 1844 book trade monthly (*Monatliches Verzeichnis der Neuigkeiten und Fortsetzungen des deutschen Buchhandels*, No.11, Monat November 1844) and in newspapers as for sale in late December (earliest found: *Nürnberger Kurier* 29 Dec.1844). Part 2 followed in 1845. Some advertisements (e.g. *Wiener Zeitung* 5 Apr.1845) include a blurb: "[tr.] This piquant collection of anecdotes (by no means a description of his tricks) characterizes the great artist very aptly, and tells us of the many wonderful deliberate misunderstandings (*qui pro quo*) which he perpetrated on his world trips to the amusement and amazement of all".

The complete edition, both parts, was advertised in *Hamburger Nachrichten* 3 Dec.1845, when Kothe was in town delivering his lectures on mnemonics.

Unlike Francesconi's book there is never any mention of this being sold at Bosco's own shows. It would appear that there is only one surviving copy, in Universitätsbibliothek, Eberhard Karls Universität Tübingen. This catalogues Part 2 as: Krieg den Schnurrbärten: Zauberposse in einem Aufzuge [with added work:] Die Visite des Teufels: eine sehr harmlose Bagatelle.

Bosco's last performance in Prague was on March 5th and he arrived in Vienna one week later,[367] his first visit since 1828, and this too was to end unhappily.

The papers were soon announcing his future plans — visits to Hungary, Paris, London, *and America*, even quoting "the New York papers" as reporting he would arrive in America in August that year; and soon stating that following his Vienna productions Bosco would leave Germany forever.[368]

An American tour had been mentioned the previous year when he arrived in Leipzig ("geht von hier nach Paris, im nächsten Frühjahr segelt er nach Amerika...": *Wiener Zeitschrift* 16 Sep.1844), and there was talk again of America in subsequent years — from Jassy to Czernowitz and Warsaw, "then probably an excursion to America"; then "...goes to St Petersburg, and from there to America": *ATZ* 22 Dec.1846; 28 Jan.1847; and in 1848 an advertisement even suggested that "Bosco may never return from America" (*Leipziger Zeitung* 6 Apr.1848).

Some obituaries were to say that he had performed in America (*Aschaffenburger Zeitung* 17 Mar.1863 says he was there "in 1845"; *Dziennik Powszechny* 18 Mar. 1863 says "recently"), but *the host of conjuring Boscos in America were all impostors* — the earliest being "Madame Bosco(1)" (BF1) in 1858. At least one of the many stories written about Bosco has him in America — 'Drei Aesopische Fabeln' by B. Heidler (*Der Wanderer* 25 Nov.1845) pictures him working wonders while strolling down "Kentuky-Street" in Philadelphia.

In Vienna he performed privately in "selected circles", including before the future Emperor Franz Josef and his mother on March 23rd (as the 14-year old noted in his diary),[369] until opening at the Josephstädtertheater on April 1st, where he had contracted to give ten shows, performing four times a week.[370]

The reviews were largely very positive, praising his skill, speed and dexterity, especially with the cup and balls, and compared him favourably with Döbler (even in the miraculous bunches of flowers act, which was regarded as Döbler's). But there were the usual grumbles about excessive prices and several reviews noted that his second show was less well attended than the first.[371]

A tongue-in-cheek piece in *Sonntagsblätter* 6 Apr.1845 sighed "Nothing new under the sun", humorously suggesting some changes in fashion and society it wished Bosco would make — more moral reading for women and girls; pianos, not dulcimers (*Hakbretter?*); more art and less exhibition in our art exhibitions; reduce the host of portrait painters to one pair of historical painters; turn our theatre directors towards art rather than profits; tragic actors to speak normally not declaim in monologues; books printed not on blotting paper but on elegant or just normal paper; and more subscribers, not just readers, for our newspapers... etc, but ending with a sting in its tail: *Bosco should change his old tricks for some new ones.*

After his second show Bosco ceased his performances. He blamed a cold, announcing he would soon resume but would move to a large room in the centre of town where he would be less exposed to draughts.[372]

On April 7th he gave a performance in the Palace of the Prince of Schönburg for the "cream" of Viennese nobility, the gorgeous room appropriately decorated for the occasion,[373] and at the end of that week he placed a notice confirming that he was giving private shows and would reopen to the public when he found a suitable venue.[374]

But all was not well. Harsher criticism was surfacing. Writing on April 5th after Bosco's second show the Vienna critic ("Odoardo Mundstück") of the Leipzig *Signale für die Musikalische Welt* was very severe: Bosco had now done his tricks ("gegaukelt") a second time before a very weak audience — the Viennese like to have dust thrown in their eyes, but when it comes too thick their patience is finally exhausted … prices increased three-fold for such worn out old tricks seen a hundred times… impudence typical of such grasping celebrities…

Even harsher was the Vienna correspondent of Leipzig's *Die Grenzboten,* who termed Bosco's two shows a "fiasco" — the public here is sick and tired of such market-place tricks and has no interest at all in looking at them at the prices Bosco wants. By the second show the house was empty and the angry magician discontinued his shows…

And the sharp-tongued Edmund Scharf, writing from Vienna on April 10th for *Der Spiegel,* published in Pest and Ofen, punned on Bosco's *cold* and the *coolness* of the public, and on *draughts* and *drawcards* ("…Kalt war das Publikum genug, aber Zug haben wir bei Boscos Vorstellungen keinen wahrgenommen, der ihm eine Erkältung hätte bereiten können").[375]

On top of all this, waiting in the wings was a performer who had been in Vienna since the start of the year and whom the public was eagerly waiting to see. *Der Wanderer* had said on April 9th that Bosco would have difficulty continuing at the Josephstadt theatre ("wird schwerlich mehr … spielen"): the theatre had already been let to a rival magician, who opened there on April 10th — not Döbler or Hofzinser, but a seven year old girl named Mathilde Bannholzer. She proved a great success, remaining in Vienna until the end of May (see *Appendix Z1*).

Bosco had now finally found a new venue, the *Kleine Redouten-Saal,* and was to open there on April 16th, but on Monday 14th the newspapers announced that his wife had died in Bologna on April 5th.[376] He cancelled his public performances but remained in Vienna until the end of the month to fulfil a command performance before the Kaiser and the royal family on Sunday 27th, which met with great success.[377] He may also have been waiting for his daughter Adelaide to join him, possibly from Warsaw where we know she often stayed, to travel together to Bologna.[378] He finally left for Bologna in early May.[379]

Bosco resumed performing on May 31st at the *Teatro del Corso* in Bologna, with further shows on June 1st, 5th and 8th.[380] The local paper *La Farfalla* published a long eulogy of him ("…to write of him sets my pulse racing…"),[381] and he was hailed as "Il vero modello di tutti i prestigiatori, *le maître, le pere de toutes les diableries…".*[382]

He then headed to Florence, performing at the *Teatro del Cocomero* on July 3rd, 6th and 10th ("sua ultima Accademia"), with a fourth show added on 17th ("sua Quarta ed ultima definitiva Accademia"), all very well attended,[383] and receiving glowing reviews.[384]

Next was Livorno, with shows at the *Teatro del Vecchio Giardinetto* on July 31st and August 1st, 2nd, and 3rd.[385]

Meanwhile, a Bosco impersonator was to be found in Vienna, but not in my list — one made of wood. "Anton Watzek, Mechaniker" was exhibiting his automata: "the jolly organ-player; the mechanical conjuror of wood, which, without any assistance on the table surprises by copying Bosco's three transformations; and the mechanical drummer who plays the grenadiers' march…".[386] Little is known about Watzek. He was in Graz in 1858 with an exhibition of the sufferings of Christ, and in Klagenfurt in 1862 with 100 movable wax figures, but this is the only reference found to his mechanical Bosco.

Bosco then returned to Bologna for a brief stay "in the bosom of his family",[387] and was then reported to be heading to Trieste.[388] But before Trieste he performed in Vicenza and in Padua, leaving there on September 15th,[389] and then in Venice at the *Teatro Apollo* on September 17th, 18th and 20th, where high prices did not deter large audiences and excellent reviews.[390]

We then lose track of him for a month or so,[391] but soon find him in Trieste. He opened there on October 24th at the *Teatro Mauroner*, a large amphitheatre holding 3,500. The *Bazar* commented that the thronged spectators found nothing new, rather a repeat of tricks seen before, but that the precision of their execution was so good that the public had to abandon themselves to loud applause. Conversely the correspondent of the *Allgemeine Theater-Zeitung* reported that he had astounded the public with "totally new presentations" and caused a great sensation. *La Favilla* lauded Bosco as the spirit of the age — "il traumaturgo del secolo decimonono … il Bosco è non solamente il traumaturgo, ma l'emblema, il simbolo, l'espressione, il rappresentante legittimo dell'epoca nostra…".[392]

At the start of November he travelled from Trieste heading to Vienna. En route he stopped in Laibach (modern Ljubljana), performing there on November 4th, 5th, 6th and 7th. The shows, all preceded by a one-act play, were crowded, his speed and dexterity greatly admired and applauded — a king of all European conjurors ("…ein König aller europäischen Escamoteure"), though in some aspects he was thought lacking in originality, and with a tinge of charlatanism, and his often repeated '*Spiriti miei obedite*' drew laughs.[393]

He then performed in Klagenfurt[394] and by November 20th had arrived in Graz, where he gave four shows in the Redoutensaal on 25th, 27th, 29th and 30th, running from 4 p.m. to 7.30.[395] Reviewers were largely positive, if not enthusiastic, commenting, as so often, that most of the tricks had been seen before, though praising Bosco's execution of them,[396] but the correspondent of the Vienna paper *Der Gegenwart* was very severe: "[tr.] …failed to live up to expectations, all the more so because of the significantly increased prices: we saw hardly any acts not familiar to us already, most of them performed hundreds and hundreds of times in inns by itinerant conjurors; and the audience inflamed all the more by Bosco's rude attitude to Döbler left the room very unsatisfied and awarded the palm to Döbler"; the Bavarian satirical paper *Gambrinus* was equally rude: "[tr.] Graz. 1 Dec. Bosco is here and doing his witchcraft ... but so far hasn't bewitched anyone. He has a distinctive artistic pride — the profane would call it arrogance. He has nothing new to show".[397]

Shortly before Bosco's arrival in Graz the Graz bookseller, publisher and writer Jakob Franz Dirnböck included Bosco in volume 4 of his ongoing whimsical *Briefe des Hans Michel aus Obersteier,* written in the local dialect.[398] A large advertisement in *Grazer Zeitung* 23 Oct.1845 listed among the contents "Der Zauberer Bosco in Bruck" (this is Bruck an der Mur, in Styria). The published work, 48pp., includes two Bosco stories, both really variations on well-worn Bosco anecdotes — Bosco finding money in a dung heap (with predictable results for two farmhands — *mit alle vier Händ haben ihn ganz durchg'wühlt ... aber — g'funden habens nix*) and of Bosco fooling a waiter, finding money but no sugar in a sugar bowl — *In Theaterkaffeehaus, da war an ordentliche Remasuri; da hat er vom Markör die Zuckerbiren begehrt...*

Two widely reprinted Bosco stories also date specifically from this time and place. One tells that when Bosco en route from Italy to Vienna arrived at an inn in Marburg (Marburg an der Drau, now Maribor) with his bulky apparatus and large elegant carriage which had a strange and Turkish appearance, his servant was asked who his master was: when he gravely replied 'A sorcerer' (*ein Hexenmeister*) they were refused admission.[399]

In the other, said to have happened in Graz on November 28th, a poor woman asks Bosco if as a magician he could give her something to calm her brutal husband who destroys everything when in a rage ("*in seiner Rabbia*"), Bosco replying: 'Poor lady, I am here only a short time, I must soon leave again, and because a cure takes a long time I cannot help'.[400]

Bosco left Graz on December 1st[401] and was eagerly awaited in Vienna where he was expected to perform at the Redoutensaal.[402] However, when he arrived he was unwell and delayed opening, announcing shows at the Redoutensaal from January 1st to 10th, every second day starting at midday; meanwhile he would give lessons and was prepared to sell items of apparatus to pupils.[403] The following week it was reported that he would open on January 1st, with further shows on 4th, 6th, 8th and 11th, the shows starting at 1 p.m.[404]

1846

The opening date then moved to January 2nd, and finally to January 4th, starting at 4 p.m, with a second show on 6th.[405]

Reviewers liked the performances, commending the choice of venue and Bosco's talent, enjoying his patter, and noting generous applause from a large and satisfied audience,[406] though *Der Sammler* felt that even the kleine Redoutensaal was too large and, being long and narrow, the wrong shape for everyone to observe his tricks closely ([tr.] "one would need to be a magician to see them") — what he needed was a small amphitheatre; it admired his cup and ball work and his speed, but "from Egypt he has brought us nothing new — except a menagerie — turkey hens, doves, canaries, siskins, guinea-pigs and rabbits for us to look at, and feel sorry for...".[407]

Bäuerle in the *ATZ* had not a bad word, highly approving the choice of venue, raving about Bosco's speed of hand (nicely suggesting he should be a surgeon), and even defending his "bird murders" — "even the most ardent member of the Society

Against Cruelty to Animals (*das rigoroseste Anti-Thierquälerei-Vereinsmitglied*) could find nothing to object to".[408]

Perhaps the most interesting review was that in the *Wiener Zeitung,* written by Hofzinser no less. Praising Bosco as the *Prästigator par excellence* , he also felt that the venue was too large to fully appreciate the subtle nuances of Bosco's art which escaped detection even by an adept who knew how they were achieved; unlike other performers, the closer one could observe Bosco's work, the more one admired it. His art is second nature to him, he eats it and sleeps it, he could not exist without it, which gives it a unique intensity. He deceives not just the eye of the body, but the eye of the soul. None can compare with him. Bosco, he concludes, possesses one simple small device; it is no secret but it is the way Bosco uses it that is so novel and astounding, and it is the one thing I envy him for — his hand.[409]

Further shows followed at the same venue on January 11th, 12th (these at 5 p.m.)[410] and another was announced for the 14th but moved to the 13th as he had to vacate the room for the *Kavalierball,* part of the Carneval. These were equally well attended and there were hopes for further shows, but the Carneval meant there were no venues available — not even he could conjure one up.[411]

Bosco then arranged to perform in the hall of the *Musikverein*, and was also working on new features for his act — with near disastrous consequences. On January 17th he was experimenting with gunpowder in his room in the guesthouse he was lodging in[412] when it exploded. A small rocket came too close to a flame, caught fire, and then set off a whole box of 300 of these rockets. He was badly burnt on the face and right hand. The windows were all broken and even the door of the next room was destroyed.[413]

He was soon slowly mending and receiving a host of visitors,[414] and on January 26th he wrote a letter reporting his gradual return to health and that the accident, with the loss of his apparatus and clothes, the damage to the hotel furniture and fittings, and his medical expenses, had cost him 10,000 francs. He lamented the misfortunes he met with every time he was in Vienna, saying next time he came he should look for an eternal home in St Marx, the cemetery.[415]

Der Wanderer confirmed he was out of danger — and he still had his principal assets (*Hauptkapital*): his hands and his ingenious head, to again entertain the public, and by early February he was giving private lessons.[416] He announced he would commence a new series of shows, 'Bosco *redivivus*', in the *Musikverein,* on February 18th,[417] and Hofzinser welcomed his impending return with a very complimentary piece, "Bosco the greatest conjuror of our time …", and approved the choice of the *Musikverein* —"He chooses ever smaller venues to produce ever greater sensations… the closer one can get to him, the more one can appreciate his colossal dexterity…".[418] Tickets were for sale at Bosco's room, interestingly still the same address.[419]

The opening was delayed until 20th, with further shows on 23rd and 27th,[420] all met with excellent reviews, welcoming his return and his whole range of tricks, plus his undiminished good humour.[421] *Der Wanderer* farewelled him with a poem ('Bosco, second Prometheus).[422]

There were hopes he might stay and give more shows, but the room was booked for concerts and Bosco had arranged to perform in Hungary.[423]

He headed first to Pest, travelling by steamer on the Danube,[424] but on his arrival could find no venue with terms to suit him.[425] He performed privately, including on March 14th for Archduke Joseph, the Palatine (as he had in 1829),[426] before opening to the public at noon on March 19th at the National Theatre (*Nemzeti Színház*). The German Theatre had wanted half of the takings of each show, another theatre wanted a quarter, and the National Theatre allowed no German, either on stage or in publicity material, so he had to use a Hungarian translator in his act: all very amusing, said *Der Wanderer,* in a city where hardly a fifth of the inhabitants understood Hungarian.[427]

He gave four shows there, the high prices not deterring large and enthusiastic audiences, though there were the usual murmurings: season ticket holders found their seats sold to others, and in his third show he promised all new tricks — yet all twenty had been seen before, and one paper said: "[tr.] ...*we have seen all twenty already! It takes a lot for someone to dare to do something like this, and we really admire the audience's patience and forgiveness. What would the same high-profile audience do if, for example, Szigligeti or another Hungarian writer, who had staged a long play under a different title, filled the theatre with this trick?".*[428]

Then on April 15th he opened at the *Stadttheater* across the Danube in Ofen (Buda). with further shows there on 17th and 19th,[429] and a final show at the *Sommertheater* (A Nyári Színház) on 27th, which included singing and a short play.[430] All were well attended and he is said to have taken 10,000 fr. in Pest alone. When he left Pest, to express his gratitude Bosco donated 200 florins to the Barmherzige Brüder (the Order of the Brothers of Mercy).[431]

He had been invited to Fünfkirchen (Pécs), 200 km north, with a guaranteed purse of 1,000 fr.,[432] and gave three shows there, on May 3rd, 7th and 10th, all full houses — so he earned far more than his guaranteed amount, with private performances on top of that.[433]

We next hear of him in Neusatz (now Novi Sad in Serbia), where he was sick for two weeks, then (all these now in Romania) in Temeswar (Timişoara) in late June, then Arad, Großwardein (Oradea), Klausenburg (Cluj-Napoca), Torda (Turda), Hermannstadt (Sibiu), Kronstadt (Braşov), Bucharest, Ibraila (Brăila), and Gallatz (Galaţi).[434]

In Temeswar he gave three shows, all sold out (despite the prices), and also performed privately.[435]

We get a glimpse of Bosco in Arad from the diary of Hungarian actor Szuper Károly who records being there with his troupe at the same time. The fair was on, there was only one other rather poor theatrical company in town, and they were expecting to do good business — but Bosco, who had had a splendid stage built at the Fehér Kereszt ('White Cross Hotel'), was attracting away all their audience. Szuper waited for a day when Bosco was not performing, and, having plastered the town with advertising for "Ál-Boscó" ("Fake Bosco"), put on a magic show parodying Bosco, with company member Futó, their handyman who knew a bit of magic, doing some tricks — and showing how they were done. The real Bosco, he says, had taken a box to watch the show and was so annoyed when the audience applauded loudly and showered the impostor with flowers that he left the theatre, and left town next day.[436]

Bosco was next in Klausenburg (Kolozsvár in Hungarian; now Cluj-Napoca in Romania). What transpired there was the subject of much comment in subsequent weeks. He was asked by the theatre owners to reduce his prices, and, offended, instead performed in a hall on July 31st for 10 and 20 fl. a seat, all for charity; he also gave a show in an arena on August 5th at 1 ducat per seat, raising 62 ducats, which again he donated for local good works. He paid all the expenses out of his own pocket and his total donation was approximately 3,000 fl. The city authorities honoured him with a splendid banquet and promised he would be made a freeman of the city. However, having decided that Bosco's magnanimity had been sufficiently rewarded, they then changed their minds and rescinded the award of 'citizenship', and instead sent him a written acknowledgement of thanks.

When Bosco received their letter of thanks, aware of its contents, he replied in Hungarian as follows —

> Honoured sir,
> It is with the greatest respect that I take the liberty of returning your esteemed letter herewith unopened, containing, as I have reason to believe, your acknowledgement of my services to the general well-being of your worthy city. If I have indeed done something deserving of gratitude, this was done not in search of praise but simply for the general good, and I am very pleased to have been able to make a contribution. I hereby solemnly declare that I sought no praise and no honorary award on the part of the esteemed magistrates and worthy elected assembly, all the less so as I can show such awards from greater cities, lords, and ministers.
> On the other hand I cannot pass over the fact that my stay in Kolozsvár was not without profit to the esteemed magistrates and the worthy elected assembly, for both bodies have rapidly learnt from me the art of t r a n s f o r m a t i o n (*changirozást*), in that they were able to change a solemnly declared award of honour by means of an equally solemn decision in a simple letter.
> It is true that I have suffered a great loss by failing to receive the honour so magnanimously conferred by the esteemed magistrates and the worthy elected assembly; on the other hand, however, the esteemed magistrates and the worthy elected assembly by learning this new method of transformation have made a significant gain, and that is a consolation to me in my considerable loss.
> In requesting your honour to read aloud this letter to the esteemed magistrates and the worthy elected assembly, I remain, sir, with respect, your humble servant,
>   Bosco Bertalan.

The Klausenburg and Hermannstadt newspapers discussed at length the merits of the award, and of the decision to rescind it,[437] and the Vienna papers soon chimed in — "These days people seem very free and easy handing out these cheap honours," said *Der Sammler*, "Liszt a *Gerichtstafelbeisitzer* (associate magistrate), Bosco an *Ehrenbürger* (freeman of the city)!", and *Der Humorist* joked that Bosco was now a *Tabla Biró* (the Hungarian term for *Gerichtstafelbeisitzer*) and what a pity that the playwright Devrient was not also made one, as we could then put a reviewer on trial before him…".[438]

Bosco soon moved on. He was in Torda (Thorenburg, now Turda) on August 7th, welcomed with a band and warm hospitality,[439] then arrived in Hermannstadt (Sibiu) on August 9th, the initial announcement in the local paper[440] calling him *Carlo Bosko* (a mistake found occasionally, no doubt arising from the numerous books credited to the mythical "Carlo Bosco/Bosko").

He opened in the Redoutensaal at noon on August 16th to great applause. A detailed review compared Bosco and Döbler, each, it said, having his individual points of excellence — Döbler performing with grace, beauty and nobility, Bosco "all nature, the fiery Italian, a born *buffo*" who does the amazing and incredible with greater dexterity and unbeatable speed.[441] There were further shows on 18th and 19th; more were hoped for, but the Room was otherwise booked and he was unable to come to suitable terms with the owner of the Theatre in the town. A two page review of his performances there lauded him to the skies — "the greatest magician who ever lived ... the magician king, Zoroaster II ... the most perfect pupil of the Egyptian priests of Moses' day...", and how wonderful that such a famous magician should agree to play in our small town...[442]

Bosco continued on his way east, his path through Wallachia a nightmare, with bad roads overturning his heavy wagon three times, and losing part of his apparatus and wardrobe when the wagon stuck in a river. He gave three shows in Kronstadt (modern Brașov), on September 6th, 8th and 10th,[443] then headed to Bucharest,[444] followed by Ibraila (Brăila) and Gallatz (Galați), and in November reached Jassy (now Iași in Romania), where he had been in 1826. He gave three shows there, on 3rd, 5th and 7th November, all sold out.

The Iași newspaper *Albina Românească* ('The Romanian Bee'), edited by poet and playwright Gheorghe Asachi, gave Bosco a long write-up and reviewed his shows (these articles, alone in the paper, are in French as well as Romanian), selecting for special mention the bird fired from the pistol and the transformed umbrella, and very taken with his language — "il parle trois langues à la fois, mais ce que chez d'autres serait un baragolu babylonien inintelligible, passe chez lui avec une grâce sentie et appréciée par tout le monde"; it also adds an apparently original detail to the story of Bosco robbing the Cossack when being robbed by him: Bosco got 9 Thalers.[445]

Another long note followed, titled 'о тъмпjіаре / un évènement', the event being Bosco's arrival to break the monotony of local life, praising Bosco at length and noting the presence at his shows of the Prince Regent (Mihail Sturdza) and his family.[446]

There are no further advertisements, but Bosco was still there in late November, as a final note in early December ('Magic and Music') reviews a combined show "last Saturday" by Bosco and a Florentine prima donna, both excelling, and Bosco performing there "for the first time" with his crystal cup and balls.[447]

From Jassy it was said he would head for St Petersburg — or for Lemberg (Lviv) — or for Czernowitz (Chernivtsi), then Warsaw... then probably America...[448]

1847

When we next sight Bosco in late February 1847 he is in Lemberg (modern Lviv),[449] and we hear he had recently performed in Kolomyia and in Stanisławów (now Ivano-Frankivsk).[450] The long trip to Jassy and back to Lemberg had taken him a little less time than in 1827 when he spent June to December on that tour.

He opened in Lemberg on February 24th, receiving an excellent review, though there were the usual comments on the prices, these justified by the reviewer in the light of Bosco's considerable expenses — not only the rent of the hall but hiring chairs and couches, carpeting the aisle, and the cost of the 400 candles.[451] Further shows followed on February 27th and 28th, and March 7th and 14th, the last a charity show for the local poor.[452]

He then left for Warsaw, via Kraków, but also intending to perform in some smaller towns, such as Przemyśl, Jarosław, Rzeszów, and Tarnów.[453]

He reached Kraków on March 30th but merely passed through, stopping over only for a meal (and a mind-reading act on a fellow-diner), "on his way to Warsaw, to spend the holidays in the bosom of his family".[454]

In early April he was in Warsaw,[455] and was immediately requested to perform for the *Namiestnik*, Field Marshall Count Paskevich, Serene Prince of Warsaw, and two hundred select guests.[456] He then opened at the Wielki Teatr on April 14th,[457] with further shows on 15th, 17th, 20th, and 23rd.[458] There was then a break, and after a week it was announced that Bosco had a fever and all shows were suspended.[459] He resumed on May 7th, billed as his last show,[460] but he gave a final benefit performance in the *Sale Redutowe* (in the Teatr Wielki) on May 16th, promising his best had been kept to the end and there would be a souvenir for each spectator.[461]

He remained based in Warsaw for some time, making occasional forays to other towns to perform. In July we find him in Sejny,[462] and the following month in Plok.[463] Then in September he was reported as leaving for Kraków,[464] but in fact first gave several shows in Radom,[465] finally, after several detours, arriving in Kraków on October 12th or 13th.[466]

He opened on Friday 22nd in the (former) Sala Knotza, with further shows on 25th and 27th, tickets available on subscription.[467] A long article preceding his opening made much of his success in Paris (back in 1832!) then came a glowing review — "…amazed, delighted and enchanted us with his unmatchable skill…"; also joking about his fondness for *Veuve Cliquot* and his need to keep his strength up, suggesting that the balls of his cups and balls were made of Strasbourg paté.[467]

At the end of October the *Allgemeine Theater-Zeitung*, catching up on Bosco's activities for the first time in six months, printed a report from Kraków on his travels through Poland. He had invitations to perform all over the country, and in towns where he had not intended to perform his wagon was sometimes stopped and further post-horses refused to make him stay over. In Kraków the hall which he redecorated and turned into an amphitheatre was compared to a fairy temple, and all the seats were sold well in advance.[469]

He gave a final show in Kraków at reduced prices on November 1st,[470] and must have left soon after,[471] as he was in Vienna by November 9th. He stayed only a few days, wanting first to perform in Preßburg (modern Bratislava) while the *Landtag* was sitting.[472]

He gave three shows there, on November 28th and 30th and December 2nd, and added a final charity show on December 5th, all held in the *fürstlich Pálffy'schen Saal*.[473]

Pannonia (really a literary supplement to the *Preßburger Zeitung*) was effusive in its praises and its coverage, opening with an anecdote (Bosco at breakfast) on November 16th, more anecdotes on November 20th (one, ascribed to humorist Louis Weyl, of Bosco in the Berlin stock exchange), a comic dialogue with Ahasuerus on

November 27th by Josef Weyl (of the *Pannonia* staff), Bosco receiving new tricks and a new magic wand from Egypt, and having Bosco say (in Bosco-ese), on the subject of high prices: "Lieber ick macken weniger Einnahme ... Bosco reicker Mann, fort bien, Bosco armer Teufel, macken auch nicks! Ein Jahr man speisen Anananas, ander Jahr man essen Herdäpfel... (*one year tasting pineapple, next year only spuds to eat*)". It published glowing reviews (30 Nov., 11 Dec.) of his first show (noting the music during the intervals by the Hungarian *Loczer Zigeuner*) and saying of the final show that he may return to Preßburg during the Carneval.

1848

In Vienna on January 6th he opened his *Zaubersalon* at "Rothenthurmstraße (Haarmarkt) Nr.733, first floor right". These were public performances, given from 5 to 7 p.m., the setting intended to be more intimate than a large theatre,[474] and anyway there were rivals in town, Robin, Baron, and soon Rappo, and the theatres were all occupied.[475]

He drew crowded houses, many unable to obtain seats.[476] Unfortunately he was forced to close for a period because of ill health — a dangerous 'Kopfentzündung' ('head infection', a term which covered anything from laryngitis to encephalitis). The papers lamented his continuing misfortunes in the city: "[tr.] Bosco just can't come to Vienna without something awful happening to him. Even *his* tricks can't stop that."[477] However, he was recovered and back performing on January 27th (postponed from 23rd), again with good crowds — despite rivals still performing in town, "a virtual congress of conjurors and athletes", but these Bosco soon "made disappear".[478]

About this time Bosco, we are told, wrote a play, with himself not merely conjuring in it but playing a character role.[479] This was 'Die Bescheerung im Serail oder Bosco überall' (see p.409), which he performed as part of his act later this year in Leipzig, Dresden and Berlin and subsequently elsewhere.

His shows continued to attract both overflowing crowds and enthusiastic reviews, not least more praise from Hofzinser, hailing him as "King of Conjurors". and using the same trope he had used two years earlier — Bosco possesses an excellent "piece of apparatus" (*Maschinchen*): his hand.[480]

The last show was announced for February 20th when he would be leaving for France via Munich,[481] but his plans changed, no doubt due to news of the February Revolution in France. He brought forward his departure to Sunday 13th so he could instead perform in Brünn (Brno) at the end of the month.[482] He reached Brünn on February 20th and performed there very successfully in the *Königl. Städt. Theater* on February 25th, 26th and 28th.[483]

We then lose sight of Bosco during March and most of April — not surprisingly, with the *Märzrevolution* suddenly flaring up in Germany and Austria. He probably travelled from Brünn to Leipzig via Prague: there is no mention in newspapers that he performed there, or even intended to, but shortly before he left Leipzig in May it was stated that he made heavy losses in Prague as well as in Leipzig.[484]

Another article,[485] soon after he left Leipzig, which is both political and satirical but clearly intended to make a *theatrical* point, complained of "outdated privileges" both in society and in the theatre, whereby foreign performers arriving in Leipzig within a set time prior to the Fair could not open there until the Fair began: this rule, said the article, had delayed Bosco (who had a staff of nine) *eight weeks* and cost him the large sun of 2331 Thaler. Certainly there is no record of him performing between February 28th and March 7th. But Bosco knew full well the rules for the Fair, as the same had happened to him in Leipzig in 1821: perhaps he had hoped for an exemption on this occasion.[486]

He arrived in Leipzig sometime during April,[486] and he remained in Germany for the next fifteen months.[487]

For this whole period his advertisements make much of the fact that he was planning to go to America, and may never return, *so this could be your last chance ever to see him in Europe:* this may well have been his genuine intention, rather than merely a sales-pitch or a humorous reference to the massive German emigration to America in 1848 and soon after.

He opened on May 7th at the *Schützenhaus*, in the Großer Saal (the ball room, later called the Blauer Saal), described as "[tr.] a tastefully decorated and brightly lit amphitheatre" with good views from all seats, "each show to be in two parts with a ten-minute break between them" (with an orchestra present), "a cycle of four shows, with 80 tricks in all".[488]

Initially he performed every night during the Fair,[489] then from May 13th he stated that daily performances were a strain on his health and he would now perform only twice a week, on Wednesdays and Saturdays, continuing until May 17th.[490] He then gave a charity show for the benefit of the poor on May 20th, and announced a penultimate show for May 21st,[491] then a final show on May 24th,[492] followed by a farewell show (*Abschiedsvorstellung*) on May 28th, which included his play 'Die Bescheerung im Serail oder Bosco überall'.[493]

His month in Leipzig went well enough, but he made little money. A review of the first show waxed lyrical over the vast number of flowers Bosco handed out to the women in the audience, *more in five minutes than a hot house could produce in eight days...* and there was *no better way of recovering from the current political troubles than in the house of King Bosco I, soon alas to cross the seas, whose subjects* (spiriti infernali) *will not so easily successfully revolt...*[494]

The political theme was to the fore again in a later note, styling Bosco the "[tr.] Autocrat (*Selbstherrscher*) of All Magicians, the Russian Alexander in the Kingdom of the Magic Arts, he whose throne, of all the thrones in this world, remains unshaken and unshakable, because it is a throne of Art, which he did not usurp, but rose onto it by his own genius, his *spiriti miei...*", and wishing he would pull off the trick of uniting all Germany... and further that the current catch-cry 'I'm not paying, you're not paying...' (*ich bezahle nicht, du bezahlst nicht, ec, ec*) would not come true for him...; ending with a poem on the same theme of Bosco's unifying powers.[495]

Another reviewer rated Bosco, the Circus Renz, and Tietz's Mechanical Museum the highlights of the Leipzig Fair that year — *Bosco never seems to age, his humour and his legendary dexterity remain unchanged, and his cup and balls work is unchallenged...*[496]

The reviewer of his charity show for the poor (noting that the audience was largely female, as the men were currently distracted by politics) acknowledged his sacrifice, saying he had lost money both in Leipzig and in Prague.[497]

Then the *Leipziger Zeitung* reviewer gave free reign to his satirical and political impulses to produce an extravagant effusion (of which this is merely an abridged paraphrase) of Bosco *leaving for Dresden, then probably America, to make comparisons between German liberty and American liberty... all other magicians bow down before Bosco, and lose their lustre before his brilliance, just as in true Germanic times, when Germany was still an Empire, all generals and petty princes paid homage to the one Emperor... Bosco is the sole-ruler of all magicians, a Russian Nicholas* [more appropriate than Alexander to whom he was earlier compared: note 495] *in the realm of magic ... Bosco is now at the zenith of his art, as the sun burns its hottest when it reaches the meridian ... Like a second Caesar, he could exclaim:* "Veni Vidi! (*more correctly* visus sum) Vici! *He had no rivals, let alone magicians who could be placed at his side: the whole train of emulators, whom he only brought into being through his brilliant performances, were mere camp-followers ... Like a shining meteor, he rose up in the southern sky... he will never be subdued or overthrown by a mighty prince of Hell; no, but one day he will descend from the throne of magic and lay down his wand of his own accord, and there will be no one who deserves to be his worthy successor ... and the empire of magic, the reins of which he steered with a single and powerful hand, will become an elective empire with hundreds of pretenders; but then, because no one is worthy of ascending the throne of magic nor able to take it by force, the electoral empire will constitute a republic... Bosco's spiritual hegemony will endure in memory forever, and miracle after miracle will be told of him, which will pass from mouth to mouth for all eternity ... A second Barbarossa, said to be in the Kysshäuser and without whose physical resurrection according to legend the German Empire will not rise again, Bosco will rest in the distant land, and he too will create the legend that only with his physical re-awakening will the true magic realm of the world one day be opened up again!*[498]

The political upheavals of 1848 continued to offer plenty of scope for the newspapers, and especially the satirical papers, to imagine a humorous role for Bosco. In June 'Bosco's Dream' of removing outdated privileges was offered as a solution to the current troubles: Bosco had got through his loss of income when unable to open before the fair began (note 486) but artists of lesser means had been ruined: it was time for privilege to lose its sway.

Oettinger in his *Charivari* joked that Bosco had recently been performing at the Austrian court and, placing a large pyramid over the head of the Emperor and tapping it with his magic wand, made the Emperor disappear: when Metternich asked where he'd gone, Bosco said: 'You've got His Majesty in your pocket'.[499]

In July a Dresden review opened by saying that Bosco had gone to the school of the diplomatic magician ("trickster") Prince Metternich, but the student has surpassed the master. Metternich, too, knew very well how to transform a living bird into a dead one, but he used a double-headed eagle for this experiment ... while Bosco uses only a canary.[500]

The radical Vienna paper *Wiener Katzenmusik* suggested several imaginary political shows and tricks for Bosco to perform and compared ministerial tergiversations and pretensions to his stage deceptions.[501]

Probably the most interesting paper was the satirical *Berliner Krakehler*, whose first issue appeared on 18 March 1848, with forty-eight issues that year published initially weekly then six per month; it was banned on November 15th but back on the streets in December until its demise in January 1849.[502] The format, with vibrant coloured (sometimes multi-coloured) titles, almost unique for the time in newspapers, was as striking as the text, with its wit, wordplay, parody, persiflage and caricatures. The editors, principally Carl Otto Hoffmann and Ernst Litfaß, put into Bosco's mouth three macaronic French-German pieces announcing '[tr.] Great Extraordinary Exhibitions of Magic' of the 'The Goddess of Freedom' (*Krakehler* 22 July 1848 p.3; 21 Oct.1848 pp.1-2; 1 Nov.1848 p.1) —

> "*Meine Herren! Attention je vous prie, ick halten hier ein Magisch-Draht-Pupp. Diese Magisch-Draht-Pupp seien holl! Ick lege hinein das kleine Göttin Freiheit in das hohle Magisch-Draht-Pupp, das soll aufheben die Freiheit! A présent ick schließen ßu, ick nix berühren, je vous donnerei la clé ...."*
> (22 July).

While this French-German mix parodied Bosco's own patter, the introduction to the reprint points out (p.xviii) a German tradition for such macaronics.[503]

There was even a booklet, a poem — *Deutschlands Einheit hergestellt durch die Zauberei des B. Bosco: Ein Dialog zwischen Faust, Mephistopheles und Bosco*. This was published in Leipzig, undated but July 1848 (for the dating see *Fiction* F59); printed by C. W. Vollrath for the publisher, C. Dederich. The booklet had two printings, one with the author given only as "Zanoni", the other naming the author as Dr. C. Zehmen.[504]

Bosco, having given his last Leipzig show on May 28th, left on June 1st[505] and arrived in Dresden on June 10th.[506] It is almost certainly this month that he married for the second time — an article 'Bosco in Dresden' in *Leipziger Zeitung* 25 June 1848 says: "[tr.] Dresden, as we learn, is now your *father-in-law town*" ("jetzt Ihre Schwiegervaterstadt ist"): see *Excursus on Family*.

The papers welcomed him, jesting that such were his powers that he could cure all the current ills ... *Bosco will get art, industry and commerce back into full swing... and conjure away the political furrows from the public's brow... and now that his advertising bills are plastered on Dresden's street corners they have magically separated the competing yellow, red and green political posters of both sides calling for action – 'Republic or No Republic'... he has come at the right time...*[507]

He constructed his 'Zauber-Salon', described (as in Leipzig) as a tastefully decorated amphitheatre, on the right of the open area by the inner Pirna Gate ("auf dem rechten Freiplatz am inneren Pirnaischen Thore"), opening there on June 26th, with performances every evening at 8 p.m.[508]

The reviews were all very positive — *extraordinary virtuosity ... the calmness (Ruhe), dexterity, and elegance of his performances... in fact, beyond reviewing — one can only review what one understands and comprehends, and with Bosco this is not the case... his tricks always changing and always more interesting... no one leaves the venue unsatisfied, but all leave wondering... puts his public at ease — it feels like being in an extended family circle...*[509]

On July 21st and 23rd he included at the end of his shows performances by athlete and equilibrist Grafina.[510] He advertised his "last three shows" (all ending with 'Die Bescheerung in Serail') for July 27th, 30th and 31st, followed by a charity show on behalf of Dresden Hospital on August 3rd,[511] and was requesting that invoices for payment be rendered by August 4th, suggesting he was now planning to depart. But he then announced that due to public demand he had decided to remain in Dresden during the *Vogelschießen*, the Bird Shooting festival (*Dresdner Vogelwiese*), which brought many out of towners to the city, and he had been allowed by the authorities to keep his Salon in place until August 15th. He advertised shows for August 6th and 7th,[512] but we then hear nothing of him until August 18th: however, he was not honeymooning, but had been unwell. The shows on 6th and 7th had been cancelled and they would be given now, two Farewell Shows on August 20th and 21st.[513]

He now finally left Dresden and headed to Magdeburg, where he performed in the Stadt-Theater on September 8th, 10th, 12th, 15th, 17th and 22nd.[514] A reviewer said simply how happy the show made him in these troubled times (not merely the political turmoil but cholera), and what most pleased the audience was Bosco magically handing out, from an "empty" box, perfumes, jewellery, watches, etc., as small mementos.[515] He then went north to Halberstadt, giving three shows in the Hotel de Prusse on September 29th and October 1st and 3rd.[516]

Bosco was still announcing his intention of soon departing for America, and he continued northwards, possibly planning to eventually leave from Hamburg.

On October 22nd he opened at Kroll's Garten in Berlin (delayed from October 18th), with further shows on October 23rd, 25th, 27th, 29th, 31st, and November 3rd (delayed from 2nd), 5th, 8th and his final show on 12th (moved from 10th), all from 7pm to 9pm.[517]

A review congratulated him on conjuring up a full house on opening night at this out of the way venue in horrible weather... *he made not just watches, rings and necklaces disappear but also time... he is master of beaker-play, the cup and balls... but he plays not with beakers, but as he pronounces it,* bakers ("nicht mit Bechern, sondern nach seiner Mundart mit Bäckern"), *but his magic is simple enough, relying on the magic words* spiriti miei obedite, *which means that anyone who realises that and uses these words correctly can do the same — that would have made Berlin three times happier last Sunday...*[518]

Bosco then headed to nearby Potsdam. As he was leaving, in Berlin a rival was opening an "Egyptisches Zaubertheater", Adolph Bils: they were to encounter each other again early the following year in Bremen. And a parody of Bosco's act continued during December and January, a "mechanical tableau with humorous transformations and funny scenes" by Sebhard, advertised as 'Bosculos Zauberreich', later 'Boscos Zaubereien' and 'Bosculos Zaubereien'.[519]

He originally announced four shows in Potsdam, on December 10th, 12th, 14th and 17th in the *Saal* of Herr Schilpp; they were packed out (over a hundred unable to find seats at one show) and he performed again on 21st and 26th.[520] Bosco was the centre of attention, said a reviewer, even silencing political debates, and a later review called him 'The Absolute Monarch in the Realm of Natural Magic', noting the presence of Prince Albert of Prussia in the audience; a poem 'To Bosco in Potsdam' followed.[521]

1849

We lose sight of him in January, but at the start of February he was in Brandenburg (the town, Brandenburg an der Havel) giving three performances there on 2nd, 4th and 6th. He is said to be en route to Cologne.[522]

In early May he was in Hannover, performing in the *Ballhofsaal* on May 5th, 6th, 7th and 12th.[523] He was next in Bremen at the *Bremer Stadt-Theater* between May 18th and 28th.[524] Also in town was the younger German magician Adolph Bils, performing at the Sommer-Theater im Volksgarten, who presumptuously challenged Bosco to a duel of skill. This Bosco ignored contemptuously as not worth his while and the rivalry, we are told, turned into a "murderous" war in the newspapers.[525]

When Bosco left Bremen is uncertain but he may have stayed on there, as his daughter Adelaide was with him, and she was there until September, when she left for Warsaw.[526]

Bosco now headed to Holland, opening in Emden on September 21st.[527] A long review in the *Emder Volksblatt* pictures *his stocky muscular figure, which with the swiftness of his movements, especially when we consider that he is over sixty [sic], is so difficult to reconcile with his litheness ... the unusual dexterity and nimbleness of his hands and feet; his black Spanish dress with the white collar, ... his piercingly restless and yet so friendly eye, which impresses everyone, but also captivates them... In an almost teasing tone he bids his spectators watch very carefully when he plays with the balls, which will disappear, but which are nevertheless clearly visible in the bright light of the wax candles; and as we fix our eyes on them — the balls are gone. An uncommon certainty, casual grace, the swiftness of all his movements, his unshakable self-confidence, these are the things that make Bosco so favourably distinguished and impressive. ...In addition, Bosco combines with his extraordinary talents finely civilized manners... The trick with which he concluded his performance yesterday was quite interesting. Bosco gives a lady a live canary, and promises that when he (Bosco) returns from the pit to the stage, the bird will come flying after him. But the bird stays away; the lady held the poor songster so well that it was impossible for him to fly away; she crushed him to death. Bosco is shocked.* "Meine Dam was ab Sie gemakt, die Vogel kost mi akzik Thaler"; *he gives the dead canary to a gentleman with the request to load it into a pistol, which he puts in his hand, and when the man pushes the ramrod too gently, Bosco tamps the load down properly — in the midst and in spite of the many ah's and oh's from the ladies present. Then Bosco takes a sword and shouts:* "Mein Er (Herr) Sie müs sik mit mir douellir; ik wer näm diesse Deg, Sie ab dis Pistol; ik zieh (*draw*) die Deg; ik wer commandir: ein, zwei, drei, und Sie schiess los auf mick. — Zielen (mik) Sie auf die Dagenspits. Merk Sie auf: Ein! Zwei! Drei! (Paf!)" ... *and the bird is hanging with bound legs flapping merrily from the tip of the sword, and the hall is in danger of collapsing from the thunderous clapping of hands.*[528]

From October 11th he performed in Groningen,[529] then in Leeuwarden on October 29th and 30th and November 3rd, attracting excellent crowds,[530] and in Harlingen on November 8th and 10th.[531]

On November 16th Bosco arrived in Amsterdam, but had not yet arranged a suitable venue. He then announced six shows in the *Hoogduitsche Schouwburg* (the 'German Theatre') in Amstelstraat, the first on November 22nd, each show preceded by a performance by the resident opera company.[532] A large audience at his first show admired the "unsurpassed swiftness with which this world-renowned artist performed his amazing and astonishing tricks", but unfortunately much of the orchestra was away at another concert and the operatic performance was "not a happy one".[533] Further shows followed on November 24th and on 27th (originally announced for 26th), but the arrangement was not a success, as he had insufficient time to set up his apparatus after the opera performance.[534]

While he looked around for a more suitable venue he gave numerous very successful private shows, and a long article paraded his achievements over the years (opening tantalisingly: *"It is indeed interesting to browse the richly filled albums of this famous artist...."*).[535] Bosco continued the private shows and offered lessons, and on December 22nd gave a charity performance for the orphanage.[536]

1850

He announced that his private shows would end on January 15th as he had received invitations from many other towns, and in a later notice stated that the number of these private shows meant he would not be able to resume public performances in Amsterdam, "otherwise the vacant *Fransche Schouwburg* would offer an entirely suitable venue".[537] But Bosco then advertised that *very flattered by the desire which the Public ... so fondly expressed to him to see him appear in a theatre... he makes it his duty to do so, and, as soon as he has fulfilled his newly made commitments (in addition to the 37 soirées already given in the principal Houses of this city), before leaving Amsterdam... he expects to give three great public performances...* However, these shows did not come to pass: we later hear that this was due to the number of private *soirées,* but he promised that the public shows would take place at the beginning of February.[538]

By mid-January he was already in Utrecht, first with private shows then in public on January 23rd in the *Gebouw voor Kunsten en Wetenschappen*, with a second show on Monday 28th.[539] He gave a private show in Vreeland,[540] and between the Utrecht performances he gave a private show in Amersfoort on Friday 25th for a Captain Voet, and planned to return there on Saturday February 2nd for a public show in the *Gebouw Amicitia*, if subscriptions (seats ƒ 1.50 and ƒ 0.75; children half price) could be raised to cover it.[541]

He then returned as promised to give a public performance in Amsterdam, at the *Fransche Schouwburg* on February 7th.[542]

Also in Amsterdam was D.L. Bamberg, father of Tobias, touring his homeland, who now confronted Bosco with a large provocative advertisement:

> [tr.] A WORD from the Court Magician BAMBERG TO BOSCO.
> It can be considered commendable at all times to pay tribute to Artists, regardless of which Country on the Earth was their Cradle, but it is also very humiliating for the Dutch to hear trumpeted the most fabulous and most exaggerated Praise to Strangers who have in no way earned this, as is now the case with BOSCO ... he only performed 12 tricks each evening, that is 36 in the three Performances here, and the same recently in Utrecht ... and among those tricks was not a single one not previously performed by me; such as the UMBRELLA, THE BIRD ON THE SWORD, HANDKERCHIEFS IN THE BREAD, THE DOVE WITH THE WATCH IN THE BOTTLE, THE FRYING OF THE BIRDS, etc. I would not make a public mention of this, were it not for the

question which my Son TOBIAS addressed to him in Amersfoort: Have you seen my Father's work yet? He haughtily replied: No! That is only good for doing Magic for Farmers at a Fair. I had not expected so much impudence from you, BOSCO; so I ask my Dear Countrymen, since 1832 as Court Magician and for 45 years known to the most important families in the Country, as Citizen of the State, have I not always fulfilled my venerable task... So, after obtaining a license from the Authorities, I will soon give a single EXTRAORDINARY PERFORMANCE in the Franschen Schouwburg, and there my first part will be done à LA BOSCO, the second Act à LA ROBIN, and the third Act the favourite Tricks à LA BAMBERG. I invite Mr. BOSCO to that Performance, and my Honoured Town and Countrymen will then best be able to convince themselves how much difference there is between the far famed Mr. BOSCO (Alias Magician) and the DUTCH FARMER-MAGICIAN.[543]

Bamberg gave his show on February 16th. A brief review reported that it "was attended with great pleasure by a large audience. Mr. Bamberg has succeeded in maintaining the reputation of Dutch magic...".[544]

The next day saw a long letter headed 'Bosco, Robin and Bamberg' signed by "Some Lovers of Magic and Conjuring" (P.K., B. K., and J.L.) suggesting that the three performers were very different — Bosco has a natural talent for his profession, which has earned him the most esteemed approval of most of the Crowned Heads of Europe, which neither Robin or Bamberg can claim. Undoubtedly these gentlemen can carry out some of BOSCO's tricks, but when they perform them will they astonish us equally? Everything comes down to the manner of execution. ROBIN possesses apparatus with which he fascinates for the first moments, but this state of wonder does not last long; when one examines the means by which such surprise has been achieved, one is convinced that dexterity in this case is more important than the best of apparatus. That's the superiority of BOSCO! ... Far be it from us to denounce BAMBERG, our Countryman, but he must put aside a little that spirit of boasting, for it exposes him to criticism... Let him submit to the judgment of the civilized public, instead of showing a manic self esteem which shines through in his conversation and writings, and in which one sees nothing but malice and envy. He works hard to do better than BOSCO and ROBIN (which we wish him heartily), and he can be sure that we will not deny him our approval.[545]

Bosco had been continuing his shows. His first on February 7th was a great success, and he advertised a second for February 9th, stressing that it featured "24 new tricks".[546] He then announced that he was remaining in Amsterdam as he had received so many invitations to give private *soirées*. After the last of these on February 16th he left for Arnhem, saying other provincial cities would follow, then The Hague, Belgium, and London.[547]

Bosco gave three shows in Arnhem in the *Stads Schouwburg* on February 26th, 28th and March 2nd, all attracting good crowds and good reviews.[548]

Next was Nijmegen, with three very successful shows in the *Schouwburg te Nijmegen* on March 9th, 12th and 13th, and a private show in nearby Grave.[549] He performed twice in Zutphen, on April 3rd and 5th,[550] twice in Deventer,[551] twice in Zwolle, in the *Concertzaal van Odéon*, on April 18th and 20th (a little later than he had planned),[552] and once in Kampen,[553] then he returned to Amsterdam, "and will rest there for a few days".[554]

Bosco now headed west to Haarlem, Leiden, The Hague and Rotterdam, but clearly had some initial problems over venues. He was in The Hague by May 3rd, staying in the Hotel Fuhri, but hopes we would perform there were not immediately fulfilled.[555]

In Haarlem he advertised two shows in the *Nieuw Schouburg,* on May 6th and 8th, but immediately changed this to a single show on 6th, "because he is prevented from giving a second by a concert on Wednesday 8 and an opera on Friday 10 May, and the large amount of work dismantling and setting up his Cabinet stops him doing this". The single show was very successful ("…the hall was crowded, and the balconies, occupied by the city's leading families, provided a beautiful sight … the famous artist was greeted with thunderous applause; at every turn the delighted spectators expressed their pleasure by bravo cheers…"), and it was hoped that he would be back there again.[556]

He then returned to The Hague where a performance had been arranged in the *Koninklijke Hollandsche Schouwburg* for May 10th, one show only, and followed by a comic play. A large audience, which included members of the Royal family, greatly enjoyed the performance, and again there were hopes Bosco would return.[557]

We next sight Bosco in Dordrecht, where he gave two shows on May 21st and 24th, warmly reviewed ("…his dexterity borders on the miraculous, while his easy manner draws a laugh from everyone…").[558]

Bamberg father and son were meanwhile performing at the fair in Dokkum, advertising "National" Magic Shows, and promising to prove that in the art of magic "they had nothing to yield to Robin or Bosco".[559]

In early June Bosco was in Leiden, giving shows in the *Schouwburg te Leyden* on June 5th, 6th and 8th. "The performance", said a reviewer, "left nothing to be desired. It can be rightly said that he surpasses everything seen in his art hitherto…".[560]

At the end of June he arrived in Rotterdam but was unable to secure a venue,[561] so performed first in Alkmaar, three shows in the *Zaal Harmonica* on July 6th, 8th and 10th; reserved seats were f 2.00 (or f 4.50 for all three shows).[562]

He opened in Rotterdam on July 17th in the *Rotterdamsche Schouwburg,* with further shows announced for 22nd and 24th.[563] All met with great success and were reviewed at length in both the Rotterdam papers. though one feature of his first show was greeted with some criticism. Bosco pulled the same stunt as he had in Berlin in 1844, pretending to fall off the stage when returning watches and to have badly cut his arm, only to reveal it was all a joke. The *Nieuwe Rotterdamsche courant* reviewer said: "[tr.] What Bosco has done with this is a masterpiece of dexterity and stage play. We must, however, dislike the thing itself, as unsuitable; we expected Bosco's taste to be a bit more refined, a bit more elegant. It is true that he made a profound impression on the public by doing this, but by very wrongly chosen means, the consequences of which, moreover, could not be calculated, since the shock and the sight of the blood could have seriously upset many ladies"; however, the overall tone of the review was very positive (*a great success … a master of magic … tricks really beautiful and dazzling*),[564] and the *Rotterdamsche courant* reviewer in describing the incident made no criticism at all, telling us that afterwards *Bosco continued his performance, amid the thunderous applause of the audience, which now also admired him as an actor.* Bosco, he said, was a real magician as despite the oppressive heat of the opening night, the air in the theatre was fresh and pleasant, and in listing several of Bosco's standard tricks he said: *We've seen the same or similar before from Linski, Bamberg or Philippi [sic], but have you ever seen a magician telling you to hold up to your ear some watches borrowed from the audience and to listen whether they were going, and if you answered yes, he ordered the watches to stop, and then immediately you no longer heard the ticking? Have you ever seen a box with a ring in it given to you, and, while the magician stood a great distance away, he commanded it to be closed for a few moments, after which he had the ring in his hand and you looked for it in the box in vain?*[565]

Both reviewers found his second show even better than the first, *our delight in his speed and his dexterity has grown even more ... the tricks were entirely new, all surprising and entertaining...* one especially liked his trick with borrowed keys that he made vanish — *are they in the flowerpot or the loaf — they are found in the loaf, but to satisfy those who thought they were in the flowerpot, he broke that and there they were, tied tightly to the roots;* the other reviewer admired Bosco's "middle path" in the art of magic, *impenetrable on the one hand and yet not bordering on the incomprehensible or supernatural... This is the part of magic that we think is the most beautiful. When Bosco, with an object between the tips of his fingers on an outstretched right arm, draws the audience's attention to it and warns that this object will disappear, a thousand eyes from all directions are fixed on the bare arm, the fingers and the object: one sees everything — and yet the object disappears from the fingers, without seeing how, without knowing where it is — it is as if it were made invisible by some magic charm or dissolved in the air...*[566]

Bosco then announced two shows in nearby Schiedam, in the *Zaal Musis Sacrum*, on July 29th and 31st, which also received excellent reviews (*...a great magician... the praise he received was exuberant but well deserved...*); he then gave a "third and last show" on August 2nd, followed by a fourth on August 3rd.[567]

The fourth show here was probably because he now knew he would not be able to fulfil an intention of giving two final shows at the *Schouwburg* in Rotterdam before he left: he had been advertising these on July 22nd and still on July 30th as to take place on August 5th and 8th and, "to add lustre to these evenings", they were to be in combination with Heer L. Faucoult, a "Hydraulic Engineer from Paris".[568] However, back from Schiedam Bosco announced that these could not now take place — "certain circumstances, completely independent of his good will, compel him to renounce several performances in the Schouwburg here", but he urged "lovers of private *soirées*, large and small", to contact him at his hotel.[569] The following week he published a *"Farewell Greeting"*: "Bosco, having had to cease his performances for lack of a venue, openly expresses his gratitude for the distinguished compliments he has received, and also offers his Farewell Greeting to the Public, hoping at a later time to shorten some winter evenings pleasantly…".[570]

In July 1850, when Bosco was opening in Rotterdam, his name was invoked into current political debate, with an imaginary comic dialogue between him and the Minister of Finance, Pieter Van Bosse, then implementing unpopular currency reforms. This piece of satire first appeared in French under the title 'Les Deux Escamoteurs' in the radical Amsterdam newspaper *Le Courrier Batave* 21 July 1850, and was written by its editor, Adriaan van Bevervoorde, under his pen name 'Asmodée'.[571]

Abridged versions of this, titled 'Bosco in Holland', wrongly dating it to *February* 1850, appear in *Satanas, Biographie und Anecdoten,* and *Il Nuovo Bosco*. These miss much of the contemporary political allusion — and some of the humour — of the original. Omissions include Bosco's pun on *Van Bosse* and *vampire*, references to Van Bosse's predecessor Van Hall, to Bosco's rival Robin (the punch line of the original), and the fact that the shower of coins Bosco produces are *all dated two years ahead.*

Van Bevervoorde makes it clear from the start that this is a piece of fiction ("unless I have been dreaming standing up..."). Bosco (wearing white pants) is summoned from his bed to Van Bosse's office. The minister has some fun with the similarity of their names, and Bosco puns on Van Bosse and *vampire*, congratulating him on his coup of taking gold coin and giving paper notes in exchange. What Van Bosse wants, he tells Bosco, is conjuring lessons — in two years he must replace the notes with real coin again. Rule one, says Bosco: magicians must always return intact what they make disappear; a problem, says Van Bosse, but, replies Bosco, not if the magician is honest... Bosco then asks him to check his pocket — found to be bulging with coins, and when they spill onto the carpet they are *all dated 1852...* You have two years grace, anything may happen by then... Bosco declines to repeat the trick — we never do the same trick twice in a row. The Minister offers to teach Bosco high finance — no thank you, there would then be two Van Bosses — and asks Bosco to teach him *le secret de vos mécaniques* — but I do not use *mécaniques*, Bosco replies — ah, yes, I'm sorry, says the Minister, it is Robin who uses *mécaniques*, and he has nothing else... he thanks Bosco and asks him if there is anything he would like done for him. Bosco now hands him the following note asking him to read it when he has the time and show it to the Minister of Police:

> Copy of the original delivered by the Commissioner of Police in Leiden — Today, June 8th 1850, appeared before me, William Kemma Jr., Commissioner of Police in Leiden, Martini Gazofski, age 40, native of Warsaw, living in The Hague, who, at the instigation of M. Bosco, has declared that he, Martini Gazofski, has been charged by M. Robin with putting into circulation, both here and elsewhere, certain booklets titled *Vérité* ('Truth'), etc., which are intended to cast a false light on the talents of M. Bosco, a copy of which booklet is attached. Finally M. Bosco declares that he never said that Robin uses an accomplice or a helper in his tricks.

The Minister, asked his reaction, says it is unworthy of Robin and tells Bosco: so far you have only conjured away (*escamoté*) Robin's audience and his takings, the next step, since he keeps annoying you, is to conjure away Robin himself.

The exact point of this final part of the article, on Martini Gazofski and the booklet titled *Truth,* is now obscure, and it — and all references to Robin — were omitted from the shortened version in *Satanas,* etc. Robin (real name Henri Donckele, a Belgian) performed in Leiden in May 1850 and the Leiden Police Commissioner is real enough, though his name was *Kemna,* not Kemma (he died in Leiden in 1854), but of Gazofski or the booklet *Truth* there is no trace (not only no recorded copy of the booklet but no contemporary advertisements either). The

Rotterdamsche courant actually reprinted this as a genuine news item ("We do not want to deny a place to a copy of the following document..."; giving the title of the booklet as *Waarheid*) on 25 July 1850, a few days after the satire appeared in *Le Courrier batave,* but significantly there is no mention of the Gazofski business in the Leiden newspapers. The likelihood is that Gazofski and the booklet were invented by Van Bevervoorde for his skit.

Van Bevervoorde's satire was itself reprinted as a booklet in Dutch, titled *Bosco en Van Bosse, of De Twee Gochelaars* ('Bosco and Van Bosse, or the Two Conjurors'). No surviving copy is known, but there is evidence in advertisements of its publication. The earliest found is in the *Middelburgsche courant* 15 Aug.1850, describing it as "[tr.] a very witty comic dialogue between the famous magician Bosco and our present Minister of Finance, to help his Excellency out of the fire in two years in exchanging the bits of paper which he has lately foisted on the country instead of precious gold". This must have sold fairly well, as three months later (*Middelburgsche courant* 15 Oct.1850) a third printing was being advertised, announced as available "from all Booksellers and Postmasters, from whom one obtains *De Ekster*", probably another hit at Van Bosse as he also privatised the postal service.[572]

From Rotterdam Bosco headed to Belgium, arriving in Antwerp by August 13th and staying at the *Hôtel St-Antoine*. He made arrangements to perform at the *Théâtre des Variétés* (*Schouwburg van Verscheidenheden*), and hoped to open by the 20th or 25th of the month.[573] After a delay — spent, we hear, making his presence felt by his usual turns, finding money (*een gouden Willem*) in eggs in the market and (*pieces de 10 fl.*) in mud from a newly dug well — he opened on September 1st.[574]

A review loved "his magnificent magic palace (*zyn prachtig tooverpaleis*) set up in the theatre" and especially liked his tricks with watches — "with one word from Bosco all the watches stop, with a second they can be heard ticking again" (*op een woord van Bosco staen al de uerwerken stil, op een tweede doen zy weder hun getik hooren*) — but then, oh dear, an accident: he has fallen off the stage and hurt himself... This went over very well — "for a moment the audience were in suspense — then apprehension turned to laughter — Bosco has played a clever trick on them" (*Bosco heeft hun en passant een knappen toer gespeeld*).[575] Further shows followed on September 3rd, 5th and 8th, then a charity show on 11th for recent victims of the floods in Brussels, his next destination.[576]

In Brussels he opened at the 'Ancien Local de la Société Philharmonique' on September 22nd, performing each day until the 29th from 8 p.m. to 10.45, with one 15 minute interval. Reserved seats were 3 fr. The venue, said to be a little run down, was "as if by magic transformed with a touch of his wand into a veritable magician's palace". Not only was it brightly lit, but Bosco performed in the centre of the audience (*...se trouvera au centre de MM. les spectateurs*) and there was even an extra row of seats installed very close to him available by special arrangement (*Vu le désir manifesté par plusieurs personages, il a été établi un rang de stalles très-rapprochées de M. Bosco, et pour la location desquelles on pourra traiter à des conditions particulières*); these close-up seats had no backs, though this was altered later.[577]

Further shows followed on October 2nd, 6th, 8th, 10th and 13th.[578] He then announced a brief break, but soon resumed similar performances, now starting at 7 p.m., every Sunday, Monday and Thursday, and offered private *soirées* on the other days.[579] A further closure followed for him to make "changes in the lay-out of the venue", but he then advertised that he had finished his run in Brussells and was about to leave.[580]

He travelled to Lièges, giving four shows with great success at the *Grand-Théâtre Royal*,[581] then on December 21st reopened in Brussells, now at the *Théâtre Royal de Saint-Hubert,* with more shows on 24th, 25th, 26th and 28th. These were accompanied by short comic plays.[582] He also advertised that he was having made and would soon have for sale "various pieces of apparatus of his own creation which would quickly make it easy to perform various entertaining tricks…".[584]

1851

We then hear of a private *soirée* for a Mme de Latour at her residence, given for her guests instead of a ball because the royal mourning period precluded dancing.[584]

In late January Bosco announced he was closing in Brussells.[585] He travelled to Antwerp, then to Ostend, to make a quick visit to England, probably to discuss business arrangements for his first tour there.[586] He sailed from Ostend to London on January 31st at 10.30 p.m. on the steamer *Triton* (a 10½ hour passage), arriving on February 1st. His "Port of London Certificate of Arrival", filled in by the Port Officer but signed by Bartolomeo himself with his name and profession, records this as his "First Arrival". Bosco signed as "*Bartolomeo Bosco (fisico)*" and the British official, presumably misunderstanding the meaning of the word, wrote down his profession as 'Physician'.[587]

Bosco stayed only briefly and arrived back in Bruges on February 7th.[588] He then gave five performances in Ghent in the *Théâtre-Minard* (*Minardsschouw*) on February 27th and March 2nd, 4th, 6th, and 8th.[589] A review of his third show praised his "agility and dexterity … one looked, watched, rubbed one's eyes, racked one's brains — all in vain, impossible to get how it was done…".[590] The theatre was then needed for plays, but "by public demand" Bosco resumed performing on March 13th and 16th, the shows now including 'Le Cadeau du Sérail'.[591]

We hear no more of him in Belgium and at the end of April he travelled to England, sailing from Ostend on April 25th, again on the *Triton,* leaving at 9.30 p.m. and arriving in London the next morning,[592] now accompanied by his wife, son Eugenio,[593] and two servants. He was met by the same Port Officer, Mr. Fabian, who filled in his Certificate of Arrival, now listing Bosco as "conjurer", native of Sardinia, with his wife and son, and naming the two servants as Pierre Andres Crola and Carlo Cazzaniga; it is signed by Bartolomeo himself with his name and the word *familia;* we also have the summary list of the day's arrivals: this is filled in by Bartolomeo as *Bartolomeo Bosco, familia, fisicho [sic]*, and under *familia* the official had added "*Madame Bosco, Eugène Bosco and Two Servants"*.[594]

He was virtually unknown to the British public,[595] and his first advertisements in the London papers announcing his arrival stress his long celebrated career and offer proof of his credentials, reading more like an appeal to theatre managers than to the public.[596]

He opened at the Royal Princess's Concert-room in London on May 28th, shows on Mondays, Wednesday and Fridays at 8.30 p.m., and offering private *soirées*.[597] The performances were widely and enthusiastically reviewed. Reviewers commented on the novelty of his bare arms (nothing hidden up his sleeve) and on his skill in mysteriously transporting the audience's handkerchiefs, watches, rings and coins — "elicited rapturous applause", *Morning Advertiser;* the *Era* hailed his "remarkable dexterity"; and the *London Evening Standard* admired his "exquisite specimens of sleight-of-hand and mechanical magic ... a little thick-set man with a roguish eye and an interminable patter... his manipulation of different sized balls... is really extraordinary"; and all were amazed at his skill at restoring to life birds he had apparently killed, either by frying or beheading or wringing their necks...[598]

The setting was judged attractive — "His contrivances are all very prettily arranged before you, half shrouded in a series of bouquets, each encircling a lamp. By means of this fairy-like forest of light and flowers ... all the experiments are clearly visible, but there is no glare upon the eyes", said the *Morning Chronicle*, though the *Era* recommended that either the seats or the stage be raised for better viewing.[599]

The first night was "rather well filled", "crowded by an assemblage of fashion and beauty",[600] but later audiences were small — the Great Exhibition was diverting people's attention and their money. Exactly when Bosco closed is uncertain but his last advertisement was in *The Times* of June 2nd, and in a notice in *The Times* of June 11th he announced he had already closed:

> LE Chevalier BOSCO begs to inform the public that he has DISCONTINUED to give REPRESENTATIONS for very obvious reasons: firstly because he finds that the public is wholly occupied with the Exhibition; secondly that the public will not go anywhere but to the Exhibition; thirdly, and chiefly, because the Exhibition skilfully draws all the money from the public, and the public dreaming of nothing else but the Exhibition, goes to see no other conjuror than the Exhibition... Le Chevalier Bosco, seeing that all the rage is for the Master Conjuror, the Exhibition, prefers to give up in time, rather than be swamped by the Exhibition. He will re-appear shortly, with a good repository of tricks of his own invention, and he hopes that the rage for the Exhibition will have greatly diminished.

Soon afterwards he stated that he would continue giving private shows and lessons until leaving England at the start of July.[601]

However, he decided to perform for the week beginning July 14th at the Prince of Wales Theatre in Windsor as part of "A Grand Musical Entertainment" given as an adjunct to the annual livestock exhibition of the Royal Agricultural Society at Windsor Home Park, part of the Royal estate.[602]

He soon returned to the Continent, the short duration of this visit meaning that Bosco left little impression in Britain.[603] He returned only once, a hurried visit to Dublin in 1856, not to perform but to denounce the "Signor Bosco" then touring Britain and claiming to be his son (in fact Epstein, B12).

However, his London sojourn did win him his first mention in a newspaper in Australia and his second in America. The review in the London *Morning Advertiser* (30 May 1851) was widely reprinted in provincial British papers and then at the other end of the world in the Hobart *Courier* of 20 Sep.1851.

In America the earliest mention found of him is the account of his reading the Czar's thoughts, in *New York Daily Tribune* 19 Dec.1842 (previously in several U.K. papers); the second is a humorous little anecdote of him in London crushing a guinea-pig — until it turns into a silk purse filled with guineas: this story first appeared in the *Brooklyn Daily Eagle* 16 June 1851 (soon reprinted in papers from Louisiana to Tennessee). The date clearly links it to his recent London run but it has not been found in U.K. papers at the time. But, oddly, it turns up in the *Exeter Flying Post* a year later, 29 July 1852, then in other provincial papers. The English version is almost word-for-word with the American version but genteelly omits the word 'beautifully' in '*his squeal growing beautifully less*'.

He is next sighted in France, where (apart from trips to Algeria and Spain) he was to perform for most of the next eight years — until the end of 1859.[604]

On September 1st he opened in Lille, and with him "Mlle Martinez, a Negress, will sing a Spanish serenade accompanying herself on the guitar".[605] This was the famous Ana María Loreto Martínez, the first black singer to perform on European stages in the mid-nineteenth century. Born in Cuba in 1820, educated in Spain, she had considerable (but not unmixed) success in France and England in 1850, billed as 'La Malibran noire' and 'The Black Malibran' (after the legendary Spanish mezzo Maria Felicia Malibran who had died suddenly at age 28 in 1836), a sobriquet considered undeserved and which was probably not of Martinez's own choosing. Martinez returned to London in 1851, performing at the Princess's Concert Rooms on April 21st,[606] where Bosco opened soon after. "One afternoon", we are told, "previous to Signor Bosco's performance at the Rooms at the back of the Princess's Theatre … he took tea with the lady", and demonstrated for her a piece of apparatus he had invented: for the source of this anecdote, and the name of the apparatus, see *Appendix Z10*.

She and Bosco may have travelled from England to Lille together. There the local paper *L'Artiste* made no comment on their performances, only quoting complaints from theatre subscribers that during the fair they had expected grand opera but instead got four shows by Bosco and Martinez and a melodrama about Frankenstein's monster.[607]

At the end of the year both Bosco and Martinez were in Paris, but not at the same venue. Her act in Paris included a short play 'La Négresse et le Pasca' set in a seraglio where she sings to amuse the bored Sultan: this was written by Charles de la Rounat and Théophile Gautier, but in London in July 1850 she had performed a similar piece titled 'Les Délices du Serail'. Now, Bosco, of course, was an expert on the serail, but there is no evidence that he met her before April 1851 and that it was Bosco who suggested this subject to her.[608]

After Lille Bosco was to perform in Valenciennes, but refused to do so when he learnt his lodging was to be downwind of the abattoir! He proceeded on to Douai, where he had great success, both on stage and in his turns in the market, finding gold coins not only in eggs but in a hare (*"what sort of hare is this — it must be a Californian hare..."*), and bringing skinned rabbits back to life.[609]

He arrived in Paris at the start of November, warmly welcomed and fondly remembered by the newspapers "after an absence of eighteen years", but was unable to find a suitable venue. He gave private *soirées* and on November 7th appeared at the *Théâtre des Variétés* in a benefit for Spanish dancer Rosa Espert. Here he was a great success, and gave a second show the following night,[610] but it was a fortnight before he began his own performances, in the *Casino des Arts* in Montmartre. This was known mainly for short farces (it was not licensed for plays) and for magicians (Adrien was recently there), but it was far from small, a "vaste salle" also hosting concerts, balls, and, immediately before Bosco, a 40 square metre relief model of Constantine in Algeria. For Bosco the theatre was transformed by electric light into *Le Théâtre des fluides animés*.[611] In the numerous ads for Bosco's long run there the admission price is never stated, and not a single mention in found in the newspapers about high prices charged by him: perhaps the price remained at the modest 1 franc the Casino usually charged?

Exactly which night he opened there is unclear. The earliest ads found are in *La République* and *Le Nouvelliste* of 26 Nov., but *La Révolution* of the same date still lists the relief model. A long piece on Bosco published in *Le Siècle* 24 Nov.1851 by its drama critic Charles de Matharel de Fiennes pictures Bosco calling at the newspaper office, regaling them with tricks and stories: he invites them to "a show for you *tomorrow*" at the Casino, and this is reviewed as already having taken place; perhaps there was an advance show for the press — or both the visit and the review are fictional.[612] *L'Assemblée nationale* 23 Nov.1851 also reviews the first show as having taken place, but that also tells us Bosco is *really the son of a magician and a fairy and lived in the 14th century under the name Nicolas Flamel...* A letter by Bosco offering an unnamed recipient complimentary entry to the shows is held at the Bibliothèque Nationale: this is dated November 23rd.[613]

He was an immediate sensation, with crowded houses night after night, week after week — and month after month. The reviews were overwhelmingly enthusiastic, praising his skill and presentation and the "infinite" selection of tricks he continued to offer: he advertised a repertoire of eighty with twenty featured in each show.[614]

1852

There were lengthy write-ups of Bosco in *L'Illustration* 29 Nov.1851 and again 17 Jan.1852, another in *Le Nouvelliste* 12 Jan.1852, and in Edmond Texier's *Tableau de Paris,* vol.2 p.299,[615] and the comic papers made much of the presence in the city of four magicians at once — Bosco, Robert-Houdin, Linski, and Lacaze, deciding they needed a degree from Heidelberg professors to practise their art — and *were there magicians at the Stock Exchange as well?...*[616]

Bosco continued to draw full houses, not getting a respite even over Easter. Finally in April a break was announced, "after 125 successive shows", blamed on an "indisposition".[617] The rest was brief. The advertisements continued uninterrupted and he soon resumed his schedule, apparently missing only a Thursday and a Friday.[618] There was a longer break in early May, said to be "after 137 shows", to allow "new arrangements".[619]

It was at this time that Bartolomeo made the contract with Eugenio: this is discussed in his son's entry (B2).

He was also distracted by a court case. In March he had been presented by an English aristocrat with a 13 year old African named Sourouth whom Bosco costumed expensively and made his stage assistant, only to have to testify against him when he was charged with theft. Bosco offered to take him back but the youth was sentenced to be detained until age twenty. The newspaper reports quote Bosco's testimony at length making fun of his fractured French ("...*Ze le faisais, z'ai quatre domestiques... ze souis artiste...* ").[620]

In late May until mid-June Bosco took "a short break in his homeland",[621] returning "nimbler and younger than ever" on June 13th. He gave a private performance at the home of Prince Callimaki, the Turkish ambassador, with an audience of Turkish high officials and several other diplomats. But despite some misleading newspaper listings Bosco did not reopen at the Casino,[622] and by June 26th he was in Rouen.[623]

On August 3rd he opened in Dieppe, finding a large and appreciative audience — "marvels, veritable marvels", said a review, "but his finest trick is to have come back to us after twenty years as young and as nimble as he was then...".[624] He remained there till the end of the month, giving several shows, a benefit, and then private *soirées*.[625]

The popular author "Roger de Beauvoir" (pen name of the novelist and playwright Eugène Augustin Nicolas Roger) honoured him both with an acrostic, which was reprinted in the Paris papers, and a story, perhaps embroidered from a real visit, 'Bosco au Manoir d'Ango', which has Bosco travelling in his carriage ("which he bought from the King") to the 15th century manor of Jehan Angot, amazing and alarming the locals with his turns and tricks.[626]

We now lose sight of Bartolomeo until early 1853. There is nothing to indicate that he left France — when he returned he was said to be *back from the provinces*.[627] There were short-lived reports that he might perform in Vienna in January ("nach Neujahr") 1853,[628] but there is no record in the Vienna papers of his presence there.

This is the period when Eugenio was beginning his career — the first definite sighting of him on stage is in Holland in July 1852 (see B2), but there is no evidence that Bartolomeo was with him.

1853

Certainly in February 1853 Bosco was back in Paris, at Les Folies-Mayer,[629] which had not flourished as a *café-concert* and now became a very successful venue for Bosco until he left in the summer.[630] The reviews universally praised Bosco and his "brillant répertoire" and the attractiveness of the venue ("jolie salle"), crowded night after night by "a public eager for miracles".[631] His shows were accompanied by concert interludes, which included four musical Swiss brothers, "artistes organophoniques", whose "artistic and musical eccentricity together with the amiable sorcerer has all Paris running, the crowds each night making advance bookings essential".[632] Bosco's success was hailed as equal to that of the previous year in Montmartre, his act always changing and going from strength to strength.[633]

On March 16th he performed at the Tuilleries before Napoleon III, the court, and the *corps diplomatique,* to great acclaim, and is said to have responded to a request by the Emperor (no mean conjuror himself) for a trick he could not fathom by correctly naming a card selected by him and then finding it in the Emperor's pocket, the card bearing a picture of a Napoleon on horseback.[634]

Bosco took part in a benefit show at the Palais Royal on May 3rd,[635] and on May 16th in another, on behalf of Paris apprentices and young workers, in the Jardin d'Hiver, where he repeated his Royal performance for the public.[636]

From late May large advertisements began to appear in the Paris papers for the summer season in Dieppe, with daily trains from Paris — the beach, the baths (recreational and medicinal), the vast glazed gallery, restaurants, music, balls, and Bosco performing twice a week.[637]

However, he did not open there until July, performing first in Le Havre, at the salle Sainte-Cécile, with a final show in a room in the Hôtel Frascati for a few close admirers who arranged for a shower of flowers to fall over him as he was concluding.[638] A retrospective report dated 24th December 1853 by the Le Havre correspondent of *Didaskalia* states that Bosco was in Le Havre for several weeks, "building a fairy palace as the fair was beginning", and giving a total of forty crowded performances. It makes much of his philanthropy while there, saying that "neither he nor his excellent wife tired of dispensing charity, especially to poor exiles who were so lucky to find such a kind benefactor on the last sod of European soil".[639]

He opened in Dieppe on July 8th at the *Grand Salon de l'Établissement des Bains,* with shows twice a week at 8 p.m.[640] On July 28th he gave (unusually) a special show for children at 3 p.m.,[641] and on September 5th a charity performance in the theatre in aid of the town of Ancourt, 8 km away, where six houses had been destroyed by fire.[642] The Emperor and Empress were there from August 20th for three weeks and the *Didaskalia* article (note 639) states he received a certificate for a performance for them.

How long Bosco was in Dieppe after September 5th is uncertain: one article reports that he gave forty shows there, which, if correct, implies he was there till late in the year,[643] possibly with a break. The next definite sighting of him is not until late December, arriving in Orléans from Blois. His daughter Alexandryna died in Warsaw on September 21st (see *Excursus on Family*) and it is probable that he travelled to Warsaw soon after that and was there for some time.

Having come "tout triomphant" from Blois, he opened in Orléans on December 21st at the *Salle de l'Institut musical*, with further shows announced for 24th and 25th.[644] A review of the first show said little about his act ("…what escapes the eye escapes the pen even more"), praised his attire ("the costume of a troubadour in mourning"), and recounted at length his encounter with the Cossack in 1812.[645] Shows were added on December 28th and January 1st, and he remained in Orléans another week, offering private *séances*.[646]

1854

We see him again in early March 1854 in Poitiers,[647] and there is again nothing to suggest that he performed outside France in the interim. In May and June he was in Bordeaux,[648] followed by two very successful months in Rennes, then gave three shows in Laval on September 17th, 19th and 21st, all well attended despite high prices, said the reviewer, and counter attractions at the Cirque.[649]

In December he was in Angers and heading for Nantes, where his plans to perform were delayed when he lost his voice.[650]

1855

He was finally able to open in Nantes on January 6th, giving shows every Saturday, Sunday, Tuesday and Thursday at 7.30 p.m., and he remained there almost three months. He redecorated a large room in the *Ancien Palais de Justice* (now the Muséum d'Histoire Naturelle) in Rue Voltaire, turning it into "an enchanted palace", which the public could come and view during the day.[651] Both the thronging public and the reviewers were entranced.[652]

His *first repertoire* was repeated until January 20th when he began his *second répertoire*, 'Durando l'Enchanteur', which included the 'Confiseur de Constantinople' and the 'Famille de Lucifer', repeating (as usual) only the cup and balls ('Les Pilules du Diable').[653] Each night sold out very early, and Thursdays became a popular night for school children, young and old.[654] On February 10th he began his *third and last répertoire* of twenty new tricks,[655] continuing to draw the crowds, though the run was briefly suspended due to snow and freezing cold weather.[656] He gave a charity show for the poor on February 13th.[657]

By late February he was advertising a selection of tricks (*quelques représentations*), some of them already seen, some new, but no less popular,[658] and "By popular demand" gave a special afternoon show for children and the aged on March 15th, promising it would include no pistol shots.[659] He announced his final show for March 18th,[660] then a second charity show followed on March 25th, on behalf of the Shelter for the Old run by the Little Sisters of the Poor.[661] He remained a while longer in Nantes to rest, but still offering lessons and apparatus for sale.

On May 1st he arrived in La Rochelle and opened at the *Théâtre de la Rochelle* on Sunday 6th, with shows to follow on 8th and 10th.[662] A long review compared him with the Bosco who was there twenty two years earlier — *a strange man this Bosco, we found him just as he was then ... unmarked by time ... the same squat, thickset person, vigorous, agile, with a sardonic smile, bristly hair... and as a magician he has lost none of his dexterity... his technique superior to Comus* (just as he was rated in the same paper in 1834) *... in the art of legerdemain* (escamotage) *Bosco has set new boundaries and we doubt if anyone will ever go further... if he has altered, it is in wisely cutting back on methods that now fool no one, excluding from his rich apparatus the multiplicity of double-bottom boxes... making him look for new and more subtle ways to baffle his audience...*[663]

He was next in Rochefort, performing with great success and lauded to the skies by the local paper — *he does things which surpass human reason ... truly astonishing, dazzling, stunning .... unique in his genre, he has no predecessor and after him there will be no other magician... in his art he is what Raphael is to painting, Paganini to the violin, Taglioni to dance, Rossini to music...*[664]

He arrived in Saintes on June 1st, giving three shows there, the last on June 6th,[665] and by the end of June he was in Bayonne, but left for Bordeaux, promising soon to return; he was back on July 16th, with plans to open there at the *Théâtre de Bayonne* the following week.[666] His first show was on July 24th, with others on 28th, 31st, and August 4th.[667] An enthusiastic review said he had the manner and bearing of an Italian comic actor, a Scaramouche, holding the audience enthralled for three hours. *His tricks are beyond belief, and if you ask him how they are done, he will reply banteringly* C'est oun prestigio! *He proudly places an old umbrella in its cover in front of the audience; a gentleman is asked to put a five franc piece in a box the size of his hand, lock it and keep the key; the box is placed on a pedestal table; on another table is an empty jar. Four scarves are loaded into a blunderbuss which Bosco holds. The man and the three objects are all ten feet apart from each other. A shot is fired, and the cover of the umbrella is in the box instead of the five franc piece which is now in the empty jar; and the four scarves have become a new and pretty cover for the umbrella...*[668] Before he left he gave a final one-hour show, preceded by a play and followed by a farce, on August 5th.[669]

We find him again in December, in Toulouse, announcing his arrival by recalling his success there 23 years earlier. He soon made the front page of the paper with some of his usual antics in the market, finding money in eggs (the money then disappearing) and a guinea-pig in the head of a cabbage. But that was virtually all that the *Journal de Toulouse* said of him during his ten weeks there: he advertised in it regularly but it published no reviews of his shows (whereas it always reviewed concerts and plays).[670]

He opened on Thursday December 27th at the *Salle du Conservatoire Philharmonique* ("redecorated, heated, and lit with gas"), giving shows every Sunday, Tuesday and Thursday.[671]

1856

In early January came Part Two of his *répertoire* ('Fata Morgana'),[672] and the following week Part Three ('Le Sorcier du XIXe siècle'). Each Part was given three times.[673] His *Tenth* and *Eleventh Soirées* promised new tricks[674] and more again in the next sequence.[675] He gave an afternoon show (promising no fire-arms) on January 31st, then a joint performance with the Sicilian violinist Silvestro Nicosia, and advertised he would be continuing to perform, with a selection of twenty tricks, "as a distraction during Lent".[676] He announced his "final show" for Sunday 17th, which was followed by a "definitive closing show" the next Sunday, and on February 28th he took part in a charity Fête, still promising "tricks which no one has yet been able to appreciate in Toulouse".[677]

Bosco now left hurriedly for Dublin — not to perform but to denounce the "Signor Bosco" then touring Britain (with great success, billed as "the Great Italian Wizard") and claiming to be his son (in fact the Pole Epstein, B12). Bosco went with "Mr Sparks, attorney" to the head Police Office in Dublin, inquiring "whether proceedings could not be taken, under the jurisdiction of the magistrates, against the Signor Bosco now performing nightly at the Rotundo, whom he asserted to be an usurper of his titles and reputation". He was told that the magistrates could not interfere and to apply to the Court of Equity.[678] Bartolomeo then sent a letter to the newspapers, no doubt composed by his lawyer:

> Sir—The first intimation I heard of a person assuming my name as "Bosco," "the Italian Wizard" was while reading a newspaper in the town of Toulouse in the south of France, and I now come at great expense and personal inconvenience to announce to the Dublin public that I have not authorized any person to assume my name, thereby damaging my present European reputation ... as the First Conjuror in the world. The only object I have is to protect my character ... I am the real Bosco of Turin.[679]

The only result was that the impostor changed his stage name (though still claiming to be a Bosco and to be Italian) to "Signor Alfred Bosco, of Mantua"; he finally got his comeuppance in 1858 in Berlin, but less for stealing Bosco's name than for falsely claiming to have the *Légion d'honneur*.[680]

Bartolomeo returned to the south of France. In June he was in Carcassonne, advertising three performances at the *Salle de la Mairie* on June 24th, 26th and 29th, promising his standard menu of sixty different tricks.[681] In fact he cancelled the third show in favour of a visiting theatrical troupe performing that night and combined with them to present a joint show on July 3rd.[682]

In early August he was reported as soon to arrive in Montpellier,[683] but performed first in the surrounding area. He was in Béziers at the end of July,[684] and gave two shows in Sète on August 29th and 30th.[685]

He arrived in Montpellier in early September, but due to a sore throat ("une indisposition d'une irritation à la gorge") could not perform for nearly a month.[686] He then announced he would give only two shows, on October 8th and 10th. Both met with excellent reviews,[687] and he went on to give a third show on 13th (billed as his last) and a fourth on 14th.[688] He then returned to Sète to give two further shows on October 27th and 28th.[689]

Bosco now travelled to Paris but it was only a short business trip in early November and he was back in Montpellier in three weeks (a 1500 km round trip).[690] On his return he announced only that he was soon to leave but would complete the course for those who had been taking lessons from him.

He was eagerly expected in Nîmes, but on his arrival had to place a letter in the paper regretting that, anxious as he was to perform here where he had been so well received twenty-three years earlier and this being the last visit that his age and health allowed him, he could not yet open, as a sore throat prevented him speaking in public. At the end of the month he was still unwell, though offering to give personal lessons.[691]

1857

A long laudatory article on him appeared in January, but it was April before he was able to perform, building a "fairy palace" styled 'Salon Bosco' (not a tent but made of wood, "le palais en planches") in the Place de la Bouquerie.[692]

He finally opened on April 12th, Easter Sunday, giving shows on Sundays, Tuesdays and Thursdays.[693] The first *répertoire* was repeated until April 26th, so seven shows in the three weeks. A reviewer particularly liked *his little scamp of an accomplice, a splendid white pigeon that took away two watches entrusted to its master, flying off out the window looking like it intended a long flight, but soon returning and hiding itself artfully in a bottle which had to be broken to set this new Asmodeus free*.[694]

The second *répertoire* (another twenty tricks, the first part ending with 'On ne saura pas l'heure qu'il est' and the whole show ending with 'La Famille de Lucifer') started on 28th.[695] This was even more popular, despite freezing cold weather, with over three hundred people unable to obtain tickets one night. *Bosco surpassed himself,* said a review, and *les Pilules du Diable* which opened his show had to be repeated by unanimous demand in part two.[696]

However, on May 12th a letter from Bosco dated May 8th was published announcing with regret that he had to "leave Nîmes for Turin on family matters", and the shows billed for May 12th, 14th and 17th, and the third *répertoire* due on 21st, would be cancelled.[697]

No specific reason is given but this must surely relate to Eugenio's accident on May 4th. Perhaps Bosco learnt fairly quickly that it was not as serious as first feared, for instead of heading to Turin he went to nearby Arles and performed there on May 13th. This was a huge triumph, netting him over 2,000 francs, said a correspondent of the Nîmes paper, which pointedly remarked that he would have found no less a welcome had he remained in Nîmes. He was in Arles a week, with further success, then returned to Nîmes to start his third *répertoire* on 21st as planned.[698]

However, after a "superhuman effort" not to disappoint his audience he advertised that ill health meant he could not continue. In early June he dismantled his *Salon,* blaming the expenses it was incurring and his ongoing poor health, but he was not leaving Nîmes, he said, only resting and hoping to recover.[699]

On July 5th he gave one final grand performance, "Représentation Vraiment Extraordinaire", in the *Arènes de Nîmes,* the Roman Amphitheatre. He would perform alone, in daylight, doing twenty tricks, and because of the size of the venue he would give his commentary by "Italian pantomime".[700]

The programme was as follows:

1re PARTIE

1. Les Pilules du Diable.
2. Le Changeur dans l'embarras.
3. Le Voyage sans locomotive.
4. Le Globe bouleversé.
5. Le Marché enchanté.
6. La Pleine-Lune (scène comique).
7. L'Ours et le Pacha, ou le Carnaval de Venise.
8. Le Revenant du tombeau de Pharaon.
9. Les Deux Boulets invisibles.
10. Le Pigeon voyageur,, ou l'Eruption de Vésuve.
  (*Entre-acte de* 15 *minutes.*)

2e PARTIE

11. Le Jardin de Flore.
12. La Marchande de modes de Paris.
13. Les Trois Pyramides d'Egypte métamorphosées.
14. Le Duel heureux.
15. Les Gardes-trésor en promenade.
16. Le Jardinier ou le Boulanger en déroute.
17. Le Trésor de Mamouth.
18. Le Parapluie de Staberl, à Vienne.
19. La Cuisine des Cosaques, ou le Banquet interrompu.
20. La Mort n'est plus la mort, grande manœuvre militaire.
  (*Scène heroïque.*)

We do not hear how many spectators attended (hardly the 24,000 it once held for gladiatorial shows) but the crowd was very large and, despite doubts that Bosco could bewitch and enthral them in such a huge venue, he succeeded admirably, with each surprise applauded from all parts of the amphitheatre; and "unusually the crowd was silent and attentive... the only sound was the directors' cash box".[701]

However, matters did not turn out to Bosco's satisfaction. The contract for the performance guaranteed him 5,000 francs net, half to be paid on the morning of the show and half *immediately* after it ended. He received only the first payment and took action against the directors in the Tribunal de Commerce in Nîmes on July 10th. The defendants' lawyer argued that the contract had been modified by a verbal agreement in which Bosco promised before witnesses that if the total proceeds did not reach

5,000 francs he would be content with the net amount taken, and that this clause was not inserted in the written agreement at Bosco's insistence, as it might reflect on his reputation by casting doubts on his success; and as the total proceeds were less than 4,000 francs he should accept this smaller net amount. Bosco's lawyer successfully argued against this and, when no reconciliation could be reached, the ruling was that the directors must pay the full 5,000 francs.[702]

Bosco headed to Alais (now Alès) at the request of "the towns of Alais, Uzès and Vauvert", giving two shows there on July 16th and 18th. He was still in that neighbourhood the following month, writing to the Nîmes paper to say his farewells to the city and that he would be giving two shows in Tarascon on 20th and 23rd August, and then leave for Algeria.[703]

In September he passed through Marseille but did not perform there, stating that "he had to comply with a pressing invitation from the authorities in Algiers" (*il a dû se rendre à une pressante invitation des autorités d'Alger*) to give shows in the capital during the annual *fêtes françaises,* held in late September at the time of the horse races when all the local chiefs would be present.[704]

This sounds like an official request from the French authorities for him to visit Algeria, and in fact such a political motive is specifically stated in a contemporary article on Muslim secret societies in Algeria, discussing attempts made by the French government to counter the influence of the Islamic mystical brotherhood, the *Aissawiyya* (`*Isawiyya*).[705]

> In order to put the natives on their guard against the *sharifs* ... the Governor-General had the splendid idea of inviting to the chief city of our colony the famous magician Bosco… it was the time of the horse races, so all the Arab chiefs of the province were together in Algiers; now, this is what one of the chiefs said to Marshal Randon as he was leaving the performance he had just seen: 'Be sure to send this man to the tribes, for, like it or not, we will proclaim him *shereef.*

The author, Alex. Bellemaire, was a French government official in Algeria and it is very unlikely that he was confusing Bosco's visit with that of Robert-Houdin, sent to Algeria the previous year by Napoleon III to "out-magic" the local sorcerers: Bosco, it seems, was sent on a similar mission and he was in Algeria for more than six months.

The Algiers paper *Akhbar, Journal d'Algérie* reported Bosco entertaining the French Prefect and bamboozling the local chief Ben-Salem on September 19th.[706]

The next report has him mystifying French officials, then includes the first appearance of the anecdote of Bosco in Marseille deciding to visit the gorges of Ollioules. There he is robbed by bandits, but ("rira bien qui rira le dernier"), while they steal his wallet, watch and gold chain, he removes from his assailant's belt three watches, several purses, two pistols and a dagger, replacing them with a flageolet and a wooden knife — which lead to the bandits' capture the next day. All highly unlikely and much too reminiscent of the old story of Bosco and the Cossack.[707]

Bosco then performed at the Algiers theatre. The *Akhbar* review, saying that many were unable to gain admission, admired his skill and technique, and, comparing him to Robert-Houdin seen the previous year, Bosco's sleeveless and tight-fitting costume, allowing no secret pockets, won approval.[708] Another report stated that for

Bosco's show on October 26th, "a large number of tickets had been distributed to the Arabs".[709]

Bosco was now said to be thinking of returning to Marseille, but was requested by the authorities in Algeria to perform in Bône (modern Annaba).[710] It was probably on this voyage to Bône that Bosco travelled with the naval officer Eugène Souville, who was sailing from Algiers to see his brother stationed in Philippeville (modern Skikda, a natural stop-over en route to Bône). Souville gives a very lively account of Bosco dining on board with the officers and several Algerian chiefs, all befuddled by his tricks with the cutlery.[711]

After Bône we hear nothing more of Bosco in Algeria until

1858

April 1858 when he writes from Algiers to a number of French papers strongly stating that the Bosco said to have attempted suicide in Manchester (actually Epstein, B12) was not Eugenio (or indeed himself).[712]

By early August Bosco was in Spain, his first tour there, soon winning the hearts of the Spanish public, if not the uncritical praise of the reviewers. Both the public and the press wanted to know: *is he as good as MacAllister?*[713]

Bosco opened in Madrid on August 15th at the *Teatro Tirso de Molina*, with further shows there on August 19th, 22nd, 26th, 29th, and September 8th, 12th (a show announced for September 2nd was cancelled because he was unwell).[714]

The papers were shown his legendary Album and obligingly paraded the highlights of his career plus the standard anecdotes, and journalists were invited to a special trial performance at *la fonda de San Luis*.[715]

There were also predictable political allusions, and an interesting (no doubt apocryphal) story of Bosco finding a long lost brother, a hat maker in Seville.[716]

As usual the first two shows, here termed *Durandeau el encantador* and *la Fata Morgana,* comprised twenty tricks each, sharing only *Las Pildoras del diablo*. He stated in his advertising that he had chosen the small *Teatro Tirso de Molina* so that he could be heard better.[717]

Reviewing his first show, *La Esperanza* politely advised him to be "more economical in his use of fire-arms", which always frighten the ladies, and to be "more lavish with conjuring tricks (*los suertes de escamoteo*) and less use of the apparatus (*mecánicas*), advice echoed by *La España* and *La Iberia; El Clamor público* was very positive, admiring the skill and variety of his tricks (rivalled only by certain Spanish politicians), asking merely that in the next show he would conjure away the heat: the theatre was full and like a sauna (*baño ruso*); *La Discusión* noted the select and distinguished audience, admired Bosco's neatness and grace, and found his language *chispeante* (sparkling) *e espiritual; El Enano* was much less taken with him, saying that the audience enjoyed the cup and balls and some other tricks, but, considering his high reputation, his tricks were rather inferior, and "we even heard some spectators rating Macalister's more highly; furthermore, Bosco gives his commentary in Italian and this does him no good".[718]

His second show on August 19th was sold out two days beforehand, and there were suggestions he should shift to the *teatro del Principe,* much larger and more comfortable.[719] *La Época* found the show "varied and interesting … among the tricks the most surprising was that of the pigeons"; *La España* commented on the large and appreciative audience and especially liked one trick, *from a box that previously contained nothing, he took out and distributed a thousand kinds of toys and trinkets that the public fought over;* El Clamor público praised his conjuring and while it felt that his act of beheading the pigeons was *not a good choice, he makes it less horrific by doing it so that not a single drop of innocent blood stains the stage, or even his fingers ...;* El Mundo pintoresco reviewing the first two shows together said he had no rival as a conjuror, rating him *even better than Macalister;* concluding that *his first show was good, but old-fashioned and monotonous; the second was better;* for *La España artística* the second show *left nothing to be desired, and was more pleasant than the previous one due to the lesser use of fire-arms;* the public *enjoyed the fate of the pigeons*, also *the surprise of seeing him cut into two a pigeon, a deserter from Sebastopol,* and *the end of the show with the flight of infinite birds that Bosco himself had just killed and fried before their eyes...*[720]

La Iberia felt that certain tricks (the cup and balls, the canary fired from the pistol, the coins which multiply or reduce in number) gave plenty of food for thought, but that in others (the bountiful flowers, the coin which jumps in the jar, and 'The dead brought back to life') Bosco lets himself down — he is *inferior to himself*, and allows the public to understand how the magic is done, completely destroying the good effect that he intends to produce.[721]

Of the third show *La Época* and *El Enano* reported a full house, well pleased, though preferring the conjuring to the other acts. They felt that the act with the mixing and separation of the wine, and that with the fried birds, were not *del mejor efecto*, "and we say the same about the box of toys, though they were much to the liking of the children — and, after all, the entertainment has a lot of childishness about it, even though Bosco may be the Astaroth of our day".[722]

La España pictured in detail Bosco's build-up to the beheading act: — Bosco walks round the stage, then suddenly holds up two sharp and terrifying knives; coming forward with a tragic expression on his face he asks the spectators: who wants to offer to have his throat cut? A general laugh replies that everyone is happy to go on living. Bosco then announces that he is in need of two victims, and heads towards a box with two doves poking their pretty heads out...[723]

Bosco now moved to *el Teatro Francés* (at that time occupying the building of *el teatro Variedades,* which held over 800), announcing "his four last shows" for September 23rd, 26th, 30th and October 3rd.[724]

On the first night he pulled his old trick of pretending to fall off the stage, emerging unsteadily and with his arm covered in blood. This time he went further, crying *Death... Death ... but it won't get me!* then doused the arm with ethanol and set it alight — and the blood disappeared. The audience soon burst out laughing and applauding. And the show went on.[725]

In his third show on September 30th a large audience were enjoying the show when something unexpected happened: the gentleman chosen by Bosco to fire the canary from the pistol refused to do so, getting up and leaving; his exit was marked with "a murmur of disapproval", said one account, or "an expressive sneer", said another.[726]

During his "last" show on October 2nd, as Bosco was making his fond farewells to the Madrid public, a spaniel trotted up to him on stage with a letter in its mouth;

this he read aloud and to his and everyone's surprise and joy the French company who were to perform next in the theatre were delayed a week and he could give two more shows.[727] These followed on October 7th and 10th[728] and before leaving Madrid he gave a private performance for señor Don Salvador Lopez and his family.[729]

By the end of October he was in Valencia,[730] giving two shows there in early November which earned him a handsome sum,[731] despite a curt dismissive review in a local journal ([tr.] "…we will only say that we have seen travelling acrobats who for two *cuartos* have done more surprising things in the streets and public squares — the management, yes, taking advantage of the gullibility of the public knew how to make good use of the skills of Mr. Bosco, and since he has so many it has done very well").[732]

He then arrived in Barcelona in late November,[733] where he was initially unwell,[734] then was announced to open at *el Teatro-Circo* on December 16th.[735] In fact he opened on December 14th,[736] receiving a luke-warm review from *La Corona*: "although he did well some sleight-of-hand that was pleasing enough, the rest of his tricks, while not without an unusual merit, offered little that was novel and appealing", concluding that it would delay judgment hoping that in his second show he would "extend his artistic range".[737]

The advertisement for his second show on 16th makes it clear that in it (and so probably also in his first show) Bosco shared the programme: the evening began with a concert (*sinfonia*), followed by a play, then a farce, then came Bosco.

We do not hear if he lived up to *La Corona's* expectations, but a third show planned for 19th was cancelled. He is not said to be unwell, simply that "the third show cannot take place" (*No pudiendo tener efecto la tercera función…*), and refunds were available. The reason may have been the problem he had encountered several times in his career when sharing the programme, having to remove his elaborate apparatus each night to free up the stage for the opening act; a letter the following night offers him the use of a room in the *Plaza de San Miguel,* but there is no mention of him remaining in Barcelona.[738]

In October a Spanish paper had reported that according to the Portuguese press Bosco intended to travel to Lisbon in the winter. No evidence has been found to confirm that he did so.[739]

1859

On January 21st 1859 Bosco arrived back in Marseille from Spain,[740] and all the evidence points to his spending the whole of 1859 in the South of France.[741]

The Marseille papers were soon running stories of him beguiling the Algerians and anecdotes of him doing the same to fellow guests in his Marseille hotel,[742] but Bosco was too unwell to perform — perhaps if the illness persisted, said one paper, he would conjure it away himself,[743] but it was not until the end of the month that *séances* were finally announced, three shows ('Durandeau l'Enchanteur', 'La Fata Morgana' and 'Tout est Bien', sixty tricks in all); and since "he had been unable to find a large venue in the centre of town" he would perform in Le théâtre Chave.[744] Shows were advertised to take place each Thursday and Sunday ("all the theatre seats have been recovered"),[745] and he finally opened on March 17th. A warm review reported a full house and praised his handiwork, but stated that, regrettably, according to a note they had received from Bosco, there would be no further shows, "for reasons he would make known later". It was subsequently stated that he had been "unable to come to an understanding with the management".[746]

Shortly afterwards *Satanas* was republished in Marseille, advertised as for sale in several local bookshops.[747]

At the end of April Bosco travelled to Aix, invited to give three performances at the *Théâtre d'Aix* on April 25th, 28th and 30th, said to be "before he leaves for Paris".[748]

Both the Aix papers published promotional biographies of Bosco when he was in town. *La Provence* quotes him as saying he will settle down in Aix, if he ever retires from working; *Le Mémorial* has him receiving many wounds in a glorious military career, including a burst of shot taking off all the toes on his left foot,[749] and summed up his visit to Aix as "a profound sensation", filling the theatre, and equally amusing the public in the streets and squares with both his marvels and his pleasant personality.[750]

This was reprinted in the Vaucluse paper,[751] but there are no references to Bosco performing there (or indeed in Paris) and when he returned to Marseille soon afterwards he was said to have come from Aix.[752]

There were hopes that he would perform again in Marseille before leaving, and, after what was described as a "mournful silence" during a "terrible struggle" with a "serious illness", he announced at the start of July that he was now fully recovered and would be giving three shows at the *Grand-Théâtre* on July 10th, 12th and 14th.[753] Enthusiastic reviews purred that he had succeeded beyond all expectation, even reducing the torrid heat to a reasonable temperature that evening, heated only by the frenetic applause...[754]

In August he gave four very successful shows in Toulon,[755] returning to Marseille at the end of the month.[756]

A nice anecdote (significantly ending *Si non è vero...*) has Bosco, dining at the *Bains de mer Phocéens* in Marseille with his family, tormenting a poor waiter by turning champagne into beer and a "bouillabaisse" into "un plat d'épinards aux croûtons"... A slightly more plausible story describes Bosco performing tricks in Marseille for some visiting Burmese who are heading for Paris: to their compliments on his skill he replies "Vous allez à Paris, eh bien!, vous y trouverez de plus grands prestidigitateurs que moi".[757]

In October he performed in Draguignan, to great acclaim,[758] then in November opened at the Théâtre Royal in Nice, performing there very successfully until the end of the year,[759] and from a correspondent writing from Nice in January we get a glimpse of him staying at the villa of "Les demoiselles Ferny" with composer François-Adrien Boïeldieu and other distinguished literary and musical guests.[760]

1860

He gave one performance in Menton on January 9th,[761] and then headed to Italy, where in 1860 and 1861 he gave his final performances.

After shows in Genoa, Florence and in Alessandria[762] in March he arrived in Turin and planned to open on March 15th.[763] Warmly greeted as a local and "King of Magicians",[764] he finally opened at the *Teatro Carignano* on May 10th, the first of four shows advertised for 10th, 13th, 17th and 20th. His repertoire remained his long standard programme: "Questa rappresentazione, divisa in due parte, sarà composita di

10 esperimenti ... *Le pillole invisibile... L'eruzione del Vesuvio* (scena diabolica) ... *I morti resuscitati...*"; the second show was *La fata Morgana*.[765]

A long chatty article, calling him "the Nestor of magicians", praised his skill and elegant manners, and "even if he no longer has the vivacity of youth, he still has that of the spirit" — but criticised his language, meaning, it seems, that even in Piedmont he used when performing his trademark mish-mash, now second nature to him. But the public, it continues, attracted by his street antics, rush to attend his shows, "crowded in like anchovies in a barrel" (*una folla di spettatori stipata nel teatro come le acciughe nel barile*).[766]

He was caricatured by Casamiro Teja in the satirical journal *Il Pasquino* (13 May 1860) juxtaposed with another great "magician", the politician Cavour, who had just signed the Treaty of Turin, which guaranteed (at the cost of ceding Savoy and Nice to France) that Napoleon III would not oppose Victor Emmanuel, Cavour and Garibaldi.

One spectator at Bartolomeo's first show was Giuseppe Canofari, the diplomatic representative at the Court of Turin of Francis II of the Two Sicilies, quoted at the Theatre that night as saying he had his passport with him and was about to leave.[767]

And anticipating Bartolomeo's first performance the Florentine humorous paper *L'Arlecchino* ("giornale umoristico con vignette") had published a pointed political piece titled 'Bosco Il Prestidigiatore. Prima Rappresentazione' ('Bosco the Magician: First Performance')[768] which imagines him regaling his audience with the story of a *sea horse... there in a corner of the room, a sad beast of burden, which has always deceived all the wretched knights who have trusted in him... he also unseated a relative of mine, who had the gullibility to get on his back to cross the sea... with my cup and balls and my magic wand I want to make him harmless, but first I wanted to tame that colossal bear that you can see there in that very remote point of the room... I soothed it, I showed it the weak side and the perfidy of the screaming sea horse, and I believe I am close to reaching the goal...* the sea-horse is heard neighing in a very sinister and frightening way, and Bosco concludes: *Gentlemen, do not disturb the demeanour of that furious beast. I have reason to believe that I will be luckier than my relative in making him in a short time quite docile to my will.*

These contemporary political allusions lose something (or everything) in translation (a very abridged paraphrase: see also *Fiction* F32) and their referents are not as apparent today as they hopefully were to readers of the time.

But Bosco's "relative" here (in fact an unrelated namesake) is presumably the Bourbon general who happened to share Bartolomeo's surname, Ferdinando Beneventano del Bosco, born in Palermo in 1813.[769] Only rarely did the satirical papers leap at the chance to pun on their names. *Kladderdatsch* published an imaginary letter signed 'Bosco the Magician': "[tr.] In the interest of my art I feel compelled to ask not to be confused with a namesake in command in Messina. I do not need to step into the gold and bread of a higher escamoteur, juggler, and sleight of hand artist, much less would I give myself up to be an accomplice to such a man. I run my business on my own, make people disappear, summon spirits, call out flowers with my magic wand, catch balls and play with cards; in short, I flatter myself to be the first in the art of enchanting people, while my namesake has already shown in Palermo that he did not pass the test". Another German comic paper, the *Münchener Punsch*, has a dialogue between its two stock characters *Marl* and *Sepperl*:

"[tr.] 'So, what do you think of Garibaldi?' — 'He's the greatest magician who ever lived' — 'Leave off, don't make a fool of yourself' — 'But it's true. He even beat Bosco, at Milazzo'—'Aha'".[770]

At the end of May Bartolomeo announced two final shows at the *Teatro Vittorio Emanuele* "before leaving this capital", giving in daylight shows of a kind previously attempted only by candlelight in the dark, the first on June 3rd, and, then on June 10th, "Bosco will give his final performance of Egyptian Magic".[771]

But it was not quite his final performance: on June 17th he gave a charity show on behalf of a local school and orphanage.[772]

And his performances in Turin were also noticed in Warsaw, where he was well remembered: "[tr.] The famous magician Bosco (the father), as reported by Italian newspapers, recently appeared in Turin, and astonished everyone with his extraordinary dexterity, as well as the range and novelty of his tricks. Bosco has been to Warsaw more than once, always making a similar impression on local audiences".[773]

There is no evidence that Bosco now left Italy. It was not him but Eugenio in Vienna in June when we hear that "[tr.] The magician Bosco had to interrupt his guest performances in Josephstädter Theater for want of an audience", blamed on the summer heat.[774]

In July Bartolomeo gave performances at the *Teatro di Santa Radegonda* in Milan,[775] and we then lose sight of him till the end of the year, when he was reported performing at the *Teatro Guillaume* in Brescia in December.[776]

1861

In April 1861 he was in Modena, where he gave two performances on April 19th and 23rd, "the spectators, amazed by the wonders produced by Bosco's magic wand, applauded him, the poets honoured him with verses, and the papers proclaimed him king of magicians".[777]

Then in June and July he was in Florence. He advertised at the end of June that he would be performing twice a week, on Wednesdays and Sundays, at the *Teatro Niccolino*, and opened on July 3rd. Shows followed on the 7th and 10th; these included his 'Le Palle Invisibili', the 'Confetturiere di Constantinopoli', 'Tiro di Guglielmo Tell', 'Famiglia di Luciforo', 'L'Orso ed il Pasciá', 'La Bottiglia del Vesuvio', and 'Morti Resuscitati'. But on the 13th he announced that owing to an indisposition his final show would be on the 14th. These are his last known public appearances.[778]

1862

He retired with his wife to a property he had bought at Gruna, outside Dresden, and we hear almost nothing of him, except brief notices in early 1862, first that if his health allowed he planned to resume his performances,[779] and then that he fully intended to do so, producing "newly invented tricks, not with the apparatus he used before but with new, still unseen resources for his craft".[780]

1863

But he died in Dresden on March 7th 1863. The cause of death was recorded as cancer of the stomach and hypostatic pneumonia; his age is given as 70 years and 2 months.[781]

He was buried on March 10th in the Alter Katholischer Friedhof (Old Catholic Cemetery) in Dresden. The grave was located and restored by Houdini in 1903, who purchased the plot, originally only leased, and handed it over to the Society of American Magicians. He states that the original inscription (confirmed in photographs), in French and with incorrect dates for both his birth and death, read: *Ici repose le célèbre Bartolomeo Bosco.—Né à Turin le 11 Janvier, 1793; décédé à Dresden le 2 Mars, 1863.*[782]

Death notices appeared in the Dresden papers on March 8th, and very quickly widely across Europe, several giving the wrong death date, wrong initial ("K. Bosco") or wrong information, such as recently in America.

His wife Friederike died on February 26th 1866 and was buried on March 1st.[783]

Soon after Bartolomeo's death *Kladderdatsch* (15 Mar.1863) had jested that hopes of finding manuscripts revealing unexplained secrets were dashed and all that was found was a note stating "[tr.] I have destroyed all manuscripts concerning my art because before my death I came to realise that compared to many diplomats I was a mere bungler in the art — of deceiving the highest authorities and the esteemed public". After Friederike's death an auction of movables ("Mobiliargegenstände") from his estate was announced to take place in Dresden, with expectations of "rings with diamonds, rose-diamonds, rubies, emeralds, broaches with pearls and coloured stones etc", from Czar Nicholas, Louis Philippe, the Sultan of Turkey and the Viceroy of Egypt. But the auction was halted by an injunction, "probably on the motion of a joint heir", and it was suggested that Eugenio had anyway probably taken the pick after his father's death three years earlier:[784] it would be interesting to know if he was mentioned in his father's will!

NOTES

[1] Reproduced in facsimile by Rusconi p.13. Some older reference works spell his first name as *Bartolommeo,* e.g. *Brockhaus Konversationslexikon,* 14. Aufl.1894-6 and *Nordisk Familjebok Konversationslexikon och Realencyklopedi* 2nd ed., 1905 (both online: url:001) — both these give his son's name as *Carlo Bosco.*

[2] See also Rusconi p.18. Interestingly the early impostor Epstein (B12) was successfully prosecuted not for falsely using the name *Bosco* but for falsely claiming (and wearing) the *Légion d'honneur.* For the later impostor "Herr Ritter von Bosco" see B18.

[3] The café was in *corso della Cittadella.* The family lived nearby in the *isola Sant' Ottavio:* Rusconi pp.11-12; Mariano Tomatis 'Blog of Wonders' 7 Feb.2018 (url:002).

[4] *Curiose avventure e brevi cenni sulla vita di Bartolomeo Bosco da Turino esimio prestigiatore ed inventore della magia egiziana...* Napoli: Fibreno, 1837 (*Books* LIt1).

[5] And of course anything genuine in the stories was gradually embroidered and elaborated. Even if one accepts that Bosco was wounded in Russia, the splendid account of him robbing the Cossack who was robbing him (in *Curiose avventure,*

etc.) is simply too good to be true. A further detail was added by a Romanian newspaper in 1846 (see note 445 below): Bosco got 9 Thaler; and a nice story in *Journal des Pyrénées Orientales* 17 Nov. (continued in 20 Nov.) 1868 has Bosco in Algeria meeting a French soldier and his wife and telling them over a meal how, as a *simple tambour du 11ᵉ léger*, he was wounded and captured after the Battle of Polotsk: "[tr.] ...the day before that I saw our Colonel fall, Casa-Bianca, and immediately replaced by our Lieutenant-Colonel Blanc, himself wounded soon after..." — "but that was my father", says his dinner companion; the story is told by the soldier's wife, Gratia Blanc. And a whole new slant on the Cossack story is first found in a Vilnius newspaper in 1935: the French army in retreat staggers into Vilnius and are told to hide gold coins in their clothing when the Cossacks attack. Amid the slaughter is "a young boy, maybe 18 years old", *voltigeur* Bosco, a drummer, wounded in the thigh. The Cossacks pay him little attention; he swallows a gold coin, approaches a Cossack, then produces the coin from his pocket... Further coins fall "as if from a cornucopia" before the astonished Cossacks, then Bosco collapses. He is taken to a Jesuit hospital where he amazes the staff with his tricks — then does the same for the visiting Czar Alexander, who showers him with roubles and has him perform in great palaces, thus launching his career... — 'Career started near Ponary' (Paneriai) *Kurjer Nowogródzki* 3 Jan.1935, online at url:003.

[6] Adding "*et Comp.*" implies he had a company with him, but this phrase is dropped from his later advertisements.

[7] *Mechanikus* had extended its meaning from "technician / inventor" to automata-maker and automata presenter, and had now become a fairly general term for any "mechanische und phisikalische Künstler" (as Bamberg billed himself).

Other performers both well-known and obscure touring Germany and Austria at this time calling themselves a *Mechanikus* include Jakob Walther; Franz Mayrhofer; Matthias Tendler ("Mechanisches Kunsttheater ... mechanische Kunstreiter und Seiltänzer" — with circus riders and tightrope walkers: see note 9); Joseph Strabel ("Reisenden Marionettenspieler, Mechanikus und Comödianten"); "ein Mechanikus Schumann" whose "Taschenspielerkünste" featured a beheading act; the famous Maelzel with his automata and spectacle of the Burning of Moscow; Professor Eberle (with the "ehemalige Dreher- und Schutz'sche Kunsttheater"); Herr Mechanikus Thieme's "Thiemische Kunsttheater und Panorama"; L.W. Witzmann ("General-concessionitter mechanischer Künstler" in Prussia); Louis Goldkette; the well-known Tschuggmall; and Weiß, "Mechanikus aus Paris", with his "magischen Belustigungen" and "magische, mechanische und optische Versuche". Interestingly, Weiß was performing with his Kunsttheater in Augsburg the week before Bosco opened there — "Vorstellungen in neuen mechanischen Künsten" in the "Saale des Gasthofes zur goldenen Traube" on November 1st and 2nd (*Augsburgische Ordinari Postzeitung* 30 Oct.1819).

[8] This is exactly the same term as used by Weiß in his advertisement for his Kunsttheater the previous week, at a different venue. "Neue mechanische Künste" is not a common term; the only others found using it are Witzmann and Goldkette.

[9] The Steinl playbill is at url:342. For Steinl's ownership of the Kunsttheater formerly belonging to "Herr Dendler" see *Münchener Tagblatt* 8 Mar.1839. Schmid was Johann Georg Schmid, "Weingastgeber, Traiteur und Kaffetier", advertising food and drink, with music and dancing, from at least 1813 to 1842. He may have bought Bosco's Kunsttheater himself, as in December 1819 he is giving marionette and "metamorphosis" shows (*Augsburger Postzeitung* 20 Dec.1819), and in 1824 there is an auction for a marionette-theatre belonging to him ("dem Traiteur Schmid dahier angehörigen Marionetten-Theaters sammt Zugehör": *Intelligenz-Blatt und wöchentlicher Anzeiger von Augsburg* 12 June 1824).

[10] And for this there are only two unconfirmed sources: the often unreliable *Curiose avventure* (p.12) says he left Turin for Poland and Russia in May 1819; and in November 1822 when he was performing in Hamburg a newspaper notice (not by Bosco himself) refers to the fame he had previously won in the leading cities of Germany *and Italy*" (see note 31).

[11] *Baierische National-Zeitung* [Munich] 10, 12 Jan.1820.

[12] *Regensburger Wochenblatt* 8 Mar.1820 ("Der bekannte Mechanikus Bartolomeo Bosco, von Turin…"; prices are 24, 12, and 6 fr.

[13] *Königlich-Bayerisches Intelligenz-Blatt des Unterdonau-Kreises* 26 Apr.1820: "Hr. Bosco, Mechanikus aus Turin" in: Fremden-Anzeige vom 14. bis 20. April 1820.

[14] *Erlanger Real-Zeitung* 11 July 1820. The claim to have been a pupil of Pinetti and Olivier was made again by Herr "Pasco" soon after in Bayreuth, and Bosco consistently bills himself as a pupil of Pinetti until 1822.

There was clearly at this time in Germany a revival of interest in Pinetti, who had been dead for twenty years. Bosco's contemporary Weiß also referenced Pinetti (advertising in 1822: "Mechanikus Weiß … neue Stücke nach Pinetti's Art"; and in 1825: "Kunstvorstellung nach der Art des berühmten Pinetti"); a long piece on him, 'Ein Meisterstreich Pinetti's', was serialised in *Der Sammler, Ein Unterhaltungsblatt* in 1820 (and reprinted in *Laterna magica* in 1823); and there were new editions of books claiming to include his tricks — advertised at this time we find *Pinetti, Philadelphia und Enslin, oder die enthüllten Zauberkräfte: eine Sammlung auserlesener leicht auszuführender magischer-chemischer- und Karten-Kunststücke...* and *Das Ganze der Taschenspielerkunst, ohne grossen Apparat und Kosten die seltensten und auffallendsten Zauberstücke zu machen: zum geselligen Vergnügen nach Ekkardshausen, Guyot, und Pinetti...*

Interestingly, when Bosco was performing in Hamburg in 1830, a reviewer who as a boy had seen Pinetti compares them: he admires the visible delight on Bosco's face at the audience's enjoyment of his tricks, never "[tr.] the trace of a smug smile, never a certain triumph (which Pinetti revealed in almost every trick)" at having fooled them; concluding that Pinetti was "far inferior to Bosco" (*Hamburger Nachrichten* 21 June 1830).

Olivier, presumably Pierre Joseph Olivier (real name Pierre-Joseph Locufier), known for his mechanical figures as well as his conjuring, lived until 1830, but there is no record of him teaching Bosco, and, as with Pinetti, who died when Bosco was a child, the statement must be taken as a respectful *hommage*, just as Abraham Blitz, and even his son Antonio, termed themselves a pupil of Philadelphia.

[15] "16. Juli von Pasco aus Turin physikal. Vorstellungen im Theater gegeben": *Bambergische Jahrbücher von 741 bis 1832...* p.785 — the copy digitised on Google Books has pages bound out of order, but our page definitely relates to 1820 as it is headed "K. Max Joseph I. 1820".

[16] *Bayreuther Zeitung* 28 July; 1, 4 Aug.1820.

[17] *Leipziger Zeitung* 5 Feb.1821 (his advertisement is dated January 30th).

[18] *Morgenblatt für gebildete Stände* 23 Mar.1821: "Ein Schüler Pinetti's, Bantol-Bosco [!], hat eine zahlreiche Versammlung in diesem Monate mehr als einmal mit seinen mechanischen und physikalischen Künsten unterhalten, und dabey in der That viele Gewandheit und geschicklichkeit gezeigt…".

[19] *Abend Zeitung* [Dresden] 10 Apr.1821, from their Leipzig correspondent dated March 1821: "Der Taschenspieler Bartolomeo Bosco … es war ihm nach bestehender polizeilicher Einrichtung nicht gestattet, seine Darstellungen ausser den Messen öffentlich zu geben…". This was to happen again later in his career.

[20] *Leipziger Zeitung* 21 Apr.; 30 Apr.; 1 May 1821; his advertisements always emphasized that he was a pupil of Pinetti, and the same newspaper included advertisements from the Leipzig publisher and bookseller Wienbrack for a new third edition of *Das Ganze der Taschenspielerkunst,* attributed to Agrippa von Nettesheim, teaching conjuring "in the style of Ekkardshausen, Guyot and Pinetti".

[21] *Leipziger Zeitung* 5 May 1821. This was run by Christian Gottlieb Klassig and rated "[tr.] the best and most popular premises of this kind in Leipzig"; the second floor was a dance and concert room: Dirk Sangmeister, 'Die Linckesche Leihbibliothek in Leipzig', *Das Archiv für Geschichte des Buchwesens* 72 (2017).

[22] *Leipziger Zeitung* 4 June 1821.

[23] *Abend Zeitung* [Dresden] 31 Aug.1821 (Magdeburg correspondent): "Am 29. Junius kündigte uns der Mechanikus Bartolomeus Bosko aus Turin, mechanisch-physikalische Kunstvorstellungen im Theater an. Ihm wurde das Glück zu Theil, die neugierige Menge herbeizulocken, worüber sein Geldbeutel gar nicht böse gewesen seyn soll".

[24] *Leipziger Zeitung* 14 Dec.1827.

[25] Held at Gottfried Wilhelm Leibniz Bibliothek (Niedersächsische Landesbibliothek) in Hannover; digitised at url:004.

[26] Also King of the United Kingdom of Great Britain and Ireland, in Hannover on a brief visit — the only visit to Hannover by any of the three Kings resident in England between 1760 and 1837.

[27] *Abend-Zeitung* 16 Jan.1822 ("...der blasse Magus mit dem Schnauzbärtchen selbst, in seinem gebrochenen Deutsch und Misch-masch von Italisch und Französich parliernd, giebt der Vorstellung noch eine wunderbarere Färbung").

[28] *Staats- und Gelehrte Zeitung des Hamburgischen unpartheyischen Correspondent* 17 Oct.1821.

[29] *Der Gesellschafter oder Blätter für Geist und Herz, Zeitung der Ereignisse und Ansichten* 23 Jan.1822. The author of *Satanas* says he saw this letter in Bosco's album, signed by the King and with the seal of his brother, the Viceroy of Hannover, Prince Adolphus, Duke of Cambridge.

[30] *Staats- und Gelehrte Zeitung des Hamburgischen unpartheyischen Correspondent* 14 Nov.1821 ("...der Mechanicus Bartholomeo Basco [!], aus Turin ... von Hannover kommend, auf seiner Durchreise nach London...").

[31] *Staats- und Gelehrte Zeitung des Hamburgischen unpartheyischen Correspondent* 30 Nov.1821. His Hamburg performances are mentioned as "agreeable and well attended" in a later review: *Zeitung für die elegante Welt* 5 Feb.1822 ("Aus Hamburg ... Basco [!], der sich 'der einzige echte Schüler Pinetti's' nennt, macht Kunststücke, die ganz artig sind und ein großes Publikum herbeiziehn..."). A later article in *Oesterreichischer Beobachter* 20 Nov.1828 (see note 97) says he gave a total of 19 shows in Hamburg.

[32] For references see url:005 (note 35). The performance for the King was on April 14th according to the compiler of *Satanas,* who saw a flattering testimonial from the King in Bosco's album.

[33] *Morgenblatt* 20 Mar.1822.

[34] *Zeitung für die elegante Welt* 22 Feb.1822.

[35] Published as the second of his 'Briefe aus Berlin' ('Letters from Berlin'), dated March 16th 1822, in the *Kunst- und Wissenschaftsblatt* (supplement to the *Rheinisch-Westfälischen Anzeiger*) 26 Apr.1822.

The annotations to the *Düsseldorfer Heine Ausgabe* at 'Das Heinrich-Heine-Portal' give references to Bosco's Berlin performances from newspapers not available online: url:005. They add a further nice contemporary comment on women spectators admiring Bosco's bare arms: "... 'v e r y h a n d s o m e   arms', as some women near me whispered" (Friedrich August Kuhn in his journal *Der Freimüthige* 1 Feb.1822).

[36] *Morgenblatt für gebildete Stände* 9 Apr.1822 (a letter from Berlin dated 15th February). The anecdote had earlier appeared in *Abend-Zeitung* 13 Feb.1822 and *Erlanger Zeitung* 22 Feb.1822. I suspect that it dates from Bosco's time in Hamburg late the previous year — several tellings of the story open "Auf dem Wochenmarkte zu H - - - erschien..." and the version in Moritz Saphir's *Konversations-Lexikon für Geist, Witz und Humor,* 1852 (url:006), is specifically set in Hamburg. It reappeared in newspapers and joke-books far and wide for many years, often calling Bosco

"Taschenspieler und Mechanikus" long after he had ceased to use the latter term. The anecdote was soon appropriated by other magicians, and from 1909 to as late as 1924 Marco (Marcus, Markus) Malini, "Zauberer und Universalkünstler" (not to be confused with the famous card manipulator Max Malini, though he no doubt hoped to be) regularly performed the "egg trick" not only in markets but as part of his stage act ("der Mann mit den verzauberten Eiern": *Salzburger Chronik* 29, 30 Oct.1909; *Tagblatt* [Linz] 27. Sep.1924).

[37] Advertisements in *Gazeta Wielkiego Xięstwa Poznańskiego* 26 June to 6 July 1822.

[38] *Zeitung für die elegante Welt* 28 Nov.1822 (dated from Königsberg Oct.6th) and *Abend-Zeitung* 14 Oct.1822.

[39] See the *Excursus* on his family for details. Rusconi (p.23 n.5) plausibly dates the marriage to 1823 or the following year. Their first child that we know of was born in May 1826.

[40] *Kurjer Warszawski* 14, 19, 29 Oct.; 12 Nov.; 1 Dec. 1822; *Gazeta Warszawska* 15, 26 Oct. 1822; *Gazeta Korrespondenta Warszawskiego y Zagranicznego* 26 Oct.; 22 Nov.1822.

[41] *Kurjer Warszawski* 29 Dec.1822.

[42] *Satanas* (1859 edition, p.9).

[43] The poster is online at this auction site url:007; the Russian section is reproduced by Rusconi p.23.

[44] *Der Gesellschafter oder Blätter für Geist und Herz* 27 June 1823. The article in *Oesterreichischer Beobachter* 20 Nov.1828 (see note 97) says he gave a total of 41 shows in Moscow and 29 in St Petersburg.

[45] He had used the same advertising technique in Hamburg with his ads signed "Some Friends of his Art".

[46] *Rigasche Zeitung* 2, 5, 9 Sep.1824.

[47] *Rigasche Anzeigen* 22 Sep.1824.

[48] *Rigasche Zeitung* 26, 30 Sep.1824. Kauffert was one of two brothers from Riga, performing in Germany and Denmark from the late 18th century (*Lexikon*).

[49] *Mitausches Intelligenz-Blatt* 14 Oct.1824; *Abend-Zeitung* 19 Nov.1824.

[50] *Rigasche Zeitung* 30 Oct.; 7 Nov.1824; *Rigasche Anzeigen* 3 Nov.1824. His Gun trick was still remembered there fifty years later: *Rigaische Stadtblätter* 6 June 1874.

[51] *Mitausches Intelligenz-Blatt* 7 Nov.1824; *Libausches Wochenblatt* 13, 17 (a very flattering review), 24 Dec.1824 (for the poem, 'An Herrn Bartholomeo Bosco' see *Fiction* F51).

[52] *Kuryer Litewski* 25, 27 Mar.; 3, 8, 15, 17, 24 Apr.1825.

[53] *Zierikzeesche Courant* 30 Dec.1824: "Eenige dagen geleden, kwam de beruchte goochelaar Bosco te Marseille aan en ging daar aan eene *table d'hote* eten…".

Similarly, the Merlin anecdote which follows in *Curiose Avventure* is attributed to "*Lione giornale di Commercio in gennajo 1825*", but there was no newspaper titled *Journal de Commerce* published in Lyon in 1825.

[54] This child died in Warsaw in April the following year age 13 months: see *Excursus*.

This raises the question of the birth date of their daughter Alexandryna, who if the information given in her death registration is correct (see *Excursus*) was born in St Petersburg between September 22nd 1826 and September 21st 1827; and since young Eugenio was born in March 1826, Alexandryna was probably not born before the start of 1827. But her sister Adelaide was born on January 27th 1828 (see *Excursus*), so the window for Alexandryna's birth is January to March 1827. There is nothing to suggest that Bosco was in Russia in early 1827: if the date is correct perhaps Antonietta was there without him, possibly with relatives? He was not with her in Warsaw when Adelaide was born.

[55] *Lemberger Zeitung* 24 Mar. ("dermal von Petersburg hier angekommen"); 31 Mar.; 5, 10, 12 Apr.1826. The review was reprinted in the issue of April 12th and a Polish translation (with the same signature, "Miłośnik i znawca szt. mech."), was published in *Rozmaitości: oddział literacki Gazety Lwowskiej* 14 Apr.1826.

[56] *Lemberger Zeitung* 24 Apr.; 1 May 1826 (a long and detailed advertisement). Another long adulatory piece in Polish appeared in *Rozmaitości: oddział literacki Gazety Lwowskiej* on April 28th. signed "A Lover of Genuine Talent", the tag Bosco had used in Riga in 1824.

[57] *Rozmaitości: oddział literacki Gazety Lwowskiej* 26 May 1826; *Lemberger Zeitung* 29 May 1826.

[58] *Lemberger Zeitung* 5, 14, 16, 21, 23 June 1826. It was presumably the birth of his son that prompted the long sojourn in Lemberg.

[59] *Lemberger Zeitung* 18, 20 Oct.1826; *Gazeta Lwowska* 18 Oct.1826. Did he ever read, I wonder, the review of his performances in Lemberg written by the local correspondent of the *Allgemeine Theater-Zeitung* and published on 17 June 1826: "[tr.] Herr Bosco …does much in his field that proves him the master, while in many performances he does tricks the reviewer has seen better done in village inns" ("…zeigt in seinem Fache so Manches, was den Meister bewährt, indessen er in manchen Vorstellungen Künste zeigt, die Referent in Dorfschenken besser gesehen hat").

[60] Probably not since 1822: "[tr.] Bosco the Mechanicus, who a few years ago entertained the local audience with his skill, will soon come to the capital", said the *Monitor Warszawski* (9 Nov.1826).

[61] *Gazeta Krakowska* 25 Feb.1827 (a puff announcing his arrival, "an artist of a rare kind … planning to open his mechanical and physical exhibitions soon…", signed "Wielbiciel i znawca Kunsztów" (*"An Admirer and Connoisseur of Art / Tricks"*); the Lwów paper, fondly remembering his time there the previous year, also noted that he was in Kraków — "[tr.] … Bartłomiej Bosco, who made so many pleasant evenings for us last year, is now in Kraków, where he was to give his first show on March 5…" (*Rozmaitości* 30 Mar.1827).

[62] *Monitor Warszawski* 5 Apr.1827; *Gazeta Polska* 20 Apr.1827: "…gave his first show the day before yesterday in the theatre here…" ("Pozawczoraj dał w tutéjszym teatrze JP. BB pierwsze wystawienie swych sztuk mechanicznych i doświadczeń bawiącéj fizyki… Przyjaciel, a w części i znawca sztuk mechanicznych, A.").

[63] *Gazeta Polska* 22 Apr.1827. An early reference to Bosco's trade mark act of "reviving" birds he has just killed (discussed by Rusconi p.197). The German writer Friedrich Gleich (born in Vogelsdorf !) in his paper *Die Eremit* (No.53, May 1829) sardonically suggested where Bosco got the idea for reviving semi-cooked birds: in 1825 the Vatican beatified a 16th century Spanish Franciscan Julián de San Agustín (Beato Giuliano di Sant'Agostino) whose miracles included similarly reviving spit-roasted birds ("…Jetzt werden unsere Leser wissen, bei wem Bosco in die Schule gegangen ist und sich nicht mehr über dessen erstaunliche Kunststücke verwundern").

[64] *Gazeta Warszawska* 30 Apr.1827. The article in *Oesterreichischer Beobachter* 20 Nov.1828 (see note 97) says he gave a total of 21 shows in Warsaw.

[65] *Gazeta Polska* 2 May 1827. From later references it is clear that Bosco's guitar was ventriloquial (see note 131).

[66] The only reference located is in a list of upcoming court cases in *Rigische Anzeigen* 27 June 1827: "Gerichtliche Bekanntmachungen … 54: die Querelsache des Mechanikus Bartholomäus Bosco, wider den Advokaten Johann Wilpert, wegen Schuldforderung".

[67] *Monitor Warszawski* 6 July 1827 ("Pan Bartłomiey Bosco okazywał swe doświadczenia na wolnem powietrzu i przy świetle dnia…").

[68] A poster dated 1 August 1827 advertising his gun trick sold at auction in October 2021 (url:344). Another dated 10 August 1827 listing his act in detail sold at auction in October 2019 (url:008; also reproduced in *Ye Old Magic Mag* 7/1, Dec.2020).

Both auctions tentatively give the location incorrectly as "Leipzig [?]" but the Leipzig *Hôtel de Pologne* was in Hainstraße and not built until 1847. (Chopin gives a humorous account of playing in 1830 in the Breslau *Hôtel de Pologne*, described by Maria Zduniak as "the Grand Hall of the Merchants' Club on ul. Biskupa, known at that time as the hall of the Hotel de Pologne" — see url: 009).

[69] *Leipziger Zeitung* 8 Oct.1827; but according to *Oesterreichischer Beobachter* 20 Nov.1828 (see note 97) he gave 35.

[70] *Tags-Blatt für München* 16 Sep.1827; *Der bayerische Volksfreund* 18 Sep.1827 (etc.).

[71] *Leipziger Zeitung* 8, 30 Oct.1827.

[72] *Leipziger Zeitung* 10 Dec.1827.

[73] *Leipziger Zeitung* 14, 18, 20, 21, 22, 24 Dec.1827.

[74] *Leipziger Zeitung* 28, 29 Dec.1827.

[75] *Leipziger Zeitung* 21 Jan.1828. These notices signed with many initials appear in the paper immediately next to the bereavement notices, often similarly signed with the initials of relatives, but it is hard to believe he was parodying those.

[76] The posters are held by the Stadtgeschichtliches Museum Leipzig; online at url:010.

[77] *Abend-Zeitung* 3 Jan.1828; *Erlanger Zeitung* 29 Jan.1828; *Zeitung für die elegante Welt* 15 Jan.1828.

[78] *Abend-Zeitung* 10, 14 Jan.1828.

[79] *Abend-Zeitung* 15 Feb.1828. Böttiger was also the paper's theatre critic until ousted by rival Ludwig Tieck. The 'cup and balls' article was reprinted in volume 3 of Böttiger's *Kleine Schriften* (1838), wherein it is easier to read. It was also published in Russian in 1828 in issue no. 11 of the journal Атеней (*Ateney*, "*Athenaeum*") — these both on Google Books; in German in *Der Spiegel* in Buda-Pest in 1829; and in Danish in *Dagen* 18 Aug.1830 when Bosco was in Copenhagen.

[80] See *Excursus on Family* for details of her birth registration.

[81] *Leipziger Zeitung* 30 Jan.1828.

[82] *Leipziger Zeitung* 1 Feb.1828.

[83] *Leipziger Zeitung* 28 Feb.1828. The article in *Oesterreichischer Beobachter* 20 Nov. 1828 (see note 97) says he gave a total of 23 shows in Dresden.

[84] *Abend-Zeitung* 1 Apr.1828.

[85] Ludwig Börne, *Berliner Briefe*: pp.93-4 in the edition by Ludwig Geiger (Berlin, 1905). Geiger's notes on the passage give some contemporary references which I have been unable to access: the first advance mention of Bosco's Berlin shows in the *Vossische Zeitung* [*Berlinische Zeitung von Staats- und gelehrten Sachen*] 17 Mar. 1828 and an adulatory article on Bosco by Ludwig Rellstab in the issue of April 18th.

[86] Long article in *Abend Zeitung* 21 May 1828 (written on May 5th). A very flattering detailed review after his third show was published in the *Lemberger Zeitung* 5 May 1828.

[87] "Circus vor dem Brandenburger Thore" — a surviving poster for the show of June 22nd is held at the Deutsche Plakat Museum (in the Museum Folkwang) in Essen: online at url:011; reproduced in Rusconi p.27. I have not been able to see Christian Theiss' article 'Boscos Zauberkünste' in *Magische Welt* 2, 2015 or the article in *Berlinische Zeitung* 31 May 1828 quoted in translation by Rusconi who states the performance was in a large tent, brightly coloured and "in the Irish style": could this be *irisierend,* 'iridescent'; and was it in fact in the promenade known as 'Die Zelte', between the *Tiergarten* and the Brandenburg Gate? However, Bosco certainly performed in a large marquee in Poland the following year.

[88] *Flora (Baierische National-Zeitung)*, 14 Oct.1828. The article in *Oesterreichischer Beobachter* 20 Nov.1828 (see note 97) says 37 not 35 and tells us "Bosco was on everyone's lips, his tricks went from mouth to mouth, and fashion created coats, scarves and perfumes *à la Bosco,* named after him" ("Bosco war das Tagesgespräch, seine Kunststücke gingen von Mund zu Mund, die Mode schuf nach seinem Namen Mäntel, Tücher, Parfums *à la Bosco*").

[89] Habitt has an entry in the *Lexikon,* but is little discussed elsewhere. He claimed in Berlin to be "from Moscow", and when last sighted, in Paris in September 1829, he is said to be Russian, age about twenty-five, orphaned at age six after his father died in the Battle of Leipzig, then taken to Egypt where he learnt the magic arts... (*Le Figaro* 17 Sep.1829). Earlier he had billed himself as Austrian, and was rumoured to be born in Brandies [*sic*] bei Prag according to the article in *Abend Zeitung* 21 May 1828, which gives an interesting survey of the controversy between him and Bartolomeo and closely compares their technique, expertise, and demeanour — much in favour of Bartolomeo (even to his opening with "*Messieurs et Dames*" and Habitt with "*Meine gnädigen Herrschaften*").

Bosco, said one paper (*Flora* 13 May 1828), appealed to the "elegante Welt" and Habitt, charging lower prices, to the "Menge", and that ridiculously high praise was bestowed upon Habitt in the papers, crediting him with unbelievable feats. Both Habitt and Bosco are parodied in a "review" of their acts in Bäuerle's *Allgemeine Theaterzeitung* 3 June 1828, which pictures Habitt shaving off men's side-whiskers, removing women's teeth, and reattaching severed marching feet (all the above miraculously restored) and Bosco borrowing a ring which he throws out the window, sending first a canary, then a dog, then his servant out to retrieve it: at last, they return – the bird with the dog in its mouth, the servant in the dog's mouth, and the ring is soon back on the owner's finger, concluding *"You won't believe it if you didn't see it"* (a phrase Habitt was fond of).

[90] Unfortunately the two main Berlin papers, *Die Vossische Zeitung* ('*Königlich Privilegierte Berlinische Zeitung von Staats- und Gelehrten Sachen*') and *Die Spenersche Zeitung* ('*Berlinische Nachrichten von Staats- und gelehrten Sachen*'), which took opposite sides on the issue, are not currently accessible online for 1828, but there were frequent references in other contemporary papers and soon a flurry of pamphlets (see note 91). A humorous article in the *Berliner Conversations-Blatt* 30 May 1828 makes fun of the rival stances taken by the *Vossische* and the *Spenersche* on "the great questions between East and West" — "Ah, you mean between Habitt

and Bosco...", referring to articles by Rellstab and 'R. v. L.'; an anonymous "Dr. Kremster" also contributed. One newspaper report compared the rivalry — "Bosco competing through skill, Habitt through the most boastful announcements" — to that between Lichtenberg and Philadelphia (*Morgenblatt für gebildete Stände* 1 Sep.1828).

[91] " ...Both seem to have bewitched several literary friends onto their side", joked the *Blätter für literarische Unterhaltung* (23 June 1828), "their notices and reviews fill the newspapers.:.".

Saphir, born Moses Saphir in Hungary in 1795, living in Berlin since obliged to leave Austria in 1825, gives a retrospective account of his association with Bartolomeo in an essay 'Alles wiederholt sich nur im Leben, oder: "Hermann" und "Löbel" (= 'Bosco und Habitt'): in this, along with a nice story about Bosco's supply of poultry for his act, he claims that Bartolomeo had come to him for advice and quotes him as saying, now that Saphir had made him the victor over Habitt, that Saphir's literary prowess was as great as his own with the cup and balls ("Dafür sein Saphir mit die Feder, was sein Bosco mit der Becher!"). The essay, first in his paper *Der Humorist* 31 Jan.1851, is reprinted in his *Ausgewählte Schriften* (1871), vol.16, online at url:012.

Other retrospective pieces on Bosco by Saphir in *Der Humorist* are:

'Die Mystifikation' (4 Nov.1843: "all Berlin was absorbed in the important question of who would deceive us best in bringing the cooked poultry back to life — Habitt or Bosco") and 'Der ewige Bosco' (15 Mar.1845), which has Bosco as 'the eternal magician' ("Ahasver, der ewige Jude, ist eine wahre Fabel gegen Bosco, den ewigen Zauberer!") putting black heads on Noah's white doves and performing Moses' magic before the Pharaoh, and much else...

Der getödtete und dennoch lebende M.G. Saphir, oder, Dreizehn Bühnendichter und ein Taschenspieler gegen einen einzelnen Redakteur: ein Schwank voll Wahrheit: in phlegmatischer Laune erzählt is at url:013 but inaccessible to me;

the summarising *Der lebende und dennoch maustodte M. G. Saphir oder: eine Salve gegen dreizehn Bühnendichter, einen Taschenspieler und einen einzelnen Redakteur*, is at url:014;

but *Kommt her! oder: Liebes Publicum, schau, trau, wem. Ein humoristischer Holzschnitt, mit Melodien versehen* ... is not online.

Habitt's pamphlet (actually by his patrons) *Habitt's aus Moskau Nothgedrungene Erklärung gegen 6 Journalisten oder die aufgeschossene Berliner Kokusnuß*, is online at url:015, but not his earlier *Habitt von Moskau contra M.G. Saphir; oder, Der für immer begrabene einzelne redakteur*.

Friedrich Christoph Förster's 'M.G. Saphir und Berlin. Besonderer Abdruck aus dem Berliner Conversations-blatt (1828, no. 78 und 79)' is at url:0169.

Also online at url:017 is a one-act farce (*Quodlibet*), arising out of the controversy, *Vosculo [sic] von Barcelona und Greif von Kasan, oder die beiden Taschenspieler in Krähwinkel* (1828) — so catalogued by German libraries, but referred to in some contemporary newspapers as *Bosculo*... and one gets the impression the publishers carefully chose a Fraktur fount with minimal difference between *V* and *B*.

[92] Rusconi p.27, source unknown; certainly the article in *Flora* 14 Oct.1828 includes "die Badestädten" among the places Bosco has successfully visited.

[93] *Unterhaltungsblätter* 9 Sep.1828 (review of first show); *Prager Zeitung* (*Intelligenzblatt*) 12 Sep.1828 (review of his second show); 18 Sep.1828 (review of his fifth show and ad for his benefit show on the 20th, featuring the Gun trick — "die große Fusillade"); 19 Sep.; 23 Sep. (shows on 24th and 27th); 5, 7 Oct.1828 (ad for show on 8th).

Adolf Bäuerle in his *Allgemeine Theaterzeitung* 11 Sep.1828 celebrated Bosco as "undoubtedly the greatest living magician" ("der erste lebende prästigatorische Künstler…"), and was soon (25 Sep.1828) shaking his head at how the reviews in Berlin and Prague tried to outdo each other in their extravagant praise of Bosco's success (even citing shows in London, Amsterdam, Stockholm… where, of course, he had not yet performed!) — "one is tempted to believe that he has more than two hands, this devil of a fellow" (*Tausendsasa;* also with connotations of 'jack-of-all-trades'— Bäuerle had written a farce with this title a few years previously, and he revived it earlier this year); *ATZ* also featured (18, 23 Oct.1828) a long very positive review of Bosco's shows by its Prague correspondent (dated start of October), and there were further equally flattering reviews in *Flora* (*Baierische National-Zeitung*) 14 Oct.1828 and in *Wiener Zeitschrift* 18 Oct.1828. Bosco gave a total of eleven shows in Prague (*Abend-Zeitung* 6 Dec.1828).

[94] "Bosco, der Matador aller Escamoteurs, ist angekommen und nun in unserm Wien…", *ATZ* 25 Oct.1828, a long paean of praise, quoting reviews from Germany, Poland, Russia (from Moscow to Odessa), no doubt from Bosco's own scrapbook.

There were the usual anecdotes — a booklet titled *Oesterreichische Senfkörner: eine Sammlung nationaler Charakterzüge und belustigender Anekdoten*, Leipzig 1833 ['Austrian Mustard Seeds: a collection of national characteristics and hearty anecdotes'] put together by Anton Gross-Hoffinger under his pen name "Hanns Normann" includes the anecdote of Bosco in a Viennese market in 1829 "finding" 20-kreuzer coins in bread: he livens up the story by quoting the reaction of the woman at the stall, one of the legendary *Fratschelweiber*, known (like "fish wives" in English) for their loud language and coarse wit, saying angrily to her neighbour 'Schaut's, Frau Gewatterin!, hat mi der schlampete Strump um d' ganzi Waare bracht; na, kummt's no wieder, kriegts a Watschen af's Maul, deeß kani Zwanziger mehr brauchst' ("*Look at that, neighbour, the useless fellow has wrecked all my stock; still, no matter, he gets a smack on the chops, so won't need any more kreuzigers*").

[95] *Oesterreischer Beobachter* 28 Oct.1828; 20 Nov.1828. The first show was titled 'Das ununterbrochene Zauberspiel, oder: Das Publicum in Verlegenheit'; *Der Sammler* 13 Nov.1828 said: "man sah, staunte und begriff nicht", though suggesting that Bosco's table was too low.

[96] 'Die große Fusillade': *Oesterreischer Beobachter* 6 Nov.1828.

⁹⁷ *ATZ* 4 Nov.1828; *Wiener Zeitschrift* 8 Nov.1828; *Oesterreichischer Beobachter* 20 Nov.1828: the last, 'On Bosco in Vienna', is a supplement to this issue — it is included in the *Google Books* version (url:018) but not on *Anno*; it reviews all three shows in glowing terms, each show better than the last, his cup and ball work perfection, his tricks with the birds amazing... (A Polish version of this article appeared as 'O wystawieniach Pana Bosco w Wiédniu' ['Bosco's Shows in Vienna'] in *Gazeta Korrespondenta Warszawskiego y Zagranicznego* 24 Jan.1829; also in *Rozmaitości: pismo dodatkowe do Gazety Lwowskiej* 6 Mar.1829).

⁹⁸ The paper was following up a note it had recently published (27 Nov.1828) on the novel French term *prestidigitation,* a reworking of *prestigiation* as if it derived not from Latin *praestigiare,* 'to practice prestige, deception' — 'conjure', but from *presto* and *digitus,* 'nimble fingered'. The earliest examples of the word in English that include the *digi* element are according to the *Oxford English Dictionary* from the 1840s, borrowed from French or Italian — except for a freak example which it cites from the *Second Characters, or The Language of Forms* of Anthony Ashley Cooper, Third Earl of Shaftesbury, written in Naples shortly before his death in 1713, left in manuscript and not published until 1914: this is the earliest example by far in any language. The passage in the 1914 edition (and in the new "Standard-Edition" I, 5 of 2001) reads: "...those who run after monsters in fairies and the θαυματοποιοί. Prestidigitators".

⁹⁹ He was even performing Bosco's *pièce de résistance,* 'Das Publicum in Verlegenheit' as an *intermezzo* during his show, says *Der Sammler* 15 Nov.1828 in a very positive review of Döbler. Some reviewers were soon rating Döbler as Bosco's equal, even superior — the following year, touring Hungary in Bosco's wake, one report concluded "he has wrenched victory from Bosco who preceded him" (*Carinthia* 25 July 1829: "...vorangegangenen Bosko den Sieg entrungen").

¹⁰⁰ These subsequent events are described in detail in several newspaper reports — *Abend Zeitung* 12 Dec.1828 said: "[tr.] Bosco did his tricks, he did them well, did them splendidly, he did them remarkably, but after such a fuss from all sides, and in retrospect the high entrance prices, the good Viennese had expected even more, indeed the impossible. The roof of the theatre did not collapse, it did not rain money, in short, the man couldn't do magic at all … There was no shortage of applause, but people did not leave the theatre well pleased. And at the same time a Herr Döbler was doing at modest prices … the same tricks Bosco was doing at twice the price. If his apparatus was not as splendid and his skill not up to Bosco's, it was cheaper and the magician himself a fellow countryman. So it happened that Bosco's second show was less well attended than the first. The third (honoured with the presence of Archdukes Franz, Anton and Ludwig) was again full, but at reduced prices, and the director Carl dismissed the magician. But the most painful blow was to replace Bosco on this stage immediately afterwards with a farce, 'Staberl as Magician', in which Carl-Staberl imitated his tricks and even his mannerisms and held them up to ridicule, revealed the secrets of his apparatus and in this way in an objectionable fashion brought the laughs to himself and the money to his pocket..."; *Morgenblatt für gebildete Stände* 23 Dec.

1828 put it: "…Gegenwärtig parodirt ihn Carl in einer Posse 'Staberl als Physiker' auf eine ergötzliche Weise, wobey er mehrere jener Kunststücke, welche Bosco mit Beyhülfe von Maschinen macht, nachamt…"; and *Allgemeine musikalische Zeitung* 14 Jan.1829 summed up: "…so ließt sich der spekulative Director Carl die schöne Gelegenheit nicht entwischen, auch für eigene Rechnung Vortheile davon zu ziehen. Er hat seinem Vorbild mehre Experimente, die nicht auf die Blitzschnelligkeit der Escamontage basirt sind, sondern durch geheimes Einverständniß bewerkstelligt werden können, mit Falkenaugen abgelernt…" — *Carl did the tricks which relied on a secret move (copied with the eye of a falcon) not those depending on speed and dexterity.*

The whole affair is discussed in:
Ferdinand Seyfried, *Rückschau in das Theaterleben Wiens seit den letzten fünfzig Jahren.* Vienna: The Author, 1864, Chapter VIII, online at url:019; and
Hans Pemmer, 'Wiener Taschenspieler im ausgehenden 18. Jahrhundert und in der Biedermeierzeit', pp.116*ff.*, online at url:020; and
Christian Gruber, *Wiener Zaubertradition. Theatrale Aspekte der Zauberkunst im 19. Jahrhundert.* Hamburg: Diplomica Verlag [2016], pp.41*ff.*

Coloured plates of 'Staberl als Physiker', and 'Staberl der konfuse Zauberer' were published in *ATZ* in the series 'Gallerie interessanter und drolliger Scenen': url:021.

In 1857 Bosco's act still included a trick 'Le Parapluie de Staberl, à Vienne'.

[101] Carl's comic parody, 'Staberl als Physiker' (the music by Franz Gläser), was very popular with audiences but soon lost its interest when the target Bosco left Vienna ("das Zugstück … hat seinen Reiz bereits verloren; die Parodie hörte schon früher auf zu interessiren, ehe der parodirte Held aus den Mauern Wiens gezogen war": *Zeitung für die elegante Welt* 24 Jan.1829). So Carl then took it on tour, Prague May 18th 1829 and Pest May 25th; and he tried it again in Vienna on December 12th 1830 (Karl Goedeke, *Grundriss zur Geschichte der deutschen Dichtung aus den Quellen*, 2nd ed., XI.2 p.37). The play was also performed in Hamburg, with local comic Karl Hechner as Staberl, in June 1830 *when Bosco was there*. The text of the show was never printed and published, but the National Library of Austria holds a manuscript of one of the songs, "Quodlibet (O Schicksal, du hast mich g'troffen)".

[102] Published in *Der Sammler* 18 Dec.1828 and in *Wiener Zeitschift* the same day.

[103] *Il Figaro* 3 June 1835; *Il Corriere delle Dame* 5 June 1835.

[104] *Preßburger Zeitung* 16, 19 (review of first show), 23 (review of second and third), 30 Dec.1828 (ad for sixth show); 9 Jan.1829 (review of final show, "[tr.] surpassing all his previous shows in variety and originality…").

[105] *ATZ* 10 Feb.1829 (report from the Raab correspondent dated January 27th).

[106] *Der Spiegel, oder: Blätter für Kunst, Industrie und Mode* 4 Feb.1829 (online at url:022); *Preßburger Zeitung* 6 Feb.1829. For Böttiger see note 79.

[107] *Der Spiegel* 7 Mar.1829; *ATZ* 28 Mar.1829 pronounced each show better than the last.

[108] *Der Spiegel* 7 Mar.1829; *Österreichisches Bürgerblatt für Verstand, Herz und gute Laune* 10 Apr.1829.

[109] *Der Spiegel* 18 Mar.1829.

[110] *ATZ* 18 Apr.1829. Astley's would have been a far from ideal venue for Bosco's performances, being an amphitheatre with a stage at one side. It did feature group variety acts such as tumblers and acrobats but the main entertainments offered were an equestrian circus with dare-devil riding, plus lions and elephants, and large scale melodramatic spectacles: the show on at this time was 'The Storming of Seringapatam', with a cast of a hundred, lots of horses, and sensational effects such as canons firing.

[111] *Biographie und Anecdoten* p.8, which is unreliable — it also states that he performed for the Palatine of Hungary on May 30th, but that was on March 5th when Bosco was in Buda.

[112] *Preßburger Zeitung* 19 June 1829; *Privilegirte Schlesische Zeitung* 30 May; 6 June 1829 (the last a plea from the locals for him not to leave but to remain during the holidays — "[tr.] The unpleasant weather means we are missing the scent of the flowers in the open air, but your little flowers, bouquets and garlands which burst into bloom thanks to your magic staff in your fairy palace spread the loveliest fragrances, just as the splendid roses and violets which you present to our ladies still enjoy a wonderful freshness in our rooms! Please stay with us…").

[113] *Gazeta Wielkiego Xięstwa Poznańskiego* 30 May; 24 June 1829.

[114] *Gazeta Wielkiego Xięstwa Poznańskiego* 27 June 1829.

[115] *Kuryer Litewski* 29 July 1829; *Gazeta Polska* 2 Aug.1829.

[116] *Gazeta Warszawska* 17 Sep.1829.

[117] *Gazeta Korrespondenta Warszawskiego y Zagranicznego* 2, 4 Oct.1829.

[118] *Hamburger Nachrichten* 18 Dec.1829: "…Er eröffnete seine Leistungen mit dem Becherspiel, das nur von ihm in solcher Vollkommenheit ausgeführt werden kann. Eben dieses Spiel ist der Prüfstein seiner Kunst und bei der Fertigkeit des Herrn Bosco, wie er hierbei Kugeln in der Luft wie Seifenblasen verschwinden und wieder erscheinen ließ, mußte das Natürliche scheinbar sich als übernatürlich gestalten…".

[119] *Rigasche Zeitung* 31 Dec.1838: "… den Sieg über Bosco davongetragen, als sie in Königsberg am 15. November 1829 eine concertirende Vorstellung gaben": originally of voices or instruments alternating, and so seeming to be in competition, *concertirend* interestingly lost its etymological sense of *competing*, still apparent here, coming to mean as in the Romance languages and English the exact opposite: harmony, in concert.

[120] Published in Munich, the paper soon banned and Oettinger expelled. He printed several Bosco anecdotes in various journals over the years, but must have formed a strong personal association with the family *as after Bosco's death he was appointed the legal guardian of his daughter Adelaide* (see *Excursus on Family*).

[121] The point of the joke is now hard to determine: Bosco took an elk, he says, which he turned into a doctor, the doctor into a demagogue, the demagogue into a crawling snake, the snake into a fawning toady, the toady into a *poète d'occasion*, the poet into a councillor, the councillor into a knight, and the knight back into an elk. This amazing trick resulted, so he says, in a magical show in Vienna by Carl Meisl, titled *Transformations of an Elk, or seven times something else but always the same* — presumably a hit at one of Meisl's plays, perhaps his 'Der delicate Tyrann'.

[122] *Allgemeines Pommersches Volksblatt*, 13 Feb.1830: "Angekommene Fremde vom 5. bis 10. Februar ... Bosco, Künstler a. Turin". The anecdote has Bosco in Cöslin asking a farmer in a market (in his poor German) for two pieces of butter — Are both equally good? — Yes, sir — Well, I think one half is bad, please cut it (*wir wollen einmol ufsneide*) — and in that half the farmer sees a "live, long-tailed rat grinning back at him".

[123] *Der Bazar für München und Bayern* 1 Apr.1830; *Wiener Zeitschrift* 4 Apr.1830.

[124] *Sundine* 25 Mar.; 1 Apr.1830. A third show announced for March 30th did not proceed.

[125] *Freimüthiges Abendblatt* 23 Apr.1830 (report dated Rostock April 19th, Bosco the only subject of conversation for the last eight days).

[126] *ATZ* 15 May 1830; *Freimüthiges Abendblatt* 30 Apr.1830.

[127] *Hamburger Nachrichten* 17, 22 May 1830. The Herzog-August-Bibliothek (Wolfenbüttel) has a letter from Bosco dated May 23rd 1830 in Hamburg, addressed to the management of the Stadttheater (url:023).

[128] Of course it is not certain that Bosco was with the mother at the time of the birth, but this does suggest that the mother was travelling with him on his tour: see Eugenio's entry (B2) for a discussion of this.

[129] *Hamburger Nachrichten* 9 June 1830. The following day this paper published a humorous poem by "Richard Roos" (Karl August Engelhardt) on Bosco finding money in bread rolls being sold by a baker who then tears up all the other rolls — to no profit, and pronounces him the devil (*"Wer kennt den Taschenspieler Bosco nicht? / Der tritt an eine Semmelbude, bricht / So ein halb Duzend Groschenzeilen an / Und, was per hocus pocus er hineingethan, / Geldstückchen finden sich darin...."*). The poem had already appeared (as 'Bosko') in an anthology, *Huldigung den Frauen*, in 1823, so was reprinted here for the occasion of his visit. It was reprinted again in 1844 in the anthology *Declamatorium: Auswahl ernster und heiterer Dichtungen zum Vortrage in öffentlichen und Privat-Gesellschaften* (ed. Ernst Littfas), Heft 18. (See *Fiction* F50.)

[130] *Staats und gelehrte Zeitung des hamburgischen unpartheyischen Correspondenten* 12 June 1830. Paganini performed at the Salon d'Apollon, tickets 4 Thaler each, to great acclaim. Later the same year his manager Georg Harrys in his *Paganini in seinem Reisewagen und Zimmer, in seinen redseligen Stunden, in gesellschaftlichen Zirkeln, und seinen Concerten* (p.58) quoted Paganini's delight that he had become more famous than Bosco. The pair had in common that both were accused of having acquired their remarkable talents through being in league with the devil, and both were said to be very wealthy: an anecdote in the *Augsburger Tagblatt* 23 Nov.1830, attributed to "an English paper", said Bosco was worth 12,000 Ducats and Paganini 58,000. Similar anecdotes told of Bosco being so rich he could live in London on his private income ("von seinen Renten"): *Rigasche Zeitung* 21 May 1834.

[131] *Hamburger Nachrichten* 21 June 1830.

[132] *Hamburger Nachrichten* 21 & (correcting that) 23 June 1830.

[133] *Hamburger Nachrichten* 26, 30 June; 3 July 1830; *Staats und gelehrte Zeitung* 25, 29 June; 5 July 1830.

[134] *Staats und gelehrte Zeitung* 6, 15 July 1830; *Hamburger Nachrichten* 10 July 1830.

[135] *Hamburger Nachrichten* 24, 26 June; 14, 22 July; 28 Sep. 1830.

[136] There is what seems a rather confused account of this in the brief section on magicians in Hamburg in *Das lustige alte Hamburg; Scherze, Sitten und Gebräuche unserer Väter* (1891) by Albert Borcherdt (Part 2 p.195; online at url:024), saying 1830 was Bosco's first visit to Hamburg and that Hechner parodied a mistake made by Bosco one night when his shredding a handkerchief act went astray. This so angered Bosco that he repeated the trick exactly, and perfectly, and "swept away" all proceeds of the show to the poor. But Hechner was in fact playing Carl's Staberl.

[137] Published in the supplement ('[tr.] Little character pictures and anecdotes of the period and for the period') in vol.4 of his *Pfefferkörner,* pp.170-173, of which I give a very inadequate abridged paraphrase; the book is online at url:025.

[138] *Hamburger Nachrichten* 16 July 1830; *Staats und gelehrte Zeitung* 22 July; 11 Sep.1830.

[139] *Danske Statstidende* 13 Aug.1830 ("Particulier Bosco med Secretair og tre Dienere").

[140] *Dagen* had a long anticipatory article on 23 June, followed by another on 17 Aug.; *Kiøbenhavnsposten* had a series of three long articles on 17, 18 & 20 Aug.1830 (the second a translation of Böttiger's 'cup and ball' article: note 79), and another on 14 Sep.1830. These were in turn drawn on by the provincial papers.

[141] *Dagen* 21 Aug.1830; *Kiøbenhavnsposten* 23 Aug.1830 (both very enthusiastic reviews).

[142] *Kiøbenhavns Kongelig alene priviligerede Adresse-Contoirs Efterretninger* 23, 26 Aug.1830; reviewed *Dagen* 30 Aug.1830 (cries of 'Dacapo' — *encore* — as he magically restored two smashed watches) and *Kiøbenhavnsposten* 31 Aug.1830.

[143] *Dagen* 28 Aug.1830.

[144] "Jomfruerne Lewin", Rosa and Flora, pantomime dancers, daughters of London-born Joseph Lewin who had settled in Copenhagen in 1800. In 1830 in Copenhagen they married on the same day fellow performers the brothers Adolph and James Price, whose father James had built the first Vesterbro theatre, later run by his widow's second husband Franz Kuhn.

[145] *Kiøbenhavns Kongelig alene priviligerede Adresse-Contoirs Efterretninge* 31 Aug.; 1 Sep.1830.

[146] *Den til Forsendelse med Brevposterne Kongelig allernaadigst privilegeret Skanderborg Amtsavis og Avertissements-Tidende* 10 Sep.1830, which quotes the 16-line poem.

[147] *Dagen* 15 Sep.1830; *Kiøbenhavnsposten* 16 Sep.1830; *Kongelig allernaadigst privilegerte Riber Stifts Adresse-Avis* 24 Sep.1830. The papers could not resist joking that he would "depart by all three ships and leave the capital by all four gates at once, like Pinetti long ago": both Pinetti and Philadelphia (Jacob Meyer) were reputedly banished from Berlin by Frederick the Great but it was *Philadelphia* who is said to have left through all four gates at the same time.

[148] *Staats und gelehrte Zeitung* 24 Sep.1830.

[149] *Staats und gelehrte Zeitung* 28, 29 Sep.; 1, 2 Oct.1830.

[150] *Hamburger Nachrichten* 28 Sep.1830. For Kerndörffer's book see *Books* p.437.

[151] *Staats und gelehrte Zeitung* 16 Oct.1830 ("...seine anderweitigen Verbindungen es ihm nicht erlaubern, hier länger zu verweilen, und die Arrangirung der von ihm neu verschriebene Sachen, welche bis jetzt seine Abreise verzögerte, vollendet ist").

[152] *Zeitung für die elegante Welt* 14 Dec.1830, noting that the Dutch magician K.M. Heesbee was also there.

[153] A poster for his fifth performance, 'Der Teufel ist Los', on February 1st is reproduced by Rusconi p.36.

[154] *Jurende's vaterländischer Pilger im Kaiserstaate Oesterreichs* vol.20, 1833, quoting "Die Abendzeitung vom April 1831, Nr.32", a rave review of Bosco's performances ("[tr.] ...he deceives us not just standing behind his magic table, but also in front of it, and even in the pit surrounded by the public...") and equating the "incredible" and "unprecedented" talents of Bosco and Paganini; also a brief reference in *Hamburger Nachrichten* 2 Mar.1831.

[155] "Extensive references and reviews" in *Kölnische Zeitung* 30 April 1831 (Beilage Nr.103 p.6) by *Kunstfreunden* of the *Kunstvorstellungen natürlicher Magie und unterhaltender Physik* given by Herr B. Bosco in the Horstschen Saal am Domhof are noted by Peter Gerlach, 'Assoziationen - Anzeigen - Ausstellungen Kunst in der Öffentlichkeit Kölns vor Gründung des ›Kölnischen Kunstvereins‹ im Jahre 1839', *Wallraf-Richartz-Jahrbuch* Vol. 50 (1989), pp.189-21 (url:026), discussing the wide application of the term 'Kunst'.

Kölns Legenden, Sagen und Geschichten, edited and published by Franz Kreuter in Cologne in 1852, has a long version pp.73-5 titled 'Bosko in Köln' of the anecdote of Bosco finding money in eggs in the market.

[156] Hermann Knispel, *Das Großherzogliche Hoftheater zu Darmstadt von 1810-1890* ..., p.357.

[157] *Abend-Zeitung* 19 Sep.1831.

[158] Poster featuring the Gun trick reproduced in Rusconi p.35.

[159] *Le Courrier de la Meuse* [Liège] 2 Dec.1831.

[160] *Le Courrier de la Meuse* [Liège] 14 Jan.1832 ("Une grande représentation de magie égyptienne (Turandot ou l'énigme)", concluding with "le repas interrompu ou la cuisine des Bohémiens enchantée" — the "interrupted meal" being the "cooking" of the birds); 15, 16, 19 Jan.; 20 Jan. (the second show, "La Volière de Papageno", including the "flying watches" and "the dead brought back to life"); 22, 23 Jan. (a show for charity, which raised 2,250 francs, reported in newspapers as far afield as Munich and Liepāja); 1, 2 Feb.; 3 Mar.1832.

[161] Antwerp is listed as visited between Liège and Brussells in *Messager de Gand* 28 June 1832.

[162] *Journal de la Belgique* 6 Mar.1832; *L'Indépendance Belge* 11 Mar.1832.

[163] *Journal de la Belgique* 15 Mar.1832.

[164] *L'Indépendance Belge* 16 Mar.1832; *Le Lynx* 18 Mar.1832; *L'Émancipation* 19 Mar.1832.

[165] *L'Émancipation* 19 Mar.1832; *L'Indépendance Belge* 23 Mar.1832.

[166] *L'Indépendance Belge* 27, 30 Mar.; 1, 3 Apr.1832. (*Grazer Zeitung* 31 Mar.1832 records a "Hr. Bosco" arriving there from Salzburg, but clearly not Bartolomeo.)

[167] *L'Indépendance Belge* 14, 16 Apr. ("*Magie extraordinaire* ... à la demande générale du public, M. Bosco voulant laisser aux habitants de Bruxelles un souvenir de sa reconnaissance pour la bienveillance dont ils l'ont honoré, se propose de redoubler de zèle..."). He also promises that during the interval will be heard "the well-known guitar amateur M. Fancello of Bologna, arriving from Italy": this is probably Maurizio Fancello (url:027).

[168] *Gazette des théâtres* 10 May 1832; *L'Émancipation* 11 May 1832, quoting a very enthusiastic review of his two shows there from the Naumur *Courrier de la Sambre* (fortunately, as the issues of April and May 1832 are not included at url:028).

[169] *L'Émancipation* 11 May; 1 June 1832 ("…est revenu dans nos murs … ce Napoléon de l'escamotage").

[170] *Messager de Gand* 28 June; 2, 3, 6, 7, 8 July 1832.

[171] *Gazette des théâtres* 12 Aug.; 9, 23 Sep.; 4 Oct.1832.

[172] *Le Figaro* 14 Sep.1832.

[173] *Le Figaro* 8 Oct.1832 (then, of course, a satirical weekly).

[174] *Gazette des théâtres* 11 Oct.1832; *Wiener Zeitschrift* 13 Nov.1832 (report dated October): "…macht uns Kunststücke vor, die an Zauberei grenzen". See note 344 for later examples of his "falling off the stage" act, not always well received by audiences or reviewers.

[175] *Gazette de France* 10 Oct.1832.

[176] *Gazette des théâtres* 28 Oct.1832: "…à laquelle j'ai assisté avec infiniment de plaisir. Mes complimens, mes éloges sont peu à côté des applaudissemens universels que vous avez justement mérités".

[177] *Gazette des théâtres* 18, 28 Oct.; 1, 4 Nov.1832.

[178] *Gazette des théâtres* 4, 8 Nov.1832; *Le Constitutionel* 17 Nov.1832; *La Quotidienne* 27 Nov.1832.

[179] *Le Revenant* 8 Oct.1832, alluding to the recent so-called Republican "coup d'État de juin 1832". For Grandville's famous caricature see Rusconi p.38 n.3 and p.43.

[180] *Le Revenant* and *La Tribune des départemens* 12, 17 Dec.1832; *Gazette des théâtres* 20 Dec.1832; *L'Eco* 8 Feb.1833. His successes there were even noted in a London paper, a rare occurrence: *Public Ledger and Daily Advertiser* 31 Dec.1832.

The autograph contracts for this engagement are held in the Bibliothèque Nationale (Collection de manuscrits d'Auguste Rondel, these deriving from Henri de Bachimont): online at url:029. This contract has now been reproduced and discussed by Pietro Micheli, 'Signing a contract with Bosco', *Ye Olde Magic Mag* 7/1 (Dec. 2020).

[181] *Gazette des théâtres* 3 Jan.1833; *Le Figaro* 4 Jan.1833; *Gazette National* 5 Jan. 1833.

[182] *Gazette de France* 29 Jan.1833.

[183] *Gazette des théâtres* 3, 28 Feb.1833.

[184] *Gazette des théâtres* 7, 10, 14 Mar.1833.

[185] *Le Constitutionnel* 15 Mar.1833; *Gazette des théâtres* 17 Mar.1833.

[186] 40,000 francs according to *Curiose avventure*, p.15. *Journal de Rouen* 3 Mar.; 2, 6 Apr.1833

[187] *Le Constitutionnel* 11 Apr.; 8 June 1833; *Le Figaro* 12 Apr.1833 (unable to resist a pun: "…la Seine a escamoté le butin du pauvre escamoteur. C'est ce qui fait qu'à Rouen il n'a pu escamoter sur la scène"). The accident was also widely reported in English, German and Polish papers. A lively account in *Curiose avventure*, pp.13-15, says it was the bridge at Le Pecq, some distance before Mantes.

[188] *Journal de Rouen* 23 Apr., 1, 15 May; 1, 25 June; 1, 4 July 1833.

[189] *Journal de Rouen* 4, 7, 10, 13, 16, 17 July 1833.

[190] *Journal de Rouen* 5, 15, 17 July 1833.

[191] *Journal de Rouen* 3 Aug.1833. In his *Histoire de la ville de Dieppe…* (Dieppe: Emile Delevoye, 1878) p.354 Alexandre Bouteiller notes Bosco among the many "celebrities" who visited Dieppe that year but says merely that he "fit de la physique amusante".

[192] Charles-Théodore Vesque, *Histoire des théâtres du Havre, 1717 à 1872… 1re partie, 1717-1836* (Havre: Impr. de Labottière, 1875), pp.271-2, quoting the poem 'Adieux aux Dames du Havre' composed by Bosco and handed out at his benefit show. Both volumes are online on Gallica.

[193] Charles-Théodore Vesque, *Histoire des rues du Havre… 2e Partie.* (Havre: Impr. J. Brenier, 1876) p.503 ("En 1833, le célèbre physicien Bosco éleva un théâtre sur cette place où il donna de nombreuses représentations. Pendant plusieurs années, la place Louis-Philippe resta à l'état de terrain nu…").

[194] *L'Auxiliaire breton* 25, 28 Oct.1833.

[195] *Lloyd nantais, Feuille commerciale et maritime* 3, 5, 7, 8 Nov.1833.

[196] *Lloyd nantais, Feuille commerciale et maritime* 9 Nov.1833.

[197] *Lloyd nantais, Feuille commerciale et maritime* 12, 14 Nov.1833.

[198] *Le Courrier de la Drôme* 14 Nov 1833; *Wiener Zeitschrift* 3 Dec.1833.

[199] *L'Écho rochelais* 7, 10, 14 Jan.1834: these comprise a brief announcement of his first show then two long and extravagant fantasies on Bosco — *How can he support the weight of his immense reputation. But Bosco is no ordinary man, Atlas carried the sky on his shoulders, and what is Atlas compared to Bosco?*

And three months later (22 Apr.1834) when Conus was there the paper published a long comparison between him and Bosco — "Bosco résume en lui le romantique du genre … Conus est le représentant du classicisme prestidigitatorial. Le premier, plein de verve, riche en tours, varié, laissait à peine respirer son spectateur, Conus est plus grave, plus rassis…".

[200] Transcribed and annotated by Michel Colle at url:030.

[201] *Gazette des théâtres* 3 Apr.1834: the charity show was on the previous Thursday, March 27th.

[202] *Gazette des théâtres* 21 Apr.1834 (noting that he had spent almost a month there recently and would now be there until at least mid-May); and 27 Apr.1834.

[203] *Gazette des théâtres* 4 May 1834.

[204] *La Gazette du Languedoc* 7 May 1834 announces he is travelling to Toulouse. I cannot see how he could have made any performances in Prussia and Vienna between being in Bordeaux and in Toulouse (Rusconi p.47).

[205] *La Gazette du Languedoc* 8, 10, 14 June 1834; *Gazette des théâtres* 15, 22 June 1834.

[206] *Courrier du Gard* 27, 30 June 1834; *Gazette du Bas Languedoc* 29 June 1834.

[207] *Courrier du Gard* 4 July 1834 ("…vu une indisposition grave et subite qui le retient au lit").

[208] *Gazette du Bas Languedoc* 6, 10, 13 July 1834 and *Courrier du Gard* 9 July 1834.

[209] *Gazette des théâtres* 20, 27 July 1834; *Le Sémaphore de Marseille* 18 July 1834.

[210] *Le Sémaphore de Marseille* 26 July 1834; *Gazette des théâtres* 31 July 1834.

[211] *Le Sémaphore de Marseille* 5, 15 Aug.1834. The Marseille correspondent of the *Allgemeine Theater-Zeitung* wrote at the end of August that Bosco had arrived there unwell and exhausted from the unbearable heat, adding that the usual venue for shows such as his had recently burnt down: *ATZ* 15 Sep.1834 (dated end of August; also in *Der Wanderer* 29 Sep.1834).

[212] *Le Sémaphore de Marseille* 15, 17 Aug.1834; *Gazette des théâtres* 28 Aug.1834.

[213] *Le Sémaphore de Marseille* 2, 3, 5, 6, 9, 13, 17, 20, 25, 26, 28 Sep.; 1, 3, 14 Oct.1834; *Gazette des théâtres* 28 Aug.; 25 Sep.; 5, 9 Oct.1834.

[214] *Le Sémaphore de Marseille* 19 Oct.; 3, 6 Nov.1834; *Gazette des théâtres* 19 Oct. 1834; 6, 27, 30 Nov.; 4, 14 Dec.1834.

[215] *Journal du commerce de la ville de Lyon* 7 Dec.1834; *Le Courrier de la Drôme et de l'Ardèche* 16 Dec.1834; then *Vert-vert* 16 Dec.1834 (the story now moved to Lyon); *Allgemeine Zeitung von und für Bayern Regensburger* 29 Dec.1834; *L'Eco* 2 Jan.1835; *L'Écho du commerce* 8 Jan.1835; *ATZ* 8 Jan.1835 (assuring us that it was reported by an eye-witness); *Le Messager de Gand* 9 Jan.1835; *Libausches Wochenblatt* 16 Feb.1835 [etc.] …

[216] *Gazette des théâtres* 14, 25, 28 Dec.1834; *Mosaïque Lyonnaise* 24 Dec.1834; *Journal de Commerce de la Ville de Lyon* 19, 21, 24, 28 Dec.1834; *Le Journal de l'Ain* 10, 26 Dec.1834.

[217] *Journal de Commerce de la Ville de Lyon* 28, 31 Dec.1834; 2 Jan.1835.

[218] *Journal de Commerce de la Ville de Lyon* 4 Jan.1835; *Gazette des théâtres* 15 Jan.1835.

[219] *Journal de Commerce de la Ville de Lyon* 11, 23 Jan.1835; *Gazette des théâtres* 29 Jan.1835.

[220] Bosco's letter is printed in *Journal de Commerce de la Ville de Lyon* 1 Feb.1835 and *Gazette des théâtres* 8 Feb.1835. Soon after (Feb.11th) the *Journal* printed a similar letter from the "lion tamer" Martin who had faced similar demands from M. Provence when planning to exhibit his menagerie in Lyon.

[221] The auction catalogue, *Catalogue d'une belle collection de lettres, autographes, manuscrits, documents historiques etc... provenant de plusieurs cabinets...* Paris, rue des Bons-Enfants, maison Silvestre, 15 avril 1858, is digitised on Gallica, url:031. It is possible that while the autograph dates from 1835 the poem is later — the title resembles that of the booklet *Deutschlands Einheit hergestellt durch die Zauberei des B. Bosco: Ein Dialog zwischen Faust, Mephistopheles und Bosco* (see *Fiction* F59), which definitely dates to 1848, and it may in fact be a copy of this.

[222] *Gazette des théâtres* 5 Feb.1835.

[223] *Gazzetta piemontese* 12 Feb.1835 ("Il celebre signor Bosco, Piemontese, valentissimo nell' arte della Prestidigitazione e della Fisica… è giunto in Italia… Egli è possessore di um Album, ove stanno inscritti gli onorifici certificati…"); *Hamburger Nachrichten* 26 Feb.1835. Rusconi (p.53) suggests he may have performed in Parma en route to Turin, on February 7th, but the source for this is uncertain and no such performance is mentioned in the *Gazzetta di Parma* either at this date or when he did perform there in April 1836.

[224] *Gazzetta piemontese* 28 Feb.1835.

[225] The date is given in *Gazette des Théâtres* 5 Apr.1835: "on the last Sunday of the Carnival" — the Carnival ended on Shrove Tuesday, which was March 3rd. *Satanas* and *Biographie und Anecdoten* say he performed for her on May 18th 1835, but that was the night he opened in Genoa.

[226] *Gazzetta piemontese* 28 Feb.; 3, 7 Mar.1835. Good Friday was April 17th.

[227] *Gazzetta piemontese* 14 Mar.1835; reprinted in *L'Eco* 18 Mar.1835, and in *Miscellanee del Cavaliere Felice Romani tratte dalla Gazzetta piemontese*. Torino: dalla Tip. Favale, 1837.

[228] *Gazzetta piemontese* 1, 18, 20, 27, 30 Mar.; 3, 7 Apr.1835.

[229] *Gazzetta piemontese* 1, 18, 20, 27, 30 Mar.; 3, 7 Apr.1835.

[230] *Gazzetta piemontese* 14 Apr.1835.

[231] *Gazzetta di Genova* 13, 16, 20, 23, 30 May 1835. A fourth show on May 20th is listed in *Il Teatro Carlo Felice: Annuario dei teatri di Genova dal 7 aprile 1828 al 15 dicembre 1844 offerto agli amatori degli spettacoli* (Tip. Teatrale dei fratelli Pagano, 1844) p.98, but the *Gazzetta* lists only three and the final notice specifically says "dopo di averci trattenuti piacevolmente e fatti maravigliare co' suoi giuochi di prestidigitazione e di fisica in tre successivi pubblici esperimenti, è partito alla volta di Milano…".

[232] *L'Eco* 15 June 1835; *Il Telegrafo* 15 June 1835; *Il Corriere delle Dame* 15 June 1835 (adding that Bosco's tricks made up for the need for this theatre to be "cleansed of its abundant filth" — this very year Marcello Mazzoni said of it (*Traveller's Guide of Milan*, p.58): "it wants cleansing, for it could not be more wretchedly dirty"); *Il Censore Universale dei teatri* 20 June 1835; *Il Figaro* 17 June 1835. All are long reviews and I hope these abridged paraphrases capture their spirit.

[233] *Il Figaro* 17 June 1835; *Il Corriere delle Dame* 20 June 1835 ("Il piccolo teatro Re…"). The *Teatro Re* held about 1,000 spectators; the *Teatro Carcano*, to which Bosco was to move, about 1500 (and *La Scala*, by comparison, about 3,000).

[234] *Il Figaro* 24 June 1835; *Il Corriere delle Dame* 25 June 1835.

[235] The opera which had been held back, *Chi dura vince* of Luigi Ricci, finally opened on July 7th, so ran concurrently with Bosco's shows. One wonders if its delayed opening was deliberate as in Rome the opera had been hissed. Bosco's sojourn at the Carcano is noted only briefly in Luigi Pilon's *Il Teatro Carcano di Milano 1803-1913,* who calls him (p.99) "un certo Bosco, personaggio pittoresco e singolare".

[236] *Il Telegrafo* 4, 8 July 1835; *Il Pirata* 7, 14 July 1835; *Il Censore* 15 July 1835; *Il Corriere delle Dame* 10 July 1835; *Il Figaro* 4, 8, 11 July 1835 (hinting beforehand that his popularity will increase *in inverse proportion to the price he puts on the entrance tickets*; praising him afterwards for *knowing how to divest his art of everything that is truly charlatanry*).

[237] *Cosmorama Teatrale* 18 July 1835; *L'Eco* 20 July 1835, *Il Pirata* 21 July; *Il Telegrafo* 22 July 1835.

[238] *Il Telegrafo* 1 Aug.1835; *L'Eco* 3, 5 Aug.1835; *Il Figaro* 8 Aug.1835; *Il Corriere delle Dame* 10 Aug.1835, following its review with a riddle whose answer was 'Bosco':
> *Selvaggio loco il nome mio ti addita,*
> *Ove dell' uomo è rado impresso il piede;*
> *Anche dell' Arno tra le voci ho vita,*
> *Ed accortezza allora in me risiede.*
> *Infin sotto un medesimo sembiante*
> *Son anche un portentoso negromante.*

[239] *Il Pirata* 11, 18 Aug.1835; *Il Telegrafo* 14, 19 Aug.1835; *L'Eco* 14, 19 Aug.1835. It is a pity that the final comment on his run in Milan should go to the Viennese *Der Wanderer*, which reported on August 26th: "[tr.] …The indifference of the public towards Bosco's magic shows is greatly increasing, and stands in almost direct relation to his perseverance, which he never tires of, in amusing the public with tricks which have already been seen often enough".

[240] *Giornale della provincia Bresciana* 3, 17, 24 Sep.1835.

[241] *Foglio di Verona* 1, 6, 10 Oct.1835.

[242] *L'Apatista* 19 Oct.; 7, 17 Nov.1835; *Il Gondoliere* 31 Oct.; 4, 11, 14 Nov.1835; a long review in the *Gazzetta di Venezia* is quoted verbatim in *Curiose avventure* pp.21-23.

[243] *Der Wanderer* 25 Dec.1835; *ATZ* 21 Dec.1835 (and also in *Neue Flora: ein Konversations- und Modeblatt für Bayerns Männer und Frauen* same date).

[244] *Il Gondoliere* 23 Dec.1835.

[245] The prices (L. 1.50) were noted almost forty years later by Alessandro Gandini in his *Cronistoria dei teatri di Modena dal 1539 al 1871* (1873, I p.350). A long write up in *Teatri, arti e letteratura* 10 Mar.1836, also quoted in *Curiose avventure*, acknowledged as "the basis of his tricks" his "stupendous agility of hand in making the most voluminous objects appear and disappear, and in making them transmute".

[246] *Teatri, arti e letteratura* 10, 17 Mar.1836. While in Bologna Bosco was honoured with a verse inscription by Luigi Muzzi, "pubblico ripetitore d'eloquenza italiana e latina nell'Università di Bologna e professore di belle lettere", published in *La Fama* 20 June 1836 (and in *Delle iscrizioni di Luigi Muzzi, accademico della Crusca*, 1836). He published a similar piece when Bosco was again in Italy in August 1845.

[247] Rusconi pp.75-6, and posters pp.73 & 77.

[248] *Gazzetta di Parma* 16, 23 Apr.1836.

[249] *Gazzetta di Parma* 4 May 1836. He is also said to have performed privately for the Queen on April 29th and for Napoleon's widow, Marie Louise, Duchess of Parma, on April 27th.

[250] *Gazzetta di Firenze* 10 May 1836 ("è giunto di recente in questa Capitale"). The evidence points to his visit to Sicily being in August-September 1837: see below.

[251] *Gazzetta di Firenze* 28 May; 2 June 1836. The Sovereign was Grand Duke Leopold II; the "King of Naples" was Ferdinand II, King of the Two Sicilies, who ruled from Naples; they were cousins: Leopold's maternal and Ferdinand's paternal grandparents were Ferdinand I of the Two Sicilies and Marie Caroline of Austria.

[252] *Gazzetta di Firenze* 2, 4, 7, 9, 11, 16 (long review of the five shows so far), 18, 21 June 1836.

[253] Published by Pietro Micheli in *Ye Olde Magic Mag* Vol.1 Issue 2; the letter is reproduced by Rusconi p.81.

[254] Published in *Il Pirata* 9 Sep.1836.

[255] This may have been the setting for the famous anecdote of Bosco, reproved by the King for arriving late, doing the impossible: successfully changing the time of every clock and watch in the palace. For the interview with Eugenio on this see p.186 & note.

[256] *Annuario storico del Regno delle Due Sicilie,* 1838, p.250, acknowledges him donating on January 21st 1837 half the profits of one evening's performance.

[257] An 1836 contract between Bosco and the owner of the *Teatro Fondo*, impresario Domenico Babaja, stipulates that the management would not charge for the orchestra but would take one quarter of the evening's takings: quoted by Paologiovanni Maione and Francesca Selle, 'Il palcoscenico dei mutamenti: il teatro del Fondo di Napoli 1809-1840' *Recercare* Vol. 9 (1997) pp.97-120: p.105 & n.47 (on JSTOR).

[258] Quoted from an unnamed giornale" by *Il Pirata* 17 Jan.1837; *Hamburger Nachrichten* 4 Feb.1837 reports him in Naples "in great demand". A colourful account of Bosco in Naples is given by Saverio Costantino Amato (*Il Globo* 23 Feb.1837), reprinted in his posthumous *Prose e versi* (1838) and by Rusconi pp.88-9, who also points out that *Curiose avventure* was published at this time, a wonderful piece of self-promotional "marketing" as he calls it (his edition, 2020, p.44).

[259] In fact the only source for Bartolomeo performing the miracle is Volume 2 of the *Grand Dictionnaire universel du XIXe siècle*, written and published after his death (and, significantly, soon after Eugenio's performance of it: p.168 below).

[260] 'Bartolomeo Bosco esimio prestigiator', *Effemeridi scientifiche e letterarie per la Sicilia* Vol.27, October [*sic*] 1839 pp.58-61; online at url:034); the article makes much of Bosco's mind reading act, and was reproduced in 2013 by Mariano Tomatis in his *Mesmer* Project at url:035.

[261] Ana Tobío Sala, *Salvatore Costanzo, Intermediario de cultura*. Florence: Alinea Editrice, 2000, p.30 n.29; p.31. The periodical is held at Biblioteca centrale della Regione siciliana Alberto Bombace – Palermo (https://opac.sbn.it/bid/PAL0081784).

[262] *La Fata Morgana* 1 Mar.1838 (p.8); this was published every 15 days (url:036). That he performed in Dresden on January 20th 1838 (Rusconi p.93) is very unlikely.

[263] *Programmi Giornali degli Spettacoli dati ne' teatri di Napoli del giorno di Pasqua di Resurrezione 1838, a tutto il Sabato di Passiono del 1839,* No.9, 23 Apr.1838 (url:037). This gives daily listings for all the Naples theatres from 15 April 1838 to 17 February 1839.

[264] *Programmi Giornali...* The play was apparently never printed.

[265] *Rigasche Zeitung* 30 May 1838; *Gazeta Wielkiego Xięstwa Poznańskiego* 23 June 1838.

[266] *Diario di Roma* 26 Apr.1838 ("previo superiore permesso", which sounds very like the ecclesiastical *cum Superiorum permissu*). The newspaper was published three times per week (usually on Tuesday, Thursday and Saturday) with every third issue (usually Thursday) being titled *Notizie del giorno* (with its own numbering sequence); all issues here are referred to as *Diario di Roma*.

[267] *Diario di Roma* 17, 29 May 1838.

[268] *Diario di Roma* 2 June 1838. The time of the show is given *alla romana*: "si darà principio ad un' ora e mezza di notte precisa, per terminare alla mezza notte" — from an hour and a half after twilight until midnight.

[269] *Diario di Roma* 7, 12, 13 June 1838.

[270] *Diario di Roma* 26 June; 5 July 1838.

[271] *Diario di Roma* 12 July 1838: he is said to have already given another show there, ("crowned with the greatest success" claims the billing), so this was probably the second of two.

[272] Belli's letters referring to Bosco are included in *Le lettere*, a cura di Giacinto Spagnoletti. 2 vols. Milan: C. Del Duca, 1961; online at url:038, and elsewhere) but not the *fischietto* letter of July 12th, which is found in *Lettere, giornali, zibaldone*, a cura di Giovanni Orioli. Turin: Einaudi, 1962 (pp.259-60). Extracts are included in Mario Verdone's article 'Bartolomeo Bosco in una poesia italiana del Belli', *Strenna dei Romanisti* 25 (1964) pp.511-6 (online at url:039), who also prints Belli's poem 'Bartolommeo Bosco soprannornato Turandò l'incantatore', which was not printed at the time, only recited, but was included in the *Versi inediti* of 1843 (on Google Books); also in Rusconi pp.226-8.

[273] Both texts were reprinted (with some minor spelling and punctuation changes) in *Giornale Scientifico-Agrario-Letterario-Artistico di Perugia ed Umbra Provincia. Dispensa Sesta dell'Anno 1863*, then as a booklet, *Intorno alcuni scritti inediti di Michelangelo Poggioli pubblicati per cura del figlio Avv. Giuseppe. Nota di Sebastiano Purgotti*. Perugia: Tipografia di Vincenzo Bartelli, 1864.

Both the *Diario* and the booklet are on Google Books, and the latter also at url:040, so I quote only the last two lines—
Namque munus agitas rapido sic undique motu,
Lynceos oculos ut superare queas.
Tua prontezza certo vince
Anche l'occhio d'una lince.

[274] Belli writes on June 23rd (letter 313): "Some say Bosco will go to the Argentina; others say Bosco will go to Sinigaglia ...it is believed that the Wizard goes to Sinigaglia in order to work there with Lanari", then on July 13th (letter 326) he puns that Senigallia will soon "enjoy in her bosom" either *bosco, o buco o selva, o foresta...*

[275] Robert-Houdin's well-known account of seeing Bosco perform in Paris in 1838 (*Confidences d'un prestidigitateur, une vie d'artiste*, 1859, Vol.1 p.297), criticising his cruelty to pigeons and his choice of the cup and balls act, is either misdated or imaginary. There is no mention in French papers of Bosco in Paris in 1838, and in fact no evidence that he was in France between 1832 and 1851. Both he and Robert-Houdin were in Paris in early 1852.

[276] *Osservatore del Trasimeno* 25, 29 Sep.; 2 Oct.1838 (a very long and encomiastic review: "…segreti incomprensibili, raggiri inexplicabili, artifizi finissimi, sveltezza di mosse, rapidità di operare, e tutto con summa naturalezza…").

Belli's fourteen year old son Ciro was at school in Perugia and probably saw Bosco perform, as his father writes back to him on October 14th (letter 350) that he knew Bosco was giving a show there and was sure that Ciro must have enjoyed it. (This letter includes Belli's poem opening "Tristo però il mortale, o filiuol mio", published as 'La Gioventu e la Vecchiezza' in *Versi* the following year.)

[277] The brief report is in *Adria* 21 Nov.1838, from its Naples correspondent, dated November 5th: "[tr.] The famous Bosco is here for some time. This black magician makes fun of everyone while laughing up his sleeve, for his motto is *mundus vult decipi,* so he deceives everyone and makes a lot of money". The editor of *Adria* was Jacob Loewenthal who had given Bosco such a good review when he performed in Trieste in 1835 (note 243).

[278] *Diario di Roma* 29 Nov.; 4 Dec.1838. This was the theatre that Belli had said in May was too far from town; interestingly, and unusually, the newspaper advertisements give the exact street address of the theatre.

[279] *Fränkischer Merkur (Bamberger Zeitung)* 21 Dec.1838.

[280] *Notizie del Giorno* 17 Jan.1839 (on Google Books this follows the issue of the *Diario di Roma* of 22 Jan.1839).

[281] Nor was he in Milan making a sensation at La Scala, no less, about this time, as stated in an unnamed German newspaper: this was ridiculed by Moritz Saphir (who may indeed have made the whole story up) in his satirical paper *Der Humorist* (7 Jan.1839), pointing out that this was actually Rugali's ballet (*ballo di mezzo carattere*) 'Il Bosco Incantato' ("The Enchanted Wood"); this was performed at La Scala on December 26th.

[282] *Programma giornaliero degli spettacoli* 11, 13, 14 Jan.1839 ("reduce dall'Italia, e dopo un silenzio di circa otto mese si riproduce con dare un altra accademia di Magia…"); these three shows are also listed in the appendix to 'Il palcoscenico dei mutamenti: il teatro del Fondo di Napoli 1809-1840' (see note 257).

The Naples weekly *Salvator Rosa* in its issue of 13 January oddly says Bosco performed at the Fondo the previous *Thursday*, which was the 10th; in the same issue it has a Word Puzzle ("Logogrifo") which it pretends that Bosco made up himself ("E voltosi a me, Bosco disse—ora, signor de L. … farò un logogrifo pel vostro Salvator Rosa…").

[283] *Programma giornaliero degli spettacoli* 25 Jan.; 1, 9 Feb.1839. The second show received a long and glowing review in *Salvator Rosa* 3 Feb.1839, which states that Bosco had moved from the *Fondo* to the smaller *Teatro Nuovo* (the stage "a kind of gallery") to avoid being accused of using his distance from the audience to his advantage. The review ends: "[tr.] …so go and see Bosco at the *Teatro Nuovo* right away, otherwise this magician who can make everyone and everything disappear will perform the ultimate trick — Bosco will make Bosco disappear".

[284] *Programma giornaliero degli spettacoli* 10, 11, 17 Feb.1839. The 17th is the final issue available online, so it is uncertain if Bosco continued in Naples.

[285] Rusconi (pp.105-6) links this appearance by Bosco at the Vatican with the anecdote of the Cardinal's platinum watch. The earliest versions of the watch anecdote (for example *Le Petit Méridional* 16 Apr.1895 and *La Gazette algérienne* 24 Apr. 1895) do not have Bosco buying the duplicate watch in Dresden but from a Rome jeweller before his engagement. The version in *L'Impartial* which Rusconi quotes adds some new features, such as the trip to Dresden and the nice touch that Bosco is performing for the Pope and Cardinals to prove he is not a sorcerer; however, that *L'Impartial* article, 'Un célèbre prestidigitateur: Bartolomeo Bosco', dates from 11 August *1942*, not 1842, and contains so much unique Bosco anecdotage that it is hard to believe it is not a twentieth century journalistic fabrication: for example, it alone says that Bosco's imprisonment in Siberia was in *Khabarovsk*, not Tobolsk, which is nonsense as the town was in China until 1858 and not even named Khabarovsk until that date; it also says he walked there after his capture — 9,000 km! (The other *L'Impartial* reference cited, 12 Sep.1895, is merely an instalment of the novel *Jacques l'honneur:* see *Bosco in Fiction* F40.)

[286] *Real Segreteria di Stato presso il Luogotenente Generale in Sicilia. Ripartimento Polizia. Repertorio anno 1839:* the indexes (only) are available online at url:041.

[287] Eusèbe de Salle, *Pérégrinations en Orient, ou Voyage pittoresque, historique et politique en Égypte, Nubie, Syrie, Turquie, Grèce pendant les années 1837-38-39*. 2 vols. Paris: Pagnerre, 1840: Vol.II pp.210-211 (available on Google Books and on Gallica).

[288] In fact Rodolphe soon headed to Constantinople and in November he and Bosco were there at the same time! Eusèbe de Salle describes recently seeing him in Athens on July 18th, "a good French conjurer, a young man of good family, who has swelled the already numerous ranks of well born educated strolling players and mountebanks…" (*Pérégrinations en Orient*, II p.209). He is first sighted in early 1837, performing at the Gymnase in Marseille, billing himself as "Physicien de la Cour d'Autriche" (*Le Sémaphore de Marseille* 1, 7 Feb.1837), and still there in March. In Constantinople he had considerable success ("…sa vogue augmente de jour en jour": *Le Sémaphore* 3 Dec.1839) and he is said to have received the Order of Glory from the Sultan (*Le Sémaphore* 2 Jan.1840; chaffed by *Le Charivari* 13 Jan. 1840 and *Preßburger Zeitung* 21 Jan.1840). He is probably the "Herr Rodolfo" described at length as running the Odeon in Pera in 1840, featuring "balls, mas-

querades, card playing, comedies and musical evenings" — and much else... (long article in *Frankfurter Konversationsblatt* 11 & 14 July 1840; also in other German papers, all crediting the article to "*Vaterländische Memoiren*" May 1840, which is the Russian-language monthly *Otečestvennyja Zapiski*).

[289] *La Quotidienne* 27 Aug.1839: "Voici la lettre de notre correspondent d'Alexandrie, elle est de 27 juillet... Le dernier pyroscaphe français nous a amené M. Bosco, de Turin...". The account in Francesconi's *Reise-Bilder* (see below under 1845, and note 366; *Fiction* F13) says Bosco landed in Alexandria on August 5th.

[290] *Satanas* dates this performance to August 15th.

[291] *Le Sémaphore de Marseille* 11 Sep.1839 (and reprinted in *La Quotidienne* 28 Sep. 1839).

[292] *Le Sémaphore de Marseille* 22 Dec.1839; and an independent and more detailed report in *Frankfurter Ober-Post-Amts-Zeitung* 23 Sep.1839. Campbell's *soirée* was reported also in the U.K. papers: "all amusements were combined in it — dancing, a banquet, Bosco, the juggler, &c.": *Morning Post* 2 Oct.1839, quoting the *Journal de Smyrna*.

[293] Scipion Marin, *Événements et aventures en Egypte en 1839*. 2 vols. Paris: Grimbert et Dorez, 1840: Vol.II p.61-2. Marin remains a rather mysterious figure. The *BNF* has no biographical data on him, but from his numerous books we learn he was from Toulon ("évoque longuement son enfance toulonnaise", says Rene Merle in his discussion of Marin's 1831 call for Provençal independence, *Aux Provençaux, sur leurs projets de séparation et de république provençale*), but was living in Paris by 1819, when he published his epic poem on the founding on Marseille, *La Massiliade, ou la Gaule poétique* — mercifully not digitised but a ten page review in *Lycée français, ou Mélanges de littérature et de critique*, Vol.I, 1819, offers abundant extracts and tells us he was then age twenty. His literary efforts found little success, and he turned more to journalism. By the mid-1830s he was living in Marseille and in 1835 and 1836 issued elaborate prospectuses to finance by subscription his collected works, *Œuvres Méridionales* in 10 volumes, offering as guarantee "a property I possess in the Valley of Dardennes"; he proposed a similar plan in 1838 to finance an educational family journal, again unsuccessful, and it is then that he travelled to the East. The result was the 2 volume *Événements et aventures en Egypte en 1839*. While it seems true that he did travel to Egypt and while the book claims to be "a faithful picture of the present state of Egypt" and ends with a detailed appendix giving Scipion's solution to the "Oriental question", it is cast in the form of a romance, with much imaginary dialogue, the adventures of a young Parisian, Alfred de Mauléon, who must rescue his beloved Rositta from the clutches of Mohammad Ali. Marin's account of Bosco in Egypt is probably factual enough, but his later claims to have engineered Bosco's success in St Petersburg in 1842 (see below) seem rather far-fetched.

[294] *La France* 20 Nov.1839 ("Le célèbre prestidigitateur Bosco ... vient de faire un long voyage dans la Haute [*sic*] Egypte. Abbas pacha qui l'avait appelé au Caire, l'a

comblé des marques de sa munificence. Bosco est arrivé le mois dernier à Smyrne, ou sa reputation l'a déjà devancé"; *La voce della verità* 23 Nov.1839: "...Scrivono dalle Smirne in data 24 ottobre ... Il celebre prestigiatore torinese Bosco è, dopo longa aspettazione, arrivato alle Smirne. Il ritardo di sua venuta nacque da ciò che Abbas pascià, figliuolo del vicerè, volle averlo per alcuni giorni al Cairo".

[295] *Diario di Roma* 19 Dec.1839 (and other Italian papers): "Constantinopoli 27 novembre... Abbiamo qui i celebri giuocolatori Bosco e Rodolfo".

[296] *Der Humorist* 3 Jan.1840 ("Sr. Excellenz Reschid-Pascha"); *Corriere dei teatri* 8 Feb.1840 ("...per mancanza di apposita sala...").

[297] The earliest account published, in *Il Corriere dei teatri* 8 Feb.1840, gives no date for the performances but the report itself is dated January 6th, so the performances must have been *before then*. The report also mentions recent performances by Bosco for the Prince of Serbia, for the Russian and British Ambassadors, and for the Directors of the Duzoglou Mint. The performance for the Russian Ambassador ("eine glänzende Soirée") is dated to "last Monday" in a report dated January 15th published in *Allgemeine Zeitung* 6 Feb.1840, making it Monday January 6th, as the standard 19th century usage was that "last Monday" indicated not the immediately preceding Monday but the Monday of the preceding week.

When the *Corriere dei teatri* report was reprinted in *Teatri, arti e letteratura* 5 Mar.1840 the report was now dated February, not January, 6th, and the shows said to have been on January 28th and 29th; similarly the report in *Gazette nationale ou le Moniteur universel* 1 Mar.1840, which is dated Constantinople February 7th, dates the two shows to "merdi et mercredi de la semaine dernière", adding that Bosco received 30,000 [*sic*] piastres".

[298] *Ausgburger Postzeitung* 23 June 1840 (report dated June 3rd of the show the previous day).

[299] *Rigasche Zeitung* 26 Oct.1840; *Folio di Verona* 28 Oct.1840.

[300] *Wiener Zeitung* 3, 11 Sep.1840; *Österreichisches Morgenblatt* 3 Oct.1840 (no smoking and no standing up); *Il Pirata* 9 Oct.1840 (posters in French, Greek, Arabic and Turkish — but Bosco himself speaking in French). The theatre was built on land owned by the Naum brothers who took it over when Bosco left, changing the name from Théâtre Bosco to Théâtre de Pera or Théâtre Naum; it survived till a fire in 1847 (Emre Araci, 'Naum Theatre: the lost opera house of Istanbul', *Turkish Area Studies Review*, Spring 2011, issues 17 & 18: online url:042).

[301] *Der Sammler* 29 Oct.1840.

[302] The article 'Souvenirs de Russie' was first published in the Paris newspaper *Le Globe,* 13 Aug.1842, as the *feuilleton* at the foot of pp.1-3; it is signed 'Scipion M . . . . .' at the end. It was not included in Marin's book *Lettres Russes* published in Paris the same year, which was only the first part (36pp) of a planned series of *Lettres*

Russes to be in 20 fascicles; the second part is advertised at the end as "sous presse" but did not appear.

The article was then reprinted

(a) in full in several French-language papers (including *Le Journal de Bruxelles* 16 Aug.1842; *Le Voleur* 20 Aug.1842, and in the literary annual *La Macédonie Littéraire,* Brussels 1842);

(b) a short anecdotal extract translated into German, merely the part about Bosco's meeting with the Czar, deliberately vague about the date ("vor einiger Zeit") and with no mention of Marin as author, appeared in Saphir's paper *Der Humorist* 22 Aug.1842 (headed "Eine Produktion Bosco's am russischen Hofe"); this was then reprinted in several German-language papers, later with the heading "Ein Kunststück Bosko's"; by the end of 1842 an English translation of this was appearing in U.K. and American papers (for example *Monmouthshire Beacon* 15 Oct.1842);

(c) a longer version in German (still less than half the original), crediting Marin and *Le Globe,* in *Wiener Zeitschrift* 1 Oct.1842; reprinted in *Frankfurter Konversationsblatt* 13 Oct.1842 (crediting *Wiener Zt.*);

(d) a version was later included (either directly from a French paper or more likely from a cutting of the article pasted in Bosco's Album) in the popular works about Bosco (with no mention of Marin as author) —

Satanas, pp.26-33 ("Nous empruntons aux *Souvenirs de Russie,* publiées il y a quelques années, le passage suivant...");

Biographie und Anecdoten aus den Reisen des alten Bosco, pp.20-5 ("Den 'Souvenirs de Russie,' welche vor eingen Jahren erschienen, entnehmen wir Folgendes...");

Il Nuovo Bosco, pp.201-8 ("Togliamo da un libro: *Rimembranze di Russia,* pubblicato alcuni anni sono, il seguenta passo...").

[303] *Satanas* and its translations quote "*Le Journal de Moscou*" ("*Moskauer Zeitung*"; "*Giornale di Mosca*") — in fact *Moskovskiye Vedomosti* (Московские ведомости) 14 Feb.1842: this issue is not included at the National Library of Russia site (url:043), but on Wikipedia Commons has been posted the January 17th issue of the paper, on p.24 of which (url:044) is an advertisement in French and Russian for this Ball and Tombola on February 14th (Bosco not mentioned).

[304] Liszt spent four weeks in Russia in April and May 1842, under the patronage of the Czarina Alexandra for whom he had played at Ems in 1840. His first concert was a sensation, with an audience of three thousand; in all he gave six public concerts in St Petersburg and several private performances.

[305] He had only just arrived in St Petersburg when the editor of the "Messager de Saint-Petersbourg" (*Sankt-Peterburgskiy vestnik*) published (26 Apr.1842) the anecdote quoted by *Satanas* of Bosco finding a purse...

[306] Interestingly Bosco says (well, according to Marin) that he had already performed for Helena in the Ukraine ("à Korshkoff [*sic*], dans la Petite-Russie" says the version in *Le Globe,* but Karkoff in *Satanas* and *Biographie und Anecdoten,* Kaskoff in *Nuovo Bosco*) — presumably Kharkov (modern Kharkiv), so it is possible that Bosco travelled through that area in late 1841 en route to Moscow (p.43).

[307] *Rigasche Zeitung* 23 May; 6 June 1842.

[308] The Institute for Artificial Mineral Water, a spa with concert room attached; *Rigasche Zeitung* 7 July 1842.

[309] *Helsingfors Tidningar* 17, 19, 20 Aug.1842; *Finlands Allmänna Tidning* 23 Aug. 1842; *Helsingfors Morgonblad* 22 Aug.1842 (a long positive review — the audience well satisfied despite the high prices).

[310] *Åbo Tidningar* 24 Aug.1842; *Åbo Underrättelser* 27 Aug.1842 (Bosco very welcome — but the prices!).

[311] *Åbo Tidningar* 31 Aug.1842 ("...Mekanikus Bosco med husfru, Modekrämerskan Delaune med dotter..."); Adele was soon to perform in Bosco's shows.

[312] *Åbo Underrättelser* 31 Aug.1842.

[313] *Aftonbladet* 5, 7, 9 Sep.1842.

[314] *Aftonbladet* 12, 16 Sep.1842.

[315] *Åbo Tidningar* 28 Sep.1842; *Åbo Underrättelser* 28 Sep.; 1, 5 Oct.1842. Two of the Turku posters for his performances are reproduced at url:045.

[316] *Finlands Allmänna Tidning* 11, 12 Oct.1842; *Helsingfors Morgonblad* 13 Oct. 1842; *Helsingfors Tidningar* 15 Oct.1842 (a full house).

[317] *Borgå Tidning* 29 Oct.1842.

[318] *Wiborgs Annonce Blad* 5 Nov.1842 (the previous issue is unfortunately not digitised).

[319] *Rigasche Zeitung* 10 Nov.; 22 Dec.1842; *Helsingfors Tidningar* 7 Jan.1843. An odd note in *Il Pirata* 2 Dec.1842, perhaps humorous, announced he was heading from St Petersburg to Persia.

[320] *Rigasche Zeitung* 26 Jan.1843.

[321] *Das Inland* 23 Feb.; 27 Apr.1843; *Der Zuschauer* 27 Feb.1843.

[322] *Mitauische Zeitung* 11, 15, 18 Mar.1843; *Das Inland* 30 Mar.1843.

[323] *Der Zuschauer* 30 Mar.; 3 Apr.1843.

[324] *Mitauische Zeitung* 8 Apr.1843.

[325] *Der Zuschauer* 15 May 1843.

[326] *Kurjer Warszawski* 10, 17, 18 June 1843; *Gazeta Codzienna* 14, 18 June 1843.

[327] *Gazeta Warszawska* 19, 26 June 1843; *Kurjer Warszawski* 22 June 1843; *Gazeta Codzienna* 22, 28 June 1843; *Dziennik Krajowy* 30 June 1843 (a long rambling essay

on magicians). A Bosco anecdote was retailed in a letter of June 1843 by Count Tomasz Łubieński, now in retirement in Warsaw — Bosco, seeing a peasant digging in a garden in Ujazdów Avenue, took the spade and, telling him to dig more carefully, started unearthing ducats: the poor boy went on digging "I do not know for how long", all in vain, of course (Roger Łubieński, *Generał Tomasz Pomian hrabia Łubieński,* II, 1899, p.345).

[328] *Gazeta Warszawska* 1, 3 July 1843; *Gazeta Codzienna* 3, 8 July 1843; *Kurjer Warszawski* 4 July 1843.

[329] *Gazeta Codzienna* 12, 14 July 1843; *Kurjer Warszawski* 15 July 1843; *Gazeta Warszawska* 19 July 1843 (a long farewell).

[330] *Gazeta Codzienna* 11, 20, 26, 27 Aug.1843; *Kurjer Warszawski* 13, 19, 27 Aug. 1843; *Dziennik Krajowy* 17 Aug.1843. *ATZ* 9 Sep.1843, quoting the *Breslauer Zeitung,* says Bosco had given *24* shows in Warsaw, which may be an error.

[331] *Dziennik Krajowy* 31 Aug.1843.

[332] *Gazeta Codzienna* 27 Oct.1843 (the write-up opening with Schiller's 'Hier stirbt der Zauber mit dem Künstler ab…', on the ephemeral magic of the theatre).

[333] *Der Ungar* 2 Dec.1843.

[334] *Breslauer Zeitung* 6 Dec.1843.

[335] The seat prices are defended on the grounds of Bosco's speed of execution and the sheer number of tricks he performed in each show in a long article in *ATZ* 16 Nov. 1843 by Hermann Michaelson, theatrical agent and editor of the *Breslauer Theater-Zeitung* (whose 1843 issues are unfortunately not digitised).

[336] *Gazeta Wielkiego Xięstwa Poznańskiego* 6 Dec.1843.

[337] *ATZ* 14 Dec.1843 (and reprinted in *Der Ungar* soon after).

[338] *ATZ* 23 Dec.1843 (reprinted also in *Donau Zeitung* 11 Oct.1847).

[339] *Gazeta Wielkiego Xięstwa Poznańskiego* 20, 24, 26, 27, 29, 30 Jan.1844; *Zeitung des Großherzogthums Posen* 20 Jan.1844; *Zuschauer* [Riga] 27 Jan.1844. There are also brief accounts of Bosco's Poznań performances in Manfred Laubert, *Studien zur Geschichte der Provinz Posen in der ersten Hälfte des neunzehnten Jahrhunderts* (1908), p.182; and in Ludwig Sittenfeld, *Geschichte des Breslauer Theaters von 1841 bis 1900* (1909) p.13 (saying he gave three shows there).

[340] *Gazeta Wielkiego Xięstwa Poznańskiego* 2 Feb.1844. Wlach gave further shows which were well reviewed, "proving what the concept of art means", but made little money, "…Mr. Bosco must have taken his toll on the public's pockets" (*Gazeta Wielkiego Xięstwa Poznańskiego* 13 Feb.1844). Also in town was the cellist Samuel Kossowski, his shows drawing good crowds, but as for the "so-called fine arts", said

the Poznań paper *Dziennik Domowy*, 31 Jan.1844, "his concerts saw ten carriages outside the theatre, while Bosco's show saw thirty!".

[341] *Neue Würzburger Zeitung* 2 Mar.1844; *ATZ* 14 Mar.1844.

[342] *Neue Würzburger Zeitung* 15 Mar.1844 ("Bosco gefällt unserm Publikum nicht mehr mit seinen Kunststücken und dürfte daher wohl bald dem Döbler den Platz räumen müssen"); *ATZ* 18 Mar.1844 (he must be the greatest magician of all if he can entice an audience at these prices!). *Der Wanderer* 11 Apr.1844 nicely suggested that one should have made the other disappear.

[343] *Frankfurter Konversationsblatt* 16, 18 April 1844 ("Aus Berlin. 9. April … Bosco, welcher von einem Ausfluge in der Umgegend, bei dem er unsern Nachbarstädten seine Zaubereien producirt hat, wieder zu uns zurückgekehrt ist…" and "Berlin, 11. April …Bosco hat heute seine erste Zauber-Vorstellung im Königsstädtischen Theater gegeben…").

[344] *Der Ungar* 17 May 1844, and in *Sonntagsblätter* 26 May 1844. The stunt usually turned out well. He had done it in Paris in 1832 and tried it again in Rotterdam and Antwerp in 1850 and Madrid in 1858.

[345] This account also appears (credited to the Berlin *Figaro*) in the 'Mode' supplement to *Zeitung für die elegante Welt* no.25 (1 June 1844; the "Jan. 1 1844" date on *digiPress* is merely a default date). It then reappears, retold largely word for word, in *Der Sammler* 6 July 1844, and in *ATZ* 8 July 1844 (crediting Berlin *Figaro*).

Years later what may be a variant of the same story surfaced: while at the Königsstädtischen Theater in the 1840s, we are told, Beckmann was away performing a guest role in Vienna; he was late returning but advised the director that he would definitely be back by "next Friday" and he was billed to appear in two plays, with Bosco performing in the intervals. On the night the director announced that Beckmann had failed to return and the plays were cancelled — when Bosco shouted from the wings: "Don't believe it — Beckmann is still in Milan — so let's help"; and waving his magic wand he called for Beckmann to appear: up he rose through the stage trapdoor, travelling bag in hand, ready for the first scene of his play. This is found in *Der Zwischen-Akt* 23 Mar.1867 and in *Tagespost* [Graz] 1 July 1867.

[346] Not digitised; url:046.

[347] *Didaskalia* 4 June 1844: "Korrespondenz. Hamburg, 29. Mai. Bosco ist hier und will nächste Woche im Stadttheater einige Vorstellungen seiner weltberühmten Zaubereien geben…".

[348] The *Hamburgischen unpartheiischen Correspondenten* in its record of recent arrivals in town listed them as "Hotel de France: die H e r r e n Bosco nebst Tochter aus Potsdam". The paper itself (no.129) is not accessible online but the implication that his daughter was male amused other papers — "[tr.] that Bosco's daughter is a gentleman is certainly no mere sleight-of-hand, but true and genuine witchcraft" (*Der Humorist* 27 June 1844; *Der Ungar* 28 June 1844).

[349] *Hamburger Nachrichten* 1, 4 (long detailed review), 10 June 1844; *Didaskalia* 14 June 1844.

[350] *Der Sammler* 27 July 1844; a longer version of the macaronic invitation in verse was quoted (with some variants) in *Münchener Tagblatt* 4 Aug.1844, *ATZ* 8 Aug. 1844, and in several other papers — "Messieurs et Dam's, ick sein, Sir wissen, / Der deitschen Sprack nit sehr bestissen...".

[351] *Hamburger Nachrichten* 19 July 1844.

[352] *Leipziger Tageblatt* 10 Sept.1844; *ATZ* 9 Sep.1844. Unfortunately *Charivari* for 1844 is not among the issues included on Google Books.

[353] *Leipziger Tageblatt* 10 Sept.1844; *Didaskalia* 15 Sep.1844; *Wiener Zeitschrift* 16 Sept.1844; *ATZ* 9 Nov.1844. The Stadtgeschichtliches Museum Leipzig has a drawing by Dr. C. Zehme of 'B. Boscos Zaubertheater im Jahre 1844, auf dem Königsplatze, Michaelismesse am 21. Oktober Leipzig', url:047. The Museum also has a painting by Zehme of Bosco's theatre there in 1848: for Zehme see notes 488 and 504.

[354] *Der Humorist* 1 Nov.1844; *Der Wanderer* 22 Nov.1844. An anecdote titled 'Bosco in Altenburg' appeared in the Leipzig weekly magazine *Der Anecdotenjäger, Zeitschrift für das lustige Deutschland* issue no.2 (listed in *Börsenblatt für den deutschen Buchhandel* 10 Dec.1844).

[355] I can find no evidence (*pace* Rusconi p.119) that he was in Dresden earlier in the year.

[356] *Morgenblatt für gebildete Stände* 14 Nov.1844: "...Man sah aber sehr häufig dieselben Kunststücke. Was mich betrifft, so muß ich unumwunden bekennen, daß Bosco's Ruhm größer ist als seine Kunst. Bedeutend und überraschend ist er bloß im Verschwindenlassen...".

[357] *Zeitung für die elegante Welt* 11 Dec.1844: "...Gewiß ist es, daß er wenig Neues bietet, und bei all seiner Geschicklichkeit meist nur auf dem niederem Gebiete der doppelten Böden und der Pistolenknalleffekte sich hält. Taschenspielerei kommt, wie die Maskeraden, immer mehr aus der Mode; es scheint, als habe man daran den Geschmack verloren..."; the *ATZ* (9 Dec.1844) said: "Bosco ... scheint aber die Theilnahme an seinen Kunststücken nicht in dem Masse gefunden zu haben, als sie von ihm erwartet wurde".

[358] *Neue Würzburger Zeitung* 10 Dec.1844.

[359] *Allgemeine Musikalische Zeitung* 18 Dec.1844; Hofmeister: *Musikalisch-literarischer Monatsbericht* 12, 1844. A copy is held in the Staatsbibliothek zu Berlin.

[360] Slg. Nebauer/S/A-D/S14; url:048 (not digitised).

[361] *Prag (Ost und West)* 4, 13 Jan.1845.

[362] *Prag (Ost und West)* 22, 25 Jan.1845; *ATZ* 13, 29 Jan.1845; *Bohemia* 19, 21, 31 Jan.1845; *Der Humorist* 29 Jan.1845.

[363] *ATZ* 15 Feb.1845.

[364] *Bohemia* 21, 25, 28 Feb.; 2, 4, 7 Mar.1845; *Ost und West* 6 Mar.1845; *ATZ* 12 Mar.1845.

[365] *Ost und West* (and *Prag*) 13, 22 Jan.1845 (reviews but largely Eastern anecdotes); 1 Mar.1845 (the harem anecdote); 8, 10 Mar.1845 ('Ein Besuch bei Bosco'; reprinted in *Der Wanderer* 19 Mar.1845).

[366] "Zweite Auflage. Wien, Prag und Venedig, 1845". Available online at url:049. The title-page (only) for *Part 2: Turkey* is included at the end, but that, and the editions in other languages, clearly never appeared. A note inside the back cover signed by Francesconi dated March 1845 announces with regret that he is unable to comply at present with requests for Part 2. The book was also advertised in Graz when Bosco was there in November 1845 (*Grazer Zeitung* 22 Nov.1845).

[367] *ATZ* 13 Mar.1845; *Sonntagsblätter* 16 Mar.1845.

[368] *ATZ* 15, 31 Mar.1845.

[369] *Der Humorist* 26 Mar.1845 ("ehevorgestern"); *Die Jugend-Tagebücher Franz Josephs (1843-1848)*… March 23 1845: "…Um halb 7 Uhr Abends producirte sich bey der Mama der berühmte Taschenspieler Bosco".

[370] *ATZ* 13, 15, 20, 31 Mar.1845; *Der Wanderer* 17 Mar.; 1, 3 Apr.1845.

[371] Reviews included *Der Sammler, Der Wanderer, Der Humorist* 3 Apr.1845; *Österreichisches Morgenblatt* 5 Apr.1845 (by F B Schindler); *Der Österreichische Zuschauer* 7 Apr.1845; *Wiener Zeitung* 11 Apr.1845; *Signale für die Musikalische Welt* [Leipzig] no.16, April 1845, report from Vienna dated April 5th (for which see p.52).

[372] *ATZ* 7 Apr.1845, sympathetically applauding his decision; *Der Wanderer* (9. 10 Apr.) agreed, suggesting he was better suited to private performances; it included a poem, 'Täuschung und Wahrheit. (An Barth. Bosco)', by A. Palme, and said that Bosco was negotiating to hire the hall of the *Musikverein*.

[373] *ATZ* 10 Apr.1845; *Der Humorist* 10 Apr.1845.

[374] *ATZ* 12 Apr.1845.

[375] *Signale für die Musikalische Welt* No.16, April 1845; *Die Grenzboten* 1845 II p.184 ("Der Entzauberte Bosco"); *Der Spiegel, für Kunst, Eleganz und Mode* 15 Apr.1845.

[376] *ATZ, Wanderer, Der Sammler* and *Wiener Zeitung* 14 Apr.1845; *Bohemia* 20 Apr.1845.

[377] *Der Humorist* and *ATZ* 29 Apr.1845. Two letters by Bosco from this period, dated April 13th and May 6th 1845, both to unknown addressees, are held by the Staats- und Universitätsbibliothek Hamburg Carl von Ossietzky; not digitised:
https://kalliope-verbund.info/de/ead?ead.id=DE-611-HS-491366
https://kalliope-verbund.info/de/ead?ead.id=DE-611-HS-491367.

[378] *ATZ* 28 Apr.1845 says: "Bosco befindet sich zwar noch in Wien, reist aber dieser Tage nach Bologna, um nach dem Tode seiner Gattin seine Kinder zu sehen und seine ältere [*sic*] Tochter, die eine ausgezeichnete Sängerin sein soll, mit auf Reisen zu nehmen". This is the first reference found to Adelaide, who would now be 17, as a singer — and where "Kleroth" learnt the fact to incorporate it in his imaginary letter (B1 pp.42, 49, and *Excursus on the Family* p.211).

[379] *ATZ* 5 May 1845 (also announcing Döbler's arrival in Vienna the same day, but a brief visit to see friends). And Frikell was now also a serious rival — noted "in the Leipzig papers as a younger and handsomer magician, outdoing Bosco, and never boring…" (*Österreichisches Bürgerblatt* 21 May 1845, quoting *Didaskalia*).

[380] *Gazzetta di Firenze* 8 July 1845.

[381] *La Farfalla, foglio di amena lettura, bibliografia, belle arti, teatri e varietà* (weekly supplement to the *Gazzetta privilegiata di Bologna*) no.23, 4 June 1845; reprinted in the Milan *Bazar di novita artistiche, letterarie e teatrali* 18 June 1845.

[382] *Teatri, Arte ed Letteratura* 24 May 1845 (*maître* and *père* so accented), with enthusiastic reviews of his shows June 5 & 12 1845.

[383] *Gazzetta di Firenze* 8 July 1845.

[384] *Il Ricoglitore fiorentino* (quoted in *Il Pirata* 11 July 1845); *Bazar di novita artistiche, letterarie e teatrali* 19 July 1845.

[385] *Gazzetta di Firenze* 19, 29 July 1845.

[386] *Wiener Zeitung* 3 Aug.1845: "…der mechanischer Taschenspieler von Holz, welcher die 3 Verwandlungen des Bosco, ohne Gehilfen im Tische zu haben, auf einmahl [*sic*] über alle Erwartung nachmacht…".

[387] *Teatri, Arte ed Letteratura* 21 Aug.1845.

[388] *Il Piccol Reno* 16 Aug.1845, printing a homage to Bosco by Luigi Muzzi from Florence on June 25th (he had written a similar piece when Bosco was in Bologna in March 1836).

[389] *ATZ* 17, 24 Sep.1845.

[390] *Il Vaglio* 13, 20 Sep.1845; *Il Gondoliere* 13, 20 Sep.1845; *Il Pirata* 26 Sep.1845.

[391] By coincidence a "Signor Bosco", of Sardinia, arrived in Folkestone from Boulogne on October 18th, but he was a merchant.

[392] *Bazar di novita artistiche, letterarie e teatrali* 1 Nov.1845; *ATZ* 29 Oct.; 4 Nov. 1845; *La Favilla* (Supplement) 26 Oct.1845.

[393] *Laibacher Zeitung (Anhang)* 4 Nov.1845; *Illyrisches Blatt* 13 Nov.1845.

[394] *Der Wanderer* 18 Nov.1845 (report dated November 14th).

[395] *Grazer Zeitung* 20, 22 Nov.1845.

[396] *Grazer Zeitung* 29 Nov.1845 (reprinted in *Der Sammler* 2 Dec.1845); *ATZ* 29 Nov.1845.

[397] *Die Gegenwart, Politisch-literarisches Tagblatt* 1 Dec.1845; *Gambrinus* No.5, Jan. 1846.

[398] Full title: *Briefe des Hans Michel aus Obersteier an seinen Göd, den Sensenschmid in der Oed über Steiermark und Gratz;* Fiction F17.

[399] *Grazer Zeitung* 23 Oct.1845; *Der Sammler* 6 Dec.1845; *Bohemia* 9 Dec.1845; *Der Wanderer* 2 Jan.1846.

[400] *Grazer Zeitung* 2 Dec.1845; *Illyrisches Blatt* 11 Dec.1845 (etc.). The *Grazer Zeitung* 4 Dec.1845 commented as he was leaving on the number of requests for help that he received making demands on his sympathetic good nature, saying he let none leave empty handed.

[401] *Grazer Zeitung* 4 Dec.1845 (also reporting an impending visit there by Döbler).

[402] *Der Wanderer* 27 Nov.1845, heralding a trio of magicians (*ein Taschenspielerkleeblatt*) in town, with Döbler and Karoline Bernhardt also still there. *Österreichisches Morgenblatt* 22 Dec.1845 made the same point — "*Figaro là, Figaro quà!. 'Tres sunt collegium?'* … Jetzt sind sie beisammen: Frau Professorin Bernhardt, Hr. Professor Döbler, und nun Hr. Professor Bosco auch noch dazu…".

[403] *ATZ* 13 Dec.1845; *Der Sammler* 13 Dec.1845 (etc.).

[404] *Der Humorist* 22 Dec.1845; *Sonntagsblätter* 28 Dec.1845 (etc.).

[405] *ATZ* 22 Dec.1845; 3, 5 Jan.1846.

[406] *Der Wanderer* 6 Jan.1846; *Der Humorist* 7, 8 Jan.1846; *Wiener Zeitschrift* 8 Jan. 1846; *Der Österreichische Zuschauer* 7, 9 Jan.1846 (the last review oddly saying that Bosco's father had the same profession).

[407] *Der Sammler* 6 Jan.1846.

[408] *ATZ* 7 Jan.1846. The Germanisches Nationalmuseum (Nürnberg) has a letter from Bosco to Adolf Bäuerle, editor of *Allgemeine Theater-Zeitung*, dated 5 Jan.1846 (url:051, not digitised).

There are two further surviving Bosco letters from this period, both written from Vienna. One (in the Harry Ransom Center, University of Texas; url:052), dated

January 14th 1846, is to an unnamed newspaper in Augsburg enclosing a cutting from a Viennese paper mentioning him and asking them to use it to publicise him. This letter may have been the source of an anecdote which was published in the *Augsburger Unterhaltungs-Blatt* on 4 Feb.1846 of Bosco fooling two young billiard players in Vienna. The other letter, in the National Library of Austria (Sammlung Wenzel La Croix von Langenheim; url:053), dated January 7th, is also to an unnamed newspaper and sounds from the description to be of a similar nature.

[409] *Wiener Zeitung* 8 Jan.1846 (reprinted in *Der Wanderer* 11 Jan.1846)

[410] *ATZ* 9 Jan.1846; *Österreichische Morgenblatt* 10 Jan.1845 ("only two more shows — don't believe it!").

[411] *Der Humorist, Der Sammler, Der Wanderer, Allgemeine Theater-Zeitung* 13, 16 Jan.1846.

[412] 'Hotel zum Erzherzog Karl', 1. Stock, Thüre Nr.31; in Kärnthnerstraße, built in 1807.

[413] *Der Wanderer* 19 Jan.1846; *ATZ* 20 Jan.1846, both quoting from letters sent to them by Bosco (which had to be written by someone else); *Wiener Zeitung* 21 Jan. 1846 added that he had the presence of mind to lie over the exploding box of rockets. The accident was widely reported in German and French papers.

[414] *ATZ* 22 Jan.1846, oddly stating that Bosco's ship had sunk between Alexandria and Constantinople and he had nearly drowned, calling him a magic-making Tamino surviving fire and water, and declaring that his recent accident showed he had gone through fire for his art; *Der Wanderer* 22 Jan.1846 also noted his recovery, and published on January 24 an effusive appreciation of Bosco by Julius Sollier, alluding to Bosco's sufferings during his early army service.

[415] Published in *ATZ* 28 Feb.1846.

[416] *Der Wanderer* 1 Feb.1846; *ATZ* 3 Feb.1846.

[417] *Der Wanderer* 13 Feb.1846; *Österreichisches Morgenblatt* 16 Feb.1846.

[418] *Der Wanderer* 16 Feb.1846.

[419] *Österreichische Zuschauer* 20 Feb.1846.

[420] *Der Wanderer* 18 Feb.1846.

[421] *Österreichische Zuschauer* 23 Feb.1846 ("…Still the old Bosco; the black powder could not put a stop to his black art…"); *Der Wanderer* 23 Feb.1846 ("…ein Salamander…") and 26 Feb. (a long paean on Bosco's character and personality); *Der Sammler* 24 Feb.1846 (wondering why he wore a dress coat and not his usual sleeve-costume — burnt arms?); *ATZ* 23 Feb.1846 (Bosco assuring the crowd that gunpowder had not done him this much harm in his army days) and 25 Feb. (a phoenix … the music union a very appropriate venue as other magic fingers had per-

formed there — Dreyschock and Liszt…); *Österreichische Morgenblatt* 28 Feb. 1846 (he hurt five fingers but now shows twenty of them, each one a magic wand… the room was full, the applause extraordinary…); *Wiener Zeitung* 4 Mar.1846 (his skills had withstood the test of fire).

[422] *Der Wanderer* 2 Mar.1846.

[423] Unfortunately *Ungar* for 1846 is not online at *https://anno.onb.ac.at* or *http://real-j.mtak.hu*, but the latter includes from this year *Budapesti Hiradó, Honderü, Nemzeti Ujság*, together with other titles (*http://real-j.mtak.hu/view/year/1846.html*): they must be downloaded as large pdf files to read or search them.

[424] *Passavia* 13 Mar.1846 gives a nice account of him entertaining his fellow passengers, teasing them with their money, rings and watches. Then a later issue (21 Mar.) quotes from *Honderü* a satirical account of his shipboard activities — turning the snuffbox of a well-known usurer into a leather boot, etc., etc.

[425] *ATZ* 11 Mar.1846; *Der Wanderer* 14 Mar.1846.

[426] *Der Wanderer* 18 Mar.1846; *ATZ* 8, 30 Apr.1846.

[427] *Der Wanderer* 18 Mar.1846; *Der Humorist* 20 Mar.1846, enjoying pointing out that Bosco's "German" was, of course, his "[tr.] mangled German (*radebrechendem Deutsch*) mixed *pêle-mêle* with French and Italian". *Der Humorist* was still laughing at this more than a year later (23 Nov.1847) in a piece headed 'Kauderwelsch ist nicht deutsch' ('Gibberish is not German'), having Bosco say to the theatre director 'Oh, Signore, sprechen ik ja nix deutsce Sprachen. sprecken ik Bißt französich, Bißt italienisch, Bißt deutsch, deutscheinand — das is nicht deutse…'.

[428] *Budapesti Hiradó* 19, 29 Mar.1846. A review in *Életképek* 28 Mar.1846 praised Bosco's "astonishing dexterity and ingenuity" (and added a story about Bosco eating a large bowl of potatoes for lunch — then later taking them out of his pocket). The Budapest weekly *Pesti Divatlap* (26 Mar.1846) used a similar phrase, Bosco's "extraordinary dexterity and speed" (*rendkívüli ügyessége, gyorsasága*), and defended his appearance at the National Theatre on the basis that his shows were at noon (meaning Hungarian plays could go on in the evening as usual). There were occasional complaints that money spent on his shows could be better spent on Hungarian artists, but then a character in a humorous story (*Életképek* 4 Apr.1846) tells us that Bosco must be Hungarian "because his name backwards is *Ocsob* — it could be *Olcsóbb* ('cheaper')…".

[429] *ATZ* 14, 20 Apr.1846; *Der Wanderer* 25 Apr.1846.

[430] *ATZ* 29 Apr.1846; *Der Humorist* 4 May 1846 ("thunderous applause"); *Passavia* 29 Apr.1846 preceded a brief review with a humorous piece ("ein Scherz") on Bosco by Josef Seidner, which has him doing wonders everywhere from England to China, telling us his first cry after his birth was an unarticulated '*spiriti miei*' and soon after said to the midwife 'I'm fine', then, when offered a wet-nurse, said he would prefer a few glasses of champagne.

[431] *ATZ* 30 Apr.1846; *Wiener Zeitschrift* 9 May 1846.

[432] *Der Humorist* 1 Apr.1846; *ATZ* 9 May 1846.

[433] *Der Wanderer* 18 May 1846; *Életképek* 30 May 1846.

[434] A summary in *ATZ* 22 Dec.1846 has the most complete list of towns he visited on this long tour, but even that omits at least Torda and Kronstadt. Amongst the appreciative audience in Kronstadt was the German traveller Ernst Anton Quitzmann who in his *Deutsche Briefen über den Orient* (1848, p.232) calls Bosco "the heartiest of companions ... conjured away the evenings for us".

[435] *Der Siebenbürger Bote* 25 June 1846 (and partly reprinted in *Der Humorist* 4 July 1846, these listing Kronstadt (Braşov) in his planned itinerary).

[436] *Szuper Károly színészeti naplója 1830–1850* (ed. Béla Váli; Budapest, 1889; reprint 1975; online at url:054): entries for June 27 and July 9 1846. No doubt to be taken with a pinch of salt, though a review of Bosco in Arad in *Életképek* 18 July 1846, written on July 8th, mentions both Szuper's company and Futó as pseudo-Bosco.

Szuper's account is quoted in the chatty book of essays *Gyorskocsin Erdélyben: Kutatások, rajzok, emlékezések* ('By Fast Coach in Transylvania: Research, drawings, memories'), published in Cluj-Napoca in 1927 by Hungarian lawyer and writer Siklóssy László (online at url:055a), in which Chap.VII is entirely on Bosco. He gives a brief account of Bosco's career, and after quoting Szuper on Bosco in Arad describes Bosco's experiences soon after in Cluj-Napoca (see below).

Another brief account of the Pseudo-Bosco in Arad appeared in Antal Váradi's *Az elzárt mennyország*, in the chapter 'Színészkaraván', 'Caravan of Actors' (online at 055b) telling us that when Bosco saw Futó revealing how he did his tricks he had a fit and not only left town but returned all his takings.

[437] The most detailed account is in the Klausenburg paper *Múlt és jelen* 13 Aug.1846, which discusses the whole business at some length. It mentions that on August 5th The Royal Cluj Academy printed at their press a portrait engraved "in memory and honour of Bosco of Turin" (*In memoriam et honorem Bartholomaei Bosco Turinensis. In lithographia R. Lycei Claudiopolitani, 1846*). Further accounts (with some minor differences) are given in *Honderü* 18 Aug.1846, in *Der Siebenbürger Bote* 20 Aug.1846 (which includes a German translation of Bosco's letter), and in *Transylvania* (supplement to *Siebenbürger Bote*) 24 Aug.1846.

An article in *Erdélyi Hiradó,* which supported the decision to revoke Bosco's freedom of the city, arguing that otherwise this great honour could go to any visiting virtuoso, actor, conjuror, circus rider, or tightrope walker who gave a few free shows, is discussed in *Der Siebenbürger Bote* 3 Sep.1846, which agreed, but felt that the revocation of the grant once made was a procedure (*Fürgang*) at best irregular, and it disagreed that the award could be rescinded on the grounds that the decision of the committee had not been publicly promulgated.

[438] *Der Sammler* 29 Aug.1846; *Der Humorist* 17 Sep.1846.

[439] *Múlt és jelen* 13 Aug.1846.

[440] *Der Siebenbürger Bote* 10 Aug.1846.

[441] *Múlt és jelen* 16 Aug.1846; *Der Siebenbürger Bote* 20 Aug.1846; *Der Wanderer* 7 Sep.1846 (report dated August 22nd).

[442] *Transylvania* (supplement to *Siebenbürger Bot*e) 24 Aug.1846. His performances in Hermannstadt saw the *ATZ* (11 Sep.1846) praise him as "at home in his profession like a fish in water", and joked that he had to perform there soon after "Maestro R. Melé", who in July had given a (poorly attended) "acrobatic-magical-physical show" and was "equilibrist, athlete, conjuror, painter, musician, polyglot, improvisor, chemist, sculptor and optician" — how much more versatile than Bosco..., who, it concluded "was leaving Hermannstadt with fewer regrets that when he left Klausenburg".

[443] *Allgemeine Zeitung* 22 Dec.1846; *Gazeta de Transilvania* 19, 26 Aug.; 2, 5, 9 Sep.1846 [this is printed in an interesting transitional Romanian cyrillic script].

[444] An unlikely story of Bosco in Bucharest was told many years later by British newspaper correspondent Joseph Archer Crowe. He was in the city in January 1854 and describing its characteristics he noted "a prevalence of gambling", illustrating this by saying that (at some date not stated) "Bosco, the eminent card-trickster, came to Bucharest with a considerable sum of money...", but in a week lost all his money "and had to go and prestidigitate elsewhere": — from a lecture he gave in London in 1855, printed in *London Evening Standard* 7 April 1855.

[445] *Albina Românească* 24, 31 Oct.; 3, 7 Nov.1846.

[446] *Albina Românească* 21 Nov.1846. The article 'Ein Ereigniß' in *Der Wanderer* 21 Dec.1846 is largely a translation of this (wrongly dating the first show to November 4th).

[447] *Albina Românească* 5 Dec.1846 ("...la musique d'Italie et la Magie d'Égypte, si hétérogènes entr-elles, se sent réunies Samedi dernier sur notre théâtre...").

Bosco was certainly long remembered in Romania. In 1875 a shop in Bucharest was selling various pieces of "Magical Apparatus", including *Disculu magicu alu lui Bosco* with a terrible old engraving of him as an illustration (*Telegraphulŭ de Bucuresci* 29 Jan.1875, etc.).

[448] *Allgemeine Zeitung* 22 Dec.1846 (quoting the Jassy "Moldauische Zeitung": so pleased to have Bosco visit "this furthest corner of Europe); *ATZ* 28 Jan.1847.

[449] He was not the "Bosco" in Marseille in January 1847 (Rusconi p.140): this was an incompetent impostor (B11).

[450] *Gazeta Lwowska* 9 Mar.1847, mentioning that he had made charitable donations when there, as he did in Lemberg. From his route it is likely that he also performed in Czernowitz (Chernivtsi).

⁴⁵¹ *Gazeta Lwowska* 27 Feb.1847, which could not resist punning on his name, saying he performed *bosko,* 'divinely' ("...i by nie nowego już wprawdzie użyć kalamburu, wykonywał sztuki swoje *bosko*"); *Der Humorist* 15 Mar.1847 said he had a cold keeping him in bed for eight days, which he spent hatching diabolical seat prices, and *Oesterreichisches Theater- und Musik-Album* 22 Mar.1847 said of the prices: "What does Jenny [Lind] say to that?".

⁴⁵² *Gazeta Lwowska* 2, 4, 6, 9, 13, 18 Mar.1847. He also gave private performances, including a very high payment for one show for two ladies who did not want to have to mingle with the locals (*Kemptner Zeitung* 26 Feb.1847).

⁴⁵³ *Gazeta Lwowska* 13 Mar.1847.

⁴⁵⁴ *Gazeta Krakowska* 3 April 1847 ("we wtorek przejezdzal przez miasto nasze slawny sztukmistrz Bosco, ktory zjadlszy tu prawie tylko obiad pod Różą, puscił się w dalszą drogę do Warszawy, dla przepędzenia świąt na łonie swéj familii"). We find his daughter Adelaide leaving Kraków a few weeks later: *Gazeta Krakowska* 2 June 1847 ("...Wyjechali z Krawkowa... Bosco Adelaida...").

⁴⁵⁵ *Gazeta Warszawska* 14 Apr.1847 says "ten days ago", and the Staatsbibliothek zu Berlin has a letter by Bosco (to an unnamed recipient) dated Warsaw 5 April 1847, url:056 (not digitised).

⁴⁵⁶ *ATZ* 29 Oct.1847.

⁴⁵⁷ *Gazeta Warszawska* 13, 14 Apr.1847 (the second quoting the long article in *Gazeta Lwowska* 27 Feb.1847: see note 451); *Gazeta Codzienna* 14 Apr.1847; *Warszawska Gazeta Policyjna* 14 Apr.1847.

⁴⁵⁸ Ongoing notices in *Gazeta Warszawska, Gazeta Codzienna, Warszawska Gazeta Policyjna*. A wonderfully extravagant article in *Gazeta Warszawska* 17 Apr. 1847 hails Bosco as "master of all mystery arts, the great dignitary of the congregation of Chaldean mages ... the Pharaoh of all magical artists ... a man who does not get old, because he believes in the transmigration of souls and today he is a transformation of a great priest of Osiris or Apis ... and in keeping with metempsychosis, we must suppose that he is enlivened by the same soul as once Pinetti, or perhaps Cagliostro... the breeze of the Nile has refreshed him completely ...now rejuvenated with new tricks learnt in Egypt...", etc., etc.

⁴⁵⁹ *Gazeta Warszawska* 1 May 1847.

⁴⁶⁰ *Gazeta Warszawska* 6 May 1847.

⁴⁶¹ *Gazeta Warszawska* 13 May 1847. His seven shows in Warsaw are said to have earned him "30,000 Polnische Gulder" (*ATZ* 29 Oct.1847).

⁴⁶² *Warszawska Gazeta Policyjna* 13 July 1847 ("Bosco Bartłomiéj mechanik", leaving) and 27 July (returning).

⁴⁶³ *Warszawska Gazeta Policyjna* 8 Aug.1847.

[464] *Warszawska Gazeta Policyjna* 13 Sept.1847 ("Bosco Bartlom. sztukmistrz").

[465] *Gazeta Krakowska* 20 Sept.1847.

[466] *Gazeta Krakowska* 14 Oct.1847. They are described as arriving "from Poland", as from 1846 Kraków had been incorporated into Austria. Two others arrived with Bosco and may have been members of his crew, Franciszek Molnar and Pierre Jaquet.

[467] *Gazeta Krakowska* 16, 19, 20 Oct.1847.

[468] *Gazeta Krakowska* 21, 25 Oct.1847 ("te kule są z pasztetów strasburskich fabrykowane". This was continued on 29 Oct. by the story 'Bosco and Death' (for which see *Fiction* F7). A poster (bilingual in German and Polish) for his three Kraków performances is digitised at url:057.

[469] *ATZ* 29 Oct.1847.

[470] *Gazeta Krakowska* 30 Oct.1847.

[471] An "Alexander Conty" is recorded as leaving Kraków for Poland in *Gazeta Krakowska* 4 Nov.1847, possibly his brother-in-law (p.208).

[472] *Der Humorist* 27 Oct.; 9 Nov.1847; *Allgemeine Theater-Zeitung* 10 Nov.1847.

[473] *Preßburger Zeitung* 22, 29 Nov., 3 Dec.1847; *Pannonia* 23, 30 Nov., 11 Dec. 1847. *ATZ* 14 Dec.1847 is incorrect in saying he gave eight shows plus the charity show.

[474] *ATZ* 18, 24 Dec.1847, commending him for allowing the audience such a close up view of his performances.

[475] Henri Robin 1811-1874, born Henri Joseph Donckele in France, is well known.
Baron, "Magician to the Great Sultan", was a pupil of Döbler according to the *Lexikon*, which quotes Hofzinser's high opinion of him, conjuror, juggler and athlete.
François Rappo, 1826-1874, another conjuror, juggler and strong man ("selten haben sich Geschicklichkeit und Stärke so sehr vereinigt"), has a long entry in the *Lexikon*.

[476] Widely reviewed in the Vienna papers, notably in *ATZ* 11, 18, 22 Jan.1848 (the last a warm appraisal by Hofzinser) and *Wiener Zuschauer* 8, 12, 22, 29 Jan.1848 — the article on the 12th (pp.43-4) is a detailed report titled 'Ein Nachmittag bei Bartholomeo Bosco', by J[uliu]s. A modern account is given by Hans Pemmer in 'Wiener Taschenspieler im ausgehenden 18. Jahrhundert und in der Biedermeierzeit', url:058.

[477] "Bosco's Fatalitäten in Wien … Bosco kann nun einmal nicht nach Wien kommen, ohne daß ihm Widriges passirt. Dies zu verhüten, ist selbst seine Kunst unzugänglich…": *Wiener Zuschauer* 17 Jan.1848, quoting *Der Wanderer*.

[478] *Wiener Zeitung* 8 Feb.1848: "…ganz Wien wird noch verzaubert werden, ein wahrer Congreß von Taschenspielern und Athleten!"; *Der Ungar* 27 Feb.1848: "Bosco hat hier sein Meisterstück geliefert, er hat noch vor seiner Abreise seine Rivalen Robin und Baron verschwinden gemacht".

[479] *Der Humorist* 20 Jan.1848: "Bosco hat ein Stück geschrieben, ein Zäuberspiel im wahren Sinne des Wortes, in welchem er sich selbst mitspielen will, aber nicht nur taschenspielen, sondern eine eigene Rolle geben, einen Charakter darstellen. Das kann jedenfalls amusant werden"; also noted in *Rigasche Zeitung* 18 Feb.1848 ("all Vienna is curious about it") and in Oettinger's *Charivari* 26 Feb.1848.

[480] *ATZ* 9 Feb.1848

[481] *Wiener Zuschauer* 29 Jan.1848; 7 Feb.1848; *Der Humorist* 12 Feb.1848.

[482] *Der Humorist* 12, 19, 19 Feb.1848.

[483] *Brünner Zeitung* 22, 23, 26, 27 Feb.1848; *Der Humorist* 1 Mar.1848; and the correspondent of the *ATZ* (8 Mar.1848) put it: "Bosco und seine *Spiriti famigliari, Che obediscono ai suoi tribunali* versetzen das zahlreich versammelte Auditorium in ein eben so großes Erstaunen, als seine *poliglotica Ciancia* die lauterste Hilarität wach zu erhalten weis".

[484] *Leipziger Zeitung* 24 May 1848.

[485] 'Bosco's Traum', *DAZ* 10 June 1848.

[486] *Charivari* 22 Apr.1848 (saying already in Leipzig for some time; very popular with the local artists and tradespeople; serenaded by a singing group); *DAZ* 29 Apr.1848 (has been there "a few days"; plans to go to America).

[487] As will be seen, there is no room for a visit to Algeria in August-September 1848 (Rusconi pp.142-3), and there is no evidence for one. The Algerian anecdote derives only from the *undated* story in the fanciful *Il Nuovo Bosco* (pp.196-8 in the 1878 edition), which also (p.176) imagines Bosco in North Africa in 1838.

[488] Large ads in *Illustrirte Zeitung* and *Signale für die musikalische Welt* 29 Apr.1848 (and elsewhere). The Stadtgeschichtliches Museum Leipzig has a painting of Bosco on stage in the Schützenhaus (online at url:059): 'Bartolomeo Boscos Zauber-theater, wie es im Monat Mai des Jahres 1848 im großen Saal des Schützenhauses zu Leipzig aufgestellt war, Farbzeichnung von Dr. C. Zehme, fertiggestellt am 22.06.1848', so the painting was completed after Bosco had left for Dresden. (For Zehme see notes 353 and 504).

That museum also has a handbill for Bosco's Leipzig farewell show on May 28th 1848, online at url:060; and a letter from Bosco (to an unidentified recipient) dated Leipzig 6 May 1848, online at url:061; the Staats- und Universitätsbibliothek Hamburg Carl von Ossietzky also has a letter from Bosco (to an unidentified recipient) dated Leipzig 6 May 1848 (url:062); as does the Harry Ransom Center

(Houdini Collection): "Letter (German) to unidentified recipient, 6 May 1848" (see url:063).

[489] Ongoing ads in *Leipziger Zeitung* and *DAZ* 29 Apr. to 12 May 1848. These ads (and the poems referred to below) in the *Leipziger Zeitung* are in the *Beilage* and *Zweite Beilage* of the paper which are included in the version on Google Books.

[490] *Leipziger Zeitung* and *DAZ* 13 to 17 May 1848.

[491] *Leipziger Zeitung* 19, 21 May 1848; *DAZ* 21 May 1848.

[492] *Leipziger Zeitung* 24 May 1848; *DAZ* 23, 24 May 1848.

[493] *Leipziger Zeitung* and *DAZ* 27, 28 May 1848 [the 27 May issue of *Leipziger Zeitung* is misdated 6 April on *Anno*); for a handbill for this final show see note 488.

[494] *DAZ* 9 May 1848; echoed, and paraphrased, in *Charivari* 11 May 1848.

[495] *Leipziger Zeitung* 13 May 1848.

[496] *Leipziger Zeitung* 21 May 1848; no mention of Mathilde Bannholzer, now said to be aged ten, who was performing daily in the Arena on the Roßplatz.

[497] *Leipziger Zeitung* 24 May 1848.

[498] *Leipziger Zeitung* 27 May 1848. Frederick Barbarossa died in Turkey in 1190 on the Third Crusade and was buried, not in Jerusalem as was hoped, but his body in Antioch, his bones in Tyre, and his heart in Tarsus. But legend had it that he lived on, a sleeping hero, in a cave in the Kyffhäuser mountains in Thuringia and would one day awake to restore Germany to its ancient greatness. A likely cave, *Barbarossahöhle* ("Barbarossa Cave") was discovered in 1865, and on June 18th 1899, the 744th anniversary of Barbarossa's coronation as Holy Roman Emperor, the German Empire dedicated the Kyffhäuser Monument, declaring Kaiser Wilhelm I, who had died in 1888, a reincarnation of Frederick.

[499] *Charivari* 23 Mar.1848. Ironically by that date Metternich was already heading off to exile.

[500] *Dresdner Journal* 3 July 1848: "Herr Bosco scheint bei einer seiner Kunstproduktionen in die Schule des diplomatischen Taschenspielers Fürst Metternich gegangen zu sein. Aber der Schüler hat den Meister übertroffen…".

[501] Later titled *Wiener Charivari Katzenmusik;* 15 July; 12, 31 Aug.; 25 Oct.1848. In Potsdam at the end of the year it was joked that Bosco had been brought there by the government to make up a quorum of deputies (*Der Wanderer* 9 Dec.1848).

[502] See the Deutsches Historisches Museum Berlin 'Bild Index' at url:064, and *Einleitung* to the 1984 facsimile reprint (which includes variant editions of some issues) at url:065.

[503] The second item was reprinted by *Der Bayerische Landbote* (29 Oct.1848) and by the *Neustadter Wochenblatt* (14 Nov.1848).

The article on Bosco at *www.jedinat-zauberschule.de* (url:066, but link now seems dead) somehow assumes these are contributions written by Bosco himself — "… Von Zeitgenossen hervorgehoben wurden die intelligenten, auf den Anlaß zugeschnittenen Wortspielereien. Das äußert sich auch in den von ihm verfaßten humoristischen Beiträgen für die satirische Zeitschrift 'Der Krakeler'" [*sic*].

[504] This is (surely) the same person as "Dr. C. Zehme" who painted the pictures of Bosco's *Zaubertheater* (notes 353 and 488): he was Dr. Carl Friedrich Zehme, a.k.a Carl Lenz, who wrote popular medical works and (with F.A.Teucher) *Das ewig denkwürdige Jahr 1845…*

[505] His final ad in *Deutsche Allgemeine Zeitung* 28 May 1848 ends with a poem 'Spiriti miei infernali' and warns "Bosco may never return from America".

[506] Listed in 'Den 10. Juni bis Mittag in Dresden angekommene Reisende': *Dresdner Journal* 11 June 1848 (he is staying at the 'Rother Hirsch' Gasthaus). Bosco travelled (so we are told by a Bosco enthusiast writing in the *Magdeburgische Zeitung* 7 July 1848) not by the magic cloak of Dr Faust or General Sybilsky of Wolfsberg, but by the Leipzig-Dresden railway.

[507] *Dresdner Journal* 16 June 1848; *Leipziger Zeitung* 25 June 1848.

[508] *Dresdner Journal* 22, 30 June 1848; *Der Dampfwagen* 23 June 1848.

[509] *Dresdner Journal* 3, 10, 16 July 1848; *Sächsiche Dorfzeitung* 4 Aug.1848.

[510] *Dresden Journal* 21 July 1848. Grafina, usually Graffina, was earlier with his brothers at the Cirque Franconi in Paris.

[511] *Dresden Journal* 25, 26 July 1848; *Leipziger Zeitung* 2 Aug.1848.

[512] *Dresden Journal* 4, 5 Aug.1848; *Sächsiche Dorfzeitung* 4 Aug.1848.

[513] *Dresden Journal* 18, 20, 21 Aug.1848; *Bohemia* 23 Aug.1848 reported him as significantly unwell.

[514] *Magdeburgische Zeitung* 3, 5, 12, 14, 16, 20 Sep.1848 (the last a large illustrated advertisement for his final show).

[515] *Magdeburgische Zeitung* 10 Sept.1848.

[516] *Magdeburgische Zeitung* 26 Sept.1848.

[517] *KPBZ* 24 Sept.; 14, 18 Oct.; and ongoing ads until Nov.12 1848.

[518] *KPBZ* 25 Oct.1848.

[519] Advertisements in *KPBZ* between 9 Dec.1848 and 14 Jan.1849.

[520] *KPBZ* 10, 14, 20, 24 Dec.1848.

[521] *KPBZ* 14, 29 Dec.1848. The poem had previously appeared as 'An Bosco in Leipzig' in *Leipziger Zeitung* 13 May 1848.

[522] "B. Bosco giebt auf seiner Durchreise nach Köln 3 Vorstellungen in ägyptischer Zauberei…": *KPBZ* 31 Jan.1849.

[523] Rusconi p.145: source unknown. Certainly when Bosco reached Groningen in September the article cited in note 529 refers to "his recent stay in Hamburg and Bremen".

[524] Two posters, listing the content of each show in detail, are in the excellent '[Theaterzettel Bremen]' collection, online at url:067.

[525] The contemporary Bremen newspapers are unfortunately not available online but a summary in *Der Sammler* 4 July 1849 gives a lively account ("In Bremer Blättern führen die Zauberer B. Bosco und Bils einen mörderischen Insertionskampf direkt und indirekt gegen einander…"), concluding humorously that the question of who was superior would be decided by the Prussia-Saxony-Hanover Court of Arbitration immediately after its creation. Bils's admission price was 12 grote; Bosco's ranged from 9 in the gallery to 36 for a box. Bils had been performing, often with his brother Carl, since at least 1838, so was by no means an unknown newcomer. He lived for some years in Denmark but was born in Potsdam (age 37 in the 1845 Danish census, url:068).

[526] "Alexandra Bosco, daughter of the famous magician well known in Warsaw, came to Warsaw from Bremen in the last few days" (*Kurjer Warszawski* 13 Sept.1849 — "Alexandra Bosco, córka wsławionego i znanego dobrze w Warszawie Magika, przybyła w tych dniach do Warszawy z Bremen").

[527] Letter from Emden quoted in *Groninger Courant* 28 Sept.1849, adding that he was soon to travel via Groningen to Amsterdam.

[528] Quoted in the *Algemeen Handelsblad* 22 Oct.1849.

[529] *Groninger Courant* 12 Oct.1849, warmly reviewing the previous evening's show, with a long humorous story about Bosco visiting the newspaper office, magically producing copy and playing havoc with all the clocks.

[530] *Leeuwarder Courant* 26, 30 Oct.; 2 Nov.1849 (large crowds not only at his shows but following him in the streets). Robin, also touring Holland, was in Leeuwarden at the same time.

[531] *Leeuwarder Courant* 2 Nov.1849.

[532] *Algemeen Handelsblad* 17, 19, 20, 21, 22 Nov.1849. Seat prices were: balcony 3 fl, box 2.50 fl, pit 2 fl, gallery box 1 fl, gallery 0.75 fl; or subscription to all six shows for balcony 12 fl, box 10 fl. The University of Amsterdam Library has an 1849 letter from Bosco to H.J. Keizer, subject unknown (url:069, not digitised).

[533] *Algemeen Handelsblad* 24 Nov.1849.

[534] *Algemeen Handelsblad* 23, 24, 26, 27 Nov.1849.

[535] *Algemeen Handelsblad* 30 Nov.; 7, 10 Dec.1849. An article on him and a portrait were advertised as appearing in the December issue of the periodical *De honigbij:* the 1849 edition has not been digitised (1850 contains only a Constantinople anecdote).

[536] *Algemeen Handelsblad* 15, 24 Dec.1849.

[537] *Algemeen Handelsblad* 27 Dec.1849; 8 Jan.1850. Tobias Bamberg was now also performing in Amsterdam (entry price *fl.* 0.50 for all) and he too gave a charity performance for the orphanage (*Algemeen Handelsblad* 12 Jan.1850).

[538] *Algemeen Handelsblad* 15, 21 Jan.1850.

[539] *Utrechtsche provinciale en stads-courant* 9, 23, 25 Jan.1850; *De Nederlander* 10 Jan.1850; *Algemeen Handelsblad* 21 Jan.1850.

[540] *Algemeen Handelsblad* 29 Apr.1850, Vreeland included in a list of his shows.

[541] *Arrondissementsbode van Amersfoort* 29 Jan.1850. Also in town was Herr Maju (for whom see note 545) performing "in imitation of Bosco"; he charged *f.* 0.49.

[542] *Algemeen Handelsblad* 1 (saying he had given a total of 43 private *soirées* when recently there), 4, 5, 6, 7 Feb.1850.

[543] *Algemeen Handelsblad* 6 Feb.1850.

[544] *Algemeen Handelsblad* 13, 15, 18 Feb.1850.

[545] *Algemeen Handelsblad* 19 Feb.1850. Meanwhile "Tobias Bamberg (de Zoon)" was performing in Haarlem, now with "various new tricks *à la Bosco*" (*Opregte Haarlemsche Courant* 23 Feb.1850). And in Zwolle L.K. Maju (born Levie Kinsbergen, 1823-1886, later better known as a science popularizer: see the interesting article at url:070) was also advertising performances of "Egyptische Tooverkunst à la Bosco" (*Provinciale Overijsselsche en Zwolsche courant* 12 Feb. 1850). Leendert Lion Kinsbergen, who later claimed to be a pupil of Bosco (C26) was Levie's cousin.

[546] *Algemeen Handelsblad* 8, 9 Feb.1850.

[547] *Algemeen Handelsblad* 11, 22 Feb.1850.

[548] *Arnhemsche courant* 28 Feb.1850 ("a master of his craft"); *Algemeen Handelsblad* 5 Mar.1850.

[549] *Provinciale Geldersche en Nijmeegsche courant* 6, 13 Mar.1850; *Arnhemsche courant* 25 Mar.1850.

[550] *Zutphensche courant* 30 Mar.; 6 Apr.1850 ("...performed with a dexterity that challenges the most trained eye").

[551] His intention (reported in *Algemeen Handelsblad* 25 Mar.1850) was to be there on April 9th and 11th, but a Deventer review quoted in *Provinciale Overijsselsche en Zwolsche courant* 16 April says his first show there was not until April 11th.

[552] *Provinciale Overijsselsche en Zwolsche courant* 12, 16, 19 Apr.1850.

[553] *Algemeen Handelsblad* 29 Apr.1850 (he had originally planned two shows there, on April 23rd and 24th).

[554] *Algemeen Handelsblad* 27, 29 Apr.1850.

[555] *Dagblad van 's Gravenhage* 3 May 1850.

[556] *Opregte Haarlemsche Courant* 4, 6, 8 May 1850; *Algemeen Handelsblad* 10 May 1850.

[557] *Dagblad van 's Gravenhage* 8, 10, 13, 14 May 1850.

[558] *De Dordrechtsche Courant* 9, 14, 23, 25 May 1850. The advertisements, signed by J.D. Van Peeren. the owner of the theatre (called the *Stadsschouwburg* by locals, even though the Council had refused the use of that name), tell us that *pleased to satisfy the desperate desire of the honoured public to have a soirée of the so highly acclaimed Physician BOSCO ... he has the honour to announce that he succeeded with great difficulty in reaching an agreement with the said Mr. BOSCO...*; prices on the first night were as high as ƒ1.99.

[559] *Leeuwardner Courant* 4 June 1850.

[560] *Algemeen Handelsblad* 3, 4 June 1850; *Leydse Courant* 3, 5, 7 June 1850.

[561] *Rotterdamsche courant* 27 June 1850.

[562] *Alkmaarsche Courant* 17 June; 1, 8 July 1850.

[563] *Nieuwe Rotterdamsche courant* 15, 16 July 1850; *Rotterdamsche courant* 16 July 1850; *Algemeen Handelsblad* 15 July 1850.

[564] *Nieuwe Rotterdamsche courant* 20 July 1850 ("...een meesterstukje van behendigheid en tooneelspelkunst. De zaak zelve moeten wij echter, als onvoegzaam, afkeeren; van Bosco's smaak hadden wij iets meer verfijnds, iets meer é[l]égants verwacht").

[565] *Rotterdamsche courant* 20 July 1850. This review is signed "C. & P."

[566] *Nieuwe Rotterdamsche courant* 24 July 1850; *Rotterdamsche courant* 25 July 1850.

[567] *Nieuwe Rotterdamsche courant* 31 July; 2 Aug.1850; *Rotterdamsche courant* 3 Aug.1850.

[568] *Nieuwe Rotterdamsche courant* 27 July 1850; *Rotterdamsche courant* 22, 30 July 1850. "L. Faucoult" (in the *Rotterdamsche courant* ads his name is misspelt "Faurault") is said in the ad to be "already well known from the newspapers" — he had been at fairs in Zwolle and The Hague in May earlier that year with his *Soirées parisiennes,* a wonderful miniature of the *Grandes eaux de Versaille,* "conjuring in the easy French style" (*het goochelspel, uitgevoerd in den gemakkelijken Franschen trant*), and with his "waterworks display ... one literally sees oneself transported to the gardens of Versailles" (*Nieuwe Rotterdamsche courant* 13 May 1850); and in Haarlem in June, "the jets of water rising and falling and forming jets, waterfalls, a crystal vase, a butterfly, a tulip, a champagne glass, then turning into a volcano erupting a shower of pearls, emeralds and rubies..." (*Le Courrier Batave* 30 June 1850).

[569] *Nieuwe Rotterdamsche courant* and *Rotterdamsche courant* 6 Aug.1850.

[570] *Nieuwe Rotterdamsche courant* 12 Aug.1850; *Rotterdamsche courant* 13 Aug. 1850.

[571] The issue is available online on Google Books (url:071). The dialogue is signed "Asmodée", pen name of van Bevervoorde, 1819-1851, who published the paper first under the title *Asmodée* (The Hague 1845-7), later as *Le Courrier Batave, et Asmodée: journal du Dimanche,* and finally as *De burger*. He had earlier been exiled and was about to serve a two year prison sentence for articles critical of the royal family when, ill and destitute, he died, age 31 in May 1851. There are biographies of him online at url:072.

[572] The printer and publisher of *Bosco en Van Bosse, of De Twee Gochelaars* and of *De Ekster* was another interesting radical, Alex. A. Crafford (Alexander Adrianus Crafford), Zeeland printer and publisher, 1816-1876, born in Bergen op Zoom and by now working in Zierikzee, soon to move to the more liberal Middelburg. He was famous for his satirical paper *De Ekster* ('The Magpie'), which he produced, despite several prosecutions, from 1850 to 1876, attacking corrupt officials, the government, the King, and any locals he took exception to. He also produced a succession of pamphlets (two prize examples are online at url:073). A number of these, known from newspaper advertisements, have no recorded surviving copy, as is unfortunately the case with his edition of the Bosco skit.

[573] *Journal de la Belgique* 13 Aug.1850; *Handelsblad* 14 Aug.1850.

[574] *Journal de la Belgique* 26 Aug.1850; *Handelsblad* 26, 31 Aug.1850.

[575] *Handelsblad* 2 Sep.1850.

[576] *Handelsblad* 3, 4, 6, 7, 9 Sep.1850. The charity show raised a healthy 169 fr. 46c. (*L'Indépendance belge* 15 Sep.1850).

[577] *Journal de Bruxelles* 12 Sep.1850; *L'Émancipation* 12, 22, 23 Sep.1850; *L'Indépendance belge* 18, 20, 21 Sep.1850; *Journal de la Belgique* 20 Sep.1850.

[578] *L'Indépendance belge* 27, 29 Sep.; 8 Oct.1850; *L'Émancipation* 30 Sep.; 1, 4, 6, 7 Oct.1850; *Journal de la Belgique* 7, 8, 11 Oct.1850.

[579] *L'Émancipation* 14, 17 Oct.1850; *L'Indépendance belge* 18, 19, 20, 21 Oct.1850.

[580] *L'Indépendance belge* 22, 26 Oct.1850; *Journal de la Belgique* 22, 28 Oct.1850; *L'Émancipation* 25 Oct. to 1 Nov.1850.

[581] *Journal de la Belgique* 15 Nov.1850; *L'Émancipation* 23 Nov.1850; *Messager des théâtres et des arts* 1 Dec.1850.

[582] *L'Émancipation* 17 Dec.1850; *Journal de la Belgique* 17, 21, 23 Dec.1850.

[583] *Journal de la Belgique* 18 Dec.1850.

[584] *Journal de la Belgique* 8 Jan.1851.

[585] *L'Indépendance belge* 26 Jan.1851; *La Nation* 27 Jan.1851.

[586] *Handelsblad* 31 Jan.1851 (adding that "Bosco has invented a new sort of gas to illuminate his room, which, it is said, has a most charming effect. He has sought a patent for this invention" (*Bosco heeft en nieuwe soort van gaz uitgevonden, waermede hy zyne zael verlicht, en die, zegt men, een allerliefst effekt maekt. Hy heeft voor deze uitvinding een brevet gevraegd*).

[587] The certificate is digitised on 'England, Alien Arrivals, 1810-1811, 1826-1869', *www.ancestry.com*. In English 'physician' in the sense of 'magician' is, I believe, unknown, whereas *fisico* in Italian and *physicien* in French are, of course, quite common in this sense in the 19th century — *though barely recognised in the major Italian and French dictionaries*. See *Appendix Z8*.

[588] *De Denderbode* 9 Feb.1851: "Den vermaerden escamoteur Bosco is vrydag te Brugge aengekomen"; then follows an anecdote which portrays his dexterity rather than his generosity — after the train halted he got a cab but dropped a gold piece as he was getting in; he picked it up immediately but saw a poor woman intending to pick it up before he did: there, he said, this is for you and gave it to her… she thought she had a gold piece in her hand, but no — the magician had turned it into a franc (*…na het afstappen van het konvooy van den yzeren weg ging hy naer eene vigilante; maer eer hy er instapte ontviel hem een goudstuk; hy raepte het aenstonds op, maer ziende eene arme vrouw, die het voor hem dagt op te raepen; daer zeyde hy, het is voor u, en gaf het haer… de oude meende het goudstuk in de hand te hebben, ntaer neen, den escamoteur had het in eenen frank veranderd*).

[589] *Messager de Gand* 21, 23 Feb.; 12 Mar.1851; *Organe de Flandres* 23, 27, 28 Feb.; 2 Mar.1851; *Handelsblad* 27 Feb.1851.

[590] *Messager de Gand* 6 Mar.1851 ("on a beau voir, beau regarder, se frotter les yeux, se torturer l'esprit, impossible de saisir le comment de la chose").

[591] *Organe de Flandres* 9, 12, 14 Mar.1851; *Messager de Gand* 12 to 17 Mar.1851.

[592] Company advertisement in *Messager de Gand* 23 Apr.1841: first class passage £1, second class 15s. She sailed right into St Katherine's Dock in London and not merely to Gravesend.

[593] There is no mention of Eugenio performing with him in England (or previously in Holland and Belgium): his son's career began after splitting with his father in May 1852 (see B2).

[594] Both documents are digitised in 'England, Alien Arrivals, 1810-1811, 1826-1869', on *www.ancestry.com*.

[595] There had been very few references to him in British newspapers over the years. In 1832 a report on Paris theatres noticed his success at the Salle Taitbout; the following year there were accounts of the loss of his apparatus when he was planning to travel to England; his performance in Alexandria in 1839 for the English consul was noted, and his building the theatre in Pera in 1840; the account of guessing the Czar's thoughts is the first 'anecdote' found. He is only once cited as a yardstick of skill — in 1846 the English magician Joseph Jacobs advertised that "the experiments of La Compt, Bosco, Philadelphia, Lodovargaziki, Herr Dobler and Phillippi are to him perfectly easy"; an 1848 letter from Constantinople referred to the Pera theatre again, and the same year an article on the French politician Thiers quotes the 'Le Bosco de la Tribune' epithet he received, which must have meant absolutely nothing to British readers: *Public Ledger* 31 Dec.1832; *London Courier and Evening Gazette* 12 Apr.1833 (etc.); *Morning Post* 2 Oct.1839; *The Atlas* 22 Aug.1840; *Monmouthshire Beacon* 15 Oct.1842, and a longer version of the Czar anecdote in *Era* 8 Jan.1843; *Manchester Courier* 3 June 1846; *Bell's Weekly Messenger* 29, 31 Jan. 1848; *Reading Mercury* 19 Feb.1848.

[596] *Morning Post; Morning Chronicle; Times* 6 May 1851; *Weekly Dispatch* 11 May 1851.

[597] *London Daily News* 20 May 1851; *Morning Post* 23 May 1851; *Weekly Dispatch* 25 May 1851. The Houdini scrapbook in the Harry Ransom Collection includes a poster for these performances, digitised at url:074 (and reproduced by Rusconi p.[157]).

[598] *Morning Advertiser* 30 May 1851; *Era* 1 June 1851; *London Evening Standard* 29 May 1851. "Many astonishing examples of illusion, executed with incomparable dexterity", said the *Illustrated London News* (7 June 1851). *Reynolds's Newspaper* (1 June 1851) summed up: "never before have we witnessed a more marvellous display of legerdemain. Other renowned conjurors sink into comparative nothingness when compared with this wonderful Italian". A later ad by Bosco in England quotes a review from the *Times,* "those who have not seen him have seen nothing", but I have

not been able to find this in the paper itself. Only one reviewer was underwhelmed on the first night: "...We did not discover in M. Bosco's performances ... anything of a novel character" (*Weekly Dispatch* 1 June 1851).

[599] *Morning Chronicle* 5 June 1851; *Era* 1 June 1851.

[600] *Express* 29 May 1851; *Morning Advertiser* 30 May 1851. It is unclear how many spectators the Concert Room held, but it was not small. It was part of the Royal Princess's Theatre which had both a large and a small concert room — "The grand Concert Room of this establishment, elegantly decorated, is one of the largest in London, and the saloon, or minor Concert Room, though not so extensive, is nevertheless of noble proportions" (*Mogg's New Picture of London,* 1844); the theatre and two concert rooms together seated about 3,000, but that tells us little. Bosco's prices were First Stalls 7s.6d., Reserved Seats 4s., Balcony 3s., Gallery 2s. None of the newspapers commented that these were unusually high; by comparison the charge at this date to visit the Great Exhibition was 5s. and 2s.6d.

[601] *Times* 11, 21 June 1851. Robin was also performing in London, in Piccadilly, and was more successful, including a command performance for Queen Victoria at Windsor Castle on April 25th (*Times* 30 May 1851).

[602] *Windsor and Eton Express* 12, 19 July 1851 ("B. Bosco, the Magician King, will arrive with Wonders and Miracles unprecedented").

[603] Bartolomeo's 1851 visit to Britain is briefly discussed by E.A. Dawes in his article 'Le Chevalier Bosco versus "The Monster Conjuror" – An Unequal Contest' (A Rich Cabinet of Magical Curiosities 148), *Magic Circular* vol.82 no. 890 (Nov. 1988) pp.210-211.

[604] Rusconi p.158 finds him performing in Rotterdam in July 1851 but there is no mention of this in the Dutch papers and it seems to be an error for July 1850.

[605] *L'Artiste: revue hebdomadaire du Nord de la France* 31 Aug.1851. Their arrival in Lille was also noted in *L'Agent dramatique du Midi* 14 Sept.1851, misspelling the singer's surname as *Martiney.*

[606] *Globe* [London] 22 Apr.1851.

[607] *L'Artiste* [Lille] 7, 21 Sept.1851.

[608] There are interesting accounts of Martinez' life and her earlier and later career (none mentioning Bosco) in an article by Arthur LaBrew and in three blog articles (url:075).

[609] *L'Echo de la Frontière* 25 Sep.1851.

[610] *Gazette nationale* 5 Nov.1851; *La Presse* 7 Nov.1851; *Le Nouvelliste* 7, 8 Nov. 1851.

[611] *La Presse* 27 Nov.1851. The *Archives Nationales* have documentation on this dated 14 and 21 November (Reference code: F/21/1155/B): "Casino des Arts, boulevard Montmartre ... Direction Beaussier. 1851.- arrêtés des 14 et 21 novembre 1851 autorisant des spectacles de fantasmagorie par la lumière électrique et des tours de prestidigitation sous le titre de Théâtre des fluides animés".

[612] There is a very similar piece in German in *ATZ* 14 Dec.1851 ('Pariser-Briefe XXIII' dated November 28th) describing a visit from Bosco who shows the writer his album and invites him to the show *tomorrow,* and there follows an enthusiastic review of the actual show.

[613] Collection de manuscrits d'Auguste Rondel: digitised at url:076. The letter is discussed by Pietro Micheli in *Ye Olde Magic Mag* 7,1 (Dec.2020).

[614] *Le Ménestrel* 7 Dec.1851, for example, admired his work with handkerchiefs, watches, cards, flowers and birds, and especially liked "le tromblon de Rinaldo Rinaldini", named for the blunderbuss of this swashbuckling robber captain. One early comment criticised his cruelty to birds: *Journal de Débats* 24 Nov.1851.

[615] A nice publicity piece, mainly the old anecdotes from Russia; includes the picture of Bosco with the bird on his sword tip which is also in *L'Illustration.* The book is online at url:077.

[616] *Le Charivari* 22 Jan.1852; *Le Journal pour rire* 20 Feb.1852.

[617] *Le Charivari* 21 Apr.1852; *Le Nouvelliste* 22 Apr.1852.

[618] *Le Nouvelliste* 22 Apr.1852 ("reprendra Samedi prochain..."); *Le Nouveau Journal* 24 Apr.1852; *Le Nouvelliste* 26 Apr.1852 ("a repris le cours de ses *soirées*..."). During his brief absence the Casino hosted the limbless mathematical prodigy Charles Grandemange.

[619] *Le Droit* 3 May 1852; *Le Nouvelliste* 6 May 1852 ("...suspendues pendant quelques jours pour de nouvelles dispositions"); again in the newspapers his listing at the Casino "tous les soirs" continued uninterrupted.

[620] *Le Siècle* 14 April 1852; *Le Droit*, 1 May 1852; *La Gazette de France* 2 May 1852 (widely reported, with some disparity in details).

[621] Said to have travelled over the Alps via Mont Cenis (Moncenisio) where he found the plant that restores youth — either that or he renewed his pact with the Devil (*Satanas*) to obtain new tricks: *Le Nouvelliste* 17 June 1852 (and word for word in other papers, so probably a "press release" by Bosco).

[622] There are ads for him there as late as *La Gazette de France* 6 July and *Le Droit* 7 July; *La Gazette* even suddenly lists him there again on 16 July!

[623] *Le Journal de Rouen* 26 June 1852 reports his arrival, and the next day, remembering his 1833 visit, says "it appears that M. Bosco is disposed once more to give a specimen of his amazing ability to the public of Rouen". I can find no ads or

reviews of these shows in *Le Journal de Rouen*, but the Paris paper *Le Nouvelliste* 2 July 1852 says he was attracting large crowds there ("à Rouen, où ses séances attirent une nombreuse affluence").

[624] *La Vigie de Dieppe* 6 Aug.1852.

[625] *La Vigie de Dieppe* 10, 17, 20, 24 Aug.1852. An autograph letter by Bosco dated Dieppe August 19th 1852 was sold by Piasa at Drouot Richelieu in March 2009.

[626] *La Vigie de Dieppe* 24, 31 Aug.1852; *Le Nouvelliste* and *Vert-vert* 31 Aug.1852.

[627] "De retour de la province, où il était allé réveiller les souvenirs qu'il y avait laissés, Bosco nous revient…": *La Gazette* 2 Feb.1853. However, he was not in Toulouse: there is no mention in the newspapers of his performing there until late 1855, so it was not in 1852, as often stated, that he took on Cazeneuve as a pupil there (for Cazeneuve see C13).

[628] *Fremden-Blatt* and *Der Humorist* 22 December 1852.

[629] The Masonic journal *Le Soleil Mystique, journal de la Maçonnerie universelle, sciences, littérature, voyages* 3 (March 1853), reviewing the Paris theatre scene, said (p.72) of the Les Folies-Mayer: "Salle comblé, voilà l'état normal des *Folies Mayer*. Le célèbre prestidigitateur Bosco l'a mise sur ce pied…".

Les Folies-Mayer, on the boulevard du Temple ("le boulevard du crime"!), became subsequently Les Folies-Nouvelles and survives as Le Théâtre Déjazet, and has attracted several historians. L. Henry-Lecomte in his *Histoire des Théâtres de Paris: Les Folies-Nouvelles…*(vol. 8, 1909) is very rude about Bosco: "Quelque temps après Bosco, émule de Philippe et de Robert-Houdin, installa dans le local vacant son matériel d'illusioniste; le public resta sourd encore aux appels du pseudo-sorcier"; the detailed article at *https://fr.wikipedia.org/wiki/Théâtre_Dejazet* similarly states: "Une vaine tentative de reprise par un magicien nommé Bosco conduit à une première fermeture", clearly assuming that Bosco took over the theatre himself and intended to run it permanently.

[630] A letter from Bosco is held in the Bibliothèque Nationale, dated Paris, February 11th, to "M. de Pommereux" (almost certainly Charles Pommereux, 1805-1857, editor of *La Revue et Gazette des Théâtres*) enclosing tickets to the Folies-Mayer for the following night (online at url:078). The letter is discussed by Pietro Micheli in *Ye Olde Magic Mag* 7,1 (Dec.2020).

The Staatsbibliothek zu Berlin has a letter from Bosco dated Paris, April 2nd 1853, written "to a theatre director" (url:079, not digitised).

[631] *La Gazette de France* 2 Feb.1853; *L'Assemblée nationale* 17 Feb.1853; *Le Siècle* 18 Feb.1853.

[632] *La Gazette de France* 12 Mar.1853.

[633] *Messager des théâtres et des arts* 27 Feb.1853; echoed by *Le Journal pour rire* 5 Mar.1853.

[634] *Le Constitutionnel* 18 Mar.1853; *Journal des débats* 19 Mar.1853; *L'Indépendance belge* 24 Mar.1853.

[635] The show, "au bénéfice d'un artiste", unnamed, was delayed from May 1st: *La Patrie* 1 May 1853; *Vert-vert* 3 May 1853.

[636] *Le Constitutionnel* 14 May 1853; *La Gazette* 15 May 1853 ("cette riche fête sera terminée par une heure de magie de Bosco, qui fera connaître au public le riche programme exécuté devant Leurs Majestés Impériales").

[637] *La Presse* 26 May 1853, etc.

[638] *La Vigie de Dieppe* 28 June 1853: "M. Bosco a quitté le Havre; déjà, depuis quelques jours, il est parmi nous…", and quoting the *Journal du Havre* for the farewell show; Vesque, *Histoire des rues du Havre… 2e Partie.* (Havre: Impr. J. Brenier, 1876), p.507, also states that Bosco was there in June 1853 ("Au mois du juin de la même année, le célèbre physicien Bosco donna plusieurs soirées à la salle Sainte-Cécile"; unfortunately the implied later section, after 1850, of Vesque's *Histoire des théâtres du Havre 1717 à 1872* never appeared (he died, *pace* http://viaf.org/viaf/5159697575603311173, which gives him as "1830-19 ", in 1899: *L'Univers* 26 Mar.1899).

[639] *Didaskalia* 2 Jan.1854: this places Bosco in Le Havre *after* he was in Dieppe, contrary to the Dieppe paper and Vesque. It is possible that he returned to Le Havre later in the year.

[640] *La Vigie de Dieppe* 1, 5 July 1853.

[641] *La Vigie de Dieppe* 26 July 1853 ("une séance spéciale, dédiée aux enfants").

[642] *La Vigie de Dieppe* 2, 9 Sep.1853.

[643] *Wiener Zeitung* 8 Jan.1854.

[644] *Journal du Loiret* 10, 17, 20 Dec.1853.

[645] *Journal du Loiret* 22 Dec.1853.

[646] *Journal du Loiret* 27, 31 Dec.1853.

[647] Known only from an anecdote in the *Courrier de la Vienne* quoted in *L'Écho de Vallées* 9 Mar.1854 of Bosco in his hotel in Poitiers saying how famished he was, and proceeding to swallow the knives, spoons, then the glasses and bottles and the plates — "astonishing his table companions who feared he might eat them". Significantly an edition of *Satanas* was published in Poitiers that year.

[648] *L'Union bretonne* 6 June 1854 has an account of him at a charity fête in Bordeaux, and the same paper the previous month (10 May 1854) had a story of him buying artichokes in a market there.

[649] *L'Indépendant de l'Ouest* 15, 20 Sep.1854.

[650] *Courrier de Nantes* 9 Dec.1854; *L'Union bretonne* 9 Dec.1854.

[651] *L'Union bretonne* 12, 21, 29 Dec.1854; 6 Jan.1855; *Courrier de Nantes* 1, 8, 9 ,10 Jan.1855.

[652] *L'Union bretonne* 10, 16 Jan.1855.

[653] *Le Phare de la Loire* 19 Jan.1855; *L'Union bretonne* 24 Jan.1855; *Courrier de Nantes* 25 Jan.1855.

[654] *L'Espérance du Peuple* 31 Jan.1855, adding that there was always something new, and "as with Nicolet, he went from strength to strength" — Jean-Baptiste Nicolet's theatre in the second half of the 18th century was proverbially productive, presenting over 9,000 plays.

[655] *Courrier de Nantes* 10 Feb.1855.

[656] *Le Phare de la Loire* 19 Feb.1855.

[657] *L'Union bretonne* 12 Feb.1855.

[658] *Courrier de Nantes* 26 Feb.1855.

[659] *Courrier de Nantes* 9 Mar.1855.

[660] *Le Phare de la Loire* 16 Mar.1855.

[661] *Courrier de Nantes* 22 Mar.1855.

[662] *L'Écho rochelais* 21 Mar.; 2, 5 May 1855.

[663] *L'Écho rochelais* 9 May 1855.

[664] Quoted from the Rochefort paper at his next stop in Saintes in *L'Indépendant de la Charente-Inférieure* 2 June 1855.

[665] *L'Indépendant de la Charente-Inférieure* 2, 6 June 1855 (the last largely word for word with articles in La Rochelle and other papers, no doubt copied from Bosco's album or from material handed out by him as press releases).

[666] *Courrier de Bayonne* 30 June; 17 July 1855.

[667] *Courrier de Bayonne* 21, 24 July 1855 (the former a long publicity piece, a biography with the usual anecdotes).

[668] *Courrier de Bayonne* 26 July 1855.

[669] *Courrier de Bayonne* 4 Aug.1855.

[670] *Journal de Toulouse* 14, 17 Dec.1855. Unfortunately the rival paper, *L'Aigle,* is not available online but we do know it included an earlier anecdote of Bosco in Toulouse: the issue of December 9 had a story of Bosco, "the day before yesterday",

finding gold coins in a bread roll ("un pistolet"), which then vanish, to be found in the pocket of another diner (quoted in *L'Écho des Vallées* 13 Dec.1855).

[671] *Journal de Toulouse* 22, 25, 29 Dec.1855.

[672] *Journal de Toulouse* 3, 5 Jan.1856.

[673] *Journal de Toulouse* 9, 12 Jan.1856.

[674] *Journal de Toulouse* 17, 19, 20, 22 Jan.1856.

[675] *Journal de Toulouse* 24, 28 Jan.1856.

[676] *Journal de Toulouse* 30 Jan.; 2, 4, 6, 10 Feb.1856.

[677] *Journal de Toulouse* 16, 23, 27 Feb.1856.

[678] 'Another Signor Bosco', *Saunders's News-letter* 28 Mar.1856.

[679] *Dublin Evening Packet* 29 Mar.1856; *Saunders's News-letter* 31 Mar.1856. The impostor had been very popular in England, Scotland, Wales, and Ireland since his arrival in 1854, whereas Bartolomeo remained almost unknown there. After this visit by Bartolomeo to Dublin in 1856 the impostor was disowned by his manager Professor Millar (B62), who soon turned his wife into the first female "Bosco" (BF1).

[680] See Epstein's entry (B12) for details.

[681] *Le Courrier de l'Aude* 18, 21 June 1856.

[682] *Le Courrier de l'Aude* 28 June; 2, 9 July 1856.

[683] *Journal de Montpellier* 26 July 1856 ("On annonce l'arrivée prochaine à Montpellier du célèbre prestidigitateur Bosco…").

[684] *L'Artiste méridional* 10 Aug.1856 quoting from *L'Indicateur de l'Hérault* of 30 July stories of Bosco finding coins in fish at the market there and mystifying diners and waiters in a café.

[685] *Le Messager du Midi* 29 Aug.1856.

[686] *Le Messager du Midi* 11 Sep.; 3, 6 Oct.1856; *Journal de Montpellier* 20 Sep.1856.

[687] *Le Messager du Midi* 8, 9, 10, 11 Oct.1856; *Journal de Montpellier* 11 Oct.1856.

[688] *Le Messager du Midi* 13, 14 Oct.1856; *Journal de Montpellier* 18 Oct.1856.

[689] *Le Messager du Midi* 27 Oct.1856.

[690] *Le Messager du Midi* 19 Nov.1856. The following month, when he was in Nîmes and unwell, the Nantes paper *Le Phare de la Loire,* reported this trip to Paris, saying it was to "organise a huge theatre in the passage Jouffroy, boulevard Montmartre". Nothing immediately came of this (and it is unlikely to relate to the *puppet* Bosco

show at the *Marionnettes du Passe-Temps* in the passage Jouffroy in 1859: see note 748).

Rusconi p.174 has Bosco performing in Paris and Berlin in summer 1856 and in Brussels in October 1856. But he was in Paris only on this short visit, and was not in Brussels at all — that was Eugenio (see B2); the statement in *Bohemia* 30 Aug.1856 that "the old magician Bosco ... intends to perform tomorrow in Cologne then will go to Berlin" cannot be correct as Bartolomeo was in Cète in the south of France on August 30th.

[691] *Courrier du Gard* 22 Nov.; 2, 25 Dec.1856.

[692] *Courrier du Gard* 22 Jan.; 28 Mar.1857; *Le Sémaphore de Marseille* 29 Mar.1857.

[693] *Courrier du Gard* 7, 9, 11, 16 Apr.1857.

[694] *Courrier du Gard* 23 Apr.1857.

[695] *Courrier du Gard* 28, 30 Apr.1857.

[696] *Courrier du Gard* 2 May 1857.

[697] *Courrier du Gard* 12 May 1857. A note by the editor hoped that he would stay longer, and ended with an account of Bosco himself telling on stage the story of his war service in 1812 and his encounter with the Cossack.

[698] *Courrier du Gard* 19, 21 May 1857.

[699] *Courrier du Gard* 23 May; 6 June 1857.

[700] *Courrier du Gard* 30 June; 2 July 1857; *Le Messager du Midi* 3 July 1857 (calling it "a spectacle ... of the kind he gave in Hungary, before thousands of spectators", but nothing he had done there rivalled this).

[701] *Courrier du Gard* 9 July 1857. The show lasted until 8 p.m. and the city theatre, where the popular Virginie Déjazet was playing, was empty that night (*Messager des Théâtres* 19 July 1857).

[702] *Courrier du Gard* 16 July 1857.

[703] *Courrier du Gard* 16 July; 18 Aug.1857.

[704] *Gazette du midi* and *Le Sémaphore de Marseille* 11 Sep.1857.

[705] Alex. Bellemaire, 'Les Sociétés Secrètes Musulmanes de l'Algérie' in *Revue Contemporaine* vol.6, 1858, pp.76-94: p.85). This issue is online at url:080.

[706] *Akhbar* 20 Sep.1857, quoted in *Gazette du midi* 23, 25 Sep.1857 and in *Le Sémaphore de Marseille* 23 Sep.1857.

[707] *La Gazette du midi* 4 Oct.1857, quoting the anecdote from *Akhbar,* which says it was "told by a traveller recently arrived from France" — Bosco himself. The story

was soon reprinted (*L'Écho rochelais* 10 Oct.1857; *Le Journal de l'arrondissement de Valognes* 23 Oct.1857; *Journal de Montpellier* 7 Nov.1857; etc.) and was reprinted again in 1859 (Rusconi pp.180-2) when Bosco was back in Marseille, then in the Naples *Gazzetta del Mezzodì* (1861?) and from that included in *Il Nuovo Bosco*, pp.191-4.

[708] Quoted at length in *Le Sémaphore de Marseille* 24 Oct.1857.

[709] *Gazette nationale ou le Moniteur universel* 5 Nov.1857, quoting *Le Moniteur algérienne*.

[710] *Gazette du midi* 16 Nov.1857; *Le Sémaphore de Marseille* 17 Nov.1857. Bône, more than 500 km east, was still fairly small, but the French had recently begun to build an iron-ore port there.

[711] E. Souville, *Mes souvenirs maritimes (1837-1863)*, Paris: Perin et cie., 1914: p.408 (online on Gallica).

[712] *La Presse* 30 Apr.1858 ("M. B. Bosco ... nous écrit d'Alger..."), and widely reprinted. Eugenio, in Leipzig at the Easter fair, also wrote pointing out that "[tr.] the Bosco frequently mentioned over the last few days who in Manchester chose such an odd way of curing his alcoholic wife" was not his father, who "travelled to Africa more than three months ago, to demonstrate his art to the Bedouins, and who lives in perfect harmony with his wife" (*Deutsche Allgemeine Zeitung* 10 Apr.1858).

[713] Andrew MacAllister, the Scottish magician, said to have trained with Philippe, had great success in Spain in the late 1840s, a favourite of Queen Isabella II, before leaving for America in 1849. His birth date is variously given but he died in Keokuk, Iowa, where he had been performing and became unwell, on September 1st 1856: a death notice in the *Keokuk Daily Post* 3 Sep.1856 (and *The Daily Gate City* same date) gives his age as "40 years, 7 months, and 21 days", which according to www.timeanddate.com calculates to *10 January 1816*, so he was very likely the Andrew McAllister born on January 10th (and baptised January 21st) 1816 in Balfron, near Glasgow, to Andrew McAllister and his wife Elisabeth, née Stevenson.

[714] His tour is recorded in the Madrid papers from 5 Aug.1858 including *La España, La Esperanza, Diario oficial de avisos de Madrid, La Época, La Discusión, El Clamor público, La América. La España artística,* and *La Iberia*, online at http://hemerotecadigital.bne.es.

[715] *La Época* 10 Aug.1858; *El Isleño* (Mallorca) 21 Aug.1858.

[716] *La Época* and *La España* 8 Sep.1858; *La España* 10 Sep.1858.

[717] *La Discusión* 13 Aug.1858 (etc.).

[718] *La Esperanza* 16 Aug.1858; *La España, El Clamor público, La Iberia, La Discusión, El Enano* 17 Aug.1858.

[719] *La Época* 19 Aug.1858.

[720] *La Época* 20 Aug.1858; *La España* and *El Mundo pintoresco* 21 Aug.1858; *La España artística* 23 Aug.1858.

[721] *La Iberia* 22 Aug.1858; also in *La Época* 26 Aug.1858 and *La España* 29 Aug.1858.

[722] *La Época* 23 Aug.1858; *El Enano* 24 Aug.1858.

[723] *La España* 24 Aug.1858; also in *La Época* 26 Aug.1858.

[724] *La Esperanza* 21 Sep.1858; *El Clamor público* 22 Sep.1858. The newspapers referred to the theatre as either *el Teatro Francés* or *el teatro Variedades* or *el teatro de la calle de la Magdalena*: a poster for the performance of September 23rd is headed solely *el Teatro Francés* (online at url:081).

[725] The same account, almost word for word, is found in *El Clamor público, La Discusión. La Época* 25 Sep.1858 and *El Isleño* 3 Oct.1858; *La Iberia* 26 Sep.1858 smiled at *how gullible we all were*.

[726] *La Época* 2 Oct.1858 (*un murmullo de desaprobación*); *La España* 2 Oct.1858 (*una risa significativa*).

[727] *La Época* 5 Oct.1858; *La Discusión* 6 Oct.1858.

[728] *La Esperanza* 5 Oct.1858 (etc.); *La Iberia* 9 Oct.1858. Several papers state under their masthead "por la mañana" or "de la mañana" and events announced as for "today" are not on the publication date printed on the paper but on the following day.

[729] *La Iberia* 14 Oct.1858 (given "the other night"; this is probably the banker Manuel Salvador López).

[730] *La Epoca* 28 Oct.1858 ("…muy pronto se ofrecerá los valencianos la ocasión de admirar su destreza imcomparable").

[731] *Journal des Pyrénées Orientales* [Perpignan] 4 Dec.1858 ("…Valence, où il a recueilli, dans deux représentations, la somme de mille napoléons").

[732] *El Guadalaviar* 7 Nov.1858.

[733] *La Corona* 28 Nov.; 5 Dec.1858. *La Corona* had been printing various anecdotes and general pieces on Bosco since his arrival in Madrid, including an article on 30 Aug.1858 on 'The Murder of the Doves', letting its readers know beforehand what to expect.

[734] *Journal des Pyrénées Orientales* [Perpignan] 8 Dec.1858.

[735] *La Corona* 7, 8 Dec.1858.

[736] *Journal des Pyrénées Orientales* [Perpignan] 29 Dec.1858. An article in *La Corona* 11 Dec.1858 seems to report a private performance for friends "yesterday evening" in an industrial building: unfortunately the article is largely illegible online due to the quality of the microfilm it is reproduced from.

[737] *La Corona* 16 Dec.1858 ("Bosco.— Esta noche da su segunda función el prestidigitador de este nombre; en la primera, si bien hizo alguna suerte de escamoteo que agradó, los demás ejercicios, aunque no estaban desprovistos de un mérito no común, ofrecieron poca novedad y atractivo. Nosotros confiamos que hoy desarrollará en mayor escala sus recursos artisticos aquel prestidígítador, motivo por el que no juzgaremos de su mérito hasta que le hayamos visto otras veces en la escena dei Circo").

[738] *La Corona* 19, 20 Dec.1858.

[739] *Diario oficial de avisos de Madrid* 15 Oct.1858: "El prestidigitador Bosco, segun vemos en los periódicos de Portugal, debe marchar á Lisboa en el invierno próximo". A search for Bosco in the 1858-9 issues online of *Archivo pittoresco* and *O panorama* at http://hemerotecadigital.cm-lisboa.pt finds no mention of him.

[740] *La Gazette* 27 Jan.1859 ("…est arrivé Vendredi dernier à Marseille … il revient d'Espagne…"); *La España* 3 Feb.1859 quipped: "*Spiriti infernale*. Ha llegado á Marsella el prestidigitador Bosco. Creíamos que aun estaba por aquí".

[741] Except technically at the end of the year: he was in Nice, which was currently part of the Kingdom of Piedmont-Sardinia until re-annexed by France on March 24th 1860 under the Treaty of Turin. Bartolomeo was not the Bosco in Berlin and Potsdam in late 1858 and early 1859 (Rusconi p.180), that was Eugenio (see B2: "…the heir of his name and fame, his son", *Berlinische Nachrichten von Staats- und gelehrten Sachen* 25 Nov.1858), and Bartolomeo was not in Paris in early February 1859, as two southern papers claimed: see note 748.

[742] *Le Sémaphore de Marseille* 25, 27 Jan.1859; unfortunately *La Gazette du midi* is not available online for 1859.

[743] *Le Sémaphore de Marseille* 5, 10 Feb.1859.

[744] *Le Sémaphore de Marseille* 25, 26 Feb.1859 (stressing that the venue was well chosen and that *le quartier de la Plaine* was no longer the remote and rural area it was seen as ten years earlier).

[745] *Le Sémaphore de Marseille* 12, 16 Mar.1859.

[746] *Le Sémaphore de Marseille* 19 Mar.1859.

[747] *Le Sémaphore de Marseille* 25 Mar.1859.

[748] *Le Sémaphore de Marseille* 16 Apr.1859; *Le Mémorial d'Aix* 24 Apr., 1 May 1859. In February two southern papers (no doubt one copying the other) had reported posters going up in Paris of Bosco soon back there in Montmartre (*Le Phare de la*

Loire 1 Feb.1859; *Le Phare de La Rochelle* 2 Feb.1859). There is no mention in the Paris papers of Bartolomeo being there and the "Bosco" in question was at the *Marionnettes du Passe-Temps*, the puppet theatre at 12 Boulevard Montmartre (the Passage Jouffroy) which on its bill this week included 'Séances de magie, par Bosko [*sic*], l'un de nos plus habiles prestidigitateurs" (*Le Messager de Paris* 6 Feb.1859).

[749] The same detail is given in the version of the story in *Fremden Blatt* 18 Apr.1866, but this elaboration is not in the earlier version in *Der Sammler* 1 Apr.1845.

[750] *Le Mémorial d'Aix* 1 May 1859; *La Provence* 5 May 1859.

[751] *Estafette de Vaucluse* 8 May 1859.

[752] *Le Sémaphore de Marseille* 20 May 1859.

[753] *Le Sémaphore de Marseille* 1, 7, 10 July 1859.

[754] *Le Sémaphore de Marseille* 12, 14 July 1859.

[755] *Le Sémaphore de Marseille* 4, 23 Aug.1859, the latter quoting a review from *Le Toulonnais*.

[756] *Le Sémaphore de Marseille* 2 Sep.1859.

[757] *Mémorial de la Loire et de la Haute-Loire* 22 Aug.1859; *L'Industrie du Nord et du Pas-de-Calais* 4 Sep.1859 (etc.).

[758] *Le Sémaphore de Marseille* 22 Oct.1859; *Le Var* 27, 30 Oct.1859.

[759] *Le Sémaphore* 2 Feb.1860, quoting the Nice paper *L'Avenir*.

[760] *Le Siècle* 24 Jan.1860: "...Qui encore? Bosco, le vrai, l'authentique Bosco, que je croyais vieux comme le comte de Saint-Germain, et qui prouve tous les jours, dans le cercle de ses amis, qu'il a hérité surtout de la sorcellerie de Cagliostro".

[761] *L'Eden, Journal de Monaco* 1 Jan.1860.

[762] Rusconi p.182, source unknown.

[763] Report dated March 12th in *Messager des théâtres* 22 Mar.1860.

[764] *Gazzetta piemontese* 2 Apr.1860: "Il celebre cav. Bosco, torinese, è giunto fra noi dopo aver percorso tutti i capitali d'Europa destando dovunque la più grande ammirazione. Meritati elogi riscosse da tutta la stampa da cui venne acclamato *re dei prestidigitatori*...".

[765] *Gazzetta piemontese* 8, 9, 10, 11, 12 May 1860.

[766] *Gazzetta piemontese* 14 May 1860 ("Una delle novità che occupa le futili ciarle del piccolo mondo Torinese è la comparsa del celebre prestidigitatore cav. Bosco ...Il cav. Bosco è il Nestore dei prestidigitatori, e in lui all'abilità della sua arte per cui da tanto tempo è famoso il suo nome, va pari la pratica conoscenza degli umori del

pubblico; ha modi forbiti e parlare acconcio; e se pur troppo non ha più il brio della gioventù, gli resta ancora quello dello spirito, di cui potrebbe far mostra migliore se invece di parlare in quell'italiano, ch'egli, non sapendo il vero, va improvvisando con multo impaccio per suo uso particolare, si esprimesse in quell'idioma che gli è più famigliare...").

[767] Report dated May 11th in *La Gazette* 14 May 1860.

[768] The article, signed "Ciliegia", is in *L'Arlecchino* 27 Apr.1860. See *Fiction:* F32.

[769] There seems good evidence that his parents were Aloisio Beneventano del Bosco and Marianna Roscio (with descendants still living in Sicily).

[770] *Kladderdatsch* 29 July 1860; *Münchener Punsch* 5 Aug.1860.

[771] *Gazzetta piemontese* 30, 31 May; 1, 6 June 1860.

[772] *Gazzetta piemontese* 16 June 1860: "...a totale benefizio della Scuola Domenicale e dell'Asilo infantile del Borgo S. Donato". For this show he was joined by a visiting Dutch "organofano" (organophonist) named Zoni, who imitated musical instruments with his voice. A final report (20 June 1860) puts it: "Il celebre prestidigitatore cav. Bosco ha voluto lasciare in Torino anche una prova di squisita beneficanza".

[773] *Kurjer Warszawski* 8 July 1860: "Znany magik P. Bosco (ojciec), występował obecnie, jak donoszą włoskie gazety, w Turynie, i zdziwił wszystkich swoją nadzwyczajną zręcznością, oraz doborem i nowością sztuk. P. Bosco był nie jeden raz już w Warszawie, i zawsze podobne wrażenie wywołał na tutejszych widzach".

[774] *Die Wiener Elegante* 7 June 1860.

[775] Undated report in *La Presse théâtrale* 22 July 1860 ("Milan ... Demain soir aura lieu à Santa-Radegonda la première séance de prestidigitation de Bosco").

[776] *Der Zwischen-Akt* 6 Dec.1860: "Der alte Tausendkünstler Bosco, Vater des Sohnes, ist nach 12jährigen Aufenthalt in Frankreich, wieder in sein Vaterland Italien gereist..." — twelve years in France is of course incorrect, though (apart from Algeria and Spain) he had been there from September 1851 to the end of 1859.

[777] Alessandro Gandini, *Cronistoria dei teatri di Moderna dal 1539 al 1871,* II p.496.

[778] *La Nazione* 28 June; 1, 3, 5, 7, 9, 10, 13, 14 July 1861. No reviews appeared in *La Nazione,* but in the issue of 2 July an article 'Rivista teatrale' by "Yorick" effuses on Bosco's upcoming shows — "...Se v'è un uomo al mondo capace di chiamare a sè quanta gente è ancora restata all'ombra della Cupola di Brunellesco, quest'uomo, senza dubbie, è Bosco il prestidigitatore ... la bacchetta di Bosco salutera le potenze infere e supere ai quattro punti cardinali".

[779] *Leipziger Zeitung* 23 Feb.1862 ("Wie uns einige Dresdner Blätter melden, gedenkt Bosco, der Nestor und König der Zauberei, sobald es seine Gesundheit ihm gestattet,

in unsern Mauern zu weilen und uns glückliche Tage unserer Vergangenheit durch seine köstlichen Productionen nochmals, ehe er seine künstlerische Laufbahn beschließt, vorzuführen").

[780] *Zwischen-Akt* 12 Mar.1862 ("In Dresden beabsichtigt der alte Bosko ... noch einmal neu erfundene Experimente vorzuführen, und zwar nicht mit Apparaten wie früher, sondern mit neuen, noch nicht gesehenen Hilfsmitteln seiner Kunst").

[781] *"Scirrhus ventriculi u[nd] schliess[lich] hypostatische Pneumonie"*. The burial certificate (digitised on *ancestry.com* under 'Bosco, Bartholomäus', url:082), signed by a Dr. Warnatz, gives his status as *privatus,* a person of financial means, living off assets and no longer needing to work to earn a living, rendering implausible Houdini's statement that "he and his wife lived in poverty". Why Houdini thought he died in poverty is uncertain, but the "fact" had appeared in newspapers over many years; for example in Warsaw in 1873 it was said that "[tr.] Bosco senior died childless in Italy and apparently in a critical financial situation"; on that occasion it was corrected by Eugenio (see *Excursus on Family*).

[782] Harry Houdini, *The Unmasking of Robert-Houdin*. New York: The Publishers Printing Co., 1908, pp.305-7. There are variant photos of Houdini at the original gravestone — url:341.

[783] Her burial registration (url:083) gives her age as 56 and the cause of death as *Schlagfluß,* an apoplectic fit, stroke (see *Excursus on Family*).

[784] *Neues Fremden-Blatt* 13 Apr.1866; *Morgen Post* 16 Apr.1866, quoting the Dresden *Konstitutionelle Zeitung.*

B2. Eugenio Bosco: son of **B1**

Name: often localised as **Eugène Bosco** in France; **Eugen Bosco** in Germany; **Eugenjusz (Eugeniusz, Eugeni) Bosco** in Poland; in advertisements sometimes billed as "E. Bosco", and when young as "Bosco jun.", "Bosco fils", "Bosco Sohn", "Bosco Zoon", "Bosco Fiz.". On his civil marriage registration in Naples in 1865 he gives his full name as **Giulio Eugenio Andrea Bosco** (and signs his name as *Giulio Eugenio Bosco*).
In Poland and Germany his surname is sometimes spelt **Bosko**.

Two unsubstantiated assumptions have led to errors in long-standing accounts of Eugenio's life.
(1) Houdini's statement (*The Unmasking of Robert-Houdin*, presumably based on Carl Willmann's article in *Die Zauberwelt* vol.2 no.7 (July 1896) pp.97-8; and see p.186 below) that "…Disabled, poverty-stricken, and respected by none, he soon disappeared from the conjuring world, and … died miserably in Hungary in 1891";
(2) Sidney Clarke's theory (*Annals of Conjuring,* 1929; earlier in *The Magic Wand;* accepted by Edward Dawes in his article on Saul Warschawski (see B63) and considered by Rusconi (p.192) as "*plausibile*") that the "Alfred Bosco" in England from 1857 was Eugenio. This was in fact the impostor Epstein (B12). Eugenio accompanied his father to England in 1851, but there is no evidence that Eugenio *ever* performed in England: the Bosco in Bangor in 1861 and the Bosco in Shelford in 1889 doing the decapitation act was not Eugenio (*pace* Rusconi (pp.214; 219) but Warschawski (accompanied in 1889 by his son Alfred, B64).

This Eugenio was the *second* son of that name born to Bartolomeo: for the first, born in Lwow in 1826 and died in Warsaw the following year, see *Excursus on the Family.*

Birth place and date: older reference works (drawing on Houdini and Willmann, *opp.citt.*) have him as illegitimate and born "Turin 1823?", and baptised in Germany "1830?" (both these denied by the *Lexikon*). The 1845 *Der Sammler* article on his father (published in Vienna, when Bartolomeo was there himself and could have provided the information at first hand: see *Excursus*) says Eugenio was born in Lübeck. But Eugenio himself in his civil marriage registration (url:084) gives his birthplace as Hamburg — and normally at this civil ceremony the bride and groom were required to submit copies of their birth records. (Further, the Fribourg newspaper, *Le Chroniqueur* 8 Sep.1866, later calls him when he was there "Eugène Bosco, de Hambourg", suggesting he described himself thus.)

The marriage took place on June 14th 1865 and Eugenio gives his age as 35, meaning (if correct) that he was born *between 15 June 1829 and 14 June 1830;* Rusconi says p.33 "nel 1829 o forse l'anno successivo" but on p.212 says only 1829 and in note 2 "forse il 6 maggio": if he was born on May 6th it must have been 1830, otherwise at his marriage he would be 36 not 35. And if he was born May 6th 1830 then it was probably in Lübeck, as Bartolomeo was still there on May 17th (and then in Hamburg, 80 km south, by May 22nd). However, Eugenio is not to be found in the listing of Lübeck births 1829-1830 on *ancestry.com* (url:085).

156

Of course it is not certain that Bosco was with his wife at the time of the birth (or indeed that she was Eugenio's mother), but this does suggest that *the mother was travelling with him on his tour.*

Setting out the arguments for and against his legitimacy, as I see them, we have:
(a) Bartolomeo was a prominent and respected figure by now and would hardly have had a pregnant mistress in tow, making it most likely that the mother was his wife
but she may have been on tour with him but following him at a discreet distance
(b) Eugenio was baptised, therefore must have been legitimate
but where is the record of his baptism as evidence?
(c) Eugenio married in a Catholic Church (at the Church of Sant'Anna di Palazzo, as the certificate states), so would have needed to prove his baptism
(d) the coincidence of Bartolomeo having a wife and a mistress with the same first name is rather unlikely
(e) on the civil marriage registration Eugenio appears to give his mother's surname as *Rosier,* and it is so transcribed on the *Antenati* site and on *FamilySearch.* Rusconi suggests very plausibly that *Rosier* is a mis-reading of *Bosco*. I would only say that to me the mother's surname in the marriage entry has an unmistakable "i" in it, and comparison of her handwritten name with that of the bride in the preceding marriage in the register, *Rosa Gaudier*, shows that the letters *Ros* and *ier* are written identically
(f) Eugenio's mother is specifically said to be "Antonina née Młynarski" in an article in a Warsaw paper in 1873 (see *Excursus*) based on statements by himself and by relatives of Antonina
(g) at the civil marriage registration the couple were normally required to submit copies of their parents' death records if they were deceased. Here Bartolomeo is correctly stated to be 'deceased', but the mother is not, yet Antonina Młynarska had also died.
I feel that he was legitimate but that with no baptism record found the verdict remains: not proven.

Eugenio himself confused the picture by his fondness for advertising himself as being, like his father, "from Turin", and even constructed a partly imaginary biography which he fed to newspapers.[1]

This has him born to Bartolomeo's wife Antoinette in 1830 "near Turin in a post coach" ("unweit Turin in einem Postwagen"), growing up in Bologna with his mother until her death when he was twelve (which would make his birth 1833), then joining his father in Russia and, after four years in a "Kadettenpensionat" in St Petersburg, spending three years reluctantly working for a merchant in Warsaw before "breaking the hated chains" in 1850 and becoming a travelling magician in Italy; he then, says this account, reconciled with his father and joined him in Holland, France and England, only to quarrel with him in 1852 and head to Holland on his own, making a precarious living over the next four years. In 1856 he was (we are told) finding success in Germany but then suffered the injury to his right hand and spent four months learning to use his left.

The only confirmed sightings of him before 1851 are: leaving Vienna to travel to Turin on September 5th 1849 (*Wiener Zeitung* 8 Sep.1849) and arriving at a Vienna hotel from Piedmont at the start of September 1850 (*Fremden Blatt* 3 Sep.1850): the males in these lists normally have their profession stated and he has none. (Why he was travelling is uncertain; he was not joining Bartolomeo who was in Holland in September 1849 and in Belgium in September 1850.)

The latter part at least of this account seems to be factual. The reconciliation with his father in 1851 accords with Eugenio accompanying Bartolomeo and his second wife to England that year (he is included on their alien arrival card, dated April 26th 1851) and the quarrel in 1852 accords with the date of the contract drawn up between father and son in Paris on May 20th 1852.[2]

In this contract both are resident in Paris, at different addresses: they agree that Bartolomeo has educated and instructed his son, providing him with the means to make an honest living, and has several times met his needs and paid his debts; now Bartolomeo will make Eugenio a final loan of 3,000 francs, enabling Eugenio to pay off his debts and leave France with "le matériel de physique", presumably magical apparatus:[3] he is to leave France immediately and continue travelling. He acknowledges that he owes his father 3,000 francs, and this amount, borrowed by Bartolomeo, is covered by a bill of exchange payable in two years by Eugenio. Eugenio must not return to France for two years, not return at all until the draft is paid off, must use only the name "Eugène Bosco fils", not bring discredit or harm on the name of Bosco in Europe, and never present himself (even if he has become a millionaire) before his father without his consent.

Houdini states in his *Unmasking of Robert-Houdin* (p.304) that he purchased the original of this contract "in a German antiquary's shop in Bonn"; he does not reproduce it there, and wrongly states that the amount was 5,000 francs *and* that it was paid "for not assuming the name of Bosco" *and* that Eugenio could not perform in Germany as well as France. A more correct version, but still with errors, was published in English translation in *M.U.M.* in 1916,[4] and an Italian version of this is given by Rusconi, pp.162-3, who states that no original exists — in fact it survives in the Houdini papers held at the Harry Ransom Center, University of Texas.[5]

The stipulation in the May 1852 contract that Eugenio leave France accords with both the *Illustrirte Zeitung* account above and with what is the earliest newspaper reference located of him performing. This first definite sighting of him on stage is in Holland in July 1852 in Leeuwarden. He is with the "Theatre Corvi van Parijs", the miniature animal circus of Jacques Corvi of Milan, famous for its "educated monkeys and dogs" (*singes et chiens savans*). Eugenio was not billed with them earlier in Paris but on this Dutch tour they added to their "trained dogs and monkeys" (*Gedresseerde Honden en Apen*) both "the Melino family from London" (father and son) and, as the opening act, "[tr.] A performance of Egyptian Magic and Conjuring by the famous [!] E. Bosco (the son)".[6] They were next in Zwolle,[7] then in Rotterdam.[8] The following month Eugenio is in Haarlem, no longer with Corvi but still with Melino.[9] Then in mid-September he is back with Corvi at the *Amsterveld* in Amsterdam.[10]

In his later advertisements Eugenio gives two different dates for the start of his career — 1853: "E. Bosco 30 ans de succès"[11] and 1857: "E. Bosco 25 ans de succès",[12] perhaps dating it from his recovery after the injury to his hand. These starting dates which he himself gives accord with the fact that he is not mentioned as performing with his father in Holland and Belgium in late 1850 or when he accompanied him to England in April 1851.

After his run with Corvi in Holland in 1852 we lose sight of Eugenio for a period. But it appears he was in Amsterdam in early 1853, as in the *Algemeen Handelsblad* of 31 Mar.1853 there is a notice warning against dealing with a lithographer named E. Winter, signed "Heer Bosco, Zoon, alhier". Rusconi says (p.212) that in 1854 he performed for the Dutch royal family in The Hague; I cannot find the source for this statement, but it would fit nicely.[13]

1856

The next sighting we have of him is performing in Tournai in Belgium in September 1856. This is certainly Eugenio (at this date Bartolomeo was unwell in Montpellier) and an anecdote pictures him as "a gentleman, young, elegant ... speaking French with a slight foreign accent".[14] Eugenio gave one show in the Théâtre de Tournai on September 25th. The programme shares several of his father's tricks — as would be expected since his father taught him — but with many new items.

REPRÉSENTATION EXTRAORDINAIRE DE MAGIE ÉGYPTIENNE, Donné par Bosco.
La séance sera divisée en deux parties par un entracte de 10 m.
Programme.
Première partie. — 1. Les boules invisibles. — 2. L'exemple du faux joueur. — 3. La société dira: arretez! arretez! arretez! 4. La plaisanterie de Christophe Colomb. — 5. Le voyage en chapeau. — 6. Le mathematicien. — 7. Le serin savant. — 8. Le duel heureux ou arme contre arme.
Deuxième partie. — 1. La fabrication instantanée.— Il y est où il n'y est pas. — La Californie. — 4. Le secret de Bosco. — 5. Rinaldo Rinaldi. — 6. Le parachute de Mme Blanchard. — 7. Métamorphose. — La soirée sera terminée par les Morts ressuscités, scène comique.[15]

A review offered lavish praise "...Dexterity, skill, a choice of tricks each more extraordinary than the last", expressing a hope he would give a second show, but he was expected in Brussels.[16]

He was in Brussels by early October, welcomed as "son of the famous magician Bosco ... though still young, he is already a worthy rival of his father".[17]

A promotional article stressed that his great skill lay in *cards,* and in this speciality he possesses a genuinely rare ability, and this is where the real talent, and, if one could say so, the most serious talent, of a conjuror lies; and the manipulation and conjuring of cards done only with the operator's hands have much more merit than so called physical tricks done with apparatus, consisting mainly of boxes with double bottoms and movable compartments, which almost win more honour for the maker than the user.[18]

He opened at the Théâtre du Vaudeville on October 18th, with a second show on 20th, both shows including a farce.[19] A reviewer noted the large and appreciative audience, which included the Count of Flanders, Prince Philippe, son of King Leopold I, and especially liked the trick of the coins in a spectator's hand increasing and diminishing — why not get M. Bosco to remedy the current European currency crisis...[20] He gave no further public performances, though had planned to do so, announcing instead he was available for private shows to families and schools.[21]

He now moved south to Charleroi, performing at the Théâtre de Charleroi on October 30th and November 2nd. Both shows were preceded and followed by short humorous plays, "to calm the strong emotions roused by this fantastic and diabolic entertainment".[22]

An enthusiastic review of the first show found his tricks *distinguished by finesse, delicacy and a rare perfection ... he conjures every kind of object with a remarkable subtlety... with the cards in his hand he is Beelzebub in person, he guesses your thoughts, and changes at will the colour and value of your card ... then he executes two pigeons, bringing them back to life with their heads exchanged... and we hear that only yesterday M. Carpentier who conjured away millions asked the magician to change his head so he could escape justice — but we don't know how well founded that story is...*[23]

Eugenio then returned to Brussells where he took part in a charity show at the Théâtre Royal on November 19th to raise money for the "pauvres honteux".[24]

1857

By 1857 Eugenio was starting to find some success. Still avoiding France as he had agreed with his father, he travelled to Vienna. Here he performed at the Circus Renz as "Bosco Fiz." or "Boscofiz." accompanying Professor Goulard's Cyclorama of North America.[25]

He ended with a show for the poor on March 18th and then headed to Germany, but it was in Weimar, on May 4th, that he famously injured his right hand with a pistol shot, threatening an end to his career.

He is said to have been loading a pistol that was already loaded and when he accidentally pulled the trigger his hand was hit by the ram-rod. News of the accident rapidly appeared in newspapers across Europe (ironically a note in *Le Siècle* 11 May 1857 was his first mention in a French newspaper). Some early reports pronounced him maimed for life and several modern accounts parrot a statement that "he shot his right hand off".[26] However, he was operated on promptly by Professor Ried, summoned from Jena by telegraph, and is later said to have lost only three fingers.[27]

On August 1st he was back on stage in nearby Erfurt, and apparently performing successfully.[28]

Eugenio now began making his way to Poland. In October a humorous story places him in Görlitz in Saxony, with two locals chatting — *did you know that Bosco's son is in our neck of the woods — Yes, I heard, but do you know if he has brought with him his father's tricks and humour — Of course — Then I'd like to see the people's faces when he does his tricks – most won't believe their eyes.*[29]

By November he was in Posen (modern Poznań), arriving there on November 23rd, billed as "Bosco from Turin" and described as "[tr.] resembling his father in his dexterity, features, and his whole character".[30]

In December he performed in Breslau (modern Wrocław), his shows there reported in the Warsaw papers: "the son of the magician Bosco, who is well-known in Warsaw, is giving performances in Wrocław *à la Bosco*", as one nicely put it;[31] another (after praising the performances there of the young Polish violinist Henryk Wieniawski) said of Eugenio: "[tr.] ... the second artist, still enjoying our place at the moment, is as successful as Wieniawski, although his art is of a completely different kind. He is Bosco, the son of the famous conjuror, a worthy successor to Pinetti and Philadelphia. From his performances it can be seen that the son not only attended a good school, but also excellently benefited from his father's teaching. His skill is remarkably great, his tricks for the most part new and surprising; he himself is very pleasant, and therefore it's no wonder they call him *Divine* instead of *Bosco*" (the same pun made on his father in 1847 in Lemberg, where he performed *bosko*, 'divinely').[32]

He also performed in Königsberg (modern Kaliningrad) in late December, attracting a good audience.[33]

1858

In early February 1858 Eugenio arrived by rail in Warsaw.[34] He demonstrated some of his skills to the *Kurjer Warszawski,* which stressed that he was "[tr.] the son of a well-known sorcerer, in no way inferior to his father", admiring his appearance and demeanour ("Bosco is young, expressive in the face, full of fire, and with great talent ... his appearance and manners are captivating and he almost charms the audience with his skill") and predicted success for him.[35]

However, he did not perform there on this occasion and after a fortnight, no doubt spent visiting relatives, he boarded the train back to Germany.[36]

We next sight him in March performing in Zwickau and soon to arrive in Leipzig for the Easter Fair.[37] In Leipzig he opened as "Bosco jun." in "[tr.] his own specially constructed *Salon*, comfortably appointed and lit by gas, on the *Königsplatz in front of the Petersthore*" (now the Wilhelm-Leuschner-Platz) — as his father had done in 1844.[38] There are four surviving posters for his shows in Leipzig, for April 19th, May 1st-2nd, May 5th-6th, and May 7th-8th. These list all his tricks in some detail, and all feature "the disappearance of a person without a screen".[39]

On June 11th the Bosco impostor Epstein (B12), recently arrived from England, opened at Kroll's Opera House in Berlin, trumpeted by the Kroll management in newspaper advertisements as "the young Bosco ... the even greater son of the great magician ... Court Magician to Queen Victoria of England and Chevalier of the Legion of Honour".[40]

Eugenio, in Karlsbad for his health,[41] wrote immediately offering proof that he was Bosco's only son and the "Pseudo-Bosco" now performing in Berlin could only be "a homonym, or, if not, an impostor".[42] Epstein was arrested on June 19th and charged the following day with using a false name and false credentials, and claiming titles and orders to which he was not entitled.

In November we find Eugenio in Bremen — very successful, *despite high prices* (the first mention found of this for him): "[tr.] the Bremen dailies cannot find sufficient praise for the young Eugenio Bosco who is giving his performances in this city. Despite the high entry prices, the theatre is always crowded with spectators…".[43]

He then headed to Berlin, where an anecdote, familiar from his father's day, has a well-dressed stranger visiting a newspaper office and bamboozling the journalists with card tricks— until one declares: *either things are not right here or you are the magician Bosco — Indeed, it was my visiting card. I have the honour to invite you to the first show to restore the honour of the name Bosco here after Markus Epstein.*[44]

If the story were true, the newspaper office would be the *Berlinische Nachrichten von Staats- und gelehrten Sachen*, from whom Eugenio was the recipient of several splendid publicity pieces, surely of his own composition. The first, when he was still in Bremen, nicely combined his inheritance from his father with the exciting novelties he himself would introduce —

Who in Berlin does not know the name Bosco? ... the elegance, the humour, the sheer wonder of his shows ...this name has an equally worthy heir, his son who without doubt will soon win as great a reputation in Europe as his father ... those who have seen his amazing shows even declare he is a master of his own master and father – all new discoveries in the chemical and mechanical sciences which have enriched the world in the last ten years he knows and exploits in the service of his art...[45]

On his arrival there was more of the same — now leaving no doubt of Eugenio's superiority over his father —

Bosco is here ... Who does not know the name of Bosco? ... But it is not the Bosco who once amused and entranced Berlin — it is the heir of his name and his fame, his son. The question asked earlier, is the pupil superior to the teacher, is now answered: Bosco the son and pupil excels his father ... using the latest scientific discoveries he enriches the field of surprises and wonders which his father opened to the world — in the elegance and assurance of his productions he surpasses his amiable and still not forgotten father and teacher, and before him stretches a shining career of fame and fortune...[46]

He opened his *Zaubersalon* in the *Hôtel de Russie* on November 28th, with shows daily. The first review recalled Bartolomeo's long run in the city thirty years earlier and the controversies that arose... *Bosco still lives, he is currently in Spain, and he lives on in his son, who, after a certain Epstein made use of his name for publicity purposes, now stands before us face to face ... for his first show he conjured up such a crowd that many could not get in, proof enough of the importance of a reputation and a name. And young Bosco is the very man to maintain that reputation and, if need be, renew it, since he is as unpretentious as he is skilful and assured, and all his performances are marked by a noble elegance... even familiar tricks have a new charm — the inexhaustible hat from which Döbler once pulled bouquet after bouquet has changed in Bosco's hands into a money-factory pouring out 500-franc notes, a nice memento of the evening and a charming advertisement. Let's hope that these continue to bear fruit and that the younger Bosco earns what his father did 30 years ago.*[47]

His *Salon* continued to attract the crowds, including members of the diplomatic corps, and he performed for the Prince Regent of Prussia, the future Kaiser Wilhelm, at a ball in his Palace, receiving a valuable diamond pin.[48] *Kladderdatsch* parodied his act, and also his language, with a long skit, ending with how to create a new ministry.[49] In all Eugenio gave 65 performances in Berlin before his departure for Potsdam.[50]

1859

After Potsdam he opened his "Vorstellung in der Chiromagique von Bosco Jun." on February 7th at the *Hôtel Stadt London* in Magdeburg, with further shows, all very successful, on 8th, 9th, 10th and 11th.[51]

He was then offered 200 Thaler to give two shows in Torgau. "Bosco-fever" gripped the town and these were crowded out, covering the promoter's costs, and he gave a third show for his own benefit.[52]

Eugenio now travelled to Vienna,[53] where he intended to perform in the *Fortuna-Saal, im Sperl*, "as soon as permission was received from the authorities".[54]

Der Humorist saluted his arrival with news of his recent successes in Berlin — "...in the *Spreestadt* he won a degree of public favour that not even his father was able to achieve", and pictured Eugenio visiting the office of the *Humorist* — "As is well known, Bartholomeo Bosco guessed the thoughts of the Russian Czar ... His son Eugen surprised us in the editorial office of this paper with a similar feat. Conversation turned to the present world situation, and the question arose as to what subject might be most occupying Count Cavour's thoughts just now. Herr Bosco quickly pulled out a set of German playing cards and told us to draw a card. Then he held the card by the corner, turned it three times, and tossed it on the nearest table. Lo and behold, the card had grown immensely in all directions, and on it was that notorious map of Europe in 1860, concocted in Paris, whose borders recently aroused Homeric laughter from all sides. It was a nice change. We also believe that Mr. Eugen Bosco correctly guessed the thoughts of the Sardinian Prime Minister".[55]

However on March 4th it was reported that he was leaving Vienna that day, unable to perform there "due to unforeseen obstacles".[56]

The following week he was sighted in Munich, but just passing through.[57] The start of April saw him in Nürnberg, where his two shows in the *Adlersaal*, though well reviewed, were poorly attended.[58]

Then came Bamberg, where the papers echoed the anthem *Who does not know the name Bosco...* he would soon equal and excel his father, employing as he did all the latest discoveries in chemistry and mechanics, excelling all others in his variety, polish, and confidence...[59] His two shows in the *Stadttheater* on April 10th and 11th both drew excellent crowds.[60] While in Bamberg he wrote to the *Illustrirte Zeitung* in Leipzig, which had published the splendid illustration of him and the (partly fictionalised) biography, requesting twelve copies.[61]

Eugenio now returned to Poland, this time to perform. On May 8th he arrived in Kraków, travelling from Leipzig.[62] Here he gave two shows, on May 17th and 18th, advertised as "only two extraordinary Chiromagic performances".[63]

An enthusiastic review in *Czas* pronounced the shows well attended and very much enjoyed. Even familiar tricks took on a novelty with his original twist, the canary fired from the pistol and landing on the sword was much admired, as were especially the novelties — *he wrote a certain number on a piece of paper, gave it to a spectator to keep hidden, and then handed out cards to the audience, who wrote down any number they wished; the sum of these numbers, added up by one of the spectators, turned out to be the exact number written by Herr Bosco given to the spectator. Also interesting was the clairvoyance. Several people wrote in pencil different sentences in Italian, French, German, Polish and Russian, which Mr. Bosco then read out with his eyes covered with gloves and double handkerchiefs tied tightly.*[64]

The correspondent of the *Zwischen-Akt*, clearly very impressed, calling him "the famous son of a famous *pater*", made several points, prestidigitational and political:

"...The world wants to be deceived, but the deception must be perfect, the liar caught out plays a pathetic role. Bosco is fundamentally different from the conjurors of our time in openly declaring his intention. Deception is his craft, misleading is his art, he deceives from the front. Others deceive by assassination, from behind... Bosco lets coins wander, stroll across the table, and makes kings disappear from the game ... this feat with the king now occupies many thousands of our brave compatriots. However, his skill of reading blindfolded is likely to remain unmatched. Our clairvoyance in similar cases mostly consists of finding ways and means to see clearly despite being blindfolded. On the other hand, we have had great practice lately in the art of reading between the lines, that is, things that have not been written at all. But now enough of this glib chatter, we won't surpass Bosco, the most amiable and smoothest talker of all magicians. His way of teasing people is as original as it is successful. The gift of the gab is all part of the craft".[65]

When he left the Hotel Rosyjski on May 23rd accompanying him were Atalida Bosco and Józefina Muntzel Bosco, who had arrived at the hotel four days after Eugenio, listed as *artistes,* having travelled from Leipzig.[66] They are then all recorded as travelling to Tarnów together, heading for Lviv, where Eugenio is said to have performed successfully.[67]

We then lose sight of Eugenio until late in the year when we find him giving a series of performances in Pest. He opened at the Stadt-Theater on November 16th — *Herr Eugen Bosco, from Turin, Magician to his Highness the Prince Regent of Prussia;* further shows followed on 19th and 20th (the last preceded by a farce); on 24th he took part in a benefit for the German actress Wilhemine Wollrabe.[68]

A widely reprinted story, illustrating the shortage of coin in the Austrian empire, told of Eugenio asking the audience for coins to use in a trick — and having to abandon it when none were forthcoming.[69]

1860

On January 30th he arrived in Vienna, heralded as "by all reports far superior to his father in his performances",[70] and opened at the Theater in der Josefstadt on February 4th, immediately attracting large crowds, and excellent reviews.

Fremden-Blatt pronounced his first show an enormous success. with his new tricks (especially the woman's hat and the watches) winning loud applause, and even familiar card tricks given a new angle; *Ost-deutsche Post* commended his skill and grace, and also the pleasant commentary he gave: *one can watch him without getting bored, which is saying a lot these days when we are used to lofty political conjuring...*; *Wiener Zeitung* approved his minimal apparatus, saying *the 'enlightened' don't go to the theatre to be deceived, the real charm is to penetrate the artist's secrets and discover his Achilles' heel ... his dexterity and apparatus leaves us perplexed when trying to spy out how he does it all...*[71]

His success saw him receive a contract for eight further shows — he was entertaining not only the public with his "rare dexterity and pleasing patter", said *Der Humorist,* but also the management with the rare pleasure of sold out houses.[72] By February 18th he had reached his thirteenth performance, advertising as the climax of the show his signature trick, 'The Appearance of a Woman from a Man's Hat'.[73]

However, at the height of his success Eugenio became suddenly unwell and was forced to discontinue his performances.[74]

Once recovered he headed to Prague, but business there was poor, as he was hot on the heels of rival Adolf Bils.[75] Further, Bils had announced he would pay 1000 ducats to any magician who could exactly reproduce one of his tricks; a local unknown named Johann Maschek had taken up the challenge, only for Bils to impose the condition that Maschek deposit 100 florins for the poor, with Bils to pay an extra 100 ducats to the poor if he lost. The 'contest' did not take place and Bils left town.[76] But the town was still excited at the prospect, so Eugenio invited Maschek to attempt his Bils imitation at the end of his own show. Maschek succeeded brilliantly before the huge and expectant audience, reproducing several of Bils's acts, possibly (some thought) after some coaching from Eugenio.[77]

On May 5th Eugenio opened in Brünn (Brno) at the Königlich städtisches Theater. A review praised his expertise and lack of pretence, and went on to pronounce that both his unadorned costume and his deliberate 'ill treatment' of German were in his favour, awarding him a leading place among modern magicians and bound to follow the celebrated path of his famous father. Further shows on 8th and 10th were no less successful and were followed by a 'farewell benefit show' on 12th, the last two culminating in his 'Appearance of a living woman out of a man's hat'.[78]

He then returned to Vienna,[79] and was back at the Josefstädter from May 25th, with large advertisements trumpeting his specialty acts —A Lady from a Man's Hat, Two Women Disappear, and The Antipodean Walk (upside down).[80]

However, this new series of shows was not a success. Reviewers commended his skill and the loud applause while also noting that "attendance should soon improve"; by the end of the month he decided to close.[81] *Figaro* now joked about "Bosco without a public — May has lost its bloom"; *Der Humorist* suggested that he add some new acts, shorten the intervals, and do away with a certain "drowsiness" (*Schlafrigkeit*) during his patter; *Die Wiener Elegante* politely blamed his demise on "the unfavourable summer season".[82]

We next find Eugenio in Frankfurt during the Fair. The newspapers welcomed him with the usual praise and implausible anecdotes — one anecdote even set in Paris, where he was yet to perform. Much was made of his talent inherited from his father, this on top of his own expertise in the new scientific discoveries, "which go hand in hand with natural magic"... He opened at the larger *Saal der Harmonie* on August 30th, attracting good crowds and receiving an excellent review (picking out for special praise his tricks with coins and rings, reading with his eyes covered, shredding and restoring a woman's hat, a bell that answered questions put to it, a duel, birds that flew to Hungary and back, and the vanishing woman...).[83] His success was not matched by the other entertainments at the fair such as the circus which suffered from being too far from town.[84]

He now made his way to Switzerland, performing in Geneva in early November,[85] then the following month began a long tour through France, his first venture there since the 1852 contract with his father. He opened in Lyon, where a glowing write-up hailed him as *heir of an illustrious name in the annals of the stage, now making his first appearance in France at the Théâtre des Célestins...* It was reported that he gave twenty performances there, and *even that number could not satisfy the public's curiosity.*[86]

1861

Next was Saint-Étienne, where he gave two shows on January 12th and 15th, both preceded by a play and followed by a farce. "He has bravely sought to outdo his father", said a review, "and this audacious attempt won the success it deserved".[87]

In February he arrived in Marseille, greeted as "the young magician who, inheriting the name of Bosco, also inherited his father's talent". The paper also printed an anecdote, no doubt apocryphal, of Bartolomeo being asked if he knew his son was better than him — "Well, I believe it", he replies, "I did not have such a good teacher as he did".[88] He opened at the *Gymnase* on February 27th, the shows beginning at 7 p.m. with two hours of vaudeville and Eugenio coming on at 9 p.m. March 1st was announced as his final show, but was followed by a benefit on March 3rd and a 'Farewell' show on 7th.[89]

We next see him in Avignon, performing on April 12th, described as very polished and attracting a good audience which included a large number of women.[90] In May the papers in Nîmes, fondly remembering Bartolomeo's successes there, reported that Eugenio was coming to perform, but there are no references to him doing so.[91]

In early June he arrived in Montpellier, where he opened on June 10th.[92] "Bosco II continues the brilliant tradition of Bosco I", said a review, and praised the simplicity of his apparatus — "a table, a pedestal table, cards, a pistol, and his ten [*sic*] fingers … these suffice for his miracles, but it is true that his ten fingers are those of an enchanter…"; if the reviewer was really unaware he had lost fingers it is a great tribute to his skill. His final show was on June 16th.[93]

By the end of the month he was in Béziers, giving his first show on June 30th.[94] After his second show on July 4th a long promotional article repeated some of the standard remarks long applied to his father — lucky not to have been born in an age when sorcerers were burnt, and his greatest trick was to attract a large audience, adding that if Bartolomeo had been in the audience that night we would not have been surprised to see him disappear through the fingers of his son…[96]

Next was Perpignan, where he gave two successful shows on July 29th and August 2nd,[96] followed by Carcassonne on August 11th.[97]

In 1883 a Pau newspaper stated that Bosco had performed successfully there in 1861 (exact date unknown).[98]

1862

We next sight him in February 1862 in Bordeaux, performing to a large audience at the *Salle du Cirque* on February 23rd. His advertising makes much of his minimal apparatus, as did Bartolomeo's, but Eugenio claims this as his own invention.[99]

On April 22nd he performed in Bayonne, again with a good audience,[100] on May 29th in Saintes,[101] and on June 12th in Rochefort.[102] He was to perform on June 20th in La Rochelle but his much anticipated show was cancelled when he refused a condition that the orchestra be allowed in free, insisting this was an exorbitant demand he had submitted to nowhere else.[103]

Eugenio moved on to Bourges, where he received a warm reception ("…a true Bosco … a worthy son of his father") and his performance on August 17th was well attended. A second show was announced for 21st but was cancelled when he was asked to give a series of shows in Lyon.[104]

We next see him performing in Draguignan on October 9th,[105] then in November in Nice, but unwell and convalescing.[106]

1863-4

During 1863 and 1864 Eugenio travelled through the East and Greece, and we have only scattered accounts. In a later advertisement[107] he claimed to have performed for the King of Greece on April 7th 1863: this cannot be correct as King Otto had been overthrown in October 1862 and while George I was elected King ("King of the Hellenes") in March 1863 he did not arrive in Greece until October 1863. Eugenio was in Greece in May *1864* and may have performed for the young King at that time.

In the same advertisement Eugenio claimed to have performed for "Sultan Abdul-Adzis and the harem on December 20th and 30th 1863". However, there are reports of this in European newspapers prior to that date, the earliest in late November; they state that he was handsomely rewarded by the Sultan but differ on the amount.[108] Unfortunately the *Journal de Constantinople* for 1863 is not online, but it is for 1864, and this has an announcement on February 19th for a performance by Eugenio that evening — a public performance:

> "[tr.] M. Bosco fils invites the public of our capital to a performance he will give this evening at the Naum Theatre. It would be superfluous to dwell at length on the merits of this distinguished magician whose abilities have already been recognized in all the great cities, it will suffice to say that his talents are equal to those of his father whose reputation was Europe-wide. M. Bosco fils, who had the honour several weeks ago to give a special performance at the Imperial palace, will show us this evening some twenty of his most amazing tricks …".[109]

Eugenio's time in Turkey — like his father's — became a rich source for anecdote. A piece of fiction titled 'Sultan Abdul Aziz in der Comödie' by "W.S. and M.S.", published some years later,[110] has Bosco fils in Constantinople in "late autumn 1864" instrumental in obtaining permission from Sultan Abdul Assiz for a performance of *Rigoletto* by a visiting Italian company, when the impresario, his singers and dancers, and even Donizetti's brother, the court musician, could not win the Sultan over. Eugenio (we are told) suggested the Sultan be presented with a barrel organ which played arias from the opera, and that did the trick… Now, *Rigoletto* was performed there in *1854* when Mahmud II was Sultan, Donizetti Pasha had died in 1861, and the barrel organ story we find only here — so, some history has been rewritten to centre the story around Eugenio's time in Constantinople in 1864. He is pictured as "a wandering daredevil adventurer, Bosco fils, as he called himself, the minor offspring of a great master, a juggler, at that time making a precarious living in the East through his very mediocre conjuring skills, but nonetheless earned a great deal of money".

What is essentially an earlier version of the same story, 'Sultan Abdul-Aziz im Theater, (Eine Reise-Erinnerung.)', signed "Z.", appeared in *Die Presse* 23 July 1867. This has no barrel organ and merely has Eugenio telling the *impresario* the layout of the small theatre near the Sultan's palace, but Eugenio is described in almost exactly the same words as in the later version, "Bosco fils, the minor offspring of a great father, a juggler, at that time making a precarious living in the East through his very mediocre conjuring skills, but nonetheless earned a great deal of money".

In May 1864 Eugenio was in Athens, but did poor business due to his high admission prices. The local papers insisted that the Athenians could do better than the "charlatanism" of the visiting *Bosko*.[111]

1865

In 1865 he was in Italy. A promotional piece on him the following year places him in Trieste in March 1865,[112] and in May he was in Naples, where he gave a series of ten shows at the *Teatro di San Carlo*.

On May 9th he was widely reported as reproducing as part of his act the "Miracle of San Gennaro". He called this trick, performed only three days after the Church liquefaction ceremony, "The Tears of Venus", no doubt adding to the irritation of the members of the Society of St Vincent de Paul who, forewarned, had gone to the theatre to protest. He is also said to have reproduced the miracle at Vicovaro of the Madonna's eyelids moving.[113]

A contemporary account appeared in the Italian liberal journal *Omnibus* on May 11th 1865: "[tr.] The tricks of Bosco in San Carlo on Tuesday evening started well and ended badly. At first they were charming and were applauded; but when he wanted to touch on the subject of making the blood of Venus liquefy, the public got angry and shouted *enough, enough!* Really, that red stuff in an open jar which became liquid is such a trifle that it is not only nothing like a miracle, but not even a joke, since any chemist knows how to make any mixture a liquid. Mr. Bosco wanted to assail an object of devotion of the Neapolitan people, and instead was assailed by the people's disapproval".[114]

Less than a month later, on June 15th, at the Church of Sant'Anna di Palazzo (in the Piazzetta Rosario di Palazzo, close to the teatro San Carlo and only 3 km from the Cattedrale di Santa Maria Assunta, home of the blood of the saint) Eugenio married Elisabetta Zanardelli. On the civil marriage registration the previous day Eugenio gives his full name, age, place of birth, and his mother's maiden name, as discussed above.

Elisabetta (Elisa), the daughter of Antonio Zanardelli and Teresa, née Iovini, had been on stage with her parents since childhood, first in their acting company, then from 1847 as a "magnetised" medium in a somnambulist and mentalist act ("sonnambula e mentalista"), a role she continued with Eugenio. Her age is given as 26 but two sources give her birthdate as April 25th 1837, making her 28.[115]

They were to have at least three children: a daughter who died on September 8th 1866, probably very soon after her birth; a son Italo (B3), born in Turin *ca.*1869, and a daughter Juliette, said to be born in 1874. Writing to *Le Figaro* 3 Apr.1882 complaining of an impostor Crémy (B21) who claimed to be his son (or Bartolomeo's) Eugenio states that he has two sons, so there was apparently a second son. In 1885 he was working in his act with "la jeune Béatrix", but she is not said to be his daughter.

They performed in Italy following their marriage, though little information is accessible on this period. We know he was in Florence in August 1865 at the *teatro Niccolini* from a poster for a performance on August 3rd.[116] Eugenio here bills himself "Il FIGLIO del Celebre BOSCO", and claims to have returned from Russia,

Poland, Prussia, Germany, Belgium, Holland, England, France, Switzerland, Austria, Greece, Turkey, Africa, America —America is certainly a false claim and he was in England only when visiting with his father in 1851.

1866

In January 1866 they were in Turin: we know this because the following year when they arrived in Neuchâtel the paper there quoted (translated into French) a glowing account from the *Gazzetta di Torino* of 16 Jan.1866, no doubt taken from Eugenio's album: "Bosco won last Tuesday at the "théâtre royal" a success worthy of Bosco père... Bosco not only possesses, executes and gives new life to the immense repertoire of his father, but has been able to create a new repertoire of his own ...". In an advertisement in France in 1868 he claimed to have given 16 shows in Turin in 1866, probably correct. And in February 1866 he was probably in Genoa, as in a later advertisement[117] he claimed to have performed for the Grand Duchess of Genoa (Princess Elizabeth of Saxony) on February 2nd 1866.

Eugenio's "anti-spiritist" demonstrations which by now constituted a large part of his act had become proverbial: a German newspaper early in 1866 joked that Bismarck in leaving the fate of the Duchy of Lauenburg (recently taken from Denmark) hanging in mid-air was imitating Eugenio hovering between the balcony and the stalls.[118]

In April he was in Lyon and it was from there that he wrote to several newspapers denying a widely reprinted report that he had recently died in Dresden (and pointing out that his father had died there several years ago).[119]

After Lyon Eugenio and Elisa began a tour of Switzerland. On their arrival in Geneva a glowing promotional piece recalled his father there, "now deceased, but he leaves a son who has followed the same career and whose reputation in Europe and America [!] is already at least as great as his father's... what particularly sets Bosco fils apart and what is totally new, are his demonstrations in so-called spiritism such as that practised by the Humes, the Davenport Brothers and others; and the fact that he illustrates to all that one can perform all the marvels of their magic without recourse to anything supernatural. That alone is of a character to attract the lively interest of the public, quite apart from the amusing tricks simply of skill which will give variety to the show".[120] They opened at the *Grand Théâtre* on May 17th, beginning with a series of "skilfully executed amusing tricks" then launching into what had become his trademark demonstration of a table rising from the ground and turning round, which won him two encores.[121]

At the end of the month they arrived in Neuchâtel, where the paper saluted his successes in "Naples, Florence, Turin, etc., etc", quoting the extract from the *Gazzetta di Torino* in January that year (above). However, the reviewer was clearly unimpressed: "M. Bosco yesterday evening was able to perform his magic tricks before a large audience with a skill worthy of the name he bears... What was perhaps less successful was the second part, though the demonstration of the turning and flying table was very interesting; still he knows how to entertain and amuse his public, a public which is pretty blasé and has already seen many excellent magicians".[122]

In early July there were in Bern and a lengthy contributed article on Eugenio rose to the level of almost ridiculous self-parody, hailing "the arrival in our midst of a new

Alexander the Great in the history of the art of magic, namely Eugène Bosco. When any human talent in one individual reaches such a height that his achievements exceed not only all previous achievements in that field, but confront them as the end does the beginning, so that even our imagination is denied the possibility of conceiving a higher development, a more accomplished method, then we welcome into our mind the noble impression of absolute perfection ... We can picture Eugène Bosco only by comparing him to the well-known greats to show how superior he is. We have seen Bosco and Habitt, Fondin [sic] and Robin, and we have heard of Pedorelli and Frickler [sic], Dobler and Hermann — all pale before him, beneath him! Great as they are they appear small next to him, for while each is great in himself, Eugène Bosco unites in his own person the great characteristics of all and exceeds all... and has reduced to nothing all the triumphs of his father...".[123] He opened on July 17th, with further shows on 20th and 23rd. All comprised three parts, the first Magic, the second Spiritism, the third "entertaining gifts, consisting of 8 surprising items, the main item being a sheep, which Herr Bosco donated to the honoured public of Bern as a souvenir".[124]

They was next in Fribourg and announced that Eugenio would be giving one show there.[125] However this was delayed because Elisa had an "indisposition",[126] and on August 8th their daughter (unnamed) died, probably shortly after her birth.[127] Eugenio finally gave his performance on September 4th; this was a great success ("the turning table turned heads") and a second and final show was given on September 6th.[128]

They continued on to Lausanne,[129] giving two successful shows at the *Casino*, on 13th and 18th.[130] Martigny followed, then Vervey on September 26th.[131]

In December they were in Treviso, which had only recently voted to join the Kingdom of Italy. They announced two shows on December 8th and 9th, "spettacoli di spiritismo e magia di Eugenio Bosco" — Elisa is not featured in the advertising here and not since Fribourg. Part I was Magic; Part II "Scientific Demonstration of Physical Experiments"; Part III "Disappearance of a Lady from Treviso who is kind enough to offer herself"; Part IV "The Mysterious Cabinet, or supernatural experiments ...". Admission prices ranged from Cent.60 to L1.50.[132]

A review pronounced the shows a *fiasco* — there was a good crowd the first night *despite the rather high prices, and expectation was high, increased by the fame of his father. But Sig. Bosco did not live up to these expectations: he performed some common tricks very skilfully, but the public wanted something new, they wanted miracles, and in this they were disappointed. And unforeseen circumstances meant the most interesting part of the show was cancelled, adding to their feeling of being misled. On Sunday the theatre was almost empty and Sig. Zanardelli who had taken the place of his son-in-law was unable to persuade a spectator to come on stage. The only novelty was the cabinet, but that lost its effect because of the slowness and repetition of the ropes being untied...*[133]

1867

They performed in Florence in March 1867 at the *Teatro nuovo*. In an advertisement in France in 1868 Eugenio claimed to have given 15 shows in Florence in 1867, probably correct. There was a humorous proposal — passed by acclamation — that Eugenio be made the next Minister of Finance: if he could produce 9,999 cigars and 9,999 bouquets from nowhere during his show he could multiply banknotes with a wave of his hand...[134]

In October 1867 they were in Turin, opening at the *Teatro Vittorio Emanuele* on October 21st, Eugenio "worthy son of the father of all magicians",[135] and on November 14th in Modena.[136]

At some date in 1867 Eugenio was also at the *Teatro sociale* in Voghera, in Lombardy.[137]

1868

A chatty account published in March 1868 of the Trieste Carneval, that year or the year before, places Eugenio there: a visitor reports her shawl and then her opera glasses missing from her box, but the culprit is soon unmasked, "Friend Bosco" ...[138]

By mid-1868 Eugenio and Elisa are travelling through France, in early July in Toulon,[140] and then in Nîmes, and with them is Dante Zanardelli.[140]

In the Nîmes papers Eugenio stresses that he is the *true* and *only* son of Bartolomeo,[141] but his advertisement for his first show contained blatant misinformation on his early career: he claims to have given 282 shows in Paris in 1854 [there is no evidence he gave *any*, and his contract with his father excluded him from France], 87 shows in London in 1857 [as stated, there is no evidence he *ever* performed in England; he was in Germany in 1857, including the period spent recovering from his hand injury], 65 shows in Berlin in 1859 [probably correct], 42 in Vienna in 1861 [that year he was only in France], 16 in Turin in 1866 [probably correct], and 15 in Florence in 1867 [probably correct]. The advertisement is signed "Tovini, *sécretaire*".[142]

They opened on August 13th at the *Grand-Théâtre*, apparently giving only the one performance. Part I of their show, 'Grand Effort des Facultés Mentales', was mind reading by Dante, Part II 'Nécromancie' by Eugenio (including the 'Headless Lady', the "victim" a *demoiselle de Nîmes*), Part III 'Spiritomanie', an exposure of the turning and dancing table tricks of the spiritualists.[143] The reviews were positive (quoting in fact much of Eugenio's own publicity material) but mentioned neither Elisa or Dante: *...Eugenio equals, if he does not surpass, his father... the levitating table new and astonishing ... dancing 50 cm above the floor...* admiring him *in the mysterious silk scarf which gave birth to crystal jars full of liquid, a field rabbit, a doll, etc.;* and *the felt hat from which came iron cannon balls and great balls of wool for a mattress, and a shower of bouquets for the ladies;* and *the trick of the decapitated pigeon which dies in a spectator's hands then comes back to life in a bottle... But he should avoid this time of year, the dog days, when the countryside and the casino are distractions and the heat is stifling (37 or 38 degrees)...*[144]

By August 20th they were in Montpellier, performing there on 22nd.[145] Eugenio was clearly now totally exasperated by impostors using the name Bosco, one claiming to be Bartolomeo's son, another his daughter. In September he wrote to newspapers lamenting his situation and asking for help in the matter. *Le Temps* advised that if he did not want to take them to court he should insist the authorities check people's credentials to confirm their identity.[146]

1869

We hear very little of Eugenio over the next few months. In June 1869 it was reported that he failed to appear as advertised to perform in a newly opened theatre in the village of Rueil, near Paris. The audience received refunds.[147]

Later that year we find him in Cesena on the Adriatic coast: "October 30th 1869 — Illusionist company directed by E. Bosco. The city band played for free during the intervals".[148]

It was during this period spent in Italy that Eugenio's son Italo (B3) was born in Turin.

1870?
1871

In mid-1871 we hear of them travelling from Italy to Austria and Germany. They performed in Villach, in southern Austria, in July,[149] then later that month Eugenio is listed staying at a hotel in Klagenfurt, apparently on his own.[150]

A few months later a story appeared in several papers, quoting from the *Temesvarer Zeitung* an account of Eugenio appearing in their newspaper office turning his hat into a feather duster then into a huge bunch of flowers by way of announcing an upcoming performance in Temesvar (modern Timişoara); but then after posters had been printed and all the preparations made he failed to appear...[151]

1872

In January 1872 Eugenio and Dante were in Lviv, recorded as arriving on January 25th and staying at the Hotel Angelski.[152]

In February 1872 'Appearance of the Magician Bosco' is item 4 in a list of entertainments to take place at an inn in Böhmisch Kamnitz (modern Česká Kamenice in the Czech Republic). The programme includes dancing harlequins, the animal quartet, the three famous monkeys (and more), and this is almost certainly not Eugenio but a local amateur Bosco imitator.[153]

We sight Eugenio again in March 1872 in Graz, performing with Dante, "E. Bosco aus Turin, Dante aus Venedig"; they are coming from Pest and have recently been performing in Bucharest and Jassy (Iaşi); this fits with their presence in Temesvar in September 1871 in suggesting they had made the same long journey that Bartolomeo had made in 1826 and 1846.[154] In Graz they announced three shows, "humoristisch antispiritische Soiréen", at the *Redoutensaal* on March 11th, 12th and 14th, comprising 'Old Magic, as performed 30 years ago by Bosco (without apparatus)'; 'Great Efforts in the Art of Memory' by Dante; and 'American Spiritism, or modern Charlatanry...'.[155] They were not a great success and it appears the third show, and possibly also the second, was cancelled, with Bosco said to be leaving immediately for Naples. One review reported a small audience due to the high seat prices, though the acts were said to be excellently done, if not all new, and the third part with the turning table was rated highly entertaining.[156] Another review approved of both the show and Eugenio's "elegant and humorous commentary", but the next day this paper confirmed that "the first show was not as well attended as he believed his reputation deserved", and that he had already left for Naples "where his family already was".[157] This suggests that Elisa and young Italo did not accompany him and Dante on the long journey to Jassy.

Presumably he did join his family in Naples, but the next sighting of him is about to perform in Esseg (now Osijek in Croatia) in August.[158]

He was apparently heading to Temesvar (Timişoara), where he had failed to appear the previous year. This time we have a report quoted from the *Temesvarer Zeitung* of their office receiving by mail ("unter Kreuzband") an advertising poster sent by Eugenio announcing his arrival, to which the paper took exception: it featured a large skull and coming out of its mouth were the words 'My son Eugen Bosco will soon arrive in this city. Bartolomeo Bosco'...[159]

1873

At the start of 1873 Eugenio was in Poland. He was first in Lviv, his initial show not well attended, but the audiences improved "as news of his fame spread".[160] The Lviv paper *Dziennik polski* apparently claimed that he was not the son of Bartolomeo, but later published a correction,[161] and when Eugenio soon arrived in Kraków[162] he was acknowledged as the famous son of the famous Bartolomeo, *attracting a large audience thanks to the great reputation of his father — the shadow of the famous magician could rejoice that the art which once served the Cagliostros and the St Germains now made a public entertainment...*[163] His two "magico-spiritualist performances" at the Hotel Saski were very successful.[164]

But the accusation that he was not the son of Bartolomeo followed him to Warsaw, where *Kuryer Warszawski* stated: "We were told that a magician Bosco was coming to Warsaw to give magical *soirées*. Some say that the magician is the son of the famous Bosco who twenty years ago charmed us here in our city, but as far as we know Bosco senior died childless in Italy and apparently in a critical financial situation".[165] This was corrected a few days later, first a notice stating that "A magician, Eugenio Bosco, has arrived in Warsaw, and he is (as we have been advised in detail) the son of the famous magician Bartolomeo Bosco and Antonina née Mlynarski, sister of Mrs. Conti, who lives in Warsaw".[166] This important family information is discussed in the *Excursus* on Bartolomeo's Family. Then followed a letter from Eugenio confirming his parentage and pointing out that his father's death and burial were in Dresden, and he had not, as stated, died destitute but on the contrary left a property with a house and a garden.[167] But Eugenio then gave some further details which are certainly not all correct, such as that he himself was "a son of Turin" (though "he has a bit of knowledge of the Polish language, because his mother was Polish, and he spent time in Warsaw in childhood"); he does not mention his older namesake, born and died in Poland age 1 (he may not have known of his existence) and does not mention Matteo, who also died young; of his two sisters, he says one, Alexandra, was "born on Italian soil" [actually in St. Petersburg], "but spent a long time in Warsaw, staying with [*or* looked after by] one of the local families and died here" [correct, in 1853]; the other sister he says was "born in Warsaw" [correct] and she "not too long ago moved to eternity" [but she was still alive ten years later: for this see *Excursus on family*].[168]

The *Kuryer Codzienny* had welcomed him as "the son of the famous magician B. Bosco" and announced that he would be giving a "completely new kind of show, the kind once attributed to spiritism, but done by him without the aid of spiritism".[169] Four shows were announced at the Theatre of the Warsaw Charitable Society (*Warszawskie Towarzystwo Dobroczynności*) for February 6th, 7th, 8th, and 9th,[170] but the theatre was not free on the first night and the shows were rescheduled to the 7th, 8th, 9th and 10th.[171]

A review praised Eugenio's conjuring skills — "Preceded by the fame of his father ... In the tricks *à la Bosco* he showed great genuine dexterity, and performing almost everything without any apparatus; he surpasses the last few magicians who have flown across the Warsaw horizon. Among other magical tricks, there were also some that we had not seen before, such as pushing an iron needle through his body and attaching a ribbon, which spectators then pulled freely back and forth...". But the mind-reading experiments were a disaster —"...Mr. Bosco's associate, Mr. Rideli, could answer 6 or 7 questions, written by various spectators and placed by them in a sealed envelope. He kept each envelope sealed, and passed it in front of Mr. Rideli, who wrote a reply, only then was the question taken out of the envelope and the answer read out if it turned out to be correct and matched the question; the audience liked: 'How in the next world will Emperor Maximilian welcome Napoleon III?'. The tables spinning, knocking, and flying in the air were the final act of the show, and (continues the reviewer) I was reminded of the table epidemic that plagued us several years ago. Mr. Rideli speaks only German, while Mr. Bosco explains his act with verve and humour in Polish and several other languages, none quite grammatical.[172]

The illustrated magazine *Kłosy* made the inevitable political joke — *apparently young Bosco famously takes off heads; what it would be if he could provide them to so many who need them! Despite his skill, he did not succeed in the kind of trick that Herr Bismarck did...*[173]

We last see Bosco in Poland later that month in Kalisz.[174]

On July 6th he opened a successful run at the *Sommertheater* in the *Pſtroß'ſchen Garten* in Prague,[175] then performed in Linz on August 1st and 2nd, his shows preceded by a farce,[176] receiving an excellent reception — *he combines elegant manners with a pleasant appearance to win over the sympathies of the public, and he understands how to spice his act with a humorous commentary, made more piquant by his foreign accent ... His development* ("Evolution") *of the old style magic (à la Bosco senior), especially the antispiritism tricks, holds the audience's attention right to the end...*[177]

From Linz he went to Brünn (Brno), performing on August 22nd and 25th.[178] They had already had in the town a previous "Bosco Junior", whose first name was forgotten, claiming to be "son of the old Bosco", and "Yesterday a second Bosco jun., a Eugenio Bosco to be precise, took the stage as a conjuror and magician before a sparse local theatre audience; a stately, agile man, but on the outside he is just the opposite of the old little, very stocky, real Bosco ... Herr Eugenio started by performing some attractive card tricks; but the water which he drew out of the silk cloth into bowls lacked the goldfish of Prof. Herrmann, who manipulated whole aquaria; this feat, like the one with the beheading, was, however, quite entertaining. The lady who was most likely to have been satisfied was the one who had to hold the supposed corpse of the bird in a bag and instead found a splendid bouquet. Of the Allan Kardek style tricks from the realm of spiritualism, only a meagre sample was performed with the help of Mr. Schmutz as writing medium; in questions and answers, however, the spirits were very sparse with their jokes; Napoleon's spirit was more help with the well done table turning, carried out with the help of six gentlemen, which, however, lacked novelty, as the majority of those present could have entertained themselves with this anyway."[179] The second show "was almost less well attended than the first. There were some new tricks in the first part, and in part two he performed the interesting Davenport act of the tied-up medium. Herr Bosco was tied hand and foot by several men, then hidden by a cover for several minutes, and when it was removed stood up free from the ropes. Table turning again closed the show".[180]

He was next in Olmütz (Olomouc), performing there on September 3rd. "He did all the usual magic tricks which we've already had the opportunity to see so often", said the local paper, "Nothing special to see. But Herr Bosco does know how to keep his audience well entertained with an amazing flow of words. And there was general hilarity when after a lot of trying he managed to entice a man onto the stage, a well know local wag, and taught him how to 'make the pass' (*die Volte schlagen*)".[181]

It also appears that Eugenio was in Piacenza this year: this must have been either late in the year or between February and July.[182]

1874

By the start of 1874 he was in Germany. An article in the Frankfurt paper *Didaskalia* notes that he planned to visit there "in the coming week", and was currently in Wiesbaden. There his first show in the larger room of the *Kurhaus* had attracted an audience of 600, "his antispiritist act well up to expectation …the little jokes which Herr Bosco still introduces as a legacy from his father confirmed his fame as a master of magic … the patter he keeps up in a range of languages is richly spiced with humour"; a second show was to follow in the White Room of the *Kurhaus*.[183]

In April he was in Innsbruck, and had also been in Mainz, where the *Mainzer Zeitung* had written of him: "We must honestly admit that we are rather *blasé* about conjuring acts, for in spite of everything the tricks are so much alike and if you have seen one or two of these performers you've seen them all. Only a very special talent, like that of Bosco, can lend the business charm, and this is the case with him to the fullest extent. Moreover, many of his acts are new. Those which are not, however, are carried out with such skill that the deception is more complete than one can imagine. In addition, Herr Bosco is a really educated man who, as an Italian, speaks German as fluently as possible and does not try to hide the complete absence of spirit and wit behind an impossible gibberish. His entertainment is light and pleasant, and we must confess that his soirees are among the most attractive to be encountered in this field".[184]

In Innsbruck he performed in the *National-Theater* on April 7th,[185] then in Bozen (Bolzano) on April 12th, securing, we are told, "a rather handsome audience. It was less the charm of the novelty than the rarity that might have attracted them; the name Bosco naturally helped. The entertainment was good. The acts as a whole, especially the spiritism, strongly held one's interest and were very amusing".[186]

On July 19th a "Performance by the world famous magician Bosko" was included in the programme of events put on by the City Rifle Corps ("das diesige bürgerl. priv. Schutzenkorps") in Saaz (modern Žatec), raising funds for flood relief. This may have been Eugenio — or, more likely, a local amateur imitating him.[187]

In France in 1880 Eugenio advertises a trick he says he performed *for the Czar in St Petersburg in 1874,* so he may well have now travelled to Russia. However, the dates in such advertisements are notoriously unreliable as evidence (either through deliberate or accidental error, or misreadings by the typesetter) and in the same advertisement later the same year he says he performed this trick not for the Czar but for the Emperor of Austria in 1874.[189]

It was probably in 1874 that his daughter Juliet was born; where is unknown, but perhaps in Italy if she was born late in the year.

1875

He was in Italy by early 1875. On January 24th he was in Cesena,[189] then in Turin in March, where he performed at the *Teatro Scribe* from March 6th to 13th.[190] Presents were offered to the audience, and Eugenio advertised a rather exotic repertoire including "the Kangoo, Chinese torture by Miss Chrystoworkeny" and "the Genuine Indian Mail".[191] His advertising stressed that he was the *true* Bosco, worthy son of the famous father.[192] Then on March 19th he took part in a benefit show at the *Teatro Vittorio Emanuele* for war veterans (*Comizio dei veterani 1848-49*), where he again performed the *Valigia delle Indie* ("Indian Mail") without a screen, "and Signor Bosco will show how difficult it is to train someone to carry out this delightful and surprising trick". This was presumably similar to John Nevil Maskelyne's *Metamorphosis* (Trunk Trick), which he invented in 1865 to expose the Davenports.[193]

In July 1875 recorded as staying in the Gasthof zum Mohren in Klagenfurt is "A. Bosko, Escamoteur von Wien". This would be the only reference found to an magician "A. Bosco", so may be a misprint for E. Bosco.[194]

At the end of the year Eugenio was in Treviso, giving a performance at the *teatro Garibaldi* on December 25th, and he has an assistant "Miss Christínn".[195]

1876-7

Over the next year or two we get few glimpses of Eugenio. In early 1876 he was in Monaco, with a performance on February 16th. A review (calling him "Bosco de Rome") reported a full house, with flowers for the ladies and sugared almonds for the children.[196]

In November a paper in the Austrian spa town of Bad Ischl revived the old Bartolomeo story of the farmer, who, having seen the swapping of the two birds' heads, wanted the same with his wife and her sister, but there is nothing to suggest Eugenio was performing there at the time.[197]

1878

In 1878 he was in Italy, and in February in Turin he is accompanied not only by Elisa but by young Italo, age 8, "a child prodigy", the earliest record found of him on stage, doing the memory and mental calculation act which was his speciality.[198]

They gave three shows at the *Vittorio Emanuele*, on February 3rd, 4th and 8th, and returned on 25th for a benefit show for the war veterans. Here Italo received great applause, "pulling off a truly extraordinary memory exercise — imagine, hearing only once the names of 35 things in numerical order, he repeated them one by one from the first to the thirty-fifth, and then in reverse order".[199]

In July they are in Trieste, opening at the *Teatro Filodrammatico* on July 2nd, Eugenio, Elisa, Italo, and "Miss Letizia", the show comprising "Olla Podrida fantastica" by Eugenio, "estasi eccentrica" by Elisa, "Stenografia della mente" by Italo, and "l'esperimento L'*inesplicabile*" by Miss Letizia, explained by Eugenio.[200] "Few people came to the entertainment last night," said a review, "and we're sorry. Both Mr. Bosco and his companions ... had the opportunity in their various acts to demonstrate all their skills, and they were warmly and repeatedly applauded. The season is solely to blame for the poor crowd last night…".[201]

They were also at the *Teatro sociale* in Voghera at some date in 1878.[202]

1879

On January 20th and 21st 1879 they performed in Esseg (Osijek),[203] then in February were back in Turin, Italo performing with them ("il suo piccolo figliuolo Italo").[204]

By mid-1879 Eugenio was in France — but 'Le Fils Bosco' who in Paris on June 7th performed in a charity Fête for the flooded town of Szegedin was not him but an imitation of him by the comic Léon Fusier of the Palais-Royal.[205]

Eugenio, Elisa and Italo were touring in the south of France — Chambéry in June,[206] Montélimar in July,[207] Avignon in August, where they were joined by American spiritist Dr May (May loudly applauded; Elisa "strongly holding the audience's attention" when in her trance),[208] then Nîmes,[209] and Montpellier. His announcements here made much of his being the son of Bartolomeo, and the show "an evocation both touching and astonishing of ghosts and spirits", reviving the "thousand resources and ingenious means" his father had used to charm and amaze the public…[210] And before the show he strolled round the town having fun with people's watches and wallets.[211] He did the same in Cette (now Sète), asking a man in a tobacconist's for a light — his watch has gone; ah, found in a box of cigars; and in a café warning a patron to be careful eating a cake — it has gold in it, and coins then fall out… He also had to establish his identity as the true Bosco, as an impostor had been there and disappointed the town.[212] The show, on August 24th, was described as a complete success.[213]

On August 27th they performed in Perpignan, "une superbe séance de thaumaturgie", Eugenio, Elisa, Dr May and Yda Mayer.[215]

1880

Early the following year Eugenio, Elisa and Italo are in Spain, still with Dr May, "el magnitizador", and now joined by magician Henry Frizzo,[215] recently very successful at the *teatro de la Comedia* in Madrid. They performed at the *Alhambra* in Madrid in February and March, the show opening with conjuring, then the "parte cientifica: magnetismo humano y sonambulismo", with Elisa "magnetizado" by May, and ending with "unas escenas llamadas fantásticas, por Bosco, Italo y la señorita Ida Romana".[216]

By May 1880 Eugenio was back in France. It is probably him (not an impostor) in Marseille on March 5th,[217] and certainly him in Nîmes later in the month.[218] The advertisement on the day of the show, May 15th at the *Théâtre d'Été,* gives a detailed programme:

Première partie. — Ouverture à grand orchestre.

Changement inattendu — expérience spéciale de poésie, Bosco.

Un ministre des finances — expérience fantastique de nos jours.

L'oeuf mystérieux de Pluton — spécialité Bosco, récompensé par S.M. l'empereur d'Autriche, 1879.

Une dépêche télégraphique — breveté par S.A.R. la duchesse de Gênes.

Le bazar universel — expérience Bosco.

Deuxième partie. — Ouverture à grand orchestre.

L'ombrelle égyptienne — expérience Bosco.

Le facteur de la malle des Indes — expérience Bosco.

Le drapeau égyptien — Amusement fantastique récompensé par le grand sultan, 1870.

Est-il, où [*sic*] n'est-il pas? — Il n'y est pas! — expérience Bosco.

Le sécretaire galant — spécialité de l'exécuteur.

La bouteille de Marsala — amusement fantastique récompensé par S.M. l'empéreur de Russie, à Saint-Petersbourg, en 1874.[219]

In June "the famous magician Bosco" was advertised as performing at the *Théâtre du Cirque* in Toulouse, but it was not Eugenio. This Bosco is part of a big line-up, the 'Folies Toulousaines' managed by M. Paul Romand, which includes "Mme Vigneau, le célèbre prestidigitateur Bosco, les incomparables Girards, le magnifique ballet d'Alessandri" and "un bataillon de jolies chanteuses".[220]

In August it appears that Eugenio was in Vichy. A diffuse article on Vichy by Philibert Audebrand in the Paris paper *Le Globe* refers to a poster by "M. Bosco fils" which mentions conjuring the Minister of Finance, an act included by Eugenio in his programme in Nîmes.[221]

In September he was at the Théâtre-Louit in Bordeaux, and was up to his tricks with people's watches the preceding week.[222] Or was he? Eugenio wrote to Paris newspapers soon after, complaining of an impostor (B21), "an individual, an Italian subject, who is presently touring round France and giving performances under the name of Bosco fils. I am the *only son* of the famous magician..."; he says he has lodged a complaint in the Bordeaux court against this person, and gives a description of himself: "*Tall, brown hair, blue eyes, bald*".[223]

And later that month the real Eugenio — real because he has Italo with him — opened at the *Gymnase* in Bordeaux. Performing with them are "M. Cascabel, l'homme caméléon" and "M. Kasj-Kalli, jongleur". There is praise for all of them, including "le jeune Italo, avec sa prodigieuse mémoire".[224]

Eugenio thus arrived in Bordeaux about mid-October, presumably after reading about the impostor performing there in late September. Eugenio himself was probably 800 km north of Bordeaux in late September in Boulogne-sur-mer: a review in the Boulogne paper *L'Impartial de Boulogne-sur-mer* 26 Sep.1880 reviews a successful show there by "le célèbre Bosco" and hopes he will be able to give a second performance.[225]

On November 11th he performed in Draguignan and in a long and detailed advertisement (a column and a half)[226] he sets out his full programme (as in Nîmes above) and stresses that this is no ordinary show, not merely old style conjuring as his father did, but includes "a series of new acts to which one can call the attention of persons interested in science and in the amazing applications that can be made of it to instruct and amuse the masses". This is signed by "Le Sécretaire, Petronio" on behalf of "Le Chevalier Bosco", the first occasion found of him claiming this title his father also claimed. He further quotes at length reports from Orléans newspapers, not of successful performances there, but of playing tricks on people round the town.

Late in 1880 an interesting snippet appeared in some English newspapers: "At the Alhambra Theatre at Rome there is a little lad of nine years of age who performs prestidigitation tricks equal to old Bosco, whose name he takes…".[227] The *teatro Alhambra* did open that year and nine is about the right age for Italo: however, Italo is never elsewhere referred to as a conjuror but always as doing a memory and mental calculation act, and this was probably the youngest Bosco impostor (B20).

In December Eugenio arrived in Paris and announced he was planning to perform there,[228] but there is no evidence in the Paris papers of him doing so. We next see him in nearby Neuilly-sur-Seine giving a benefit show in late February.[229]

1881

He, Elisa and Italo then headed to Normandy and Brittany, and continued to tour France until late in 1885. In June 1881 we find them in Rouen and Elbeuf,[230] the following month in Aix,[231] in October in Angers,[232] November in Saumur,[233] and December in Nantes, where Italo is billed as "the new Pico de la Mirandola", and Elisa's act is here termed "*L'Extase hors centre*": Eugenio attracted a good audience, said a review, but they made a game of his show ("en ont fait un jeu"), refusing to lend him the objects he requested for conjuring and refusing to go on stage.[234] However, he gave ten shows in Nantes, the last on January 10th, which was pronounced "a true success, before a well filled room."[235] That year they had also visited (at unknown dates) Le Havre and Caen.[236]

1882

From Nantes they travelled to Vannes,[237] where his performance on January 14th received a long review recalling a visit there "about twenty years ago" by Bartolomeo, "*Bosco 1er, le grrrrand Bosco*",[238] shaving, and regrowing, beards with his wooden sabre… now "Bosco II" who, "[tr.] despite his tall stature and fine bearing calls himself the little Bosco out of respect for his father's fame and no doubt from modesty, has shown his skill in cards and sleight-of-hand; he shows he went to a good school and benefited from it. Forcing a card and making a pass are the ABC of the art, but he, a new Moses, under a magic handkerchief makes an inexhaustible fountain well up with its source in his waistcoat — that's more difficult; and, more difficult still, pours from a carafe of pure water drawn from the same source Vermouth or Madeira, Burgundy or Bordeaux. The wine at the wedding in Cena is only small beer to Bosco… Look at this empty basket… in it he finds and unrolls a long ribbon, so long, so long… he makes a knot, and out of the knot comes a pigeon, a real pigeon… he cuts its throat, wraps the dead bird in paper, and gives it to a willing lady in the audience, telling her to unwrap it … and the corpse has turned into a bouquet of flowers… Haven't you seen him conjure away his son? The young man escapes, he chases him, picks him up, folds him in half like a rag, and, like it or not, crams him in the magic box… the boy struggles… one, two! the box is opened… he's gone… then runs up from the depths of the room and does an act of his own. Next to a series of numbers from 1 to 40 the audience write any words they like – drum, turnips, Naples… the father reads the list aloud, and the boy then repeats it, then again backwards…"; and he did it in French, Italian and Spanish.[239]

On January 18th they arrived in Lorient, performing there between January 23rd and 29th.[240] We next see them in Laval in late February, and the newspapers there imply they had also been to Le Havre, Brest and Rennes. They performed in Laval on February 23rd,[241] and Eugenio's advertisements here are interesting on several points. The acts are the same — "GRANDE SOIRÉE Inoptique, Spirite, de Science occulte et de Sténographie mentale, par E. BOSCO ... Sténographie mentale par le nouveau Pic de la Mirandole, ITALO agé de 11 ans... Expériences Psychologiques sur l'Ipnotisée Mlle ÉLISA...", but there are several new points.

First Eugenio says he is the author of a book: *La Prestidigitation de l'Avenir*. I can find no trace of this: he probably wrote it in Italian but again neither *La prestidigitazione del futuro* nor *La prestigiazione del futuro* are recorded. Perhaps he intended to write the book but never published it? However this may have been a later or revised edition of his earlier book, *La magia di viaggi e avventure di Eugenio Bosco: cenni biografici di Prrrr*. Two surviving copies of this are recorded, both of the 3rd edition (Milano: Tipografia di Alessandro Gattinoni, 1865), held in Biblioteca civica di Arco and in Biblioteca nazionale Vittorio Emanuele III – Napoli.

Eugenio now also describes himself as "Membre honoraire de la Société d'Encouragement, *Le Diable Rose* de Florence", and Italo is said to have been "décoré de 3 Médailles des Sociétés d'Encouragement de Milan, Vienne et Naples". These are the various *Società di incoraggiamento,* some of whose records may still be available...

From Laval they headed further north, performing in Amiens on April 16th, in conjunction with the local society *Harmonie d'Amiens,* and receiving an excellent review.[242] Eugenio meanwhile had been writing to the papers again, complaining of the impostor Crémy (B21), probably the same he had set his sights on in 1880 for claiming to be Bosco's son.[243]

We do not catch sight of Eugenio again until November when we find "représentations de magie et de prestidigitation donnés par M. Bosco, le fils du célèbre Bosco bien connu" in Pontivy on November 18th.[244] However, it is hard to believe that this is not the impostor as this is over 500 km south, near Rennes, and only a few days later on November 25th we have the real "Eugène Bosco" still in the north, performing in Saint-Quentin.[245]

Eugenio then did move south, he, Elisa and Italo giving one show in Troyes on December 16th. Here he makes much of his long career ("25 ans de succès") and qualifications, and his act includes "grand vol souterrain à travers la salle".[246] The following week they arrived in Dijon, with shows at the *Salle Guillier* on December 30th and 31st, Eugenio magnetising not only "his subject" Elisa but members of the public.[247]

1883

Bourg-en-Bresse followed in the new year,[248] and in late January they were at the *Théâtre Bellcour* in Lyon,[249] then in early March in Geneva.[250]

We next find "M. Bosco" back in the north, in Coulommiers at the end of the month,[251] then in Nogent-sur-Seine[252] and in Bas-sur-Seine.[253] However, none of these last three shows mentions Italo and Elisa and in Bar-sur-Seine this Bosco is accompanied by a "M. Joann" doing a memory act *à la Italo*, so these may well be the impostor (B21).

Eugenio, Elisa and Italo were not far south in Chalon-sur-Saône, performing there on May 6th, which unfortunately coincided with a local fête, reducing the audience. But Italo was particularly praised for his mental abilities and compared to Henri Mondeux and Giacomo Inaudi.[254]

In late May Eugenio was in Nevers, then on June 6th in Bourges,[255] building up to his performance with the old ploy of asking a stranger for a light, then for the time, only for the other's watch to be mysteriously missing…[256] In August they were in Limoges and Poitiers,[257] then in La Rochelle — "a great success, the hall crowded and many unable to obtain seats… for two hours the clever magician held the audience under his spell…", Elisa "…douée d'une puissance divinatoire étonnante", the closing act "a demonstration of catalepsy in a girl of 12 or 13 … *extase hors centre*", which excited great interest. This is the right age for his daughter Juliette so she may have been the subject.[258]

On September 1st they performed in Rochefort, with a second show added on 6th; Eugenio here advertises his "30 years of success", dating his career from 1853; the previous year in Troyes he had stated "25 years of success", probably dating from his recovery in 1857.[259]

At the end of September they arrived in Saintes, Eugenio "with his wife and two children", deciding to rest for a few days before performing.[260] Their show on October 5th went off so well that they stayed and gave a second on October 9th. The review of the first show exhibits a genuine admiration and enthusiasm: "…his conjuring tricks — *"des tours, (qu'on nous passe le mot) de prestidigitation"* — were of such skill, such dexterity as to deceive even the most perspicacious. We have seen many masters in conjuring but none possessed the subtlety of fingering shown by Bosco the incomparable, the equal of, the superior to his father", describing as an example the same trick which had so impressed the Vannes reviewer in 1882 — unrolling dozens of metres of ribbon from a small cup, winding it into a ball, out of which emerges a live pigeon, he cuts its head off, wraps it in a newspaper, which he unwraps immediately — and out comes a bouquet of flowers — "the trick is done with such astonishing speed and skill that the illusion is complete … Bosco's success was huge with loud applause after every trick, the public awarding a veritable ovation to the most famous thaumaturge and magician of the present day".[261]

On October 7th Eugenio performed in the town of Jonzac: we know this because he wrote to local newspapers soon after, complaining that an impostor using his name (and his good newspaper reviews) had performed at the same time in Saint-Jean-d'Angély, about 70 km north (and with twice the population). He says he has laid a complaint with the police and hopes "this audacious rogue" will soon be unmasked.[262]

At the end of the month he was stated in a Toulouse newspaper to be about to perform there "in a few days",[263] but nothing seems to have come of this, and we lose sight of him till the start of December, when he was reported to be in Pau and to have had recent success in Auch (and also, earlier that year in the summer, to have performed in Royat for Dom Ferdinand II, the former King of Portugal).[264] He was also in Agen about this time, probably prior to Auch.[265]

On December 13th he performed in Oloron-Sainte-Marie. The local paper described the show as well attended, but it was clearly a major disappointment: "M.

Bosco expected fewer spectators and the spectators expected more — he had prepared his *soirée* too poorly; did our friends in Pau tell him that we were not very difficult and above all not very well-informed? Lenient, perhaps, but blind, never!".[266] He was next in Baignères-sur-Bigorre, welcomed as "no less skilful, no less amazing, no less famous than his father",[267] and at the end of the month gave a single performance in Carcassonne.[268]

1884

A nice Bosco anecdote appeared in a Bordeaux paper at this time, in an article on ventriloquists. Bosco was walking downstairs with an old friend, a ventriloquist, chatting together; when they got to the bottom, Mme Bosco was heard from upstairs calling her husband back. But when he got back up, she hadn't said a word, so he realised what was going on. He rejoined the ventriloquist and they continued their walk, till the ventriloquist asked him triumphantly: 'So what did Mme Bosco want?'. 'Oh nothing really', replied Bosco, 'just to return your snuffbox and handkerchief which you left on our table', and he gave these back to the amazed ventriloquist.[269]

Eugenio arrived in Montpellier at the start of 1884, but did not perform there until March;[270] and there was again a report that he would "immediately" perform in Toulouse, again apparently coming to nothing.[271] On January 21st he gave a show in Béziers, "the room was crammed … M. Bosco has a sympathetic demeanour and a good-natured manner … all his tricks were excellently performed".[272] He was in Pézenas on February 13th, performing in the *Salle du spectacle*, then on 15th gave a further show in the premises of the *Cercle catholique*: "I can say, without fear of contradiction, that he literally enchanted his audience…".[273]

In early March they arrived in Cette (Sète) and gave a successful show on March 8th:[274] Eugenio "magnetised" several locals and Italo repeated back a list of forty items. A further show followed on March 15th at the *Cercle catholique*.[275]

They then returned to Montpellier,[276] performing first on March 16th at the *Cercle catholique,* drawing an audience of 400 to 500 people, then at the *théâtre du Gymnase* on March 20th.[277] On the same night another hypnotist, Eugene Verbeck, gave a rival show at the *Grand théâtre*,[278] but Eugenio, despite the *Gymnase*'s reputation of being unlucky,[279] had a very successful night, both he and Italo warmly applauded.[280]

On March 28th they arrived in Marseille.[281] In the years since he was last in Marseille, said one newspaper, "M. Bosco has toured all the European capitals, and speaks almost all known languages … In Germany he saw the magnetiser Jansen and in Paris often went to see the great doctor Charcot, which gave him the idea of introducing demonstrations of hypnotism into his performances".[282] He began by giving a special presentation to the local press on April 5th,[283] then opened to the public on April 24th at the *Théâtre des Nations*,[284] giving only a single performance, "the vast room completely filled" (it held 4,000), and his greatest trick: "making us forget his father".[285]

The following week they were in Aix,[286] where they performed on March 13th,[287] a review praising the wide variety of the acts in the show, conjuring to catalepsy, and the audience enthralled.[288]

In June in Nîmes[289] they gave a single performance on June 13th to a full house who "did not spare their applause".[290] They were still there on June 26th, Eugenio taking part in a gala benefit show for the theatre manager.[290] July saw them in Montauban, where they performed on July 12th, and on July 14th Eugenio also took part in a benefit show for the poor.[291] On August 8th they performed in Arcachon.[292]

In Royan on September 15th at the *Casino* Eugenio suffered the ultimate wardrobe malfunction. Part one of the show went well, but when he called for five members of the audience to come on stage and rotate a table, one noticed that Eugenio had **a hook hidden in his sleeve**: "a lively discussion ensued, the man was manhandled and at Bosco's instigation was about to leave the stage when voices shouted out 'Let him stay. he's a Frenchman'. Bosco, realising he was not going to get the last word, said 'The gentleman stays, but the show is over', and lowered the curtain".[293]

They finally performed in Toulouse in October,[294] Eugenio, Italo, no mention of Elisa, but with *Emma* Zanardelli and Dr May (described as Eugenio's brother-in-law) and Miss Béatrix. They opened at the *théâtre des Nouveautés* on October 30th.[295] A review reported a large and receptive audience, enjoying equally the conjuring, hypnotism and spiritism acts, but the undoubted highlight, "the really amazing thing", was the performance by Italo (billed as "premier mnémoniste du monde").[296] A show on November 7th promised "invisibility illuminated by a light with the power of 100 candles",[297] and on November 13th a special afternoon show was given at a boarding school by Eugenio, Italo, Dr May and M. Kapper, a conjuror.[298] Kapper joined Eugenio again at a matinée and soirée on November 30th at the theatre featuring young local singers and Eugenio with a pantoscope.[299] According to a later report they gave ten shows in Toulouse and their receipts totalled 2,600 francs.[300]

1885

In early 1885 they were back in Montpellier, Eugenio, Italo, Dr May, Emma and Béatrix, with a performance at the *Grand-Théâtre* on January 14th, Dr May promising to reveal the secrets of *false* magnetism and demonstrate the secrets of *true* hypnotism.[301] Eugenio and Italo (apparently without the others) gave a further show on January 23rd at the *Théâtre du Gymnase*,[302] then another for children on 29th for the *Cercle catholique* (grown-ups 1 fr., children 50 cent.), which included a hand-out of sweets, flowers and toys, and a "monster Agioscope, lit by Carlevaris light, with the power of 400 candles".[303]

They then headed to Montélimar, performing there on February 19th.[304] A fortnight later (28 Feb.1885) the local paper printed a biography of Bartolomeo by an anonymous local, but it is merely a collection of anecdotes (one nice one of how he *aced* three Russian officers in St Petersburg).

In June we find Eugenio and Italo in Nîmes, still with Emma and Dr May, performing at the *Grand Théâtre* on June 10th,[305] at the end of the month in Nice,[306] and on July 18th in Draguignan.[307]

By August Eugenio (now with Italo only) was in Turin. *La Stampa* made much of the name and skills he had inherited from his father, "a patrimony of ability", and Italo too would carry this on... Eugenio, still afflicted, we are told, by continuing thefts of his name, and while these may be a source of pride for him, they do cause him harm.[308]

They performed at the *Teatro Vittorio Emanuale* on September 13th but it was not a great success, with part of the audience soon losing interest in Eugenio's now well-worn tricks. A large crowd was eager to enjoy "his demonstrations of magic, illusion (a lot of illusion!), hypnotism, enchantment (not much enchantment!)", and the prodigious mental efforts of Italo: "We do not deny", said *La Stampa*, "that signor Bosco has shown dexterity and elegance in performing some tricks, but, on the other hand, these had whiskers on (*la barba lunga un metro*) and did not arouse any interest. Matters proceeded well enough up to a certain point, then the public became indifferent and began to make a noise. On the one side there was shouting: *enough!* on the other there was applause; in short, it was a stormy and not very amusing evening".[309]

Later this year they performed in Fiume (now Rijeka in Croatia), as we learn from a report on the new theatre there which opened on October 4th: since opening the theatre had hosted operas, plays, and "three Bosco performances".[310]

1886

Early in 1886 they were in Verona and on January 12th Eugenio while standing outside the theatre in the *Piazza Navona* (the *Teatro Nuovo*) talking to Italo suddenly turned pale and held on to the door frame for support saying 'I don't feel well' (*mi sento poco bene*); before he had finished speaking he fell heavily, hitting his head on the footpath. There was a lot of blood and Italo rushed into the theatre for help, the attendants and some passers-by coming to assist. Eugenio, pale as a corpse, was still bleeding heavily from the fall and showed no signs of life. Italo called a cab and took him to where they were staying in the *via San Tommaso*. Two doctors were called and soon realised it was a stroke. Then after an hour Eugenio regained consciousness, insisting he no longer felt any pain — on the contrary he joked about it. The head wound was said to be of no consequence.[311]

Later in the year Eugenio and Italo travelled to Algeria, performing there for several months. From various local papers we get glimpses of them on their travels — August in Guelma[312] and in Batna,[313] September in Oran, and October in Sidi Bel-Abbès.[314]

1887

By early 1887 they were back in France, performing to acclaim at the *casino* in Menton on February 4th.[315]

They now returned to Italy, and while there Eugenio was reportedly asked to give a private performance for Pope Leo XIII in the Vatican. He is said to have knelt before the Pope and to have assured him the Devil had no part in his act. The Pope, we are told, was briefly bewildered when a key which he kept in his pocket was found in the possession of one of the Swiss Guard, and there was laughter all round when Bosco changed a portrait of the Pope's niece into a painted bouquet of roses.[316]

In May 1887 we hear that he was heading to Naples and then to Lecce.[317]

Later in the year they made a second visit to Algeria. From Algiers, where he was said to have had great success in hypnotising both people and animals, they moved on to Mascara,[318] then two shows in Tlemcen, where the paper joked that with hypnotised animals "we feel that the idea of accomplices should be dismissed" ("Nous pensons que l'idée de compères doit être écartée !").[319]

From Algeria they travelled to Spain, giving three performances in Barcelona in early December,[320] before arriving in Perpignan on December 14th.[321]

1888

They remained several months in the south of France, performing in Béziers on January 17th with great success,[322] but Lodève on January 29th did not turn out well. Not only was the carneval a distraction, but the locals remembered being deceived some years earlier by a visiting magician calling himself "Lopez-Bosco" (possibly C31) who, after carefully collecting the takings, gave one sleight-of-hand trick then disappeared by the back door. So the audience for Eugenio was small, and those who missed it, said the local newspaper, need have no regrets — *He is, it appears, a descendant of the famous Bosco, but he has not inherited his talent. He did a few tricks, nothing out of the ordinary, that were reasonably interesting and pleasant, but he had promised too much to be able to satisfy the audience.*[323]

They were in Clermont-l'Hérault on January 31st,[324] then in early February in Montpellier, with the animal hypnotism billed as a novel feature (again: "no accomplices here!") and another new act he and Italo had been working on in Algeria, an execution by the guillotine — with the victim brought back to life if found innocent.[325] The shows on February 8th and 10th were labelled "brilliant successes".[326]

They were next in Nîmes, where both Bartolomeo and Eugenio had done so well over the years, performing at the *Théâtre d'Été* on March 5th.[327] In the nearby commune of Les Aires a recent local election had been called void due to fraud and a new date announced, but even for this, said the local paper, *our Boscos have more than one trick up their sleeve.*[328]

On March 8th Eugenio and Italo performed at the *Folies Arlésiennes* in Arles,[329] and on 21st at the *Eden-Théâtre* in Avignon, having failed to come to terms with the management of the *Grand-Théâtre*.[330]

In April they were in Lyon, a *grande séance* preceding a ball at the *Villa des Fleurs*, with part of the takings going to charity.[331]

At the end of the year Eugenio was in Italy. On December 24th 1888 he performed, by his own account, before the Queen of Italy, Margherita of Savoy.[332]

1889

In September 1889 he arrived in Trieste from Gorizia. He performed in Trieste on October 5th and 6th at the *Anfiteatro Fenice* and was well written up in *Il Piccolo*, which hailed him as "the Nestor of Italian magicians".[333] But when it came to review his show, while conceding that the public enjoyed his human and animal hypnotism act, *Il Piccolo* said bluntly: "…But Bosco has a very great defect, a defect to which we are all unfortunately subject and from which not even he, with all his magical art, can escape: Bosco has aged, and a lot…".[334]

1890

The following year we find him in Graz in April[335] and in Laibach (Ljubljana) in June,[336] then at the end of the year back in Turin. where Eugenio did not give a series of public performances but on November 28th took part in a charity show on behalf of the children's hospital at the *teatro Scribe* which included plays by pupils of Cav. Bassi of the scuola Maria Lætitia. Alas: this "did not have the desired outcome: the expenses exceeded the takings by 178 lire".[337] However, the following week Eugenio gave a very successful private performance at *La conferenza all'Alleanza Mutua Cooperativa*.[338]

1891

In early February 1891 an "E. Bosco, Wien" is listed as staying in Budapest at the Hotel Europa. This was almost certainly not Eugenio as we know he was in Genoa on January 25th. But interestingly at the head of the same page is a list of Deaths in Budapest ("Verstorbene in Budapest"). Could it have been a cursory misreading of this page by Wellmann or by Houdini (or presumably his researcher) that led to the erroneous statement that Eugenio "died miserably in Hungary in 1891"?[339]

On January 25th 1891 Eugenio took part in an "Evening of Magic on behalf of Prof. Eugenio Bosco" put on as a benefit for him by members of the *Unione Illusionisti Herrmann* at the rooms of the Genoa *Società degli Impiegati Civili dello Stato* (Union of Civil Servants). The evening included acts by local magicians — then followed (said a review by Orazio Eton in *L'Illusionista*) "[tr.] Prof. Eugenio Bosco who was to be the highlight of the evening. First of all, I am not competent to criticize Bosco, but I will limit myself to expressing my opinion. One sees in Eugenio Bosco the artist, the artist, I would say exhausted by his great work, exhausted by the many misfortunes of which he was the target but which did not succeed in making him lose the cheerfulness that is due and necessary to the magician nor his interesting patter intertwined with jokes and anecdotes that keep an audience happy. The customary *bon mot* is part of what makes the show amusing, and Bosco knows this. But Bosco must confess that he is no longer the magician of twenty or thirty years ago. We see in him the glimpses of the true, great, unsurpassable artist, but his age, the accumulation of his misfortunes, have now rendered him barely suited to the art of prestidigitation. This is only natural. He no longer possesses the necessary agility and dexterity that one has in youth… However, he possesses an ease of mastering his audience, which is difficult, indeed very difficult. Some of his tricks were well appreciated… Overall, he received thunderous applause and several encores…".[340]

Soon afterwards an interview with Eugenio was published in the same periodical on the subject of Bartolomeo's feat in famously making all the watches at the German Emperor's court strike the same time.[341]

Perhaps Eugenio took the criticisms of his performance as a challenge, for he was soon back on the road, touring the south of France where he and Bartolomeo had both been so successful over the years. In June 1891 he was in Nice, performing at the *théâtre Français* on June 11th,[342] the following month in Marseille, at the *Alcalzar* on July 30th,[343] and in August in Béziers. This is announced as "his final tour in Europe" and he is accompanied by his pupil Callet.[344] He and Callet then performed in Toulouse at the *Théâtre des Nouveautés* in September.[345]

1892

By February 1892 Eugenio was back in Turin, where he announced a forthcoming performance by himself and his pupils "as the start of his last artistic tour of Europe — despite bad luck, his hair turned white with age, and considerations of his health".[346] This performance, it seems, never eventuated.

However, we catch a final glimpse of him three months later. In May that year he signs a testimonial for Bartolomeo Marchelli (C34), affirming that he was Bartolomeo Bosco's apprentice for two years from 1854. Eugenio signed this on May 12th in Diano Maurizio (Provincia di Porto Maurizio), witnessed by the mayor.[347]

Diano Marino is in Liguria, south-west of Genoa, and it is probably there that Eugenio was living when he disappears from sight after this date.

His death date is unknown. He is described as deceased when Italo married in 1906, but Elisa is still alive.

NOTES

[1] Printed in the *Illustrirte Zeitung* [Leipzig] 2 April 1859. Eugenio wrote to the paper from Bamberg thanking them for this article and the splendid illustration of him and requested to be sent twelve copies (for the letter see note 61 below).

[2] It is in French: perhaps it had to be in French to be valid under French law.

[3] It is uncertain whether Eugenio already had this or whether Bartolomeo was now giving it to him to launch a professional magic career. I believe the latter.

[4] *M.U.M., Society of American Magicians Monthly*, vol.7 no.60, March 1918, p.3, online at url:086.

[5] Harry Houdini papers, Container 21.17: "... Agreement (French) between Bosco and his son Eugene with several typed English translations, 20 May 1852", url:087. (Not digitised but they will provide a copy.)

[6] *Leeuwarder Courant* 16, 20 July 1852: "Séance de Magie Egyptienne et de Prestidigitation, door den beroemden *E. BOSCO (Zoon)*".

[7] *Provinciale Overijsselsche en Zwolsche courant* 30 July 1852.

[8] *Rotterdamsche Courant* 10 Aug.1852. *Nieuwe Rotterdamsche courant* 12 Aug. 1852.

[9] *Opregte Haarlemsche Courant* 4 Sep.1852: "... De Pyramide van Cristal, uitgevoerd door den Heer Melino van Londen. Séance de Magie Égyptienne et de Prestidigitation, door den beroemden *E. BOSCO* Zoon".

[10] *Algemeen Handelsblad* 13 Sep.1852; also mentioned in Maria Keyser *Komt dat Zien!, De Amsterdamse kermis in de negentiende eeuw*, pp.40, 162.

[11] *Les Tablettes des Deux-Charentes* 1 Sep.1883.

[12] *Le Petit Troyen* 17 Dec.1882.

[13] In his later advertising (such as *Intelligenzblatt für die Stadt Bern* 17 July 1866) Eugenio claimed he performed for the King of Holland on December 8th 1863 [*sic*] but he was in the Middle East at that time.

[14] *Courrier de L'Escaut* 22 Sep.1856. The anecdote has him, predictably, buying eggs in a market — but this time they start to dance, floating like balloons...

[15] *Courrier de L'Escaut* 25, 26, Sep.1856 (*arrètez* so accented).

[16] *Courrier de L'Escaut* 27 Sep.1856.

[17] *L'Émancipation* 2 Oct.1856: "fils de célèbre prestidigitateur ... quoique jeune encore, M. Bosco est déjà le digne émule de son père"; *Algemeen Handelsblad* 4 Oct.1856: "De zoon van den beroemden goochelaar Bosco is alhier aangekomen. Ofschoon nog jong, is hij reeds een waardige mededinger zijns vaders".

[18] *L'Indépendance Belge* 16 Oct.1856.

[19] *L'Indépendance Belge* 20 Oct.1856.

[20] *L'Émancipation* 20 Oct.1856.

[21] *L'Émancipation* 22 Oct.1856; *L'Indépendance Belge* 27 Oct.1856.

[22] *Journal De Charleroi* 28, 29, 30 Oct.1856.

[23] *Journal De Charleroi* 1 Nov.1856. Carpentier, cashier of James Rothschild's railway company, stole 3 million francs; he was caught in America and sentenced to three years in the galleys.

[24] *L'Émancipation* 19 Nov.1856; *L'Indépendance belge* 21 Nov.1856.

[25] *Fremden Blatt* 6 to 18 Mar. 1857: "...Soirée amusante des Herrn BOSCO *Fiz.* (Prestidigitateur)": *Morgen Post* 11 Mar.1857 ("Boskofitz").

[26] *Deutsche Allgemeine Zeitung* 7 May 1857 (and widely reprinted).

[27] *Würzburger Stadt- und Landbote* 7 May 1857; *Vereinigte Laibacher Zeitung* 15 May 1857.

[28] *Fränkischer Kurier* 3 Aug.1857; *Würzburger Stadt- und Landbote* 5 Aug.1857, quoting the *Erfurter Zeitung* ("has the use of seven fingers").

[29] *Nordböhmischer Gebirgsbote* 24 Oct.1857: "Du Ratz, weeßte och schun, daß der Suhn vom ahlen Tausendkünstler Bosco ißt in unserer Gegend is? / Jo, das ha ich gehiert. Weeßte aber, ob er och seines Vater's Kunststücke und witz mit gebracht hat? / Das verstieht sich von selber, das weeß mer ißt schun. / Do will ich aber die Gesichter bei uns sahn, wenn er seine Kunststücke den Leuten vor macht, do wär'n Manchem de Ogen uff doer übergiehn".

[30] *Gazeta Wielkiego Xięstwa Poznańskiego* 24, 25 Nov.1857 ("...Przybył w tych dniach do Poznania syn sławnego Bosco, który i zręcznością i rysami i całą postacią przypomina ojca swego...").

[31] *Kurjer Warszawski* 11 Dec.1857: "*Bosco*. syn znanego w Warszawie Sztukmistrza *Bosco*, daje przedstawienia w Wrocławiu à la Bosco".

[32] *Kronika Wiadomości Krajowych i Zagranicznych* 7 Dec.1857: "Drugi artysta, w téj chwili jeszcze u nas bawiący, ma tyle co i Wieniawski powodzenia, choć sztuki jego innego zupełnie są rodzaju. Jest to *Bosco*, syn słynnego kuglarza, godnego następcy

Pinetego i Filadelfji. Po tém, co wyrabia, widać, że synaczek nie tylko był w dobréj szkole, ale że i wyśmienicie korzystał z nauk przez ojca dawanych. Zręczność jego nadzwyczaj jest wielka, sztuki po większej części nowe a zadziwiające, on sam bardzo miły, a zatem nie dziwota, kiedy zamiast Bosco nazywają go *Boskim*".

[33] Survey of theatrical activity in Königsberg dated December 31st in the Klaipéda paper *Memeler Dampfboot* 6 Jan.1858: "…Ferner haben wir einen Taschenspieler Bosco jun., den Sohn des berühmten Zauberers und eine Kunstreiter-Gesellschaft in unseren Mauern, die beide stets ein zahlreiches Publikum anziehen".

[34] *Kurjer Warszawski* 4, 5 Feb.1858.

[35] *Kurjer Warszawski* 8 Feb.1858" "Już donieśliśmy o przybyciu do Warszawy P. Bosco, magika. Winniśmy przeto Czytelnikom, objaśnienie, to jest, że przybyły pod tem imieniem magik, jest to Eugenjusz Bosco (syn znanego czarnoksiężnika), w niczem nienstępujący Ojcu swojemu. Nie przytaczamy tu na dowód żadnych gazet zagranicznych, które oddaja mu nadzwyczajne pochwały, gdyż mieliśmy sposobność widzenia go sami, a raczej niektóre z sztuk jego. dowodzące nadzwyczajnej zręczności. P. Bosco jest młody, pełen wyrazu w twarzy, pełen ognia, i z wielkim talentem, zabawiający widzów. Powierzchownością swoją i manierami ujmuje, a zręcznością czaruje prawie, patrzących na niego. Po tem wszystkiem cośmy dotąd widzieli, możemy rokowoć powodzenie u uas P. Bosco, jeżeli tylko wystąpi".

[36] *Kurjer Warszawski* 16, 18 Feb.1858.

[37] *Deutsche Allgemeine Zeitung* 18 Mar.1858.

[38] Advertisement in *Deutsche Allgemeine Zeitung* 10 Apr.1858; in the same issue Eugenio points out that the Bosco who attempted suicide in Manchester was not his father (see B12 p.232).

[39] Held in the Stadtmuseum Leipzig; online at url:088 (and elsewhere).

[40] *Vossische Zeitung* 10, 11, 12, 13 June 1858: "…des jungen Bosco … des großen Magiers größeren Sohn … *soirée fantastique* des Signor A. Bosco jr., Hofkünstler Ihrer Majestät der Königin Victoria von England u. Ritter der Ehrenlegion …".

[41] Receiving treatment on his injured hand according to *Magdeburgische Zeitung* 4 Feb.1859.

[42] *Vossische Zeitung* 16 June 1858:
"Geehrter Herr Redacteur!
    Ich habe so eben in einem Artikel Ihres Journals gelesen, welchem zufolge ein Sohn des berühmten B o s c o Vorstellungen in Krolls Etablissement giebt. Natürlicher Weise finde ich mich zu der Anfrage veranlaßt, wie dieses sein kann, da der einzige Sohn B o s c o ' s sich diesen Augenblick seiner Gesundheit wegen in Karlsbad befindet. Der Herr, der sich für einen Sohn des berühmten B o s c o ausgiebt, würde ein Pseudo-Bosco sein, da der Unterzeichnete vollgütige Beweise in

Händen hat, daß er der einzige Sohn jenes B o s c o ist, der zu seiner Zeit die Welt in Erstaunen setzte.

Der gegenwärtig in Berlin anwesende B o s c o kann daher nur ein Homonyme, wenn nicht, ein falscher B o s c o sein. Der name B o s c o wurde übrigens schon von vielen mißbraucht, um sich dadurch ein Publikum zu verschaffen, welches sie sich keineswegs durch Talente oder Geschicklichkeit zu verschaffen gewußt hätten.

Uebrigens überlasse ich es dem Interesse der Polizei, diesen B o s c o bei Kroll zu veranlassen, den Beweis zu führen, daß er wirklich sei, für den er sich ausgiebt. Ich will zugeben, daß Ihrem Artikel zufolge dieser Herr wirklich B o s c o heiße, aber nimmer kann noch werde ich gestatten, daß er sich für einen jüngeren Sohn des berühmten B o s c o ausgebe.

Eugêne B o s c o fils.

[43] *Kurjer Warszawski* 21 Nov.1858: "Dzienniki Bremeńskie nie mogą się nasycić pochwałami nad młodym Eugenjuszem Bosco, który daje swoje przedstawienia w tem mieście. Pomimo wysokich cen wejścis, jedosk teatr zawaze jest przepłoiony Publicznością".

[44] *Ost-Deutsche Post* 25 Nov.1858 (and elsewhere).

[45] *Berlinische Nachrichten* 5 Nov.1858. I give only abridged paraphrases of these encomia.

[46] *Berlinische Nachrichten* 25 Nov.1858.

[47] *Berlinische Nachrichten* 30 Nov.1858.

[48] *Berlinische Nachrichten* 7, 21 Dec.1858; *Gazeta Codzienna* 24 Dec.1858. In a poster produced in 1860 Eugenio states he performed for the Prince Regent twice, on December 12th and 23rd. One performance was illustrated in the article on Eugenio in the *Illustrirte Zeitung* [Leipzig] 2 April 1859 (see note 1); the illustration is online at url:089.

[49] *Kladderdatsch* 12 Dec.1858 (reprinted *Augsburger Anzeigeblatt* 19 Dec.1858; and elsewhere) — "Mesdame et Messieurs! Sie sehen in mir keine gewöhniklike Taschenspieler, was macken seine Stücke, um zu nehmen der Geld ..."

[50] *Der Humorist* 26 Feb.1859, and Eugenio also gives the same number in his later advertisements.

[51] *Magdeburgische Zeitung* 4, 6 , 8 , 9, 10, 11 Feb.1859.

[52] *Magdeburgische Zeitung* 23 Feb.1859.

[53] *Fremden-Blatt* 26 Feb.1859, staying at the Hotel National; *Ost-Deutsche Post* 3 Mar.1859 ("arrived last Saturday").

[54] *Zwischen-Akt* 26 Feb.1859 ("sobald die obrigkeitliche Bewilligung erhalten").

[55] *Der Humorist* 26 Feb.1859.

[56] *Ost-Deutsche Post* and *Zwischen-Akt* 4 Mar.1859 ("eingetretene Hindernisse").

[57] *Münchener Tages-Anzeiger* 10 Mar.1859 ("Bosco, Künstler v. Turin": this is certainly Eugenio; Bartolomeo was in Marseille).

[58] *Fränkischer Kurier* 4 Apr.1859.

[59] *Tag-Blatt der Stadt Bamberg* 7, 8 April 1859.

[60] *Bamberger Zeitung* 8 Apr.1859; *Tag-Blatt der Stadt Bamberg* 11 Apr.1859.

[61] The letter is in the Stadtgeschichtliches Museum Leipzig. Eugenio oddly misdated it "6.4.1856" instead of "6.4.1859". The letter is now digitised on the Museum's website: the direct url is too long to reproduce but it can be found by searching for "objekt A0000973".

[62] *Czas* 6 May 1859: "Eugeniusz Bosko artysta z Lipska" at the Hotel Rosyjski.

[63] *Czas* 15, 17 May 1859; *Krakauer Zeitung* 16 May 1859.

[64] *Czas* 20 May 1859. He clearly knew some Russian despite not having performed there yet, lending credence to the details in his *Illustrirte Zeitung* biography that he had gone there with his father as a boy and spent "four years in a 'Kadetten-pensionat' in St Petersburg".

[65] *Der Zwischen-Akt* 27 May 1859.

[66] *Czas* 10 May 1859: "Józefina Muntzel, Atalida Bosco artystki z Lipska"; *Czas* 24 May 1859: "Wyjechali… Eugeniusz Bosco, Atalida Bosco, Józefina Muntzel Bosco". See *Excursus on Family*: *Atalida* is a very uncommon name and it is hard to believe this is not his sister Adelaide, the singer. Józefina Muntzel Bosco remains unidentified but surely a relative.

[67] *Czas* 20 May 1859: "…We have heard that this chiromagician is going to Lviv, where he is to give his performances". No mention is found of him in *Gazeta Lwowska,* but the Cieszyn paper *Gwiazdka Cieszyńska* (25 June 1859) reported under 'Correspondence from Lviv' that *Bosco, son of the grandmaster, has been floating clouds of dust before our eyes…*

[68] *Pesth-Ofner Localblatt und Landbote* 16, 19, 20, 23, 24 Nov.1859.

[69] *Fränkischer Wald* 23 Nov.1859; *Le Journal des Débats* 1 Dec.1859; *Gazeta Warszawska* 4 Dec.1859 (etc.).

[70] *Ost-deutsche Post* 31 Jan.1860; *Zwischen-Akt* 1 Feb.1860 ("…überdies in seinen Leistungen nach übereinstimmenden Berichten seinen Vater weit übertrifft").

[71] *Fremden-Blatt* 5 Feb.1860; *Ost-deutsche Post* 6 Feb.1860; *Wiener Zeitung* 10 Feb.1860.

[72] *Fremden-Blatt* 10 Feb.1860; *Der Humorist* 20 Feb.1860.

[73] *Fremden-Blatt* 18 Feb.1860; *Der Zwischen-Akt* (23 Feb.1860) joked that he had been seen at the shop of hat-maker Herr Flebus, whose famous 'hat-machine' turned hares into hats, while Bosco conjured hares out of hats, and if Flebus decorated hats *for* women, Bosco decorated hats *with* women.

[74] *Fremden-Blatt* 22 Feb.1860.

[75] *Der Humorist* 26 Mar.1860; *Tetschner Anzeiger* 21 Apr.1860. In later advertisements Eugenio also claimed to have performed for the Austrian Emperor on April 9th this year.

[76] *Fremden-Blatt* 14 Apr.1860; *Zwischen-Akt* 17 Apr.1860.

[77] *Tetschner Anzeiger* 28 Apr.1860.

[78] *Tagesbote* 5, 8, 10, 11, 12 May 1860.

[79] Listed as recently arrived at his Vienna hotel, E. Bosco from Prague, in *Fremden-Blatt* 15 May 1860. (Two days later, arriving at a different hotel, are "E. Bosco, Artiste" and "Fr. J. Bosco", both from Paris, *Fremden-Blatt* 17 May 1860; they were singers and were not relatives of Eugenio.)

[80] *Der Zwischen-Akt* 25. May 1860: "…Gastvorstellung des Herrn Eugen Bosco in drei Abtheilungen… Das Erscheinen einer Dame aus einem Männerhute … Das Verschwinden zweier Dame … Der Spaziergang der Antipoden (Gegenfüßler")…".

[81] *Fremden-Blatt* 27 May 1860; *Zwischen-Akt* 28 May 1860 (enjoying his idiosyncratic German); *Morgen Post* 30 May 1860 (noting the three new tricks: The Two Ladies Vanishing, The Cards Torn and Restored, and the Antipodean Walk); the last advertisement found is in *Ost-Deutsche Post* 31 May 1860.

[82] *Figaro* 2 June 1860; *Der Humorist* 4 June 1860; *Die Wiener Elegante* 7 June 1860.

[83] *Frankfurter Nachrichten. Extrabeilage zum 'Intelligenz-Blatt der freien Stadt Frankfurt'* 22, 29 Aug., 2 Sep.1860.

[84] *Mannheimer Anzeiger* 8 Sep.1860.

[85] *Journal de Genève* 30 Oct., 6 Nov.1860.

[86] *L'Entr'acte lyonnais* 16 Dec.1860; *Le Sémaphore de Marseille* 23 Feb.1861.

[87] *Mémorial de la Loire et de la Haute-Loire* 11, 14, 15 Jan.1861.

[88] *Le Sémaphore de Marseille* 12, 16 Feb.1861; the anecdote was widely reprinted.

[89] *Le Sémaphore de Marseille* 27 Feb.; 1, 3, 7 Mar.1861; *La Presse théâtrale* 10 Mar.1861.

[90] *Estafette de Vaucluse* 14 Apr.; 5 Mar.1861.

[91] *Courrier du Gard* 23 May 1861; *L'Opinion du Midi* 29 May 1861.

[92] *Le Messager du Midi* 9 June 1861 (now listing Russia amongst the countries he had performed in, which was untrue).

[93] *Le Messager du Midi* 12, 16 June 1861.

[94] *Le Publicateur de Béziers* 28 June 1861 (again claiming to have "arrived from Germany and Russia").

[95] *Le Publicateur de béziers* 5 July 1861.

[96] *Journal des Pyrénées Orientales* July 3, 27, 31 1861.

[97] *Le Courrier de l'Aude* 10 July 1861; 10 Aug.1861; *Panurge* 18 Aug.1861.

[98] *L'Indépendant des Basses-Pyrénées* 1 Dec.1883.

[99] *La Gironde* 17, 23, 24 Feb.1862 ("Escamotage sans cabinet et sans instruments, genre nouveau crée par M. Ch. Bosco").

[100] *Courrier de Bayonne* 9, 23 Apr.1862.

[101] *L'Indépendant de la Charente-Inférieure* 27 May 1862.

[102] *L'Écho rochelais* 18 June 1862.

[103] *Le Nouvelliste de La Rochelle* 18, 21 June 1862, quoting his letter to the newspaper ("…on voulait m'imposer des conditions exorbitantes, que je n'ai subies dans aucune ville…") with a note by the editor on his "bad grace"; the letter was also reprinted in *L'Indépendant de la Charente-Inférieure* 26 June 1862.

[104] *Le Courrier de Bourges* 15, 17 Aug.1862; *Journal du Cher* 16, 21 Aug.1862.

[105] *Le Var* 9 Oct.1862.

[106] *Le Phare de la Loire* 18 Nov.1862.

[107] *Intelligenzblatt für die Stadt Bern* 17 July 1866.

[108] *Le Sémaphore de Marseille* 27 Nov.1863 (8,000 francs); *Fränkischer Kurier* 17 Dec.1863 and *Fremden-Blatt* 18 Dec.1863 (50,000 piastres for two performances).

[109] *Journal de Constantinople* 19 Feb.1864 (p.169). There follows an extract from the evening's programme, which I reproduce as printed:
  Bosco, fontaine, volaille et nourrice (expérience présentée pour la 1re fois en habit par Bosco devant S.M. le roi de Saxe.)
  La Société dira: *Arrêtez arrêtez, arrêtez !*; expérience de Bosco père;
  4,500,000 francs.
  On ne saura pas l'heure qu'il est, (expérience créée et présentée pour la première fois au théâtre Alexandre à Saint-Petersbourg.)
  Les morts (ressuscités par Bosco père.) [*the opening bracket should probably precede* par]
This year of the *Journal de Constantinople* is online at url:090.

[110] *Wiener Sonn- und Montags-Zeitung* 24 July 1876; also in *Wiener Theater-Chronik* 28 July; 3 Aug.1876 (*Fiction:* F37).

[111] *London Daily News* 25 May 1864 (report from an Athens correspondent dated May 9th); reprinted in other U.K. papers.

[112] Anecdote of Eugenio making mischief when buying a roll of ribbon in a dress shop, quoted from "a Trieste paper of 29 March 1865" in *Le Chroniqueur* [Fribourg, in Romandy] 30 Aug.1866.

[113] *Journal de Génève* 21 May 1865; *Le Temps* and *Le Siècle* 22 May 1865; and soon widely reprinted in papers as far afield as England and Poland. The Lausanne paper *L'Estafette* summed up: "This piece of audacity caused a sensation. Some of the public protested; most clapped".

[114] "I giuochi di Bosco anche a san Carlo martedì sera cominciarono bene e finirono male. I primi erano graziosi e furono applauditi; ma quando volle toccare un tasto, cioè quello di voler fare liquefare il sangue di Venere, il pubblico se ne indispetti e gridò *basta, basta !* Veramente quella roba rossa in un vasetto aperto, poi venuta liquida è tale inezia da essere non solo non paragonabile a un miracolo, ma neppure ad uno scherzo, sapendo fin l'ultimo farmacista, come si rende liquido un qualunque impasto. Il signor Bosco volle affrontare una divozione del popolo napoletano, ed affrontò invece la sua disapprovasione". This is quoted in an article in the Catholic periodical *Fiori Cattolici* (Anno Quarto, Vol.VII, Naples 1865) pp.128-9 (part of a longer article, 'Il Sangue di S. Gennaro' pp.121-9, by Giovanni P. Maestro Vitelli): on Google Books. One wonders if Eugenio's recipe for fake blood matched that in the *Gabinetto magico* (LIt9-15 below; not, of course, actually written by Bartolomeo).

[115] Napoleone Pietrucci, *Biografia degli Artisti Padovani* (Padua, 1858) pp.284-5; *Biographisches Lexikon des Kaiserthums Oesterreich* vol.59 (Vienna, 1890) pp.154-5.

[116] Reproduced in Rusconi p.220.

[117] *Intelligenzblatt für die Stadt Bern* 17 July 1866 (though several of the dates he lists there are clearly incorrect).

[118] *Nürnberger Journal* 2 Feb.1866.

[119] *Neue Freie Presse* 14 Apr.1866 ("Der bekannte Zauberkünstler Bosco (Sohn) ist in Dresden gestorben"); then *Mémorial de la Loire et de la Haute-Loire* 24 Apr.1866; *Le Petit Journal* 26 Apr.1866; etc.

[120] *Journal de Génève* 15 May 1866. Here and elsewhere in Switzerland they were on the heels of Moreni (C39), billing himself as "Bosco's sole pupil", whose act had grown very similar to Eugenio's, with electrical effects, exposing the Davenports, and his wife doing a clairvoyance and memory act.

[121] *Journal de Génève* 20 May 1866.

[122] *L'Express: feuille d'avis de Neuchâtel* 30 May; 2 June 1866.

[123] *Intelligenzblatt für die Stadt Bern* 16 July 1866.

[124] *Intelligenzblatt für die Stadt Bern* 17, 20, 23 July 1866. This paper printed no reviews, but *Der Bund* 20 July 1866 reported a full audience and hearty applause.

[125] *Le Chroniqueur* 31 July; 2, 5 Aug.1866.

[126] *Le Chroniqueur* 7 Aug. 1866 ("une indisposition de Madame Bosco" — often a euphemism for pregnancy or parturition).

[127] List of recent deaths in Fribourg in *Le Chroniqueur* 8 Sep. 1866: "Un enfant féminin d'Eugène Bosco, de Hambourg".

[128] *Le Chroniqueur* 30 Aug.; 6 Sep.1866.

[129] *L'Estafette* 3, 10 Sep.1866; *Le Nouvelliste vaudois* 6, 11 Sep.1866; *Gazette de Lausanne* 11 Sep.1866; *Le Confédéré* and *Gazette du Valais* 16 Sep.1866.

[130] *L'Estafette* 13, 17 Sep.1866; *Gazette de Lausanne* 18 Sep.1866.

[131] *Le Confédéré* 16 Sep.1866; *Nouvelle Feuille d'Avis des districts de Vevey, Aigle et Oron* 25 Sep.1866.

[132] *Gazzetta di Treviso* 8 Dec.1866.

[133] *Gazzetta di Treviso* 11 Dec.1866.

[134] Florence correspondent of *Gazzetta di Treviso* 21 Mar.1867.

[135] *La Stampa* 21 Oct.1867: "degno figlio del papà di tutti I prestidigitatori".

[136] Gandini, *Cronistoria dei teatri di Moderna dal 1539 al 1871:* "sera straordinaria di prestigio sul sistema Americano data da Eugenio Bosco".

[137] Noted in 'Teatro Sociale di Voghera 1800-1912': Archivio Storico Civico di Voghera (url:091).

[138] *Leitmeritzer Wochenblatt* 14 Mar.1868.

[139] *Le Var* 9 July 1868.

[140] There is abundant contemporary and modern discussion of the Zanardellis, but no one, as far as I am aware, has clarified how Dante was related to Elisa and her father and to Emma Zanardelli, who performed with her husband Domenico. Dante's book, *La verità sull'ipnotismo, Rivelazioni* (Rome, 1886) includes a portrait of Emma.

Dante was born *ca.*1856 (we know this from Italo's marriage registration: see B3), so being twenty years younger than Elisabetta he is probably not her brother. In 1879-1880 and 1884 Eugenio and Elisa were joined by "Dr May", and in Toulouse in 1884 Dr May is performing with Emma Zanardelli (and young Béatrix) and he is stated to be Eugenio's brother-in-law. This suggests he was married to the sister of

Eugenio's wife Elisa, so perhaps Emma was Elisa's sister and Béatrix the daughter of Emma and May. So could Dr May also be Domenico?

[141] *L'Opinion du Midi* 19 July 1868; *Courrier du Gard* 21 July 1868.

[142] *L'Opinion du Midi* 22 July 1868. The secretary is presumably the G.B. Tavini [*sic*] noted in *Ye Olde Magic Mag* 7,3 (June 2021) as writing the promotional booklet on Antonio Zanardelli.

[143] *Courrier du Gard* 31 July; 13 Aug.1868; *L'Opinion du Midi* 2, 12, 14 Aug.1868.

[144] *Courrier du Gard* and *L'Opinion* 19 Aug.1868.

[145] *Le Messager du Midi* 20, 22 Aug.1868.

[146] *Le Temps* 1 Sep.1868.

[147] *Le Petit Journal* 24 June 1869; *Le Figaro* 25 June 1869.

[148] Alessandro Raggi e Luigi Raggi. *Il Teatro comunale di Cesena; memorie cronologiche, 1500-1905* (Cesena: G. Vignuzzi, 1906); online at url:092.

[149] *Süddeutsche Post* 20 July 1871: "[tr.] The magician Herr Eugen Bosco (son of the famous old Bosco), who in Naples publicly imitated the miracle of St Januarius, is here…".

[150] *Klagenfurter Zeitung* 22 July 1871.

[151] *Süddeutsche Post* 16 Sep.1871. The same account appeared in *Die Presse* 13 Sep.1871 and *Klagenfurter Zeitung* 17 Sep.1871 but setting it in Hermannstadt (modern Sibiu); a note in *Die Presse* 6 Oct.1871 makes it clear that Temesvar was correct.

[152] *Gazeta Narodowa* 26 Jan.1872: "Przyjechali do Lwowa, d. 25. stycznia: [...] Hotel Angelski: [...] E. Bosco z Turynn, D. Zanardelli z Neapolu".

[153] *Böhm.-Kamnitzer Anzeiger* 10 Feb.1872: "Turner-Jux-Abend am 13. Feber 1872 in der städt. Keller-Restauration in Böhm. Kamnitz…". The following week's entertainment was "the magician and card-performer Herr C. Hofmann from Munich", who I suspect is probably the same as "K. Hofmann" (C23) advertising himself in the 1860s as "[tr.] artist in magic and pupil of the famous Bosco": it may even have been him doing the Bosco act the week before.

[154] *Grazer-Zeitung* 6 Mar.1872; *Grazer Journal* 7 Mar.1872; *Tages-Post* [Graz] 7, 10 Mar.1872.

[155] *Grazer Volksblatt* 10, 12 Mar.1872. Dante's 'Great Efforts in the Art of Memory' suggests he was Italo's mentor in his future act.

[156] *Grazer Volksblatt* 13 Mar.1872.

[157] *Grazer Journal* 12, 13 Mar.1872.

[158] *Die Drau* 22 Aug.1872 ("[tr.] will give one or two shows here next week; brilliantly executed conjuring tricks together with his imitation of the cabinet and table tricks of the Brothers Davenport…").

[159] Quoted *Deutsche Zeitung* 21 Sep.1872.

[160] Mentioned in Warsaw papers in February: *Kurjer Codzienny* 4 Feb.1873.

[161] The January issues of *Dziennik polski* are not accessible online, but reported by *Gazeta Narodowa* 13 Jan.1873.

[162] *Kraj* 14 Jan.1873: "Eug. Bosco prof. mag. z Neapolu" staying at the Hotel Victoria.

[163] *Czas* 18 Jan.1873.

[164] *Kraj* 18 Jan.1873.

[165] *Kurjer Warszawski* 24 Jan.1873. The original text is given in the *Excursus on the Family*.

[166] *Kurjer Warszawski* 27 Jan.1873.

[167] *Kurjer Warszawski* 29 Jan.1873.

[168] *Kurjer Codzienny* 4 Feb.1873, p.2.

[169] *Kuryer Codzienny* 30 Jan.1873.

[170] *Kurjer Warszawski* 3, 5 Feb.1873; *Kuryer Codzienny* 4 Feb.1873.

[171] *Kurjer Warszawski* 6 Feb.1873.

[172] *Kuryer Codzienny* 8 Feb.1873. Eugenio's confederate here, Mr Rideli who spoke only German, was possibly from Temeswar, where listings on *ancestry.com* suggest that the name Rideli was common.

[173] *Kłosy* 13 Feb.1873.

[174] *Kaliszanin: gazeta miasta Kalisza i jego okolic* 18 Feb.1873.

[175] *Prager Abendblatt* 4, 10 July 1873.

[176] *Linzer Volksblatt* 1, 2 Aug.1873.

[177] *Tages-Post* [Linz] 5 Aug.1873.

[178] *Brünner Zeitung* 18 Aug.1873; *Illustrirtes Wiener Extrablatt* 21 Aug.1873.

[179] *Brünner Zeitung* 23 Aug.1873.

[180] *Brünner Zeitung* 26 Aug.1873.

[181] *Die Neue Zeit: Olmüzer politische Zeitung* 31 Aug.1873; *Deutsches Volksblatt für Mären* 8 Sep.1873.

[182] The only evidence is a record in the Archivio di Stato di Piacenza (url:093), where the online index lists "Programma della serata del celebre mago Bosco (1873)".

[183] *Didaskalia* 7 Feb.1874, quoting Wiesbaden *Rheinischer Courier* 13 Jan.1874.

[184] Quoted by *Innsbrucker Nachrichten* 7 Apr.1874.

[185] *Innsbrucker Nachrichten* 3, 4, 7 Apr.1874; *Der Bote für Tirol* 7 Apr.1874.

[186] *Bozner Zeitung* 8, 11, 13 Apr.1874.

[187] *Saazer Hopfenzeitung und Lokal-Anzeiger* 16 July 1874.

[188] *Le Midi* 15 May 1880; *Le Var* 14 Nov.1880.

[189] Raggi, *Il Teatro Comunale di Cesena, memorie cronologiche, 1500-1905* p.255.

[190] *La Stampa* 5 Mar.1875 ("un bellissimo trattenimento umoristico di prestidigitazione").

[191] *La Stampa* 6 Mar.1875 ("... presentando fra gli altri esperimenti il Kangoo, tortura chinese, eseguito da miss Chrystoworkeny (nome facilissimo a scriversi), e la vera valigia delle Indie"). The humorously named Miss Chrystoworkeny is probably identical to the "Miss Christínn" who is with him in December.

[192] *La Stampa* 10, 13 Mar.1875.

[193] *La Stampa* 18, 19 Mar.1875.

[194] *Klagenfurter Zeitung* 10 July 1875.

[195] *Gazzetta di Treviso* 23 Dec.1875 "...il prestigiatore Bosco darà una serata a programma variatissimo. Miss Christínn si presenterà pure co' suoi esperimenti".

[196] *L'Éden, journal de monaco* 15, 22 Feb.1876 ("soirée thaumaturgique, humoristique et spirite").

[197] *Ischler Wochenblatt* 19 Nov.1876.

[198] *La Stampa* 3 Feb.1878 ("il famoso mago Bosco, colla *estatica* signora Elisa Zanardelli ed il suo figlio di anni 8, che si dice un piccolo prodigio").

[199] *La Stampa* 7, 25 Feb.1878.

[200] *L'Indipendente* 2 July 1878.

[201] *L'Indipendente* 18 July 1878.

[202] Noted in 'Teatro Sociale di Voghera 1800-1912' (url:091).

[203] *Die Drau* 19 Jan.1879.

[204] *La Stampa* 27 Feb.1879.

[205] *Vert-vert* 19 May 1879; *Le Temps* 6 June 1879; *Le Figaro* 19 June 1879; the programme for the event, *Fête de l'Opéra donnée par le Comité Français de Secours aux Inondés de Szegedin et organisée par le Figaro ... 7 juin 1879* is online at url:094.

[206] *Le Courrier des Alpes* 26 June 1879; *Les Petites annonces théâtrales et musicales* 5 July 1879 ("la soirée n'a été qu'une longue suite de surprises et d'étonnements").

[207] *Journal de Montélimar* 26 July 1879 ("un intéressant spectacle de thaumaturgie fantastique et spiritisme américain").

[208] *Le Petit Méridional* 1 Aug.1879. May remains unidentified; performing with him next month is the equally obscure Yda Mayer, and in Feb.1880 he is with Ida Romana, probably the same lady. One of May's acts, said to make the audience shudder, was *le tour des crânes* (*le* tour, not *la* tour), 'the skull trick'.

[209] *Le Midi* 9, 11 Aug.1879.

[210] *Le Messager du Midi* 14, 18 Aug.1879.

[211] *Le Petit Méridional* 15 Aug.1879.

[212] *Le Nouveau Cettois* 19, 21, 24 Aug.1879.

[213] *Le Progrès artistique* 29 Aug.1879.

[214] *Le Petit méridional* 13 Sep.1879.

[215] Enrico Longone; born in Milan 1852, died in an asylum in Montevideo in 1894.

[216] *El Popular* 17, 20 Feb.1880; *El Eco de Madrid* 20 Feb.; 8 Mar.1880.

[217] *Le Petit Marsellais* 5 May 1880: "Gymnase ... rep. de M. Bosco, physicien ... Séances de prestidigitation par M. Bosco".

[218] *Le Midi* 13 May 1880; *Le Petit Méridional* 14 May 1880.

[219] *Le Midi* 15 May 1880.

[220] *La Dépêche* [Toulouse] 1, 12, 16 June 1880. Possibly Crémy (B21).

[221] *Le Globe* 21 Aug.1880.

[222] *La Petite Gironde* 14, 26 Sep.1880 (named as "E. Bosco" and "M. Bosco fils, prestidigitateur").

[223] *Le Gaulois* 8 Oct.1880.

[224] *La Petite Gironde* 25 Oct.; 2, 6 Nov.1880.

[225] *L'Impartial de Boulogne-sur-mer* has not been digitised but the review is included in a scrapbook compiled by Maurice Valet which is digitised on Gallica, url:095.

[226] *Le Var* [Draguignan] 14 Nov.1880 (published subsequent to the show),

[227] *American Register* [London] 20 Nov.1880; *Worcestershire Chronicle* 4 Dec.1880.

[228] *La France* 4 Dec.1880.

[229] *L'Intransigeant* 28 Feb.1881.

[230] *Journal de Rouen* 29 June 1881.

[231] *Mémorial d'Aix* 3 July 1881.

[232] *Le Courrier d'Angers* 26 Oct.1881 ("…M. Bosco …son fils, bambin de 11 ans … Mlle Elisa, dans ses expériences esthétiques").

[233] *L'Écho Saumurois* 25 Nov.1881 (drawing only a small audience).

[234] *Le Phare de la Loire* 5, 7, 10 Dec.1881.

[235] *Le Phare de la Loire* 10, 11 Jan.1882.

[236] Referred to in *Courrier de Bretagne* 11 Jan.1882.

[237] *Le Petit Breton* 10, 14 Jan.1882; *L'Avenir de Morbihan* 14 Jan.1882.

[238] I could find no record in the local newspapers of Bartolomeo ever performing in Vannes, but he could well have done so in the late 1850s.

[239] *L'Avenir de Morbihan* 18 Jan.1882.

[240] *Le Morbihannais* 8 Jan.1882; *Courrier de Bretagne* 11, 18, 21, 28 Jan.1882.

[241] *L'Avenir de la Mayenne* 20, 24 Feb.1882; *L'Ouest-Éclair* 24 Feb.1882.

[242] *Le Progrès de la Somme* 26 Mar.; 13, 16, 18 Apr.1882.

[243] *Le Figaro* 3 Apr.1882.

[244] *Le Journal de Pontivy et de son arrondissement* 19 Nov.1882.

[245] *Journal de la ville de Saint-Quentin et de l'arrondissement* 24 Nov.1882.

[246] *Le Petit Troyen* 17 Dec.1882.

[247] *Le Progrès de la Côte-d'Or* 23, 28, 29 Dec.1882.

[248] *Le Journal de l'Ain* 19 Jan.1883.

[249] *Le Salut Public* and *Bavarde* 25 Jan.1883.

[250] *Journal de Genève* 4, 10 Mar.1883.

[251] *L'Éclaireur de l'arrondissement de Coulommiers* 28, 31 Mar.1883.

[252] *L'Écho nogentais* 1 Apr.1883.

[253] *Le Petit Courrier de Bar-sur-Seine* 6 Apr.1883.

[254] *Courrier de Saône-et-Loire* 4, 7 May 1883. Both these calculating prodigies were much written about in their own time and are still discussed today, whereas Italo has attracted no modern interest at all. Inaudi was only three years older than Italo and also born in Piedmont; their acts were similar and a reviewer who had seen them both did not hesitate to say in 1884 that Italo left him far behind (*Le Messager du Midi* 16 Mar.1884).

[255] *Courrier du Berry* 1, 6 June 1883; *Journal de Cher* 2 June 1883.

[256] *La Démocratie de Cher* 3, 5, 6 June 1883.

[257] Limoges is mentioned in *L'Indépendant de la Charente-Inférieure* 27 Sep.1883; the Poitiers review is quoted from "a Poitiers paper of August 9th" in *L'Écho rochelais* 15 Aug.1883.

[258] *L'Écho rochelais* 11, 15, 18 Aug.1883 ("...Après qu'une jeune fille qu'on endort est tombée en catalepsis, M. Bosco lui fait faire un tour d'équilibre absolument renversant").

[259] *Les Tablettes des Deux-Charentes* 29 Aug.; 1, 5 Sep.1883. The first includes an anecdote of Eugène "the other day in Metz", but that must have been several months earlier.

[260] *L'Indépendant de la Charente-Inférieure* 27, 29 Sep.1883.

[261] *L'Indépendant de la Charente-Inférieure* 6, 9 Oct.1883. Italo also amazed, now repeating back forty five items.

[262] *L'Indépendant de la Charente-Inférieure* 11 Oct.1883; *L'Écho de Jarnac* 14 Oct.1883. It is possible that this impostor was Julio Bosco (B118) who was in France at this time.

[263] *La Dépêche* 30 Oct.1883.

[264] *L'Indépendant des Basses-Pyrénées* 1 Dec.1883.

[265] *L'Éclair* 17 Jan.1884.

[266] *Le Glaneur d'Oloron et des Basses-Pyrénées* 15 Dec.1883.

[267] *L'Avenir des Hautes-Pyrénées* 20 Dec.1883.

[268] *Le Bon sens* 25 Dec.1883; *La Fraternité* 29 Dec.1883.

[269] *La Petite Gironde* 26 Jan.1884.

[270] *Le Messager du Midi* 1 Jan.1884.

[271] *La Dépêche* 10 Jan.1884.

[272] *L'Éclair* 17, 23, 27 Jan.1884; *Le Petit Méridional* 19 Jan.1884; *Le Messager du Midi* 19 Jan.1884.

[273] *L'Éclair* 11, 19 Feb.1884.

[274] *Le Petit Méridional* 5 Mar.1884; *Le Petit Cettois* 7 Mar.1884.

[275] *L'Éclair* 9, 12 Mar.1884; *Le Petit Cettois* 9 Mar.1884.

[276] *L'Éclair* 13 Mar.1884; *Le Petit Méridional* 13 Mar.1884; *Le Messager du Midi* 13 Mar.1884.

[277] *L'Éclair* and *Le Messager du Midi* 18 Mar.1884; *Le Lez* 20 Mar.1884.

[278] "If Montpellier is not at this moment the most magnetised city in France and Navarre it is because its inhabitants have a very lymphatic temperament", thought *Le Messager du Midi* 23 Mar.1884 in its review.

[279] The reviewer in *Le Messager du Midi* says: "cet infortuné théâtre du Gymnase" was "*désenguignoné* pour un soir" — 'it lost its bad luck for one night'; *désenguignoné*, a rare word, perhaps a piece of theatrical jargon, is not in the dictionaries and Google and Bing find only one example in a book (in the 1885 novel by Alexis Bouvier, *La belle herboriste:* "…Voilà le Théâtre-Italien désenguignoné"); however *Retronews* finds over 800 examples in newspapers, nearly all in a theatrical context.

[280] *L'Éclair* 22 Mar.1884 was equally enthusiastic, and regarded Italo very highly because he could recite perfectly not some text he could have spent years learning by heart but phrases he had just heard, and only heard once.

[281] *Le Petit Provençal* and *Le Sémaphore de Marseille* 29 Mar.1884.

[282] *Le Sémaphore de Marseille* 4 Apr.1884.

[283] *Le Petit Marseillais* 5, 6 Apr. 1884 ("ladies will be admitted"); *La Vedette* 13 Apr.1884.

[284] *Le Sémaphore de Marseille* 20 Apr.1884; *Le Petit Marseillais* 24 Apr.1884.

[285] *Le Petit Marseillais* 27 Apr.1884 and *Le Sémaphore de Marseille* 29 Apr.1884. According to a later report they took 4,200 fr. in Marseille, "the same takings as Sarah Bernhardt" (*Journal de Montélimar* 14 Feb.1885).

[286] *Le Mémorial d'Aix* 4 May 1884; *La Provence* 4 May 1884 (telling us that Eugenio not only inherited his father's abilities but these have gone from strength to strength — so how great will they become in Italo, quoting a comment on him in a Budapest newspaper: "His secretary Italo's memory really amazed everyone").

[287] *Le Mémorial d'Aix* and *La Provence* 11 May 1884.

[288] *Le Mémorial d'Aix* 18 May 1884.

[289] *Le Midi* 10, 13 June 1884.

[290] *Le Midi* 21 June 1884.

[291] *La Dépêche* 12, 13 July 1884.

[292] *La Gironde* 3, 8 Aug.1884.

[293] *Les Tablettes des Deux-Charentes* 18 Sep.1884.

[294] *La Dépêche* 10, 22 Oct.1884.

[295] *Journal de Toulouse* 30 Oct.1884 ("grande soirée extraordinaire de magie ancienne et moderne, de chimie, de faculté mentale, transcendentalisme et de spiritisme … voyage à travers la monde des merveilles, une série d'expériences nouvelles, surprenantes, amusantes et instructives").

[296] *La Dépêche* 1 Nov.1884.

[297] *La Dépêche* 7 Nov.1884.

[298] *Journal de Toulouse* 9 Nov.1884.

[299] *Le Midi artiste* 7 Dec.1884. The pantoscope, invented in 1865, was hardly a novelty; it showed wide-angled views. Here it is presumably refers to the same lantern-slide projector which Eugenio the following month calls the "Monster Agioscope" (note 303).

[300] *Journal de Montélimar* 14 Feb.1885.

[301] *Le Messager du Midi* 13, 14 Jan.1885; *Le Petit Meridional* 13, 14 Jan.1885.

[302] *L'Éclair* 21 Jan.1885; *Le Messager du Midi* 22 Jan.1885.

[303] *Le Messager du Midi* 28 Jan.1885. 'Agioscope' was a type of lantern-slide projector showing dissolving views first used by Henri Robin in 1852 in London, but largely out of fashion by the 1880s. This may have been an improved version, as *Carlevaris light*, using a salt of magnesium, was invented by Prospero Carlevaris only in 1865.

[304] *Journal de Montélimar* 14 Feb.1885: special praise for Italo ("étonnant") and for Béatrix ("vraiment extraordinaire dans son expérience *hors centre*").

[305] *Le Petit Méridional* 9 June 1885; *Le Midi* 10 June 1885.

[306] Known from an anecdote in the Nice paper *Le Phare du Littoral* 29 June 1885 of its reporter sent to interview Eugenio being hypnotised by him in a café; quoted in *Le Var* 16 July 1885.

[307] *Le Var* 9, 18 July 1885.

[308] *La Stampa* 31 Aug.1885.

[309] *La Stampa* 16, 17 Sep.1885.

[310] *Neue Freie Presse* 31 Dec.1885 (also quoted in *Allgemeine Theater-Zeitung* 15 Jan.1886).

[311] *La Stampa* 15 Jan.1886 (quoting "le gazzette di Verona"). A short account of the incident was printed in several French papers (*Le Figaro* 20 Jan.1886; *La Croix* 21 Jan.1886; *L'Intransigeant* 22 Jan.1886), clearly taken from a Milan paper.

[312] *La Mahouna: journal de l'arrondissement de Guelma* 1 Aug.1886 ("des soirées absolument charmantes").

[313] *L'Écho du Sahara: Journal de l'arrondissement de Batna* 5 Aug.1886 ("… Italo un prodige de mémoire véritablement inouï").

[314] *L'Avenir de Bel-Abbès* 22, 29 Sep.; 6 Oct.1886.

[315] *Le Littoral Illustré* 1, 7 Feb.1887.

[316] *Wiener Allgemeine Zeitung* 7 Apr.1887. This account was reprinted in many other papers, including *Die Presse* of 12 April and *Kurjer Warszawski* 15 April, with a note expressing reservations as to its credibility, and the Austrian satirical paper *Der Floh* (10 Apr.1887) joked that Bosco was very rash performing magic tricks in Rome where there were so many black magicians. *Le Figaro* reprinted the story (11 Apr. 1887) from the Viennese paper as 'Un Sorcier au Vatican', wrongly stating that Bosco was in Vienna when he received the invitation to perform for the Pope.

[317] *Gazzetta delle Puglie* 14 May 1887 ("Sappiamo che, fra non molto e dopo che sarà stato a Napoli, verrà a Lecce…").

[318] *Courrier de Tlemcen* 12 Aug.1887; *L'Indépendant de Mascara* 14 Aug.1887 ("M. Bosco vient d'Alger où il a obtenu un très grand succès, avec l'hypnotisme et magnétisme sur les personnes et les animaux vivants"). The following year a French paper was to say of his act that while seeing a human being under hypnotic control was disquieting, there are not the same reasons for pitying a duck or a rabbit that has "abdicated its will": *Le Petit Marseillais* 8 Mar.1888.

[319] *La Tafna, Journal de l'arrondissement de Tlemcen* 31 Aug.; 7 Sep.1887; *Courrier de Tlemcen* 2, 9 Sep.1887 (summing up: "…tout le monde a été ravi et enchanté d'une multitude d'expériences humoristiques qui paraissent toucher au merveilleux").

[320] *La Vanguardia* 16 Nov.; 6, 7, 8 Dec.1887 ("juegos de escamoteo y prestidigitación por el profesor señor Bosco").

[321] *Le Petit Marseillais* 14 Dec.1887.

[322] *Le Petit Marseillais* 16 Jan.1888; *Le Messager du Midi* 17 Jan.1888 (Italo "absolument extraodinaire dans 'Les Micropiles du cerveau'").

[323] *L'Indépendant de Lodève* 28 Jan.; 4 Feb.1888.

[324] *Le Petit Marseillais* 31 Jan.1888.

[325] *Le Petit Méridional* 21 Jan.; 5 Feb.1888; *Le Messager du Midi* 4, 8 Feb.1888. This, "L'expérience de la Guillotine ou l'Innocent ressuscité", became a feature of their act but, as stated above (p.156), it was not Eugenio and Italo performing this act in England in 1889 but the "Signor Bosco" whose real name was Saul Warschawski (B63): it was a regular feature of Saul's performances in Britain between 1882 and 1894, and was still performed by his son Alfred (B64) in 1901.

[326] *Le Petit Méridional* 9, 10 Feb.1888.

[327] *Furet nîmois* 18, 25 Feb.1888; *Le Petit Méridional* 25 Feb.1888.

[328] *Le Petit Méridional* 25 Feb.1888.

[329] *Le Petit Marseillais* 8 Mar.1888.

[330] *Le Petit Marseillais* 20, 21 Mar.1888. The *Eden-Théâtre* was actually a concert hall, with Eugenio performing in the "jardin couvert". On March 23rd at the same theatre appeared another Bosco, a singer with the local choral society.

[331] *Le Salut Public* 20 Apr.1888.

[332] He states this in an announcement in Trieste the following year (*Il Piccolo* 5 Oct.1889): his show will include "*Il ritratto delle Signore,* eseguito per la prima volta dinanzi a S.M. la regina d'Italia il 24 dicembre 1888".

[333] *Il Piccolo* 29 Sep.1889 ("… il nestore dei prestigiatori italiani"); 5 Oct.1889 ("… Bosco promette una serie di novità fra le quali: *Il ritratto delle Signore* … e *Saggi d'ipnotismo sopra animali vivi…*").

[334] *Il Piccolo* 6 Oct.1888: "Però Bosco ha un difetto grandissimo, difetto a cui tutti purtroppo siam suggetti ed al quale nemmeno lui con tutta la sua arte magica può sottrarsi: Bosco è invecchiato, e di molto; non pertanto in parecchi giuochi ha saputo farsi applaudire. Il pubblico ha riso parecchio a certi saggi d'ipnotismo su animali viventi, non troppo docili a lasciarsi ipnotizzare e su esseri umani docilissimi a questo esperimento".

[335] *Grazer Volksblatt* 25 Apr.1890 (his shows still billed as "des Sohnes des weltberühmten Escamoteurs Bosco").

[336] *Laibacher Zeitung* 1 June 1890.

[337] *La Stampa* 14, 27 Nov.; 9 Dec.1890.

[338] *La Stampa* 11 Dec.1890.

[339] *Pester-Lloyd* 8 Feb.1891.

[340] *Illusionista* Anno II, Num 6, January 1891: "La serata di Prestidigitazione a beneficio del Prof. EUGENIO BOSCO…".

The journal *L'Illusionista*, edited by Riccardo Ardito, was the organ of the *Unione Illusionisti Herrmann*, founded in Genoa by Enrico Rubatto, son of the sculptor Carlo Rubatto.

[341] *L'Illusionista* Anno II, Num.8-9, March-April 1891. The interview in the *Illusionista* is signed simply "Blitz": this cannot be Antonio Blitz (Rusconi p.83), who had died in America in 1877. From an online version of the interview at 'Club Lanterna Magica Genova' (url:096) I take it that it was reprinted in *Il Prestigiatore Moderno* 1893 with the name as "Emilio Blitz", not a relative of Antonio; perhaps a member of the *Unione Illusionisti Herrmann*.

[342] *Le Petit Marseillais* 11 June 1891.

[343] *Le Petit Marseillais* 30 July 1891.

[344] *Le Messager du Midi* 7 Aug.1891 ("sa dernière tournée qu'il fait en Europe").

[345] *Le Sud-Ouest* 16 Sep.1891; *La Dépêche* 17 Sep.1891. Nothing further has been found on Callet (C11); there is no evidence that he went on to make a career in magic.

[346] *La Stampa* 24 Feb.1892.

[347] The document is quoted by Emilio Costa in his biography of Marchelli, *Bartolomeo Marchelli, Capitano Garibaldino, 1834-1903* (Ovada 1961), p.13 (online at url:097).

B3. Italo Bosco: son of B2

Name: His marriage registration (below) gives his full name as *Eugenio Italo Libero Bosco*. He is always referred to as Italo.

Birth: At his marriage he gives his birthplace as Turin and his age as 37 on 24 September 1906, meaning (if correct) that he was born between 25 September 1868 and 24 September 1869. This birthdate accords reasonably well with the many references to his age given in his father's advertisements. He is first found on stage with his parents in February 1878, said to be age 8; in 1880 age 10; in 1881 and 1882 age 11; in 1884 age 14.

He was at various times an assistant to his father in the 'Indian Mail', Decapitation, and Mind Reading acts, but his main role was performing feats of Memory and Mental Calculation, billed as a "child prodigy" and for a period as "the new Pico de la Mirandola". Eugenio would ask the audience to write random words next to each of a series of numbers, as many as 45; he would read the list aloud to Italo once, and Italo would repeat it faultlessly, forwards, backwards, and in several languages. He was compared favourably to the famous Henri Mondeux and Giacomo Inaudi but unlike them has attracted no modern interest at all (for references to his act see B2 and especially note 254).

Italo is last mentioned performing with his father in 1888. There is no evidence he then continued his career. In 1906 when he married he is listed as a clerk, but, significantly, to Dante Zanardelli who is now a stockbroker, so Italo was his human computer.

His civil marriage registration on September 24th 1906 in Rome is online at the *Antenati site* (url:098):
Italo is age 37, born in Turin, resident in Rome, a clerk (*impiegato*), and never married;
Eugenio is recorded as deceased but Elisa is alive and resident in Rome.
He married Livia Farina, age 19, resident in Rome, spinster.
The witnesses are Dante Zanardelli, stockbroker (*agente di cambio*), age 55, and Celestino Grea, age 60, a tramways manager (*direttore tramway*).

No record has been found of Italo's death.

Excursus: Bartolomeo's Marriages and Children

Bartolomeo's first wife was Polish, Antonina Młynarska (Antonina née Młynarski; known also as Antoinette Mlinarska, and in Italian records as Antonietta Mlinarski and Antonietta Molinascha), born in Bologna in 1803 or 1804, daughter of Andrzej Młynarski and Gertruda Ceratti.

We know that Antonina had a sister whose married name was Conti and lived in Warsaw. This was stated in a Warsaw paper when Eugenio was performing there in January 1873, correcting a statement that he could not be Bartolomeo's son as Bartolomeo had died childless in Italy: "Some say that the magician is the son of the famous Bosco who twenty years ago charmed us here in our city, but as far as we know Bosco senior died childless in Italy and apparently in a critical financial situation".[1]

The paper then published a note correcting this, acknowledging that he was "the son of the famous magician Bartolomeo Bosco and Antonina née Młynarski, sister of Mrs. Conti residing in Warsaw",[2] and also published a letter written by Eugenio confirming this and pointing out that his father died in Dresden, not Italy (and not in a poor financial state), "and his grave is there in the Catholic cemetery in the suburbs, with a stone monument in the shape of a cross and the inscription 'Bartolomeo Bosco † 1868'"[*sic*].[3]

The name and marriage of Antonietta's sister are confirmed by Polish genealogical records. Her name was Marianna and according to her death registration she was born *ca.*1799 in Bologna "in the Papal States" and her marriage registration gives her parents' names as Andrzej Mlynarski and Gertruda Ceratti.[4] In Warsaw in 1815 a young Marianna married Alexandre (Alexandra, Aleksander) Augustyn Kajetan Conti, born *ca.*1791, son of Julian and Teresa Conti.[5]

Alexandre ran a well-known café and patisserie, "with a garden, known for its excellent ice cream", in Miodowa Street.[6] He is listed in Warsaw records as a 'traktyera' (defined as 'traiteur'; 'restaurateur' in *Słownik polsko-francuzki*, 1843) or as 'obywatela' ('citizen'). They had eight children in Warsaw; Marianna died there in 1847 age 48[7] and Alexandre in 1871.[8]

That Antonina was also, like her sister, born in Bologna is stated in the 1845 *Der Sammler* article (see p.156 above) and in the registration of the birth of her son Matteo in 1837 (below) which names her as "Donna Antonietta Molinascha di Bologna di anne trenta tre sua Moglie legittima e con egli domiciliata".

She and Bartolomeo are said to have married in Warsaw, probably when he was in Poland for an extended period from October 1822 and returned through Poland from Russia in 1824.[9]

Bartolomeo and Antonina had at least five children, three sons and two daughters. We know the names of these five children and the exact birthdates of two, but there is some contradictory information. The 1845 *Der Sammler* article states that Bosco at that date had a daughter age 19 born in St Petersburg; another daughter age 16 born in Warsaw;[10] and a son age 17 born in Lübeck (discussed in B2). Their two other sons, both deceased, are not mentioned in the article.

The oldest was born in Lviv in March 1826 and was named **Eugenio (Eugeniusz Bosko di toryno)**; he died in Warsaw on April 16th 1827, age 13 months, of "tooth ache" (commonly given pre-20th century as a cause of death). We do not have his birth registration but his death registration is available online (url:104) —

Transcription (a few possible minor errors do not affect the meaning)
Działo się w Warszawie Dnia Szesnastego Miesiąca Kwietnia, Tysiąc osiemset
dwadziestego siódmego roku, o godzinie w pół do dziewiątej n rano stawiła się Bar
tlomiey Bosco di toryno, Mechanik, lat trzydzieści pięć maiący, przy Ulicy Mia
dowej pod liczbą czterysta osiemdziesiąt dwa, y Alexander Konti Obywatel lat trzy
dziesci sześć maiący, przy Ulicy Miodowej pod liczbą czterysta dziewięćdziesiąt dwa
obydwaj w Warszawie zamieszkały y oświadczyła się w dniu piętnastym Miesiąc
ca Kwietnia roku bieżącego, o godzinie w pół do piątej popołudnie, przy Ulicy Mia
dowej pod liczbą czterysta osiemdziesiąt dwa, Umarł na ból zębów Eugeniusz Bos
ko di turyno, Rok ieden y Miesiąc ieden maiący, Rodem z Miasta Lwowa, Syn
Bartlomieja wyżej wspomnianego y Antoniny Młynarskich lat dwadzieścia
trzy maiący Małżonkow Bosko dy toryno, Po przekonaniu się naocznie o Zej
ściu Eugeniusza Bosko di toryno Akt ten przeczytany stawaiącym zktorych
pierwszy iest oycem zmarłego syna przez Nas, wraz i oycemi y Alexandrom Kon
ti podpisany został.
[*signed by the priest and witnesses*] Xiądz Michail [*surname illegible*] Jana
Bartolomeo Bosco di Torino   Alexandre Conti

A literal translation:
It happened in Warsaw on the sixteenth of the month of April, one thousand eight hundred and twenty-seven, at half past nine in the morning, there presented themselves Bartlomeo Bosco di Torino, Mechanic, thirty-five years old, of Miodowa Street number four hundred and eighty-two, and Alexander Conti, Citizen, thirty five years old, of Miodowa Street number four hundred and ninety two, both resident in Warsaw, and declared that on the fifteenth of the month of April this year, at half past five in the afternoon, at Miodowa Street number four hundred and eighty-two, Eugeniusz Bosco di Turin, died of toothache, aged one year and one month, a native of the city of Lviv, son of the above-mentioned Bartlomeo and

Antonina Młynarska, twenty-three years old, husband and wife. Bosco di torino having witnessed with his own eyes the decease of Eugene Bosco di toryno this document was read to those present of whom the first is the father of the deceased son and was signed by us together.

Their son **Matteo Fortunato** was born in Naples (registered in Quartiere San Giuseppe) on April 30th 1837 at 6.30 "Italian time" at Bosco's place of residence in the Largo del Castello and baptised on May 12th.[11] He probably died very young, as Rusconi suggests (p.92).

The daughter said in *Der Sammler* 1845 to be born in St Petersburg and then age 19 was **Aleksandryna** (known as Aleksandra and Alexandra). We do not have her birth record but her death registration is online (url:106) and there are newspaper notices of her death.

She died at age 26 in Warsaw on September 21st 1853 "after a severe illness" and was buried with a Catholic service on September 23rd.[12]

Her death registration reads

Transcription:
Dzialo się w Warszawie dnia dwudziestego drugiego
Wrześnią Tysiąc osiemset pięćdziesiątego trzeciego
Roku ogodzinie czwartey popołudniu stawił się Mi
chal Conti własciciel cukierni i Alexander Ję
drzejewski Artysta Teatru pełnoletni w Warszawie
zamieszkali i oświadczyli się w dniu wczorayszym ogodzi
nie jedenastey rano przy ulicy Senato
rskiey Czterysta siedemdziesiąt jeden umarla Alexandra
Bosco Panną przy familii zostającą lat dwadzieścia
sześć zyiącego urodzona w mieście St Petersburgu
Córka Bartłomieja sztukmistrza i Antoniny z
Młynarskich małżonków Bosko. Przekonawszy
się naocznie o zejściu Alexandry Bosko Akt ten
po przeczytaniu podpisany został.
Xiądz…
[signed by the priest and Michal Conti and Alexander Jędrzejewski]

Literal translation:
It happened in Warsaw on the twenty-second day of September one thousand eight hundred and fifty-three at four o'clock in the afternoon, Michal Conti, the owner of a bakery, and Alexander Jędrzejewski, an actor, both of full age and resident in Warsaw, presented themselves and declared that yesterday at eleven o'clock in the morning at four hundred and seventy-one "Senator Street" died, Alexandra Bosco, age twenty six, born in the city of St Petersburg, daughter of Bartolomeo Bosco, magician, and his wife Antonina, née Młynarski; having witnessed the death of Alexandra Bosco with their own eyes, the document was read by them and signed...

Alexandryna lived in Ulica Senatorska ("Senator Street") which crosses Miodowa Street and also *placu Teatralnego* ("Teatralny Square"), said to be "the centre of the city's life".

The witnesses were Michal Conti and Alexander Jędrzejewski, a well-known actor, 1811-1886 ('Encyclopedia of the Polish Theatre', url:107).

There was a memorial service on the first anniversary of her death.[13]

Alexandryna's death at age 26 on September 21st 1853 would make the date of her birth in St Petersburg between September 22nd 1826 and September 21st 1827. And since young Eugenio was born in March 1826, Alexandryna was probably not born before 1827. But her sister Adelaide was born on January 27th 1828 (see below), so the window for Alexandryna's birth is *January to March 1827*.

Eugenio, talking of his sisters to the Warsaw newspaper in 1873 (above) states[14] incorrectly that Alexandryna was "born on Italian soil". He also says correctly that "she spent a long time in Warsaw, staying with one of the local families and died here". He then says "The second daughter, born in Warsaw, not long ago moved to eternity." So he is saying that Alexandryna was the elder and born in Italy, and the second (unnamed, but Adelaide) was born in Warsaw; and by 1873 both have died. So, he is wrong about Alexandryna's birth and he is wrong about Adelaide being dead: she was still alive in 1882.

The daughter born in Warsaw was **Joanna Adelayda Kaietaną** (known as Adelaide or Adele) and was definitely born in 1828 (see below), so her age is correct in *Der Sammler*. But she is said to be the *elder* daughter in 1845, when she joins her father in Vienna to travel to Bologna together after Antonina's death, and also in the 1887 court decision (*Annali della Giurisprudenza Italiana* XX, below) — and we know that she was still alive in 1882.

Adelaide's birth registration is available online (url:108; and is reproduced by Rusconi on p.30). It states clearly that she was born in Warsaw on January 27th 1828 at 6 p.m. and registered and baptised on February 5th. The entry gives a lot of interesting information: Bartolomeo is away, performing in Dresden, and those appearing before the priest are the midwife, Krystyna Wagner; Alexander Conti (Bartolomeo's brother-in-law, above); Jan Celli(?), a professor at the Conservatory of Music; and Antonino Anderlini; Celli and Anderlini are the godparents.[15] The "Kaietaną" in her name is probably a gesture to the Conti family, after Alexandre Augustyn *Kajetan* Conti; Alexandre also named one of his sons Konstanty Maksymilian Kajetan Conti: the family may have had links to Gaeta in Latina. The full text reads:

Działo się w Warszawie dnia piątego Miesiąca Lutego Tysiąc Osiem/
set dwudziestego Osmego Roku o godzinie piątej wieczorem stawi/
ła się Krystyna Wagner Akuszerka licząca lat sześćdziesiąt/
sześć przy ulicy podwale pod liczbą pięćset jedanaesta zamiesz-/
kała w obecności Inni Panów Jana Celli professora Konser-/
watorium Muzycznego liczącego lat trzydziesci osm przy ulicy/
Miodowej pod liczbą czterysta dziewięćdziesiąt dwa tudzież Ale-/
xandra Contti Obywatela liczącego lat trzydziesci siedem/
przy ulicy Miodowej pod liczbą czterysta dziewięć-/
dziesiąt dwa zamieszkałych i okazała Nam Dziecię płci/
Żeńskiej urodzone tu w Warszawie pod liczbą wyż rzeczony/
na dniu dwudziestym siódmym Stycznia roku bieżącego/
o godzinie szóstej wieczorem z Antoniny z Mlinarskich/
Bosco maiący lat dwadzieścia cztery pod tą z liczbą miesz-/
kaiący i jej małżonka Bartlomieia Bosco maiącego lat trzy-/

dzieści siedem Mechanika na teraz w Mieście Drezno w Saxony/
znajduiącego się Dziecięciu temu na Chrzcie Świętym odbytym w/
dniu dzisiejszym nadane zostały Imiona Joanna Adelayda/
Kaietana a Rodzicami jego chrzestnymi byli wyżej wspomniany Jan/
Celli z Antonino Anderlini. — Niniejszy Akt stawaiący i Świadkom prze-/
czytany podpisanym został przez nas wraz z stawiająca Akuszerka i Obecnie Świadkami./
  Xiądz Walenty Greiffenberg Proboszcz Kościoła Parafialnego Świętego Jana/
[*signatures*] [Anderlini?]   Giovanni Celli   Alexandre Conti

Literal translation:
In Warsaw on the fifth day of the month of February in the year one thousand eight hundred and twenty-eight, at five o'clock in the evening there presented themselves Krystyna Wagner, midwife, sixty-six years old, residing at number five hundred and eleven Podwale Street, in the presence of the gentlemen Jan Celli, Professor at the Conservatory of Music, thirty-eight years old, residing at number four hundred and ninety-two Miodowa street, and Alexandra Contti, a citizen, thirty-seven years old, resident at four hundred and ninety-two Miodowa street, and she showed us a female child born here in Warsaw at the address mentioned above on the twenty-seventh day of January of this year at six o'clock in the evening to Antonina née Mlinarski Bosco, twenty-four years old, resident at this address, and her husband Bartlomieja Bosco, thirty-seven years old, at present found in the city of Dresden in Saxony. At the baptism held today the names Joanna Adelayda Kaietana were given to this child and her godparents were the above-mentioned Jan Celli and Antonino Anderlini. - This [present] certificate was read to the witnesses present and signed by us together in the presence of the midwife, as witnesses.
Father Walenty Greiffenberg Priest of the Saint John Parish Church.
[*signatures*] *Anderlini, Antonio,   Giovanni Celli,   Alexandre Conti*

There are references in Polish newspapers over the years to Adelaida Bosco and to Alexandra / Alexandryna Bosco — hardly common names in Poland, and one reference to Alexandra specifically names her as Bartolomeo's daughter, arriving in Warsaw in September 1849: "Alexandra Bosco, daughter of the famous magician well known in Warsaw, came to Warsaw from Bremen in the last few days".[16]

Of her sister Adelaide we hear more. In April 1845 when Bosco in Vienna learnt of Antonina's death in Bologna several days earlier, he did not leave immediately but remained in Vienna until the end of the month, cancelling his public performances (except a command performance before the Austrian royal family on Sunday 27th),[17] waiting for Adelaide to join him, probably coming from Warsaw, and to travel to Italy with him. He left for Bologna soon after Monday 28th "to see his children after the death of his wife and to travel with his elder [*sic*] daughter, who is said to be an excellent singer".[18]

This is the first mention found of Adelaide as a singer. At this time "Kleroth" was writing his sketch 'Der Dämon der Magie' (see B1 p.42; F11) and in his fictional "1839" letter from Antonina to Bartolomeo he has her mention young Adelaide's musicality as a nice touch of verisimilitude — "Adelaide ... has a most charming voice, an excellent musical ear, and a peculiar talent for impersonation...".[19]

There is a further curious reference to "Signor Bosco's daughter" as a singer, but fictional and allusive — a comment by A. de Rovray in *Gazette nationale ou le Moniteur universel* 6 June 1858: "Jamais Rossini n'a donné de leçons de musique à la fille du prestidigitateur Bosco" — *Rossini never gave music lessons to the daughter of the magician Bosco*; this is in a critique of the recently published French translation of Eduard Maria Oettinger's book *Rossini, L'Homme et l'Artiste*. It refers to a scene in the book in which the author meets Rossini in 1845 in Bologna (where Rossini lived from 1835 to 1848) and asks him if he has read his novel written about him: "only extracts...", replies Rossini, "but the daughter of Signor Bosco, whom I give singing lessons to here, has told me a lot about you and your book" (p.152: "... mais la fille de M. Bosco, à laquelle je donne ici des leçons de musique, m'a beaucoup parlé de vous et de votre livre..."), and de Rovrary says that Oettinger has blown smoke in the eyes of his readers. So, the book merely calls her "la fille de M. Bosco (and in the German original "die Tochter des Signor Bosco, der ich hier Unterricht in Gesang gebe": vol.2 p.272), not saying her father was the magician Bosco. The comic nature of Oettinger's book is best seen from its German and Italian titles, *Rossini: komischer Roman* and *Rossini: romanzo comico*,[20] and we might be tempted to dismiss the above story as a canard, or a misinterpretation by de Rovray — except that *Oettinger was appointed Adelaide's legal guardian after the death of her father* (see below).

There are some further glimpses of Adelaide in the next few years. In April 1847 we hear that Bartolomeo on a tour of Poland stopped only briefly in Kraków then rushed on to Warsaw "to spend the holiday in the bosom of his family",[21] then in June 1847 Adelaide Bosco is travelling from Kraków.[22] In November 1850 there is a record of Adelaide Bosco, noted as an Italian subject, arriving in Kraków from Warsaw,[23] and in February 1857 Adelajda Bosco leaving Warsaw by rail.[24] Then in January 1859, travelling from Warsaw to Berlin (where her father was) she is now described as a 'governess'.[25] Later that year she is probably the *artiste* "Atalida Bosco" arriving from Leipzig in Kraków (where Eugenio was performing) with Józefina Muntzel; the two women leave for Tarnów together with Eugenio a fortnight later, Józefina Muntzel now listed as Józefina Muntzel Bosco, so presumably a relative.[26]

In 1863, following the death of Bartolomeo, legal notices from Dresden lawyers were published in several German newspapers to the effect that in Adelaide's absence her affairs had been taken over by a legal guardian in absentia (*Abwesenheitsvormund*), implying she was unmarried, that she had been living with her father and stepmother, and *probably* also that she was no longer capable of managing her own affairs.[27]

What is most interesting here is who her legal guardian was. The guardian did not have to be a lawyer and the appointee is "Herr Eduard Maria Oettinger", the journalist and writer who had mentioned Adelaide in his Rossini novel years earlier, and had dined with Bartolomeo in Leipzig in 1844. He was living in Dresden from 1861, and published his massive 6 volume reference work *Moniteur des dates* (with a million entries, including one for Bosco) in Dresden between 1866 and 1868.[28] Oettinger died in Blasewitz, a borough of Dresden, in 1872.

Adelaide's condition clearly deteriorated after 1863, and in August 1865 she arrived in Livorno from Florence, "an unknown woman using the name Giovanna Baldi", and after "showing signs of madness" was admitted to the city hospital; then on November 2nd the Livorno court ordered her held in the S. Bonifacio Asylum in Florence, where she was taken on November 8th.[29] She was subsequently identified and on April 8th 1867 the Livorno court declared that she was "Adele (or Adelaide) Bosco, daughter of the magician Bartolomeo Bosco of Turin". The Florence asylum now requested payment for her keep from the Livorno Provincial Administration, which in turn requested it from the province of Turin on the basis that Adele "belonged there by domicile". In July 1882 she was moved to the asylum in Turin, with court cases continuing over which province was to pay, based on questions whether the Warsaw marriage of her parents was proven, so making her legitimate, and whether Bartolomeo had maintained a domicile in Turin. It was not until July 1887 that the Florence Court of Appeal delivered a final decision which established several precedents. Adele presumably died in the Turin asylum, date unknown.[30]

Antonina had died in Bologna on April 5th 1845, when Bartolomeo was performing in Vienna.[31] Bartolomeo married again, almost certainly in Dresden in mid-June 1848 — he left Leipzig for Dresden on June 1st 1848 and arrived on June 10th: an article 'Bosco in Dresden' in *Leipziger Zeitung* 25 June 1848 says: "Dresden, as we learn, is now your father-in-law town" ("jetzt Ihre Schwieger-vaterstadt ist"). He married a widow, Friederike Auguste Pfeiffer (née Luther), born *ca*.1810, whom he may well have met in Dresden before Antonina's death in 1845.[32] Friederike died of a stroke on February 26th 1866, age 56, and was buried on March 1st.[33]

STRAYS AND IMPOSTORS

There are references over the years to several so-called relatives of Bartolomeo, either (a) described as such in newspapers, or (b) performers claiming to be related.

(a)
In Spain in 1858 Bosco is said to have met an unknown or long-lost brother, a hat maker from Seville (B1 p.83).

Staying in the same Hotel as Eugenio in Kraków in 1859, and all leaving together, are Atalida Bosco and Józefina Muntzel Bosco. Atalida may well be his sister Adelaide; Józefina Muntzel Bosco remains unidentified, possibly an aunt of Adelaide's...?

The well-known baritone G.F. Beneventano ("Cavaliere Beneventano"; Francesco Giuseppe Federico Beneventano Del Bosco, barone della Piana, 1823-1880), when singing in Trieste in 1860 with Mario and Angiolina Tiberini was first thought to be a cousin of General Bosco (Ferdinando Beneventano del Bosco), but is later described as "the cousin and not the brother of Bosco, the magician" (*La Presse théâtrale* 4, 11 Nov.1860; 20 Jan.1861).

Houdini stated in 1906 that he met a second cousin of Bartolomeo in Dresden (see Rusconi p.152); and Houdini met Mrs Mueller, the niece of Bosco's second wife, at Frikell's funeral.

(b) *These have individual entries in the 'Impostors' list (B) or in the 'Pupils and Relatives' section (C).*

Hermann Bosco (B8) in Nantes in 1846 claimed to be Bartolomeo's son.

August Günther (C21), found performing as a magician ("magisch-physikalischer Künstler") in the Baltic and northern Germany 1848-1853 advertised himself as "brother-in-law of the famous Bosco" ("Schwager des berühmten Herrn Bosco").

Bernard Marius Cazeneuve (C13) claimed to be Bosco's son-in-law.

The magician Professor St. Roman, (real name Samuel Thiersfeld, *ca.*1830-1913) (C49) long advertised himself as Bartolomeo's nephew ("Neffe Bosco's"; "der große Neffe seines großen Oheims Bosco"), claiming he was born in Milan not Poland. He made much of this across Europe from around 1864, soon after Bartolomeo's death.

The magician "Madame Schulz" (C46) performing in France in 1868 consistently advertised herself as Bartolomeo's daughter.

The English impostor "Morton Bosco" (B69) is said in 1872 to be "son of the original world-renowned magician of this name, who has inherited all his father's skill in the magic art" (*Ulverston Mirror* 27 Jan.1872).

The "Bosco" in Brazil in 1876 (B115; probably José Curvello D'Avila) claimed to be Bosco's son.

In Bosen (Bolzano) in 1879 a magician "Herr Bosco" (B18) claims to be Bosco's grandson ("der Enkel eines berühmten Mannes"), having earlier claimed to be his son.

Leotard Bosco (B77) is found claiming to be the son (or son and successor) of "the late original Signor Bosco".

In Reval (modern Tallinn) in 1883 Herr Professor Giordano advertised an exhibition of Magic and Antispiritualism, accompanied by his daughter Frl. Antoinette and a "Somnambule", Frau Nina Bosco (BF7), billed as "einzige Tochter des berühmten Bartolomeo Bosco" (only daughter of the famous Bartolomeo Bosco).

In Nîmes in 1891 a magician "Leonardo Bosco" (B35) advertised himself as "son of the famous magician" ("le fils du célèbre prestidigitateur").

"The clever Italian magician, Bernardo Bosco" (B113) performing in New York in 1920, claimed to be the "grandson of the original Bosco, and … the only genuine Bosco alive today" (*Billboard* 18 Sep.1920).

NOTES

[1] *Kurjer Warszawski* 24 Jan.1873: "Mowiono nam, że do Warszawy ma przybyć magik Bosco i urządzać wieczory czarodziejskie. Niektórzy głoszą, że rzeczony magik jest synem słynnego Bosco. który przed dwudziestu laty czarował w naszem mieście, o ile zaś wiemy, Bosco senjor umarł beżdzietnie we Włoszech i podobno w krytyczuem położeniu majątkowem".

[2] *Kurjer Warszawski* 27 Jan.1873: "Przybyły do Warszawy magik Eugenjusz Bosco, jest jak nas o tem dokładnie objaśniono, synem słynnego magika Bartłomieja Bosco i Antoniny z Młynarskich, siostry zamieszkałej w Warszawie pani Conti".

[3] *Kurjer Warszawski* 29 Jan.1873. The error "1868" for 1863 was probably a misreading by the editor of Eugenio's handwriting.

[4] Marriage registration see url:099. The father was said to be a Polish officer — credibly, as Młinarski was a *szlachta* name, the class from which army officers were drawn. This is stated in an article giving an apparently factual account of Bosco's life, devoid of many of the fanciful anecdotes, that appeared in Vienna in 1845, when he was actually in Vienna himself and could have provided the information at first hand: *Der Sammler* 1 Apr.1845 (also in *Der Österreichische Zuschauer* 14 Apr.1845 and in *Bild und Leben, eine Unterhaltungs-Lektüre* vol.2, Prague 1845). The article was later reprinted with elaborations in *Fremden Blatt* 18 Apr.1866.

[5] When their daughter Regina was born in 1820 Alexandre's age is given as 29, Marianna's as 20. An older son Michal, 1816-1863, signed his father's death registration.

[6] Adolf Starkman, *Cukiernie warszawskie* (Warsaw, 1895), p.8; online at url:100.

[7] Marianna's death registration is online at url:101.

[8] Alexandre's death registration is online at url:102 (after 1868, so in Russian).

[9] Rusconi (p.23 n.5) plausibly dates the marriage to 1823 or 1824. The Warsaw marriage is specifically stated in the report on their daughter Adelaide in *Annali della Giurisprudenza Italiana* XXI, 1887 (see below) and in the 1845 *Der Sammler* article: "…1822 in Berlin, ging er von da nach Warschau, wo er sich mit Antoinette Mlinarska, einer polnischen Offizierstochter vermählte, welche, in Bologna geboren, eben so schön, als gebildet war. Die Honigsmonate in Warschau verlebend, zog er von da weiter…"): however, it is odd that the marriage is not indexed in Warsaw, or elsewhere in Poland, on *Geneteka* (url:103).

[10] "Er hat zwei Töchter; eine neunzehnjährige, in St. Petersburg geboren — eine sechszehnjährige in Warschau geboren…".

[11] His birth registration is online at the *Antenati* site (url:105) and reproduced by Rusconi p.91. There is also a transcription on *FamilySearch*.

[12] *Kurjer Warszawski* 24 Sep.1853: "Wczoraj, o godzinie 3ej z południa, przewiezioho a Kaplicy XX. Bernardynów na smętarz Powązkowski, zwłoki zmarłej w BOGU dnia 21 b.m., po ciężkiej chorobie ś.p. Alexandryny Bosco. Wzniosłość umysłu i serca, gotowość do poświęceń, cierpliwość w znoszeniu przeclwności, łagodność w przebaczaniu uraz, oto przymioty, które cechowały ś.p. Alexandryne w pielgrzymce po zasłanej najboleśniejszemi cierniami drodze żywota. Spokój jej duszy!" ("…Sublimity of mind and heart, readiness to sacrifice, patience in enduring adversity, gentleness in forgiving injury, these are the qualities that marked the late Alexandryna on a pilgrimage along the path of life covered with the most painful

thorns. Peace on her soul"); and also a brief note in *Gazeta Codzienna* 25 Sep.1853: "W dniu 21 b.m., po ciężkiej chorobie zakończyła życie Aleksandryna Bosco" ("On 21st., after a serious illness, ended Aleksandra Bosco's life").

[13] *Kurjer Warszawski* 20 Sep.1854: "Jutro, jako w rocznicę skonu ś p. Alexandriny Bosco, odbędzie się w Kościele XX, Bernardynów o godz: 8 ej z rano żałobne Nabożeństwo; na które, zaprasza się Krewnych i Przyjnciót".

[14] *Kurjer Codzienny* 4 Feb.1873: "Bosco ojciec mial dwie córki jeszcze, z tych jedna Aleksandra, zrodzona na wloskiej ziemi, dlugi czas przebywala w Warszawie, bawiąc przy jednej z rodzin tutejszych i tu umarla. Druga córka urodzona w Warszawie, niezbyt dawno przeniosła się do wiecznosci".

[15] Anderlini was also a witness at the birth registration of Conti's daughter Regina where he signs himself Giordani Antonio Anderlini. A Karolina Anderlini, probably his sister, was married to Michal Conti, probably Alexandre's brother or son, so they and the Boscos were all related by marriage. Anderlini married Marianna Perepelnicka and they had four children in Warsaw between 1818 and 1827.

[16] *Kurjer Warszawski* 13 Sep.1849: "Alexandra Bosco, córka wsławionego i znanego dobrze w Warszawie Magika, przybyła w tych dniach do Warszawy z Bremen".

[17] *Der Humorist* and *ATZ* 29 April 1845.

[18] *ATZ* 28 Apr.1845: "Bosco befindet sich zwar noch in Wien, reist aber dieser Tage nach Bologna, um nach dem Tode seiner Gattin seine Kinder zu sehen und seine ältere Tochter, die eine ausgezeichnete Sängerin sein soll, mit auf Reisen zu nehmen".

[19] "...Adelaide ist voll lustiger Einfälle, sie hat ganz das Temperament des Vaters, und zwingt mich ungeachtet meines öftern Trübsinns doch zum Lachen. Dabei hat sie ein allerliebstes Stimmchen, ein vortreffliches musikalisches Gehör und ein eigenthümliches Darstellungstalent. Wenn sie einer frappanten Persönlichkeit begegnet, so weiß sie dieselbe in allen Einzelnheiten so überraschend nachzuahmen, daß ich den kleinen Schelm oft anzustaunen gezwungen bin".

[20] Oettinger's novel first appeared in his satirical periodical *Narren-Almanach* vol.3, 1845, and the 'Bosco's daughter' episode was reprinted separately in *Signal für die musikalische Welt* Nov.1845 and in *Brünner Zeitung der k.k. priv. mähr. Lehenbank* 25 Nov.1845; it was then published as a book: German edition in 2 volumes, 1847 and 1851; Danish, French and Swedish translations followed.

[21] *Gazeta Krakowska* 3 Apr.1847: "...puscił się w dalszą drogę do Warszawy, dla przepędzenia świąt na łonie swéj familii".

[22] *Gazeta Krakowska* 2 June 1847: "...*Wyjechali z Krakowa... Bosco Adelaida...*".

[23] *Czas* [Kraków] 11 Nov.1850: "Przyjechali do Krakowa od dnia 8 do 9 listopada [...] Bosco Adelajda pod. rzymska, z Warszawy".

[24] *Gazeta Codzienna* 1857 13 Feb.1857.

²⁵ *Kurjer Warszawski* 18 Jan.1859: "Wyjechali koleją selazną: Bosco Adelajda Guwernantka do Berlina".

²⁶ *Czas* 10, 24 May 1859.

²⁷ Published in *Leipziger Zeitung* 26 Sep.1863, *Allgemeine Zeitung* [Augsburg] 2 Oct. 1863, and elsewhere: "Nachdem für das abwesende Fräulein Adelaide Bosco, hinterlassene Tochter des am 7. März dieses Jahres in Gruna bei Dresden verstorbenen Herrn Professors Bartolomeo Bosco, welche den Geschlechtsnamen ihrer Mutter Mlynarski führen soll, Herr Eduard Maria Oettinger hierselbst als Abwesenheitsvormund bestätigt und in Pflicht genommen worden ist, so wird solches hierdurch zur öffentlichen Kenntnis gebracht. Dresden, den 21. September 1863. Königliches Gerichtsamt. Bauer, Assessor. Schlegel, Act. [*Actuar*]". Her stepmother was still alive, aged about 53, but she died of a stroke early in 1866 and may already have been unwell. Eugenio at this date was in, or on his way to, Constantinople.

²⁸ *Moniteur des dates, contenant un million de renseignements biographiques, généalogiques et historiques...* [title in French but the text is in German], 'Bosco' in Vol.1 p.111, online at url:109.

²⁹ 1865 was the very year that Telemaco Signorini painted his 'La Sala delle Agitate a S. Bonifazio di Firenze' ('The Ward of the Madwomen at St. Bonifazio'), url:110.

³⁰ The most detailed account of the legal decision, which also involved wider questions of jurisdiction by various courts, is in *Annali della Giurisprudenza Italiana*, XXI, 1887, pp.396-400 (url:111); shorter account in *La Legge: Monitore Giudiziario e Amministrativo del Regno d'Italia,* XXVII,2, 1887; summaries in *Rivista Amministrativa del Regno*, XXXVIII, 1887, and in *Atti del Consiglio Provinciale di Livorno*, 1886 (the last misdates Adele's institutionalisation in Livorno to 1861).

³¹ Announced in the Vienna papers *Wanderer, Wiener Zeitung* and *Allgemeine Theaterzeitung* 14 April 1845; *Bohemia* 20 April 1845.

³² Houdini reproduces a photograph of her in *The Unmasking of Robert-Houdin* "given to the author by Mrs. Mueller, Madame Bosco's niece, at the funeral of Wiljalba Frikell"; also in Rusconi p.185.

³³ Houdini (*The Unmasking of Robert-Houdin*) states from "municipal and cemetery records" that she was buried in the same grave as Bartolomeo, and is no doubt correct. The burial record is digitised on *ancestry.com,* giving date of death and of burial and cause of death, but not the plot number: these are the weekly summaries sent by the sextons to the Dresden municipal authorities (*Kirchliche Wochenzettel, 1685/1703-1902. Stadtarchiv der Landeshauptstadt Dresden, Dresden, Deutschland*); each entry does include a "Signatur", Bartolomeo is *2.1.3.C.XXI.20/148* and Friederike *2.1.3.C.XXI.20/150a*, but these apply to all the burials in the respective years.

B4. Giovanni Melchiorre Bosco. Italian Roman Catholic priest (not related to Bartolomeo).
Name: Often referred to as San (Saint) Giovanni Bosco (with Giovanni localised to John, Jean, Johannes, Joannes, Jan, Juan, João…) or as Don Bosco (Don the Italian form of the honorific Dom, for *Dominus*); Latin name: Ioannes Melchior Bosco.

Born 16 August 1815 in the Biglione farmhouse (*Cascina-Biglione*)[1] in Becchi[2] (*I Becchi,* a small cluster of houses, now renamed Colle Don Bosco), in the village (*frazione*) of Morialdo, in the municipality (*comune*) of Castelnuovo d'Asti (now renamed Castelnuovo Don Bosco), in Piedmont (then in the Kingdom of Sardinia); died 31 January 1888, Turin, Italy; buried there in the Basilica di Santa Maria Ausiliatrice;[3] founder of the Salesian Order (*Società Salesiana di San Giovanni Bosco; Societas Sancti Francisci Salesii*); beatified 1929 (url:112); canonized 1934 (url:113). In 2002, Pope John Paul II was petitioned to declare St. John Bosco the Patron of Stage Magicians (url:114).

As a young child by observing performers at markets and fairs he became a skilled conjuror (and acrobat), and with his street performances (accompanied by a sermon and prayers) he attracted children and the poor:[5] he has entries as a magician in the *Lexikon,* Whannell, *Magicpedia, ZauberPedia*. He may well (as Rusconi nicely suggests: p.57) have seen Bartolomeo performing in Turin in 1835 but by November that year he was in the seminary and he himself states that he ceased to perform magic tricks in 1836.[5]

Sources:
The primary source is Don Bosco's own *Memorie dell'Oratorio di S. Francesco di Sales dal 1815 al 1855,* written in the 1870s at the command of Pope Pius IX; first published from the manuscripts as *Memorie dell'Oratorio di S. Francesco de Sales dal 1815 al 1855.* Turin: Società Editrice Internazionale, 1946, edited by Eugenio Ceria SDB.
Various versions digitised at url:115 [and elsewhere]
English translation as *Memoirs of the Oratory of Saint Francis de Sales from 1815 to 1855: The Autobiography of Saint John Bosco.* Translated by Daniel Lyons SDB. (New Rochelle, N.Y.: Don Bosco Publications, 1989); digitised at url:116 [includes errata noted in the sympathetic but critical review of the book by Arthur Lenti SDB in *Journal of Salesian Studies* vol.1 no.1 (Spring 1990), digitised at url:117, which details many errors in translation (and makes clear that the infiltration of the word 'Autobiography' into the title is inappropriate).]

The numerous popular biographies of the Saint inevitably rest largely on the detailed memoir of his life compiled (Vols I-IX) by Fr G.B. Lemoyne; Vol.X [in fact the final volume published] by Angelo Amadei; Vols XI-XIX by Eugenio Ceria, published as *Memorie Biografiche di Don Giovanni Bosco* [later as: *…del Venerabile Servo di Dio Don Giovanni Bosco;* as *… del Venerabile Don Giovanni Bosco;* as *…del Beato San Giovanni Bosco;* as *…di San Giovanni Bosco*], 19 vols. Turin & S. Benigno Canavese: Scuola Tipografica Libraria Salesiana [*later* Tipografia S.A.I.D., *then* Società Editrice Internazionale], 1898-1917, then resumed 1930-1939 (plus Index volumes). Digitised at url:118 [and elsewhere]

English translation as *Biographical Memoirs of Saint John Bosco*. 19 vols (in progress). New Rochelle, N.Y.: Salesiana Publishers, 1965-. Digitised at url:119.

The background to Lemoyne's massive work, itself largely a distillation from his preliminary 45 volume collection of *Documenti*, is given by Arthur Lenti in his article 'Don Bosco's "Boswell": John Baptist Lemoyne — the Man and his Work', *Journal of Salesian Studies* vol.1 no.2 (Fall 1990), digitised at url:120.

Interesting material on his birthplace and later places associated with him is found in:
Aldo Giraudo & Giuseppe Biancardi, *Qui è vissuto don Bosco* (url:121); English version, *Don Bosco Lived Here* (url:122).

The popular religious biographies of him tend to say little of his conjuring, though it is made the focus of some modern books and comics about him intended for children, such as (url:123) the Flemish comic Guido Grilli, *Don Bosco, De kleine goochelaar* (Brussells 1953), Catherine Beebe, *Saint John Bosco and the Children's Saint, Dominic Savio* (San Francisco: Ignatius Press, 1955), and Dolores Ready, *John's Magic, A Story about John Bosco* (Minneapolis: Winston, 1978).

A statue of him performing, *Il monumento a Giovannino giocoliere*, was put up at Becchi in 1929, since replaced by a bronze version (url:124). Another is included in the Museo della Magia of the Salesian Catholic priest and magician Silvio Mantelli ("Mago Sales") in Cherasco (url:125).

One might have expected the anti-clerical press in the 19th century to have made much of the coincidence of his name and Bartolomeo's, but I have found very few examples. In a humorous piece in *Le Progrès de la Somme* 27 May 1883 the writer pretends to mix up the two when people refer to Don Bosco in Paris at that time, and *La Presse* 21 Mar.1883 says, referring to Chambord, the Legitimist pretender to the French throne: "La presse cléricale announce que don Bosco, le thaumaturge qui obtient à cette heure un si grand succès dans les églises du noble fauborg vient d'être mandé à Goritz auprès du comte de Chambord. On espère que le moine italien voudra bien renouveler, en faveur du fils de saint Louis, un de ces miracles qu'il sème un peu partout, avec une facilité qui rappelle les procédés merveilleux de son célèbre homonyme, le prestidigitateur Bosco".

NOTES

[1] Where his parents were living in 1815, and where his grandfather had settled in 1793 as a share farmer (*mezzadro*) of the Biglione Farm. It was only in 1972 that this was shown to be his birthplace, previously believed to be the family's later house further up the hill (in *Canton Cavallo*) where he grew up. The farmhouse had been demolished in 1957-8 and replaced with a huge Basilica.

[2] *Becchi* is usually given as his birthplace; he himself in his *Memorie* says Murialdo (spelling it the way he pronounced it), and similarly in the Decretal Letter announcing

his canonisation "Egli nacque in Murialdo, piccolo borgo campestre, e propriamente nella frazione detta volgarmente dei Becchi, vicino a Castelnuovo di Asti".

[3] Except for part of his brain, kept as a relic in the Basilica; stolen in 2017 but recovered.

[4] His own accounts of the tricks he performed are in his *Memorie dell'Oratorio* I, 3, 11, 12, and similarly in *Memorie Biografiche* Chapters 13, 17, 35 and 39.

[5] *Memorie dell'Oratorio* II, 1, 3; *Memorie Biografiche* Chapter 42: he specifically states that he will never again perform "i giuochi dei bussolotti, di prestigiatore, di saltimbanco, di destrezza, di corda", which is only paraphrased in the English version.

However, Michel Sedlow in his chapter on Dom Bosco in *Les Illusionistes et leurs Secrets* quotes from Auffray's *Un Saint traversa la France* (1937) an account of him extracting a donation by magic in Paris in 1883.

B5. Carlo Bosco.
For the Russian Karla Bosko *see B6; for the American* Carl Bosco *see B98-99.*

There appears to be no reliable evidence for *any* magician performing under the name Carlo Bosco, which is found with three main references:

(1) = Bartolomeo (B1). The *Lexikon* lists Bartolomeo as "Bartolomeo (Carlo)" presumably misled by Carl Willmann's article 'Carlo Bosco' in *Der Zauberwelt* August 1896. Bartolomeo is very occasionally referred to as "Carlo Bosco" (or "Carlo Bosko") in newspaper reports (for example, "Carlo Bosko, der weltberühmte Taschenspieler ist gestern … hier eingetroffen": *Die Siebvenbürge Bote* 10 Aug. 1846), probably from confusion with the many books under that name, but never in his own advertisements.

(2) = Eugenio (B2) is occasionally wrongly said to be named Carlo, perhaps influenced by the 1838 book *Carlo Bosco des Jüngern Das Ganze der Taschenspielerkunst*. This is found both in contemporary newspapers (for example, "Der Tausenkünstler Carlo Bosco hat in Weimar Unglück gehabt…", *Zurcheriesche Freitagszeitung* 15 May 1857) and in later references — both *Brockhaus Konversationslexikon,* 14. Aufl. 1894-6 and *Nordisk Familjebok Konversationslexikon och Realencyklopedi* 2nd ed., 1905 give his name as *Carlo Bosco,* and as late as 1927 a Dutch newspaper article (*De Nieuwe Koerier* 29 Jan.1927) calls Bartolomeo's son Carlo: "[tr.] His son Carlo Bosco continued the business shortly after his father died…" ; 'Magier der Welt' gives **Carlo Bosco Junior** as the name of "einzigster Sohn von Bartholomeo Bosco", with "Künstlername: **Carlo Bosco**".

(3) "Carlo Bosco" as the attributed author of *Carlo Bosco's Zauber-Cabinet* (1840) and other 19th century titles on conjuring (still being reworked in the 20th century, ultimately as *Carlo Bosko* [sic]*, der weltberühmte Zauberkünstler und Taschenspieler…*1922). These are listed in the *Books* section. There is no evidence that any of these were written by Bartolomeo (or Eugenio) and the earliest was by Heinrich August Kerndörffer (who himself died in 1846): Kerndörffer probably made up the name based on the old book *Carl der Tausendkünstler,* which he re-edited in 1825.

The attribution is simply a literary forgery — "mystification" a politer term — using the name of a famous person to promote book sales ("una strumentalizzazione, non propria legittima, di un cognome che era ormai sinonimo di magia", as Rusconi puts it, p.211). The interesting question is: who did contemporary readers think was the author of these books? Presumably most believed "Carlo Bosco" was a real person and many no doubt equated him with Bartolomeo, and there are occasional references to this mythical "Carlo Bosco" as

(a) a specific famous magician — "... die schwarze Kunst, die Kunst des Carlo Bosco..." (article in *Neue Jenaische allgemeine Literatur-Zeitung* 22 Aug.1844), and "[an empty flask] ist dasjenigen Instrument, auf welchem Carlo Bosco sich nach den Mühen der Produktion erholt..." (story in *Nürnberger Trichter* I: 4; 1849); the Dutch impostors "Professor Bosco Jr." (B39) and "Robertus Bosco" (B40) even claimed to be "son of the late Carlo Bosco"; and Charles Mirano (C38) claimed to be a pupil of Carlo Bosco!

(b) a generic term for magician — "ein angehender Carlo Bosco" (story in *Morgenblatt für gebildete Leser* 12 Mar.1854), and "some Carlo Bosco exploit in the line of *Taschenspielerkunst,* as the Germans call it..." (political article in *Londonderry Standard* 25 Nov.1868).

B6. Karla Bosko (Карла Боско).

The 1849 book, *Opyty natural'noy magii i volshebnyy kabinet Karla Bosko...* [tr. *Experiments in natural magic and the magic cabinet of Karla Bosco...* see *Books* section LRu3] is said to state that the famous Italian magician Giovanni Bartolomeo Bosco was a soldier in the army of Napoleon during the Patriotic War of 1812, captured in the battle of Borodino and sent to Tobolsk, where he first began to show artistic inclinations. After the exchange of prisoners in 1814 he returned to his homeland and toured all European capitals, enjoying tremendous success. *Later he returned to Russia and performed under the name Karla Bosco for nine or ten years* and was extremely popular. Before the end of the tour in Russia, in 1849 he published [the above] book in Moscow with a full description of his repertoire.

It is safe to say that there was no "Karla Bosko" touring Russia for nine or ten years (and that the book is a translation not an original).

B7. "Bosco der Zweite"

A person under this name is mentioned in *ATZ* 31 Oct.1838 as performing recently in Aachen, "ein Wundermann", predicting the fall of dice, determining the path of billiard balls, prophesying cards in whist and ombre, etc, causing a sensation and well deserving the name "Bosco the Second".

"Bosco der Zweite" was later used (like Carlo Bosco) as the name of an imaginary author of books on conjuring (see *Books* LGe98-101).

B8. Hermann Bosco (1)

A magician performing under the name "Hermann Bosco" is found only in Nantes in 1846 and claiming to be Bartolomeo's son. He is at the Grand Théâtre on January 19th — "Tout Nantes se rappelle M. Bosco, ce prestidigitateur fameux; c'est aujourd'hui de son fils qu'il est ici question…" (*Le Breton* 19 Jan.1846); his act, we are told, is in two parts 'La Pêche Miraculeuse ou la Naissance d'une Ménagerie' and 'Un Concert imitatif de plusieurs oiseaux' (*Courrier de Nantes* 19 Jan.1846).

The reviews were excellent — he made coffee and an omelette in a hat, first making the eggs dance on his wand, his arms and on his body, then suddenly produced from nowhere fish in a bowl and half a dozen rabbits, imitating bird song wonderfully, and ending by handing out sweets and presents (*Le Breton* 20 Jan.1846); "feats of legerdemain done with incredible skill" (*L'Hermine* 20 Jan.1846). He was hailed as "a worthy son of his famous father, and a worthy rival of Comte and Philippe" (*Courrier de Nantes* 20 Jan.1846);

A second show followed on 22nd with no less success, but he then suddenly disappeared — "après avoir escamoté tant de choses, il a fini par s'escamoter lui-même" (*Le Breton* 22 Jan.1846; *Courrier de Nantes* 22, 24 Jan.1846).

Another "Hermann Bosco" is found in London in 1863 (B67).

B9. Mignard-Bosco.

Active in France 1846-1850. First sighted in Limoges in 1846, opening on February 23rd — "M. Mignard Bosco, physicien … aura l'honneur de donner quelques séances de physique et scènes de ventriloquie mimique et polyphonique…"; this was well received and further shows followed (*L'Ordre* 15, 22 Feb.; 1 Mar.1846).

On October 4th he opened in Toulouse, the newspapers promoting him as "le célèbre physicien" and "…privilégié de toutes les maisons d'instruction de France et de l'étranger … M. Mignard-Bosco, dont le nom est si universellement connu". His "Grande Soirée mystérieuse et instructive" promised to "promener l'imagination des spectateurs sur une variété d'objets dont on chercherait en vain à se donner une juste idée, et qui tous, différant les uns des autres, en produisant tour à tour de nouvelles surprises, charmeront les yeux du public occupé à pénétrer les mystérieux prestiges qui lui seront offerts.—La séance sera divisée en six parties: 1. Prestidigitation; 2. physique expérimentale; 3. tours d'illusion; 4. scène de mécanisme; 5. scènes mimiques et comiques; 6. scènes de l'homme à la poupée"; with the programme including "Le Cagaro — Le magicien sortant des enfers. — Le chemin de fer ou le nouveau siècle. — La petite cuisinière. — Le parapluie à la polka. — La danse des sorciers. — Le galop du démon. — Les mouchoirs voyageurs. — La boule sympathique. — Les boulets de 48 et de 96. — Le cercle magique dévoilé. — Création de fleurs enchantée seule en Europe" (*Journal de Toulouse* 14, 15 Sep.; 3 Oct.1846; *La Gazette du Languedoc* 15 Sep.; 2, 4 Oct.1846).

The following month in Nîmes he was hailed as "le célèbre Mignard Bosco dont la réputation est depuis longtemps européenne…" (*Courrier du Gard* 24 Nov.1846).

In 1848 we find him in the north, announced to appear in Méaux, now "accompagné de ses deux demoiselles, l'une professeur de physique, et l'autre élève du conservatoire de musique", but the *Soirée* was delayed (*Journal de Seine-et-Marne* 18, 25 Mar.1848).

Finally, in 1850 we hear that a magician named *Mignart*-Bosco (presumably the same person) is coming to La Rochelle, "la prochaine arrivée du prestidigitateur Mignart-Bosco…" and, as his promotional piece ironically puts it: "Le nom seul de Bosco est une recommandation puissante auprès du public…" (*L'Écho rochelais* 8 Feb.1850).

B10. 'Petit-Bosco'

This epithet was adopted for a period by Victor Houdmon, active 1847-1860. He is first sighted in Toulouse in 1847 — "soirée extraordinaire de physique, magie, prestige, nécromancie et tours d'adresse … donnée par M. Victor Houdmon, élève de M. Conte, de Paris" (*Journal de Toulouse* 14 Apr.1847).

In 1851 he is performing at a fair in Chalon-sur-Saône, "Victor Houdmon, surnommé le petit Bosco … ce qu'il y a de plus merveilleux, de plus étonnant, c'est la suspension dans l'air d'une personne complètement isolée … Il faut voir pour juger, la plume est inhabile à décrire un semblable phénomène … et puis ces tours de passe-passe, cet escamotage d'une grande personne…" (*Courrier de Saône-et-Loire* 25 June 1851).

Over New Year 1852 we find him in Bourges with his "Temple d'Illusion" during the fair, "le célèbre Victor Houdmon, qui se laisse modestement surnommer le *petit Bosco,* bien que le *grand Bosco,* lui-même, n'ait pas grand chose à lui revendre en fait d'inventions de physique amusante, de prestidigitation et de ces tours subtils qui font crier tout un auditoire *à la sorcellerie…*" (*La République de 1848* 26 Dec.1851; 7 Jan.1852).

In June 1854 he was at the Foire du Mail in Orléans, and had recently been in Rennes and Tours. He has now dropped his 'petit Bosco' tag, promoting himself as a "disciple de Bosco et de Robert-Houdin". The local paper rated him above Bartolomeo: "Nous avons vu Bosco cet hiver et nous pensions qu'il était impossible de pousser aussi loin l'art de la prestidigitation. M. Victor Houdmon nous a bien vite convaincu du contraire. Tous les soirs il étonne, par la variété et la nouveauté de ses tours … Nous engageons nos lecteurs à aller faire comme nous, la comparaison entre les deux artistes, et nous sommes assurés que M. Houdmon parviendra à leur faire oublier le magicien italien … nous citerons particulièrement les tours du mouchoir aux oeufs, de la bouteille aux rubans et de la pêche miraculeuse" (*Journal de Loiret* 20 May; 6, 8, 15, 24 June 1854).

In 1855 at the fair in Clermont-Ferrand in the Auvergne he was rated a "prestidigitateur d'une rare adresse et d'une grande habilité", and equally skilful is the "ecamotage de Mme Victor, dont l'agilité personnelle est certainement à la hauteur du talent de son mari…" (*L'Ami de la Patrie* 22 Aug.1855).

June the following year saw him in Nevers (*Nevers Médiathèque Jean Jaurès - Ms 001 à Ms 199 - Manuscrits et dessins - Inventaire 2015*, p.32) and the last we see of him is in Luxemburg in May 1860, "Grande Soirée Caméléonienne, ou les enchantements modernes … les merveilles de l'art et de la nature …continué par le

Comicorama Américain..." (*Courrier du Grand-Duché de Luxembourg* 16, 20 May 1860).

See also Viarizio (B26) who for a period used the epithet 'Le Petit Bosco Modern'.

B11. "Bosco" (Marseille 1857)

An unidentified impostor calling himself *Bosco* performed at the *Théâtre du Gymnase* in Marseille on Saturday 9th January 1847 (see Rusconi p.140, taking him to be Bartolomeo) and had played earlier in Brive-la-Gaillard. His unfortunate Marseille performance is wittily described at some length in the *Le Journal des théâtres* 23 Jan.1847: from his advertisements a large and eager audience was expecting Bartolomeo, whom they fondly remembered from his 1834 visit, but instead of "l'embonpoint réjouissant et la figure épanouie du véritable Bosco" they were disappointed to see "un grand messieur vêtu de noir, aux allures de fântome" who spoke French "comme une vache de Séville ou de Madrid". He did some card tricks "avec une dextérité de rhinocéros", using a plant from the audience, and ended by fleeing the stage after throwing oranges at the audience, who were enraged he had beaten them to it.

B12. "Signor Bosco"; Alfred Bosco (real name Marcus Epstein)

This covers Marcus (Markus, Marek, Sigmund, Sigismund, Zygmunt, Marianus) Epstein (Eppstein, Epzstain; *aka* Salomon Engländer), *which I believe are all names used by the same person.*

Discussed at the end are:
B12a. "Adam Epstein" (H.A. Epstein; Henry Adams; real name Brøndum)
B12b. "Professor Sigismund Epstein" (Finland 1875)
B12c. "Dr A. Epstein" (Finland 1880; England 1881)
B12d. "Professor Epstein" (Holland 1870) = Heksch
B12e. "Professor Epstein" (Holland 1883)
who are Epstein impostors not Bosco impostors

Probably the most interesting of the Bosco impostors, and certainly the most annoying to Bartolomeo. His repertoire included not only conjuring but ventriloquism, playing several musical instruments, a decapitation act, the gun trick, and plate-spinning (the plates on their *edge*, not flat on a stand or stick: see *Appendix Z7*). When he is first seen in England in November 1854 he is clearly already a very accomplished performer, but of his previous career in Europe we get only a glimpse.

From events soon after he left England in 1858 we know his real name was Marcus Epstein, and in June 1851 we get our first sighting of him: a wanted notice from the police in Prague for "Markus Joseph Epstein, also known as Salomon Engländer", magician from Leutschitz in Russian Poland, age 23; religion Jewish; stature medium, slim; hair black; eyes grey. Convicted of inducement to misuse of official power and sentenced in Kraków to be deported to his native country.[1]

So, he had already used at least one false name, and he was born in 1827 or 1828 in Leutschitz (in Kalisch, now Kałusz), which is probably modern Łęczyca.

The only other evidence, for what it is worth, for his activities prior to his arrival in England in November 1854 are his own claims made in later advertisements, and these claims are inconsistent (and implausible).

In the *Era* 13 June 1857 he claims to have performed before
    King of Prussia December 16th 1849
    King of Hanover May 11th 1851
    King of Sweden and Norway March 4th 1852
    Emperor of France and family October 15th 1854;
in the *Rochdale Pilot* 20 Feb. 1858 he claims
    King of Prussia at Berlin May 11th 1851,
    King of Hanover December 16th 1852
    the Emperor Napoleon, no date given;
in the *Sussex Agricultural Express* 5 Dec. 1857 he claims
    King of Prussia at Berlin May 11th 1851,
    King of Hanover Dec. 16th 1852;
in the *Chester Chronicle* 23 Jan. 1858 he claims
    King of Prussia at Berlin May 11th 1852,
    King of Hanover December 16th 1852

In the *Dublin Evening Post* 4 Mar.1856 he also claims to have performed before the Sultan of Turkey.

Some of the inconsistencies in these dates may be due to misread handwriting or to typesetting errors — or was he being deliberately vague? He is, however, consistent in claiming to have performed at Balmoral before Queen Victoria on September 24th 1855, which he in fact did; after he left England this was claimed by a number of other magicians (see *Appendix Z12*).

One reason for his departing for Britain may have been his impending liability for compulsory military service. An edict published in the Kraków paper, *Czas* 28 Mar. 1856 (and elsewhere), actually names a 'Markus Epstein' among Jews who had not reported for service, but that is in Dukla, and the name may have been common.

His arrival in England is recorded in some detail:
"The Bremen barque *Westphalia,* from Bremen, bound to New York, put into Falmouth a few days since, short of water, having on board the son of the celebrated Bosco, whose talent as a magician and ventriloquist is so well known throughout Europe; he was obliged to land in consequence of his suffering so much from the long and tedious passage from the above port in order to restore his health" (*Royal Cornwall Gazette* 10 Nov.1854; the ship's arrival is confirmed by the *Shipping and Mercantile Gazette* 2 Nov.1854, which gives the exact date: "Falmouth ... Put in, Oct. 30—The Westphalia, Mensing, from Bremen for New York, for water"). The ship sailed again on November 3rd (*Lloyd's List* 4 Nov.1854) but the self-proclaimed son of Bosco remained in England. His age is uncertain but the following year he was described as "young yet" (*Aberdeen Herald* 22 Sep.1855) and when he married in July 1856 (see below) he gave his age as 23.

A few weeks later he was performing in Penzance — "Legerdemain — Signor Bosco, who made his appearance in a curious fashion at Falmouth a few weeks since, has been giving two or three of his entertainments at the Prince's Hall during the week. Very clever his sleight-of-hand tricks have proved, and most amusing, apparently, to the audiences, who, however, have not been large. In dexterity we have never seen Signor Bosco surpassed, and he varies his performance by a clever use of the concertina and certain ventriloquial powers..." (*Cornish Telegraph* 13 Dec.1854).

He was fairly safe in his choice of the name "Bosco". Bartolomeo had not returned to England after his short-lived 1851 venture and had left little impression; nor did the British papers report on Bartolomeo's European performances or notice the incipient career of Eugenio. Epstein finally left England in 1858 and while there had the name "Bosco" to himself — until "Madame Bosco" (BF1) appeared in 1857, and by the following year there was another Madame Bosco (BF2) and at least two further Signor Boscos (B63, B65) sporting the name in Britain, and more to follow.

From Penzance he moved on to Bristol — "Signor Bosco, the Great Magician and Ventriloquist, who has had the honour of Performing before all the Crowned Heads in Europe... Feats of Magic, at the Albert-Rooms, College-Green, on his way to London ... The Trick, denominated the 'Barber's Trick, or Magic Soap-Box,' is really almost beyond belief..." (*Bristol Mercury* 23 Dec.1854). This trick, with different coloured lathers and a shaved beard reappearing, must have been popular as he was still in Bristol well into January ("...the Great Italian Wizard, Who has given his Astonishing Entertainments before the Kings of Hanover and Prussia...": *Bristol Mercury* 6 Jan.1855); he then added a new feature to his act, "the Surprising Trick of Cutting Off the Human Head" (*Bristol Mercury* 13 Jan.1855). His advertisements now included a striking illustration (which seems to be original) of himself holding his severed head under his arm and holding a large knife in the other hand.[2]

From Bristol he headed to Wales and from February to May is found performing in Newport, Cardiff (cheekily promising to "spare no exertion to attain the renowned reputation of his father, Professor Bosco, the Greatest Magician in the World"),[3] and in Carmarthen, Haverfordwest,[4] Pontypool, Milford, Pembroke,[5] Tenby, and Wrexham.

He now went north to Chester, then Birmingham in June, and Scotland in July, opening in Glasgow on July 18th, with some success despite the season,[6] Next in Dundee, he performed under contract to George W. Cassidy who had been showing his 'Diorama of the Overland Route to India' at the Circus in Lindsay Street since June 4th. Bosco's entertainment was "well attended ... exhibiting a large amount of inventive faculty" (*Dundee, Perth, and Cupar Advertiser* 14 Aug.1855), and while in Dundee he met the man who was to be his manager for the next eight months, the colourful American, William John Lauderdale Millar (B62).

Millar had come to England only the previous month, as manager of the conjoined "African Twins", whom he soon lost. He describes his first meeting with Bosco (whose claim to be the son of Bartolomeo he insists he initially believed to be true) in an 1892 article, 'How I Brought Bosco before the Queen'.[7]

"... After the Twins were stolen I felt rather depressed, and to change the scene I went to Broughty Ferry, a lovely watering-place near Dundee, to rest for a few days previous to returning home to America. About eleven o'clock on the night of my arrival ... a well-dressed dark gentleman came forward and said — 'I am Signor Bosco, and I came here to make business with you...'".

Millar and Bosco agreed to start working together in two weeks' time in Aberdeen. Millar arranged a hall, plastered the town with advertising, and Bosco opened to a packed house. Queen Victoria had now arrived at nearby Balmoral, says Millar in his article, and he naively asked the proprietor of his hotel to give him a letter of introduction to Her. He made the same request to the editor of the *Aberdeen Herald* and received from him a letter to Dr. Robertson, manager of the Duchess of Kent's estate, and Robertson introduced him to Colonel C.B. Phipps at Balmoral.[8] Phipps "agreed to mention the subject to Her Majesty this evening". A letter duly arrived from Phipps dated September 18th commanding him to bring Bosco to perform before Her Majesty on Monday evening next (24th). Bosco, Millar continues, "looked perfectly wild with excitement". The performance was to take place in the ballroom after dinner was over about a quarter past nine, with the Queen's carpenter to make a suitable small stage. Special engraved programmes were printed (url:343) and the pair arrived at Balmoral at 3 p.m. "I asked Colonel Phipps in what language Signor Bosco should speak during the performance, as he spoke seven"; "Most definitely in English", Phipps replied. "That happened to be the one with which Bosco was the least acquainted with [*sic*], and his mistakes were often very amusing...". The audience, Millar tells us, included the Prince Consort, the Royal children, the Crown Prince of Prussia, various nobles, and several local farmers and their children invited by Phipps, and the show went on for about an hour and a half. Millar ends by giving the text of a letter from Phipps dated September 25th enclosing a cheque for fifty pounds.[9]

Phipps's first letter of September 18th was printed in a note about Bosco in the *Aberdeen Herald* of September 22nd, and on the 29th he advertises his "final performance at the Mechanics' Hall ... on his return from Balmoral Castle, where he has had the honour...[etc., etc.]". The Balmoral performance was widely reported in other papers at the time (e.g. *Inverness Courier* 27 Sep.1855), and was featured in Bosco's future advertisements — in Edinburgh later in the year he declares: "Signor Bosco ... had the distinguished honour of performing at Balmoral Castle on the 24th September, 1855, before Her Most Gracious Majesty the Queen..." (*The Scotsman* 5 Dec. 1855).

From Aberdeen Bosco moved on to Inverness (where his advertisement stated he "was trained from infancy to the art, by his father, who himself had no mean reputation as a magician" [indeed!]: *Inverness Courier* 4 Oct.1855), then Brechin, Montrose, Forres, Stirling, Greenock, and Edinburgh in December (advertising special terms for schools "by making application to Professor Millar..."). There he was giving four performances a day, with an "*exposé* of spirit rapping" added to the show and presents given to the audience, both probably Millar's idea.

They now headed to Ireland, opening in Belfast in January ("...to Professor Millar is due the credit of all the business arrangements connected with Signor Bosco's exhibitions..."), then performing with great success in February and March in Dublin, where his final show was announced for March 18th. This featured 'The

Necromancer's Polka', played during the interval, newly composed and dedicated to Bosco by his accompanist T. Barbor Might.[10]

But Millar and Bosco were increasingly at odds over the terms of their business arrangement and this came to a head when Millar beat and dismissed Bosco's black servant. Millar was charged with assault and Bosco appeared as a witness against him. The most detailed account of the trial names the servant as John Mathews, "the negro lately employed at Bosco's entertainment", and quotes Millar as claiming he had used "insulting and filthy language" to Mrs Millar[11] when she had suspected him of stealing a woman's veil. Millar had dismissed him but Mathews insisted Bosco was his master and refused to go. Millar's lawyer stated that "there happens to be a difference at present between Mr. Millar and Signor Bosco, who are partners, and this circumstance will account for this business". The magistrate ruled the assault proved, and unjustifiable, and Millar was to pay the outstanding wages, and court costs.[12]

Immediately afterwards they ended their business association and joint notices were published side-by-side, dated March 19th, stating that their partnership was now "dissolved, by mutual consent" (*Saunders's News-Letter* 21 Mar.1856).

Millar embarked on a new theatrical venture, purchasing the Diorama of India which had been touring England and Scotland for several years and had been on show in the Concert Room of the Rotunda in Dublin since August 1855; he took this to Cork. (For Millar's later career see B62).

Bosco, rather than moving on as planned to Cork, since Millar was now there with the Diorama, continued to perform in Dublin, taking over the Concert Room at the Rotundo which had been vacated when Millar purchased the Diorama. He reopened under his own management on Monday 24th, now with added features he had announced earlier in the month —"10,000 Presents to be Given Away during the Easter Holidays", plus "New and Gorgeous Paraphernalia", new apparatus from Paris and Birmingham at a cost of over £400 "which forms in itself a complete Temple of Enchantment" (borrowing a term long used by Joseph Jacobs) and a new series of "Astounding Wonders" including "the new Gun Trick, first time here" (ad in *Catholic Telegraph* 2 Mar.1856, and in at least five other Dublin papers the same day). He does not mention his ventriloquism in his current advertisements, which was the one feature of his performances that reviewers had found less than great; and a rival ventriloquist was in town, "Mr Gallaher, the unrivalled Solo-Dramatic and Transformatic Ventriloquist", advertising himself as "Gallaher versus the Foreigners, alias the Russians — Multiloquism versus Boscoism…" (*Saunders's News Letter* 25 Mar.1856).

Bosco's act, and the "trinkets and toys" for the children (from one inexhaustible hat), went off well — then on March 27th *who should arrive in Dublin but Bartolomeo*, having rushed over from Toulouse where he had been performing. Producing his album as proof of his identity, he went with a lawyer to the head Police Officer in Dublin, inquiring "whether proceedings could not be taken, under the jurisdiction of the magistrates, against the Signor Bosco now performing nightly at the Rotundo, whom he asserted to be an usurper of his titles and reputation". He was told that the magistrates could not interfere and to apply to the Court of Equity. Bartolomeo then wrote to the newspaper: "…I have not authorised any person to assume my name, thereby damaging my present European reputation ... as the First Conjuror in the world" (*Saunders's News-Letter* 28, 31 Mar.1856).

The only result was that the impostor changed his stage name (though still claiming to be a Bosco and to be Italian) to "Signor Alfred Bosco, of Mantua",[13] and he continued performing in Dublin until April 5th.[14]

Alfred, as it now convenient to call him, then resumed his tour of Ireland, and opened in Limerick on April 7th,[15] still billing himself as "Signor Bosco" or "Alfred Bosco", but no longer claiming to be Bartolomeo's son. He is next sighted in Waterford, where his "exposure" had clearly done nothing to discourage the public: the show was a great success — "the Town Hall ... was crowded to excess, and the performance was applauded through every stage by the spectators..." (*Waterford Mail* 17 Apr.1856).[16]. Then came Cork,[17] Clonmel, and Kilkenny, followed by Liverpool in June ("Signor Alfred Bosco, the eminent Italian magician and ventriloquist"). An article on his performance there remarks on "the Chinese plate and dish dance" (*Liverpool Daily Post* 11 June 1856), a regular feature of his shows (and his opening act at Balmoral). He drew excellent crowds in Liverpool and moved from the Queen's Hall to the more capacious Theatre Royal.

During July he was in Birmingham, exhibiting his "cabalistic and ventriloquial powers", and while there he got married, after a three day courtship. On July 25th at the Anglican Church of St Thomas under the name Alfred Bosco, Artist, age 23, and giving his father as Alexander Bosco, Artist, he married Hannah Waldron, age 22, spinster, daughter of Thomas Waldron, Green Grocer.[18]

On August 11th he began a long run at the Exchange Rooms in Manchester, again described as very successful ("...certainly deserves to be styled the wizard of wizards"). He was fined in court soon after for not paying a toll (*Manchester Daily Examiner* 23 Aug.1856; the avoidance ended up costing him 7s4d. instead of 10d.), and in September he was sued by his former secretary Braham Jacob for unpaid salary and a gold watch. When they were in Liverpool Alfred had obtained the watch from Jacob and pawned it to pay for "advertisements, hand-bills, &c". Jacob had then resigned after hearing that Alfred "had spoken slightly both of himself and his sister, to whom the defendant was paying his addresses". Alfred "was cross-examined as to his real name, and also the name of his father: He believed that he was born in Poland, but claimed to be an Italian, because he had resided there for some time; had not seen his father for some years; spoke eleven languages; and on being asked as to his religious belief, defendant said that 'he believed what he saw'." The judge awarded Jacob his salary and expenses, but found for Alfred as to the watch (*Manchester Courier* 20 Sep.1856).

Alfred moved on to Huddersfield, advertising his shows there and in Leeds as "for a short time only ... previous to his departure for America on 15th October" (*Manchester Times* 13 Sep.1856). But instead of America he headed to Halifax (*Bradford Observer* 16 Oct.1856). He then opened in Leeds on October 21st, preceded by several weeks of tantalising placards plastered around the town announcing "Bosco is coming". On arrival he received a verse greeting in the *Leeds Times,* clearly inserted by a local shop-keeper who combines it with a poem on his own business:

SIGNOR BOSCO THE GREAT WIZARD OF THE WORLD. Bosco's coming ! Bosco's coming ! Is the universal cry ; And we hear it all around us, From the lowest to the high. Bosco ! he who works such wonders, With his feats of sleight-of-hand; He whose fame extendeth widely, And throughout the mighty land. Bosco's coming! Bosco's coming! Who the greatest wizard beats ; Fame, it gives him world-wide honor, For his hundred splendid feats ; Royal heads have watched his magic, With both pleasure and delight; Here, no doubt, he'll show his prowess, And surprise on Tuesday night;

The Manchester Guardian in speaking of this clever gentleman says:—"There can be no doubt that there is but one wizard, Bosco, and he is the greatest man in the world in his art."

There only is one Bosco, true, And that is clearly known; There only is one Hyam, mark ! And see his great renown. For wondrous dress, both cheap and good, Substantial, new. and smart; Whoever wants to save their cash Should purchase from his mart.[19]

His 'Temple of Magic' was hailed as "one of the most dazzling we have seen for some years, and is almost unique in the beauty and completeness of its furniture and machinery, and a negro attendant, resplendent in plush and gold ... certainly not an ordinary everyday wizard". His act included conjuring and legerdemain, ventriloquism and the accordion; no mention here of plate-spinning (*Leeds Intelligencer* 25 Oct. 1856). His shows drew large crowds, and the crowds drew the local pickpockets.

Next was Batley, then Bradford, York, Preston, and south to Bristol. In February he was back in Glasgow, followed by Greenock, and Edinburgh, where he did especially well over the Easter Week as he was exempt from the ban on plays and concerts during Lent.

It was at this time that reports began appearing in the British papers of Eugenio's injury to his hand in Weimar. Alfred had not billed himself since Dublin as the son of Bartolomeo, but at least one paper (the *Limerick Chronicle* 20 May 1857) assumed the victim was their recent visitor.

Alfred was once again advertising as "prior to his departure for America" (*Caledonian Mercury* 3 Apr.1857), but again this did not happen (and may have been merely a promotional ploy). Instead he finally opened in London, performing at the Strand Theatre from June 1st. Audiences and reviewers were enthusiastic, the *Era* (7 June 1857) especially welcoming the inclusion of plate-spinning in his act — "the dance of the dinner plates and the *pas-seul* of the wash-hand basin, that Signor Blitz introduced into this country a quarter of a century since, but which we have never since seen so well accomplished, displays a nimbleness of the present professor's fingers to very great advantage".

The *Era* went on to admire his legerdemain, less enthusiastic about "the famous Gun Trick, a disagreeable and possibly a dangerous experiment", though "very dexterously performed"; and praised "his powers as a ventriloquist ... producing the apparent voices of children of all ages... But his great skill, and that on which his fame may securely rest, is his wonderful dexterity of manipulation. Years of practice — though he is still very youthful-looking — must have been bestowed on this...".

"The palmy days of magic and sleight of hand seem revived", said the *Morning Chronicle* (15 June 1857), but one reviewer felt obliged to comment that this was not "the Chevalier Bosco whose marvels have long delighted high continental circles... the name has become quite common property among conjurors abroad... The 'Signor Alfred Bosco' ... at the Strand Theatre wants the delicacy and *finesse* of that renowned juggler ... but his sleight of hand is truly astonishing..." (*John Bull* 6 June 1857).

His London run won him great acclaim and publicity — but no money: the lessee of the Strand, Thomas Payne, was declared bankrupt soon after, leaving Alfred and a host of theatricals well out of pocket.[20]

Alfred's advertising was now even more exaggerated, proclaiming in the *Era* (14 June 1857) that at Balmoral "the title of the Great Wizard of the World was graciously bestowed upon him", and he was now calling himself "Signor A. Bosco, Chevalier of the Legion of Honour" — a claim which was soon to cause him trouble. He then announced (*Era* 21 June 1857) that he would next appear in Portsmouth on June 29th, "in honour of Her Most Gracious Majesty's Coronation, by express command".

Portsmouth went well. He was now accompanied by Anton Kratky-Baschik, billed here as a musician (playing "a novel and grotesque combination of instruments") rather than as a conjuror)[21] and they then continued on to Sherborne, Southampton, Ryde, Newport, Ventnor and Cowes on the Isle of Wight, where the season was at its height. The *Isle of Wight Observer* (15 Aug.1857) called Alfred's "tricks ... very interesting and clever ... a good musician and a tolerable ventriloquist", saying he began his performances "in a gay, full dress, decorated with the badge of the Legion of Honour" then changed to his bare-armed robe. He later claimed to have performed before the Queen a second time, at Osborne House on August 27th 1857, and further that among those present was the Emperor of the French who had presented him with the Star of the Legion of Honour "as a token of his great satisfaction with the entertainment gave their Majesties" (*Leeds Intelligencer* 27 Feb.1858). Victoria and the Emperor were indeed at Osborne earlier in August 1857, but there is no mention of "Bosco" performing before them at that time — and of course he had been sporting a Legion of Honour since June

His card in the *Era* now trumpeted: "...Signor Alfred Bosco and his Fairy Temple of Magic.— Bosco travels from town to town with Ten Tons of Luggage, Fifteen Assistants, and Full Band" (*Era* 30 Aug.1857).

However, he was forced to cut short his itinerary after breaking his leg when thrown from a horse while doing some amateur riding at Bowcombe Down.[22] While he was laid up Professor Millar, who was touring through Wales with his brother and "Madame Bosco", briefly put her on hold and himself performed as "Signor Bosco", impersonating the impostor — with a singular lack of success (p.278).

It was October 26th before Alfred was back performing (now without Kratky-Baschik), still in the Isle of Wight, then, finally able to travel again, in Hastings, and from November 23rd in Brighton ("astonishing good houses"). He was next in Lewes, then opened in Liverpool on December 14th, billing himself as "The Greatest Wonder of the Age". His ad in the *Liverpool Mercury* of 1 Jan.1858 is headed by the Royal cypher V.R. in large letters and announces that "1000 Presents will be Given Away, By Express Command of the Great Wizard of the World, Sig. A. Bosco..."; and at his next venue, Chester, where he opened on January 23rd, his advertising was even cheekier, not only with the cypher but the Royal coat of arms between the initials and a list of 40 gifts valued at £60 "In Honour of the Marriage of ... the Princess Royal and ...Prince Frederick William of Prussia" (*Chester Chronicle* 23 Jan.1858).

Professor Anderson was also performing in Chester and made himself unpopular locally with comments on the illegality of "lottery" prizes, both those offered at recent 'People's Concerts' and those by Alfred; and of Alfred he stated that he was "on intimate terms" with Bartolomeo and that the Bosco in Chester was not his son, but in fact "a Polish Jew, named Rosenthal, and no relation to the real Bosco".[23] Local feeling was that "Whether he be Bosco or not we are convinced ... that he possesses Bosco's talent, and that he is a remarkably clever magician" (*Chester Chronicle* 30 Jan.1858; 6 Feb.1858).

Alfred moved on through Bolton, Rochdale, Bury, Burnley, Todmorden, Leeds (billing himself as "Signor A. Bosco", implying but not claiming a relationship with Bartolomeo). While at Leeds he was warned by the police not to proceed with the "lottery", and a near riot ensued when he announced this during the show; a "jury" selected by the audience voted that entrance money should be returned ('A Warning to Wizards', *Globe* 22 Mar.1858, etc: widely reprinted, even in U.S.A.: *Brooklyn Daily Eagle* 15 Apr.1858).

On Tuesday March 30th he opened in Manchester, to a good audience, but following the show on the Thursday night, having returned to his lodgings, he went out again about half past two in the morning, followed by his wife, and threw himself into a pit. Her screams brought a policeman who extracted him, and on the Saturday he was charged with attempted suicide. In court he explained that he and his wife had quarrelled and he was only trying to frighten her, saying she was bad-tempered and drank too much. He was reprimanded and discharged (*Morning Post* 3 Apr.1858; *London Evening Standard* 5 Apr.1858, noting that they had married after a three day courtship). This was widely reprinted, with headlines such as "Attempted Suicide by Signor Bosco". In Britain it was assumed that the ill-tempered wife was the "Madame Bosco" (BF1) they had recently seen performing (Mrs Millar), and expressed surprise: "...the lady certainly did not appear to be a shrew..." (*Merthyr Telegraph* 17 Apr.1858), and the "attempted suicide" was soon picked up by the foreign press, who assumed it was either Bartolomeo or Eugenio — "le fameux magicien Bosco" (*Le Constitutionnel* 5 Apr.1858) — "Der famöse Zauberer Bosco" (*Zürcherische Frei-tagszeitung* 9 Apr.1858) — "De beroemde goochelaar Bosco" (*Handelsblad* 8 Apr. 1858) — "znany czarnoxięznik Bosco" (*Tygodnik Petersburski* 8 Apr.1858), etc. Eugenio, performing in Leipzig (*Deutsche Allgemeine Zeitung* 10 Apr.1858), then Bartolomeo in Algiers (*La Presse* 30 Apr.1858), both wrote to European papers denying it was either of them, Bartolomeo describing the Bosco in England as "un Polonais qui se sert de son nom pour établir à son profit"; by early May this was being widely reprinted in British papers — "a Pole, who had assumed his name in order to attract the public to his exhibitions" (*Morning Post* 3 May 1858, etc); interestingly, some English papers were sceptical: "No one who saw the Bosco who was recently at Leeds, would believe that he was a Pole", said the *Leeds Mercury* 6 May 1858.

Nothing daunted, Alfred was already back on stage in England, with a grand farewell benefit in Manchester on April 15th, followed by Ashton from April 22nd to 26th, Hull from April 27th to May 8th (the gun trick, "the original inexhaustible bottle", and selections from 'Norma' on his accordion on the final night), then Sheffield from May 17th to 20th, where "in spite of his talismanic powers he has failed in drawing together remunerative audiences", said the *Era* 23 May 1858. This same issue of the *Era* has a letter he wrote in reply to a notice in the issue of 2 May that luggage left in Worcester by Madame Bosco as security would be sold: he writes "my wife has never been in Worcester ... the person travelling under the name of Madame Bosco has no connexion with the establishment of Alfred Bosco, The Great Wizard of the World". This (surely tongue-in-cheek) repudiation of a person using "his" name is almost the last we hear of him for now in Britain, followed only by a week in Harrogate (*Wetherby News* 27 May 1858).

Three rival "Boscos" were already hovering in Britain vying to assume the name — Louis Susser (B65) in the north of England, Saul Warszawski (B63) in the south (forced to change his stage name from "Signor Bosco" to "Saul Bosco" in October when he was arrested in Scarborough on suspicion of being Alfred), and a second Madame Bosco (BF2, Mrs Ball), currently touring Ireland.

Harrogate is some distance from the Channel, but by June 19th Alfred was already in Berlin — and under arrest.[24]

He had opened in the Königssaale at Kroll's Opera House on June 11th, with further shows on 12th and 13th, trumpeted by the Kroll management in advertisements as "the young Bosco ...the even greater son of the great magician"...[25]

Then three days later the paper printed a letter from Eugenio, in Karlsbad for his health, offering proof that *he* was Bosco's only son and the "Pseudo-Bosco" now performing in Berlin could only be "a homonym, or, if not, an impostor".[26]

He was arrested on June 19th and charged the next day with using a false name and false credentials, and claiming titles and orders to which he was not entitled ("British Court Magician", and the Legion of Honour). From a letter found in his possession which he intended to send to his father he was identified as **Markus Epstein, or Eppstein**, Jewish, from Warsaw.[27]

In court he claimed he was not Prussian and so not subject to Prussian law, and that false names and false claims were common practice among magicians, but was sentenced to a fine of 100 Thaler or 3 months' imprisonment. His situation attracted some sympathy and donations enabled him to pay the fine and court costs and leave for Warsaw.[28]

He did not use the name "Bosco" again. He performed successfully in Warsaw for several months, billed as "M. Epstein, magician and ventriloquist, a native of Warsaw and coming from England, having visited almost all of Europe and Asia, and learnt the secrets of the Chinese...".[29]

In March 1859 he was in Lublin, April in Radom, May in Łódź, Łęczyca, Kalisz, and Plock, and June in Lowicz.[30]

Then no more is heard of him as Marcus Epstein. But it may be him the following month as **Zygmunt Epstein**, magician and ventriloquist, performing in Kalisz "with great success" and his wife making her debut as a pianist, both "received not only with applause but bouquets of flowers". From Kalisz he was announced to go to Konin for two performances, then to Ciechocinek, and from there to Warsaw.[31]

Next we find a **Marianus Sigismund Epstein** on tour in the Baltic region, in early 1860, and it is hard to believe this is not Marcus, for his specialities include not just conjuring but ventriloquism and even plate-spinning, and he claims to have performed before the King of Prussia on May 11th 1852, before Queen Victoria at Balmoral on September 24th 1855, and (also at Balmoral) before Napoleon III on August 27th 1857.[32]

In April 1860 he is in Riga, leaving in May,[33] in July in Pernau (modern Pärnu),[34] then in August in Reval (Tallinn).[35] Here two large and detailed advertisements[36] give a list of his tricks (including "Die lustigen Geschirre" — *the merry crockery,* his plate-spinning), and an unlikely biography which boasts of 21 years of travelling through Europe, the United States, Mexico, Egypt, India, China, and gives some precise dates — before the Prince Regent of Prussia on September 16th 1859, before the heir to the Prussian throne on June 27th and July 9th in Libau (Liepaja), and he talks of seventy-nine performances the previous year in Warsaw and twenty-one in Riga.

A review reported great anticipation and a full house with Epstein skilfully building up suspense from one show to the next , in complete control of "both the *spiriti infernales,* whose help he invokes, and the minds of the audience"; especially enjoyed were the tricks with cards and coins, the egg-laying purse, and the three magic bouquets. In his ventriloquism he performed splendidly, drawing many laughs as "Friedrich im Keller" and as "der kleine Franz in der Schieblade" (*Friedrich in the cellar,* or more likely *tavern*, and *Little Franz in the drawer*).

We next catch sight of him in August 1863 in Vienna as "**Sigmund Epstein**, known as the Midnight Magician", performing at the Theater an der Wien; the show also included a short burlesque play. The reviewer praised his dexterity but criticised his "sackful" of languages, and was worried that the plank he used to move into the audience from the stage was insecure and in danger of becoming "a Bridge of Sighs".[37]

The next sighting is in July and August 1865, a run in Vienna at the Thalia-Theater by "the Midnight Magician", variously named (often in his advertisements on the same day in different papers) as **Sigismund Epstein, Siegmund Epstein** or **Sigmund Epstein**; it is hard to believe that this variation was not deliberate on his part. There are short burlesque plays again, ventriloquism (with ten different voices), plate-spinning, and the decapitation act.[38]

In August he is off to the "Austrian provinces", then back in Vienna in October at the Blumensaal until that was taken over by a rival, Muhamed Ismail,[39] and he moved to the Hotel zum weissen Ross, where he made much of his decapitation act[40] and was doing his old multi-coloured lathers and regrowing beard trick.[41]

From late November performing with him is Mathilde Bannholzer "who many years ago had great success in Vienna" when as a seven year old "Wunderkind" she almost upstaged Bartolomeo.[42]

We then lose sight of him until June 1867 when, while performing in Lemberg (modern Lviv), "Sigismund Epstein, known as the Midnight Magician", was convicted of a sexual assault ("Gewaltthat") on a 17 year old girl he had hired as a servant for his wife.⁴³ He was sentenced in July to two years' hard labour and to pay compensation to the victim, but lodged an appeal. This "Sigismund Epstein" is a "Taschenspieler" and said to be age 30, married, born in Warsaw, but *Roman-Catholic*, however he does seem to be the same person.⁴⁴

His appeal was apparently successful, for in October he is performing in Czernowitz (modern Chernivtsi), where he was greeted with a long and glowing report in the newspaper — his name, we are told, is famous in all parts of the world, and a biographical puff has him born the son of very rich parents in Poland; completed a medical degree, but was drawn away by a love of the natural sciences, especially chemistry and magnetism, and a desire for freedom; travelled through Europe, Asia, Africa and America; speaks eleven languages; among the gifts and awards he has received are a wand tipped with diamonds from Sultan Abdulaziz and the Persian Order of the Lion and the Sun — a safer claim than the Legion of Honour.⁴⁵

The following year he was in Betschkerek (modern Zrenjanin) in July,⁴⁶ then on November 10th he opened in Munich at the Aktien-Theater,⁴⁷ and "despite considerably higher prices ... drew a very respectable audience"; the show opened with an amusing operetta, then after a long delay which led to signs of impatience, "the curtain went up and a man in a black dress-coat richly decorated with medals announced that he was the expected magician and asked for their indulgence as he was Polish and spoke German poorly...". He started with well-known tricks with rings, watches and canaries, and impressed with his sleight of hand work, then proved himself "bullet-proof", shot at by six soldiers on stage and holding up the bullets and inviting the audience to bring their own pistols and rifles to the next show...⁴⁸ His four shows, the next featuring ventriloquism with seven voices, were all very successful.

He moved on to Stuttgart and Augsburg, now "Dr Epstein ... der Matador der Escamotage". There the papers admired his elegance and dexterity — but "nothing new", even the bullet trick, and with his boring lecture he was regarded as arrogant towards his audience, which, while enthusiastic, was rather sparse — blamed on the "abonnement suspendu" notice in his advertisement, meaning that even theatre subscribers had to pay.⁴⁹

"Docteur Epstein" was soon in Paris, and before long his name was in newspapers all over Europe. He opened at the *Salle Herz* on January 28th 1869, attracting excellent audiences and the usual comments — great skill in his fingers, very pronounced accent, talented on the harmonica, but nothing not seen before and nothing exceeding the marvels of "the Parisian Robert-Houdins".⁵⁰

In February he shifted to the *Fantaisies-Parisiennes* and the introduction of the decapitation act excited interest, disgust, and criticism for alarming the audience.⁵¹

He performed three times at the Tuilleries Palace for the Emperor's family, especially the Prince Imperial, thirteen year old son of Napoleon III, not of course doing the decapitation act, and not allowed to bring in guns for the gun trick. For the second performance, on April 4th 1869, he received a letter of acknowledgment from the Vicomte de Laferrière, the First Chamberlain, dated April 13th: this is included in Epstein's album which was sold by Bloomsbury Auctions in 2017. The album was described as comprising "21 letters ... from various Royal courts around the world ...

London, Scotland, Persia, Russia, Germany, Crimea, Paris, Bulgaria, Austria and the Ottoman Empire".[52]

Le Monde illustré on April 3rd published a lengthy biography of him by Maxime Vauvert, with a splendid illustration of him performing before the Emperor's family at the Tuilleries.[53] The biography is similar to that in *Bukowina* in 1867 (above) — born of rich parents in Warsaw in 1827 and after completing a medical degree in 1848 he travelled through Europe, Asia and America until 1853. But it then adds that in 1855 he wrote a book on the last days of Czar Nicholas, published in four languages, dedicated to his successor Czar Alexander, who awarded him a medal.

The only book that fits this description is titled (in Russian): 'The last hours of the life of Emperor Nicholas I': it is anonymous but Epstein's claim to have written it is preposterous. It was written as an official account of the Emperor's death, compiled to emphasise that he died a firm Christian and did not commit suicide. Further, he died on March 2nd 1855 and the book was published in St Petersburg before the end of that month — when Epstein was in Wales![54]

Late on Friday April 23rd,[55] when performing at the Cirque-Napoléon, Epstein fell victim to one of his own tricks, the '*carabine au mouchoir*'. The act involved using a rod to insert into a carbine a handkerchief which he recovered intact on the end of a sword when the gun was fired at him by a volunteer from the audience. He failed to remove the rod and when the gun was fired the rod broke, part entering his chest just above the lung. He staggered and fell, the audience initially thinking it was part of the act; he pulled out the rod himself, then after initial treatment was taken to where he was staying, L'Hôtel d'Espagne et de Hongrie.[56]

There he was visited soon after by journalist "Timothée Trimm"[57] of the *Petit Moniteur*. His account is summarised in the *Gazette nationale ou le Moniteur universel* of April 27 — shown the waistcoat with hole front and back, saw the victim ("un beau garçon, d'environ 33 à 35 ans, au front large, aux yeux expressifs, à la physionomie ouverte"), in pain and too weak to speak, and met his brother who we are told was his usual stage assistant.

He recovered slowly and on May 6th wrote to the papers thanking them and the French people, the most spiritual and generous in the world, for the expressions of sympathy towards him.[58]

On Tuesday June 1st he resumed at the Cirque.[59] He was warmly applauded when he appeared on stage, thanked the crowd profusely, then began performing with his usual dexterity. The audience gasped when he went to load a pistol — there is no rod, he announced, and flourished a small gold-tipped cane made of the shaft which wounded him. All very successful, and one review ended with the remark that he no longer regretted an accident that will add to his fame and give rise to future successes.[60]

His career in fact prospered. In July he performed in Brussells at the Alcazar Royal theatre and gave a show at the Royal Palace for the Viceroy of Egypt, for which he received a valuable diamond pin.[61]

In August he was in Dijon,[62] then over the following months in Dole,[63] Geneva,[64] Saint-Étienne,[65] Bourges,[66] Tours,[67] Nantes,[68] Poitiers,[69] La Rochelle,[70] Saintes,[71] Bordeaux,[72] Marseille,[73] Nice,[74] and in January 1870 in Neuchâtel...[75]

In April 1870 he may be the "Dr. S. Epstein, the celebrated prestidigitateur", briefly in England. On April 27th he gave "a private séance ... in the presence of a select company" at Hanover-square Rooms in London. "His performance," we are told, "included many feats altogether new to English professors of sleight-of-hand, and he also exhibited a series of 'passes' on a principle of his own, the quickness displayed completely surprising several gentlemen present well qualified to give judgment in such matters"; it was predicted that he "will be extensively patronised on his appearance in public",[76] but all that came of it was three afternoon performances at the Crystal Palace on April 30th and May 2nd and 3rd.[77] He returned to the Continent, performing for a week at Dover before he left.[78]

Later that year probably the same "Dr S. Epstein, Court Magician of the Emperor of France", made a long tour of Holland, his act featuring "Finger-Tooverij" (without apparatus), plate dancing, ventriloquism, and the gun trick. From July onwards we find him in Arnhem,[79] Zwolle,[80] the Hague, and next in Amsterdam, where he announced in September he was teaming up with a well-known opera baritone, Johann Jacob Heksch, to give concerts combining their talents during the fair.[81]

Epstein moved on to Leiden[82] and Delft[83] in October, and then we get our first sight of an impostor (B12d): an advertisement in the *Heldersche en Nieuwedieper Courant* of October 21st announces that performing in Den Helder on October 22nd and 23rd will be *Dr S. Epstein fils:* he will be doing "Indian and Egyptian finger-magic", no plate-dancing, ventriloquism, or gun-trick, and the show includes two opera singers, one of whom is Heksch.[84] And Heksch was also the impostor, perhaps an amateur magician or he had picked up some tricks from Epstein.

In the same issue of the newspaper Epstein, advertising a performance in Nieuwediep on October 26th, added that he was obliged to make it known to his honoured public that there is a person in the provinces under the name *Epstein fils*, with whom the famous Dr Epstein has no connexion.[85] Heksch duly replied with a statement signed "Dr EPSTEIN fils" stating that his performances would definitely go ahead, while that announced by a certain Dr Epstein next Wednesday at the Tivoli would positively not proceed, as the gentleman referred to does not dare to come here because Dr Epstein fils would prosecute him.[86]

A review of Heksch's performance on 26 October complimented him on his "unrivalled, swiftness and dexterity" and commended the two singers.[87] He continued to perform as Epstein fils until the end of the year, found in Schagen, Hoorn, 's-Hertogenbosch (on November 12th and 13th),[88] Antwerp,[89] and the last sighting of "Dr. Epstein fils" is in Amsterdam in December.[90] Heksch then returned to his singing career.

"Dr. S. Epstein" had meanwhile continued his tour, sighted in Groningen, Assen, Leeuwarden, and at the start of December in 's-Hertogenbosch, where, a fortnight after Heksch, he stresses that he is "the famous, the *real* Dr Epstein" who has performed at royal courts all over Europe.[91] He next performed in Breda on December 3rd, his advertisement emphasising his skills in ventriloquism.[92]

The following year he was touring the Baltic countries, arriving in Reval (Tallinn) from Dorpat (Tartu) in September and giving four successful shows, culminating in ventriloquism and the decapitation act.[93] In November he is probably the Dr S. Epstein arriving in Riga from Vilna (Vilnius)[94] and we now lose sight of him for several years.[95]

Then in March 1875 we have a "Doktor Sigmund Epstein" performing in Vyborg (Viipuri), and then in Finland. He is twice described as Hungarian ("ungare till nationen", "unkarilainen tohtori Epstein") but in all other respects including the specifics of his act appears to be the same Epstein. We are told that during recent years he was in Persia, travelling with the Shah in 1873, and after that in Russia, having now recently left St Petersburg.[96]

The following week he is in Helsinki,[97] then in Riga, remembered for his performances there in 1860 (strongly suggesting this is Marcus), and said also to have recently been in Astrakhan, Constantinople, and Egypt.[98]

Then in August we find an impostor (B12b), calling himself "Professor Sigismund Epstein" (Sigmund preferred "Dr.", but see below) performing in Vyborg (Viipuri), at Huusniemi Park. His act features magic, ventriloquism, playing the Aeolian harp, plus fireworks (no gun trick, decapitation, or plate spinning) and he is said to be "a new Epstein".[99] A week later this "Epstein" is in Helsinki with a musical-magic *soirée* at Brunnshuset (Kaivopuisto Park). One review describes him as "a well-known friend from a previous stay", but another specifically states "The wizard, Mr Epstein (not the same one who entertained Helsinki with his visit last winter)…".[100] He organised a final firework show on August 25th, criticised for its high prices and poor fireworks which fizzed for a few seconds then left a cloud of stinking smoke ("first and foremost bad, secondly very bad, and thirdly, unforgivably bad … As a magician, Mr Epstein is in some way justified and accustomed to leading the audience by the nose, but it should not be done in such a clumsy and inconsiderate manner as yesterday".[101] We may get a final glimpse of this "Epstein" in Reval in 1878 (below).

Sigmund meanwhile was performing in Reval (Tallinn), where he opened on August 20th — it is probably him, even though here he is billed as "Professor der Magie, Zauberei und Bauchredekunst Sigismund Epstein", because the impostor was still in Helsinki on this date. He gave three performances at the Stadt-Theater and a final grand show at Schweickerdt's Salon in Catharinenthal (Kadriorg Palace), which was followed by "Bengal flames and electric lights" in the gardens.[102]

The following month Sigmund, said to be coming from Russia, began a long tour of Scandinavia, first Norway — Bergen, Kristiansund, Haugesund, Frederikshald (Halden), ending in Christiania (Oslo) in early 1876.[103] He spent March to June 1876 in Sweden — Stockholm,[104] Norrköping, Jönköping, Göteborg, Lund, Malmö, including a performance before the King and Queen.[105] He was next in Denmark until February 1877 — Copenhagen, Roskilde, for the royal family at Fredensborg, Kjøge (Køge), Kalundborg, Odense, Kolding. But on January 18th in Randers he was injured when shot in the cheek.[106] Epstein, unable to eat or speak for some time, issued an explanation blaming the accident on his own forgetfulness. He was back performing in late February, in Aarhus, described as "completely healed" and could even resume ventriloquism with seven voices.[107]

We next see him in July, in Hamburg, where we hear an odd story of how "Dr Epstein, 'King' of Magicians" was "plucked" of a large sum at billiards by one Dr Reimers, having to pawn his magical apparatus to pay his rent, and was given back 500 marks by Reimers so he could leave Hamburg… Epstein and another victim took Reimers to court but the verdict was that Reimers did not do this for a living and it would be like prosecuting a great pianist for practising his skill.[108]

In November in Kulm he was again a victim of his own bullet trick when a mechanism designed to remove the bullet from the barrel before firing failed and he was hit in the chest, the bullet lodging near his spine.[109] By late December he was reported "healed" and in Copenhagen looking for a venue, and soon to perform in Kiel.[110]
. In August 1878 in Reval (Tallinn) "Magiker S. Epstein", just arrived from Grodno, advertises a "Soirée mystérieuse brillante … bestehend in der höheren Magie, Bauchredekunst und im Spiel auf der Aeolsharfe". This may be Sigmund but he is promising the audience presents and that and the Aeolian harp suggest the impostor and former "Professor" (B12b).[111]

Either way no more is seen of Marcus-Sigmund / Sigismund Epstein. There is no evidence that he went to America and performed there as a "Bosco" — his dates and act fit none of the American Boscos.

I see no reason to doubt that (impostors aside) this was the same Epstein — conjuror, ventriloquist, musician, and in his younger days plate spinner, never a "spiritist"; in England in the 1850s, and, despite some modern references to him as Adam Salomon Epstein, he is *never* called by that name in contemporary sources.

NOTES

[1] *Allgemeiner Polizei-Anzeiger* 28 June 1851 p.260: "Epstein, Markus Joseph, auch Salomon Engländer gen., Taschenspieler aus Leutschitz in Russisch-Polen. Alter: 23 J.; Relig.: jüd.; Statur: mittel, schlank; Haare: schwarz; Augen: grau. Er is wegen Verleitung zum Mißbrauche der Amts-Gewalt bestraft u. am 5/6. 51. an die k. k. österr. Stadt-Hauptmannschaft in Krakau zur Weiterbeförderung in seine Heimat abgeschoben worden. Prag, 5/6. 51".

[2] An example from the *Pembrokeshire Herald* 16 Mar.1855 is reproduced by Rusconi p.172 (but he was not in Liverpool at Queen's Hall on January 14th, as Rusconi states: anyway, January 14th was a Sunday with no performances, and at that venue over this period was "Gallaher's Prize Entertainment").

[3] *Cardiff and Merthyr Guardian*, 9 Feb.1855, saying in its review (17 Feb.1855) "old tricks, nevertheless, well executed". In Newport *The Star of Gwent* (17 Feb.1855) praised the "ease and elegance" with which he performed his tricks, and listed amongst them "the inexhaustible bottle … the dish and plates dances, the inserting a knife into a bottle and then gradually drawing it out, the eating of common wadding and then producing fire therefrom, the great knot trick, the London cook, the magic dagger … Signor Bosco stands unrivalled".

[4] In Haverfordwest March 16th and 20th: *Pembrokeshire Herald* 16 Mar.1855 and poster in Rusconi p.174.

[5] Review in *Pembrokeshire Herald* of March 23rd: "On Friday and Tuesday last Signor Bosco, the celebrated Italian Conjurer, gave his extraordinary entertainments at the Townhall, in this town… he surpasses in 'slight of hand' and other tricks

anything we ever before have seen"; Rusconi quotes this in translation, but this is not the "vero Bosco", as he argues.

[6] *Era* 22 July 1855: "...we have fears for his success ... as the gentry ... are at the coast, and the working classes prefer out-door amusements at this season of the year"; but the *Caledonian Mercury,* 20 July 1855, reported: "The theatre was well filled. The performances of Signor Bosco equal, if they do not surpass, those of the far-famed Wizard of the North".

[7] *Dundee Evening Telegraph* 8 Sep.1892. He also published his account as a booklet which I have not seen, *How an American brought the great Italian wizard before H. M. Queen Victoria.* London Andrew Churchman, 1899 (16 pages), referred to in *Ye Olde Magic Mag* 7,3 (June 2021) p.140 n.10.

[8] Sir Charles Beaumont Phipps, K.C.B., 1801-1866, Privy Purse, was indeed in the Royal suite at Balmoral at this time ('Court Circular', *Morning Chronicle* 7 Sep. 1855).

[9] Victoria recorded the performance in her Journal (url:128), commending Bosco's performance but not his poor English.

[10] Might self-published it in 1856: "extremely pretty" and "danceable", said the Irish papers, but *The Musical World* pronounced it "ungrammatical"; no surviving copies are recorded.

[11] This is the first we hear of his wife: she was soon to be the first "Madame Bosco" (BF1).

[12] *Freeman's Journal* 19 Mar.1856; the *Dublin Daily Express* report of the same day gives the servant's name as Charles Battie, and quotes at length both Bosco (replying, when asked "Did you not horsewhip him yourself?", "He is my servant") and Millar ("I am an American by birth, and not accustomed to insolence from negroes").

[13] *Saunders's News-letter* 2 Apr.1856, and in other papers: this is the first time he is found as "Alfred". The "Mantua" was soon dropped.

[14] And he had his "sable featured attendant" (dismissed by Millar) again on stage with him (*Evening Freeman* 7 Apr.1856).

[15] Here his advertising went up another notch, promising "New and Gorgeous Paraphernalia" and "The Extraordinary, Inexplicable, Mystic, Magic Programme will contain upwards of Fifty Distinguished Feats in Magic and Ventriloquism nightly…" (*Limerick Reporter* 8 Apr.1856), and he had boys in the streets holding placards announcing his arrival (upsetting the council: *Limerick Reporter* 11 Apr.1856). But Bartolomeo, or probably his lawyer, was keeping track of him. Soon after he opened in Limerick a notice by Bartolomeo was published in the local paper — "Signor Bosco, of Turin, has lately arrived in Dublin, and begs to inform the Citizens that he has received a letter from Professor Millar, now in Cork… Mr Millar admits that his

late partner is not named Bosco ... the name was assumed ...": *Limerick Chronicle* 9 Apr.1856.

[16] A long advertisement in the *Waterford Mail* 12 Apr.1856 quotes at length from his reviews in Ireland, carefully avoiding any claim of being Bartolomeo's son.

[17] In Cork he was challenged to a Conjuring Match by magician "Rignoldi" (Thomas Rignold), who renewed the challenge soon after, but was again ignored: *Southern Reporter and Cork Commercial Courier* 9 May 1856; *Era* 18 May 1856: "Challenge to the Would-be Bosco...". The following year Rignoldi was lecturer for Millar's Diorama.

[18] "Artist" was a standard term for anyone working in the theatre. An image of the marriage registration is online at url:129.

[19] *Leeds Times* 18 Oct.1856. The shop-keeper is named Hyam but this is not the family of B66, a future "Signor Bosco".

[20] *London Gazette* 2 Oct.1857; detailed accounts *London Evening Standard* 14 Oct.; 14 Nov.1857.

[21] Ottokar Fischer's article in *The Sphinx* 10 May 1937 shows that he must have actually sighted the contract signed between Kratky-Baschik and "Alfred Bosco" in June 1857, but he concluded from the similarity of Alfred Bosco's signature with that of Bartolomeo that this in fact *was* Bartolomeo touring England under that name! The contract gave K-B £10 a week plus free board and travel for performing at all Alfred's public shows and half the profits from their private shows: for Kraty-Baschik see *Appendix Z6*.

[22] *Isle of Wight Mercury* 6 Sep.1857; an account in *Southern Reporter and Cork Commercial Courier* 7 Sep.1857 says his leg was broken by kicks from the horse.

[23] *Chester Chronicle* 6 Feb.1858. Where the name Rosenthal came from is uncertain: he may have been thinking of Orginski *Rosenfeld* who performed in Britain from 1846 to his death in 1869 as "The Polish Wizard" and later "The Polish Necromancer". There is no evidence that Anderson and Bartolomeo knew each other but both were in London in May 1851 and they may well have met or at least watched each other perform.

[24] Whether he took his wife with him we do not know; perhaps not: in the 1861 census a Hannah Epstein, age 25, born Stourbridge, married but on her own, is running a boarding house in Birmingham. There is no matching death registration for a Hannah Epstein (or Bosco) in England, but she may have remarried. Certainly when he was convicted in Berlin Epstein said he had no money to pay the fine and no money to support his wife if he went to prison — but it seems this was a wife in Warsaw (*Oesterreichische Zeitungshalle* 22 June, 2 July 1858).

²⁵ *Vossische Zeitung* 10, 11, 12, 13 June 1858: "...des jungen Bosco ... des großen Magiers größeren Sohn ... *soirée fantastique* des Signor A. Bosco jr., Hofkünstler Ihrer Majestät der Königin Victoria von England u. Ritter der Ehrenlegion ...".

²⁶ *Vossische Zeitung* 16 June 1858: "...Der gegenwartig in Berlin anwesende Bosco kann daher nur ein Homonyme, wenn nicht, ein falscher Bosco sein...", signed "Eugêne Bosco *fils*". See B2 p.161 for further details.

²⁷ In the Polish newspapers, where the case was widely reported, he is referred to as *Markus Eppstein, Markus Epstein*, or *Marek Eppstein* — *Gazeta Wielkiego Xięstwa Poznańskiego* 25 June 1858: "Pokazało się, że inniemany Bosco byl Markusem Eppsteinem synem kupca a Warszawy"(*It turned out that the supposed Bosco was Markus Eppstein, son of a merchant in Warsaw*); *Czas* 3 July 1858: "...że jest on żydem z Warszawy i nazywa się Marek Eppstein. Między papierami jego znaleziono list jego, który miał przesłać ojcu swemu do Warszawy. W nim zawiadamia ojca, aby tenż pisywal do niego pod adresem 'Signor Bosco'" (*... that he is a Jew from Warsaw and his name is Marek Eppstein. A letter was found among his papers, which he was going to send to his father in Warsaw. In it, he tells his father to write to him as 'Signor Bosco'*).

²⁸ *Fremden-Blatt* 23, 25 June 1858; *Hamburger Nachrichten* 24 June 1858; and reported in Dutch, French and Polish papers; oddly no mention of the trial is found in any British paper. *Kladderdatsch* (4 July 1858) amused itself by announcing "1200 new wearers of medals and crosses, for example in Berlin ... Alfred Bosco... with the Legion of *Horror*": "An die 1200 neuen Medaillen- und Kreuzträger, z.B. in Berlin. Spielet nicht mit Kreuz und Stern, Sonst fühlt ihr wie ich den Schmerz! Alfred Bosco, genannt Marcus Eppstein mit der Légion d' horreur [*sic*]".

²⁹ Ongoing announcements, reviews and advertisements in *Kurjer Warszawski* and *Gazeta Warszawska* 4 Sept.1858 to 30 Jan. 1859.

³⁰ *Kurjer Warszawski* 5 Mar., 15 Apr., 7 May, 11 June 1859. A criticism was made by the *Warschauer Zeitung* 11 May 1859 that, while his tricks were clever and the audiences good, he gave his patter, so important for a magician, in a mish-mash of four different languages ("...allein wir bedauern, daß es ihm an der Rednergabe mangelt, welche für einen Escamoteur so wünschenswerth ist. Namentlich gefiel uns nicht, daß er seine Escamotagen in einem Mischmasch von vier verschiedenen Sprachen erläuterte...".

³¹ *Kurjer Warszawski* 7 July 1859. Probably him: he later used the names Sigismund and Sigmund.

³² The last had been claimed by "Alfred" at *Osborne*, but almost certainly took place at neither.

³³ "Große Vorstellung des berühmten Magisters und Bauchredners M. Sigismund Epstein in der Ägyptischen Fingerzauberei": *Rigasche Zeitung* 23 Apr. 1860; *Livländische Gouvernements-Zeitung* 6 May 1860.

[34] "... der berühmte Magiker und Bauchredner Marianus Sigismund Epstein...": *Pernausches Wochenblatt* 30 July 1860.

[35] Arrivals at the Hotel zum Goldnen Löwen "Hr. Sigismund Epstein mit Familie", travelling from Hapsal (Haapsalu): *Revalsche Zeitung* 5 Aug.1860.

[36] *Estländische Gouvernements-Zeitung* 8, 11 Aug.1860 (url:130).

[37] "Sigmund Epstein, bekannt unter dem Namen: 'Der mitternächtliche Zauberer'...": *Fremden-Blatt* 24, 25 Aug.1863; *Der Zwischen-Akt* 24, 26 Aug.1863. The plank suggests he might have tried Bartolomeo's "falling off the stage act" but he is never mentioned as doing so.

[38] "Außerordentliche Production des berühmten Magiers Sigismund Epstein, bekannt unter dem Namen: „Der mitternächtliche Zauberer." Programm: Das indische Pir, oder: Mahomed's Paradies. Magische Vorstellung in der egyptischen Fingerzauberei...": *Die Presse* 9 July 1865; "Siegmund Epstein, Magiers und Ventriloquen...": *Neue Fremden-Blatt* 23 July 1865; "Siegmund Epstein" ... long list of his tricks, opening with "Der chinesische Tanz, oder: Das lustige Geschirr..." and ending with "Das Bauchreden mit 10 verschiedenen Stimmen": *Neues Fremden-Blatt* 29 July 1865.

[39] Ismail billed himself as Court Magician of the Shah of Persia: *Neue Fremden-Blatt* 25 Oct.1865; *Die Debatte* 27 Oct.1865. Brief entry for him in the *Lexikon*, and in *Magier der Welt* for his brother-in-law who succeeded him.

[40] His advertisements (e.g. *Fremden-Blatt* 30 Oct.1865) feature a large illustration of himself holding a head under his arm (similar to, but not the same as, the illustration that he used earlier in England). His shows started a "decapitation-mania" in Vienna, with humorous attempts by amateurs to perform the same act ("eine wahre Kopfabschneidungsmanie": *Tages-Post* [Linz] 19 Dec.1865).

[41] 'Wiener Silhouetten', *Tagespost* 5 Nov.1865.

[42] *Fremden-Blatt* 21 Nov.1865. For Mathilde see *Appendix Z1*.

[43] *Fremden-Blatt* 18 June 1867; *Gemeinde-Zeitung* [Vienna] 22 June 1867.

[44] 'Ein Zauberer — auf zwei Jahre in's Gefängnis gezaubert': *Gemeinde-Zeitung* 30 July 1867.

[45] *Bukowina* 16, 18 Oct.1867.

[46] "Der Physiker Herr S. Epstein, genannt der „mitternächtliche Zauberer,"... Der in den weitesten Kreisen der Monarchie durch seine Leistungen bestrenommirte Künstler...": *Gr.-Becskereker Wochenblatt* 11 July 1868.

[47] "...Der rühmlichst bekannte Escamoteur und Bauchredner, Dr. S. Epstein, bekannt unter dem Namen der mitternächtliche Zauberer und berühmt als einzige dastehender Meister bei den Höfen von England, Rußland, Oesterreich, Preußen, Frankreich,

Türkei, Bayern, Persien, Serbien…": *Münchener Anzeiger* 7 Nov.1868, His advertisement in *Münchener Tages-Anzeiger* 18 Nov. 1868 spells his name "Dr. S. Eppstein" and includes "das lustige Geschirr".

[48] *Münchener Bote für Stadt und Land* 12 Nov.1868.

[49] *Augsburger neueste Nachrichten* 23, 27 Nov.1868; *Augsburger Tagblatt* 25 Nov. 1868; *Neue Augsburger Zeitung* 26 Nov; 1 Dec.1868.

[50] "Le docteur Epstein … est un très habile prestidigitateur, mais il n'a rien fait … qui sorte des prodiges auxquels les Robert-Houdin parisiens nous ont habitués": *Le Gaulois* 29 Jan.1869; "…Grande adresse dans les doigts — accent très prononcé — un talent particulier sur l'harmonica — spectacle curieux": *Le Figaro* 29 Jan.1869.

[51] "Le truc de la tête coupée n'a produit qu'une impression de dégoût général…": *Le Gaulois* 19 Feb.1869. On the first night the audience were not taken in and hissed the act: *Le Figaro* 20 Feb.1869, calling it "enfantin". A long article on him in *Le Constitutionnel*, 22 Feb.1869, listing his tricks — and revealing how each was performed! — praised his skill at palming and at forcing, putting into effect Robert-Houdin's axiom 'L'escamotage est l'esprit des doigts', but thought little of the gun trick and even less of the decapitation act which it considered should be shown the door. In March he withdrew it from his show: "Le docteur Epstein a sagement fait de renoncer à sa tête coupée…": *Gazette nationale* 2 Mar.1869.

[52] The letter is viewable at url:131. We have now learnt more about the album from the interesting article in *Ye Olde Magic Mag* 7, 3 (June 2021): the album, embossed "ALBUM S. E.", covers solely his career after dropping the name "Bosco" and the contents date from 1860 to 1869. Other contents mentioned are a silk programme for a performance before Ludwig II of Bavaria; and requests in 1865 for British consuls in Russia to ask Charles Phipps for confirmation that Bosco performed for Victoria at Balmoral.

[53] Online at url:132.

[54] The book's Russian title was Послѣднie часы жизни императора Николая Перваго [that is in the modern alphabet; in the original the e in bold italic was the old letter *yat;* the bold italic ие was IE; and ПЕРВОГО was ПЕРВАГО]; variously transliterated in modern library catalogues as *Posledniye chasy zhizni Imperatora Nikolaya Pervago* or *Poslědnie časy žizni imperatora Nikolaja Pervogo* [etc.]; copies are online at url:133.
 Also printed there in 1855 were editions in
French (*Les derniers moments de l'empereur Nicolas I*, held RSL);
English (*The last hours of the life of the emperor Nicholas I*, held RSL, BL)
Polish (*Ostatnie chwile życia Cesarza Mikołaja Pierwszego*, held RNL etc)
and probably editions in Armenian and Georgian.
 After describing the Czar's last days it prints his will, and a new edition in 1856 was titled Завѣщание и послѣднiе дни жизни императора Николая Перваго

(*Zaveshchaniye i posledniye dni zhizni imperatora Nikolaya Pervogo* = 'Testament and the last days of the life of Emperor Nicholas I').

A French edition was also published in Vienna in 1855, *Les dernières heures de la vie de l'Empereur Nicolas I. Traduit du russe.* Vienne: imprimerie de M. Auer, 1855 (online at url:134); and a German translation (by M. Joel), *Die letzten Lebensstunden des Kaisers Nicolaus des Ersten nebst seinem Testament,* in Berlin by J. Schneider in 1855.

Another edition in English was apparently printed in London by Goulburn in 1855 (held Lambeth Palace Library).

The book, quoting at length from Archypresbyter Basil Bajanov, the Czar's confessor, and Dr Arndt, his doctor, is usually attributed to Count Dmitry Bludov, 1785-1864, one of the people closest to the Czar.

[A similarly-titled French work, *Les dernières heures de sa Majesté l'Empereur Nicolas. Méditation par l'auteur des pélerins russes a Jérusalem*, published Leipsic: Francois Wagner, 1855 is a completely different book; it is, as it says, a "meditation" and was written by Elisabeth Bagreef-Speranski (online at url:135).]

[55] Not the 24th or 25th as stated in several accounts old and new.

[56] He was performing each night at the *Fantaisies-Parisiennes* at 8.30pm then later at the Cirque, which opened at 8, with his *séance* as the final act of the night and this the final trick, around 10pm. The accident occurred too late to be reported in the morning papers of Saturday 24th. Contemporary accounts are found in *La Presse, Le Petit Journal, Le Siècle, Journal des débats* and *Le Figaro* 25 April 1869. These are fairly consistent, though call the handkerchief either *mouchoir* or *foulard,* and either one or three of them. The accident was widely reported with variations and elaborations in provincial and foreign papers (he was dead; or he was hit by a bullet from a pistol; or the gun had a hidden second barrel). Two of the three doctors who treated him published a correction in *Le Figaro* 29 April, and *Le Français* 30 April confirmed that the rod was wooden, not metal, as had been stated.

[57] Léo (actually Antoine Joseph Napoléon) Lespès, 1815-1875.

[58] *Le Gaulois* 10 May 1869; *Gazette nationale* 11 May 1869; etc.

[59] The ongoing listing for his shows at the *Fantaisies-Parisiennes* had continued uninterrupted in *Le Français.*

[60] *Gazette nationale ou le Moniteur universel* 3 June 1869. There had already been suggestions that the whole episode was merely a publicity stunt and his greatest trick of all would be his resurrection — so said *Le monde illustré* 5 June 1869; and *Le Rappel* 11 May 1869 had wondered if it was all "…une immense mystification". Much was made of this by H.J. Burlingame in a very inaccurate account many years later in his *Herrmann the Magician,* and others, notably Houdini, saw Epstein's "deceit" as soon ending his career and leading to a sad death: references in Joshua Jay, 'Tragic Magic' site (url:136).

[61] *Le Figaro* 4, 18, 20, 27 July 1869; *Leidsch Dagblad* 7 July 1869.

[62] *Le Progrès de la Côte-d'Or* 5 (a teaser: "Epstein viendra!"), 17 Aug.1869.

[63] *Album dolois* 14 Aug.1869.

[64] *Journal de Genève* 20, 22 Aug.1869, his advertising making much of his recent narrow escape from death, now recovered "after six weeks of suffering".

[65] *Mémorial de la Loire et de la Haute-Loire* 27, 28 (the biography again), 30 (delayed by illness) Aug.1869.

[66] *Le Courrier de Bourges* 8 Sep.1869 (his conjuring, ventriloquism and music-making all warmly applauded); *Journal du Cher* 9 Sep.1869.

[67] *L'Union libérale* 10 Sep.1869.

[68] *Le Phare de la Loire* 29 Sep.1869 (his tunes played on a tiny Pan flute, 25cm long).

[69] *La Réforme politique et sociale* 4 Oct.1869.

[70] *L'Écho rochelais* 6, 9 Oct.1869.

[71] *L'Indépendant de la Charente-Inférieure* 4, 7 Oct.1869.

[72] *La Gironde* 19 Oct.1869.

[73] *Le Sémaphore de Marseille* 28 Nov.; 7 Dec.1869; 21 Jan.1870; *Le Petit Marseillais* 11 Dec.1869; 11 Jan. (unwell) 1870.

[74] *Le Gaulois* 31 Dec.1869.

[75] *L'Express* 23 Feb.; 3 Mar. 1870 (still closing the performance with the gun trick, "les armes enchantées").

[76] *The Sportsman* 30 Apr.1870.

[77] *Pall Mall Gazette* and other London papers 30 Apr.; 2, 3 May 1870.

[78] *Dover Express* 14 Apr. (announcing his imminent arrival from Paris); 29 April 1870; *Era* 8 May 1870.

[79] *Arnhemsche courant* 13, 16, 18 July 1870 ("De Opstanding, De Luchtreis, Het Erfdeel der Grootmoeder, Dr Regen der Danaïden, Chineesche Dans, De verbazing der Dames, De eigenzinnige Dame, De verboden vrucht, De Tuinmann, De Diergaarde, De Kaarsen van den Duivel, Het ongeloofelijke Concert").

In 1883 when the later impostor "Professor Epstein" (B12e) was in Arnhem, he was thought at first to be the *S. Epstein* who had performed there in 1870 — Sigmund. In 1883 the papers stated that in 1870 he attracted only small crowds in those tense days "because it was said that he had come to our country to spy on our defence system!": *Arnhemsche Courant* 20, 26 Apr.1883. I could see nothing to that effect in the 1870 newspapers.

[80] *Provinciale Overijsselsche en Zwolsche courant* 13, 19, 28 July 1870.

[81] *Algemeen Handelsblad* 7 Sep.1870: "...De Wereldberoemde Prestidigitateur en Ventriloque DR. S. EPSTEIN neemt de vrijheid aan het geëerde Amsterdamsche Publiek beleefd bekend te maken, dat hij in verbinding met den hier alom zeer geliefkoosde Operazanger en voormalig Hoofdregisseur van het Volkspaleis, DEN HEER JOH. JAC. HEKSCH, in het lokaal Diligentia, in de Kalverstraat, tijdens de KERMIS Concerten geven zal...".

[82] *Leydse Courant* 10 Oct.1870.

[83] *Delftsche courant* 14, 16 Oct.1870.

[84] "...Groote Phisische en Magische Voorstelling in de Egyptische en Indische Vinger-Tooverij, uitgevoerd door den wereldberoemden Prestidigitateur Dr S. Epstein fils": *Heldersche en Nieuwedieper Courant* 21 Oct.1870.

[85] "... De directie acht zich verpligt het geëerde publik opmerksam te maken, dat er nog een persoon in de provinciën onder den naam van EPSTEIN fils, doch die met den beroemden Dr. Epstein volstrekt niet in betrekking staat": *Heldersche en Nieuwedieper Courant* 21 Oct.1870.

[86] "De angekondigde voorstellingen van Dr. Epstein fils ... GAAN BEPAALDELIJK DOOR. De voorstelling, door zekeren Dr Epstein tegen a.m. Woensdag in Tivoli aangekondigt, zal stellig geen voortgang hebben, daar bedoelde heer hier niet durft te komen, uithoofde Dr EPSTEIN fils hem door de politie doet vervolgen": *Heldersche en Nieuwedieper Courant* 23 Oct.1870.

[87] *Heldersche en Nieuwedieper Courant* 26 Oct.1870.

[88] Here (this one time only) he advertises himself as "Dr Epstein Heksch (fils), de Wereldberoemde Prestidigitateur": *Provinciale Noordbrabantsche en 's Hertogenbossche Courant* 11 Nov.1870.

[89] As "Dr S. Epstein (Fils), accompanied by the pianist Jacques, and the opera singer M^r. John. Jac. Heksch...": *De Grondwet* 17, 20 Nov.1870.

[90] *Algemeen Handelsblad* 30 Dec.1870. Tivoli Theatre, Friday 30 Dec. ... two comic plays interspersed with extraordinary performances by Doctor Epstein fils and the Hoftheater singer Heksch".

[91] "Dr. Epstein, de beroemde, de *echte* dr. Epstein, zal vrijdag avond eene voorstelling in den schouwburg alhier geven. Voor de vorstinnen en vorsten van Engeland, Pruisen, Griekenland, Rusland, Turkije, Beijeren, Oostenrijk, Wurtemburg, België, Egypte, Frankrijk, enz. gaf hij voorstellingen, die steeds onverdeelden bijval mogten inoogsten, even als in alle steden waar hij optrad; alle kunstkenners bragten hulde aan zijne talenten in de vakken, waarin hij werkzaam was": *Provinciale Noordbrabantsche en 's Hertogenbossche courant* 29 Nov.1870.

[92] *Bredasche courant* 1 Dec.1870.

[93] *Revalsche Zeitung* 21 Sep. to 7 Oct.1871. Soon after his departure the comic Robert Guthery (having placarded the town with 'Guthery geht!' posters in the style of Epstein's 'Epstein kommt!') parodied his shows as 'Epstein der Zweite': *Revalsche Zeitung* 29 Sep.1871).

[94] *Livländische Gouvernements-Zeitung* 26 Nov.1871.

[95] A possible sighting is "Herr Sigmund Epstein, Privat, mit Gattin, aus Ungarn" arriving in Bad Ischl on September 8th 1873 (*Ischler Bade-Liste* 25 Sep.1873): however he later claimed he was in Persia in 1873.

[96] *Wiborgs Tidning* 13 Mar.1875: "...Doktor Sigmund Epstein, enligt utländska blad en celebritet i escamotage, magi och buktalarekonst, som haft förmonen att uppträda för de fleste europäiske regenter och åtföljt schachen af Persien på dess resor 1873, kommer på genomresan till Helsingfors i morgon att gifva en representation å härvarande teater. ...". His advertisement in the same issue lists the acts in the three sections of his show, ending with his familiar ventriloquial piece 'The thief caught'.

[97] *Finlands Allmänna Tidning* 22, 23, 25 Mar.1875; *Hufvudstadsbladet* 23 Mar.1875; *Åbo Posten* 30 Mar.1875 has a 'Letter from Helsinki' largely on Epstein's gun trick; plus a nice ventriloquial anecdote of two men sitting eating and approached by a dog — who suddenly asks them for something to eat.

[98] *Eesti Postimehe lisaleht* 26 Mar.1875.

[99] *Wiborgs Tidning* 7, 10 Aug.1875: "en ny Epstein... Det är denna gång 'professor Sigismund Epstein'".

[100] *Helsingfors dagblad* 15 Aug.1875: "...den redan sedan en föregående vistelse härstädes bekante hr Epstein"; *Morgonbladet* 16 Aug.1875: "Trollkarlen hr Epstein (icke den samme, som senaste winter fägnade Helsingfors med sitt besök)...".

[101] *Helsingfors dagblad* 25 Aug.1875; *Finlands Allmänna Tidning* 26 Aug.1875.

[102] The acts in each show, all different, are listed in detail in four large advertisements: *Revalsche Zeitung* 19, 21, 23, 26 Aug.1875.

[103] There are anecdotes of him as far north as Tromsø (and one even has him coming back from Archangel).

[104] Several of his advertisements here list him consistently as "E. Epstein", e.g. *Aftonbladet* 18 Mar.1876.

[105] A contemporary Swedish illustration shows him performing the gun and other tricks; it is reproduced widely, including on the Russian *Magicpedia* site (url:137) which has other interesting gun trick material.

[106] The act involved Epstein being fired at by two *Bøsse*, probably smooth-bore shotguns. The first night went off well, but on the second night one gun splintered beneath the lock and part of the discharge, probably from the other gun, entered his

right cheek just in front of his ear, passing through his nasal cavity and hard palate. There was a lot of blood but he was able to remain upright and to sit down in a chair: *Nationaltidende* 19 Jan.1877; the most detailed account found is in *Dagbladet* (Copenhagen) 20 Jan.1877, quoting the *Randers Dagblad og Folketidende*.

[107] *Jyllandsposten* 22 Feb.1877; *Kallundborg Avis* 23 Feb.1877.

[108] *Thisted Amtsavis* 31 July 1877; *Kjøge Avis* 1 Aug.1877.

[109] Widely reported — *Würzburger Stadt- und Landbote* 23 Nov.1877; *Helsingfors Dagblad* 30 Nov.1877 (both saying Kulm, either the town in Germany or modern Chełmno); *Leydse Courant* 27 Nov.1877; *Heldersche en Nieuwedieper Courant* 28 Nov.1877 (both saying Keulen — Cologne).

[110] *Kjøge Avis* 22 Dec.1877; *Morgenbladet* 2 Jan.1878.

[111] *Revalsche Zeitung* 5 to 8 August 1878.

B12a. Adam Epstein; H.A. Epstein; Henry Adams; Adam Brøndum

The next Epstein is the interesting character who performed as (Mr., Dr. or Professor) **Adam Epstein**, **Adams Epstein**, **Adam Epstein (jun.)**, **H.A. Epstein (junior)**, and **Henry Adams**,[1] who has long been a source of confusion,[2] which I do not pretend to fully clear up.

From newspaper controversies and from obituaries we know that he was Danish, born in Copenhagen, his birth name was Adam Brøndum,[3] his father was a "deceased Copenhagen baker", and "the well known spirits distiller Brøndum was his grandfather".[4] The distiller was Anders Anton Brøndum (1790-1861), whose third child was Niels Christian Brøndum, born 1822; he is a "Bagersvend" ("baker") in the 1845 Danish census. Niels married Betty Laurentze Roede in 1849 and their children included **Hans Adam Julius Brøndum**, born Copenhagen 21 July 1862, baptised 21 September 1862.[5]

Adam made various assertions during his career when charged with making false claims and using a false name, one being that his father had died and his mother remarried to the magician Epstein, and he claimed he had adopted his stepfather's name![6] He further claimed he had gone with his stepfather on a tour to America when he was fourteen, but had returned home and graduated from Efterslægtens School — "[tr.] since then the world has been his homeland; he is currently an American citizen.[7] After earning a great deal of money in America, he became Co-Director of a Company that travelled around the United States with approximately 100 ballet girls. The company went bankrupt and he started conjuring again. Later he assumed the name of his stepfather, Epstein, and is now known throughout most of Europe under that name".[8]

His father died in 1875 (*Dagbladet* 22 March 1875) but the stepfather story is nonsense; however, he did go to America — at age 15 (arrived May 2nd 1878) and did become an American citizen, naturalised in New York on July 23rd 1882. However, his occupation at this time is given as "carvin [*sic*] in wood" and his

249

witness, Hans Gabryel Christenson, was a New York piano-maker, and presumably his employer.[9]

In May 1884 he was back in Denmark at the head of a large variety company, the first sighting of him on stage, but presumably he travelled with this company the previous year "around the United States", as he claimed, and brought at least some of the "100 ballet girls" with him. He calls himself Henry Adams "from New York" (and "Prof. i den højere Magi") and the company is the "Henry Adams Première Varieté Compagnie", including "Miss Lizzie", a serpentine dancer, said to be a Creole; "Miss Cora", singer and imitator of animal sounds; plus dancers, acrobats, a wire walker, and Negro comedians.

They opened in Aarhus on June 3rd 1884,[10] followed by Horsens, where the reviewer commended the dancing, the animal noises and especially the negro comedians, but found that "Mr Adams's experiments in the higher magic" were disappointing and did not live up to the promise of the programme.[11] Randers and Aalborg followed, then they left from Frederikshavn for Sweden, performing in Landskrona, Helsingborg, Malmö, Norrköping — where, in their final week, in early July, "Henry Adams" is first billed as performing "Det Gröna Huset", the spirit-cabinet act,[12] which was to become a staple of his show as he turned more to Anti-Spiritism performances. Linköping was next,[13] then Stockholm, and finally, with some changes in personnel, back to Norrköping and Linköping, where they closed in early October.

We next find him later that month in Örebro, no longer with the variety company but wearing a new hat — *impresario*, managing a mind-reader named "Emil Franzisco". A notice signed "Henry Adams, Impressario, New York" announces that private and public seances by Franzisco, delayed due to his ill-health, will soon take place.[14] The arrangement proved to be short-lived. There were performances in Nora and in Arboga, but the pair went their separate ways at the end of the month in Eskiltuna. Franzesco was sued in court for their board and lodging, prevented from leaving and his wardrobe and apparatus held as surety: he blamed it all on the contract signed by "Mr Adams".[15]

This partnership is of some interest, both for the identity of "Emil Franzisco"[16] and for the course that the career of "Henry Adams" now took. At the end of 1884 he reappears in Helsinger as Hr Henry Adams "a new mind reader", who has been "travelling for a long time with Mr Bishop".[17]

He continued, as *Hr., Prof.*, or *Prof. Mr.* Henry Adams, in Aarhus, claiming that he was a pupil of Bishop when he (Adams) was "was still a travelling actor in America".[18] A scathing review of his "Anti-Spiritisme og Psycophysik" said he "claimed he was born in America, and began by making an apology in English for not speaking good Danish, but then he began to speak Danish ... spiced with a bit of a Swedish accent. He opened by playing the magician, with no success. The tricks he knew were poor, and those that weren't poor he couldn't do ... lacking any dexterity ... the mind reading act is best not mentioned. The best thing about the performance was the countless thrilling lectures he gave to the audience, they were at least comical. Mr. Adams should kindly take a couple of courses with Mr. Bishop before trying to lure people to his shows".[19]

He was next through Randers, Aalborg, Hjørring, with little success (not helped by reprints of the Aarhus review following him round), and then in Skive, where he declared in his ad: "Although Professor Henry Adams is only 25 years old, the entire English and Swedish and part of the Danish Press have unanimously declared him to be the best and most talented current Professor in the higher Salon Magic... he will perform all the experiments done by his colleagues Mr. Cumberland and Mr. Bishop..."; however he failed to appear for the show, the newspaper deciding it was an April Fool's joke and probably no great loss.[20]

He travelled on — Morsø, Holstebro, Thisted, Lemvig, Horsens, and Vejle, and then to Sweden, with a show in Malmö in June. In August he is listed as staying in a hotel in Öresund, but no mention of him performing there,[21] and we now lose sight of him. He may have gone to Russia, as he later made the very unlikely claim of performing for the Czar on September 1st 1885 (the geography but not the audience perhaps correct).

In October and November 1885 he was back in Denmark as Henry Adams with a variety troupe, in Frederiksborg (Hillerød) and at the Thalia in Copenhagen,[22] but he then drops out of sight once again. Among his later claims were performances this year for King Oscar II of Norway and Sweden in Stockholm on August 17th 1886 (possible, and claimed only one year later) and for President Cleveland in Washington on October 13th 1886 (highly improbable).[23]

The truth is found in the Copenhagen Poor Relief Records which list him in 1886, age 24, as sick and receiving assistance.[25]

In November 1886 he is in Norway, still as Henry Adams, in Fredrikshald (Halden) as lecturer on a diorama and soon after in Bergen.[25] We see him again in Bergen in February 1887 with "Spiritist Seances" ("Mr Adams, who spoke very good Danish [!], announced that he wanted to expose Spiritism..."),[26] then in Stavanger with the seances and the diorama,[27] followed by Kristiansand on March 13th.[28]

It all came apart a week later when the Stavanger paper printed a long account headed "Warning against the 'antispiritist' Mr. Henry Adams" — *he claims to be American, but according to Danish sources he is Danish, a former merchant in a small town, and his genuine and unadulterated Danish also left no doubt as to his nationality. After the glowing account in the Bergen papers of Mr Adams's performance there, we introduced this gentleman to our audience as a virtuous man in his profession, and a not entirely small audience attended his performance. However, it was a disappointment to the spectators and the next show let down both himself and the audience. And then this "American" gentleman disappeared, leaving behind a small crowd of creditors who no doubt remember him, though not fondly. Our colleagues at the Christiansand paper report that he also left there with unpaid debts.*[29]

"Mr. Henry Adams" now drops out of sight until December 1887. In the interim **"Mr. H.A. Epstein (junior)"** suddenly appears, performing in Kristiania (Oslo) only a month after Stavanger and Kristiansand. The act is very like that of Henry Adams, spiritist shows (never including ventriloquism, playing a musical instrument, plate-spinning, or the gun-trick), and there is no specific mention even of conjuring, and everything points to this being "Henry Adams" in a new guise. The strongest evidence is that later this year **"Dr. H. Adam Epstein"** appears, not only with a very similar act but this name alternating with "H.A. Epstein" even in the same town on successive days, and it was as "Adam(s) Epstein" that Brøndum was outed.[30]

"Mr. H.A. Epstein (junior)" first appears in April 1887 at the Victoria Theater in Kristiania (a wise choice as he had not previously performed in Kristiania), accompanying one of the regular concerts by the "skandinaviske Damekvartet"; he describes himself as "a spiritist and a magician".[31]

Then in September we first find "Dr. H. Adam Epstein" in Fredriksstad (modern Fredrikstad), advertising an evening of spiritism and mind-reading, and offering to show the audience how the mind-reading was done.[32] In September he was in Moss and Sarpsborg,[33] and from October touring Sweden. In Göteborg he is first billed as "Herr Doktor H. Adam Epstein" then as "Doktor H. A. Epstein", and is first found claiming the prior performances in England, Russia and Washington.[34] In November in Hässleholm as "Hr D:r Adam Epstein (jun.)" he makes the same claims, adding that he hopes to perform before King Oscar at the end of the month.[35] Later that month he is in Landskrona as "Herr Adam Epstein",[36] and continuing on to Borås ("Hr. Dr. Adam Epstein (jun.)" and Hässleholm, first as "Herr Doktor H.A. Epstein" then as "Hr D:r Adam Epstein (jun.)" in early November 1887,[37] when he leaves Sweden for Copenhagen.

Here he reverts to the name "Henry Adams" that he was known by there with his Variety Company in 1884, and opened a "Great Variety Performance" at the Thalia Theatre on December 7th 1887. He billed himself as "den berømte Salon-magiker og Tryllekunstner Prof. Henry Adams" and is accompanied a bevy of young ladies — Olga, Mimi Nielsen, Lilli Remia, Mathilda Andersen.[38]

He reappears in Frederiksborg (Hillerød) on March 23rd 1888, now for the first time in Denmark as Dr H.A. Epstein, jun.[39] Here he advertises as before his claimed performances for Queen Victoria, the Czar, and President Cleveland, but his act is largely new, now including "the dancing skeleton" (*det dansende skelet*), which was to become his trademark act.[40]

A week later he is in Lund advertising on March 29th with the same name, same claims, and same act (*det dansande skelettet*). A promotional piece in this issue calls him "dr Adam Epstein jun." with the remark: "if he is to some extent comparable to his older name, he may well merit a large audience".[41]

In April 1889 a rather odd account appeared in a Copenhagen paper, which is the earliest reference found to "Ebstein's" [*sic*] real name being Adam Brøndum. Headed "Thrown out!", it appears that a carpenter Alfred Born and "magician Adam Brondum, called Ebstein", had for the past couple of weeks been showing the Transformation Lady 'Iphigenia' in the Hotel Tivoli, but had been neglecting their obligations both to the owners and to the public who often had to wait hours for the performance, leading to constant uproar in the room. The gas was turned off and the two were left in the dark.[42]

At the end of May 1889 he is in Helsinki as Henry Adams ("… The dancing skeleton, Spirit arts, The art of getting rich, Mind reading, etc."), joined by other performers,[43] then a similar act in Landskrona, Karlshamn, Karlskrona. In October he gave a performance for Vesterbro school children in Copenhagen,[44] then was in Malmö in December.[45]

The following year saw him first performing in Sweden as H.A. Epstein, then from April he worked his way south through Denmark under that name. In September he reached Holstebro, where he incurred a very harsh review — "Dr. (?) H.A. Epstein jun. performed here on Friday. Since they wished to avoid a review by not providing us with tickets, we would in principle have confined ourselves to that mere announcement, if the good doctor had not made an attempt to dupe the audience with a new name and a very boastful programme, which he failed to live up to. For it is not the first time that the good Doctor has appeared here with his wretched and worn out acts; we remember his first performance here a few years ago under the name 'Professor Henry Adams'; it was just as wretched as ever. That he has now appeared under another, more familiar name, and with a remarkably boastful programme, and has thus attracted some people to his show, must be forgiven; What's done can't be undone!; however, we should not recommend another attempt in that direction; for the moment let's forget all about it".[46] The review was also in the Lemvig paper so he gave Lemvig a miss, heading straight to Aarhus.[47] His performance there did not end well — the climax of the show was to be the disappearance of a horse and rider before the audience's eyes; this went "pitifully", and he was hissed off the stage.[48]

He himself now disappeared and we lose sight of "H.A. Epstein" for some time. However in October the following year we find a "Mr. Adams Epstein" with a very similar act in Mülhausen (Mulhouse) in Alsace. He is the "Imperial Russian and Royal Swedish Court Magician"[49] and besides the dancing skeleton he offers the clairvoyant skull, rapping ghosts, the spirit cabinet, levitating chairs and tables, and thought-reading, ending with his own mysterious disappearance.[50] The following month in Rosenheim in Bavaria is "Dr. H. Epstein". similarly billing himself as "Imperial Russian and Royal Swedish Court Magician" and with the same list of acts; he is "assisted by Miss Lotti Epstein".[51] In March 1892 he is in Linz;[52] followed by Graz, first as Doktor Herr Adam Epstein, then as Mr Adams Epstein;[53] and in May 1892 in Olmütz (Olomouc), first as Dr Adam Epstein then as Dr H. Adams Epstein, billing himself as American.[54]

By April 1893 he is in Denmark and in May in Sweden, performing in Lund as Dr H.A. Epstein with "Miss Mary Epstein", then in August in Höganäs, September in Halmstad (Dr H. Adams Epstein, still with the dancing skeleton). In October he was in Norway (as Dr Adam Epstein), where his show went well enough but it was remarked that this "was not the old Epstein", a lady jokingly suggesting that he had given the old Epstein (presumably meaning Sigmund) so and so much to be allowed to use his name and continue his business.[55]

Performing in Sweden later in the year, he was questioned by the police in Köping after his performance for claiming in Arboga that he was an American and was an honorary doctor: forced to admit that both the name and the title were borrowed, it was confirmed that his real name was Bröndum and he was born in Copenhagen, though he persisted with the claim that he was the stepson of the "old Epstein". Having no papers he was gaoled for the night, along with his manager, the gaol proving "more solid than his Green House".[56]

He was again Henry Adams in Stockholm in January 1894, then later that year travelled through Norway with some success (in Trondheim referred to as both H.A. Epstein and Adam Epstein). Back in Sweden in December, he was severely criticised in Sundsvall, "Henry Adams or Adam Epstein, as he also calls himself" ... nothing new, no unusual skills ... and his "Green House" act was a disaster.[57]

He is found in Norway from late 1895 to February 1896, and then headed to England, where he toured for several months as "Dr Adam Epstein" promising to expose spiritism and its exponents. He opened in Ipswich in early March, where a long review[58] noted "neither a very large or a very enthusiastic audience ... popular interest in this kind of thing seems to be dying out". He was not fluent in English, but "his courteous and unassuming manner made an extremely favourable impression" and his act, especially the skeleton, was then described in some detail — he opened with a prodigious feat of memory, then came "a curious and exceedingly comical trick, which kept the house in roars of laughter. He produced and handed round for inspection a figure cut in card-board to the resemblance of a skeleton. There was apparently no machinery by which it could moved, but on the stage that figure cut some extraordinary capers — standing bolt upright, dancing with lively agility, and refusing to lie still like any properly-constituted skeleton, even when ordered so to do, and weighted down with different articles. The figure was afterwards placed again in the body of the Hall, and it was funny to see the suspicion with which it was regarded. Some people evidently thought that the 'thing' might get up again of its own accord, and go waltzing all over the room". Next came "a number of neatly-executed conjuring feats ... together with striking evidences of what may perhaps be called unconscious muscular force". In the second part, "a really wonderful exposition of table-turning was afforded, an ordinary square table — standing by itself on the platform with nobody near it — rising up and answering questions put to it in the approved 'spiritualistic fashion'". He concluded by responding to unseen questions in sealed envelopes and escaping from ropes.

The tour continued through Bury St Edmonds, Beaconsfield, Lancaster, Morecombe, largely summer holiday spots, ending in Bridlington in August.

In October he was back in Denmark as "Dr Epstein jun.", then in Sweden in 1896-7, where in Landskrona his manager Rodhe fled with the takings of 100 kronor.[59] He continued on through Sweden and Finland (as "Adam Epstein, from New York") and in February in Helsinki was confronted by rival Danish magician "Faustinus".[60] In an article headed "There are false wizards in Finland!", Faustinus declared how disappointed people were in Tampere that the Epstein they came to see was not the "old honourable Epstein" and not even a mediocre conjuror, but a person who simply took that name and who was really Adam Bröndum.[61] Epstein replied: "Is it jealousy or stupidity that has dictated Mr Faustinus' comments...", saying that the name of "Mr. Faustinus, alias Capriello" on his baptismal certificate is Petersen, and about 10 to 12 years ago he was working as a waiter at the theatre restaurant in Randers, when I was there as an antispiritist and magician, and was very interested in my shows. Voilà tout!...".[62] The controversy continued with Faustinus labelling "Brøndum-Epstein" a poor performer, not entitled to the titles he claimed, and calling humbug his statement that his mother had married Epstein; he maintained his own name was genuine and denied being a waiter in Randers but a friend of the owner's son and assisted there to get a free look at the show by Epstein, "then Prof. Henry Adams".[63] Other papers were not slow to express an opinion and it was generally felt that Faustinus was a far more skilled magician than Epstein.[64] Epstein left Helsinki before completing his announced series of shows, and his manager Le Fort was said to have threatened *Nya Pressen's* editor with a revolver over a poor review.[65]

Epstein resumed his touring — in Poland (as Dr Adam Epstein) in 1898; in Hamburg in early 1899, then in Sweden (June in Oresund as Dr Henry Adams with a troupe including Miss Lilly Edison) and Helsinki (July as Dr Adam Epstein). In March 1900 he gave several shows in Munich (as Adam Epstein) then from July in Sweden (as Adam Epstein, with "Lilly Edisson").[66] He is found touring Scandinavia 1900-1903 (as "Adam(s) Epstein" and once as "Dr Henry Adams Epstein"), still proclaiming his right to the name Epstein through his mother's remarriage.[67] In Germany in 1905 he had an embarrassing episode when with the lights off he summoned up a spirit for the audience, then the lights suddenly went on and it was revealed as a mannequin decorated with luminous paint.[68] In 1906 many French papers enjoyed reprinting a story of "a certain Doctor Epstein" performing in Straßburg where police objected to his poster on the grounds that it was not entirely in German as the law required: it contained the French word *séance,* and this, they demanded, should be replaced with the German word — *soirée.*[69]

He was in Bern in July 1906, still with his "dancing skeleton, clairvoyance, spirit-cabinet, spirit-apparitions",[70] and on September 7th that year he opened in the Imthurneum in Schaffhausen.[71] He never left. There were several reports in Danish papers of his death in Schaffhausen, the earliest on September 19th (*Fredericia Dagblad*, et al.). Most gave his real name and many mentioned his grandfather. A long and sympathetic obituary in *Viborg Stifts Folkeblad* 21 Sep.1906 said "[tr.] ...He never became a significant Artist in his profession. His sorry, awkward figure seemed without sympathy, and he was constantly feuding with his happier and more inventive colleagues... He also fought hard for existence, but the belief that he was a 'real' wizard never left him. Epstein was one of the naive wizards who, in their happiest moments, blindly believe in the presence and existence of supernatural beings ... Now he's dead... Adam Epstein's misfortune was that he 'believed' in himself, his dancing skeletons, the spirit writings, and the talking head. Now he has found the Artist's death, and will be buried, a stranger and unknown, in a tomb in a foreign land".

NOTES

[1] That "Henry Adams" and "Adam(s) Epstein" were identical is shown by the very critical note on him in *Sundsvalls Tidning* 4 Dec.1894: "[tr.] Henry Adams or Adam Epstein, as he also calls himself" ("Henry Adams eller Adam Epstein, som han ock kallar sig..."); and in 1897 Faustinus Capriello in his dispute with him calls him "[tr.] Mr Epstein alias — that time — Prof. Henry Adams" (*Nya Pressen* 2 Mar.1897: "hr Epstein alias – den tiden – prof. Henry Adams...").

[2] The *Lexikon,* for example, referring to Dammann and Whannell, equates this Epstein with the so-called *Adam Salomon Epstein,* further confusing matters by saying that *Sigismund Epstein* may be the same person.

[3] Not Bröndrum or Bröndrumin, as variously stated. The name is printed Bröndum in some non-Danish papers (whose founts would not have included ø).

[4] Obit in *Viborg Stifts Folkeblad* 21 Sep.1906: "'Doktor' Epstein ... hvis borgerlige Navn var Adam Brøndum, var en Søn af forlængst afdøde Bager Brøndum i Kjøbenhavn, og den kendte Brændevinsbrænder B. var hans Bedstefader".

[5] Birth and baptism record on *FamilySearch* (url:138). His father's older brother, Thomas Christian Brøndum, 1812-1892, who founded the Copenhagen *Hippodrom* in 1846, which became the *Folketeater* in 1857, is the only member of the family known to have a theatrical connexion.

[6] He was claiming this in early 1897 when attacked by Faustinus (see below) and by 1901 it was a staple of his promotional material.

[7] *Figaro* [Stockholm] 9 July 1900.

[8] *Aalborg Tidende* 21 Oct.1901.

[9] Hans Adam Julius Brondum, born Denmark 21 July 1862, in 'New York, State and Federal Naturalization Records' digitised on *Ancestry.com* (url:139).

[10] *Jyllandsposten* 25 May 1884; *Aarhuus Stifts-Tidende* 28 May 1884.

[11] *Horsens Folkeblad* 7 June 1884.

[12] *Norrköpings Tidningar* 9 July 1884. The cabinet act, first introduced by the Davenport Brothers in the 1850s and frequently exposed by Antispiritists, was performed in Scandinavia under the name "Det Gröna Huset" by the Italian "Professor Roberth" from 1881 (*Norrlandsposten* 27 May 1881) and again by him there in 1884. "Henry Adams" was one of many magicians touring Scandinavia who at this time added it to their repertoire, including Max Alexander, Joseph Buatier, Emil Paxton, Fr. de Blanche and Sidonie Roman.

[13] A promotional piece, no doubt supplied to the paper by them, preceding their arrival in Linköping states that the company has received the highest praise not only in Denmark and Sweden but in Germany ("...Från såwäl Tyskland och Danmark som olika platser i Swerige — senast från Norrköping — medför sällskapet de wackraste loford": *Östgöta Correspondenten* 15 July 1884): no other evidence has been found for them performing in Germany prior to Denmark.

[14] *Nerikes Allehanda* 15, 17 Oct.1884. Both Franzisco, from Bergen, and "Henry Adams", from New York, are listed staying at the Centralhotell in Örebro, each with manservant.

[15] Detailed accounts are given in *Eskilstuna Tidning* 4 Nov.1884 ("Sjelfpantning..."); *Norrköpings Tidningar* 22 Nov.1884 ("Skuldfordringsmål...").

[16] "Emil Franzisco" was one of the early stage names of the protean character variously known as Frants Forsberg, Frantz Emil Cetti, Francesco Alexandro Cetti, Francesco Cetti, Francisco Cetti, and Frans Frandsen — *in fact baptised Frantz Emil Frantzisco Settisen*, successively actor, musician, magician, mind-reader, starvation artist, and balloonist: see *Appendix Z3*.

[17] *Dagens Nyheder* 13 Dec.1884. Washington Irving Bishop, 1855-99, who in his stage mind-reading act claimed no supernatural powers, saying that he followed unconscious bodily cues, toured Scandinavia in September and October 1884, but there is no mention of Brøndum/Epstein accompanying him and in fact at that date he was still with "Franzisco". In 1885 "Franzisco", now as "Franzisco Cetti", was also touring a mind reading act, claiming "secrets known only to Cumberland and Bishop" and calling himself a former "pupil" (sometimes "companion") of Prof. Epstein [*sic*].

[18] *Jyllandsposten* [Aarhus] 15 Feb.1885 (but he was an actor in America only *ca.*1883 and at that time Bishop was in Europe).

[19] *Aarhus Amtstidende* 16 Feb.1885.

[20] *Skive Folkeblad* 1, 4 Apr.1885.

[21] *Öresundsposten* 13 Aug.1885: "...Professor Henry Adams och handl. L. Breiting, Köbenhavn."

[22] *Frederiksborg Amts Avis* 31 Oct.1885; *Dags-Telegraphen* [Copenhagen] 25, 29 Nov.1885.

[23] Claimed, for example, in his advertisements in *Göteborgsposten* 7 Oct.1887. Needless to say there is no record of this in American newspapers: Cleveland was indeed in Washington on that date (he went hunting in West Virginia later that week) but if anyone performed for him it was The Great Herrmann who opened in Washington on October 11th (*Washington Evening Star* 13 Oct.1886). The Stockholm performance is possible, but no mention is found in newspapers — and he further claimed to have performed before Queen Victoria and the Prince of Wales at the Crystal Palace in London on November 14th 1881, which is certainly false as he was then in America.

[24] "Brøndum, Hans Adam Julius. Artist, 24 Aar, Kbhvn., Udh. Sj. B. 33/86.": Fattigvæsenets Hovedregistrant 1881-1887 A-K (url:140).

[25] *Fredrikshalds Tilskuer* 4 Nov.1886; *Aftenposten* [Oslo] 14 Nov.1886; *Dagbladet* 15 Nov.1886; *Bergens Tidende* 24 Dec.1886.

[26] *Bergens Tidende* 11, 14 Feb.1887.

[27] *Stavanger Amtstidende og Adresseavis* 26, 28 Feb.; 4 Mar.1887.

[28] *Fædrelandsvennen* 11 Mar.1887.

[29] *Stavanger Amtstidende og Adresseavis* 19 Mar.1887.

[30] A fatal objection would be if any two of "Henry Adams", "H.A. Epstein (junior)", or "Adam Epstein" were found performing in different places at the same time, but that is never the case.

[31] *Dagbladet* and *Aftenposten* 23 Apr.1887: "Optræden af Aandespiritisten og Magikeren Mr. H.A. Epstein (junior). Forvandlings-Tableauer, Aandemaning m.m.".

[32] *Fredriksstad Tilskuer* 6 Sep.1887: "...en spiritisk Seance (Aandemaning og Magi). Aande-Manifestation, (Tilsynekomst). Klartsynede medier. Aande-Kabinettet. Stoffets Glennemtrængellhed (4 forskjellige Experimenter). Aande-Sækken. Tankelæsning. Tankeoverføring. Med Afslering og Anvisning, saa at enhver af Publikum kan udføre dem.".

[33] "Tankeleseren Epstein har i denne Uge givet Seancer...": *Smaalenenes Amstidende* 9 Sep.1887.

[34] *Göteborgsposten* 7, 11, 17 Oct.1887 ("en framstående tankeläsare och magiker" ... "den vidtberömde Trollkonstnären och Tankeläsaren").

[35] *Norra Skåne* 10 Nov.1887 ("...och hoppas att i slutet af November månad tå äran uppträda inför H.K. Majestät Konung Oscar").

[36] *Korrespondenten* 10 Nov.1887 ("[tr.] famous for his skill as a magician").

[37] *Norra Skåne* 8, 10 Nov.1887.

[38] *Social-Demokraten* 4, 7, 9, 10 Dec.1887.

[39] *Frederiksborg Amts Tidende og Adresseavis* 23 Mar.1888.

[40] He almost certainly acquired this from "Max Alexander" (Carl Max Alexis Rhodin, 1848-1924): he and his young son had recently been touring Scandinavia with it as a feature of their act.

[41] *Lunds Weckoblad* 27 Mar.1888.

[42] *Social-Demokraten* 24 Apr.1889.

[43] *Helsingborgs Dagblad* 28, 29 May 1889. Posters for these performances are included at url:141.

[44] *Nationaltidende* 10 Oct.1889 ("Henry Adams Taagebilleder").

[45] *Arbetet* 30 Nov.1889 ("D:r Henry Adams från Köpenhamns Tivoli").

[46] *Holstebro Dagblad* 16 Sep.1890; also in *Lemvig Folkeblad* same date.

[47] He is recorded (*Aarhuus Stifts-Tidende* 17 Sep.1890) as staying at a hotel with his wife, the first mention found of her. In the *Politiets registerblade* (listing all Copenhagen residents) dated May 1 1899 his wife is named as Julie Marie Isabella Brøndum, born in Reval 21 September 1878 (url:142) — clearly that is a later wife.

[48] *Aarhuus Stifts-Tidende* 22 Sep.1890; and widely reprinted.

[49] A previous "Professor Epstein" (B12e) with a spiritist act and calling himself "Russian [but not Swedish] court magician" was performing on tour in Holland in 1883. He is not B12 and very unlikely to be the young Brøndum (B12a), then age 23 and as far as we know still in America and not yet a magician.

[50] *Express* 10 Oct.1891.

[51] *Rosenheimer Anzeiger* 28 Nov.1891.

[52] *(Linzer) Tages-Post* 29, 30 Mar.1892.

[53] *Grazer Tagblatt* 8, 9 April 1892.

[54] *Mährisches Tagblatt* 10, 12, 14 May 1892.

[55] *Dagbladet* 6 Oct.1893.

[56] *Dagens Nyheter* 15 Dec.1893; *Agderposten* 8 Jan.1894/

[57] *Sundsvalls Tidning* 4 Dec.1894.

[58] *East Anglian Daily Times* 11 Mar.1896.

[59] *Social-Demokraten* 22 Jan.1897, the report calling him "…the Danish magician Adam Epstein, whose birth name is Brøndum…".

[60] Faustinus' name was one of the points at issue between him and Brøndum. He was born in Fredensborg, Denmark, on February 15th 1868 (parents Kristian Petersen and Johanne Regine Kristensen), and baptised on November 15th as *Faustinus Petersen*. On April 23rd 1882 he was confirmed under the name *Faustinus Petersen*. By a Royal Grant on March 17th 1900 his name became *Faustinus Pedersen-Faustinus* (url:143) and he is listed under that name in the 1925 census.

[61] *Nya Pressen* 20 Feb.1897.

[62] *Nya Pressen* and *Aftonposten* 25 Feb.1897, signed Adam B. Epstein.

[63] *Nya Pressen* and *Aftonposten* 2 Mar.1897.

[64] *Tammerfors Nyheter* 27 Feb.; 6, 11, 25 Mar. 1897; *Åbo Tidning* 28 Feb.1897; *Borgå Nya Tidning* 2 Mar.1897.

[65] *Aftonposten* 6 Mar.1897; *Nya Pressen* 10 Mar.1897; *Program-bladet* 14 Mar.1897; *Tammerfors Nyheter* 1, 4, 6 May 1897; *Åbo Tidning* 3 May 1897.

[66] The Stockholm *Figaro* 1 Sep.1900 published a splendid illustration of him.

[67] Interviews with him are found in *Bornholms Tidende* 7 Apr.1902 (nice picture of him playing cards with a skeleton; he used this picture in his advertisements) and *Fredriksstad Tilskuer* 21 Nov.1902.

[68] *Berliner Tageblatt* 15 Nov.1905, and widely reprinted.

[69] *L'Aurore* 26 Apr.1906 (etc.).

[70] *Bern Intelligenzblatt* 20, 21 July 1906.

[71] *Schaffhauser Nachrichten* 7 Sep.1906.

B12b. "Professor Sigismund Epstein" (Finland 1875)

As discussed in B12, in August 1875 we encounter an impostor calling himself "Professor Sigismund Epstein" (a title seldom used by Sigmund who preferred "Dr.") performing in Vyborg (Viipuri), at Huusniemi Park. His act features magic, ventriloquism, playing the Aeolian harp, plus fireworks (no gun trick, decapitation, or plate spinning) and he is said to be "a new Epstein".[1]

A week later he is in Helsinki with a musical-magic *soirée* at Brunnshuset (Kaivopuisto Park). One review describes him as "a well-known friend from a previous stay", but another specifically states "The wizard, Mr Epstein (not the same one who entertained Helsinki with his visit last winter)…".[2]

A final firework show on August 25th was criticised for its high prices and poor fireworks which fizzed for a few seconds then left a cloud of stinking smoke ("first and foremost bad, secondly very bad, and thirdly, unforgivably bad … As a magician, Mr Epstein is in some way justified and accustomed to leading the audience by the nose, but it should not happen in such a clumsy and inconsiderate manner as yesterday".[3]

That seems to be the end of that Epstein, though he may be the "Magiker S. Epstein" in Reval (Tallinn) in August 1878 just arrived from Grodno, advertising a "Soirée mystérieuse brillante … bestehend in der höheren Magie, Bauchredekunst und im Spiel auf der Aeolsharfe".[4] As he is promising the audience presents and plays the Aeolian harp it is more likely to be this impostor than Sigmund.

NOTES

[1] *Wiborgs Tidning* 7, 10 Aug.1875: "en ny Epstein… Det är denna gång 'professor Sigismund Epstein'".

[2] *Helsingfors dagblad* 15 Aug.1875: "…den redan sedan en föregående vistelse härstädes bekante hr Epstein"; *Morgonbladet* 16 Aug.1875: "Trollkarlen hr Epstein (icke den samme, som senaste winter fägnade Helsingfors med sitt besök)…"

[3] *Helsingfors dagblad* 25 Aug.1875; *Finlands Allmänna Tidning* 26 Aug.1875.

[4] *Revalsche Zeitung* 5 to 8 August 1878.

B12c. Dr. A. Epstein (said to be brother of B12)

Dr. A. Epstein is first sighted in Vyborg (Viipuri) in April 1880.[1] He advertises "Magical-Physical Performances after a new system" (including the beheading; but he is not a ventriloquist and plays no instrument, so is probably not B12b; and he is not a spiritist). Later that month he is in Helsinki and he is now described as the brother of Sigmund (B12).[2] We know that Sigmund's brother was his stage assistant in 1869 (when the accident occurred at the Cirque Napoleon) so this could be true, but there is no other supporting evidence. The reviews in Helsinki were polite rather than enthusiastic ("a skilled magician, no worse and no better than others of the profession"), and he then added decapitation to his act ("Dr. Epstein will use a knife to cut off the head of a living human being", with the audience invited to hold and inspect the severed head).[3] He next performed in Tampere on May 2nd and 4th, in Åbo (Turku) on May 9th and 11th, and in June was in Reval (Tallinn).[4]

We then lose sight of him until the end of 1881, when a "Dr A. Epstein" with a very similar act began a long tour of England. He opened in Eastbourne on Boxing Day — "Dr A. Epstein, Court Prestidigitateur to H.I.M. the Emperor of Russia ... Four Grand Performances in the Mysteries of the Natural Indian and Egyptian Saloon Magic, Consisting of Magic, Physic, Chemistry, Spiritism, Somnambulism and Magnetism", with his "extraordinary performances" including "the beheading of a living person, the wonderful bottle of the 19th century, the enchanted cigar, and many other magical exploits".[5] He moved on to Hastings, a review praising his decapitation act and stressing that "anyone present in the body of the Hall can undergo this pleasant (?) operation"[6] — so his "victim" was not an assistant but a spectator chosen from the audience (a plant?). Next we see him in Kingston, Acton (the closest he was to get to London),[7] Leicester in May,[8] and then in Rugby, where he is joined by "The Original Bosco, the Royal Illusionist". Rugby was not a success ("a very inferior house", said *The Stage*) and a planned second night was cancelled due to lack of patronage.[9]

"Bosco" was again with him in Coventry at the end of May (with "Bosco" claiming to have performed before Queen Victoria at Balmoral) and in Southampton in June.[10] This "Bosco" was **Saul Warszawski** (B63) who at this time lived in Leicester and probably made contact with Epstein when he was there. Saul had billed himself as "The Royal Illusionist" since 1876 and also as "The Original Bosco" and had long claimed (falsely) to have been the Bosco at Balmoral (see *Appendix Z12*). In 1882 Saul added a very successful decapitation act to his show, so it is likely that he learnt this from Epstein.

This Epstein's two final appearances in Britain, both without "Bosco", were in Folkestone in mid July and Eastbourne at the start of August.[11]

NOTES

[1] *Östra Finland* 7 Apr.1880 ("...den verldsberömde Dr. A. Epstein, hofkonstnär, endast 2 stora Magisk-Fysiska Föreställningar, alldeles efter nytt system..."); *Wiborgs Tidning* 13 Apr.1880.

[2] *Helsingfors Dagblad* 16 Apr.1880 ("Magikern A Epstein, icke att förblanda med hans broder, som här förut uppträdt..."); *Morgonbladet* 17 Apr.1880 ("Magikern A. Epstein, broder till den skicklige prestidigitatör med samma namn, som uppträdde härstädes för fem år sedan, och sjelf vidtbekant för sina 'trollkonster'...").

[3] *Helsingfors Dagblad* 22 Apr.1880 ("Dr E. kommer att med en knif afhugga hufvudet på en lefvande menniska. Hvarje åskådare utan undantag kan taga hufvadet i hand för att öfvertyga sig om att det verkligen är hufvudet af en lefvande menniska..."). The ad includes an illustration of a beheaded conjuror holding his head under his arm and a bloody knife pointed upwards (similar to but not the same as that used earlier by Sigmund).

[4] His Reval advertisements in *Revalsche Zeitung* 10, 18 June 1880 make much of his decapitation act: the second ad. includes the same illustration he used in Helsinki in April.

[5] *Eastbourne Gazette* 21, 28 Dec.1881.

[6] *Hastings and St Leonards Observer* 7, 21 Jan.1882.

[7] *Surrey Advertiser* 21 to 28 Jan.1882; *Acton Gazette* 25 Jan.1882 (good reviews but small audiences).

[8] *Leicester Journal* 28 April to 19 May 1882.

[9] *Stage* 26 May 1882; *Nuneaton Advertiser* 27 May 1882.

[10] *Coventry Standard* 19 May 1882; *Hampshire Advertiser* 17 June 1882.

[11] *Folkestone Express* 8 July 1882; *Eastbourne Gazette* 2 Aug.1882.

B12d. "Professor Epstein" (Dr S. Epstein fils, Holland 1870) = Heksch

As discussed in B12, when Sigmund was touring Holland in 1870 he teamed up in Amsterdam in September with a well-known opera baritone, Johann Jacob Heksch, to give concerts combining their talents during the fair (references in B12). The following month Heksch began performing in Den Helder as *Dr S. Epstein fils* doing "Indian and Egyptian finger-magic".

Epstein, annoyed, advertised that he was he was in no way connected with him. Heksch duly replied with a statement signed "Dr EPSTEIN fils" stating that his performances would definitely go ahead, while that announced by a certain Dr Epstein next Wednesday at the Tivoli would positively not proceed, as the gentleman referred to does not dare to come here because Dr Epstein fils would prosecute him.

A review of Heksch's performance complimented him on his "unrivalled, swiftness and dexterity" and he continued to perform as Epstein fils until the end of the year. The last sighting is in Amsterdam in December and Heksch then returned to his singing career.

B12e. "Professor Epstein" (Holland 1883)

As discussed in B12, in 1883 there is a "Professor Epstein" performing on tour in Holland. He calls himself "Russian court magician" and in May is specifically billed as "Professor A. Epstein". He is unlikely to be the same person as B12b as his act is mainly spiritism and there is no mention of beheadings, ventriloquism, or the gun trick, and is almost certainly not Adam Brøndum (B12a) who was then age 21, probably still in America and not yet a magician.

He is first seen in April in Arnhem[1] with successful "Groote Spiritistische Toover-Soirées" of "Indian-Egyptian Salon Magic, Spiritism, Poltergeistry, and Illusions". He then moved on to Tilburg ("…den Keizerlijk Koninklijken Hofkonstenaar Professor A. Epstein"), and The Hague, and Delft, ending in Rotterdam in June.

[1] "Der K.K. Russ. Hof-Prestidigitateur Professor EPSTEIN kommt!!!". He was thought at first to be the *S. Epstein* who had performed there in 1870 — Sigmund, who is oddly said to have attracted small crowds in those tense days "because it was said that he had come to our country to spy on our defence system!": *Arnhemsche Courant* 20, 26 Apr.1883. I could see nothing to that effect in the 1870 newspapers.

B13. Charlemagne Bosco.

Found in Maubeuge and Valrnciennes in Northern France in 1861. "Un habile prestidigitateur, M. Charlemagne Bosco, en ce moment à Maubeuge, se propose de venir donner quelques séances à Valenciennes …" (*Courrier du Nord* 30 Jan.1861).

B14. Bosco: unidentified, Dutch?, *ca*.1860.

The *Lexikon* (p.56) lists an unidentified "Bosco", Dutch?, performing with David Leendert Bamberg *ca.*1860. No source is given and though Bamberg advertised extensively in Dutch papers of the period I have been unable to find a reference to him performing with a Bosco.

B15. "Bosco", unidentified, France 1868

An unidentified impostor active in France in 1868: Eugenio Bosco (B2) wrote to *Le Monde* (1 Sep.1868) complaining of "les usurpateurs du nom de Bosco … il y a en ce moment en France un individu qui se dit fils de Bosco, et qui escroque le monde…".

B16. Herr Bosco — Wolf Wilhelm Blumenfeld, 1849-1906.

"Herr Bosco" was one of several stage names for the magician best remembered for being fatally shot performing the bullet trick in Switzerland in 1906; listed by the *Lexikon* as "Blumenfeld, Louis = Louis Blanc; Blanc sr.; Bosco-Blumenfeld; St. Jean Bosco"; by Ben Robinson in *Twelve Have Died* as "Professor Blumenfeld"; and at *http://www.bulletcatch.com* and *https://www.magictricks.com/biographies-of-magicians-B.html* as "Otto Blumenfeld".

He was **Wolf Wilhelm Blumenfeld**, born in Limberg, Germany, on March 28th 1849, one of sixteen children of Emanuel Levy Blumenfeld of the Blumenfeld circus dynasty (whose history is treated at length by Gisela & Dietmar Winkler in *Die Blumenfelds, Schicksale einer jüdischen Zirkusfamilie: eine Dokumentation*, 2012, and at *https://blennowgenealogy.wordpress.com*).

Wilhelm, as he was known, married Gottliebin Nagele in Berlin in 1875 and they had ten children, four born in England where they settled in 1886 and where he used the name William Bloomfield. He began his career as an acrobat and strong man, and as late as 1889 he was still "…Professor Blumenfeld … described in the bills as 'Sampson' … a wizard, conjurer, and juggler of considerable merit, and, in addition, possesses wonderful strength. In some of his conjuring tricks, such as the umbrella, the electric chair and mesmerising, and the ring and the dove trick, he was very successful, and his performances in balancing 36lb cannon balls and eggs was very interesting ... he also gave some capital acrobatic feats, in company with his son...": *Bournemouth Guardian* 21 Dec.1889. In 1886 he was "Herr Boscoe ... a truly marvellous juggler and balancer on the slack wire" (*South Wales Echo* 12 Aug.1886) and from 1900 was performing as "The Great Herman" ("stated to be the greatest card and cigar manipulator in England": *Herts & Cambs Reporter* 6 Feb.1903), then as "The Great Herman & Family's Novelty Company", now joined by his children, including Annie, who married the conjuror John Brignall, and William Otello Samson Blumenfeld, born in Brighton in 1889, who became the actor and magician "Oscar Stirling". Wolf had been working in Europe for about six months when on January 24th 1906 in a music hall in Basle he removed as usual the false barrel on the pistol he used for the gun trick, but failed to remove the bullet also, and was killed instantly. The news did not reach his family in England till long after his burial (*Neue Zürcher Nachrichten* 25 Jan.1906; *Era* 3, 10 Feb.1906). Gottliebin died in Wandsworth in 1928.

B17. "A. Bosko" in Klagenfurt 1875.

Staying at the Gasthof zum Mohren in Klagenfurt in July 1875 is "A. Bosko, Escamoteur von Wien" (*Klagenfurter Zeitung* 10 July 1875). No performance there is mentioned, and no performer of this name is known; it may be a misprint for E. Bosco — Eugenio was in Turin in March that year and in Treviso in December, so it could possibly be him just passing through.

B18. Herr Ritter von Bosco, "Hof-Prestidigitateur"; Herr Bosco jun.

Found in Brno, Vienna, Laibach (Ljubljana) and Bolzano 1878-9 billing himself as "einzige Erbe der Talente seines Vaters", so claiming to be the son of Bartolomeo.

He is first sighted performing in Brno on September 29th 1878, advertising a single performance of his "staunenerregenden, unerklärlichen Kunststücken", and claiming to have performed before the royal family in Vienna on July 28th. However his show, announced as "extraordinary", was, said a review, indeed "extraordinary" — the expectation of the public, the size of the crowds — and their disappointment... all extraordinary. Moreover, he did not speak German and an interpreter was required.[1]

And a performance soon after in Vienna, where he plastered the town with posters billing himself as "der einzige Sohn des seinerzeit berühmten Bosco", was equally disappointing: any "Prater-Taschenspieler", performing for free in the park, could have done as well, said one review.[2]

The following month he performed in Ljubljana, announced as "der berühmte, bekannte, überall beifällig aufgenommene Tausendkünstler". A review lamented his lack of originality (and lack of German) and even his act 'Satan's Trunk' was not new, performed previously by Professor St. Roman (C49), and from the construction of the box it could easily be seen how the trick was done.[3]

He is last sighted in 1879 in Bolzano, performing in the intervals between one-act plays. now wisely claiming to be the grandson rather than the son of Bartolomeo ("der Enkel eines berühmten Mannes"), as Eugenio had played there in 1874. He performed for two nights and was well applauded, but the reviewer felt that he did not know how to entice an audience to the theatre.[4]

NOTES

[1] *Tagesbote* [Bruno] 28, 29 Sep.; 1 Oct. 1878.

[2] *Die Presse* 10 Oct.1878; *Jorgel-Briefe* 12 Oct.1878 (making fun of his posters headed "Bosco v'arrivez!"); *Tagesbote* [Bruno] 13 Oct.1878 ("Tout comme chez nous").

[3] *Laibacher Tagblatt* 14, 18 Nov.1878 ("…' Der Koffer des Satans' … die an der äußeren, unteren Bodenseite des Koffers befindlichen Leisten ließen das Geheimniß Bosco's so ziemlich deutlich errathen").

[4] *Bozner Zeitung* 13, 16 Oct.1879 ("… verstand Herr Bosco nicht, unser liebes Publikum in's Theater zu locken").

B19. H. Bosko, Rumburg 1874

In 1874 we find the versatile "H. Bosko" advertising three performances by his "large company" in Rumburg (now Rumburk in the Czech Republic), comprising 'Physic, Gymnastics, Singing, Comedy and Ballet', of which the first ("Fysik") is probably a magic act as he bills himself as Court Artist to H.M. the King of Bavaria ("Hofkünstler Sr. Maj. des Königs von Baiern"), currently the eccentric and artistic Ludwig II (*Rumburger Zeitung* 27 June 1874.

B20. Bosco: unidentified, performing in Rome, age 9, in 1880.

Late in 1880 an interesting snippet appeared in some English newspapers: "At the Alhambra Theatre at Rome there is a little lad of nine years of age who performs prestidigitation tricks equal to old Bosco, whose name he takes…" (*American Register* [London] 20 Nov.1880; *Worcestershire Chronicle* 4 Dec.1880).

The *teatro Alhambra* did open that year and nine is about the right age for Italo (B3): however, Italo is never elsewhere referred to as a conjuror but first as an assistant in his father's tricks then doing a memory and mental calculation act, and he and his father were performing in Spain and France right through 1880, so this was probably not him but the youngest Bosco impostor.

B21. "Bosco fils" (France ca.1880-83: Crémy and probably others).

Eugenio wrote to the French papers in 1880 and 1882 complaining of an impostor (or impostors) using the name "Bosco fils" who claimed to be "sole heir of the name Bosco"; the second letter names him as Crémy, "an Italian subject" (*Le Gaulois* 8 Oct.1880 and *Le Figaro* 3 April 1882).

In June 1880 "the famous magician Bosco" was advertised as performing at the *Théâtre du Cirque* in Toulouse; this was not Eugenio (and perhaps not Crémy: *La Dépêche* 1, 12, 16 June 1880; B2 p.178).

In April 1883 we find "M. Bosco" in the north of France, in Coulommiers at the end of the month (*L'Éclaireur de l'arrondissement de Coulommiers* 28, 31 Mar. 1883), then in Nogent-sur-Seine (*L'Écho nogentai*s 1 Apr.1883) and in Bas-sur-Seine (*Le Petit Courrier de Bar-sur-Seine* 6 Apr.1883). In none of these shows are Italo and Elisa mentioned and in Bar-sur-Seine this Bosco is accompanied by a "M. Joann" doing a memory act *à la Italo* (B2 p.180) so these may well also be the impostor.

Again, in October 1883 an impostor (possibly Crémy) performed in Saint-Jean-d'Angély when Eugenio was in Jonzac (B2 p.181): Eugenio wrote to the local papers (*L'Independent* 11 Oct.1883 and *L'Écho de Jarnac* 14 Oct.1883) denouncing the "audacious rascal" and stating he had proof he was the only son of Bartolomeo.

B22. Hofschwarzkünstler Bosko, Linz 1879

An unidentified Eugenio impostor using the title 'Hofschwarzkünstler Bosko' ("Bosco, Court Black Magician") appeared in Linz in September 1879, then in October in Meran (Merano, in the South Tyrol), first as *Bosko* then as *Bosco* (*Linzer Volksblatt* 30 Sep.1879; *Meraner Zeitung* 15 Oct.1879). He makes the claim to be the "only heir of the talents of his late father".

Eugenio never used the term *Hofschwarzkünstler*; indeed the only other occurrence of the word traced is a humorous newspaper reference in Vienna in 1926 to magician Alfredo Uferini (Alfred Ufer, 1863-1934), because he billed himself as "[tr.] Holder of numerous awards from most European courts" (*Der Tag* 18 Jan. 1926).

B23. "Le Fils Bosco", Paris fête, 1879

In June 1879 a large charity fête was held in Paris to raise funds for flood victims in the town of Szegedin. The programme included 'Le Fils Bosco', not Eugenio but an imitation of him by the comic Léon Fusier of the Palais-Royal (details B2 p.177 & note 205).

B24. "Bosco", Znaim 1880.

In February 1880 when Eugenio was in Spain an impostor was performing in Znaim in Moravia (modern Znojmo), said to be "[tr.] doing his tricks, many of which are new, with great skill" and with "a very pleasant patter" (*Znaimer Wochenblatt* 28 Feb.1880).

B25. Le Bosco Moderne (1), M. Auguste L.

At least five performers in France used the title "The Modern Bosco".
The earliest is found in Toulouse in 1846, a "**M. Auguste L.**," (surname unknown), "now back amongst his compatriots … King of Magicians…" with an elaborate programme of magic and ventriloquism, and a musical interlude by Mme Auguste (*La Gazette du Languedoc* 3, 7 May 1846).

B26. Le Bosco Moderne (2), Antoine Viarizio

Antoine Viarizio, describing himself as "of Turin" and variously as "pupil of the famous Renaldi *père*" and "sole pupil of Philippe", is found in France and Switzerland between 1843 and 1868, sometimes using the title "Le Bosco moderne" or "Le Petit Bosco moderne". He is first sighted in Marseille in March 1843, "professeur de physique amusante et de jeux d'adresse" (*Le Sémaphore de Marseille* 2 Mar.1843). In 1847 he is in Dole in Burgundy, "M. Viarizio, dit le Petit Bosco moderne", fresh from successes in Salins, St-Claude, Arbois, Champagnole and Poligny (*Album Dolois* 3 Feb.1847); later that year he was in Geneva (March and again in October) — "M. Viarizio, dit le *Bosco moderne*", and back there again in 1857 (*Journal de Genève* 16 Mar., 23 Oct.1847; 17 Dec.1854). In 1859 he is in Bourges (*Journal du Cher* 6 Jan.1859; *Le Courrier de Bourges* 12 Jan.1859), and in 1866 an anecdote has him in Marseille, playing tricks on a policeman until he shows him his card: "Antoine Viarizio prestidigitateur"; his then age is said to be "about 45" (*Courrier de Saône-et-Loire* 15 Nov.1866). He is last sighted in Switzerland in 1868, still *"le Petit-Bosco moderne"*, donating some of his profits to help flood victims (*Gazette de Lausanne* 29 Oct.1868; *Journal de Genève* 17 Nov.1868).

B27. Le Bosco Moderne (3), Enghien-les-Bains, 1878

An anonymous performer named only as "le Bosco moderne" is performing at the Casino du Jardin des Roses in Enghien-les-Bains, the Paris spa, during July 1878 (*La France* 3 July 1878; *L'Ordre de Paris* and *La Lanterne* 21 July 1878).

B28. Le Bosco Moderne (4), Émile Alphonse Duval, 1896

In 1896 arriving in Bordeaux is "Anderson, le Bosco moderne, le véritable enchanteur parisien", who "had the greatest success at the *Musée Grévin* in Paris" (*La Gironde* 29 Feb.1896). This is **Émile Alphonse Duval**, 1858-1933, alias **E. D. Anderson**, who used the stage names "Professeur Anderson" and "Professeur Omo", but only here found as "le Bosco moderne". He performed as a magician at the *Cabinet Fantastique* in the Musée Grévin until 1892 when he began travelling with his "Théâtre-salon Anderson", and in 1903 founded the "Cirque féérique Anderson".

B29. Le Bosco Moderne (5), Professeur Félix, Algeria 1903

A "**Professeur Félix,** *surnommé le Bosco moderne*" is found performing in Djidjelli (modern Jijel) in Algeria in 1903 — "grande séance de prestidigitation, d'escamotage et de cartomancie…", magic, legerdemain, cartomancy, followed by "the appearance and disappearance of animals and other objects", thought reading by cards and second sight, and ending with "the human volcano" — "He who has not seen Professor Félix has seen nothing" (*L'Impartial* 26 July 1903). The same person is probably the "Professeur Fedick" doing a "séance de prestidigitation" in the same town in 1900 (*L'Impartial* 29 Apr.1900).

Manuel Lopez (C31), who claimed to be a pupil of Bartolomeo, is also once referred to as *Le Bosco moderne*.

B30. Gacou, le Bosco helvétique, Nîmes 1880

Performing under this title, "the Swiss Bosco", in Nîmes in June 1880 is "M. Gacou, le Bosco helvétique", offering "une grande *soirée* de prestidigitation". He was probably a local amateur as the show is free with a collection for the poor (*Le Petit Mériodional* 2 June 1880).

B31. Bosco II, Salzburg 1879

In Seekirchen am Wallersee, in Salzburg, in February 1879 the annual entertainment by the local amateur fire brigade included a magic show by "Bosco II" (*Salzburger Volksblatt* 4 Feb.1879).

B32. Josef (Jozef, Jószef) Bosco (Bosko); Herr J. Bosco; Bosco der Jüngste; Herr Josef Racskay-Bosko

These are very likely the same person, found performing as a magician in Austria, Poland and Hungary 1884-1913.

In February 1884 he is in Hermannstadt (modern Sibiu in Romania) as *Bosco der Jüngste*, more successful with his ventriloquism than his well-worn magic tricks, but well received the next afternoon (as *Herr J. Bosco*) with a show for schoolchildren. And in May we find "der Magier Josef Bosco" again performing for children in Marosvásárhely (modern Târgu Mure).[1]

In March 1887 in Lugosch (now Lugoj in Romania) as *Jószef Bosco* he "[tr.] gave an interesting magic performance this week at the Lugos Theatre. The performance on Sunday was sparsely attended, but this time Mr. Bosco won the audience's favour with his skilful tricks… On Wednesday afternoon there was a children's performance, at which time the theatre was quite full … The audience's enthusiasm for ventriloquism culminated in a pleasant and amusing performance… Also worth mentioning is the beautifully performed national dance performed by Miss Emma Bosco, for which the audience rewarded her with a dense storm of applause."[2] He was in Lemberg (Lviv) later that year ("Józef Bosko magik i prestidigitator..."),[3] then in Czernowitz (Chernivtsi), where one newspaper gave him a splendid write-up, saying that in his case the statement "Geschwindigkeit ist keine Hexerei" — speed does not imply witchcraft — did not apply, so great was his amazing skill in magic, hypnotism, somnambulism...[4] But another newspaper wondered whether he would live up to the name he was using:

> "[tr.] Sailing the world under the flag of a famous name is not infrequently a less beneficial, but very arduous task, especially when the man in question lacks the necessary qualities to meet the expectations raised by his famous name. The black magician Herr Josef Bosko did not shrink from the difficulty of this task, and with fresh courage, and the ease with which you put on a hat, he put on himself the name of the master in black magic ... We must therefore assume that Mr. Bosko has actually achieved the mastery in his art that is expected from a bearer of this famous name. Tomorrow will give an answer on whether the courage discussed was justified or not".[5]

A review judged that he fully lived up to the expectations raised by the name he had chosen; he gave four shows in all in Czernowitz, the audience enjoying and applauding all his varied skills and those of his wife as a clairvoyant.[6]

In 1888 staying at the Bad Ischl spa is "**Herr Josef Racskay-Bosko**, conjuror, with daughter, from Hungary",[7] and in 1894 "Josef Racskay-Bosko, artiste" is arriving with family in Graz from Vienna.[8] This is probably him and probably his real name, *Racskay*.

He is performing in Klagenfurt in 1903,[9] and finally sighted in 1913, "the famous illusionist and ventriloquist Josef B. Bosko", now accompanied by the sisters Ida and Emma Esmeralda with their clairvoyant and memory act, in Innsbruck[10] and in Klagenfurt.[11]

NOTES
[1] *Siebenbürgisch-Deutsches Tageblatt, allgemeine Volkszeitung für das Deutschtum in Rumänien* 28, 29 Feb.; 6 May 1884.
[2] *Krasso-Szörenyi lapok* 3 Mar.1887.
[3] *Kuryer Lwowski* 5, 15 Nov.1887.
[4] *Czernowitzer Presse* 1 Dec.1887.
[5] *Bukowinaer Rundschau* 29 Nov.1887.
[6] *Bukowinaer Rundschau* 1, 4 Dec.1887.
[7] *Ischler Bade-Liste* 2. Oct.1888.
[8] *Grazer Volksblatt* 10 Aug.1894.
[9] *Freie Stimmen* 11 July 1903
[10] *Innsbrucker Nachrichten* 13 Jan.1913; *Allgemeiner Tiroler Anzeiger* 15 Jan.1913.
[11] *Freie Stimmen* and *Kärntner Zeitung* 16 Sep.1913.

B33. "Oscar Boulay, dit Bosco", Oran 1884

A certain Oscar Boulay, "magician", is found in Oran, Algeria, in 1884 — breaking a bottle over the head of a chef ("Oscar Boulay, dit Bosco, prestidigitateur a, le 24 février, frappé à la tête, avec une bouteille, le chef de cuisine de M. Bédai...": *L'Avenir de Bel-Abbès* [Oran] 8 March 1884).

B34 "Bosco", in Forbach, Moselle, 1887.

In October 1887 *Le Messin,* published in Metz, quoted an account from a paper in Forbach of two wandering artistes, one claiming to be "the famous magician Bosco", performing in an inn. Having received some payment, they then announced "the very popular trick of the disappearance of two living people", and promptly disappeared, leaving the spectators happily amused (*Le Messin* 14 Oct.1887).

B35. Leonardo Bosco.

Performing in Nîmes in 1891 is magician "Leonardo Bosco", claiming to be "son of the famous Bosco", and "accompanied by a talented pianist, Mme Chési Fenza". The show, on August 31st, between the first and second acts of a play, was not well received, the magician clearly short of "both skill and dexterity". The pianist would have been enjoyed but by then the audience were merrily shouting out rude remarks, then began singing the 'Marseillaise'. The magician returned but "his preparation of an omelette and some similar tricks did not win the attention of the audience who continued their fun" (*Le Petit républicain du Midi* 27, 30, 31 Aug.; 2 Sep.1891; in the first their names are misspelt but corrected subsequently).

There are a number of Dutch "Boscos" in the 1880s, several hard to differentiate and some probably the same person

B36. Professor Theodor Bosco

Found performing in Lekkerkerk in November 1883 ("Groote Goochel Soirée": *Schoonhovensche Couran* 3 Nov.1883) and in Delft in April 1884 ("…Grand Café Concert et Amusant, ter benefice van den Heer P.T. Kousbroek, zal, met medewerking van de Heeren Sauvlet en Professor Theodor Bosco in de hoogere Goochelkunst, plaats hebben… 27 April 1884": *Delftsche Courant* 25, 27 April 1884).

B37. J. R. Borkini Bosco

Active in the Netherlands (Assen, Zwolle, Steenwijk, Hilversum, Leeuwarden) 1884-1886, and claiming to have played in "Austria, Germany, Switzerland, Belgium, etc.", "Hof-Prestidigitateur, het nieuwste op het gebied der Magie, Physique en Spiritisme". He is billed as "élève de Heer E. Basch" (as is B44), and "Directeur en arrangeerder van Kinderfeesten uit Utrecht", but was advised by one reviewer to give his patter in German, "which according to Mr Bosco's speech would to be his mother tongue, rather than last night's peculiar language" (dat volgens de tongval des heeren Bosco zijn moedertaal schijnt te zijn, dan het eigenaardig taaltje van gisteravond: *Provinciale Drentsche en Asser courant* 17 May 1884).

He is often found performing with *either* "de Wonderdame Mej. **Emma Bosco**" (BF7) *or* Mej. **Baretta-Dorst** ("de zwevende dame", variously as "uit St. Petersburg" or "uit Berlijn"), who played the verraphone (glass harmonica).

Baretta-Dorst is probably Augustine Baretta Zanfretta of the circus family who married Ernest Dorst in 1870 and founded the Baretta Dorst Company; and "Emma Bosco" is probably Emma Valdran (Valdren) who in 1878 married the famous showman and clown Alexander Zanfretta, Augustine's brother: "Borkini Bosco" was likely a member of the same family.

In May 1886 Borkini-Bosco is playing on his own in Leeuwarden (*Leeuwarder Courant* 24 May 1886). A fortnight later Baretta Dorst is playing there with "den wereldberoemden Herr **Professor Bosco Jr.**, de grootste Toovenaar, Geestenbesweerder en Illusionist onzer Dagen" (*Leeuwarder Courant* 7 June 1886): whether this is Borkini-Bosco under another stage name or yet another Bosco impostor (perhaps B41) is uncertain.

B38. "Professor" Bosco, Leiden 1888

Performing in Leiden 1888, advertising as "the famous magician", with conjuring and magic lantern slides — "…den heer 'Professor' Bosco uit Leiden, den beroemden prestidigitateur, voor dezen avond geëngageerd om zijne goocheltoeren en lichtbeelden ten beste te geven…": *Leidsch Dagblad* 5 Sept. 1888.

B39. Professor Bosco Jr.

Performing in the Netherlands 1887-1888, and probably 1893, claiming to be "son of the late Carlo Bosco" (!) is "Professor Bosco Jr., bijgenaamd De Toovenaar, is op komst!!!": *Nieuwe Tilburgsche Courant* 24 Apr.1887; "Brillante Elite-Soirée. Fantastische Experimenten op het gebied der Sensatie-Tooverij door den WelEd. Heer Prof. Bosco Jr., van Leiden…": *Leeuwarder Courant* 27 Jan.1888; "…Professor Bosco Jr., zoon van wijlen den Heer Carlo Bosco … eene enkele Voorstelling … Zijn werken werd bekroond met een Gouden Medaille op de tentoonstelling te Brussel in 1888, en verkreeg het grootste succes in de voornaamste steden van Europa…": *De Nieuwe Koerier* 14 Feb.1889; and (the same person?) "Tijdens eene Woensdag te Amersfoort gegeven voorstelling deelde de goochelaar, zich noemende Bosco Junior, mede, dat hij met de werkzaamheden niet kon voortgaan, omdat zijne vrouw met het geld, dat hij noodig had voor preparaten om eene tooverlantaarn te vertoonen, er vandoor was gegaan…": *Leidsch Dagblad* 22 Feb.1893.

B40. Robertus Bosco

Performing in Amsterdam 1893, this one show only, also claiming to be son of the late Carlo Bosco (so perhaps the same person as B39); his advertisements (*Algemeen Handelsblad* 16 Aug.1893 and other papers) read: "Tolhuis. Woensdag 16 Augustus … Groote Voorstelling door den beroemden Prestidigitateur Robertus Bosco, Zoon van wijlen den Heer Carlo Bosco…".

B41. J. Bosco Jr.
Performing in Alphen aan den Rijn, 1887 — "Vrijdagavond gaf de bekende goochelaar J. Bosco Jr. eene voorstelling, in het hotel St. Joris te Alfen...": *De Rijnbode* 20 Nov.1887.

B42. Professor J.G. Bosco Jr.
Performing in 's-Hertogenbosch 1888, said to be from Leiden — "de gunstig bekende Professor J.G. Bosco Jr., uit Leiden ... eene hoogst interessante uitvoering met zelf uitgevonden mysterieuse experimenten. Dat een talrijk publiek deze uitvoeringen van den grootsten illusionist der 19s eeuw zal komen bijwonen, lijdt geen twijfel": *Provinciale Noordbrabantsche en 's Hertogenbossche courant* 8 Oct. 1888.

B43. Professor Bosco, 1890
Touring the Dutch East Indies (Java, Sumatra, Aceh, and more) 1890. Billed as "Prof. Bosco de grootste goochelaar van de wereld ... verschillende wonderbaarlijke stukken op het gebied van Magie, Wetenschap en Spiritualismus"; said to be planning to take a vaudeville company to India: *Sumatra-courant* 30 Aug.; 4 Sep.1890 (long positive review). Possibly identical to B120.

B44. Professor Don Giovanni Bosco
Performing in the Netherlands 1886 to 1924; also (when performing to children) as **Don Giovanni, Jr**. and **Professor G. Bosco, Jr.**; later as **Don Bosco**, **G. Bosco**, or simply **Bosco**, billing himself as "Egyptischen Magiër" and "Salon-Humoristische Goochelaar en Illusionist". In 1892 he is advertising a 'Kinder- en Familiefeest' with his 'groot succes: De Feeën-Koningin'. He may be the Bosco performing in Schoonhoven in 1892 — "...Elite-Voorstelling, optreden van Bosco, de grootste Illusionist dezer Eeuw..."; well reviewed, and also a show for children that followed, but a small audience (*Schoonhovensche Courant* 23, 27, 30 Apr.1892). And possibly also the Bosco Junior in Amersfoort in 1893 who announced he could not continue as his wife had run off with the money set aside for lantern slides... (*Schoonhovensche Courant* 22 Feb.1893).

Newspaper references describe him as "uit Amsterdam" and state that his real surname was **Bork** ("een goochelaar, de heer Bork, alias Don Bosco": *Haarlem's Dagblad* 10 Feb.1902; "Giovanni don Bosco (J. van Bork)": *Tielsche Courant* 5 Mar.1905); "Professor Don Bosco (J. Bork, Albert Cuypstraat 51, Amsterdam), de Koning der Goochelaars": *De Soldatencourant* 22 Jan.1915; "...Het was de heer J. Bork, meer en beter bekend onder den naam Don Bosco uit Amsterdam, gewezen assistent van den beroemden Basch...": *Utrechtsch Nieuwsblad* 15 Nov.1921; B37 was also "a pupil of Basch").

He may have been **Jan Bartholomeus van Bork**, 1853-1926.

In one show only, in Tiel in 1887 (*Nieuwe Tielsche Courant* 12, 15 Jan.1887: "Buitengewone Voorstelling"), he is accompanied by **Mlle Sellina Bosco** (BF8).

B45. Professor Bosco, Schoonhoven 1891

In Schoonhoven in 1891 is a "Professor Bosco", said to be American, doing a "Magic, Spiritism and Magnetism" performance with a clairvoyant "Mdlle de Marguerit". He trumpets successes in The Hague and Amsterdam and quotes at length from a review in an unidentified Amsterdam paper: "[tr.] …We once saw him work in London and found him a much more skilled magician than Miss Fay. What he does is well suited to give a shudder of awe at the unseen to those who like to see something supernatural in spiritistic miracles — because they want to believe in something anyway. What Hr. Bosco knows how to do, he does not do in a cupboard behind green curtains, but he walks among the audience in the full gaslight; he fools their eyes and deceives their perception standing right in front of them. This American magician makes coins disappear from the closed fist of one of the spectators themselves; a deck of large cards shrinks and melts as he shuffles them into a deck of microscopic cards. His experiments with animal magnetism in the second part of the evening are also very fascinating. He puts Miss Margaretha into magnetic sleep and then lets her guess in the most curious way the thoughts of everyone in the audience who so desires. We were most struck by the way in which she managed to remain silently in the same position, keeping her arm stretched out, or resting on one knee, bent over and off balance … Bosco is a master of his craft…".

A review found that he lived up to expectations — "the first two sections were devoted to magic tricks. Mr. Bosco must be admired for his extraordinary swiftness, especially with 'the enchanted beer glasses' … The third section 'The Bound and Sealed Medium' presented by Ms. Margaretha, also provoked much applause…" (*Schoonhovensche Courant* 29 Apr.; 2, 6 May 1891).

B46. La Troupe Bosco.

Performing in Vevey in Switzerland in 1896 is "La Troupe Bosco", advertising "Tours de physique et d'escamotage — Transmission de la pensée — Duos et chansons — Grande succès de Mlles Jeanne et Suzanne" (*Feuilles d'avis de Vevey et des districts d'Aigle et d'Oron* 10, 11 Apr.1896).

It is presumably the same group the following year in Marseille — "grande concert … donné par l'excellente troupe Bosco" (*Le Petit Marseillais* 27 Nov.1897).

B47. Bosko, Rosenheim, 1897

An unidentified "Bosko" is listed to give "a performance with a concert" in Rosenheim in Bavaria in November 1897 — "der berühmte Sensations-Illusionist und Zauberkünstler Bosko"; he is on tour and said from newspapers in neighbouring towns to have a good reputation (*Rosenheimer Anzeiger* 26 Nov.1897).

B48. Faustinus as Bosco

The Danish magician Faustinus (B12a note 60) included in his act "Magical Acts by Magicians of the Past" — Prof. Bosco, Bellachini, Dr Epstein, Max Alexander (advertised *Buskeruds Amstidende* 8 Mar.1900, etc.).

B49. Mikhail Pavlovich Trachtenberg (1873-1943)
B50. Gennady Mikhailovich Trakhtenberg (1917-2000)

The article on the 'Russian Association of Magicians' site (url:144) states that both the father and the son of this famous circus family performed as illusionists under the name 'Bosco' — the father "[tr.] illusionist, manipulator, founder of the famous circus dynasty Trachtenberg", and the son then "continued to perform as an illusionist under the name 'Bosco'".

The origin of the Bosco stage name is quoted from Mikhail's grandson — "[tr.] ...Our circus story began very unusually and, one might say, unexpectedly ... my grandfather, being the son of a rich and famous bread maker from St. Petersburg, decided not to continue in his father's profession, but to become a magician ... young Mikhail was sent to America with a load of grain, but spent the proceeds on magic apparatus ... his enraged father called him a good-for-nothing 'Clown! Circus artist!', and threatened to disinherit him; when the son argued that circus artists in America are very respected people, and, for example, Bartolomeo Bosco is the most illustrious illusionist in Europe, the inexorable father replied: 'Well, let this Bosco be your father!' ... From then on my grandfather took the stage name 'Bosco' for his performances, and his show, titled 'Illusion, Telepathy, Hypnosis', won him fame first in St. Petersburg, and then throughout Russia...". Mikhail died in the siege of Leningrad.

B51. Ludwig Krieger ("Pop Krieger", Louis Krieger), 1851-1934.

German, worked largely in America from 1885, known as "King of the Cups and Balls" and "The American Bosco". Well-known, with entries in *Lexikon,* 'Zauber-Pedia', 'Magicpedia', etc.

B52. Olivero Bosco

Found performing in Martigny, Valais, Switzerland, 1906 is "M. Olivero Bosco, de Milan, sujet psychique renommé... liseur de pensée, peintre, prestidigitateur, équilibriste, cartomancien ... fantaisiste et le Roi des Illusionistes ... electro peinture...": *Le Confédéré* 14 July 1906.

B53. Bosco, Avignon 1921

Performing at the spring fair in Avignon, April 1921 — "Foire de printemps à Avignon ... 26 ... 28 avril ... Séance de prestidigitation par le célèbre illusioniste Bosco...": *Le petit méridional* 21 Apr.1921.

B54. Józef Pokrywka-Brzeziński, 1877-1951.

He is listed in the *Lexikon* p.266 (from Whaley) as an illusionist who used the name "Bosco". The article on him in 'Encyklopedia Teatru Polskiego' (online at http://www.encyklopediateatru.pl/osoby/5068/jozef-pokrywka-brzezinski) records him only as an actor and theatre director.

B55. Stuller-Bosco, 1885-1962

Real name Joseph Stuller; German, performed as Joe Stuller, Joe Bosco, José Bosco. Detailed entries in *Lexikon* and 'ZauberPedia', with further references/

B56. "John Olms", 1888-1955

Real name Richard Lischke; the famous German "Uhrenkönig", "The King of Clocks". After 1945 as "Bosco" he had a comedy act parodying a late 19th century conjuror. Detailed entries in *Lexikon,* 'Magier der Welt', 'Zauber-Pedia' (with photo of him in his Bosco act).

B57. Jean Bosco, Belgian conjuror, in England in 1915

Performed at a concert in Barnsbury, north London, on May 20 1915 — "…the professional artists were … M. Jean Bosco , a Belgian conjuror of considerable dexterity who submitted some original tricks" (*Stage* 27 May 1915).

He is mentioned again in the same issue: "Bosco, 'the human aquarium,' himself a Belgian, on Tuesday evening gave, in addition to his usual performance, a two-hour entertainment of conjuring to the Belgian refugees at Earl's Court. Bosco will open at the Rendezvous, Margate, on Saturday, under the management of C. C. Bartram".

B58. Fritz Bosko

Performing at the "Zirkus-Busch-Varietee" in the Wiener Prater in June 1915 with "some amazing tricks" (*einigen verblüffenden Tricks*) is "der geniale Taschenspieler Fritz Bosko" (*Die Neue Zeitung* [Vienna] 6 June 1915; *Wiener Sonn- und Montags-Zeitung* 7 June 1915).

B59. Bosco (Berlin, 1948)

The *Lexikon* lists (p.56), from *Klett's Künstler-Adressen-Nachweis,* a German magician named 'Bosco' resident in Berlin in 1948.

B60. Theodor von Schledorn, 1896-1975

German; stage names Bosco, Bellini, Bellachini Jr., "Der große Bellachini". Detailed entries in *Lexikon*, 'Zauber-Pedia'.

B61. Bernard Bosco, aka Bernard Voinson
Contemporary French *prestidigitateur.*
https://www.weezevent.com/conference-8-fevrier-bernard-voinson (etc.)

Boscos in Britain
(*see also Epstein* B12)

B62. Professor W.J.L. Millar, 1825-1910
Millar, a very colourful and interesting character, made four interesting contributions to the 'Bosco' story in Britain and America —

(1) he became the manager of the first 'Bosco' in Britain ("Alfred Bosco", actually Epstein B12) and was instrumental in his performing before Queen Victoria at Balmoral (an honour later falsely claimed by three other 'Boscos': see *Appendix Z12*);

(2) after falling out with Epstein, he himself performed briefly as 'Signor Bosco' when Epstein broke his leg;

(3) he launched his wife as the first female 'Bosco' (BF1), then took her to America, the first magician to perform in America under that name; and

(4) in the 1870s he performed in America as "Bosco Millar".

Born William John Lauderdale Millar on Broadway in New York in 1825,[1] by the age of thirty he had opened the first theatre in New Jersey, been a Professor of Penmanship at several universities, founded a commercial college in Pittsburg with his younger brother, Kennedy Millar, and went on to become a successful magician and theatre manager.

In 1855 in Philadelphia he and a partner William Thompson secured the rights to exhibit the famous African-American conjoined twins known as "Millie-Christine", born as slaves in North Carolina in 1851.[2] To avoid the Refugee Slave Act in the northern states Millar and Thompson took them to Canada, billing them as "The United African Twins", and concocting a story that they were born in Africa and taken to Cuba as slaves. From Canada they took them to England, arriving in Liverpool on July 25th 1855. They exhibited the twins in Liverpool then headed to London. But there on August 4th Millar broke with Thompson and spirited them away to Dundee. Thompson tracked them down and with four "prizefighters" violently snatched them back. He soon had them on stage in London.[3]

Millar, after losing the twins in August 1855, describes in an 1892 article[4] how he then formed his association with Alfred Bosco, whose claim to be the son of Bartolomeo he insists he initially believed to be true. He remained Bosco's manager (their association is detailed in B12) until March 1856 when they fell out in Dublin and ended their business association; joint notices dated March 19th were published side-by-side in *Saunders's News-Letter* 21 Mar.1856 stating that their partnership was now "dissolved, by mutual consent". The following month, after Bartolomeo denounced Bosco, Millar immediately sought to exonerate himself in a letter published in several Dublin papers on April 5th: "…came to me under that name, and I always believed him to be the son of Signor Bosco … I am now fully convinced that his name is not Bosco, and he is not the son of the great Italian Wizard".

Millar now embarked on a new theatrical venture, purchasing the Diorama of India which had been touring England and Scotland for several years and had been on show in the Concert Room of the Rotunda in Dublin since August 1855.[5] His purchase of the diorama was announced in early March,[6] and he opened it in Cork in April as 'Millar's Grand Diorama of India, and Voyages up the River Ganges'.[7] It was advertised to close there at the end of the month, "after which it will leave for America",[8] but instead Millar took it to England, opening in Bristol on May 19th, followed by Bath, Cheltenham, a long run in Birmingham, then Leeds in December.

However, Millar had not forgotten the African Twins, "stolen" from him in August 1855 and still being toured round England by Thompson. He was determined to regain them, and got his brother Kennedy Millar, in Newark, New Jersey, to locate their mother, Monemia. After lengthy negotiations with Joseph Pearson Smith, who had now bought the twins from McKoy, their owner, Kennedy, Smith and Monemia arrived in England on January 1st 1857. The twins were in Birmingham with Thompson. The local police agreed to their being handed over to the mother, and this was confirmed by a subsequent court decision. Millar and Smith then exhibited them in Edinburgh and Leeds, now claiming that part of the proceeds would be used to free their parents from slavery; they then headed to Newcastle, but on February 17th soon after they opened there Smith whisked the twins and their mother back to America, so that Millar lost them yet again.[9]

Kennedy had meanwhile taken over the management of the Diorama of India from his brother and himself played the flautina during the intervals.[10] The Diorama closed in Leeds on January 31st and then opened in Newcastle as advertised on February 9th,[11] where the twins also opened the following week — only to be taken away by Smith on February 17th.

The Diorama continued in Newcastle, and March 28th saw the first appearance with it of "Miss Annie Kemble, the Pleasing Ballad and Serio-Comic Vocalist".[12] However on May 3rd the Diorama was seized "under a distraint for rent" and sold at auction.[13]

William, now bereft of both the Twins and the Diorama, had already planned his next venture: he had trained his wife as a magician, and decided to bill her as "Madame Bosco". Annoyingly *we do not know her first name or maiden name*, or when or where they married: before this she is mentioned only once, during the court case in Dublin in March 1856 when Epstein's black servant was said to have used "insulting and filthy language" to her. After her death she was said to be from Yorkshire, implying they probably met and married in Britain after William's arrival in July 1855, but there is no record of a marriage that matches. Perhaps they had previously married in America; perhaps they were not legally married at all.

"Madame Bosco, the Wonder of the Age" is first sighted in May 1857 advertised as soon to appear in Bristol,[14] but the earliest actual performances traced were in Wales — Newport on June 1st, during the Whitsuntide festivities,[15] then Cardiff (billed as "...the unrivalled Pythonist, in her Gorgeous Palace of Magic" and as "Madame Bosco, The great and Only Female Magician in the World", appearing with "Prof. K. Miller [*sic*], the celebrated American Flutinist" and "Miss Florence Kemble, the highly popular Vocalist"),[16] and a good run in Merthyr, where she declares herself "Patronized by the Queen and Royal Family".

Audiences were consistently good, helped by the "Monster Gift Nights" and good reviews — "Madame Bosco, as a female magician, is herself a novelty, but her experiments are still more novel, many of them being her own introduction, and never performed by any other magician ... the orange tree feat ... placing a small tree upon a table before her audience she contrives by some wonderful mechanical process to conduct it gradually through the various stages of the bud, blossom, and the full ripening of the fruit, and finally plucks and distributes the oranges among the astonished spectators...".[18] They toured on successfully through Aberdaire, Neath, Swansea, Carmarthen, Tenby, Haverfordwest...[18]

All was going well, but Millar was also keeping an eye on Alfred Bosco's success, and when Alfred had to cease performing after breaking his leg in early September, Millar seized the opportunity to perform under the name "Signor Bosco", impersonating the impostor — with a singular lack of success. "Madame Bosco" was briefly put on hold and Millar, together with Kennedy and Kemble, opened in Pontypool on September 7th. It did not go well and clearly Millar's skills as a magician were at this time rather poor — though he seems to have taught "Madame Bosco" well enough.[19] To quote the local paper

> A SIGNOR Bosco made his appearance in the Town-hall, on Monday, and also announced himself for Tuesday and Wednesday. The bill of fare presented would have been most welcome had it been carried out in anything like the manner proposed: beyond the few tricks of legerdemain, not exceeding mediocrity, and two ballads by a Miss Florence Kemble, the few who formed the audience had nought to thank the signor for. We presume M[r.] Millar (called professor,) the great flautist, was an embry[o] personage. One visit was sufficient for us.[20]

And it may just have been Millar again the following week in nearby Chepstow, where the outcome was even worse. Placards were plastered round the town announcing "Signor Bosco is Coming" but the large crowd was soon disappointed by the quality of the "common tricks" and two men who had seen "the real Bosco" [*viz.*, ironically, Alfred] and knew that he was laid up after the accident demanded their money back; this was refused and the police were called; confusion and fighting followed; the manager fled with the cash box; "Signor Bosco" was left to explain that "although he was not the Italian Bosco, still he was a Pole of that name", promising another performance and an explanation the following night; needless to say, by then he had slipped away, leaving the hall hire and printer's bill unpaid.[21]

It was not until late October that "Alfred Bosco" could resume his performances, but Millar now prudently returned to promoting Madame Bosco, and on September 19th she opened in Pembroke, followed by a short return run in Haverfordwest from September 23rd.[22] In October she had a long run in Gloucester, where the newspaper quoted a review so laudatory that it was surely penned by Millar himself:

> ... Her experiments are most unique and astounding, and were performed with an ease and dexterity which we have never seen equalled. Professor Anderson ... is a bungler when compared to her, while Robin ... could never remove from the mind of the spectator the impression of collusion and of probable failure. Madame Bosco, on the contrary, performs with all the ease of an experienced master, or rather mistress, of the 'art deceptive,' and is without any comparison the cleverest manipulator we have ever seen or heard of. There is no dallying in her experiments — no talking to gain time —

no mingling of tricks so as to enable a confederate to collude and deceive. Everything is performed off hand, and with a quickness and skill which are almost incredible.[23]

Stroud and Cheltenham followed in November, but despite promises of "New and astounding marvels never before witnessed. Four Grand Gift Nights. Splendid presents given away...", she initially "met with anything but success".[24] However, once more Gift Nights were added to her show, and the "Illustrations of the American Spirit-Rapping Delusion", she performed there successfully until December 19th.[25]

She was next in Worcester at the end of the year, advertised for six nights beginning December 28th. She remained there until January 15th but again "the audiences ... have not been so good as the performances have merited", and when she closed the *Era* reported: "Her short stay has been anything but a paying one".[26]

Millar now decided that the novelty had worn off and it was time for greener pastures. Madame Bosco (well, this one) now disappears from the U.K. papers as she and Millar headed to the U.S.A.[27]

The first we hear of them there is in early September, living in Rondout, New York, near Kingston, and looking to perform: "Madame Bosco, the celebrated female magicianess, just arrived from Europe, is 'susceptible' to engagements through the West and South".[28] She opened in Connecticut later that month, the first magician to perform in U.S.A. under the name "Bosco",[29] though not, of course, as claimed, the first ever female magician — "Madame Bosco, of whom the New Haven papers speak in the very highest terms of praise, opens her 'enchanted palace' at Touro Hall this evening. She is the first female who ever appeared before the public in the character of a magician, and is said to surpass most of the male 'conjurers' of the day. Prof. Millar, who accompanies her, will deliver an interesting lecture upon 'Natural Magic' in the course of the evening".[30]

She then toured widely — over the next few months we find her performing in Ohio (Cincinnati, Columbus),[31] Pennsylvania (Pottsville, Philadelphia),[32] Maryland (Frederick), West Virginia (Wheeling),[33] Indiana (Evansville, Bloomington, New Albany), Kentucky (Louisville), Illinois (Chicago),[34] and Wisconsin (Janesville, Madison, Milwaukee, Racine).

On Friday July 29th 1859 she failed to appear as advertised in Ottawa, Illinois, where she had arrived on Saturday 30th, "very much indisposed — indeed in a dying condition ... she lingered until Sunday morning, when she died. Her husband, who lives somewhere in New York, had been telegraphed for from Morris, and arrived on Saturday night. His name is Miller [*sic*], and as he gives entertainments of the same kind, is known as Professor Miller ... Mrs Miller (for that was her real name) was buried on Tuesday in the Ottawa Cemetery".

William, explaining that his sudden need to travel and then bury his wife had left him "in straightened circumstances" and that he wished to "leave the city honorably", gave a performance similar to hers; then a second, including his lecture on 'Natural magic' and 'Spirit Rapping', which, the local paper said, it "would be an act of humanity" to patronize. His advertisement for this spells him name as "Millar".[35]

A note in the *Racine Journal* of 17 August quoted the *Chicago Journal:* "...She was for years a great sufferer from paroxysms of the spine; to allay or deaden this intense pain, she resorted to great doses of ether and chloroform, which at times so worked upon her to make her nearly crazy..."; a brief obituary in the *New York Clipper* (20 Aug.1859) described her as "inhaling sulphuric ether for temporary relief", and stated she was a native of Yorkshire, England.

Millar continued his performances as a magician, and in 1860 married singer Margaret Cochran; their five children, Willie, Clyde, Katie, Jessie, and Bertram, all went on stage. He lived and worked both in England and America, touring with his wife and children in the 1860s and 1870s, then turning to management. Rarely in America (never found in Britain) he called himself "**Bosco Millar**" — "Bosco Millar, the world-renowned prestidigitateur and his little son Willie are in the city ... the Bosco Millar Prestidigitateur Entertainment Company". In Fort Wayne in 1873 his advertising stresses the value of the prize gifts as much as the "superior excellence of the entertainment", which included panoramas, songs and dancing as well as his magic act.[36]

After Margaret's death in 1878, he married a widow Clara Wagner, née Rossiter, in London in 1880, and their three daughters (the eldest of whom was given the name Flora Telula Leighton Lauderdale Rossiter Millar) also went on stage.

Millar died in Newport News, Virginia, 26 July 1910.

NOTES

[1] An obituary in *New York Dramatic Mirror* 16 July 1910 gives his birthdate as 28 Jan.1825; it describes him as "in his prime ... a man of striking appearance... He was a man of great culture and ability and possessed a most engaging personality. His life was one of ceaseless activity..."; other obituaries (containing some minor errors) appeared in *New York Times Herald* 27 June 1910; *Brooklyn Daily Eagle* 1 July 1910; and in U.K. in *The Stage* 14 July 1910. His surname is sometimes spelt *Miller* in newspapers but never in his own advertising.

[2] The twins were joined back-to-back, shared several body parts, and had one heart and one nervous system, always referring to themselves as "I" not "we". They had been exhibited as a curiosity since before their first birthday, managed first by John Pervis, then by a Mr Brower, backed by Joseph Pearson Smith, who had made a deal with their owner, Jabez McKoy, to share the profits. Brower then lost them to a swindler and after a spell with Barnum's Museum in New York the twins ended in Philadelphia where they were secured by Millar and Thompson.

[3] Millar wrote his version of his part in the Millie-Christine story many years later, 'Two-Headed Nightingale. How I Found and Lost Her', *Dundee Evening Telegraph* 28, 29 Nov.1894. Millar's son Bertram presented Millar's own scrapbooks relating to the twins to the State Archives of North Carolina, and the finding list, online at url:145, includes many contemporary newspaper references. A pamphlet sold at their shows is online at url:146, and another allegedly giving Millie-Christine's own account at url:138. Useful modern works on the twins are Sarah E. Gold, 'Millie-Christine McKoy and the American Freak Show: Race, Gender, and Freedom in the Postbellum Era, 1851-1912', online at url:147; and Joanne Martell, *Millie-Christine:*

Fearfully and Wonderfully Made. Winston-Salem, N.C.: John F. Blair Publisher, 1999.

[4] 'How I Brought Bosco before the Queen' *Dundee Evening Telegraph* 8 Sept.1892. See also B12 note 7.

[5] The diorama had been for sale since the end of 1853. Large advertisement (with list of the scenes) for its Dublin opening in *Dublin Evening Mail* 17 Aug.1855. Dioramas, a precursor of the motion picture, were a very popular Victorian entertainment, regarded as educational and as suitable for families — a series of consecutive large paintings, usually of foreign travel or battle scenes, on a giant roll of canvas which was slowly unrolled with an accompanying commentary and interludes with variety acts, sometimes magicians. This Diorama, which had opened at the Asiatic Gallery in London in 1851 as the 'Diorama of Hindustan', was 1500 feet long and 18 feet high, comprising 28,000 square feet of canvas and billed as "5000 square feet larger than any other Diorama ever exhibited". It illustrated the course of the Ganges upstream from the sea to its source in the Himalayas — 'Grand moving diorama of Hindostan, displaying the scenery of the Hoogly, the Bhagirathi, and the Ganges, from Fort William Bengal, to Gangoutri in the Himalaya ... painted by Mr. Philip Phillips, the figures and animals by Mr. Louis Haghe, the shipping by Mr. Knell...'. An illustrated booklet sold to viewers is digitised at url:148.

[6] *Dublin Evening Packet* 4 Mar.1856; *Dublin Evening Post* 6 Mar.1856: "The Diorama of India ... is now the property of Professor Millar, a native American — a man of singular ability, and adaptation of talent to everything in the arts and sciences calculated to be facile in the conveyance of solid instruction, recreation, and amusement to the masses, as well as to the more enlightened and refined ideas of those in affluence and the enjoyment of aristocratic and courtly life" — *presumably he wrote that pæan himself.*

[7] *Southern Reporter* [Cork] 23 Apr.1856. The variety interludes were provided by an unnamed "Young Lady Vocalist (A native of Cork)".

[8] *Cork Constitution* 26 April 1856.

[9] Millar says in his 1894 article (above note 3) that he was in Germany making arrangements for a tour there by the twins when he received a telegram from Kennedy saying that Smith planned to take them back to America, ostensibly as their mother preferred America. He returned to England with all speed but the twins had sailed from Liverpool the previous day. They went on to a successful career, later billed as "The Two-Headed Nightingale", fluent in five languages and accomplished pianists, singers, and even dancers, performing until the 1890s; they died in 1912. Coincidentally in 1884 their manager was another Bosco impostor, Leotard Bosco (B77).

[10] "Great Excitement! — Hundreds Nightly Unable to Gain Admission ... The Grand Monster Gift Nights ... Monday, January 12th, 1857 ... First appearance of Professor

K. Millar, the celebrated Flautina performer from America... 400 Splendid Presents...": *Leeds Times* 10 Jan.1857.

[11] *Newcastle Journal* 7 Feb.1857. Millar had originally retained the former lecturer, Watkins, but he had now been replaced by "Rignoldi" (Thomas Edmund Rignold), better known as a magician (he who had tried to challenge Alfred Bosco a year earlier). At the end of March Rignoldi was advertising that he had ended this engagement and "he purposes very shortly to reopen in Magic and Ventriloquism...": *Era* 22 Mar.1857.

[12] *Newcastle Journal* 28 Mar.1857; later billed as "Fanny Kemble". I think it probable that behind these stage names was Kennedy Millar's new wife: on March 19th in nearby Sunderland he married Sarah Ann Moses (*Newcastle Weekly Courant* 3 Apr.1857), born in Manchester in 1835. She and Kennedy subsequently remained in England, he both teaching penmanship and managing dioramas, she a singer; in 1861 he was managing a 'Grand, Colossal Diorama of America' and she was singing with it as "Sarah Isaacs". Sarah died in Gravesend in 1878 ("...the beloved wife of Kennedy Millar, professionally known as Miss Isaacs": *Era* 24 Nov.1878); Kennedy died in Yarmouth in 1887, age 52.

[13] *Newcastle Guardian* 9 May 1857: "...sold to Mr B. Fenwick, North Eastern Hotel, Neville Street, for £105". It reopened in Liverpool on May 25th (with no mention of the Millar brothers) and was re-auctioned there. It appears that Millar regained ownership for a period, as in March and April 1858 we find "Millar's Grand Views of the Great Revolt in India" on tour in Cornwall, apparently the same diorama, as with it are Kennedy Millar and Miss Kemble singing. By the end of the year it had been bought by the Hamilton family of diorama exhibitors who added new scenes and showed it for many years as 'Hamilton's Grand Historical & Colossal Moving Panorama of India' (and, with fresh scenes) as 'Hamilton's Panorama of the Indian Mutiny' (see my forthcoming 'The Hamilton Family and their Dioramas').

[14] *Bristol Mercury* 23 May 1857.

[15] *Monmouthshire Beacon* 6 June 1857 ("the famous magician of the age"); *Era* 7 June 1857: "....Madam Bosco is no relation to the M. Bosco now in London" [*viz.* Alfred].

[16] *Cardiff and Merthyr Guardian* 6 & 13 June 1857.

[17] *Cardiff and Merthyr Guardian* 13 June 1857. Not, of course, a new trick — Robert-Houdin also claimed it as his invention, but Houdini in his *Unmasking of Robert-Houdin,* Chapter II, attributes it as "the Apple-tree" to Christopher Pinchbeck as early as 1730.

[18] The show now included "Wonderful Illustrations of the American Spirit Rapping Delusion". She was now advertised as "MADAME BOSCO! the Great Original and only Female Magician in the World, and the only person in this country of the name" (*Pembrokeshire Herald* 21 Aug.1857) and reviews remained positive — "...large

audiences. Her tricks are astonishing, and must be seen to be believed. Indeed they surpass anything of the kind ever exhibited in this place. After each performance valuable articles of jewellery, watches, clocks, china tea services, &c. are presented to the company by lottery" (*Pembrokeshire Herald* 4 Sep.1857).

[19] Later, especially when back in England in the 1860s, Millar was very successful as a touring magician, with the orange-tree trick a favourite in his repertoire. But prior to his arrival in England in 1855 he is found only as a teacher of penmanship and before that as a theatre manager: as such he must have seen magicians' acts close up — for example at his Newark theatre in 1847 there was "Young Alexander: This famous Necromancer, lately arrived from Paris..."; and he would have seen Alfred Bosco's repertoire at close hand.

[20] *Monmouthshire Merlin* 12 Sep.1857; a brief report in the *Usk Observer* 19 Sep. 1857 was more polite but no less critical: "Signor Bosco last week gave two entertainments, but no great sensation was excited by the performance of either himself or his company".

[21] *Chepstow Weekly Advertiser* 19 Sept.1857; similar account in *Monmouthshire Merlin* 26 Sep.1857. As this Bosco claimed to be Polish this was probably *not* Millar but the possible first sighting of either Warszawski or Susser (B63, B65); however, it was definitely Millar and his brother in Pontypool.

[22] *Pembrokeshire Herald* 18 Sep.1857.

[23] Quoted from the *Haverfordwest Telegraph* in *Gloucester Journal* 10 Oct.1857.

[24] *Cheltenham Chronicle* 1 Dec.1857. And the *Cheltenham Examiner* 2 Dec.1857 remarked: "... Madame Bosco is in every respect, whether as a professor of magic or as the occupier of a public platform, perfectly at her ease, and conducts her business with the greatest possible quiet and ladylike propriety". Of course, as a lady, there is never any suggestion that, like Bartolomeo, various other Boscos, Blitz, and Frikell, she performed bare armed.

[25] *Cheltenham Journal* 12 Dec.1857.

[26] *Worcester Journal* 19 Dec.1857: 2 Jan.1858; *Era* 17 Jan.1858.

[27] They may have left in some haste as a notice appeared in the *Era* of 2 May 1858 that luggage earlier left in Worcester by Madame Bosco as security would be sold. (This provoked a cheeky response from Alfred Bosco in the *Era* of 23 May stating "my wife has never been in Worcester ... the person travelling under the name of Madame Bosco has no connexion with the establishment of Alfred Bosco, The Great Wizard of the World").

[28] *New York Clipper* 4 Sep.1858.

[29] The second is not found until 1862, in Milwaukee (B90).

[30] *Hartford Courant* 27 Sep.1858.

³¹ In Cincinnati she was billed as "Madame Bosco, The original, World-Renowned and Only Magicienne ... Mad. Bosco will make selections from the most 'recherche' of her experiments, many of which are entirely new...": *Daily Press* 14 Apr.1859. (The term "recherche" in such ads was not common; it was used by Epstein in Ireland in 1855 so may have been a term conjured up by Millar: see also *Appendix Z11* note 12.). The *New York Clipper* joked (23 Apr.1859): "Madame Bosco is doing the magical at Melodeon Hall, Cincinnati. She is said to boss the whole co. of magicians".

³² Her advertisement there lists among her acts: "...she makes an Orange Tree blossom and bear fruit at command. Makes a bell answer questions without touching it, and allows a gun to be fired at her, and catches the marked bullet in her hand": *Pennsylvania Daily Telegraph* 11 Dec.1858. This would make her only the second woman (following the lamented Madame DeLinsky, accidentally shot dead by her husband in 1820) known to perform the "gun trick".

³³ Here and elsewhere her advertisements make the specific (false) claim that her entertainment was "presented by her before Queen Victoria and the Court, at Balmoral castle, Scotland, September 24, 1855" [once misprinted as "Baltimore [!] castle, Scotland"]: *Appendix Z12*. The splendid large advertisement in the *Wheeling Daily Intelligencer* 19 Jan.1859 includes a woodcut illustration of her at work.

³⁴ William Pack includes brief notes on her, mainly her time in Chicago, in his blog 'ChicagoMagic' (url:149).

³⁵ *Ottawa Free Trader* 6 Aug.1859.

³⁶ *Fort Wayne Gazette* 5, 7 Dec.1873.

B63. "Signor Bosco": Saul (Solomon) Abram Warschawski, 1833?-1906

B64. Alfred Bosco (2) (Alfred Herbert Jacob Warschawski, 1864-1932, his son)

Saul is the subject of two articles by E.A. Dawes in *Magic Circular:* 'Signor Bosco and Son: The Story of Saul Abram Warschawski and his Son Alfred', vol.95 no.1014 (January 2001) pp.152-155; and 'Signor Bosco and Son: The Story of Son Alfred', vol.95 no.1019 (June 2001) pp.198-200.

These have a great deal of information as he was in contact with the family; I have summarised them here, followed by additional comments on Saul's life and career.

First article: Born Poland 1833, Jewish, son of a jeweller; left country age *ca.*15; said to have trained in Italy under an elderly conjuror named Bosco [!], eventually arrived in England; settled in Hull, then worked with John Moseley jeweller in Spalding; eloped with his daughter Elizabeth and married (Church of England) in Sculcoates 1860; states wife converted to Judaism; seven children, including Alfred who was born

1864. Saul performed as a society conjuror, never in music halls [*not correct*]; played before Queen Victoria at Balmoral 24 Sept.1855 [*not correct*]; living in [*in fact only passing through*] Carnoustie 1863; Exeter 1864; Farnham 1866, performed at army camps in that area. With compensation from railway accident *ca.*1884 [*actually 1876*] bought house at Winchelsea; daughters Priscilla (Pessa; "Miss Madge Virgo") and Rebecca (Belle) singers; they and son Alfred performed with father. Testimonial from Sir Henry Irving 1892.[1]

Second article: Alfred was the only child to become a magician, performing with Saul as "Signor Bosco and Son" until at least 1895; he was also father's agent as "Alfred Abrams" and "Dr Alfred Herberts". Family moved to Blackpool 1890s, opened boarding-house and small shops. Alfred married local milliner Fanny Firth in 1907; four children;[2] he died 1932.

Some additional comments on Saul's career

While music halls were not his preferred venue in his later years, Saul did play in them on numerous occasions early in his career: two examples are 28 November 1862 in Glasgow; 11 January 1863 in Airdrie.

His naturalisation application in June 1862 (below) gives his age as 28 and states he has been in England for thirteen years, meaning he arrived about 1849, age 15. Any time spent training in Italy en route is very implausible.

Saul later claimed that he began performing in 1852,[3] but the earliest confirmed sighting of him is in Hull in June 1858,[4] referred to variously as "Signor Bosco", "the Celebrated Bosco", "Bosco, the Great Wizard". Epstein (who had now just left England) had performed in Hull as "Bosco" as recently as the previous month, so there is no likelihood that Saul was passing himself off as Epstein. However when he opened in Scarborough on October 28th that year he was apparently arrested or at least accosted immediately after the performance as he was thought to be Epstein. Notices in the paper make it clear that it was not because he gave a disappointing performance but that Epstein was wanted there on some charge. There is no record of Epstein ever performing in Scarborough but it is possible he passed through there in May when leaving Harrogate for Berlin. A Public Notice headed "Professor Saul Bosco" explained that "the unpleasant occurrence which took place at the close of last night's performance was a mistake — the person wanted being ALFRED BOSCO, and **NOT** SAUL BOSCO". He announced a morning performance on 30th, "… it is to be hoped that the visitors and townspeople of Scarborough will out of sympathy for this talented man, give him their utmost support…".[5]

He was soon calling himself simply "Signor Bosco" once more, though not consistently. In June 1859 he is found performing in Newcastle ("Signor Bosco, the highly accomplished Polish 'wizard' … may lay undisputed claim to the title of the 'Wizard of Wizards' … We have seen Mr Anderson … and the talented Signor Freikel … Signor Bosco far surpasses both…".[7] In January 1860 we find him both working as a jeweller in Hull and also performing there, and that year in Sculcoates he married Elizabeth Moseley. In May he was performing in Beverley and Norwood in Yorkshire: "Signor Saul Bosco, The greatest Wizard in the World, will have the honour of opening his Enchanted Palace of Illusions…".[7] In June he made what seems to be first venture south, to the Isle of Wight in the summer season: "Signor S. Bosco, the highly accomplished Polish wizard, gave two entertainments…", claiming to be "the brother of that celebrated individual who some years back astonished the natives with his illusions…[Epstein]".[8] He then gave several performances in Aldershot, where he was later to settle.[9]

Saul is the "Signor Bosco" performing in Devon from November 1860 ("Sig. B. will avail himself of all the recent discoveries of Natural Science…"), then from February in Cornwall where he has added an exposure of "spirit rapping" to his repertoire. In Truro he was praised for his "astonishing sleight of hand tricks" and for "the gentlemanly *naïveté* with which he gives utterance to his broken English". He remained in Devon until April 1861, then later that year is found in Chester, Wales,[10] and Shropshire, rendering impossible his later claim to have performed before the "Emperor of Russia" on September 8th 1861 and the King of Prussia on November 17th.

He was touring widely in central England in early 1862 —"Signor S. Bosco, the Prince of Wizards…" in Nottingham in March, Hereford and Rugby in April, making equally false his later claim to have performed before the Emperor of Austria on April 9th 1862. In May he was advertising in Bradford as "Signor S. Bosco" then from June[11] bills himself as "Warschawsky, the Polish Wizard" and in Lincolnshire later that month as "Professor Warschawski". This change of stage-name coincides with his naturalisation on June 16th 1862.[12]

In November in Hull he sued a Mr Hopwood for failing to repair his "inexhaustible bottle"… "the bottle was produced in court, and caused considerable amusement".[13]

Performing in Scotland in March 1863 he added the Polish honorific title "Pann" to his name, and is first found doing plate-spinning ("…Pann Warschawski displays the most astounding tricks … linked together heavy and solid rings … restoring a broken plate … making whisky toddy out of burnt handkerchiefs, and spinning heavy plates at a prodigious rate…"),[14] with some new feats then added, including "successful experiments in electro-biology".

There was some embarrassment at the end of the month when it was reported that he performed in Dundee and at Broughty Ferry at exactly the same time ("…it looks as if there was some 'conjooring'' in the matter…", said the *Dundee Courier*): he wrote apologetically to the paper explaining that he felt constrained to continue in Dundee, "and accordingly sent my partner, who is equally able in the various tricks of legerdemain, to the adjoining towns".[15]

Who this partner (B63c) was is a mystery: The whereabouts of Louis Susser (B65) are unknown at this time and it is possible they briefly worked together — at the height of their rivalry in the 1870s Saul claimed he had employed Louis and Louis claimed Saul passed himself off as his brother.

Interestingly, on February 24th 1863 there was a show for "the Catholics of Edinburgh" by "the Brothers Bosco of Poland, entitled 'Natural Magic'" (B68): possibly Saul, and possibly with Louis Susser, or a different pair altogether? (A further "Signor Bosco", unidentified, was playing in Leeds from February 23rd 1863, who must be someone else again, possibly an early appearance by Morton, B69).

Saul was still in Scotland in late October 1863,[16] always billing himself as "Pann Warschawski" not "Bosco", then in Northumberland on October 29th and in Oxford on November 13th. He later claimed to have performed for Prince Alfred at Holyrood Palace in Edinburgh on November 12th, the night before his Oxford appearance, so Holyrood too must be another fabrication. On November 23rd he performed in Bicester, but left without paying the printer's bill: the local paper published a 'Wanted' notice — "An individual, speaking imperfect English, about five foot eight inches in height, and about thirty-five years of age, with a Jewish cast of countenance, well dressed, and with a show of jewellery...".[17]

He worked his way south and was in Brighton in late December and in Hastings in January. Here his advertisement[18] claimed he had performed at Balmoral (for the Queen), at Curragh Camp in Ireland, and at Holyrood, all on specific dates, and all untrue. He was next in Dover, Southsea, Bridport, then north to Bristol in May. In June he was back at Aldershot, then south to Devon and Cornwall until late October (playing before Russian aristocracy in Torquay in August).[19] His son Alfred (B64) was born in Exeter on October 7th 1864.

We then lose sight of Saul until June 1865, in Aldershot, where he last bills himself as "the Polish Wizard", then in Winchester in August, last as "Pann Warszawski", and is henceforth "Signor Bosco" again.

In 1872 Saul claimed to have been away for seven years, but it seems to be him performing in Aldershot in September 1865 (now offering gifts) and certainly him sued by a printer in Aldershot in October 1865: "after pleading on behalf of a large family and other circumstances, the defendant was ordered to pay the amount by monthly instalments".[20]

Saul is not found performing again until January 1866 when he advertises a show at the Royal Pump Room in Leamington Spa. Louis Susser was also due to perform in Leamington, at the Royal Music Hall, and in the end Saul withdrew ('Rival Wizards', the local paper headed an article, "...one disappeared, the other remained...").[21]

The next we hear of Saul is that he is building three cottages at Aldershot[22] and in September 1866 he is advertising as a watchmaker and jeweller in Aldershot: "... S. Bosco ... has purchased and succeeded to the Business of Mr. Melson ... 11 Wellington Street, Aldershot". But in November he is offering lessons in conjuring and has "made arrangements" for Maskelyne and Cooke to perform there; and he has an advertisement in *The Times*: "Signor Bosco, the great magician is ... at liberty to attend private parties ... Propect-villa, Victoria-road, Aldershot".[23]

On December 26th and 27th 1866 a "Signor Bosco", almost certainly Saul, performed in Gravesend, then on 31st in Dartford. This was advertised and reviewed in the *Gravesend Reporter*[24] ("...some wonderful and startling illusions"). A poster for the Dartford performance[25] features the "Enchanted Palace of Illusions", including Emperor Napoleon's Enchanted Card Case, Enchanted Talking Monkey, Hindoo Knot Trick, Flower Vase, Prolific Bird, Flying Bonnet.

The following year Saul is advertising as a Manufacturing Goldsmith and Jeweller and has erected workshops.[26] Then in January his premises and living quarters were destroyed by fire; a nephew, children, and a servant barely escaped. His loss was said to be up to £2000, but insured. In February he is calling for tenders for a salvage sale.[27]

Saul then travelled on the Continent; on his return he settled in Peterborough, and next in Goodman's Fields in London — we know this from a bankruptcy declaration he made in June 1869:
"Saul Warschawski, of No. 20 Great Alie-street, Goodman's-fields, Middlesex, before then of Chapel-street, Peterborough, Northamptonshire, before then travelling on the Continent, before then of Warsaw Villa, Victoria-road, Aldershot, Hants, in no business or employ, before then of No. 10, Wellington-street, Aldershot, aforesaid, Jeweller, and before then travelling in the United Kingdom as Professor of Legerdemain, and while exercising this art known as Signor Bosco, having been adjudged bankrupt...".[28] In August he agreed to pay his creditors two shillings and sixpence in the pound within fourteen days; and obtained a release.[29]

A "Signor Bosco" gave a performance in Aldershot at the end of December 1869, probably Saul, but in February 1870 he was working as a jeweller in Yaxley (charged when his dog attacked a sheep).[30] However he was also touring and performing (as far afield as Bath and Lincolnshire). His rivalry with Susser soon resurfaced and performing in Cheltenham in late November 1870 Louis had to defend himself against "handbills stigmatising him as an impostor", asserting that "he has adopted the name of 'Bosco' for the last 15 years...".[31] Their advertisements are often hard to differentiate, but it is certainly Saul in Colchester in December 1870 with "the Great American Wizard, Professor Hill". He and Hill were then announced to play in Melton Mowbray but failed to appear, and then in Bristol at the Victoria Rooms, Clifton. Here his rivalry with Louis again flared up as Louis was also due to appear soon in Bristol. Louis placed a notice saying "Signor Bosco intends shortly to visit Bristol, and has no connexion with the Person now advertised to Perform at the Victoria Rooms Clifton. That Person tried to pass himself off as Signor Bosco's brother in Bath. His proper name is Salomon Warschawski. (Signed) Louis Bosco".[32] Saul replied: "...The Person signing himself 'Louis Bosco,' whose real name is 'Louis Susser,' of 63, Chorlton-road, Manchester, was formerly connected with Signor Bosco's establishment, and is challenged to deny the fact; he, the said Louis Susser, being furthermore in no way equal to Signor Bosco as a public professional. (Signed) Saul Bosco".[33] Louis was soon in Staines and again advertising that "S. Warschawski, travelling ... under the name of 'Bosco' ... is not my Brother, nor is he in any way connected with me";[34] and again in Glossop in March.

Saul and Hill performed in Norwich in January 1871, "Bosco begs to announce he will perform his great feats, entitled — Defiance to the Chasse-Pot and Needle Gun, and extraordinary Manoeuvre with a Prussian Bombshell...".[35]

On census night 1871 both Saul and Louis were at home with their families, Louis in Chorlton, Saul in Yaxley (profession: "Professor of Legerdemain").

Both Morton Bosco (B69) and Leotard Bosco (B77) were also now on the road, so there were four major Boscos active in Britain at this period.

Saul and Louis clashed again in August 1871 when Saul performing in Bangor was denounced as an impostor by Louis who had also planned to perform there. Saul then published, apparently here for the first time, a testimonial he claimed was signed by "C.B. Phipps, Privy Purse" dated September 25th 1855 stating that "Signor Bosco performed by Her Majesty's command at Balmoral Castle, yesterday evening". It is odd Saul never cited this testimonial earlier if he was the Bosco referred to (which he was not). Saul continued touring, still parading his Balmoral appearance and stating he was back after seven (sometimes as eight) years overseas.

A typical Saul ad is this in March 1872: headed "A Night with the Original Bosco", it offers "Two Hours of Illusion; or Magic, Mirth and Music" by "Signor Bosco, the Great Monarch of Legerdemain", who had the honour of performing for Her Majesty (claiming to have the Original Testimonial from the Queen), and all the crowned heads of Europe, now returned to England after seven years, having had a highly successful tour, visiting France, Russia, Prussia, Switzerland, Austria and Denmark; listing his tricks in detail, and ending with a notice that he has "No Connection with a 'Manchester' Bosco ... A Person who has lately been travelling though some towns in England and Wales under the name Signor Bosco, and signed himself Louis Bosco, but whose real name is Louis Susser..."[36]

Performing in Chippenham in November 1872 Louis similarly advertised that "A Person formerly in my employ is now travelling about the Country (together with a Mr. Rosenthal) and represents himself as Signor Bosco, who is also copying my Bills and Programmes. I hereby state that his real uame is Solomon Warschawski, and is in no way connected with me".[37]

In Cheltenham in 1873 Saul proclaims himself "the greatest and only Prestidigitateur in the World who performs entirely without Apparatus" and launches a new trick, one which he was apparently the only "Bosco" to perform. He originally calls it "Dr Lynn's Great Blood Trick"[38] and over the next two years calls it variously "the blood trick" or "the Great Blood Illusion".[39]

In August 1874 Saul performed at Sandown for the fortieth birthday of Princess Charlotte of Prussia,[40] proudly quoting this as he toured through the south for several months billing himself as "Professor Saul Bosco" and including 'The Watch Trick', 'Blood Trick' and 'Dark Seance'. Slowly heading north, in September 1874 he reached Ripon, to be met by Louis: Saul again declared Louis an impostor, who replied as usual, denouncing Saul as Solomon Warszawski formerly in his employ, and "having been exposed in various towns through the press and handbills", now adding "His statement that he performed before Her Majesty is not true".[41] The rivalry ended only in 1875 when Louis left England for good.

A long review of Saul's performance in Yeovil on October 13th, which left "a moderately large audience ... much gratified and amused", described in detail three of his tricks which "were of an extraordinary nature". Three men were asked to write four-digit numbers on cards and the total when read out was the same as that in a locked box which a boy had been holding on stage the whole time; a watch was placed in a box which a boy from the audience held to his ear; when he said he could no longer hear it ticking it was found in the innermost of half a dozen locked boxes which fitted inside each other; and a man was asked to select a card, name it aloud, shuffle the pack, and throw the pack at Saul who was standing "at the angle of his entertainment screen" and impaled the correct card on a sword. The reviewer suspected the same boy was behind the screen with a duplicate pack of cards...[42]

Again, in Bedford in December it was "the watch trick" that struck a reviewer as the most remarkable act of the night; later in the show he "explained" the "clever rope trick" of the Davenports, though he never seems to advertise that as a highlight.[43] But the following year the watch trick had to be put on hold as "a certain small box ... for performing his celebrated watch trick" was broken when an audience member in Helpringham (worried that his brother was to be mesmerised) came on stage, and assaulted Saul and his son, who retaliated. Saul said he "had given six guineas for it, but he valued it at £10"; Saul's coat was torn, they had had to refund the £3 15s taken at the door, and "there had been several complaints at places where they had since exhibited because the watch trick was not performed". The defendant was fined 10s for assault and had to pay £5 for the box, and costs.[44]

In early 1875 while Louis was in Scotland then in Cumberland, and Leotard in Yorkshire, Saul was touring Lincolnshire, billing himself as "Signer Warschawski (S. A. Bosco), The Wizard of the Age";[45] the following month he was in his home town of Peterborough and now calling himself "The Royal Illusionist",[46] and the following year he adds to this "The Monarch of Legerdemain", advertising as "The Royal Illusionist ... Signor Saul Bosco, the Monarch of Legerdemain ... his Enchanted Palace of Illusions, and will give his New and Original Entertainment Entitled 'Magic!'", and still claiming to have performed at Balmoral.[47]

He was again touring Lincolnshire and Warwickshire in 1876, Alcester in October, Ramsey in November, and in King's Cliffe, near Peterborough on December 6th (with the watch trick back in his repertoire), but it was on December 23rd 1876 that he was in a serious railway accident.

This occurred at Arlesey, on the Great Northern Line, near his home in Peterborough. In February 1878 he sued the Company, claiming that his right arm and hand had become paralysed, meaning he could not practise his art; he had been obliged to sell his clothing business in Peterborough managed by his wife as she had to devote her complete attention to him; medical and other expenses had been £300 to £400; and such was the shock to his nervous system that he was unable to walk out unattended. The jury awarded him damages of £1500.[48]

Saul certainly resumed performing, on his own and later with his son Alfred: exactly when is uncertain, but probably by late 1881. He is a "clothier" in November and December 1878 (minor court cases), a clothier in June 1880 in an apparent settlement of his old bankruptcy,[49] and a clothier in the 1881 census, staying in a hotel in Lutterworth with his sons Joseph and David, also clothiers. But he is almost certainly "Signor Bosco, the Royal Illusionist", also as "The Original Bosco" and "The Monarch of Legerdemain", performing in Leicester in December 1881 (contact address Claremont Villa, Aylestone Park, Leicester).[50]

Saul is found on tour in the 1880s as "the original Bosco"[51] and as "Signor Bosco, the only genuine Artiste of that name, who has travelled since 1852".

By 1882 he had developed a very successful beheading act, holding up the head and making it laugh or grimace, This act he probably learnt from "Dr A. Epstein" (B12c) with whom he performed in England in 1882.[52]

We get a personal glimpse of Saul, with some quoted remarks by him, in 1887 when he was sued by a landlord in Horsham for not paying rent for the hired room as the takings were so poor; Saul, swearing in court on an Old Testament he brought with him, declared he was "head over heels in debt" and that paying the amount at 4s. a month was "the hardest judgment I've ever heard".[53]

An advertisement in October 1887 listed among his tricks "his entirely new Watch trick ... The Supper of the Magicians, or the Three Graces from the Fire; the Spanish Salad and enchanted Transformation Scene ... the enchanted Brewery ... the obedient cards and the Star of Siberia; a man changed to a hen by enchantment; Amusing Experiments in Mesmerism" and concluding with "the Beheading of a Living Person".[54] In November 1888 we find Saul performing his beheading act and "on the following afternoon Bosco jun. entertained a large number of school children"; and the following year "the Original Bosco and Son" are appearing together in Aldershot. In November 1889 he is also telling the future by palmistry. He and Alfred are performing the beheading of a mesmerised young lady in Goudhurst in November 1891: the head is removed and made to smoke, dance, and blow out a candle before being replaced, all while the pianist plays Handel's 'Dead March in Saul'.[55]

Saul's daughters were performing as "the Sisters Boscoe" by 1883 ("...Sparkling, Fascinating, Young, Pretty, and Clever Duettists, Opera Bouffe Artistes, and Dancers")[56] and later travelled with their father and brother variously billed as the "Sisters Bosco", "Misses Warschawski" and "Sisters Warschawski"; Alfred was also the manager, as "A.H.J. Bosco".

In December 1891 "Signor Bosco and A.H.J. Bosco, Jun., The Royal Illusionists & Mesmerists" were advertising in Hastings (address: Paragon House, and the troupe were soon billed as the "Paragon Combination Company").

Alfred in 1894 was advertising as "Professor A.H.J. Bosco (son of the Original Signor Bosco)", but in 1897 in Leamington Saul was still on the road ("Signor Bosco and his company"), and in 1898 ("the Original Signor Bosco" in Rugeley), and still in January 1900 ("Signor Bosco and Son"). In public life both father and son were now using the surname Abrams — in 1900 "Samuel Abrams, better known as Signor Bosco" sued a timber merchant (one farthing damages)[57] and the following year in Blackpool Alfred was prosecuted under the shop hours' trading act as "Alfred Abrams".[58] By 1901 Alfred is performing the beheading act as "Signor Bosco (son of the original Bosco)" but in 1901 they are still advertising as "Signor Bosco or Son".

When Saul last performed is uncertain: he died in Blackpool on April 22nd 1906, reported in the *Era* as "Bosco, magician, aged 72", and registered as "Warschawski, Abram Solomon". age 69.

Alfred (possibly B89 below in 1916) was still advertising in the *Rugby Advertiser* in 1919 — "Signor A. Bosco, 'The Royal Society Entertainer' ... Manager: A. Abrams" (himself!); last sighted performing in Birmingham in 1924. He died in Birmingham on May 12th 1932.

NOTES
[1] Dawes wonders who was the "Signor Bosco, Prince of Wizards" at the Mechanics' Institute in Hull in December 1866 — this was definitely Morton Bosco (B69).
[2] Alfred and Fanny named their children Lord Leopold David Abrams Bosco-Warschawski; Lady Winifred Bessie Abrams Bosco-Warschawski; Baron Edward Louie Abrams Bosco-Warschawski; and Edward Daniel Abrams Bosco-Warschawski; Edward later changed his surname to Adams and settled in New Zealand.

[3] "Signor Bosco, the only genuine Artiste of that name, who has travelled since 1852" (*Leicester Journal* 1 Dec.1882). The statement also features on the poster at url:158.

[4] *Hull Packet* 25 June 1858; *Hull Advertiser* 3 July 1858; etc. It is possible he was the "Signor Bosco" who previously failed miserably in Chepstow in September 1857, saying, when it was found he was not Epstein, that he was not the "Italian Bosco" but the "Polish Bosco" (*Chepstow Weekly Advertiser* 19 Sep.1857). However this may have been Susser or even Millar, or an unknown.

[5] *Scarborough Mercury* 30 Oct.1858.

[6] *Newcastle Daily Chronicle* 17 June 1859.

[7] *Beverley Guardian* 19 May 1860.

[8] *Isle of Wight Observer* 30 June; 14 July 1860.

[9] *Aldershot Military Gazette* 28 July; 18 August 1860.

[10] Performing in Denbigh in September as "Signor S. Bosco" he received an excellent review: "…It would be impossible to convey a description of the wonderful and astonishing illusions performed by the clever Wizard; suffice it to say, that he is not a pretender but a first-class artist, ranking with Anderson and Frikell. Many of the tricks were quite new. His thorough exposure of the tricks of the spirit-rappers and table-turners was very appropriate at the present time…": *North Wales Chronicle* 28 Sep. 1861.

[11] *Era* 8 June 1862.

[12] National Archives HO 1/105/3845: "…Saul Warschawski, professor of Legerdemain, age 28, has resided 13 years, married to an English Woman, with one child". The Home Office official noted: "All regular but the Professorship does not sound well".

[13] *Hull Packet* 14 Nov.1862.

[14] *Dundee Courier* 25 Mar.1863; the *Dundee Advertiser* of the same date called it the "Chinese plate and dish dance".

[15] *Dundee Courier* 1, 2 Apr.1863.

[16] His daughter Rachel was born in Carnoustie on September 9th 1863.

[17] *Bicester Herald* 11 Dec.1863.

[18] *Sussex Advertiser* 19 Jan.1864.

[19] *Western Times* 19 Aug.1864.

[20] *Aldershot Military Gazette* 21 Oct.1865.

[21] *Leamington Spa Courier* 20, 27 Jan.1866.

[22] *Aldershot Military Gazette* 7 July 1866.

[23] *The Times* 26 Dec.1866.

[24] *Gravesend Reporter* 22, 29 Dec.1866.

[25] Sold at auction by Potter and Potter in August 2016, item 409 (url:150).

[26] *Aldershot Military Gazette* 7 Sep.; 9 Nov.; 7 Dec.1867.

[27] *Aldershot Military Gazette* 25 Jan.; 29 Feb.1868.

[28] *London Gazette* 8 June 1869.

[29] *London Gazette* 24 Aug.1869.

[30] *Bedfordshire Times and Independent* 12 Feb.1870.

[31] *Cheltenham Looker-On* 3 Dec.1870.

[32] *Bristol Daily Post* 27, 29 Dec. 1870.

[33] *Bristol Daily Post* 27, 29 Dec. 1870.

[34] *West Middlesex Herald* 21 Jan.1871.
[35] *Norfolk News* 14 Jan.1871.
[36] *Tadcaster Post* 14 Mar.1872.
[37] *Devizes and Wiltshire Gazette* 7 Nov.1872.
[38] *Cheltenham Examiner* 19 Nov.1873.
[39] *Boston Guardian* 9 Oct.1875 (the last time he mentions it). See also *Appendix Z2: Bill Matter*.
[40] *Hampshire Advertiser* 1 Aug.1874.
[41] *Knaresborough Post* 19 Sep.1874. For Louis's ad see B65 note 35.
[42] *Western Gazette* 16 Oct.1874.
[43] *Bedfordshire Mercury* 12 Dec.1874. Saul is described as "Warschawski — a very clever member of the Bosco family".
[44] *Grantham Journal* 27 Nov.1875; another account in *Sleaford Gazette* same date.
[45] *Grantham Journal* 27 Feb.1875. He also resumed the use of his old title of "The Russian Wizard" (*Central Somerset Gazette* 15 Feb.1875; etc.).
[46] *Peterborough Standard* 6, 13 Mar.1875.
[47] *Peterborough Standard* 12 Feb.1876.
[48] His passenger train struck a derailed goods train. Four people were killed and several seriously injured: *Nottinghamshire Guardian* 29 Dec.1876; details at url:151. For Saul's court case see *Pall Mall Gazette* 7 Feb.1878; *Western Mail* and *Yorkshire Post* 8 Feb.1878; *Era* 10 Feb.1878.
[49] *London Gazette* 8 June 1880.
[50] He had billed himself as "The Royal Illusionist" in October 1876 when the title was already in use by Leotard Bosco, and in the 1890s he or Alfred used that title in Hastings. A number of other magicians had adopted the term in England, first Bernardo Eagle in the 1830s, and notably Evanion and Maskelyne and Cooke in the 1870s.
[51] In Leicester in 1882 he bills himself as "BOSCO, (The Original Bosco)" in a special performance "In aid of the Fund for the Persecuted Jews in Russia": *Leicester Journal* 17 Feb.1882.
[52] For example: "TOWN HALL, RUGBY. The Original Bosco, The Royal Illusionist, and DR. A. EPSTEIN, The World Renowned Russian Court Prestidigitateur and Magician, will give THREE GRAND PERFORMANCES ...": *Rugby Advertiser* 6 May 1882.
[53] *West Sussex County Times* 22 Jan.1887.
[54] *Sevenoaks Chronicle* 7 Oct.1887.
[55] *Hastings Agricultural Gazette* 14 Nov.1891. The Harry Ransom Center has a playbill (url:152) for Saul performing in Broadstairs (with Alfred named as his manager) on "Tuesday August 14th and Wednesday August 15th", so probably 1893 (though possibly 1888 or 1900). He makes much of his performance before the Queen and because of "many impostors" he includes a photograph of himself. There is also a later playbill, including "the Sisters Warschawski", at url:153.
[56] *Aldershot Military Gazette* 12 May 1883.
[57] *Coventry Evening Telegraph* 28 July 1900.
[58] *Lancashire Evening Post* 9 Sep.1901.

B63a. Saul Warschawski's unknown partner.

When touring Scotland in 1863 Saul Warschawski (B63) was "exposed" as performing in both Dundee and nearby Broughty Ferry at the same time. He wrote apologetically to the Dundee *Courier and Argus* (2 Apr.1863) explaining that he felt constrained to continue in Dundee, "and accordingly sent my partner, who is equally able in the various tricks of legerdemain, to the adjoining towns".

It was probably also the partner performing at Ferry-Port-on-Craig (Tayport) soon after, or so the *Dundee Advertiser* assumed (4 Apr.1863), but "he proves himself a most expert conjurer, and excited the wonder of the audience to a great degree, whose risible faculties he also tickled amazingly"; and probably the partner again in Cupar the following week (*Dundee, Perth, and Cupar Advertiser* 10 Apr.1863).

It is possible that this partner was his later arch-rival Louis Susser, whose whereabouts at this date are uncertain; certainly when they were denouncing each other as impostors a few years later each claimed to have employed the other.

B65. Louis Bosco (Louis Susser), 1836-1908

Real surname **Susser,** his first name in U.K. is Lewis or (usually) Louis.

He was born Leibel Susser (Zysser) in Kraków, Poland, on April 25th 1836, fourth of twelve children of Henoch Susser and Freindel Kelner-Szlamowicz who married in Kraków in 1831.[1] He probably arrived in England in 1853 — he states in his Naturalisation application in 1869 that he has been there 16 years.[2] His parents and several of his siblings died in Poland, so it appears he emigrated alone.

Louis had a long career as "Signor Bosco" in Britain and later in America, and in Britain an ongoing rivalry with "Saul Bosco" (Warschawski, B63), both using the title "Signor Bosco", and at times they cannot to differentiated (see *Appendix Z2: Bill Matter*). Both used similar terms and claims in their advertising and any new catchphrase used by one as bill matter was often copied by the other — Saul was the first of the two to use the phrase "Enchanted Palace of Illusions"[3] but Louis (followed by Leotard Bosco, B77) adopted it. Both Louis and Saul claimed to have performed before Queen Victoria at Balmoral in 1855: in fact it was neither of them but Epstein (B12), an example of Louis and Saul laying claim to Epstein's reputation after his departure. Louis is sometimes identifiable (early in his career) as *L. Bosco, Herr L. Bosco*, or as "The German Wizard", while Saul early on billed himself as "The Polish Wizard", though Louis later also adopted this title.[4]

The first definite sighting of Louis performing is in Havant in the south of Hampshire at the end of March 1858:[5] here he is "Herr Louis Bosco, the great German wizard … his sleight of hand feats are truly astonishing"; with him is Professor Buckingham, a local favourite with his performing dogs.[6] They then appeared in Emsworth, Chichester, Fareham, Winchester, Arundel, Bognor, Godalming… this limited area in which he at first operated suggesting he was living at home, not on tour, and probably still had a "real job". There was plenty of competition for him in England at this date — not merely Anderson, Frikell and Herr Dobler,[7] but John Blitz, Professor Jacobs ("the English wizard"), Professor Ewart ("the Great Wizard of the Orient"), Mr Phillips ("the Wizard of the East"), Antonio

Poletti ("the Roman Wizard"), Hartz ("Wizard of the World"), Madame Bosco (BF1), and of course the other "Signor Bosco", Saul Warschawski (B63), initially in the north of England as "the Polish wizard" while Louis worked the south.

In October 1858 Louis is now performing on his own and a little further afield in Maidstone ("…will appear unaided by…any Tinselled Paraphernalia … without the use of Apparatus, the arms and table free from any covering");[8] then we find him in Horsham, Tonbridge, Worthing (with "Mr Simmonds, comic vocalist"), Rogate, Winchester, Romsey, Horndean, Hambledon, Poole, Weymouth… Reviews were generally good, but audiences were often small — in Bridgwater in June 1859 despite "extensively placarding the town" he attracted only eight people, cancelled the show, and left town "without paying the cost of the printer's bill".[9] He is probably the "Herr Bosco" who performed at St John's College in Hurstpierpoint, West Sussex, on February 11th 1859 — Epstein had now left England and Warschawski was in the north. The Rev. Sabine Baring-Gould noted that

> …he performed with great success, amid deserved applause, his marvellous series of conjuring tricks. Such exhibitions of manual dexterity are not only interesting as shewing the skill that practice and perseverance may achieve, but they suggest in answer to any who may cavil at the supposed uselessness of such pains, whether, besides the refreshment and pleasure they afford to many spectators, they do not serve a purpose in helping us to realise the wonderful mechanism of our frame, when we see its delicate operations leading to such perplexing and baffling results — the gross material flesh endowed, as it were, almost with the elasticity and subtle motion of spirit itself.[10]

Louis is next sighted in Sherborne and Crediton, then in August in Tavistock, no longer merely "The Great German Wizard" but "the celebrated Professor of the unique and Fashionable Science of Natural and Philosophical Magic", and now first claiming (or implying) he had performed at Balmoral — "Herr Bosco will perform his two astonishing tricks (as shown before the Royal Family at Balmoral,) entitled 'The Queen's Handkerchief,' and 'The Prince Consort's Card.'" And we have "The Terpsichorean Delf![11] The Posing Plateau!! Telegraphic Conveyance of Cash! A Concatenation of Curiosities, embodying the Fruitful Canary, in the Illustrations of which Herr Bosco will be found Outwizarding all Wizards".[12] And the same in Exeter and through Cornwall — Torpoint, Bodmin, Truro, Falmouth, Penzance, then "disengaged over the Christmas Holidays" and offering private entertainments, January 1860 in Holsworthy, February in Barnstaple ("will also introduce Natural Magnetism, which has never been performed by any other person, as it is the Professor's own invention"),[13] South Molton and Bideford, March in Ilfracombe and Bath, and April at the Zoological Gardens in Bristol. His advance publicity was small and audiences sometimes sparse.

On April 13th 1860 he played before the Duchess of Beaufort at Badminton, receiving an excellent testimonial which he was soon parading in his advertisements (and still doing so in America in 1897). He moved on to Chippenham, Weston-super-Mare, Clevedon (where "the attendance was good … he has the happy gift of not only astonishing his visitors, but of keeping them in a roar of continuous laughter").[14] Next came Wells, Shepton Mallet, Frome, Warminster, Trowbridge, Devizes, Gloucester, Cirencester, and Stroud (where the local newspaper stated that he "some three years ago, made a sojourn of several months at Bristol":[15] if correct this has not been traced and would be his earliest known performance). He is next found in Lydney, Newnham, Coleford, and Chepstow, and then spent some time in Wales, opening in Cardiff on September 24th and still in Carmarthen in late November.

While Louis was moving north, the other current "Signor Bosco", Saul Warschawski, was heading south, playing in the Isle of Wight in July, then in Aldershot and in Plymouth (where he claimed to have performed at Balmoral on the same date as claimed by Louis), then through Devon and Cornwall for several months. Louis had gone to Ireland and was touring there from January 1861, opening at Cork, where a warm review noted the range of his act, including plate-spinning — "card tricks, gun tricks, handkerchiefs that were burnt to ashes and afterwards phenix-like, re-appeared... he made sundry dishes perform wonderful gyrations ... table turning ... spirit manifestations...".[16] He seems to have found better audiences in Ireland and continued touring there until late 1862.

His advertisements proclaimed that his performances "have been patronised by the several Courts of Berlin, Vienna, Munich, Naples, St. Petersburgh, and London; and have been given in all the principal towns in Europe and America":[17] all nonsense. On September 4th 1861 he performed in the Grenadier Guards Officers' Mess at Curragh Camp before the Prince of Wales — soon quoted proudly in his advertisements, and still almost thirty years later in Nebraska.[18]

In Londonderry in January 1862 he still bills himself as "the Great German Wizard" but in February in Armagh he is "Signor Bosco, of Poland", and so for the rest of his tour of Ireland. In July 1862 he was back in Dublin, playing before the Lord Lieutenant, whose testimonial he was also to quote in future advertisements.

He is last found in Ireland in Carlow in December 1862, then from February 23rd 1863 Louis is probably the "Signor Bosco" performing in Leeds (Saul was touring Scotland at this time; but this could possibly be an early appearance of "Signor Morton Bosco", B69).

A "Signor Bosco" claimed in 1864 that he performed for Prince Alfred at Holyrood on November 12th 1863 — this was Louis, as Saul was in Oxford the following day, but Saul also later claimed this performance and "Prince Alfred" became a particular bone of contention between them.[19]

In late 1864 Louis is in Norfolk,[20] Saul in Cornwall, and Morton in the north. Louis has now added to his repertoire "the Davenport Brothers' rope feat", either himself or sometimes an assistant bound by an audience member and freeing himself behind a screen. He gradually worked north until reaching Cumbria in July 1865, then turned south, and in Birmingham he got married.

His bride was Annie (or Hannah) Hyam (or Hyams), Jewish, born in Newport on the Isle of Wight in 1848 to Hyman (also Henry) Wolf Hyam (born in Kraków like Louis), and his wife Amelia (also Julia), née Lazarus. (For the Hyam family see under David Hyam, Hannah's brother (B66): born in Portsea in 1843 David became another "Signor Bosco").

Louis was naturalised in 1869 and by 1870 he and Annie were living at 63 Chorlton Road in Manchester (and living at no.60 were Annie's mother, brother David, and youngest sister Kate).

A son Harry (Enoch) was born in Birmingham in 1866; another, Jacob Isaac, when they were on tour in Dublin in 1867 (died in Buffalo in 1899); Albert Samuel in

Chorlton in 1870 (died in infancy); Hilda Flora in Chorlton in 1871; Leah (Lillian) in Chorlton in 1873; then after they left Britain a daughter Sidonie was born in Austria in 1876; then in America another Albert about 1879; and Miriam Grace in 1880. (This is confirmed by the 1900 US census: eight children born, six living.)

None of their children went into show business.[21] In the 1871 census Louis's profession is "dealer in fancy goods" but this was a back-up as he was still on the road conjuring. As was Saul, both using the name "Signor Bosco". They successfully avoided each other until January 1866, when both were announced to perform in Leamington at the same time, Louis at the Royal Music Hall and Saul at the Royal Pump Room, both quoting in their announcements their appearances (real and alleged) before royalty and distinguished patrons. In the end Saul withdrew and Louis gave a successful performance and then resumed touring, returning to Leamington in April: "Rival Wizards", said the *Leamington Spa Courier,* "...one disappeared, the other remained...".[22]

Their advertising remained very similar and deliberately deceptive, both using the tags "Enchanted Palace of Illusions" and "without apparatus, without covered tables..."; both still claiming to have performed at Balmoral in 1855 and before Prince Alfred at Holyrood Palace in 1863. Louis made another prolonged tour of Ireland from July 1867 to April 1868, then moved gradually south from Scotland to Cornwall, now offering "the Great Japanese Top and Butterfly Illusions", and "the Instantaneous Growth of Flowers ... the only European who can perform this marvellous and beautiful Feat".

Saul ceased touring for a period, working as a jeweller, but resumed performing in 1871 ("Professor of Legerdemain" in the 1871 census), advertising as "The Original Signor Bosco" and touring with "the Great American Wizard Professor Hill". The rivalry between Louis and Saul had soon resurfaced and performing in Cheltenham in late November 1870 Louis had to defend himself against "handbills stigmatising him as an impostor", asserting that "he has adopted the name of 'Bosco' for the last 15 years...".[23]

Matters came to a head in December when both Saul and Louis were to perform in Bristol. Louis placed a notice saying "Signor Bosco intends shortly to visit Bristol, and has no connexion with the Person now advertised to Perform at the Victoria Rooms Clifton. That Person tried to pass himself off as Signor Bosco's brother in Bath. His proper name is Salomon Warschawski. (Signed) Louis Bosco".[24] Saul retaliated: "...The Person signing himself 'Louis Bosco,' whose real name is 'Louis Susser,' of 63, Chorlton-road, Manchester, was formerly connected with Signor Bosco's establishment, and is challenged to deny the fact; he, the said Louis Susser, being furthermore in no way equal to Signor Bosco as a public professional. (Signed) Saul Bosco".[25] Louis was soon in Staines and again advertising that "S. Warschawski, travelling ... under the name of 'Bosco' ... is not my Brother, nor is he in any way connected with me";[26] and again in Glossop in March.[27] On census night 1871 both were at home with their families, Louis in Chorlton, Saul in Yaxley.

Saul, touring through Wales in August and September 1871, was met with handbills calling him an impostor. In August Louis was in Kent, Broadstairs on 2nd, Seaford on 7th.[28] Louis then had four months in Ireland, and on his return Saul was soon warning people against this "Louis Bosco" — and now includes among his tricks Louis's "Oriental Top Spinning, The Instantaneous Growth of Flowers" and "the World Renowned Japanese Butterfly Trick".[29]

Morton Bosco (B69) and Leotard Bosco (B77) were also now on the road, so there were four major Boscos active in Britain at this time, including two L. Bosco's, provoking a notice in 1873 from Louis, as "Signor Bosco", denying any connexion with "a person performing at a music hall in this city under the same name";[30] and Leotard soon adopted the same phrase "Enchanted Palace of Illusions" used by Saul and Louis. After Morton Bosco missed his show through drunkenness in April, Louis wrote to the local paper stating that this was not him.[31] But his main bugbear remained Saul. In Oxford in November 1872 a large ad announced a performance by Louis at the Town Hall, but "just before the commencement of the performance another person, giving the name of Bosco, came on the scene, and claimed to be the Bosco whose agent had engaged the room. He was, however, ultimately persuaded that he had no right to the possession of the room that night".[32] The other 'Bosco' was probably Saul (not Leotard: he was in Scotland), because soon after in nearby Chippenham Louis advertised that "A Person formerly in my employ is now travelling about the Country (together with a Mr. Rosenthal) and represents himself as Signor Bosco, who is also copying my Bills and Programmes. I hereby state that his real uame is Solomon Warschawski, and is in no way connected with me".[33]

In 1873 Louis is advertising for an advance agent: "Wanted a Smart, Active, and Intelligent Young Man, to go ahead of Signor Bosco's Entertainment, Address, 64 Chorlton road, Manchester".[34]

Louis and Saul had not crossed paths for some time when in September 1874 Louis was about to perform in Ripon on September 14th and placed a large ad on page one of the *Richmond & Ripon Chronicle*: immediately below it was published a "Notice to the Public" by Saul, then in Hampshire but himself due to perform in Ripon on October 1st. Saul's notice listed his credentials (including his Balmoral claim) and stated that "Signor Bosco, the Royal Illusionist … is in no way connected with the person advertised as Signor Bosco to give an entertainment on the 14th of September. The person is no other than a man he had in his Establishment, and whose real name is Louis Susser… .[35] Louis replied[36] as usual denouncing Saul as Solomon Warszawski formerly in his employ, and "having been exposed in various towns through the press and handbills", now adding "His statement that he performed before Her Majesty is not true". Louis continued north and Saul was soon busy in the south west, still claiming his Balmoral appearance.

In early 1875 Louis was performing in Scotland and the north of England, and is last found in Britain in Wigton on March 17th ("the audience appeared to be well pleased as the applause was frequent").[37] He is never sighted in Britain again.

We know he first headed to the Continent, as a daughter Sidonie is listed in the 1880 US census as age 4 and born in Austria (probably in Poland, where Louis's family still were), and as age 16 born Austria in the 1892 NY State Census. There is a record of Annie Susser, 31, and her five children (variously misspelt) arriving in New York from Liverpool as cabin passenger on the 'Adriatic' on June 5th 1876. It would appear, then, that Louis's wife and children travelled soon after March 1875 to Europe, where Sidonie was born, and they then returned to England before heading to America; Louis, not listed with them, went separately, probably a little earlier. The first confirmed sighting of him performing in North America is almost certainly this, in Galena, Illinois, in April 1876, where it is said: "Signor Bosco has been in this country but seven months, and has in his possession testimonials from very many distinguished Europeans, as to his proficiency as a magician".[38] If correct, this means he arrived about October 1875, leaving him ample time to have travelled to Europe first after leaving England soon after March 1875.

The performance in Galena was not a great success, so much so that he decided to cancel a second and third night. However he changed his mind and instead reduced his admission price from 75 cents, to 25 and 35 cents.

Prior to Galena he is probably the "Sig. Bosco" reported as touring through Illinois earlier that year — in Henry in February; Minonk, Winona, Amboy, Galesburg, Rock Island, Moline in March,[39] then Genesco, Muscatino, Peoria,[40] and Chicago in May.[41]

A month after he was in Galena the paper there quoted remarks from other Illinois papers that "the Bosco sleight-of-hand troupe now traveling in Illinois, is a fraud";[42] this may or may not be Louis (but see note 44!).

The family had settled in Buffalo, N.Y., where David Hyam (B66) and family were also living. Louis is listed in the 1877 Buffalo City Directory living at 196 Sixth Street; the following year they are at 269 Niagara, and still there in the 1881 U.S. census, Louis's profession "prestidigitateur"); later they moved to 708 Elmwood (there in the 1900 census, Louis with the same profession).

In 1877 Louis is touring N.Y. state — in May he "gave three of his legerdemain performances in Cazenovia, we understand to crowded houses";[43] but less well received in Marshall in June where the local newspaper (one of many to object to the prize draws associated with these shows) summed up: "A tramping wizard, who calls himself Signor Bosco, has bulldozed many of our people out of all their loose change. He stopped here for three days, and it was wonderful how he gulled them. Rich and poor, young and old, all rushed to the show to secure a prize… Now that he has gone his victims begin to realize their stupidity, and 'fraud, humbug, cheat, swindler', and such gentle epithets are offered by them…'.[44] He was more welcome in August that year in Cobleskill: "Signor Bosco, the celebrated conjuror, will give a series of entertainments in the Opera Hall… Signor Bosco shows excellent testimonials from England, where he has recently been giving exhibitions".[45]

He had similarly diverse receptions the following year. After he left Groton, N.Y., in April the paper said: "Signor Bosco, as he terms himself, humbugged the citizens of our quiet village last Friday, Saturday and Monday nights…",[46] while in September Camden was very sympathetic — "Signor Bosco. The entertainment given by this gentleman … last Thursday … was of a very superior order, and deserving of a more liberal patronage than it received. The presents were numerous, and many of them of actual value … Signor Bosco is an Austrian and a gentleman, and we were sorry he should meet with such luck here".[47]

In 1879 he was touring Ontario, "Signor Bosco, wizard", playing in Belleville, Napanee and Kingston, immediately provoking a complaint in the *New York Clipper* from another "Signor Bosco" who had been touring America and Canada for some time, that "some magician, who had assumed his name, is now playing in Canada".[48] The *Clipper* then stated it had received a letter from L. Bosco in St. Marys, Ontario, enclosing programmes for shows by him in England and Scotland, and the *Clipper* suggested each use an initial or first name to distinguish themselves. When this did not happen the *Clipper* then designated the Bosco in Ontario "Signor L. Bosco" and the other, currently touring Ohio, as "Signor D. Bosco",[49] with Louis soon advertising that "Sig. L. Bosco, Wizard, Claims to be the Original of that Name".[50]

All this may well have been contrived for publicity, for "D. Bosco" was David Hyam, older brother of Louis's wife Annie, and he and his parents were living in Buffalo only a few streets from Louis and his family. David had arrived in America by 1873 and Louis by 1876, so in 1879 both had already been touring in North America as "Signor Bosco" for several years.

Louis is probably the "Signor Bosco" on a long tour of Vermont in early 1880, sighted in St. Albans, Montpelier, Newport, Barton, St Johnsbury, and Springfield, where he was told to "get out" following a complaint that no one had won the gold watch in his prize draw.[51] He continued on to New Hampshire and Massachusetts, then it is probably him announced as the Sig. Bosco who is "to close his traveling season of forty-nine weeks in Wappinger Falls, N.Y." in June.[52]

Early in the next season he was in Friendship, N.Y. in September, where the local paper was certainly a lot more friendly, saying "we guarantee the citizens of this place a fine entertainment", and found room for "an incident in connection with one of Signor Bosco's performances ... Signor Bosco spent the winter of '58-9 in Berlin, and was one day announced to appear at the palace...", retailing the *Bartolomeo* anecdote (no doubt supplied by Louis) of Bosco making Prussia appear larger on the globe...[53]

"Signor Bosco" is found over several years with an advance agent named "Joe Simons" (or Simmons).[54] He is with him in Oswego and Ottawa, Kansas, in May 1882, and now has a "Bosco troupe" and is travelling with "Madame Bosco".[55] They are still in Kansas with Simons as agent in September, performing in Wichita, Nickerson, Strong City, Cottonwood Falls, Osage City, Carbondale,[56] and by December have reached Missouri.[57] We know that in early September David was in Colorado and at the end of the month in Albuquerque, so this Bosco with Simons is Louis. However, in the following and subsequent years the evidence points to Simons being with David Hyam.

In 1885 "Signor Bosco" in the west is David Hyam and his namesake in the east is Louis. In March 1885 when David Hyam was in Montana, Louis was in Vermont. His advertising is very similar to David's, both using the phrases "Original and Only Signor Bosco" and "Enchanted Palace of Illusions". In Guildhall, Vermont, Louis's ad reads: "Grand Appearance of the Original and Only Signor Bosco, The Greatest Wonder of his Age, who will open his Enchanted Palace of Illusion..."; the newspaper describes him as "Austrian" and his wife as "a refined English lady, so there is no doubt as to his identity.[58]

"Signor Bosco ... in his Enchanted Palace of Illusion" in Oakland in 1885 is probably David as he was touring California later that year, now advertising "Monster Gift Concerts". In late 1885 the *Clipper* again reported there were "two Signors Bosco", one in the far west "who came here from England ten years ago" (David) and one, L. Bosco, touring Maine, whose agent is J.H. Hewett.[59] In December to avoid confusion the *Clipper* resumed its policy of designating one as Sig. L. Bosco (who it pointed out was ill in Dover, Maine) and the other as Sig. D. Bosco, still in the far west.[60]

Louis's long tour of Maine continued into June 1886,[61] then several months in Canada.[62] He was in Quebec in early September, then it also seems to be him 4,500 km west in British Columbia by September 25th — possible as the Canadian Pacific Railway was now completed.

In May 1889 Louis is touring Kansas, still with Hewett as agent,[63] but when Hewett arrived in Joplin, Kansas, he "was much chagrined to learn that a spurious 'Bosco' had been there only last week. Mr Hewett has been agent for Bosco for nine years. Several times within the past year the impostor 'Bosco' has dropped in their route to realize on the reputation of Bosco ... Mr Hewett was justly indignant at the repetition of this dishonest trick". But the following week the paper received a letter from the "spurious" Bosco stating that he was the genuine article and "the other Bosco is a fraud and dissembler"... so "if Bosco isn't Bosco who the devil is Bosco?".[64]

The rival was not David, for he was not on the road at this time, but taking a "much needed rest" at home in Buffalo".[65]

A Signor Bosco appearing in Kearney, Nebraska, in January 1890 quotes testimonials for shows in Dublin in 1862 and before the Prince of Wales at Curragh Camp in 1868 [*i.e.* 1862], which was Louis — David and Louis may have copied each other's advertising but there is no evidence that David stole any of Louis's testimonial claims.

Sig. L. Bosco is listed as in Alberquerque in March 1890, so probably also him in Santa Fe in April 1890.[66] Then in May 1890 in San Bernardino L. Bosco is listed as staying at the Stewart Hotel, with Mrs Bosco, Miss L. Bosco (daughter Lillian), and two days earlier arrived Henry Bosco, Louis's son now in his 20s, "advance agent of the weird and wondrous magician 'Bosco' ... the modern Faust...".[67] In June 1890 they are in Los Angeles, in August in Folsom ("The Greatest of All Magicians in His Palace of Illusions and Gift Entertainment, 100 beautiful and Costly Presents given away nightly..."); then on through Nevada in September and October (following David's route in 1886); in Elko, Nevada, in October 1890 he bills himself as "the original and only Signor Bosco, The Greatest Wonder of the Age, Who will open his Enchanted Palace of Illusions, and will introduce his new and original entertainment, entitled 'Magic', As performed by him over three hundred consecutive nights at Egyptian Hall, London Eng. ... The Royal Magician". [68] He was then in Utah until February 1891, [69] probably him in Minnesota in April,[70] and in North Dakota in May.

He was back on the road later in the year, and Louis is probably the "Signor Bosco" in Chicago in December 1891 offering testimonials from the Prince of Wales and Charles Dudley Warner. He quotes Warner's commendation in his advertising regularly (from Nevada in 1891 to Carmel, N.Y. in 1894): "Our party saw Signor Bosco's performance last night with a great deal of pleasure, not less on account of his dexterity than his genial wit and agreeable manner. May 23 1890".

David was also touring under the same name, but in Shreveport, Louisiana, in February 1894 we hear of Harry Bosco, advance agent, so this is Louis and his son. And probably him again, citing Warner, in Putnam, New York, in 1894. Louis is touring Alabama late 1895 to early 1896, and in Buffalo and area later in 1896, accompanied by son Harry and a boy named Victor or Victor Leon, "clever in his imitation of a phonograph". In December 1896 Victor Leon, "the ten-year-old phonograph imitation prodigy" and the "Bosco Troupe", including "Bosco" and "Mrs Bosco" are in Kentucky. "Signor L. Bosco" was in Pittsburgh, Kansas, with the Bosco Troupe and Victor Leon, also known as "Bosco, Junior" in July 1897. There the boy "gave them the slip", but rejoined them later as their tour continued through Kansas, Nebraska and South and North Dakota. Then we are told that the boy's real name was W.J. Ross: he had run away from home about 1894 and the following year "he fell in with professor Bosco, who … took him under his wing… and taught him to sing and dance and play the banjo".[71] Meanwhile another Signor Bosco, presumably David, was performing in Buffalo.

In 1897 Louis in Mount Morris, N.Y., advertises as "the great French Prestidigitator", with "his unique, refined, amusing and instructive entertainment, entitled Magic … new and entirely on the Indian and Egyptian Principles…"; he refers to his testimonials from the Prince of Wales, Prince Alfred, and the Duchess of Beaufort, dating back to 1860, with a long list of his tricks.[72]

In August 1898 Louis, his wife and son were travelling from Rapid City to Keystone, South Dakota, when their carriage overturned. His wife was injured and they decided to go back; soon afterwards the dray carrying all their luggage met the same fate… How soon they can resume their tour is unknown, said the *Rapid City Journal*.[73]

In late 1899 and early 1900 Louis, still touring, is in Reynoldsville, Pa.,[74] his act billed as all "on the Indian and Egyptian principles", and still with plate-spinning.

A Bosco performed for three nights in La Plata, Missouri, in May 1901, possibly a last sighting of Louis, though it could be David (but he had by then probably turned to theatrical management) — or another Bosco altogether, as the local paper summed up the show as "a snide affair".[75]

Louis died in Buffalo on November 18th 1908[76] and was buried there in Forest Lawn Cemetery; his gravestone reads "Father / 1836-1908". His wife Annie and the children Flora, Jacob and Sidonie are buried nearby.

NOTES

[1] Details of his family are at Dan Hirschberg's Kraków site (url:154), and also on *https://www.jewishgen.org*. In the US censuses he gives his birthplace as Austria, in which Kraków was incorporated 1846-1918. His exact birthdate is from a family tree on *ancestry.com* (url:155), and probably from family information.

[2] Reference HO 1/155/6149 (digitised on *www.ancestry.com*).

[3] "Enchanted Place of Illusions(s)" was used in England from 1859 by Herr Dobler (*Oxford University and City Herald* 12 Feb.1859, etc.), taken over by Warszawski the following year (*Beverley Guardian* 19 May 1860, etc.) then by Louis, and by Leotard Bosco and his wife (see *Appendix Z2: Bill Matter*), and also used in Great Britain in the 1860s by Herr Herrmann, Professor Devono, Mons. Luigi Hiodini, and others — and by several Boscos (and others) in America.

[4] The tag "The Polish Wizard" was also used by Orginski Rosenfeld who performed in Britain from 1846 to his death in 1869: he was "The Polish Wizard" to at least June 1854, then "The Polish Necromancer".

[5] Unless he was the "Signor Bosco" who failed miserably in Chepstow in September 1857, saying, when it was found he was not Epstein, that he was not the "Italian Bosco" but the "Polish Bosco" (*Chepstow Weekly Advertiser* 19 Sep.1857). However this may have been Warszawski or even Millar. There is also a reference to him (not confirmed) performing in Bristol in 1857 (see p.295 above and note 15).

[6] *Portsmouth Times* 3 Apr.1858.

[7] For this Dobler see *Appendix Z5*.

[8] *Maidstone Journal* 9 Oct.1858.

[9] *Bridgwater Mercury* 22 June 1859.

[10] 'Transactions of the Sabine Baring-Gould Appreciation Society, Volume 8 (2008)', url:156.

[11] Although not noted by the *OED* there are abundant examples in English newspapers of 'delf' used in the sense of 'delft', and this refers to his plate-spinning. In 1861 a reviewer noted: "he made sundry dishes perform wonderful gyrations" (note 16). He was still doing this act in 1874 ("Chinese plate-spinning": *Lancaster Gazette* 14 Mar.1874), and still using the phrase "enchanted delf" in America in 1879 (note 48).

[12] *Tavistock Gazette* 19 Aug.1859.

[13] *North Devon Journal* 16 Feb.1860.

[14] *Bristol Daily Post* 16 May 1860.

[15] *Stroud Journal* 28 July 1860.

[16] *Southern Reporter and Cork Commercial Courier* 5 Feb.1861. The Houdini Scrapbook in the Harry Ransom Center has a poster of Louis performing in Cork on February 8th and 9th [1861], url:157.

[17] *Tralee Chronicle* 22 Mar.1861.

[18] "His Royal Highness expressed himself greatly pleased with the performance and signified his intention of presenting Signor L. Bosco with a testimonial": *Kearney Daily Hub* (Kearney, Nebraska) 30 Dec.1889.

[19] Louis years later stated in an advertisement: "In consequence of some unprincipled person having in several towns represented himself as Signor Bosco, S.B. begs to draw public attention to his testimonials which he publishes in his programme, especially those of H.R.H. the Prince of Wales, H.R.H. Prince Alfred, which no one else dare copy under penalty" (*Rochdale Observer* 16 Mar.1867) — all to no effect. He was still quoting Prince Alfred's testimonial in America in 1897.

[20] The Houdini Scrapbook in the Harry Ransom Center includes posters of "Signor Bosco" performing in Royston and Fakenham on November 7th and 25th 1864. These are both Louis (url:158).

[21] Harry was for a period his father's advance agent but became an investment broker; he married in Ohio in 1900 and died there in 1922; Flora became a nurse and died in Hamburg, New York, in 1930; Lillian, who married Dr Colfax Long, then after his early death, Albert Dodge, died in 1927; Sidonie was a teacher in Catholic schools and died in Buffalo in 1944; Albert was an engineer in the US Army; Miriam married

first Abraham Bluestein in 1907, then in 1928 Albert Dodge, widower of her sister Lillian.

[22] *Leamington Spa Courier* 20, 27 Jan.1866.
[23] *Cheltenham Looker-On* 3 Dec.1870).
[24] *Bristol Daily Post* 27, 29 Dec.1870.
[25] *Bristol Mercury* 31 Dec.1870.
[26] *West Middlesex Herald* 21 Jan.1871.
[27] *Glossopdale Chronicle and North Derbyshire Reporter* 4 Mar.1871.
[28] The Harry Ransom Center has a poster and a handbill for these two performances (url:159).
[29] *Tadcaster Post* 14 Mar.1871.
[30] *Manchester Guardian* 22 Jan.1873.
[31] *Lancaster Gazette* 6 April 1872.
[32] *Jackson's Oxford Journal* 2, 9 Nov.1872.
[33] *Devizes and Wiltshire Gazette* 7 Nov.1872.
[34] *Era* 26 Oct.1873.
[35] *Richmond & Ripon Chronicle* 12 Sep.1874.
[36] *Knaresborough Post* 19 Sep.1874. The *Ripon Chronicle* refused to print his reply, stating (19 Sep.1874): "Louis Bosco — We cannot admit the controversy to our columns".
[37] *Wigton Advertiser* 20 Mar.1875.
[38] *Galena Daily Gazette* 5, 7, 8, 12 Apr.1876. Among his tricks are listed "The Enchanted Sword, the Shower of Gold, the Globe of Fire", all featured by Louis in his performances in Britain. He has an advance agent, T.K. Burke.
[39] *Henry Republican* 17 Feb.1876; *New York Clipper* 11 Mar., 1 Apr.1876.
[40] *New York Clipper* 22 Apr.1876.
[41] *Chicago Tribune* 7 May 1876: "Signor Bosco, a star representative of the legerdemain fraternity, opened his series of entertainments at Kimball Hall, Thursday night, to a slim house … As a magician Signor Bosco is unrivaled in his specialties … the globe of fire and shower of gold were among the best of his performances".
[42] *Galena Daily Gazette* 27 May 1876, quoting "Brick Pomeroy's Democrat", and adding: "The Sandusky Register is less mild, and says that the signor is — well no matter. The appellation is by no means complimentary".
[43] *Cazenovia Republican* 24 May 1877.
[44] *Rome Sentinel* 12 June 1877.
[45] *Cobleskill Index* 19 Aug.1877.
[46] *Groton Journal* 11 Apr.1878.
[47] *Camden Advance* 5 Sep.1878; in the 1880 census he gives his birthplace as Austria, see note 1). The *Rome Sentinel,* which had been so hostile to him the previous year, said (10 Sep.1878): "Signor Bosco, a sleight-of-hand gift show performer, was very poorly patronized in Camden recently, and left the town in disgust".
[48] *New York Clipper* 23, 30 Aug.1879.
[49] *New York Clipper* 30 Aug.; 6 Sep.1879.
[50] *New York Clipper* 13 Sep.1879. He was still in Ontario in November (*New York Clipper* 15, 22 Nov.1879).

[51] *St. Albans Daily Messenger* 5 Feb.1880; *Vermont Christian Messenger* 5 Feb.1880; *New York Clipper* 7 Feb.1880; *Vermont Standard* 19 Feb.1880 ("we have no sympathy for these humbugs").

[52] *New York Clipper* 19 June 1880.

[53] *Friendship Register* 16 Sep.1880.

[54] Brother of comedian Jake Simons.

[55] *Ottawa Daily Republic* 5, 16 May 1882; *Oswego Daily Republican* 24 May 1882; and *The Daily Eclipse* (Parsons, Kansas) 15 June 1882 reports staying at an Oswego Hotel "Signor and Madam Bosco and Mr C. Fox, pianist, J. Simons, advance agent, and Mr. C.G. Earnest, assistant agent". Simmons was also in Warrensburg, Missouri, in May, "advance agent for Boscoe, the Illusionist ... but failed to secure dates": *The Journal-Democrat* 5 May 1882.

[56] *Wichita Daily Times* 14 Sep.1882; *Wichita Weekly Beacon* 20 Sep.1882 ("pretty good houses"); *Nickerson Argosy* 27 Sep.1882; *Chase County Leader* 28 Sep.1882 ("...to say that his performance was meritorious is the least that can be said..."); *The News-Courant* 28 Sep., 5 Oct.1882; *Strong City Independent* 29 Sep.1882 ("crowded house"); *Osage City Free Press* 5 Oct.1882; *Carbondale Independent* 19 Oct.1882.

[57] *Fulton Gazette* 1 Dec.1882.

[58] *Essex County Herald* 20, 27 Mar.1885.

[59] *New York Clipper* 24 Oct.1885. *The Somerset Reporter* (Skowhegan, Maine) 11 Nov.1885: "Grand Appearance of the Original and Only Signor Bosco ... In his Enchanted Palace of Illusions ... I.H. Hewitt, Agent".

[60] *New York Clipper* 5 Dec.1885.

[61] *New York Clipper* 22 May, 29 May, 12 June 1886.

[62] *New York Clipper* 10 July 1886 (Truro, Nova Scotia); 28 Aug.1886 (Sherbrooke, Quebec); 4 Sep.1886 (Drummondville, Quebec).

[63] *Galena Weekly Republican* 4 May 1889; *The Smelter* (Pittsburg, Kansas) 4 May 1889; *Parsons Daily Sun* 10 May 1889.

[64] *The Smelter* (Pittsburg, Kansas) 10, 17 May 1889 (both quoting the *Joplin Herald*).

[65] *New York Clipper* 6 Apr.1889.

[66] *Santa Fe Daily New Mexican* 31 Mar., 3 Apr.1890 ("...the audience was large, and there was great sport when it came to the distribution of presents").

[67] *San Bernardino Daily Courier* 8, 10 May 1890.

[68] *Daily Independent* 14 Oct.1890; same ad. in *The Daily Appeal* (Carson City, Nevada) 7 Oct.1890. Claims of long runs at Egyptian Hall were now a cliché in magicians' advertising. In 1891 in North Dakota Louis claims 300 nights at Egyptian Hall and 200 nights in New York (*Dickinson Press* 23 May 1891).

[69] *Salt Lake Herald* 2 Nov.1890; *Iron County News* 3 Jan.1891; *Salt Lake Tribune* 21 Feb.1891.

[70] *Buffalo Morning Express* 3 Apr.1891; *NY Clipper* 4 Apr.1891 ("dangerously ill")

[71] *Omaha Daily Bee* 26 Aug.1898.

[72] *Mount Morris Union* 16 Sep.1897.

[73] *Rapid City Journal* 4 Aug.1898.

[74] *The Star* 6 Dec.1899; 12 Jan.1900.

[75] *La Plata Home Press* 23, 30 May 1901.

[76] Death notice *Buffalo Courier* 19 Nov.1908, giving his age as 72.

B66. David Hyam, 1843-1914

David Hyam(s), brother of Louis Susser's wife Annie (Hannah) Hyam, performed as "Signor Bosco" in America from the early 1870s.

He was born in Newport on the Isle of Wight in 1843 to Hyman (Henry) Wolf Hyam (born in Kraków in 1816) and his wife Amelia (Julia), née Lazarus, who married in Portsea in 1840. There is no definite evidence of him performing as a magician in Britain before he left for America, but it is hard to believe he did not do so, and it is likely he learnt from Louis who had been performing for at least seven years when he married David's sister in 1865. In an 1885 interview (below) David said he had been on the road for seventeen years, which, if correct, would mean two or three years performing in Britain before he left. In Edinburgh in May 1868 a review[1] praises Louis's "most wonderful tricks ... which are so cleverly executed by himself and assistant", but there is no proof that the assistant was David. It is quite possible that David was briefly one of the several "Signor Boscos" in England in the late 1860s but, again, there is no confirming evidence.

In the 1851 census he is living with his parents in Portsea; in 1861 the same, now listed as an auctioneer's assistant; in 1871 he is unmarried and "dealer in fancy goods" (but that is the profession Louis also gives that year, and he had been a magician for more than ten years); David in 1871 was living with his mother and sister Kate at 60 Chorlton Rd, Manchester (Louis Susser and Annie were living at no.63).

By 1877 he was resident in Buffalo, New York, listed as a travel agent in the city directory, living at 110 Delaware Street with his parents, and Louis and Annie are a few streets away. In the 1880 U.S. census, taken on June 11th, he is living in Buffalo with his parents; he now has a wife Sarah and a stepson Harold Adlauff and is listed as a "Magician". In Buffalo directories from 1888 to 1893 he is living at 365 Niagara Street with his mother and sister. His father died in 1881 and his mother in 1896. David's wife Sarah died in 1909 and in the 1910 census he is living on his own in Buffalo, "theatrical book keeper", and he is on his own in the 1913 directory.

A death notice in the *Buffalo Times* 30 Nov.1914 describes him as "a well-known theatrical manager ... For many years Mr Hyam was a manager of several theatrical enterprises, but more recently he had been associated with 'The Times' [the Buffalo newspaper]..."

In the 1880 U.S. census he says he has been in America since 1870, but he must have arrived a little later as he was still in England in the 1871 census.

An interesting interview with David when he was on tour in California in 1885[2] speaks highly of his act — "...His tricks all bear the stamp of originality and are cleverly done. He does not use much paraphernalia, but does his tricks in plain sight of the audience. He is assisted by Prof. Hillyer, a ventriloquist. The prizes are of a better quality than those usually given by traveling shows". It states that he has been on the road for seventeen years and has played before three million people. His present trip began in Florida, but each year he travels through a different part of the country. His home is in Rochester, N.Y., but "he prefers to live in California near the coast". He then volunteers some biographical information: born in Portsmouth, England, and "was intended for the English navy, in which his brother is now a

Lieutenant", and, we are told, David left the navy when drawn to his present profession. Needless to say there is no record of David or a brother serving in the Royal Navy.

I believe this is David in Haverstraw, N.Y., on the Hudson River, in early October 1873 and, if so, it is the earliest record found of him performing in America:[3] "Signor Bosco, the renowned Magician has been giving a series of amusing entertainments in Swift's Hall during the last week. The feats of Legerdemain are new and wonderful, and the Signor is said to be the best performer that has ever visited the town. The audience being highly entertained and convulsed with laughter. The large number of beautiful presents which he has nightly given away, has been an additional attraction".[4] Soon after this he is in nearby Cold Spring on October 17th, 18th, and 20th: "Grand Appearance of the Original and Only Sig. Bosco, who will open his enchanted palace of illusion and give Three Monster Gift Nights…";[5] then at the end of the month in Nyack,[6] and still in New York state, in Sing Sing, in December that year.[7] Subsequent advertisements over many years referring to "the Original and Only Sig. Bosco" are not necessarily him as Louis also used the phrase, but David appears to be the "Sig. Bosco" often described as genial and known for his wit.

It is probably David as "Sig. Bosco" in Waterloo, N.Y., in May 1874: "…He is considered the greatest Wizard, Wit, Humorist and Illusionist of the age. His entertainment is moral and intellectual. He also gave away a large number of useful and costly presents…";[8] and, still in the same area in August that year, in Springville and Cattaraugus.[9]

In early 1875 he was in Canada — in February "Prof. Anderson[10] and Bosco, both wizards, are showing in opposition to each other in the small towns of Canada"; in April "Signor Bosco, wizard, with gift show, performed at Paris, Ont. … Dundas … Hamilton";[11] then later that year in U.S.A. — in May "Signor Bosco, wizard, with gift-show, was at Modina, N.Y. … Brockport …Albion"; and in August "Signor Bosco, wizard, with gift-show, performed in Petrolia, Pa. …Karns City … and is billed at Millerstown … Titusville…", and "The new opera-house, Millerstown, Pa. … was opened on Aug.13 by Signor Bosco, wizard … Bosco performed at Butler … Kittaning …Rouseville…".[12] He was in Pennsylvania until September — "Grand appearance of the Original and Only Signor Bosco … nightly in his Enchanted Palace of Illusions … Selden Hillyer, agent"[13] in Clearfield, and "Signor Bosco, the wizard, performed in Brookville, Pa. … Reynoldsville … and will show at Clifton …".[14] In October he was in New Jersey — "Grand appearance of the Original and Only Signor Bosco …" [etc.] in Freehold;[15] then in November touring widely in Michigan;[16] and December in Indiana.[17]

The above are surely all David, but by early 1876 similar notices in the *Clipper* and in local papers can equally refer to Louis who probably arrived in America about October 1875[18] and was touring Illinois in early 1876. For example, the Sig. Bosco in Michigan in January 1876 could be either of them.[19]

David is found touring Pennsylvania in 1877-78, opening his "fifth annual tour" in July, and his advance agent is C. Fox,[20] and we know he was in Harrisburg, Pa., on December 19th 1877, as he recalled this when back in Harrisburg in 1905 (below).

As detailed in the entry for Louis, the *New York Clipper* published a complaint from David in 1879 that "some magician, who had assumed his name, is now playing in Canada", the *Clipper* then stating that it had received a letter from L. Bosco in St. Marys, Ontario, enclosing programmes for shows by him in England and Scotland. The *Clipper* suggested each use an initial or first name to distinguish them. When this did not happen the *Clipper* then designated the Bosco in Ontario "Signor L. Bosco" and the other, currently touring Ohio, as "Signor D. Bosco"; Louis now advertised: "Sig. L. Bosco, Wizard, Claims to be the Original of that Name".[21] It is hard to believe this was not contrived for publicity by the brothers-in-law, whose families were living a few streets apart in Buffalo.

It is probably David touring Indiana in early 1879, "the renowned wizard, wit and humorist".[22] We know he was in Ohio in late 1879 from the *Clipper* statement above, so probably also him in Ohio in June that year[23] and in West Virginia,[24] and back in Ohio in September.[25]

He was in Pennsylvania in late 1880,[26] where he fell foul of one particular newspaper, *The Indiana Progress* —

> Bosco, advertising himself as the greatest wizard, wit and illusionist in the world, performed in this place on Friday and Saturday nights of last week and Monday night of this week… we cannot resist the opportunity of saying something — for the benefit of communities they may visit in future. We say to such that in patronizing this fellow they are giving countenance to a humbug of the first class, as well as a liar, a cheat, and a swindler. His tricks are of the most common description, while he advertises impossible feats. He promises to give away silver ice-pitchers, gold and silver watches, lace shawls, sets of furniture, etc. But the car containing the furniture and shawls never arrived, while the watches, which were displayed on the stage, left this place with him. He gave away a few cheap articles… Our brethren of the press will favor their readers by advising them to attend Bosco's entertainment if they wish to be thoroughly swindled, supremely disgusted and hear some execrable English roll from the mouth of this charlatan…

and the paper tracked him as he toured on —

> Bosco, the miserable illusionist, visited Tionesta, Forest county, but found that the people took no stock of such humbugs, and failing in two nights to get an audience to his taste, he lit out for more verdant pastures[27]

We know that he was in Michigan in early 1881 as when his father died in February that year he fell down the stairs in a hotel in Blissfield, Michigan, and was said to be accompanying his son on his tour.[28] David was still in Michigan in June,[29] and later in South Bend, Indiana.[30]

By July he was in Wisconsin;[31] September in Michigan;[32] and by November again touring Pennsylvania. We know he was in Hazleton, Pa., on November 24, 25, 26 1881 (he said this when back there in 1905, below). and he is the Bosco in various Pennsylvania ads around that date,[33] billing himself as "the Only Original Signor Bosco, the World Renowned Wizard, Wit and Humorist. One Hundred Large and Costly Presents will be Given Away Nightly"; one review said of him: "the hall has been crowded to overflowing each evening of his appearance, and his sleight-of-hand tricks and magic wonders were far ahead of any performance of the kind ever before presented to our people, and gave universal satisfaction".[34]

In August and September 1882 David, preceded by advance agent W.C. Waite, is in Colorado, sighted in Fort Collins, Golden City, then in Boulder, and at the end of the month he is in Albuquerque.[35]

We next see him in February 1883 in North Carolina,[36] and South Carolina.[37] By March he is in Virginia, and heading for Tennessee,[38] in April in Alabama,[39] then due in Asheville and Salisbury, N.C., "and there close his season. He expects to reopen in Wilmington, Del., May 1".[40] In July 1883 he reached Sharon, Pa.[41] and it may be David in Howell, Michigan, in September.[42]

In May 1884 David is reported as closing "a successful season of forty-eight weeks in Richmond, Va., May 30".[43] This points to him being the Signor Bosco with Simons as advance agent in April 1884 in Charlotte, N.C., despite this being described as "his first visit South", adding "there is no fraud about him. He is the one and only original Bosco;"[44] and also him back in Charlotte in May,[45] and performing in Richmond, Va., May 22nd-24th — "Signor Bosco's Enchanted Palace, commencing Thursday night, Signor Bosco, assisted by Professor J. Simons...", said to be his first appearance in Richmond.[46]

Then in early 1885 it is probably him in Miles City, Montana, and recently in Fargo and Bismark, N.D., travelling with "Prof. Hilliard, who will introduce his happy family of marionets".[47] Soon after he is in Livingston, Montana (recently in Jamestown, N.D.), preceded by "Joe. Simmons, advance agent";[48] and still in Montana in March, sighted in Butte.[49]

A Signor Bosco with "J. Simons" as business manager in Sacramento in July 1885 is certainly him,[50] as we know David was in California in late 1885 from the interview in Santa Cruz in October; so he is likely also the "Signor Bosco ... in his Enchanted Palace of Illusion" in Oakland in July 1885, and then in Cloverdale in November, Folsom in December, and Rocklin in February 1886.[51]

This accords with the statements in the *Clipper* in late 1885[52] that there were "two Signors Bosco", one in the far west "who came here from England ten years ago" and one, L. Bosco, touring Maine.

In early 1886 Louis is still in Maine and David now in Nevada and Utah. Nevada audiences were good in the large towns,[53] but they toured far and wide. A report from Sierra City, where they performed in April, sums up: "Signor Bosco and his party are playing the mining-towns between Nevada City and Truckee, covering an overland line of one hundred and forty miles. While on their way here, between Forest City and Downierville, their sleigh was overturned on the mountains, the roads of which have been in a terrible condition. The party escaped serious injury, but were well shaken up and scared. Mrs. Bosco just missed fracturing her skull by contact with a rock.[54]

In Ogden, Utah, we hear that he "executed some very pleasant and dexterous tricks" but "his audience was very small". On the second night he announced gifts for all and a dance to follow with prizes for the best dancers. He was still in Utah in July.[55]

Finally he announced the end of his epic journey, his "Fifteenth Season ... One hundred and twenty-five consecutive weeks, from Tampa, Florida, to Portland, Oregon; from San Francisco to New York — twenty-seven thousand miles. Will close season July 24. Successful everywhere".[56]

He continued performing for several years before turning to theatrical management. In Knapp, Wisconsin, on January 26th 1891 David lost all his apparatus (worth over $1000) and almost his life when Place's Hall caught fire soon after his performance.[57]

In Shreveport, Louisiana, in February 1894 we hear of Harry Bosco, advance agent, but this was probably Louis's son (born 1866) rather than David's step-son (born *ca.*1868).

David then made a long tour of Mexico and Texas in 1896, and it is probably him in Wisconsin in 1899 — "Prof. Bosco, the great magician, for twenty years the Michigan and Wisconsin favorite showman, manager and entertainer, will play a three nights' engagement at Pierce's Opera House ... Speaking of him the *Ashland Daily News* of February 22nd says: 'Prof. Bosco, who appeared here in 1884, 1887, and 1892, appeared here ... last night ... to a packed house and standing room only. The performance was refined, clever and amusing. Bosco, with his wonderful deception and wit and humor kept the large audience in almost a continuous roar of laughter throughout...'".[58]

An ad in Maryville, Missouri, in April 1901 bills "Prof. Bosco, the celebrated Magician and World's 'King of Fun Makers'", announced as on "his farewell tour of the West, being his 27th year",[59] which sounds very like the swan-song of David as a touring magician. Nearby in La Plata, Missouri, the following month we find a Bosco performing ("many useful presents") but his shows were described as "a snide affair": a shame if that is the last we hear of David performing.[60]

In 1905 David was now a theatrical agent and on the road as "advance representative of the Fays" travelling in their medium act. We catch sight of him in March in Hazleton, Pa., recalling his performances there in 1881 when "he was a famed magician and traveled under the name of Signor Bosco";[61] later that month in Wilkes-Barre, Pa., he described recently piloting the Fays round Mexico, saying it was his first trip there.[62] In May he was in Harrisburg, Pa., where he had performed in 1877 — "years ago he was one of the most successful and widely-known wizards on the stage, his stage name being Signor Bosco".[63] By September he was in Kansas with the Fays, saying he had been in England in the interim and had received a cablegram to return to America: he left Liverpool on September 15th, reached New York on 23rd, Boston on 24th, Syracuse on 25th, Chicago on 26th, Davenport on 27th, and Topeka on the morning of the 28th: "about 4,000 miles in 13 days".[64]

David died suddenly in Buffalo on November 29th 1914 and is buried there.

NOTES
[1] *Edinburgh Evening Courant* 29 May 1868.
[2] *Santa Cruz Sentinel* 8 Oct.1885.
[3] Not necessarily, of course, his very first performance there, but this date fits well with the report in July 1877 that he is "now on his fifth annual tour" (*New York Clipper* 14 July 1877). However he called a tour ending in July 1886 his "Fifteenth Season" (below). An advertisement in April 1901 announces "his farewell tour of the West, being his 27th year".
[4] *Rockland County Messenger* 2, 9 Oct.1873 (the third sentence, with no main verb, seeming a deliberate attempt at lively journalese).

[5] *Cold Spring Recorder* 18 Oct.1873.
[6] *Rockland County Journal* 1 Nov.1873.
[7] *The Republican* 18 Dec.1873 (the same wording: "Grand Appearance of the Original and Only Sig. Bosco, who will open his enchanted palace of illusion…").
[8] *Waterloo Observer* 13 May 1874.
[9] *Springville Journal* 8 Aug.1874; *Cattaraugus Republican* 27 Aug.1874.
[10] John Henry Anderson, the son, 1843-1878.
[11] *New York Clipper* 13 Feb., 17 Apr.1875.
[12] *New York Clipper* 22 May; 14, 28 Aug.1875.
[13] Hillyer was with him for many years — a note in the *Clipper* 13 Mar.1886 states: "Prof. S. Hillyer says he will quit Sig. Bosco about March 20 to return to his Pennsylvania farm…", but David had a different agent named C. Fox in 1877-8.
[14] *Clearfield Republican* 8 Sep.1875; *New York Clipper* 11 Sep.1875/
[15] *The Monmouth Inquirer* 7 Oct.1875.
[16] *New York Clipper* 6, 13, 27 Nov.1875; *Hillsdale Standard* 16, 24 Nov.1875. He was not well received by the locals in Pontiac: *Pontiac Weekly Gazette* 5, 12 Nov. 1875; *Pontiac Weekly Bill Poster* 24 Nov.1875.
[17] *New York Clipper* 11, 25 Dec.1875.
[18] See B65 p.299.
[19] *New York Clipper* 15, 22 Jan.1876.
[20] *New York Clipper* 14 July; 25 Aug.; 1 Sep.; 24 Nov.; 22 Dec.1877; 5 Jan.; 13 Apr. 1878. A "C. Fox" is with Louis in 1882 but as pianist, not advance agent.
[21] See B65 pp.299-300.
[22] *The South Bend Tribune* 6 Feb.1879; *New York Clipper* 1 Mar.1879 (in Ligonier and La Porte, Ind.).
[23] *Belmont Chronicle* 5 June 1879 ("…his performance was rather tame in some respects"); *New York Clipper* 14 June 1879 (in Cadiz).
[24] *The Wheeling Daily Intelligencer* 19 June 1879.
[25] *New York Clipper* 20 Sep.1879: "Signor D. Bosco, magician is to exhibit in Burton, O., … and Cuyahoga Falls…"
[26] *New York Clipper* 30 Oct.1880 ("Signor D. Bosco, magician" recently in Dubois and Kittaning).
[27] *The Indiana Progress* (Indiana, Pa.) 4 Nov., 2 Dec.1880.
[28] *New York Clipper* 5 Mar.1881.
[29] *New York Clipper* 18 June 1881 ("Signor D. Bosco" due in Hancock, Houghton, Calumet); and also him earlier that month, "The Signor Bosco Troupe, magician, ventriloquist and grotesque specialty people … showing to reported large business in the Lake Superior copper country": *New York Clipper* 4 June 1881.
[30] "Signor Bosco, the world-renowned Wizard, Wit, Humorist", preceded by agent "Mr S.M. Hillyer": *The South Bend Tribune* 6, 8 June 1881.
[31] *Green Bay Press-Gazette* 13, 16, 18, 19 July 1881 (a full house on a very hot night); *New York Clipper* 13 Aug.1881: "Signor D. Bosco, magician, who will not close his season this year, is due in Warsaw … Jenny…".
[32] *New York Clipper* 10 Sep.1881.

[33] *Wyoming Democrat* (Tunkhannock, Pa.) 4 Nov.1881; *The York Daily* (York, Pa.) 21 Nov.1881 …
[34] *The York Dispatch* 19 Nov.1881.
[35] *Fort Collins Coloradoan* 29 July, 1 Aug.1882 ("The Signor Bosco troupe has arrived…");*The Daily Express* (Fort Collins, Co.) 1, 2 Aug.1882; *New York Clipper* 2, 30 Sep.1882.
[36] *Goldsboro Messenger* 1, 5 Feb.1883 (both the performance and the presents warmly reviewed). In Fayettesville, as well as gifts, a silver cup was awarded to "the most beautiful lady in the hall"; a committee (of three men) choosing "a piquant, charming brunette" (*Fayetteville Weekly Observer* 22 Feb.1883).
[37] *Sumter Watchman and Southron* 20 Feb.1883 ("Grand Appearance of the Only Original SIGNOR BOSCO. The World Renowned WIZARD, WIT AND HUMORIST…"; *The Times and Democrat* (Orangeburg, SC) 1 Mar.1883: "a gala week with Bosco the magician, and the Wizard Oil Company, who give day and night open air concerts".
[38] *New York Clipper* 31 Mar.1883.
[39] *The Opelika Times* 6 Apr.1883; *Union Springs Herald* 11 Apr.1883 (but cancelled there).
[40] *New York Clipper* 21 Apr.1883.
[41] *New York Clipper* 7 July 1883.
[42] *Livingston County Daily Press and Argus* 6 Sep.1883.
[43] *New York Clipper* 31 May 1884.
[44] *The Charlotte Observer* 25 Apr.1884.
[45] *The Charlotte Observer* 20 May 1884 ("return engagement").
[46] *Daily Dispatch* 21 May 1884.
[47] *Daily Yellowstone Journal* 17 Feb.1885.
[48] *The Livingston Enterprise* 21 Feb.1885.
[49] *The Semi-Weekly Miner* 18 Mar.1885.
[50] *Sacramento Daily Record* 6 July 1885.
[51] *Oakland Tribune* 28 July 1885; *Cloverdale Reveille* 21 Nov.1885; *The Folsom Telegraph* 5 Dec.1885; *The Placer Herald* 20 Feb.1886;
[52] *New York Clipper* 24 Oct.; 5 Dec.1885.
[53] *The Daily Appeal* (Carson City, Nevada) 14 Apr.1886; *Reno Gazette-Journal* 14 Apr.1886; *The Silver State* (Unionville, Nevada) 23 Apr.1886.
[54] *New York Clipper* 17 Apr.; 22 May 1886.
[55] *Ogden Standard* 5 May 1886; *New York Clipper* 10 July 1886.
[56] *New York Clipper* 24 July 1886.
[57] Reported in his hometown newspaper: *Buffalo Evening News* 10 Feb.1891.
[58] *Iron County Republican* (Hurley, Wisconsin) 30 Sep.1899.
[59] *Maryville Republican* 11 Apr.1901.
[60] *La Plata Home Press* 23, 30 May 1901. But this could be Louis — or some other unidentified 'Bosco'.
[61] *The Plain Speaker* (Hazleton, Pa.), 4 Mar.1905.
[62] *Wilkes-Barre Times* 24 Mar.1905.
[63] *Harrisburg Daily Independent* 4 May 1905.
[64] *The Topeka Daily Capital* 29 Sep.1905.

B67. Hermann Bosco, active London 1863

Found twice in December 1863, advertising as "Europe's Greatest Magician", not performing but advertising magical apparatus for sale in *Lloyd's Weekly Newspaper.* He is unlikely to be one of the well-known *Hermanns* and the name is clearly a pseudonym; his address is 2a Upper Church St, Chelsea, but I cannot trace who lived at that address.

On December 13th he offers "the complete apparatus for 8, and directions for 16, wonderful Magical tricks" and the same the next week, specifying them as "Beheaded Birds Alive Again, A Snake out of a Stick … Fortune-Telling Cards…" [etc.]

B68. "Brothers Bosco of Poland"

On February 24th 1863 there was a show in Glasgow for "the Catholics of Edinburgh" by "the Brothers Bosco of Poland, entitled 'Natural Magic'" (*Glasgow Free Press* 28 Feb.1863).

This may have been Saul Warschawski who was in Scotland at the time, possibly with the partner (B63a) he tried to pass off as himself in Broughty Ferry, and possibly this partner was Louis Susser.

These "Brothers Bosco of Poland" are not found again.

B69. Morton Bosco = William Morton, *ca.*1840-1887, *and sons*
B70. Leopold Bosco, 1864-1901
B71. Mastrilio Bosco, 1868-1946[1]

Real name **William Morton**, born probably in Stockton, Yorkshire, *ca.*1840 (father named as James Morton, "traveller", "necromancer").[2] William was touring the north of England as "'Signor Morton Bosco,[3] the Celebrated 'Wizard of the World'" by late 1863,[4] and is found performing only in the north of England and the south of Scotland for the first ten years or so of his career, which, to judge from reviews, was quite successful, apart from an unfortunate incident or two — in Lancaster in 1872 when he failed to appear and the impatient audience broke up much of his apparatus, greeting him "with a mingled ovation of hisses and applause" when he finally showed and admitted he had been "indulging rather too freely";[5] and a performance in Romsey in 1878 "did not … seem to satisfy the audience, and by the time it was half over … a good many of the patrons left the hall … on the performers leaving the hall they were saluted with hooting and shouting … Mr. Bosco had his hat knocked about, and he narrowly escaped being knocked down…".[6] More typical is a review such as: "…This distinguished necromancer visited Padiham during the past week, and for evenings enchanted, bewildered, and astonished his audiences by his marvellous feats of magic. There was also Madam Bosco, the Clairvoyant…".[7]

Though from 1866 he largely billed himself simply as "Signor Bosco" (one of at least four in Britain at this time), he is fairly easy to identify in newspapers as he was usually accompanied by his wife, billed as "Madame Morton Bosco", or "Signora Bosco".[8] He married Mary Roberts Walmsley in Manchester in 1863,[9] and by 1865 they are regularly performing together, she as "the Clairvoyant Lady … all the wonders of the second sight" and "the Clairvoyant Lady, who can see clearly into abysses of the profoundest darkness with her eyes blindfolded…". He was also the only Bosco to use the phrase "Mysteries of Wonderland" in his bill matter.

In March 1864 his programme promised "some most astounding feats, such as have been performed by command *before Her Majesty, the Prince Consort, and the Royal Family*"[10]— implying, but not claiming, that *he* performed before them

His repertoire included the "Great Indian Basket Illusion",[11] the "gun trick";[12] and also plate spinning — "… he first introduced his dancing plates, which he made spin round a table and keep time to music … thunderous applause".[13]

By 1872 he and Mary have been joined by their son, registered as **Leopold Bosco Morton,** born in 1864 in Chorlton (not in Belgium as they state in the 1881 census), billed as "La [*sic*] Petite Leopold, the Marvel of Mecca, sleeping in the air!".[14] Another son, registered as **Mastrilio Bosco Morton**, born in 1864 in Kirkstall, Leeds (not in Geneva as they state in 1881), also joined the act.[15]

In 1879, now as far south as Newport Pagnell, we hear: "Signor Bosco, the great wonder-worker and necromancer, gave his grand entertainment entitled 'Mysteries of Wonderland', assisted in the second part by Madame Bosco, the world renowned clairvoyant … The programme commenced with dancing plates and dishes, a performance requiring no mean amount of skill… Madame Bosco exhibited remarkable powers… …The great sensation, entitled 'The Rajah of Singapore', performed by Le petit Leopold and Mastrillo, was a remarkable performance…".[16]

Mary died in Barrow in 1882, age 36 ("On the 12th inst., at Barrow, Mary Morton, wife of Mr. Wm. Morton, Bosco, a wizard, aged 36 years").[17] On August 1st the following year William remarried in Dewsbury to Eliza Pennington, age 27.[18] He gives his age as 39 and his profession (and his father's) as "Necromancer"; he again signs his name with a cross.

By February 1884 Eliza was performing with him as a clairvoyant — "exhibited her extraordinary powers of second sight and thought-reading…".[19]

William died in Melbourne, Derbyshire, on July 14th 1887, registered as William Bosco Morton and his age given as 42. An urgent notice appeared in the *Era* of 16 July: "Wanted, Leopold and Mastrillo Bosco to communicate with Prof. Trevori … immediately. Signor Bosco father dead". He was well enough known for his death to be mentioned in the *New York Clipper* ("Sig. Bosco Morton, conjurer, etc…": 6 Aug. 1887).

The sons both made very successful stage careers.

Leopold after his early trance performances ("The Marvel of Mecca, or the angel's flight through the air") became a versatile showman, inheriting apparently both his father's skills ("The Illusion King and Card Expert … the man of many mysteries and premier prestidigateur" [*sic*])[20] and his mother's ("materialised trance medium, séances, and cabalistic esotericism").[21] He performed both with travelling troupes and in music halls — in 1898 he is touring with "the P. and T. Collins crowd" as "The Only Bosco, the Great Leopold of magic fame, the prince of sleight-of-hand artists",[22] and in 1899 is performing at fairs in his "Temple of Esoteric Mastery".[23] By 1900 he was running "Leopold Bosco's African Menagerie",[24] but died suddenly at Miles Platting Fair Ground in Manchester in 1901, age "38".[25]

Mastrilio, performing with his parents by age 14 as "the youngest clairvoyant in the world"[26] had a long and varied career and a large family (he and his sons are all listed as "Showman" in the 1901 and 1911 censuses). In 1907 the *Music Hall and Theatre Review* (27 Sep.1907) called him "the magician and king of cards … one of the cleverest men at his business to be found in the country". He lived until 1946.

Later members of the family often used the surname Bosco Morton or Morton Bosco.

NOTES

[1] In official records his name also appears as Mastrillo and Mastrillio.
[2] His age as given in censuses and marriages suggests he deducted a few years and his birth may be William Morton Morton, mother née Watts, registered in Stockton and Sedgefield in first quarter 1838.
[3] According to an obituary of the clown James Rhodes, who died age 81 in 1904, Rhodes was a circus "colleague of young Billie Morton, whom one night he announced as 'Bosco', a name which has stuck to that famous conjurer to this day": *Yorkshire Evening Post* 12 Sep.1904.
[4] *Preston Herald* 1 Aug.1863. He might just be the unidentified "Signor Bosco" playing in Leeds from February 23rd 1863.
[5] 'Extraordinary Scene in a Music Hall', *Manchester Evening News* 7 Mar.1872.
[6] *Hampshire Telegraph* 30 Oct.1878.
[7] *Burnley Gazette* 18 Jan.1873.
[8] Leotard Bosco's wife (B77, BF3) who was also a conjuror was occasionally referred to as "Madame Bosco", but soon took the stage name "De Lonna".
[9] On the registration he gives his own and his father's profession as "Traveller"; he signs with his mark.
[10] *Burnley Gazette* 19 Mar.1864.
[11] *Walsall Free Press* 2 Feb.1867.
[12] *Era* 6 Jan.1867, in Hull.
[13] *Dundee Courier* 7 Apr.1869 (on a night when his apparatus had failed to arrive).
[14] *Lancaster Gazette* 2 Mar.1872, worried that they gave the eight-year old chloroform to induce rigidity.
[15] A daughter Pauline, born in 1872, died in infancy.
[16] *Croydon's Weekly Standard* 15 Mar.1879.
[17] *Soulby's Ulverston Advertiser* 18 May 1882.
[18] *Dewsbury Chronicle and West Riding Advertiser* 4 Aug.1883; marriage register entry on *www.ancestry.com*.
[19] *Huddersfield Chronicle* 21 Feb.1884.
[20] *Era* 6 Aug.1898.
[21] *Era* 25 Feb.1899.
[22] *Era* 20 Aug.1898.
[23] *Era* 6, 13 May 1899.
[24] *The Showman* 1 Dec.1900.
[25] *The Showman* 12 Apr.1901.
[26] *Dewsbury Reporter* 28 Apr.1883.

B72. Sig. I. Bosco

A "Signor I. Bosco" is found once, performing at the Alhambra Music Hall in Wakefield in 1866 — "...we have a Signor I. Bosco and wife, the former of whom attempts conjuring tricks similar to the illustrious wizard of that name, and the lady is a pleasing vocalist": *Era* 18 Nov.1866.

B73. Signor Bosco (Junior)

Performing at the People's Music Hall in Hartlepool in 1866 is a "Signor Bosco (junior)", who "opened on Monday last, and gave his performance. Though evidently somewhat under a disadvantage from the nearness of the audience to the stage, many of his legerdemain tricks and feats were effective … the result … was a very fair house on Monday evening, and they were all warmly applauded": *Era* 4 Mar.1866.

B74. Alfred Bosco, Jun.

Possibly the same person as B73, he is listed in *Era* 31 Mar.1867 as co-signatory of a letter re the Princess' Concert Hall, Leeds. His field is not stated but he is listed with Morton Bosco — however, he is not a known relative of his and not mentioned with him elsewhere.

B75. Lawrence Bosco

A performer of this name is found working in West London 1867-70, advertising only in the *West London Observer,* published in Hammersmith.

On August 17th 1868 he is part of the entertainment, along with popular singers and bands, at a Grand Summer Fete on behalf of the West London Philanthropic Society — "Lawrence Bosco the Magician and his Endless Hat Supply" (*West London Observer* 15 Aug.1868).

The following year he is advertising his services: "Excursions, Fetes, &c. Attended by Lawrence Bosco" — no charge is mentioned so perhaps he performed solely for charity. He gives his contact address: 2 Providence Place, Farm Lane, Walham Green [now West Kensington to the north and Parsons Green to the south] (*WLO* 26 June; 3, 10 July 1869) and a catchy little notice: "George, where did you get that Large Drum from? Why, Pa! I got it from Lawrence Bosco's Inexhaustible Hat" (*WLO* 7, 21, 28 Aug.1869).

He was also in the 1869 fete — "a very clever manipulator in the mystic art", said the review (*WLO* 17 July 1869); and again in 1870; at the end of that year he is advertising with a changed address "Mirth, Magic, and Mystery. Juvenile or Evening Parties Attended by Lawrence Bosco, Professor of Natural Magic, 3 Devonshire Cottages, Farm Lane, Walham Green, S.W." (*WLO* 24, 31 Dec.1870).

From the 1871 census we find from his address that "Lawrence Bosco" was George Shaw, age 39, born Westminster, who gives his profession as "Professor of Natural Magic". In the 1861 census he is in Manchester and gives the same profession. He died in 1875.

This career of at least ten years suggests he was probably more than a local amateur. If he was performing when in Manchester in 1861 at census time, it was not under the name Bosco. He is mentioned by the inventor John Feggetter in a letter to the *New York Clipper* 28 July 1877 who says "...I have made automatons a study since 1858. When I was traveling with Lawrence Bosco, the English magician, for whom I made several automatons, I conceived the idea of making an automaton chess player, which I named Namole..." [etc.]
[Feggetter, born John William Blake, 1845-1911, settled in America in 1872: see url:160].

B76 Henri Bosco

Found once, performing in Newbiggin in October 1874 — "Professor Henri Bosco the clever ventriloquist and conjuror gave an entertainment at the national school of Newbiggin, on Friday evening last": *Morpeth Herald* 3 Oct.1874.

B77. Leotard Bosco (real name James Frederick Greathead), 1851?-1895

The subject of two *Magic Circular* articles by E.A. Dawes: 'Leotard Bosco, Conjurer and Entrepreneur' vol 76 no.824 (April 1982) pp.58-60, and 'Magicians in Hull in the 18th and 19th Centuries Part 7. Madame de Lonno, and Leotard Bosco Re-visited' vol. 107 no. 1165 (August 2013), pp.240-243.

The first article notes 'Signor Leotard Bosco, the Great and Famous Conjuror, in his beautiful Enchanted Palace of Illusions' in Bristol in the early 1880s; and as lessee of the Empire Palace of Varieties in Hull from December 1888 until sometime between 1892 and 1895.

The second article records Leotard's life and career in detail: born in Bristol to unmarried Mary Greathead (also as Greethead) in 1850 or 1851; in the 1861 census he is in the Bristol workhouse with his mother and handicapped sibling Louisa; Mary was prosecuted in 1862 when she abandoned them there; with Cook's circus age 16; with Rubini age 20 (see *Appendix Z9* for Rubini); then joined Mark Wheeler's company; married Mary Relph (Ralph) in 1869, giving his profession as "singer"; living Birmingham 1871 census, he a ventriloquist, she a singer; she is found as "Mme Bosco" only once, Dec. 1873, and then it is almost certainly her as "Madame De Lonno, the Queen of Wizards", last sighted under that name May 1883; "his career seems to have commenced in 1872 with engagements traced in Derby and Scotland..."; card in the *Era* 3 Nov.1872 as 'Mons. Leotard Bosco' (provoking a complaint from another "Bosco"); 1881 census as Bosco, on tour in Sheffield, both he and wife as "Magician"; later in theatrical management; 1891 census as Bosco, living Cottingham, a "Music Hall Proprietor"; he died 1895, she 1897.

There is also a biography of him by Jan Cooper on the Greathead family website (url:161); for his career this draws on obituaries in *Era*; *The Handsworth Chronicle*; and *The Handsworth Herald and North Birmingham News* 27 July 1895.

Some additional comments:

Birthdate: If his mother Mary was the daughter of Robert and Sarah Greathead (as the family website states (url:161) the fact that young James is not listed on the 1851 census (where Mary is a "shoe binder" still living at home with her widowed mother, a "dealer in antiquities") suggests it is likely that he was born *after* the census, so 1851 not 1850; however when he married in Bristol on 26 June 1869 he gave his age as 19, meaning (if correct) he was born between 27 June 1849 and 26 June 1850.

Career: He is found a little earlier in the newspapers than Dawes says — card in *Era* 24 Dec.1871: "Leotard Bosco, the Great and Famous Conjuror, Mimic, &c., is now open to accept Engagements...". And this is probably him performing in Chester-le-Street in September that year: "...Bosco, the conjuror, ventriloquist, mimic, and vocalist... succeeded in drawing a very good audience, his various tricks evoking loud applause..." (*Era* 24 Sep.1871).

In early 1872 he is performing in Cardiff (*Cardiff Times* 27 Jan.1872): "...the greatest Necromancer and Ventriloquist of the day, from the Egyptian, St. James's, and St. George's Halls, London". He is then found performing at the Mechanics' Institute in Hull in March 1872 (*Era* 3 Mar.1872), Sheffield in July (*Sheffield Daily Telegraph* 23 July 1872) and selling a set of conjuring apparatus there (*Era* 28 July 1872). Then in Scotland, where in Alloa (*Alloa Advertiser* 26 Oct.1872) he is advertising "his celebrated INDIAN SWORD FEAT, BOSCO'S Wonderful Umbrellas, BOSCO'S Shower of Money, BOSCO'S Miraculous Production of Gold and Silver Fish, in his Enchanted Palace of Illusions" and declaring "positively no connection with any other entertainment of its kind travelling. All other parties advertising themselves as Leotard Bosco are simply impostors" — there were, of course, no other Leotard Boscos but plenty of Boscos and this provoked a counter attack in the *Era* of the following week (quoted by Dawes).

The earliest ad found for his 'Fairy Fountain' is in *Era* 25 Feb.1877: "...Herr Zangermann's [?] Fairy Fountain of Real Water and Living Statuary ... 200 gallons of water per minute, from nine to 35 feet high... Introducing Madame De Lonno's *Troupe* of Statuary in the Fountain whilst the water is playing...". Shortly afterwards Leotard was advertising for "a Lady of Fine Figure, for Bosco's Fairy Fountain and *Troupe* of Statuary (a Tall Lady preferred). Must have a First-class appearance (*Era* 6 May 1877). The fountain was destroyed when the South of England Music Hall in Portsmouth caught fire in 1878 (*Portsmouth Evening News* 13 Sep.1878) but Leotard bounced back with a new fountain in Southampton in October, and in *Era* 19 Oct. 1879 was announcing an improvement "after a Successful Engagement of Nine Months on the Continent".

In 1879 he has a large touring variety company named "the Great American Combination", billed as "the largest and most talented Company travelling on this side of the Atlantic ...". The show included "gifts" and he was charged with running an illegal lottery in York in 1882 (*Yorkshire Gazette* 14 Jan.1882; 28 Jan.1882; *Era* same date): dismissed as there was no evidence that he was the proprietor; but again in Leeds (*York Herald* 29 Apr.1882): fined 1 shilling and costs.

In late November he was advertising for acts to contact him at the Odd Fellows' Hall, Middlesborough (*Era* 21 Nov.1880), so Leotard was presumably the "magician named Prof. Bosco" there when a gas bag exploded during a lantern slide exhibition; windows were blown out and people blown off their seats, but no major casualties (*Sheffield Independent* 24 Dec.1880; *Darlington & Stockton Times* 25 Dec.1880; widely reported, some papers stating this "Prof. Bosco" was an acrobat).

In 1883 he added boxing matches to his conjuring show, both amateurs and a professional display bout (*Nottingham Evening Post* 11 June 1883; *Yorkshire Herald* 11 June 1883)

By 1878 Leotard was regularly claiming to be the "son (sometimes "son and successor") of the original Bosco" (*Walsall Observer* 19 Oct.1878; *Bicester Herald* 14 Mar.1879; *Todmorden Advertiser* 29 Apr.1881: "son of the original Bosco, the Spanish magician"), which must have particularly annoyed Saul Warszawski (B63) who had been billing himself since 1872 as "the Original Bosco" (and from 1874 as "the Only Original Bosco"). In a large ad in the *Era* 8 Jan.1881 Leotard proclaimed "To Proprietors, Managers, *Artistes,* and the Public generally. I, Signor Leotard Bosco, acknowledged by everyone in the profession to be the original Bosco, beg to caution the above not to be misled by boasting outsiders titling themselves as the original Bosco, as the original Bosco has been dead only fifteen years", and offers £20 to anyone who can prove they have a better claim to the name than he has. He lists his venues over the last fifteen years, all over Britain, and "France, Germany, and America".

An article in the *Era* 19 Jan.1901 on the early career of theatrical manager W.E. Potts says he spent three years touring with the "original Bosco", who preferred travelling by road rather than rail — "he was the owner of several good trotting horses; one of these put in a light American buggy soon carried them from one town to the other". This may be behind Leotard's claim in 1882 (*Bristol Magpie* 14 Dec.1882) to have a carriage which had been presented to him by President Ulysses Grant at Niblo's Gardens, New York, in 1879. There is no record of his being in America that year, however in 1883 (*Era* 9 June) he was offering for sale the rights to the title of "Bosco's American Minstrels" — "owner going abroad", and the following June the *New York Clipper* (30 June 1883) announced that "Mme. De Lanno [*sic*] ... in conjunction with Sig. Leotard Bosco ... will shortly leave England and make their first appearances in America ... will be pleased to hear from responsible managers..."; this was repeated to late July (*New York Clipper* 21 July 1883), but must have been cancelled as there are no references to them performing there, and in August 1883 Leotard was in Middlesborough announcing the start of a British tour (*Era* 18 Aug.1883).

The following year he was manager for Millie-Christine, "the Two-headed Nightingale", the two conjoined twins, one a soprano the other a contralto, singing simultaneously in different languages (for whose earlier career see Professor Millar, B62).

He was still conjuring in Devon in 1888 — "First Appearance this Season of SIGNOR LEOTARD BOSCO, The Great and Famous CONJUROR, his world-renowned ENTERTAINMENT of Startling and Mysterious WONDERS..." (*Western Times* 2 Apr.1888)

He and Mary moved from Cottingham to Hull in December 1891.

Madame de Lonno (BF3):

She is billed with Leotard as both *Mdlle* and *Mme* De Lonno, and they conjured conjointly — "Neat and puzzling legerdemain tricks were executed by Madame De Lonno and Leotard Bosco" (*Era* 24 Oct.1875) and "Madame de Lonno, The greatest female conjuror, travelling in conjunction with Leotard Bosco. The most wonderful sleight of hand performer now before the public. These artistes have no equals..." (*London and Provincial Entr'acte* 24 Feb.1877).

Dawes says she is last sighted in *Era* 12 May 1883, but she come out of retirement for a benefit performance in Hanley in December 1885, as "Madame Bosco" — "Madame Bosco had a most cordial reception, and her clever sleight-of-hand tricks were watched with keen interest..." (*Era* 26 Dec.1885). This come-back appearance by a conjuring Mary Bosco strengthens the case for her and De Lonno being one and the same.

Miss (or *Mdlle*) *de Lonn:*

Madame De Lonno had another performer using a name very similar to the stage name she had been using since at least November 1873, and the rival first appears under that name when playing on the same bill as De Lonno in a music hall in Barrow in October 1875. Alongside "Madame De Lonna [*sic*] and Leotard Bosco (Wizards)" are "Pio Whautkins, Madame Whautkins, and Miss De Lonn (Jugglers)". Madame Watkins is Elizabeth Washbrook Baptist Delain (the surname variously spelt) who married "Whautkins" (Thomas Poniah Watkins) in 1852. "Miss De Lonn" was their daughter Harriet Elizabeth Watkins, born 1858. Harriet is then found in Hull in January 1876 as "Signorina De Lonn"; with her mother in November: "Madame and Miss De Lonn... introducing the great Umbrella Trick... Miss De Lonn being the only Female Artiste that performs this Trick; also juggling on the running Globe"); and with her father in 1878. From August 1882 she is performing on her own as Mdlle de Lonn, tightrope walker and juggler (card in *Era* 2 Dec.1882: "the greatest Lady Juggler and Balancer"), including several tours with Joseph Hamilton's diorama. In 1884 she married theatre owner Thomas Barrasford and they had three sons. She continued performing (last sighted in January 1893) and died in 1894.

This similarity in names was surely at least a minor annoyance to De Lonno (Bosco), not merely for the inevitable newspaper misspellings, and she wrote to the *Era* (16 May 1875) correcting a statement that "Mdlle De Lonno" recently performed in Huddersfield: "I am the only De Lonno in the profession", and in 1883 (*Era* 12 May 1883) she was advertising "...There are many imitators, but only one De Lonno...".

The careers of the Watkins family are described in more detail (Harriet's brothers became the famous "Valjeans") in my forthcoming book on Hamilton's Diorama.

A holograph letter to a printer probably by Leotard is online at url:162

B78 Nelson Bosco

On August 7th 1880 the *Rugby Advertiser* published a death notice reading: "Death of Boscoe — This well-known magician died at his lodgings in Coventry on Monday night, For the last two months he has been in receipt of outdoor relief. Boscoe died at the age of 42". (The paper thought this interesting enough to reprint on August 1st 1930 in its 'Fifty Years Ago' section).

These dates, 1838?-1880 do not correspond to any of the otherwise known Bosco magicians. The death was registered as BOSCO, NELSON age 42. There is no corresponding birth record for him under this surname, so he was one of the many performers who "died" under their stage-name.

Later that year in Coventry (in the October to December quarter) an Elizabeth Anne Bosco married a watchmaker Edward Grundy. A family tree on *Ancestry.com* lists her as the widow of Nelson Bosco. She and Edward are in Coventry in the 1881 census, she is aged 46, he 33. Elizabeth died in 1884; Edward in 1897.

B79. Bosco Wylde

A magician named as "Bosco Wylde" is found performing in 1876 and as "Bosco Wyld" in 1892 and 1893, all in Birmingham, so likely the same person.

In December 1876 he is at the Steam Clock Music Hall — "Mr Bosco Wylde (wizard), who performs a number of clever tricks which have elicited the applause of the audience" (*Era* 3 Dec.1876). In July 1892 he is at a Bank Holiday show at the Reservoir in Edgbaston ("Bosco Wyld, conjurer": *Birmingham, Daily Post* 30 July 1892) and in August 1893 he is entertaining at a show by the Harborne Horticultural Society — "Bosco Wyld in his Magical Illusions, and Miss Jessie May, in her second-sight Séance" (*Birmingham Daily Post* 5 Aug.1893).

B80. Professor Bosco = Richard Reynolds

"Richard Reynolds, alias Professor Bosco, itinerant conjuror" was prosecuted in Warminster in Wiltshire in August 1881 for borrowing from a local draper a table-cloth and other items to use in his performance and failing to return them: *Western Gazette* 12 Aug.1881; the account in the *Wiltshire Times* 13 Aug.1881 refers to him as "Richard Reynolds, a travelling legerdemainist" and states an order had been made against him on this charge in May 1877, so the offence presumably took place then.

B81. Bosco, 1881

In December 1881 in Shenstone in Staffordshire a girl named Swindonia Wesley was prosecuted for breaking into and stealing from her father's house. She was currently with "a rough-looking man giving the name of Thomas William Trew Longmore", her co-accused. She had left her father some months earlier "to travel with a man named Bosco, who goes from one public-house to another earning money as a conjuror" (*Lichfield Mercury* 16 Dec.1881; *Worcestershire Chronicle* 17 Dec. 1881).

B82. "Herr Bosco", 1877

An unidentified conjuror is found performing under this name in England in 1877. In April he is in Trowbridge for two nights, "Herr Bosco, The renowned Wizard, Conjurer, and Ventriloquist, in conjunction with Mons. Salmar, The Marvellous Acrobat in his Drawing Room Entertainment", and in June two nights in Stanford in the Vale, "an entertainment very superior to those generally presented in country villages by travelling companies ... the ventriloquial part of the entertainment was very amusing...", and two nights in nearby Wantage — "legerdemain, ventriloquism, &c. In these illusions Herr Bosco proved himself a proficient, his conjuring tricks being especially meritorious".
(*Wiltshire Times and Trowbridge Advertiser* 28 Apr.1877; *North Wilts Herald* 11 June 1877; *Berkshire Chronicle* 16 June 1877)

B83. Bosco Brothers

The Bosco Brothers, "conjurors, mesmerists, etc." are found performing in the early 1890s. In Kingsthorpe in 1891 they "gave an entertainment ... amusing, and concluded with 'a hypnotic séance'" (*Northampton Mercury* 22 May 1891) and later that year "visited Aylesbury ... and gave mesmeric performances" (*Bucks Herald* 14 Nov.1891).

The following year in Newport Pagnell their advertising is deliberately similar to that of Saul Warschawski and son — "Bosco Bros., (Sons of the original Bosco) are coming, and will give their Grand and Original Entertainment, Entitled Magic, Mirth, and Mystery ... See the Bosco Bros. in their great Beheading Trick. They will select a person from the audience (with permission) and take his head from his body and place it upon a plate, and bear it to view among the assembled company, that it is actually the head of a living person. This Trick alone is worth all the money. Anatomists should not miss seeing this, as it excites extraordinary interest in the science of anatomy..." (*Croydon's Weekly Standard* 1 Oct.1892).

Finally, in 1893 when Saul and son Alfred were on tour in Rugby and Nuneaton they were so annoyed that they stated in the local papers: "Signor Bosco & Son beg to inform the Public of this Town and surrounding neighbourhood that it has come to their notice that two persons travelling in the name of Bosco Bros., with a poor imitation of our Entertainment, have no connection with us, or any claim to that name, one being named Daniel Fisher, late of the Blue Anchor Beerhouse, Castle Street, Northampton. Not satisfied with using the name of Bosco, they have the audacity to copy our Bills and Testimonials..." (*Rugby Advertiser* and *Nuneaton Advertiser* 28 Oct.1893).

Fisher was publican of the Blue Anchor in 1891 and is listed there in the census that year — age 35, born Northampton, wife Ellen and several children.

From August 1893 to August 1897 Fisher was licensee of the Fox Inn in Gas Street in Rugby; in 1894 he was assaulted by a customer, and in court the customer stated "Fisher and 'Professor' Bosco attacked him" (*Rugby Advertiser* 21 Apr.1894).

There were later Bosco Bros. in 1906 but they were acrobats.

B84. Lyndale Bosco

Dr Lyndale Bosco is first sighted in 1894, advertising in the *Era* (11 Aug. 1894):"Sleight-of-Hand Performer; Madame Bosco, Military Sword Performer, Liberty 20th. 66 Belmont-avenue, B'pool". He is found performing only in Huddersfield, in February 1896 at a private function "Prof. Bosco entertained the guests with clever conjuring and legerdemain"; again in March ("gave a splendid show of legerdemain"); and they are performing together in a concert in Huddersfield in October that year — "Professor Bosco gave a very clever illusionist, conjuring, and sword feat entertainment, in which he was ably assisted by a young lady, who also wielded the sword with great dexterity"; also at a concert there in January 1897 "Professor Bosco did some 'fair to middling' conjuring tricks, and afterwards went through some very clever sword feats, such as cutting an apple in two on a girl's neck…", and in February "Professor and Madame Bosco succeeded in completely deceiving the audience by the way they performed their numerous tricks, and the sword performance was very good"; and later the same year in nearby Cumberworth ("an Australian sword performance by Professor and Madam Bosco, and a wizard and illusionistic performance by Professor Bosco").

Huddersfield Daily Examiner 15 Feb.; 28 Mar.; 19 Oct.1896; 2 Jan.; 4 Feb.; 5 Mar.1897

A similar combination of conjuring and sword play was earlier performed by "Professor Sinclair assisted by Madame Sinclair, in his great Australian sword performance" (Surrey Palace of Varieties, *Era* 8 Feb.1890); also at Lewis's Music Hall the following year: "Professor Sinclair does some clever sword-cutting feats" (*Era* 21 Mar.1891). This is not Professor Sinclair "the Queen's Ventriloquist" of earlier in the decade and may be the same person as "Lyndale Bosco".

Professor Sinclair Bosco (B85) may also be the same person.

Lyndale Bosco's contact address, 66 Belmont Ave, Blackpool, was also used in 1895 by "Professor Gleave" for the sale of copies of a popular pseudo-medical book, *The Magic Wand and Medical Guide*, and in 1897 by "Thomas Gleave" for a self-help book *The Silent Helper*. The first book, which is only 8 pages, states "This book can only be obtained from the compiler, Professor Gleave" but Gleave is unlikely to exist and the book seems to be a reprint of a much older American book.

Living at 66 Belmont Ave round this time are a succession of railway workers but at no.62 Belmont Ave in 1901 with wife Hannah and 3 young children is **Arthur Harper Swales**, age 27, born Bradford, who gives his profession as "Professional (ventriloquist)". He was an "electric tram guard" in 1891 but "ventriloquist" by 1896 when he married, "theatre manager and entertainer" in 1911, "Public Entertainer" in 1918; he died in Blackpool in 1943. He does seem a potential candidate for being "Lyndale" Bosco.

B85. Professor Sinclair Bosco

"Professor Sinclair Bosco" is found once, giving "an exhibition of legerdemain" at a lodge concert in Shipley in Yorkshire (*Shipley Times and Express* 25 Nov.1899). Possibly the same person as B84.

B86. William Mortimer Bosco

Not to be confused with William Morton Bosco (B69), William Mortimer Bosco was described as a "conjurer" when he was fined 2s6d. and 16s. costs in Bradford in 1901 for alighting from a moving train ("… dragged along the platform and fell onto the line … a miracle defendant was not killed": *Bradford Daily Telegraph* 15 Feb. 1901; *Bradford Observer* 16 Feb.1901).

His address is given as 131 Tong Street and living at this address in the 1901 census is indeed "William Bosco", "Music Hall artiste", age 42, born Keighley, and his wife Lena, same profession, age 29. This is clearly his stage name — there are no birth, death or marriage records for him under this name.

He is possibly the "Billy" Bosco referred to in an ad in *Era* 8 & 15 Feb.1880: "Wanted For Proctor's Great Illusion, a Good Conjuror, with New Tricks, or any other Single-handed Performer that can make an impression in Thirty Minutes. Will Professor Anderton and "Billy" Bosco send address? J.C. Proctor".

B87. Leon Bosco

"Leon Bosco", 1863-1923, who performed with Le Roy and Talma from 1901 or 1902 (replacing James Fox) was probably born Alexander Van Gelder in England. When he left them in 1912 he was succeeded by Dr. James William Elliott who took over both the role and the name Bosco. There are said to have been a total of nine of these successive Boscos with Le Roy and Talma, including F Drummond Nisbet, Wilmot Hastings, Thomas Mullens, and Charles Zazell.

Leon Bosco's family and his earlier and later career are discussed in detail by Peter Brunning in Y*e Old Magic Mag* 7,1 (Dec.2020).

B88. Allan Bosco

A person named as "Alan Bosco, conjuror" was fined in Nuneaton in 1926 for "allowing his child Joan, aged four years and ten months, to perform with snakes at Nuneaton fair ground", and apparently for the same offence earlier in Warwick. (*Warwick and Warwickshire Advertiser* 30 Oct.1926; *Lancashire Evening Post* 30 Nov.192; and widely reprinted, naming him various as Alan and Allan, Bosco and Boscoe).

There is no trace of him doing any actual conjuring and, as Houdini lamented in *The Unmasking of Robert-Houdin*, "Bosco" had become a popular stage name for snake handlers and snake-eaters, especially in America (see section below, pp.392-3).

In Sheffield in 1935 a fire destroyed the circus tent of "Mr Alan Bosco, whose family have been in the show business for generations as illusionists" (*Sheffield Independent* 8 Aug.1935). He may also be the "Prof. Alan Bosco" promoting female boxing matches in 1950 (*Bradford Observer* 26 July 1950).

B89. The Original Bosco.
Touring through the north of England in 1916 was "John A. Walker's Great Comedy Revue 'Oh! Dear'" featuring plenty of singers and "the Crinoline Girls, a bevy of beauties". The show included vaudeville acts which varied from town to town, sometimes a conjuror. In Liverpool in June this was "Ching Woo" (Alfred J. Banks) but in Cheltenham and Chesterfield in July and August it was "the Original Bosco", described as "The Mirthful Conjuror" (*Gloucestershire Echo* 29 July to 4 Aug.1916; *Derbyshire Courier* 12 Aug.1916).

Leotard Bosco and Saul Warschawski had both billed themselves as "the Original Bosco" but both were by now dead. It is possible this was Saul's son Alfred, but according to Dawes's article on him (see B63-64) he was called up in 1914 to do war work in a factory.

Boscos in U.S.A.
There are a few references to Bartolomeo's exploits in Europe in American newspapers from at least the 1840s, but the earliest conjuror to perform in America under the name Bosco was **"Madame Bosco"(1)** (BF1)*, wife of* **Professor Millar** (B62), *from 1858 until her death the following year; Millar himself performed in America as "Bosco Millar" in the 1870s. Two Boscos from England performed in U.S.A. and remained there,* **David Hyam (B66)** *from about mid-1873 and his brother-in-law* **Louis Susser (B65)** *from late 1875.*

Several other Boscos are found in America from the 1860s onwards, most hard to identify and many difficult to distinguish.

B90. Professor Bosco, Milwaukee 1862
Professor Bosco, "the world-renowned magician and prestidigitator", is found performing in Milwaukee in late 1862, the earliest male "Bosco" traced conjuring in U.S.A. He advertises "Two Grand Magic Soirees" at the Academy of Music, and an accompanying article states "The Professor comes well recommended, and his exhibitions have been extensively patronized in neighbouring cities"; a review tells us "He performed a great number of tricks, some of them entirely new and unique" (*Milwaukee Daily Sentinel* Nov.18, 19 1862).

B91. Prof. Otto Bosco, Indiana 1862
"Professor Otto Bosco" is offering performances of "natural magic" on behalf of wounded soldiers in Bloomington, Indiana in December 1862 and gave a public performance while there (*The Pantagraph* 1 Dec.1862, adding: "We can distinctly state that he is no Hambujer [for whom see *Appendix Z4*]. While in this office, and as a matter of course without preparation he performed a few tricks which were superior to anything we have lately seen"). Possibly the same as B101.

B92. "Herr Bosco", Missouri 1863

In March 1863 the German language newspaper *Westliche Post* in St. Louis, Missouri, announced an "Extra Performance in Magic" that evening (*Extra-vorstellung im Gebiete der magischen Zauberei*) by "Herr Bosco, member of the company of Herr Pfeiffer. He will present some of the most amusing tricks. A young Parisian who has appeared in France with great success will assist him" (*Westliche Post* 3 Mar.1863).

Alexander Pfeiffer had been a successful actor in Germany but his liberal views led him to emigrate to America. He played in Henry Boernstein's German company in St. Louis, then formed his own company when Boernstein headed off to the Civil War in 1861. Which member of Pfeiffer's company played "Bosco" is unknown.

This performance was, by chance, only a few days before Bartolomeo died in Dresden and the *Westliche Post* published an obituary of him on April 6th: "…with [his] death hundreds of secrets go to the grave. We don't know if he wrote 'Memoirs' or 'Disclosures' (*Aufschlüsse*), but how interesting they would be…"; in fact this obit. is reprinted from a European paper and wrongly says Bartolomeo performed in America.

In 1865 when Hermann (Herrmann) played in St. Louis the paper pronounced that "[tr.] Bosco's former mantle as the foremost of magicians has now fallen on Hermann's shoulders and he knows well how to wear it" (27 Dec.1865)

B93. Signor Bosco with Kate Weston

A "Signor Bosco" billing himself as "First Prestidigitateur of the 19th Century" is first sighted in Poughkeepsie, N.Y. in July 1864. He advertises "his New Entertainment entitled 'The Mystification of the Senses, or a Night among the Mystic, Weird and Wonderful'", including 'The Davenport Brothers Exposed', with Miss Kate Weston performing 'The Vision of the Inward Eye' and as pianist (*Poughkeepsie Eagle-News* 13, 16 July 1864).

Kate Weston is found earlier that year in Hartford as "The Pleasing Pianist and Balladist" accompanying a touring panorama (*Hartford Courant* 27, 29 Feb.1864).

In August 1864 they are in Brooklyn, where he is now "Bosco, the Greatest Illusionist of the 19th Century" and promising "total eclipse and defeat of the Davenport Brothers by Signor Bosco", with "Miss Kate Weston, the beautiful Retro-Reminiscent Clairvoyante". Bosco's reputation, we are told, "stands pre-eminent … his wonderful feats and illusory miracles … defy the comprehension of the most astute… Prominent among the novelties is the magical frying pan, which frys into life whatever inanimate object he places in it…" (*Brooklyn Daily Eagle* 29, 30 July; 1, 2, 3, 5 Aug.1864).

B94. Bosco, Troy, N.Y., 1864

An ad in the *Troy Daily Whig* 8 Sep.1864 announced: "For Six Nights Only. Signor Bosco's Promenade Entertainments of Prestidegitateurism [*sic*], Escamotison [*sic*], Necromancy, &c., &c., the whole to conclude with A Social Hop…".

The result was described in the *New York Clipper* 1 Oct.1864: "A Professor of Magic, calling himself Bosco, showed in Troy last week. He advertised to stay a week, but got sick and left sooner than expected. The performance each evening closed with a hop, from 9 to 11, all for the small sum of 25cts. It was not appreciated by the Trojans, and he got sick of his bargain and left for 'ye ancient city of Albany'".

Possibly the same as B95 who once advertises a hop after his show.

B95. Bosco with the "Cyclopean Gift Show", 1865

A "Signor Bosco" with the "Cyclopean Gift Show" is found in upstate New York (Geneva, Syracuse, Oswego, Rochester) January to February 1865, then in Massachusetts, and in March in Connecticut. In Oswego (only) there is a hop following one show, so he may be the same as B94. He bills himself as "the Escamoteur and Greatest Arch Illusionist Living, who has been the wonder and astonishment of all Europe and America".

He was announced to perform in Geneva, "one of the most expert Magicians of the age" with 'The Cyclopean Gift Show' in late 1864, then this was postponed until early January due to illness, and he does not seem to have performed there at all (*Geneva Gazette* 6 Jan.1865). He opened in Syracuse on January 17th, and both the tricks ("…"the production of the globe with gold fishes is the finest of his efforts") and the gifts (a grand piano on the last night) were well received (*Syracuse Daily Courier* 18, 20, 23 Jan.1865; *Syracuse Daily Standard* 23 Jan.1865).

He gave three successful evening shows and a matinee in Oswego at the end of January, one show followed by "a social hop" (*Oswego Daily Palladium* 26 to 31 Jan.1865). Five nights in Rochester followed (*Evening Express* 6 Feb.1865), then a short run in Pittsfield, Massachusetts later in the month (*Berkshire County Eagle* 16 Feb.1865), and six nights in Hartford, Conn.; again the gifts were judged very acceptable and overall "an entertainment of a superior order. His feats of legerdemain are in many respects wonderful…". When he left he was heading for New Haven (*Hartford Courant* 27 Feb. to 8 Mar.1865).

B96. Signor Bosco in Long Branch, N.J., 1865

A chatty article in the *New York Times* 8 Aug.1865 on 'Our Watering Places' describes seeing a "Signor Bosco" performing to holiday makers in Long Branch — "… I confess I was wonderfully amused with Bosco … eye-catching sleight-of-hand tricks … standing on his hands on the table and drinking off three glasses of soda-water, 'upside down'; blindfolding his eyes, putting a tall glass of ale on his forehead, and with it balanced there crawling under and through the rounds of a chair, backwards, etc. The vote of that parlorful was unanimous that the Signor Bosco beat Heller, Herman, Houdin and all the rest … he was a comical little Italian…".

B97. Prof. Bosco, 1868-9

"Prof. Bosco, Prestidigitator" is found in Salt Lake City ("having arrived from the east") in October 1868, opening on 23rd in "a Grand Soiree Diabolique": "Many of his tricks are perfectly new, and all are performed with a finish which proves him not only a 'professor', but well qualified in practice". On show would be "the Egyptian Miza Sphynx, the Instantaneous Growth of Flowers, the great Davenport Rope Feat, the Piscatorial Paradox, producing a number of living Fish from the atmosphere, and the Great Indian Basket Feat". He "has lately arrived from his great European tour", and the show will conclude with "a comic Shadow Pantomime, in which he will be assisted by Mrssrs. [*sic*] Graham and Merritt, Miss Clive and Mrs. Roberts". The last mentioned were members of a theatrical company, who played the melodrama 'Gunmaker of Moscow!' on October 31st, followed by the 'Shadow Pantomime' with Professor Bosco as Pantaloon (*Deseret Evening News* 13, 21, 22, 23, 28, 30 Oct.1868).

It is probably the same "Prof, Bosco" in California in 1869, "The Great Conjuror, Wizard, and Prestigator [*sic*] … in "a Grand Soiree Diabolique", with a similar (but not identical) list of tricks "to conclude with the great Mystery of the Sphynx" (*Los Angeles Daily News* 18 Feb.1869).

He may also be the "Prof. Bosco [who] gave a performance in magic in San Bernardino on Feb.26th" (*New York Clipper* 3 Apr.1869), and also the "Professor Bosco" giving his "Soiree Magique" in San Luis Obispo at the end of 1869: "… a very creditable [entertainment]… The Professor's hands are far too quick for the eyes of the audience. Go and see him. We have never had a better dollar's worth of fun and diversion in this town. We have seen Heller, Herr Alexander and Anderson, but Bosco is up with them all" (*San Luis Obispo Tribune* 25 Dec.1869).

It is probable that these are early appearances by Carl Bosco (B98), especially as both perform the otherwise uniquely named trick the "Piscatorial paradox".

(The term "Soiree Diabolique" was perhaps borrowed from Heller who had used the term in America in 1866.)

B98. Carl Bosco, 1845-1878

"Carl Bosco", magician and photographer, is first found performing as Charles Bosco; his real name is said in obituaries to be Charles Isaac; in Utah in 1873 his name was said to be Mortimer, "son of Mr. Mortimer, juggler of Yorkshire, England", but in 1876 he is registered as Carl Bosco as a voter in San Francisco, resident at Lick House, photographer, age 30, born Germany ("Reg. on proof of nat. of father").[1]

His photographic career is detailed in Thomas Robinson's *Oregon Photographers: Biographical History and Directory, 1852-1917*.[2] Robinson finds him first as "Bosco & Penelon" in Los Angeles June to September 1869; however, prior to that he was in partnership with the well-known photographer Charles Gentile.[3] Gentile was Italian and had changed his first name from Carlo, perhaps inspiring Charles Bosco to do the same in reverse. Bosco was next in Portland in 1870 where he first travelled for Joseph Buchtel taking scenic photographs, then in February 1875 he opened his own business "Bosco and Megler, Photographers" offering portraits, scenic views and stereoscopic cards. The business lasted only until August that year. Bosco now worked again for Buchtel and resumed his travelling magic show.

He toured his show mainly on the West Coast between California and British Columbia, extending to Montana, Nevada, Utah, Idaho, and (finally and fatally) Louisiana. He is first definitely sighted on stage in late 1869, but I believe he is probably B97, the "Prof. Bosco" performing from at least October 1868. He is probably also the Bosco performing in San Luis Obispo in December 1869. The same month he performed in Los Angeles, very inauspiciously: "Mr Charles Bosco, a photographer and illusionist, is said to have absconded from Los Angeles, leaving numerous creditors behind. He has latterly given entertainments in legerdemain and feats of magic".[4] He then performed in Gilroy, again disappearing rapidly,[5] but soon resurfaced as "Carl Bosco" in Maguire's Opera House in San Francisco, with a show featuring "an *exposé* of the Davenport Brothers", and "a miscellaneous entertainment of magic, and the humorous feat of resuscitating a skeleton and cause it to walk on the stage".[6] On the first night "he was unable to extricate himself from the rope. He did better the second evening, but the public failed to appreciate his efforts…".[7]

He headed to Sacramento, where his performance was "a decided success", both the legerdemain and the rope business going down well.[8] Marysville, his next stop, was equally successful — "gave excellent satisfaction".[9] For a performance in Almaden he had 500 programmes printed in Spanish by the *San Jose Mercury-News,* which concluded it was ":simply one of his tricks" when he failed to pay, but apologised when he turned up and paid the next day.[10] He continued on through Healdsburg, Grass Valley, Stockton, Shastas (all with reasonable audiences except in Shasta, where his agent offered free tickets on the first night), Trinity, Weaverville, Eureka… In October his agent "Prof. Griffith" deserted him and did a rival show of his own, "exposing" Bosco's tricks.[11]

By the end of the year he was in Nevada — "Herr Carl Bosco … performed a series of very clever tricks with cards, and feats of legerdemain… His exposure of the Davenport Brothers… was the most interesting part of his doings … Bosco then explained the whole thing to the audience…"; and after his next show: "…we consider him among the best in the sleight of hand and legerdemain line, and fully entitled to the cognomen of the Electric Wizard…".[12] In October he was very successful in Oregon — "as a magician and conjuror we have never seen his equal, and as an affable and clever gentleman he has no superior…".[13]

In May 1871, now settled in Portland, he announces: "Having determined to retire from my profession as Magician and Illusionist and to cast my fortune before the people of Portland, before doing so I wish to present to them several illusions never witnessed on this Continent": these include 'The Piscatorial Paradox' and the show culminates in 'The Great Mystery of Transmogrification'.[14] He is assisted by "Miss Annie Pixley", here age 20, the oldest of the three Pixley sisters who all made stage careers.[15]

If he really intended to retire from magic and concentrate on his photography this did not happen. He took photographs during his travels but his magical shows continued until his death . In October 1871 he was at a fair in Salem, Oregon, with his 'Temple of Mystery' offering Illusions, Transmogrifications, Blood-curdling East

Indian Basket Feat, plus his photography,[16] and later that year he was in Canada — "Magic Prestidigitation! Ancient Diabolism! Modern Spiritualism! ... Carl Bosco, the great explorer of the world of wonders...".[17] and in Seattle.[18]

Performing early the next year in Olympia, Washington,[19] he announced he "will also present to each of his audience a copy of his book on Magic". This has not been traced.[20]

A review of his show in Owyhee, Idaho, that year[21] has a long list of his tricks — "The Enchanted Cards; Candles and Handkerchief; Wreath and Rings; Coin and Decanter; Aerial Bell and Frame; Mystic Clock; Demon Hat...; Floating Stick; Mysterious Water; The Hindu Chain; Lessons in Legerdemain; Mystic Ball; Turkish Handkerchief; Treasures in the Air".

He then spent several months in Utah,[22] a successful tour apart from some problems in Salt Lake City in March. His legerdemain went off well but when it came to his being tied with ropes in the cabinet, the locals (who included Dr Congar who had been the Davenports' agent) had brought their own long rope; Bosco refused to allow this and tied himself. Here his true name is said to be Mortimer, "son of Mr. Mortimer, juggler of Yorkshire, England".[23]

Back in Portland at the end of the year he is assisted in his "Soiree Magique" by Miss Lucy Pixley, the third of the three Pixley sisters, two becoming well-known actresses and Lucy a singer.[24]

In 1877 on tour in Nevada the *Yerington Times* remembered him from Gilroy: "an illusionist (particularly so when he has a printing bill to pay)".[25] He is then found performing in San Francisco, and from May is "supported by Miss Ada Joliet" on long tours through Nevada and Montana. She, we learn from the Helena *Independent-Record*,[26] "appeared in tablaux [sic] of aerial suspensions, presenting Prayer, Red Riding Hood, Dancing Girl ... Goddess of Liberty, and Columbia, which were admirably executed", and *The New North-West* in Deer Lodge[27] tells us she was his wife. They continued on through dozens of small towns and mining camps, often arriving unannounced but well received. "The Professor is a showman of note, being a descendant of the great Bosco of the old world", fibbed the *Rocky Mountain Husbandman* in Diamond City.[28] In November they were performing together in Salt Lake City,[29] but she is not listed with Carl the following year on a tour of Louisiana where he was exhibiting his photographs. At a gallery in New Orleans in April 1878 he was described as "recognised as a very superior artist by the leading photographers in the United States".[30]

He died of yellow fever in Donaldsonville, Louisiana, on September 18th 1878. Death notices in several papers gave his name as Charles Isaac.[31] A longer obituary appeared in the Seattle *Daily Intelligencer*:[32] "Died — We have heretofore neglected to mention that among the victims of the yellow fever scourge, well known on this coast, who have recently been carried away at New Orleans, was Carl Bosco. Mr. Bosco was a photographer by profession, but is better known as a showman in the magic art. He made a tour of the Sound in this line of business in 1871, and made friends and acquaintances".

NOTES
[1] California, U.S., Voter Registers, 1866-1898: *www.ancestry.com*.

[2] Portland: The Author, 1993, and updated at his website url:163.

[3] Advertisement in *Los Angeles Daily News* 23 Mar.1869: "Gentile, Bosco & Co., Photographers, Downey's Block, Main Street"; Gentile had shifted from Arizona to California in January that year (*Weekly Arizona Miner* 23 Jan.1869). A notice dissolving their partnership by mutual consent (signed "Charles Gentile and Charles Bosco") appeared in the *Los Angeles Daily News* 13 Apr.1869, and in the same issue is an ad for Bosco & Penelon at the same address.

[4] *Sacramento Daily Union* 30 Dec.1869; *Sonoma Democrat* 1 Jan.1870.

[5] *New York Clipper* 29 Jan.1870: "…some very good tricks, the principal of which consisted in disappointing the citizens in general and leaving the city".

[6] *San Francisco Chronicle* 15 Feb.1870; *Daily Alta California* 17 Feb.1870 ("Herr Carl Bosco, the Eclectic Wizard").

[7] *New York Clipper* 12 Mar.1870.

[8] *Sacramento Daily Union* 25, 26 Feb.1870; the *Daily Alta* correspondent said: "Bosco has fully and satisfactorily exposed the Davenport cabinet tricks" (27 Feb.1870).

[9] *Marysville Daily Appeal* 1, 2, 3 Mar.1870.

[10] *San Jose Mercury-News* 23, 24 Mar.1870.

[11] *Trinity Journal* 15 Oct.1870.

[12] *Gold Hill Daily News* 17, 19 May 1870 (but he billed himself as "the Eclectic Wizard", not "the Electric Wizard"). This was a vindication for Bosco. A few months earlier the Davenports had performed in Gold Hill and their advertising declared that "their 'seances' were crowded by the highest order of citizens while at San Francisco, and one emulous individual, Carl Bosco, afterward appeared in an 'expose' of their feats, but his attempt, like all others, proved a disgusting failure. The Davenports still remain the great mystery": *Gold Hill Daily News* 14 Mar.1870.

[13] *Albany Democrat* [Albany, Oregon] 4 Nov.1870. In Corvallis, Oregon, a review called him "the finest magician we have ever seen" (*Corvallis Gazette-Times* 5 Nov.1870).

[14] *Morning Oregonian* 5 May 1871.

[15] Née Shea, they took their stepfather's name: see url:164. They moved from San Francisco to Nevada in the 1860s then to Olympia and were in Portland by 1870: *Washington Standard* (Olympia, Wa.) 17 Nov.1893.

[16] *Statesman Journal* [Salem, Oregon] 19 Sep., 7 Oct.1871.

[17] *Victoria Daily Standard* 15 Dec.1871.

[18] *Puget Sound Dispatch* 25 Dec.1871.

[19] *Washington Standard* (Olympia, Wa.) 20 Jan.1872.

[20] There are of course three conjuring titles with the author named as Carl (as opposed to Carlo) Bosco:
Carl Bosco's Zauberkünste... Berlin: Mode, 1865 (reprinted till 1903);
Carl Bosco's Kartenkünste... Berlin: Mode, 1866 (reprinted till 1907);
Carl Bosco's Zauber-Geheimnisse... Berlin: Mode, 1877 (reprinted till 1900);
(See *Book* section LGe59-66 for details). Even though the American Carl Bosco was said to be born in Germany it is hard to believe that he was the author of these or that he would be offering his Olympia audience a book not in English. No 'Bosco Books' were published in U.S.A. in English — only in Polish and Swedish.

[21] *Owyhee Avalanche* 23 Nov.1872.

[22] *Deseret Evening News* 16 Dec.1872; 1 Mar.1873; *Salt Lake Tribune* 27 Feb.1873; *The Ogden Junction* 1 Mar.1873.
[23] *Salt Lake Tribune* 4 Mar 1873; reprinted *Gold Hill Daily News* 6 Mar.1873.
[24] *The New Northwest* [Portland, Oregon] 18 Dec.1873. For the Pixleys see note 15.
[25] *Yerington Times* [Yerington, Nevada] 16 May 1877.
[26] *Independent-Record* [Helena, Montana] 15 Aug.1877. In October, back in Helena, Ada received a benefit (*Independent Record* 2 Oct.1877). She was with him earlier that year in Reno: *Daily Nevada State Journal* 15 May 1877.
[27] *The New North-West* [Deer Lodge, Montana] 31 Aug.1877.
[28] *Rocky Mountain Husbandman* [Diamond City, Montana] 2, 15, 18, 30 Aug.1877.
[29] *Salt Lake Tribune* 3 Nov.1877 ("Carl Bosco, Assisted by the beautiful and accomplished Miss Ada Joliet, In their new Cabinet of Wonders: Marvels of Mecca, Flying Cage and Fairy Bird, Spiritual Manifestations").
[30] *New Orleans Daily Democrat* 7 Apr.1878; *Times-Picayune* 28 Apr.1878.
[31] *The Independent-Record* [Helena, Montana] 13 Oct.1878 (etc.).
[32] *Daily Intelligencer* [Seattle, Wa.] 19 Oct.1878.

B99. Carl Bosco (2), 1879

Soon after the death of the first Carl Bosco (B98) a namesake appeared in the mining town of Idaho City. He is listed on April 15th 1879 as "Carl Bosco, Cal." staying at the Luna House Hotel, but his show soon after was not well received: "'Carl Bosco's' show didn't succeed here. Two boys and one man went to see him perform his 'wonderful tricks'… The people of Idaho City are not easily 'taken in' by bilks" (*Idaho Semi-Weekly World* 15, 18 Apr.1879; how big the population then was it would be interesting to know — it was no longer the boom town of the 1860s).

Another Carl Bosco appears in Louisiana in 1880 but not, it seems, a magician. A large troupe performing in St Joseph includes "Prof. Carl Bosco's Russian Hussar Brass and Reed Band of 20 Solo Musicians" (*Tensas Gazette* 3 Jan.1880).

B100. John Bosco, fils

In New York in February 1869 Leonard Grover's 'Tammany Amusement Co.' was announcing in its upcoming "Mammoth Attractions" in Tammany Hall "First appearance of the World Renowned John Bosco, fils, in his very celebrated feats of Prestidigitation, effected entirely without aparatus [*sic*], and his wonderful and unequalled Musical Performance, entirely without instruments" (*NY Daily Herald* 22 Feb.1869; similar ads in *Brooklyn Daily Eagle* 23 Feb.1869, etc.)

The result was reported in the *New York Clipper* 6 Mar.1869: "Tammany certainly gives us variety. 'John Bosco, fils' was extensively carded to open there on the 22d, and 'John Bosco, fils' did appear and so he did on the following night, but there an end. John is an alleged prestidigitateurist, and he was under contract for a two weeks' engagement, but his style was too weak, and he was let off. His tricks were queer, and the public did not take to them or him kindly, and he was let down after the second night".

B101. Prof. Bosco, Chicago 1869

A "Prof. Bosco" said to have "just arrived from Paris" performed in Uhlich's Hall in Chicago on November 10th and 11th 1869. He offered a "grand exhibition of Magic and Prestidigitation" and "will also introduce to the audience the Rapping, Musical, and the other 'Spirits' imported from Paris" (*Chicago Tribune* 10 Nov. 1869).

This might have been interesting as the Davenport Brothers were opening in Chicago four days later. However, there are no other mentions of this Bosco or his performance. (The Davenports reaped a large and curious audience but a poor review: *Chicago Tribune* 16 Nov.1869.)

B102. Prof. Otto Bosco, 1870

Another (or the same as B91?) Prof. Otto Bosco is in Salt Lake City in 1870 (*Deseret Evening News* 29 Oct. to 4 Nov.1870) lecturing "On Magic, Mystery and Miracles", including 'Magic Ben and the Magic Rooster', 'The Spirit in the Drum', 'The Bewitched Orange', etc.

He is probably also the "Professor Bosco" later that month in Corinne, Utah, where "after successfully exhibiting his wonderful magicious power over a circuit of forty thousand miles, and before all the crowned heads of Europe, [he] gives his first lecture at the Opera House to-morrow evening exposing the magician's secrets" (*Corinne Daily Reporter* 30 Nov.; 1, 2 Dec.1870).

B103. Bosco, Wisconsin 1871.

"Bosco, the magician" is listed to give a performance in Fond du Lac, Wisconsin, on July 4th 1871 (*The Appleton Crescent* 1 July 1871).

B104. Dr. Bosco

"The Man of Mystery. Dr. Bosco, the Wizard, Illusionist, Psychologist, Mesmerist, is now open to engage with responsible parties, either in variety or gift business. Address Harry Day, 309 Park ave., Brooklyn": advertisement in *New York Clipper* 4 Apr.1874. ("Harry Day" is presumably his agent rather than himself; this is not the well-known Harry Day (Edward Lewis Levy); he was born 1880.)

B105. Bosco, died 1877.

The Forest Republican in Tionesta, Pennsylvania, stated (18 Apr.1877): "'Signor Bosco', the sleight-of-hand performer, who recently gave a series of entertainments here, is reportedly dead. It is said that he dropped dead, of heart disease, while performing. Where he was at the time, or how the news got here we are unable to learn".

One would have expected such an event to have been widely reported but no other mention has been found. And a search back through the previous three months of *The Forest Republican* finds no references to a Bosco performing in Tionesta.

B106. Paul and Nellie Bosco, 1879

In Bozeman, Montana, in 1879 we find "Paul and Nellie Bosco, the renowned 'Illusionists and Ventriloquists'" — "those who were present at the entertainment, pronounced it quite a success" (*Bozeman Avant Courier* 6 Nov.1879).

B107. P. Bosco, 1883.

In Oakland in 1883 at the Tivoli Opera Garden is "P. Bosco" (perhaps half of B106), "the Greatest Living Magician, in his wonderful illusions, in conjunction with the Miniature & Vaudeville Opera Co., including Miss Theresa Lingwood, Messrs A. Messmer and C. St. Martin" (*Oakland Tribune* 3 Feb.1883). The following month they appeared in Dashaway Hall in San Francisco (*San Francisco Examiner* 9 Mar. 1883; *San Francisco Chronicle* 10, 11 Mar.1883).

B108. Mons. Bosco, Arizona 1882

Performing in Tucson, Arizona, in 1882 is "Mons. Bosco, The world renowned Magician", accompanied by Miss Kitty Wilson and Lena Modesto Rodriguez, and "assisted by the whole company". His act includes the gun trick and a beheading act, the only Bosco in U.S.A. known to include beheading — "Prestidigitation, Magic, Impalpable Phantasms, Sleight of Hand, Cutting a Man into Pieces, The Phantom Child, Invulnerable Man or Bosco Shot … The Beheading of a Live Man, concluding with the Mammoth Kaleidoscope, or the new Silforam, Produced with Electric Light!!!" (*Tucson Citizen* 26 Oct., 6 Nov.1882; *Arizona Daily Star* 9 Nov.1882).

The list of tricks and especially the "silforam" [*i.e.* silforama], a magic lantern, strongly suggest this to be **Julio F. Bosco** (B118), who was in France in July 1882 and back in America later that year: however, he was definitely in Brazil in September, October and November 1882.

B109. Fiasco Bosco, 1889

An ad in the German-language St Louis, Missouri, paper *Anzeiger des Westens* 2 June 1889 announces an upcoming fair on Easter Sunday which will include "[tr.] the black magician Fiasco Bosco [who] will amaze the public with his tricks" (*Am Abend wird der Schwarzkünstler Fiasco Bosco das Publikum durch seine Künste in Verwunderung setzen*), no doubt a local amateur.

(This and other St Louis papers have ads in 1892 for a "Dr. Bosco" just arrived from Berlin, "better known as 'The Guiding Star'", but he is a clairvoyant, fortune teller and medium, not a conjuror: *Westliche Post* 28 Aug., 6 Sep.1892; *St. Louis Post-Dispatch* 3 Sep.1892.)

B110. Professor Bosco, Kansas 1889.

An unidentified "Bosco" was touring Kansas in 1889, much to the annoyance of Louis Bosco (B65) and his agent Hewett — "Several times within the past year the impostor 'Bosco' has dropped in their route to realize on the reputation of Bosco...". The impostor then insisted he was the genuine Bosco and "the other Bosco is a fraud and dissembler"... so "if Bosco isn't Bosco", said the newspaper, "who the devil is Bosco?" (*The Smelter* (Pittsburg, Kansas) 10, 17 May 1889; both quoted from the *Joplin Herald*).

B111. "Professor Bosco and his versatile wife Louise"

A performer so described is found with a "magic and variety show" in New Orleans in December 1891. He was travelling from Texas and the *Times-Picayune* (27 Dec.1891) quoted the *Fort Worth Gazette:* "...Bosco's Present Show gave a very entertaining performance. The audience was large and very appreciative... The first part was a roaring Dutch farce, in which the principal characters were Professor Bosco, and his versatile wife, Louise. Every movement of the couple produced mirth... [then] a wonderful wire act ... Professor Bosco closed the entertainment by bewildering the audience with his lightning sleight-of-hand work and mesmerism".

B112. Bernardo Bosco (1)

There appear to be (at least) two illusionists who used this name in America.

In Cardondale, Pennsylvania, late in 1911 a vaudeville act includes "Bernardo Bosco's Successor in his Great Cremation and Illusion Acts"; the following year Bernardo Bosco is mentioned (a letter for him) in North Tonawanda; then in 1913 in Utica he was charged with assaulting a former employee Bernard Gigliotti; Bosco is described as "a sleight of hand artist".
(*The Carbondale Leader* 1 Dec.1911; *North Tonawanda Evening News* 28 Aug.1912; *Utica Herald* 11 Apr.1913; *Utica Daily Press* 12 Apr.1913).

Another (possibly the same) "Bernardo Bosco" was arrested in San Antonio, Texas, late in 1913 for violating the Mann act ("White Slavery!", said the headlines). He is variously described as "a traveling magician and hypnotist", "a violinist and magician", and as the snake-eater known as "Eats-'Em-Alive Bosco".
(*San Antonio Express* 11, 14 Oct.; 20 Dec.1913; *Niagara Falls Gazette* 7 Nov.1913; *Buffalo Times* 9 Nov.1913).

B113. Bernardo Bosco (2)

In San Francisco in 1915 is "the famous Italian illusionist, signor Bernardo Bosco" on his tour of the United States, tomorrow giving a grand performance of "magnetism, spiritism and sleight of hand" (*Il celebro Illusionista italiano, signor Bernardo Bosco è arrivato ier nella nostra città insieme colla sua signora dopo i continui successi ottenuti nella sua tournée attraverso gli Stati Uniti e farà la sua prima comparsa domenica 21 marzo, al Nuovo Teatro in Broadway, con un grande spettacolo di magnetismo, spiritismo e giuochi di prestigio: L'Italia* [San Francisco] 19 Mar.1915).

In 1920 he is performing in New York — and claiming to be Bartolomeo's grandson: "...The clever Italian magician, Bernardo Bosco, grandson of the original Bosco, and, as he claims, the only genuine Bosco alive today, is presenting some remarkably fine magic at the Harlem Museum here and gives a performance well worth seeing. He is a clean worker and holds the crowds well" (*Billboard* 18 Sep. 1920).

B114. De Bosco Hughes

De Bosco Hughes was not a conjuror but travelled in America in 1877-9 with an optical illusion device he called "The Great Egyptian Mystery", which like the 'Sphinx' used a concealed series of mirrors to make objects and people appear and disappear in whole or in part.

De Bosco Hughes was his real name, born to Matthew and Marry Ann Hughes in Birmingham *ca.*1834. He is listed as De Bosco Hughes in the 1841, 1851, 1861 and 1871 censuses and married under that name in 1854. He became a scenic artist, like his father, but in 1863 is also found exhibiting "his startling and wonderful illustration of The Ghost" in conjunction with "Mr. Birkhead's Stereopticon" (*Liverpool Mercury* 17 Aug.1863). He was bankrupted in 1866 and again in 1869, but had some success with a Panorama of the Franco-Prussian War in 1870 and was working in a studio in Birmingham in 1873.

By January 1875 he was engaged as a scenic artist in New York, having left his wife and children in England. Then in October 1876 he went into partnership (by his account) with Colonel Warren in New York, who renamed the Thirty-fourth Street Theatre "Egyptian Hall" and from December 23rd included Hughes's "Great Egyptian Mystery" among his variety acts (*New York Clipper* 23 Dec.1867). When this did not attract, Warren's manager J. Charles Davis dropped the act. Hughes promptly left, taking his "Mystery" and all his lithos and art-work with him and, to use these, started what he called "The Egyptian Hall Traveling Combination". He opened his "Mystery", a half hour show combined with variety acts, at the Howard Athenaeum in Boston in February 1877; he claimed to have invented it, advertising it as "from Egyptian Hall, London", but he is never mentioned in connexion with the London Egyptian Hall. It ran there until the following month, and Hughes then reopened it at the Beethoven Hall on March 12th. The first night there was a disaster, with the complicated "Egyptian Hall" mechanism not working and most of his advertised variety acts failing to appear (*New York Clipper* 24 Mar.1877); he closed soon after.

Then in the *Clipper* (7 Apr.1877) two rival ads appeared cheek-by-jowl, one by Davis accusing Hughes of departing unannounced and taking Warren's property, the other by Hughes, declaring himself "Original Inventor of the Egyptian Mystery" and entitled to what he took. He opened it in Baltimore in April, Buffalo in May, then Toronto, Cincinnati, Detroit, Chicago, Philadelphia and Indianapolis (all while a rival "Egyptian Mystery" company toured the west coast).

Hughes settled in Indianapolis, married there in 1879, and resumed as a scenic artist; he also toured exhibiting a giant painting of the Battle of Vicksburg (with live fireworks) and a Biblical Tableau after Doré.

He died probably in Indianapolis and probably in the 1890s.

Central and South America

B115. Bosco, Brazil 1876 (Avila)

Performing in the province of Rio Grande do Sul in Brazil in 1876, having come from Argentina, is "o filho do célebre Bosco, que é como seu pae um habil thaumaturgo humoristico" — *the son of the famous Bosco, who like his father is a skilled humorous magician.*[1]

He is also referred to just as "Bosco" — performing in Mercedes the following year,[2] and as both "Bosco" and "son of Bosco" in São Paulo and Campinas in 1879. These performances are both for charities, the Smallpox hospital and the *Santa Casa di Misericordia*, but he is no amateur and advertises a very elaborate programme, *Grande e variado espectaculo de Thaumaturgía Humoristica,* including Os Últimos Esforços da Thaumaturgia, Dez Minutos de Catoptrica, Palingenesia, O Que Sera' a Hesperidina de Bagley [*making fun of the favourite Argentine apéritif*], O Golpe de Jarnac [*a sword cut to the thigh — with cards*], Ideas de um Homem Esclarecido, Experiencia da Velha Escola, Os Relampagos e os Trovões da Thaumaturgia, Um Segredo da Creação, Um Emulo de Brillat-Savarin ['*phantasia gastromica'*], Um Novo Promotheo, Maravilhhsa [*sic*] Bibliotheca, A Mesa Gyratoria.[3]

This list of tricks is rather distinctive, While *Thaumaturgia Humoristica* is not unique (it was used, for example, by Faure Nicolay and Conde Patrizio when in Brazil) it became a favourite phrase of the local magician and ventriloquist "Avila" (José Curvello D'Avila) and I believe the 1876 and 1879 "son of Bosco" performances are early appearances by him.

In 1882 he took part in a "Sarau Artistico-Dançante" put on in Rio de Janeiro by the "Alumnos de Minerva" which featured "Thaumaturgia Humoristica" by Sr. Avila Junior.[4]

In November 1885 as "Avila' he gave a series of performances of "Ventriloquia, Thaumaturgia Humoristica e Prestidigitão" in Rio de Janeiro,[5] and a single show on December 16th, the large advertisement including his picture.[6] And more of the same in São Paulo the following year, again "Thaumaturgia Humoristica e Ventriloquia", the show opening with "Os ultimos esforços da thaumaturgia" and including "A Bibliotheca maravilhosa" and now "O Gabinete maravilhoso ou a mulher encantada, esperiencia de catoptrica" as presented in "Palacio de Crystal in Sydenham by Maskeline and Cooker" [*sic*] and now for the first time in Brazil.[7]

He is found performing in Maranhão in 1894 now as "Curvello D'Avila, célebre ventriloquo e prestidigitador portugez" with Dickson's Theatric Company; in Rio de Janeiro in 1895; and later that year with Dickson's in Santa Catarina. A large advertisement there has an updated picture of him, leader of the Dickson's Company of ten artists. They then left for Laguna and Tubarão.[8]

Later that year they were in Porto Alegre,[9] and he was back there the following year with magic, ventriloquism and lantern slides.[10]

He published *Segredos da Magia Branca* (Rio de Janeiro: Eduardo & Henrique Laemmert 1873; new ed.1882) and *O Magico Moderno* (Rio de Janeiro: Livraria popular de Cruz Coutinho, 1882; copy held at Brown University; this may be a new edition of the 1873 book)

He may have been the José Curvello d'Avila Maciel born in the Azores (Angra Do Heroísmo, Terceira), 11 Sep.1846 (brother of João Curvello d'Avila Maciel, 1848?-1919; parents: José Curvello d'Avila Maciel and Marquise Adelaide Maciel).

NOTES
[1] *Correio Paulistano* 11 Nov.1876.
[2] *O Despertador* 26 Oct.1877.
[3] *Correio paulistino* 25, 27, 28 Sep.1879 (also in *Jornal da Tarde*, etc.); *Monitor Campista* 18, 24 Oct.1879 (in Campinas he also took part in a variety benefit, *Espectaculo Magico Phantastico Acrobatico*, for Mlle Maria Jossand).
[4] *Gazeta de Noticias* 3, 26 Sep.1882.
[5] *O Programma-Avisador* 11, 14 Nov.1885; *Gazeta de Noticias* 20 Nov.1885.
[6] *O Fluminense* 16 Dec.1885.
[7] *Mercantil* 21 Feb.1886 (with his picture).
[8] *Diario do Maranhão* 29 Sep.1894; *Cidade do Rio* 26 June 1895; *Republica* 8, 10 Aug.1895.
[9] *A Federação* 21 Nov.1895.
[10] Alice Dubina Trusz, *Entre lanternas mágicas e cinematógrafos: As origens do espetáculo cinematográfico em Porto Alegre, 1861 - 1908* (São Paulo: Terceiro Nome/Ecofalante, 2010); with references.

B116. Bosco, Argentina, 1888

The *New York Clipper* reports (2 June 1888) in Argentina: "the National Theatre opened with Bosco, the magician, and his troupe of Japanese".

B117. Bosco, Mexico, 1896

The *New York Clipper* reports (16 May 1896): "Mexico. A magician named Bosco has opened a new small theatre devoted to illusions". This may well be the same performer succinctly described in *El Diario del Hogar* [Mexico City] 14 Aug. 1896: "[tr.] Magician.— There is a very bad one who calls himself Bosco, in Laredo, Mexico, but he works with little success" (*Prestidijitador.—Se encuentra uno muy malo que se hace llamar Bosco, en Laredo, México, pero trabaja con pequisimo éxito*).

B118. Julio F. Bosco (Jules F. Bosco)

I believe he was French rather than Spanish, Argentinian, or Italian as variously stated. He is first sighted as "M. *F. Jules,* élève du célèbre Bosco" performing a "séance de prestidigitation de physique et de magie" in Rio de Janeiro in June 1863 as part of a French variety troupe of actors and singers at the *Alcazar Lyrique Fluminense.* The performers are all French and their show and their advertising are in French.[1]

He later used the name Jules F. Bosco in South America and Julio F. Bosco in France, presumably to appear exotic; in South America he often billed himself as *'Cagliostro do Rio da Prata'* in Brazil and as *'Cagliostro del Río de la Plata'* in Spanish-speaking countries.[2]

The next confirmed sighting is not until March 1868 at the *Theatro Philo-Dramatico-Apollo* in Jaguarão in the southern Brazilian state of Rio Grande do Sul. Here as **Julio F. Bosco**) in a large advertisement in the *Onze de Junho* of 27 March 1868[3] he promises "Prestidigitacões, Fisica, Magia, Adevinhações, Escamotagens", and more, from the "Prestidigitador" known as 'Cagliostro do Rio de Prata'.

Carmen Luz Maturana,[4] calling him "Italiano", notes him performing in Chile in late 1869 — Valparaíso, Santiago and La Serena, and refers to a poster stating he had previously played in Rio de Janeiro, Montevideo and Buenos Aires, and that his show included a decapitation with a talking head, together with ghosts and 'diamond fires', the last his magic lantern show of optical effects, *Silforama*.[5]

In December 1872 we find him in Mazatlán in Mexico,[6] very successful with the decapitated talking head and the *silforama*. He was in Durango in March; in Aguascalientes in May,[7] Querétaro in August,[8] Guanajuato in September,[9] and Michoacán in October.[10] In the capital in November, finding the *Teatro Nacional* unavailable, he announced he was heading first to Puebla, Jalapa, Orizaba, and Veracruz.[11]

Back in Mexico City in early January he waited for the end of the Carnaval masked balls before opening at the *Teatro Nacional*.[12] Meanwhile he offered private performances and was selling copies of *El Gran Fisico, ó el arte de aprender varias pruebas de naipes y otras,* and also a periodical titled *El Brujo,* which one paper termed "este periódico órgano oficial del célebre prestidijitador".[13]

He opened on March 5th and ran until 26th. With one exception the newspaper reviews were positive and flattering, praising his dexterity and affirming that he lived up to his reputation.[14] The exception was *El Monitor Republicano* which had been hostile or at best sceptical of him since January, with a sarcastic greeting ("[tr.] Welcome to the capital the new Cagliostro") then quoting a review from *La Tierra de los Oprimidos* which had said that he "[tr.] did a few well known, cheap, and easy tricks" (*ejecutó unos escamotos tan conocidos, tan vulgares, tan faciles*), dismissed the silformama as merely a collection of dissolving views, and found the decapitation act so laughable that the following week a comedy company had produced a farce titled 'The Beheading' (*La Degollación*). We shall see, concluded *El Monitor,* if the sensible and enlightened Mexico City public is astounded by these easy and well-known tricks of the so-called Cagliostro of the Rio de la Plata.[15]

When it published its review the result was possibly the worst review imaginable of any conjuring performance, criticising his "simple and disgusting tricks", and tabulating a detailed list of nine faults (then adding a tenth)....[16]

He left on April 14th. *El Monitor* wished him a good voyage.[17]

September 1875 found him in Puerto Rico — "el famoso prestidigitador D. Julio Bosco",[18] and November 1876 in San Fernando in Trinidad.[19]

We next see him in September 1879 in Kingston, Jamaica. The Theatre was in such a dangerous condition that it could not be used, but he performed instead in Wallack's Gallery.[20] He was back in Kingston in February 1880 — "Jules F. Bosco ... his Great Novelties ... the Pinnacle of Thaumaturgy...".[21]

In July 1882 he turns up in France, with the *silforama*. Oddly he is sighted only in Bayonne[22] and Bordeaux (perhaps on his way from Spain) — advertised first as "Jules F., le Bosco américain" then as "Julio-F. Bosco", performing with "beaucoup de souplesse et de désinvolture".[23] It is just possible that he was the Bosco impostor who so annoyed Eugenio in France in late 1882. He claimed in Rio de Janeiro the following year that he had performed in Bordeaux and at the *Théâtre de Nouveatés* in Paris, but I can find no record of the latter. However, two advertising lithographs of his (not localised, but one printed in Paris) are held in the Coll. Dutailly in the *Maison du livre et de l'affiche*, Chaumont.[24]

One would think he was the "Mons. Bosco" performing in Tucson, Arizona, in October 1882 (B108) as the acts listed correspond closely to his, but Brazilian newspapers have him performing there from September 1882 onwards.

He now began a long tour of Brazil, billing himself as "Jules F. Bosco". He had arrived in Recife from Europe in early September 1882,[25] and performed there on September 19th.[26] In October he was in Portaleza,[27] then in Belém in November.[28]

He arrived in Rio de Janeiro on February 11th 1883 and opened at the *Imperial Theatro Dom Pedro II* on 18th, with further shows on 24th and March 3rd, the last a benefit for Sra. Eugenia, and including a musical interlude by her sung in French.[29]

In his advertising here he cites performances in Bordeaux, in Paris at the *Théâtre de Nouveatés*, and at the 1876 Philadelphia Exposition; the first is genuine so perhaps the others are too but I can find no references to these.

On March 25th he opened at the *Theatro S. José* in São Paulo, "Grande Soirée Misterioso", with "Sra. Eugenia" now as "Eugenie, a mulher phantasma", and further shows on 29th, 31st (now including the decapitation act), and April 1st, 5th and 8th.[30] Soon after was published in São Paulo the 'Silforama-Valsa', which had been played by the orchestra during his shows.[31]

He was next in Campinas,[32] with shows in Taubaté and Urupês also mentioned, then Itu in June,[33] and Juiz de Fora in early September.[34] By the end of September he was back in Rio de Janeiro, now at the *Theatro Recreio Dramático*,[35] and in November in Campos dos Goytacazes, at the *Theatro S. Salvador* and in Macahé.[36]

This long second tour of Brazil continued — Ouro Preto in May 1884,[37] São Paulo in June 1884,[38] Bragança Paulista in August,[39] São Paulo again in October 1884,[40] Curitiba[41] and Antonina in November;[42] and still in 1885 — Santa Catarina in January and February,[42] Rio Grande do Sul in March,[44] Porto Alegre in April.[45]

In February 1886 he was in Argentina, in Córdoba en route to Tucumán, parading recent successes in Montevideo, Buenos Aires and Rosario, and featuring "[tr.]

Display of the great and unrivalled Silforama, produced by electric light and executed by the famous artist A. Filhon".[46] His act included the gun trick; the ghost child (a boy on stage is covered by a bag; two shots are fired and he is in the stalls); the female question: *What do the girls like the most?* in which the public are asked to choose one of three handkerchiefs placed on a table, the piece of paper with the question is fired from a gun and the answer is on the chosen handkerchief: *Marry a good husband;* and Bosco's Black Book of Accounting, its pages changing from black to white, to squares filled with numbers, to pictures of women, or to devils...

He was back in Mexico in 1887, six shows in Mexico City in May at the *Teatro Principal,* with 'La Mujer Fantasma', 'El Jarabe Mexicano', 'El Kaleidoscopio Gigante', '¡El Fusilamiento!', and more...; a great success, with his run extended, closing finally on June 6th.[47]

We get a glimpse of him in Argentina in 1888, at the *Teatro Nacional* in Buenos Aires,[48] then again in Brazil (Cachoeira) in 1891,[49] and in December 1891 in Tacuarembó in Uruguay.[50]

At the end of 1892 he arrived in Puerto Rico from Guadaloupe and performed in several towns there. He is said to have last been in Puerto Rico in 1874 and he has the silforama, so everything points to this being the same person. He is "accompanied by his family, who are all artists".[51]

February 1893 in Puerto Rico is the last known sighting of him.

NOTES

[1] *Diário do Rio de Janeiro* 30 May, 1 to 4 June 1863.

[2] In this choice of title he was no doubt inspired by '*Cagliostro das Antilhas*' used in Brazil in 1864-6 by J.B. Linski, who claimed to be Polish — possibly Chrétien-Jean-Baptiste Linski, 1827-1882.

[3] Reproduced by Carlos Otoniel Pacheso da Cunha in his 2015 thesis '"Nos Julgamos Compensados com o Regosijo de Ver Nossa Terra Natal Dotada com um Theatro": A Trajetória do Teatro Esperança (1886-1929)': online at url:165.

[4] Carmen Luz Maturana, *La Comedia de Magia y los efectos visuales de la era pre-cinematográfica en el siglo XIX en Chile*, online at url:166.

[5] On this she refers to Mauro Fernández, *Historia de la Magia y el Ilusionismo en la Argentina.* Buenos Aires: Producciones Gráficas, 1996, which I have not seen.

[6] *Iberia* 11 Jan.1873; when quoting this the Francophone *Le Trait d'Union* 12 Jan. 1873, published in Mexico City, expressed doubt that this was "[le] fameux Bosco, déjà célèbre en France ... nous serions plutôt tentés de croire que c'est un faux Bosco...". His performances in Mazatlán are the subject of Antonio Lerma Garay, 'El Cagliostro Rioplatense Llega a Mazatlán', online at url:167.

[7] *La Iberia* 29 Mar.; 29 May 1873.

[8] *Le Trait d'Union* 21 Aug.1873 quoting *La Sombra de Arteaga* which added that a local priest had pronounced Julio's act to be "diabolique".

[9] *El Monitor Republicano* 25 Sep.1873; *Le Trait d'Union* 26 Sep.1873 (here, as in previous shows, he gave part of the proceeds to charity).

[10] *El Eco de Ambos Mundos* 26 Oct.1873.

[11] *El Correo del Comercio* 14 Nov.1873.

[12] *El Siglo Diez y Nueve* 12 Feb., 3 Mar.1874.
[13] Neither of these has been traced.
[14] *La Rivista Universal* 7 Mar.1874; *El Foro* 8 Mar.1874; *La Voz de México* 10 Mar. 1874.
[15] *El Monitor Republicano* 23 Jan.1874.
[16] *El Monitor Republicano* 13 Mar.1874. The review is accessible online at url:168.

His Mexico City performance is briefly discussed by Chester Urbina Gaitán, 'Nigromancia, prestidigitacion e hipnotismo en la ciudad de Mexico (1864-1910)', *Revista de Ciencias Sociales* 1 September 2014; online at url:169.

[17] *El Monitor Republicano* 15 Apr.1874 ("...Deseàmosle un viaje feliz").
[18] *Boletín mercantil de Puerto Rico* 26 Sep. to 10 Oct.1875.
[19] *San Fernando Gazette* 18 Nov.1876 ("this week has been enlivened by several performances of the far-renowned M. Bosco ... this far-famed Prestidigitator..."); 25 Nov.1876 ("left here this week taking away golden opinions").
[20] *Budget* 16 Sep.1879; *Kingston Gleaner* 19, 20, 24, 30 Sep., 2 Oct. 1879.
[21] *Kingston Gleaner* 21 Feb.1880.
[22] *Courrier de Bayonne* 5 July 1882.
[23] *La Petitie Gironde* 19, 22 July 1882.
[24] These are online at url:170
[25] *Diario de Pernambuco* 8 Sep.1882: "Companhia Bosco — Ao bordo do paquete *Niger* chegou da Europa o Sr. Julio F. Bosco e seus auxiliaries, que constituem uma companhia de prestidigitação e magica branca...".
[26] *Jornal de Recife* 19 Sep.1882.
[27] *Gazeta do Norte* 11 to 17 Oct.1882 (a series of large ads illustrated with blocks which he must have carried with him).
[28] *O Liberal do Pará* 23 Nov.1882; *Diario de Belém* 25 Nov.1882.
[29] *Gazeta de Notícias* 11, 18 Feb.; 2 Mar.1882. Her name is given as *Eugénie Labat* in *O Estado de S. Paulo* 23 & 27 Mar.1883.
[30] *O Estado de S. Paulo* 21, 23, 25, 27, 28 Mar.; 4, 6 Apr.1883; *Correio Paulistano* 25, 29, 30 Mar.; 7 Apr.1883.
[31] *O Estado de S. Paulo* 15 May 1883.
[32] *O Estado de S. Paulo* 12, 15, 18 Apr.1883.
[33] *Imprensa Ytuana* 14 June 1883.
[34] *Pharol* 5 Sep.1883.
[35] *Gazeta de Notícias* 30 Sep.; 14, 21 Oct.1883; *Gazeta da Tarde* 3 Oct.1883.
[36] *Monitor Campista* 20, 30 Oct.1883; 8, 9, 12, 13, 14 Nov.; 8 Dec.1883.
[37] *Jornais de Ouro Preto* 8 May 1884.
[38] *Correio Paulistano* 27 June 1884.
[39] *O Estado de S. Paulo* 17 Aug.1884.
[40] *O Estado de S. Paulo* 16, 17 Oct.1884.
[41] *Gazeta Paranaense* 15 Nov.1884; *Dezenove de Dezembro* 28 Nov.1884.
[42] *Gazeta Antoninense* 16 Nov.1884 (url:171).
[43] *O Despertador* 31 Jan., 4 Feb.1885; *A Regeneração* 4 Feb.1885; *Conservador* 7 Feb.1885.
[44] *O Despertador* 21 Mar.1885.
[45] *A Federaçao* 16, 20, 24 Apr., 11 May 1885.

[46] Víctor Ramés 'El ilusionista en Córdoba, 1886' (url:172, with references).
[47] *The Two Republics* 11, 21, 22 May, 5 June 1887; *Trait d'Union* 11, 14, 15, 18 May 1887.
[48] *El Mosquito* 29 Apr.1888.
[49] *A Federaçao* 5, 9 Sep.1891.
[50] Martina Iñíguez — url:173.
[51] *La Correspondencia de Puerto Rico* 24 Dec.1892; 7, 12, 13, 14, 15, 16 Jan.; 1, 3 Feb.1893.

B119. Bosco Ruchwaldy.

The well-known Professor Ruchwaldy is found only briefly performing as "Bosco Ruchwaldy", in Mexico in 1896.

His birth name was almost certainly Bernhard Ruchwald. Ruchwald is not uncommon as a surname but *Ruchwaldy* is unique — used only by him and his descendants; he adopted it early in his career (the suffix *-y* added to a Hungarian surname has the same meaning ('from') and the same implication (nobility) as *von* in German; later he also added the -y to his first name, *Bernhardy*); *Ruchwaldy* also has an Indian ring about it, an impression he cultivated, especially in Europe and America.

His death registration gives an implied birthdate of *ca.*1844; however when joining a Masonic Lodge on June 19th 1865 (see below) he gave his age as 26, implying *ca.*1839, though he may have wanted to leave no doubt that he was at least 21. The death registration gives his birthplace as "Hungaria" and his parents' names as Isaac and Julia. His son's birth registration (below) and his own burial show that he was Jewish.

He is first sighted in India, joining the Morning Star Lodge in Lucknow on 19th June 1865, his name spelt as *Bernhard Richwold,* and significantly joining with him are "Joseph Venek" and "John Wessely", all giving their profession as "Artist". Wessely was Vanek's manager and Ruchwald his assistant. Later that year they moved on to Simla and there on August 28th they joined the Lodge of Himalayan Brotherhood, all three giving their profession as "Conjuror"; his name is given there as *Bernhard Ruchwald* and his age as "full".[1]

This lends credence to a claim he later makes in his advertising: "Professor B. Ruchwaldy, *partner of the late Professor Vaneck*".[2] Vaneck, usually Vanek, about 25 years older than Ruchwald, is said by the *Lexikon* to have fled to Turkey with Kossuth in 1849. I'm not sure what evidence there is for this, but it seems unlikely, as by 1854 when the Hapsburgs were still demanding Kossuth back for summary punishment, Vaneck was performing in Hungary with his magic and lantern slide show (*"physikalisch-phantastisch-optische Vorstellung"*),[3] and in 1857 was touring far and wide in the Austro-Hungarian empire, accompanied by Wessely — Agram (Zagreb), Graz, Laibach (Ljubljana), Vienna (at the *Josephstädter Theater*), Brno, Kraków, Leitmeritz (Litoměřice), Außig (Ústí nad Labem)…

By early 1860 Vaneck was in Egypt,[4] then we next see him five years on in India, when Ruchwald is first confirmed as with him. After Lucknow and Simla (Shimla) they performed in Lahore in late 1865, Bombay (Mumbai) February to March 1866, and Baroda (Vadodara) in April. Vaneck then returned to Europe (performing for Napoleon III in Paris on August 12th 1866), but was back in India at the start of 1867. Vaneck and Wessely are now accompanied by a "Mr Philipps" and it seems that Ruchwaldy has parted company with them.[5]

Certainly by July 1868 Ruchwaldy and his wife are in Bombay,[6] and we find the earliest record of him performing under his own name. He bills himself as Hungarian and as having arrived from Vienna. If he did return to Europe there is no record of him performing there: "Professor Ruchwaldy, the Hungarian Wizard, Pupil of Professor Anderson, [!] and Madame Ruchwaldy, the celebrated Pianiste, Pupil of Liszt, [?] have arrived from Vienna, and intend shortly to give a series of performances in Bombay". They opened their "First Grand Magical and Musical Performance" on August 22nd, with further shows on 27th and September 5th (with Ruchwaldy now also playing the "Violon claron, or wizard violin").[7]

They travelled widely. In April 1870 he was in Ceylon (Sri Lanka),[8] and in July that year his wife had a son in Calcutta (Kolkata).[9] In 1872 he was touring India, "advertising himself in the up-country papers".[10] In early 1873 they were performing in Penang and soon in Singapore — "...a very thin audience. The best part of the entertainment was the musical, in which Mme Ruchwaldy appeared both as a pianist and singer, and Prof-essor Ruchwaldy as a violinist. The evening closed with a series of dissolving views...".[11]

Later that year they returned to Europe, and a son Alfred was born in Wies in Austria on September 30th.[12] They appear to have remained in Europe until about 1879.

In May 1875 he performed in Warsaw, which proved a disaster. He claimed to be Court Magician to the King of Siam (Thailand), and recipient of the *Pusamala* medal.[13] He stated that "he has not yet introduced himself in Europe and comes direct from India, and as proof he showed us the local newspapers, from Singapore. He speaks several languages, preferably English, and speaks Serbian well".[14] He plastered Warsaw with posters of himself holding his own severed head in his hand, which caused some amusement.[15]

He opened on May 20th, "to an almost empty house", said one newspaper, continuing sarcastically: "... Despite his success in India, La Plata, Tierra del Fuego, and the waterless Sahara ... the Professor could not please barbaric Warsaw ... such a giant miracle worker that in Central Africa the kings gaped when he worked his magic... Mr. Ruchwaldy, although, as he claims, this is his first time in Europe, knows all the tricks of European magicians, with watches, cards, etc. and does them no better and no worse than the others..." The weather was hot and the prices were high, which did not help, but there were *four paying spectators*, and some others with free tickets. Deciding, we are told, that those four had got enough for their money he did not bother with part two of the advertised show but proceeded straight to the music, playing "an instrument of his own invention brought from India, made of bamboo strung together...".[16]

He advertised a second show for May 23rd, "a Great Magic Performance combined with an Instrumental Concerto by Professor Ruchwaldy and his wife..." — "Undaunted by our indifference, the magician lowered the prices to half and gave a second show. Despite this, the pews were empty ...". He then called it a day.[17]

We next catch sight of him in 1877, now in the Baltic. His wife had a daughter in Mitava (Jelgava) on August 19th 1877,[18] and the *Lexikon* (per Sven Hirn) records him ("der siamesische Hofkünstler") performing in Finland that year. In November he was in Riga, billed as "[tr.] Imperial East Indian and Royal Siamese Court-Magician".[19] There is no news of how he fared, but six months later a notice in the official gazette states that "boxes and pictures" he had pawned are to be sold by auction.[20]

By early 1880 he was back in India, performing in Lahore in April, "A Grand Comic, Vocal, Instrumental, and Legerdemain Performance ... by Professor L. [*sic*] Ruchwaldy, Wizard of the North, Hungarian Star Violinist and Comic Vocalist, assisted by Miss Annie Orlande, The Celebrated Clairvoyance [*sic*]...";[21] and later that year in Singapore, now with the children involved: "Professor Ruchwaldy The Celebrated Hungarian Sorcerer, with Troupe of Variations, consisting of Necromancy, Musical, Optical, Vocal, and Comical Performances with three children of 5, 7, 9 years old...", and in Penang ("...two entertainments in music and magic to appreciative, but not over large, audiences").[22]

They travelled extensively. In 1881 he is in Bombay, performing with Miss Annie Orlande ("the Parisian lady Clairvoyante"),[23] in April 1882 he, his wife and their now five children are sailing from Hongkong (Hong Kong) to Singapore.[24] In Bombay in 1883 the family are now "The Hungarian Anglo-Variety Troupe, consisting of four wonderful children, aged 3, 5, 7, and 9 years, Madame Malwin Ruchwaldy ... and Professor B. Ruchwaldy, partner of the late Professor Vaneck" — the first time he is found advertising this connexion; he clearly believed that Vanek was dead.[25]

In 1884 we find them again in Lahore, "Professor Bernhardy [*sic*] Ruchwaldy, with his clever family ... the programme embraces Necromancy and Music...",[26] and in 1887 in Singapore, where there was a fuss over his not "allowing military under the rank of a Sergeant to enter his premises".[27] And in 1889 in Karachi he and his wife are part of the entertainment following the haggis on Burns Night.[28]

By February 1890 the family are living in Hongkong. Two of their children are buried there,[29] the parents' names given on the tombstone as *Bernhard and Malvine Ruchwaldy*.

In 1890, testifying that his Chinese cook had threatened to stab him, he was described as a "professor in music and foreign languages";[30] in 1891, testifying for a friend, he was said to be "a naturalised British subject".[31] He would hardly state this in a legal hearing unless it were true but there is no record of him being naturalised — not under the name Ruchwald or Ruchwaldy.[32] The last sighting of him in the East is in Shanghai in 1892 where he sued "Mr. Redmond, of the Central Hotel, for the proceeds of two performances given in the Lyceum Theatre". Ruchwaldy had paid out $54 but received only $15 from his two performances: "His Worship, as plaintiff had no evidence, found that he had no cause for action and dismissed the suit".[33]

He now decided to travel to Hawaii, arriving in Honolulu from Yokohama in May 1893, and saying on arrival that he planned to remain there if possible; his wife and children did not accompany him.[34] He advertised for some time as a music teacher,[35] and announced a "grand magical, psychical, and musical entertainment" for June 10th, making much of his decoration received from the King of Siam.[36] The reception was at best luke-warm — "The professor's efforts seemed to meet with favor although most of his tricks had a 'chestnutty' flavor",[37] and he soon left for San Francisco.

He arrived there on July 19th but we hear nothing of him until late 1895 when he first performed there. He opened at the Bush Street Theater on November 11th after some expensive advertising the preceding week in at least three papers, *San Francisco Call*, *San Francisco Examiner* and *San Francisco Chronicle*. All reviewed his show on the 12th, the verdicts running from poor to worse — "Professor Ruchwaldy, the Siamese sorcerer, gave a magic performance … last night. There is some novelty in it" (*SF Chronicle*); "Professor Ruchwaldy … opened at the Bush-street to a very slim audience. Some of the tricks he performed were good, but they cannot be said to be very new" (*SF Call*); "A man announcing himself as Professor Bernhardy Ruchwaldy, Sorcerer to the King of Siam, made his San Francisco debut … last night. There were about twenty people in the house. The sorcerer gave some bad imitations of several time-worn tricks of Herrmann" (*SF Examiner*).

There is no mention of a second show, and he continued on his travels. At the start of 1896 he has arrived in Mexico City, and managed to attract some interest, perhaps helped by his new stage-name "**Bosco Ruchwald**y" (which probably owed more to B118 than to B1). The Anglophone paper *Two Republics* noted his arrival in town: "Prof. Bosco Ruchwaldy, the famous painter [!], and for years portrait painter to the king of Siam, is at the Central Hotel for a few days".[38] He returned to Mexico City in March and apparently took a lease on the *Orfeum* theatre, which became the *Orfeum Bosco Ruchwaldy*. "Profesor Bosco Ruchwaldy. prestidigitador de la corte do Siam" gave shows of "Legerdemain and Indian Jugglery" each evening with an afternoon show of Optical Illusions ("la ilusión óptica *Abdulin Melosin* y el sorprendente y maravilloso *busto vivo*").[39] Then in April came the announcement: "A New Theatre. Ruchwaldy's Orpheum to Be Transformed into a Concert Hall … [it] will soon be metamorphosed into a concert hall, after the style of similar resorts in the United States. A permanent exhibition of legerdemain performances, just as the well-known magician had contemplated, not having met with the successes the enterprise deserved, and the introduction of novel attractions has been planned … all the available talent in the variety line … there will be a refreshment counter and pretty girls will be engaged to wait on the patrons… the proprietors and managers, Messrs Pablo L. Royal, Prof. Ruchwaldy, and Francisco Duran, expect to throw open the doors of their new theatre, which is to be known under the name of 'Folies Bergeres' a week hence".[40] This enterprise even wins a mention in the massive *Reseña Histórica del Teatro en México*,[41] but neither that nor the newspapers reveal what became of this Mexican *Folies Bergeres*. However, the fact that by October he was living in New Orleans suggests it did not survive long.

In late October he was giving shows for the Y.M.C.A., but even for this audience his performance won little appreciation — "…a small audience …the performance consisted of about fifteen odd tricks, card tricks, palming, and a repetition of Bancroft's coffee trick. A violin solo … was perhaps the only redeeming feature… he is more acceptable as a violin performer than as a wizard…". And we see him playing the violin in concerts until the following February, though there is one further magic show mentioned, a charity performance for the Seamen's Bethel, preceded by a piece claiming that he not only performed for the King of Siam but was tutor to his son, performed in "Jaypore, Nizam, Tunk and Ulunar" in India, appeared before the Mikado in Japan, and taught German to Queen "Lillonkalani" of Hawaii.[42]

By 1901 he was living in New York, getting in the newspapers a couple of times. In November that year a headline said it all: 'Robbed by Woman He Helped. King of Siam's Friend of Seventy Thinks New York Belles Ungrateful'. Described as "a bland and innocent person", "a music teacher", he appeared in court wearing his "gorgeous decoration" from the King of Siam, to lay a complaint of robbery against "an attractive young woman" he had met in the street and "she was willing to talk to him, though they had not been introduced"; they had a drink in the back room of a saloon and he offered to teach her the mandolin. While there another woman and two men entered; the woman was taken ill, and he assisted her to the train. He later found that $30 was missing from his pocket. The woman was found and on being searched by the police matron had on her Ruchwaldy's gold eye-glasses which he had not noticed were missing..."[43]

In 1903 he sued the Manhattan Railway Company in the New York Supreme Court in a drawn out case, the eventual result being "judgment in favor of the defendant dismissing the complaint, and for $146.12 costs".[44]

He is listed (*Bernhard Ruchvaldy*) as a French and Violin teacher in a 1902 NY City directory.

He died in New York on June 1st 1909, registered as *Bernhart Ruchwaldy*, "widowed", address 121 W. 105th St,[45] which was the "Home for Aged and Infirm Hebrews of New York". His age was given as 65 but he was surely older than that. He was buried on June 3rd in Mount Zion Cemetery in Queens, recorded as *Bernhard Ruchevaldy*.[46]

NOTES

[1] Both the registers are online on *ancestry.com* in 'England, United Grand Lodge of England Freemason Membership Registers, 1751-1921'.

[2] *Times of India* 20 Jan.1883. Vanek was in fact still alive.

[3] *Pesth-Ofner Localblatt und Landbote* 16, 19 Sep.1854 (with favourable comments — "[tr.] Herr Vanek needs only to make his name in Europe for the general public to rank him with the celebrities in his field, Döbler, Bosco, Hermann, etc.").

[4] Letter written from Alexandria where he is "[tr.] amusing the Arabs", quoted in *Grazer Zeitung* 4 Mar.1860.

[5] *Englishman's Overland Mail* 7 Nov.1865; *Bombay Gazette* 11, 24 Feb.; 10, 17, 26 Mar.; 24 Apr.1866; 7 Jan.; 13 May 1867.

[6] He was married by 1864 when their eldest child was born; his wife's name is variously given as Malvina (Malvin, Malwin, Malvine) Peck or Peska.

[7] *Bombay Gazette* 30 July, 17, 25 Aug.1868; *Times of India* 1 Sep.1868.

[8] *Morning Post* [London] 2 June 1870.

[9] *Homeward Mail from India, China and the East* 19 Aug.1870.

[10] *Indian Statesman* 5 Apr.1872.

[11] *Straits Times Overland Journal* 30 Jan.; 13 Feb.1873.

[12] The birth registration (which confirms his wife's name and that they were Jewish) is online on *FamilySearch*. He gives his profession as "Magier Professor".

[13] Possibly he had been to Bangkok but the claim is very reminiscent of Vanek's, who performed for the King earlier that year (*London and China Telegraph* 24 May 1875).
[14] *Kurjer Codzienny* 3 May 1875.
[15] *Gazeta Polska* 18 May 1875.
[16] This is an abridged amalgam of the four reviews in the *Gazeta Handlowa, Kurjer Codzienny*, and *Kurjer Warszawski* of 21 May 1873 and *Tygodnik Illustrowany*.22 May 1873.
[17] *Wiek* 22, 24 May 1875; *Kurjer Warszawski* 22 May 1875; *Gazeta Polska* 24 May 1875; *Ognisko Domowe* 28 May 1875; *Gazeta Warszawska* 31 May 1875.
[18] "Sakhanine Ruchvaldi", parents Bernard and Malvin (née Peska): Latvian births on https://www.jewishgen.org.
[19] *Rigasche Zeitung* 19 Nov.1877; *Libausche Zeitung* 20 Dec.1877.
[20] *Kurländische Gouvernements Zeitung* 14, 28 June 1878.
[21] *Civil & Military Gazette* 30 Apr., 1 May 1880.
[22] *Singapore Daily Times* 30 June, 2, 12 July; 20 Nov.1880.
[23] *Times of India* 22 Apr., 1 June 1881.
[24] *Overland China Mail* 18 April 1882.
[25] *Times of India* 20 Jan.; 8 Mar.1883.
[26] *Civil & Military Gazette* 24 Dec.1884.
[27] *Straits Times Weekly Issue* 7 Sep.1887.
[28] *Civil & Military Gazette* 2 Feb.1889.
[29] Online at url:174. Helmuth died when he fell off a cliff flying a kite, Julia died of the plague. A son Nathan became a successful composer, publishing songs and music (mainly waltzes), but committed suicide in Singapore in 1901.
[30] *Overland China Mail* 19 Feb.1890.
[31] *Overland China Mail* 19 Mar.1891.
[32] Based on searches of *https://discovery.nationalarchives.gov.U.K.* and of 'UK, Naturalisation Certificates and Declarations, 1870-1916' on *ancestry.com*.
[33] *North China Herald* 5 Aug.1892.
[34] *Honolulu Advertiser* 10, 13 May 1893. His wife was still alive in 1898 (sailing from Hongkong to Singapore with three of the children); her furniture was auctioned in May 1905.
[35] *Pacific Commercial Advertiser* 17 May to 22 July 1893 (the final ad. appearing after his departure).
[36] *Evening Bulletin* 29 May 1893; *Honolulu Advertiser* 3, 7 June 1893.
[37] *Honolulu Advertiser* 13 June 1893.
[38] *The Two Republics* 2 Jan.1896.
[39] *The Two Republics* 12, 16, 19 Mar.1896; *El Nacional* 12, 16 Mar.1896.
[40] *The Two Republics* 4 Apr.1896.
[41] By Enrique de Olavarrria y Ferrari (2nd ed., 1895) Vol. IV p.621: online at url:175.
[42] *Times-Picayune* 31 Oct., 3 Nov.1896; 27 Feb.1897; *Times-Democrat* 31 Oct., 20 Nov.1896.
[43] *New York Press* 24 Nov.1901.
[44] *New York City Record* 10 Mar.1905.
[45] Death registration online at url:176,
[46] Burial record online at url:177.

Asia

Many European, especially British, theatrical troupes toured Asia and the far east in the 19th century, but none of the Boscos are known to have performed there apart from Ruchwaldy (who was not calling himself 'Bosco' at that time), B43 and B120 (and Madame Schulz, C46, who called herself Bosco's daughter).

B120. Professor Bosco in Darjeeling

A "Professor Bosco" (possibly = B43) was performing in Darjeeling in 1892. The first report "from our own correspondent" reads: "Professor Bosco, the great wizard, has given two performances, but the result cannot have been satisfactory". But of his show on April 30th we are told: "Professor Bosco, the Wizard, astonished a large audience with his clever feats of skill and sleight of hand. Some of the tricks were truly wonderful, and we hope the Professor will give many more entertainments before leaving Darjeeling" (*Englishman's Overland Mail* 20 Apr.; 11 May 1892).

Boscos in Australia

B121. "Bosco" (Philip Dent, Dinte, Schpinesky).

The colourful career of this conjuror and ventriloquist who performed widely in Australia between 1874 and 1882 is told in fascinating detail by Kent Blackmore at http://sydneymagic.net/bosco.html.

Despite advertising from 1877 as "Bosco! Bosco! From the principal Theatres in Europe…" it is unlikely he ever performed outside Australia. He billed himself as "Bosco", "Monsieur Bosco", and for a period (using his mother's maiden name) as "Bosco Schpinesky"; he was often referred to by newspapers as "Professor Bosco" and less often as "Signor Bosco", but did not use these titles in his own advertising.

He was born to Hyman Dinte and his wife Mulyazetcha, née Schpinesky, probably in Kalisz, Poland, in 1846; his original first name is unknown, but he took the name Philip James Dent when he and his father settled in England after his mother's death. In 1860 they migrated together to Melbourne and both worked as tailors.

He died in prison (on a charge of vagrancy) in Sydney on June 14th 1892, registered as Philip Bosco Schpinesky.

B122. Bosco impostor, Brisbane 1874.

When the "Mammoth Company" including B121 arrived in Brisbane at the start of May 1874 they were faced with a rival company calling itself the "Mammoth Troupe" which featured an impostor billed as "The Great Bosco! Bosco! Bosco!" — plus "the Great Somatic Conjurer and Fire King, Herr W. Frikell!".

The impostors advertised in the *Brisbane Courier* 30 May 1874 announcing they were in town but had not opened when the genuine Mammoth Company arrived: the latter advertised on 1 June that "The Legitimate Mammoth Company, with the real Bosco … are in no way connected with the persons advertised to appear in South Brisbane…". They opened on June 3rd and on 15th were still stressing in their advertising that *they* had the real Bosco…

B123. Signor Bosco, Australia 1891-3

Found performing in New South Wales in 1891-1893: "Signor Bosco in his Marvellous Feats of Legerdemain and Thought reading", part of a large variety troupe at the Coogee Palace Aquarium (*Sydney Daily Telegraph* 24 Jan.1891).

He promises "an exposé of so-called 'Spiritualistic phenomena,' including 'Spiritual Fire and Lightning', 'The Transmutation of Wine and Water', and 'The Great Metempsychosis or Transmigration of the Spirit', at the Royal Standard Theatre in 1892 (*Sydney Morning Herald* 20 Aug.1892). In Bowral he is billed as "Signor Bosco, the original and world-renowned Wizard of the South" (*Bowral Free Press* 12 Oct.1892), but the fact that he performed for two years in this limited area strongly suggests he was a local.

Last sighted as Bosco "the king of miracle workers", in January 1893 at the Aquarium (*Evening News* [Sydney] 27 Jan.1893).

Among other Australian theatricals who took the name 'Bosco', non-conjurors, were
- Professor and Madam Bosco, advertising as "the well-known palmists" in Sydney in 1891;
- Bosco Wilson, agent and "old time variety pro"; real name William John Folkeston Wilson;
- Major Bosco, "wonderful midget" in a comedy act with Harry Sadler.
- In Melbourne in October 1889 "a man named Charles Moore, *alias* Charles Duncan Valentine, *alias* Charles Russell", a bogus theatrical promoter, was prosecuted for obtaining money by false pretences (*Argus* 13 Sep.1889, etc.): one report (*Otago Daily Times* 26 Oct.1889), by the usually well-informed "Scalfax" (Harry Wilby Taylor) listed "Professor Bosco" among his aliases; if so, he is unlikely to have been one of the above,

Boscos in New Zealand

None of the overseas Boscos toured New Zealand apart from Le Roy, Talma and Bosco in 1905 and 1914.

At least two unidentified local magicians took that name.

B124. "Prof. Bosco", New Zealand 1884

Found once, performing at a Rowing Club concert in Hamilton in 1884 — "Feats of Legerdemain by the Great Prestidigitateur, Prof. Bosco" (*Waikato Times* 25 Sep., 7 Oct.1884).

B125. "Professor Bosco", New Zealand 1893

Another is found performing in the "Professor Bosco and Otto Herz Company" at several concerts in 1893 (Herz did a ventriloquist act), but all in the Wairarapa district — a charity concert in Woodville, "illusionary entertainment by Professor Bosco" (*Bush Advocate* 9 Mar.1893); soon after at a school concert — "Professor Bosco went through conjuring and slight-of-hand [*sic*] feats which brought down the house …

performed with a definite skill and address which at once proclaims Professor Bosco to be a professional" (*Woodville Examiner* 8 May 1893). And he is indeed performing professionally in a variety show a week later in Dannevirke — "Prof, Bosco, Illusionist and Conjurer, in his startling illusion, 'Stroubika'"[1] (*Bush Advocate* 11 May 1893). He gave a show on his own in Pahiatua as well, "…it consisted of sleight of hand tricks and songs for the first part, and the second part was made up with a startling illusion where a boy was placed on a board and padlocked down by the hands, feet, and head. On firing a pistol the boy disappeared and in his place a girl made her appearance" (*Woodville Examiner* 12 May 1893).

NOTE
[1] It would be interesting to know where he learnt this, *La Stroubaika persane* of Georges Méliès.

A bogus "Signor de Bosco" got some free hotel accommodation in New Zealand in 1893 by claiming to be touring a circus. One of the many 'Bosco' snake charmers (Captain Greenhalgh) was in New Zealand in 1922; and "Bosco the Ventriloquist and his Pal Jerry" is found in 1939.

FEMALE BOSCOS

BF1. Madame Bosco (1) (Mrs Millar)

The earliest Female Bosco was the elusive "Mrs Millar"; elusive not as regards her career which can be traced in detail, but as regards her early life. We do not know her first name or her maiden name, or when and where she and Professor Millar married. We first hear of her, simply as Millar's wife, in Dublin in March 1856 when Epstein's (B12) black servant was said to have used "insulting and filthy language" to her. After her death she was said to be from Yorkshire, implying they probably met and married in England after Millar's arrival in July 1855, but there is no record of a matching marriage (in England, Scotland or Ireland). Perhaps they had previously married in America; perhaps they were not legally married at all.

Her career is for convenience here described in her husband's entry (B62). As a performer, "Madame Bosco, the Wonder of the Age", she is first advertised in Bristol in May 1857 but her earliest actual performances traced were in Wales, starting in Newport on June 1st that year. They left England for America in 1858 and in September they are living in Rondout, New York State, and "Madame Bosco, the celebrated female magicianess, just arrived from Europe" is looking for business. She performed in America with some success but died in Ottawa, Illinois, on July 31st 1860. Obituaries stated that she was "a great sufferer from paroxysms of the spine; to allay or deaden this intense pain, she resorted to great doses of ether and chloroform".

BF2. Madame Bosco (2) (Marian Ball)

The last we see of the original Madame Bosco (BF1) in England is in Worcester in January 1858. Two other female magicians were currently performing in Britain. One was "Mdlle Vernone", performing since 1856, who had just adopted the stage-name Veroni (see *Appendix Z11*). The other was "Miss Marian", also performing since 1856, and she now adopted the vacant stage-name "Madame Bosco".

She was first seen in Liverpool in August 1856, billed as "Miss Marian, the American Enchantress" and "the first and only Lady performing the Black Art",[1] then in Wigan,[2] Bolton,[3] Blackburn,[4] Leigh,[5] Bury,[6] Chester, all with some success — "…all that 'Bosco', 'Anderson' and all the other wizards perform, she executes with ease, grace, and the utmost sang froid…".[7]

In January 1857 she was in Wrexham,[8] but then "Miss Marian" drops out of sight, reappearing in May 1858 in Ireland under the name "Madame Bosco". She is first found under this name in Cork,[9] then touring Ireland — Waterford in October,[10] Wexford in November, Kilkenny in December and the following February, Carlow in July 1859, and a long successful run in Dublin in early 1860.[11]

She was still there in April, and in May her husband and manager was involved in a court case over payments to their printer, and we learn their real name: he was charged as "James Bosco", stating when asked: "James Bosco is not my real name, but is the name I have used for years"—"Is it not the name of a celebrated actor in the necromantic line that you have seized on."—"It is."—"Now, for the benefit of posterity, let us know what your name is."—"Ball …".[12]

"Madame Bosco" is then sighted performing in Leeds in December 1860, April 1861 in Dudley and West Bromwich, Aldershot in May, usually in music halls. Touring Berkshire on her own later in the year, audiences were often poor — in Reading the *Era* correspondent sympathised: "Madame Bosco, the female *magicienne*, has met with wretched business, and no likelihood of improving, having dismissed Saturday night's audience, not numbering seven persons. The lady is particularly clever, and well calculated to draw good houses, and worthy of the notice of enterprising Managers".[13]

When we see her at the Royal Pavilion in Brighton in July 1862 she has reverted to the name "Madame Marian Ball", still "the Great Original Magicienne".[14] She was next in Portsmouth and then in Ryde, where her repertoire is listed as "Table and Spirit Rapping, the Love Token, the Fiery Goblet, the Protean Bottle, the Enchanted Plume, the Lilliputian Hornpipe, the Inexhaustible Bottle, the Crystal Pyramids. To conclude with the Enchanted Tree; or, Botany Extraordinary".[15] She is accompanied for a period by a young trapeze artist, Hubert Meers, "the only Rival of Leotard", whose act concluded in "a Terrific Leap of One Hundred Feet".[16] Reviews were good — Meers on the trapeze "truly astounding and very clever" and Marian's "conjuring tricks were of a high order" — but there were so many entertainments on at that time of year that audiences were small.[17]

Later that year she was touring Wales, still with Meers, and advertises as "Madame Marian Ball (late Bosco)".[18] In December she had a long run in Birmingham, billed as American as she had been in 1856 — "Madame Marian Ball, the Great American Magicianne…".[19]

She was in Wolverhampton in early 1863, again in Birmingham at the end of that year, then the last sighting of her is in Birmingham in early 1865, "Madame Marian Ball in her World of Magic".[20]

NOTES

[1] *Liverpool Mercury* 23 Aug.1856; *Liverpool Daily Post* 17 Sep.1856.

[2] *Wigan Observer and District Advertiser* 11 Oct.1856: "… Some of Miss Marian's tricks were very good, but, on the whole, the performances were not of that superior character we were led to expect from the extraordinary amount of puff which ushered in her appearance".

[3] *Bolton Chronicle* 18 Oct.1856: "Miss Marian's Enchanted Evenings… the first and only enchantress in the world… selections from the most recherche of her experiments…": for this catchphrase see *Appendix Z11* on Vanoni, note 11.

[4] *The Weekly Standard and Express* 5 Nov.1856: "…mechanical delusions as well as … sleight of hand tricks".

[5] *Leigh Chronicle and Weekly District Advertiser* 15 Nov.1856: "…fifty distinct feats of Magic and Sleight-of-hand…".

[6] *Manchester Courier* 29 Nov.1856.

[7] *Chester Chronicle* 27 Dec.1856.

[8] *Wrexham Advertiser* 24 Jan.1857. A lengthy advertisement making much of her elaborate apparatus… and "she will endeavour to restore the science of Magic to its ancient dignity, to present it to the Illustrator of the laws of Nature, to arouse the reflective faculties of her audience, rather than to illude them only and cause them bewilderment…".

[9] *Cork Constitution* 4 May 1858; *Era* 9 May 1858.

[10] "Madame Bosco, the Great Original and only Female Magician in the World…": *Waterford News* 8 Oct.1858.

[11] \ "…the great original and only magicienne in the world": *Freeman's Journal* 9 Feb. 1860.

[12] The case was reported at some length in *Irish Times* 18 May 1860. The jury found for the defendant and the judge agreed: "…I think it is as impudent an action as ever I tried".

[13] *Era* 25 Aug.1861.

[14] *Brighton Guardian* 16 July 1862.

[15] *Isle of Wight Observer* 2 Aug.1862.

[16] Hubert Meers, born in Birmingham in 1844, was a member of the famous circus and equestrian family.

[17] *Isle of Wight Observer* 9 Aug.1862.

[18] *Merthyr Telegraph* 4 Oct.1862.

[19] *Birmingham Daily Gazette* 24 Dec.1862.

[20] *Birmingham Daily Post* 21 Jan.1865.

BF3. Madame Bosco (3) (Madame de Lonno)

De Lonno, wife of Leotard Bosco (B77), is billed with him as both *Mdlle* and *Mme* De Lonno, They conjured conjointly — "Neat and puzzling legerdemain tricks were executed by Madame De Lonno and Leotard Bosco" (*Era* 24 Oct.1875) and "Madame de Lonno, The greatest female conjuror, travelling in conjunction with Leotard Bosco. The most wonderful sleight of hand performer now before the public. These artistes have no equals…" (*London and Provincial Entr'acte* 24 Feb.1877).

Dawes (see B77) says she is last sighted in *Era* 12 May 1883, but she come out of retirement for a benefit performance in Hanley in December 1885, as "Madame Bosco" — "Madame Bosco had a most cordial reception, and her clever sleight-of-hand tricks were watched with keen interest…" (*Era* 26 Dec.1885).

BF4. "Signora Bosco" (Albina di Rhona)

The well-known actress, dancer and singer Albina di Rhona performed in a farce 'Wie man Künstlerin wird' ('How to become a female magician') at the *Münchener Aktien-Volkstheater* in Munich in 1868 playing a female "Bosco". The play included singing, dancing and "experiments in natural magic" (*Schwank mit Musik, Tanz und Experimenten in der natürlichen Magie*). It was in three scenes, the third being: "Signora Bosco, or an Hour of Deception in the Theatre" (*Eine Stunde der Täuschung im Theater*). The dancers included her as "Fräulein Bosco, Taschenspielerin". Advertised: *Süddeutscher Telegraph* and *Münchener Tages-Anzeiger* 23 Apr.1868

Described as "the celebrated Danseuse soubrette from St. Petersburg" when she first performed in England in 1860, she has an entry in *Biographisches Lexikon des Kaiserthums Oesterreich* saying she was born Albina Hron in Bohemia *ca.*1837.

BF5. Unidentified female Bosco in France 1868

Eugenio wrote to *Le Monde* 1 Sept.1868 complaining of male and female Bosco impostors, the latter even claiming to be Bartolomeo's daughter: "…il y a en ce moment en France un individu qui se dit fils de Bosco, et qui escroque le monde… Puis il y une prestidigitatrice qui se fait appeler fille de Bosco; celle-là ne se contente pas seulement d'escroquer les personnes en s'appuyant sur ce nom célèbre, mais aussi elle vole."

BF6. Mme Bosco, Dijon 1881

Performing in Dijon ("Grande représentation de physique et de prestidigitation moderne, sans préparatifs") in October 1881 is "Mme Bosco", claiming to have given 75 shows in Paris, 47 in London, 15 in St Petersburg, 20 in Constantinople, 14 in Athens, 10 in Tunis, 13 in Madrid, 16 in Rome, 20 in Naples, 15 in Milan and 10 in Turin, and in "all the great cities of Europe and America" (*Le Progrès de la Côte-d'Or* 13, 14 Oct.1881).

No more is heard of her, before or since.

BF7. Frau Nina Bosco, Estonia 1883.

In Reval (modern Tallinn) in April 1883 Herr Professor Giordano advertised an exhibition of Magic and Antispiritualism accompanied by his daughter Frl. Antoinette and a "Somnambule", Frau Nina Bosco, billed as only daughter of the famous Bartolomeo Bosco.

(*Grosse Vorstellung des Magikers und Antispiritisten Herrn Professor Giordano und seiner Tochter Frl. Antoinette und der Somnambule Frau Nina Bosco, einzigen Tochter des berühmten Bartolomeo Bosco*: Revalsche Zeitung, 7 Apr.1883)

BF8. Emma Bosco

Found performing on several occasions with **J. R. Borkini Bosco** (B37) in the Netherlands in 1884, as "Mejuffrouw Emma Bosco" or "de Wonderdame Mej. Emma Bosco". She is probably Emma Zanfretta (later Anderson), née Valdran (Valdren), 1860-1913.

BF9. Lina Bosco

Frl. Lina Bosco is found 1881 to 1892 accompanying Max Rössner, "Hofkünstler aus Berlin", who travelled with his own *Zaubertheater*. (Rössner, 1852-1906, has an entry in the *Lexikon*). Her role was to perform a series of transformations in various costumes billed as 'Dreams from the 1001 Nights' and she herself may not have done conjuring in the act.

1881 in Zug, Switzerland (*Neue Zuger Zeitung* 30 July 1881);

1882 in Berlin (*Berliner Börsenzeitung* 11 Feb.1882);

1884 in Gleiwitz (now Gliwice) in Silesia (*Der Oberschlesische Wanderer* 25, 27 Mar.1884);

1888 in Berlin (*Berliner Börsenzeitung* 14 Jan., 11 Feb.1888)

1892 in Prague (*Prager Tagblatt* 5 Mar.1892)

BF10. Giovanna Bosco

Found in Hilversum in Gooi in 1885 is Giovanna Bosco with dissolving views — "Extra Groote Voorstelling van Giovanna Bosco. Met zijne Dissolving Views (Verdwijnende Gezichten), en Stella! Wat is Stella! Wat is Stella! Het ondoordringbare geheim van de 19de eeuw…": *De Gooi- en Eemlander* 20 Nov.1885.

BF11. Mlle Sellina Bosco

Found only once, performing in Tiel in 1887 with Professor Don Giovanni Bosco (B44).

BF12. Hedwig Bosco (Hedwig Stuller)
She has an entry in the *Lexikon,* married to Joseph Stuller (Joe Bosco, B55),

The partners of Morton Bosco (B69) and of Lyndale Bosco (B84) also appeared on stage as "Madame Bosco" but not as conjurors; they were clairvoyant and sword performer respectively.

A stage performer of unknown genre "Miss Bosco", real name Sarah Ann Norton, "known in the travelling show world as Miss Bosco", was sent to gaol for 14 days at Chesterfield in 1901 for having abandoned her two children, Evelyn and Victoria, aged 12 years and fifteen months (*Shepton Mallet Journal* and *Leigh Chronicle* 16 Aug.1901; a similar report in *Derbyshire Times and Chesterfield Herald* 14 Aug.1901 gives her stage name as "*Mrs* Bosco").

"PUPILS AND RELATIVES"
Some stole Bosco's name, others merely claimed to have been his pupil, associate, follower, or even relative. Some may have genuinely used the term "pupil" as a mark of homage and respect, as Bartolomeo described himself as a pupil of Pinetti and Antonio Blitz himself as a pupil of Philadelphia. And at times the term "pupil of Bosco" was used by newspapers virtually as a synonym for magician. However, many of these are clearly laying claim to an actual apprenticeship, one they did not have. It is just possible that a few had actually paid Bosco for a little tuition but even that hardly qualified them to claim to be his "pupil".

They are listed here, male and female in one alphabetical sequence, with brief biographies where possible, either newly composed or referring to standard sources if they exist.

This list also includes those who claimed to be related to Bartolomeo but did not use the name "Bosco" – if they did the latter they have an entry in section B.

Not included are the countless descriptions in reviews or advertisements of performances as "*à la Bosco*", or magicians as "a worthy rival of Bosco", or "another Bosco", or "outdoes Bosco", where he is the yardstick of perfection; nor humorous examples of wily politicians being termed "a pupil of Bosco", where he is the yardstick of duplicity.

C1. M. Abadie-Gasparin
Several newspapers in 1844 reprinted an account of "M. Abadie-Gasparin", a captain in the 68th Regiment stationed in Toul in northern France, who gave a charity magic show, demonstrating great skill; he is described as "a pupil of Bosco" (*élève de L'italien Bosco, et comme lui aussi adroit, ses tours d'escamotage laissent surprise qui eût été enviée des Comte, Olivier, Comus, Chalon, Conus et autres de leurs fameux devanciers..."*).
(originally in *L'Impartial de la Meurthe;* reprinted *Gazette nationale* 7 Jan.1844; *Der Humorist* 20 Jan.1844; etc.

C2. Giovanni Barbarigo-Clementini.

Found performing in Split in 1885 ("Qui si trova il rinomato professore di prestidigitazione e fisica, sig. Giovanni Barbarigo-Clementini": *Narod. Das Volk* 7 Mar.1885) and the following year in Marburg, where he is described in general terms as "a pupil of Bosco and Hermann", not a claim he is making himself (*Marburger Zeitung* 15, 18 Aug.1886: "...Professor der Magie aus Verona ... ein Schüler Bosco's und Hermann's...").

C3. Ferdinand Friedrich Becker, 1813-1835

Becker (entries in the *Lexikon* and *Zauber-Pedia*, etc.) certainly advertised himself as a "former associate of Bosco" (*ehemaliger Compagnon des Hrn. Bosco*). As Rusconi says (pp.68-9), when Bartolomeo left Germany for Italy in 1835, young Becker filled the vacancy, performing tricks very similar to Bosco's, and to legitimise this imitation he claimed to have worked with Bosco. There is no evidence for that (and, as Rusconi says, p.69 n.8, no evidence for Houdini's statement that Becker had been Bosco's pupil and revealed some of his secrets).

He is announced as "ehemaliger Compagnon des Hrn. Bosco" in (for example) *Museum der eleganten Welt* 26 Mar.1836; in his detailed 1837 Leipzig Fair poster (held in the Stadtmuseum, Leipzig; online at url:178), and still in *Fränkischer Merkur* in 1839.

He also referred to himself as "**Bosco II**" — this occurs regularly in newspaper announcements of his forthcoming arrival and was clearly part of his own publicity material — examples include: *Zeitung fur die Elegante Welt* 21, 26 Feb.1835; *Augsburger Postzeitung* 8 Apr.1836; *Augsburger Tagblatt* 17 Apr.1836; *Paderbornsches Intelligenzblatt* 19 Dec.1838.

A review of Becker in *Bohemia* 4 Oct.1835 made some salient points: "[tr.] He appeared in a very tasteful costume and with bare arms, continued to speak uninterruptedly during the production, until he asked the audience to take a short break, and in all these aspects reminded one of Escamoteur Bosco, whose former companion Herr Becker announced himself to be ...a pity that Herr Becker works more with apparatus than with his hands, and the cup and balls, this touchstone of an Escamoteur, he does not perform with the calm and elegance of a Bosco ... he does not yet know, like Bosco, how to create excitement in the audience, to lead them astray, and to surprise them all at once..."

C4. MM. Belval, père et fils

M. Belval from Bordeaux is first found performing in December 1846 in his home town, and performed there regularly over the years with an act including "Le Palais des Enchantements, Le Charivari des Montres, La Décapitation, Le Jardinier-Fleuriste, La Boule de Syracuse, and Les 500 Cadeaux et autres expériences aussi surprenantes qu'extraordinaires".[1] At the fair in 1847 he set up his own theatre titled *Illusions fantasmapolemoscopiques,*[2] and continued over the years to perform in Bordeaux in public and in private homes.

By 1848 he is calling himself "élève de M. Comte" and travelling more widely; in 1849 he is in Rochefort, "au salon, une séance de magie";[3] back in Bordeaux in 1851 and again in 1853. In 1852 he is in Avranches, still billing himself as "élève du célèbre Comte" with "une séance de prestidigation dans le genre des Bosco, des Conus, et du fameux Robert Houdin".[4] He received a warm review in Pau in 1855, and in La Rochelle in 1858 he is said to have astonished the audience there back in 1854 by "sa dextérité prestigieuse et par la variété de ses tours ingénieux".[5]

In Dieppe in 1860 he is first found calling himself "seul élève de Bosco",[6] as he did for many years. In 1861 in Valenciennes he is "élève de Bosco" and "seul élève du célèbre Bosco" and indeed "le dernier prestidigitateur de France".[7] The following year in Saint Quentin he is "physicien, prestidigitateur et magnétiseur ... seul élève du célèbre Bosco, qui parait en avoir fait aussi le seul héritier de son incomparable talent" — the sort of claim that so annoyed Eugenio.[8]

In Seine-et-Marne in 1865 he is offering "une Soirée de Prestidigitation et de Fantasmagorie ... élève du célèbre prestidigitateur Bosco...",[9] and the same claim in Bellac in 1868 and in Bagnères-de-Bigorre in 1869.

Back in Bordeaux in 1868 he claimed not only to be vaguely "a pupil" of Bosco but that he had actually taken lessons from him, and from Conte,[sic] — "le prestidigitateur bordelais ... un habile disciple de Conte et de Bosco, dont il a, d'ailleurs, reçu des leçons".[10]

Then in April 1870 in Gaillac we have **Belval father and son** performing together, "MM. Belval père et fils, élèves de Conte et de Bosco..."[11]

In Finistère in 1876 is "M. Belval, prestidigitateur" offering private shows en route to Brest, then in Bellac in 1878 we have "M. Belval Fils" with a "Soirée de haute Prestidigitation".[12] In 1880 we again have "M. Belval, physicien" with a "séance de prestidigitation" in Bordeaux, presumably the son,[13] and the last sighting is "M. Belval, prestidigitateur" in Meaux in 1899.[14]

NOTES
[1] *Le Mémorial bordelais* 6 Dec.1846; *L'Indicateur* 10 Jan.1847.
[2] *Le Mémorial bordelais* 23 Mar.1847.
[3] *Les Tablettes des Deux-Charentes* 26 May 1849.
[4] *Le Journal d'Avranches* 21 Nov.1852.
[5] *Le Mémorial des Pyrénées* 18 Jan.1855; *L'Écho rochelais* 26 June 1858.
[6] *La Vigie de Dieppe* 9 Nov.1860.
[7] *L'Echo de la Frontière* 5, 6, 7 Sep.1861; *Le Courrier du Nord* 20 Sep.1861.
[8] *Journal de la ville de Saint-Quentin et de l'arrondissement* 29 May 1862.
[9] *Journal de Seine-et-Marne* 25 Mar.1865.
[10] *La Gironde* 10 Jan.1869.
[11] *Le Mémorial de Gaillac* 30 Apr.1870.
[12] *Le Républicain de Finistère* 21 Dec.1876; *Le Nouvelliste de Bellac* 24 Mar.1878.
[13] *La Petite Gironde* 8 Feb.1880.
[14] *Journal de Seine-et-Marne* 5 Feb.1899.

C5. Francesco Benevolo, 1865-1939

Benevolo, who Gallicised his name as **François Bénévol** when in France in 1894, has a brief entry in the *Lexikon* and a French wikipedia article which refers to the biography *Bénévol: le maître du mystère* by Jacques Garnier (Orléans, 1969), and the exhibition catalogue *Bénévol, 1865-1939: exposition, Musées d'Art de la Ville de Clermont, 2 mars-30 avril 1982* (Clermont-Ferrand, 1982).

A contemporary article on him, 'F. Bénévole' in the Roubaix newspaper *La Revue* (22 Nov.1894) said: "[tr.] From a very young age, Bénévole dedicated himself especially to the study of this science [*viz.* prestidigitation]. His singular natural aptitude caught the attention of Bosco who regarded him very highly and made him his pupil" (*...ses rares dispositions appelèrent l'attention de Bosco, qui le prit en grande estime et en fit son élève*).

From the date this could only be Eugenio, of course, and there is no evidence for this.

C6. E. Bentheim.

Found performing at a charitable private show in Prague in 1885, said to be a citizen of Prague and to have costly apparatus, he is described as "a pupil of Bosco" ("...der durch seine Wohlthätigkeits-Vorstellungen seit Jahren als Prestidigi-tateur bestens bekannte Prager Bürger Herr E. Bentheim, ein Schüler Bosco's, dem die kostbarsten Apparate für die Salon-Magie zur Verfügung stehen...": *Prager Abendblatt* 16 Nov.1885).

C7. Karoline Bernhardt (Caroline Bernhard)

This well-known performer advertised an 1838 show as "Wunder der natürlichen Magie dargestellt: eine Reihe überraschender Kunststücke aus dem Gebiete der unterhaltenden Physik, Chemie und egyptischen Zauberei" and herself as "Frau Caroline Bernhard, Kollegin von Bosco, Königl. Preuß., K. K., Oesterr. und K. K. Russ. Hofkünstlerin und Professorin, Schülerin des berühmten Eskamoteurs Pinetti und Künstlerin der natürlichen Magie ..." — *colleague of Bosco; magician and professor to the Prussian, Austrian and Russian courts; pupil of the famous conjuror Pinetti...*".

A Danzig paper termed her the "weibliche Bosco" (quoted with a smile by *Der Humorist* 19 June 1841, not because of the Bosco comparison but because she was said to be Viennese). Her skills were highly regarded, the *ATZ* (3 Dec.1833) saying she deserved an honoured place beside Bosco, Comus and Döbler.

C8. August Broëta

August Broëta, who billed himself as "pupil of Bosco" from 1860, is first found performing as a magician and ventriloquist in 1854, though was probably active long before that.[1] In Salzburg in 1854 he is billed as having won great applause in the most important theatres in Germany and America,[2] and continued to make grandiose claims throughout his long career. There is no trace of him in America under the name Broeta. In Klagenfurt in 1854 he announces ventriloquism with three voices, magic without apparatus, Madame Broeta blindfolded as a clairvoyant, and the climax of the show a "Hiolosus or Gakalak" and a boa constrictor fed live rabbits on stage.[3]

Then in September that year we get some interesting information: a report from the Chief of Police in Agram (modern Zagreb) describes him as born in Peigarten (a village in Thaya in Austria), an itinerant conjuror and ventriloquist, who had worn unauthorised military decorations, claiming he had served in the Greek army and that a crippled foot and several other wounds were from military service. However, it had been reliably established that Broeta had never served in a foreign army but in the Austrian military, and had been sentenced to two years in the Fortress of Comorn for a serious theft. Dismissed from military service, he was in custody because of a burglary in a parsonage near St. Pölten, where he tried to escape and damaged both feet so severely that he was left lame. He was accompanied by Clara Zahradnik from Moravia, whom he claimed was his wife, and a fifteen year old apprentice Rudolph Weiß, probably an orphan. Broeta's past showed him to be a dubious individual, a risk to property, impudently deceiving the public for profit, and all authorities should be made aware to keep a close watch on him.[4]

He resurfaces two years later and has successfully resumed his career, arriving in Krems, "August Broeta, with family, Professor of Ventriloquism and Magician"; the following year we find him in Melnik, reported as having travelled all over the world, and here performing "higher ventriloquism" and exhibiting a mummy which had been in the Sahara Desert for 1200 years.[5]

By 1860 he has begun claiming to be a pupil of Bosco —"ein Schüler Boskos":[6] but some papers were sceptical — in Iglau (Jihlava) he was described as "angebliche Schüler des berühmten Bosco" (*alleged pupil of the famous Bosco*).[7]

A long and very positive review of him as a ventriloquist and a conjuror in 1860 lists some of his repertoire — "die Uhr in tausend Trümmern, das wandernde Blatt, der Zauberhut, der fliegende Ring, die vier untrennbaren Aß, der englische Koch, die Cigarrenspende, die fleißig Eier legende Henne".[8]

Over the next few years he is found in Innsbruck, Linz, Bolzano ("Zögling des berühmten Bartholomäus Bosco"), back in Klagenfurt (imitating five people, a parrot and a dog), Ljubljana (said not to be a real ventriloquist but an imitator of animals and people), Děčín, Brno (claiming silver apparatus, Bosco as his teacher, and military service), Jihlava, Znojmo, Teplice, and in 1865 back in Innsbruck, now calling himself Baron Broëta and claiming to be travelling from Russia to London. Later sighted in Bolzano ("Schüler des berühmten B. Bosco"), Lindau, Kempten, Lviv, and in 1867 Chernivtsi, where the paper published a long account of his life and career, apparently completely fabricated: "von Broëta", we are told, having travelled across much of America and Asia, especially Arabia, had taken part in the fighting of 1809 and in the Battle of Leipzig (1813) and had spent a lifetime as a soldier, then as a doctor after being wounded; later with the Indians in America and the Bedouin in Arabia; a natural history researcher, collector, and owner of a menagerie; before deciding to retire to his estates in Moravia — when the Prussians arrived, "burnt his belongings and emptied his granaries", forcing him to return to his life of wandering — now aged eighty —suggesting he was born c.1786.[9]

In 1870 he is in Znojmo (calling himself Herr August *Ritter v.* Broeta), Krems, and Graz (now speaking in eight voices and singing a duet with himself); in 1871 in Marburg and Klagenfurt; 1873 in Teplice (still "Zögling des berühmten Bartholmäus Bosco");[10] 1875 in Litoměřice (now with dissolving views) and Žatec; 1877 in Krems, said to be age 84, performing "with the elasticity of a youth", and then heading to Weitra and elsewhere in the Waldviertel region...[11]

That is the last we hear of August Broëta.

But in 1912 there is a report of the death in Freistadt and burial in Vienna of Franz Broeta, said to be his son,[12] age 69 and a conjuror, who had gone blind suddenly some years earlier while performing his juggling act. Franz was known in his hey-day as the 'Zaubererbaron', because he claimed to be of an aristocratic family which had emigrated from Belgium to Austria.[13] His grandfather, we are told, still owned estates, but Franz's father August led a wandering life and lost both the estates and the right to his noble title.[14]

Franz is buried in Friedhof Meidling, together with an Anna Broeta, died 1916.

NOTES

[1] He is probably the Hr. Boëta [*sic*] giving a charity "Kunstvorstellung" in Graz in 1846 (*Grazer Zeitung* 3 Feb.1846).

[2] "...der berühmte Bauchredner und Kunstpfeifer Hr. August Broeta, welcher auf den bedeutendsten Theatern Deutschlands und Amerika's den größten Beifall erwarb" (*Neue Salzburger Zeitung* 12 Jan.1854).

[3] *Klagenfurter Zeitung* 18 Mar.1854 ("... ein Hiolosus, oder Gakalak gennant, sich mit der Abgotts oder Königs-Schlange zeigen, welche dann mit lebenden Kaninchen ... gefuttert wird").

[4] *Eberhardts allgemeiner Polizei-Anzeiger* 14 Sep.1854.

[5] *Kremser Wochenblatt* 12 July 1856; *Bohemia* 8 Nov.1857.

[6] *Salzburger Zeitung* 24 Nov.1860 (his imitations of a parrot and of sleigh-bells highly appreciated).

[7] *Sonntags-Blatt für Gewerbe, Industrie, Handel und geselliges Leben* 29 July1860.

[8] *Gmundner Wochenblatt* 6 Nov.1860.

[9] *Bukowina* 11 Oct.1867.

[10] *Teplitz-Schönauer Anzeiger* 29 Nov., 6 Dec.1873.

[11] *Kremser Wochenblatt* 3 Nov.1877.

[12] But was he the apprentice Weiß, born c.1839?

[13] The implied link is to the family of Joseph-Guillaume de Broëta, ennobled by Empress Marie Thérèse in 1768, but there is no evidence that August or Franz were related to this family.

[14] *Deutsches Volksblatt* 3 Mar.1912; *Illustrierte Kronen Zeitung* 5 Mar.1912; *Illustrierte Kronen Zeitung* 5, 9 Mar.1912 (with a picture of Franz).

C9. Matteo Bassi

Little has been found about Bassi, who described himself as *a pupil of Pinetti and a former companion of the no less famous Bosco* ("Schüler des berühmten Pinetti und vormaligen Gefährten des nicht minder berühmten Bosco"). A note on him in a Polish newspaper (*Gazeta Warszawska* 27 Oct.1837, when he was performing in Vienna) said he was from Trieste and by then had performed in "Europe, Asia, Africa and America, and recently for the Sultan in Constantinople".

Magier der Welt records him in Innsbruck in 1833 and also his appearance in the *Theater in der Josephstadt* in Vienna in 1837, of which there are three interesting detailed reviews.

Der Humorist (28 Oct.1837) pointed out he was too young to have been Pinetti's pupil, and that, while he did perform with bare arms as announced, the sleeves of his jacket (*Spenser*) kept falling down, and that he did only five tricks but had promised ten — but no matter about all that, were they all *ein Taschenspielstreich,* playing tricks on us? But he did do one trick that was unfathomable, and alone worth the effort, and his patter was droll and amusing, though more suited to a hotel waiter than to the stage.

Allgemeine Theater-Zeitung (same date) was disappointed that the show did not live up to its bombastic promotion, expecting "something better and newer than these worn out *Taschenspieler-Schwänke*", describing Bassi as a "pretend imitation Italian" who speaks Viennese dialect the way only a local can; he is not without skill but puts more effort into his humorous talk than dexterity into his tricks; the cup and balls, torn handkerchiefs, cooked birds are all old as the hills, and to produce this stuff you don't need to have travelled to the four quarters of the globe and performed for the Dalai Lama; but he did have one good trick, with the bag of eggs…

Wiener Zeitschrift (same date) also liked the bag of eggs but found his other acts ordinary, and the audience soon got bored with the long wait required for setting up; it praised his skill but thought him better suited to private shows than to the theatre.

C10. Valentin Burzinski

Valentin Burzinski, described as a Polish refugee, a former army office, born in Warsaw, is found performing mainly in France, also in Germany and Switzerland, between 1839 and 1855, consistently claiming to be a pupil of Bosco.

He is first sighted in the north of France, in Saint-Quentin, Aisne, in September 1839,[1] then soon in Paris,[2] and the following year in Lausanne ("élève du célèbre Bosco").[3] He made quite a stir in Dieppe in 1841 where "Bosco-Buzinski" [*sic*], we hear, "did all sorts of marvels, an omelette cooked in a hat, a rhinoceros hatched from a hen's egg" and promising to remove the shirt of some local celebrity without touching his tie and to swallow half a kilo of English eels washed down with nitric or prussic acid…[4]

He travelled extensively — sighted in 1843 in Düsseldorf;[5] 1844 in Marseille and Aix; 1846 in Brussels, Paris, Bern; 1847 in Florence[6] and in La Rochelle ("l'élève et le rival de Bosco"); 1849 in Bourges; 1851 in Aurillac;[7] 1852 in Dieppe[8] and touring Switzerland; 1853 in Saumur, Nantes, and Alençon; 1855 in Loiret and Meaux, where he is still "élève du célèbre Bosco"; but when last sighted, in Saint-Germain-en-Laye in 1856, he is calling himself "l'élève de Robert Houdin".[9]

NOTES

[1] *Journal de la ville de Saint-Quentin* 8 Sep.1839: "…polonais, natif de Varsovie, élève de Bosco, physicien, se propose de donner une Soirée de physique amusante, de mécanique et de prestidigitation expérimentale…".

[2] *Le Siècle* 19 Sep.1839.

[3] *Gazette de Lausanne* 7, 24 July 1840.

[4] *La Vigie de Dieppe* 8 May 1841.

5 *Düsseldorfer Zeitung* 25 Jan.1843 ("…M. Valentin Burzinski aus Warschau, früher Offizier der polnischen Armee im Friedenheitskampfe, Schüler des Herrn Bosco…").

[6] *Oesterreichisches Theater- und Musik-Album* 8 Feb.1847 ("Bużynski, Schüler Bosco's aus Paris, wird hier Vorstellungen geben. *Jam satis*".

[7] Two of his programmes are recorded as held in the *Archives départementales du Cantal* (*https://francearchives.fr/agent/18805102*); not digitised.

[8] *La Vigie de Dieppe* 12 Oct.1852: "…une séance de physique amusante, donnée par M. Durzinski [*sic*], prestidigitateur, élève de M. Bosco…".

[9] *L'Industriel de Saint-Germain-en-Laye* 4 Nov.1856.

C11. Callet

Callet, whoever he was, performed with Eugenio in France in 1891 and was described as his pupil.

Eugenio was touring the south of France that year, Nice in June, Marseille in July, then he has Callet with him in Béziers in July, and in September they performed together in Toulouse. No more is heard of him as a magician.

(*Le Messager du Midi* 7 Aug.1891; *Le Sud-Ouest* 16 Sep.1891; *La Dépêche* 17 Sep. 1891)

C12. Maximilian Ritter von Caspary

Maxim. Ritter von Caspary is first sighted in Prague in 1849 ("Eskamoteur"), and the following year in Innsbruck, where he is described as "a pupil of Bosco", said to have performed widely and in Prague for Kaiser Ferdinand. He is again said to be "pupil of Bosco" in Vienna later the same year.

(*Bohemia* 26 Oct.1849; *Der Bote für Tirol* 25 Apr.1850; *Grazer Zeitung* 9 Aug.1850)

He was again in Vienna in 1852, then in Pest in 1853, where, said *Der Humorist*, his performances attract limited interest, because for all his skill he lacks the right *savoir faire* necessary for success, the magical *je ne sais quoi* that makes the performances of a Döbler or a Herrmann so appealing.

(*Fremden Blatt* 25 Mar.1852; *Der Humorist* 2 Mar.1853)

He is last seen in Hermannstadt (Sibiu) in Transylvania in 1854, with his wife as a clairvoyant.

(*Der Siebenbürger Bote* 12, 17 May 1854)

C13. Bernard Marius Cazeneuve, 1839-1913

Much has been written on Cazeneuve's life and career, by himself and others, including articles in *ZauberPedia*, *fr.wikipedia*, and (as Cazaneuve) in the *Lexikon*.

It is often said (on what evidence?[1]) that it was late in 1852 that Bartolomeo took on Cazeneuve, age 13, as a pupil in Toulouse, his home town. That cannot be correct as Bosco did not perform in Toulouse until the end of 1855 (see B1), and Cazeneuve, born in 1839, spent time after leaving school with the Spanish riding academy and directing the Lyric Theatre in Lyon before training as a magician: there is no record of him performing until 1859.[2]

Certainly Cazeneuve is found invoking Bosco's name in his advertising over the years. In Nancy in 1860 he is announced as "[tr.] This eminent artist, of whom his teacher M. Bosco is rightly proud",[3] then soon after in Nantes he is even claiming to be Bosco's son-in-law.[4] He is still billed as a pupil of Bosco in 1867,[5] and "un digne élève du fameux Bosco" in 1871.[6]

In an 1868 newspaper there is an unlikely story of Bosco meeting a French officer and his wife in Algeria: "… Bosco talked to us of a pupil whom he cherished and who would take his place…"; they realised that this was Cazeneuve, and the story, in a Perpignan paper, goes on to sing Cazeneuve's praises at some length — he was (not coincidentally) performing in Perpignan at the time.[7]

Cazeneuve's claims were long remembered and his obituaries described him as "pupil then rival" of Bosco.[8]

NOTES

[1] According to Rusconi (p.164) Cazeneuve states that it was at the "teatro Moncavrel in Toulouse" and (note 8) that he states this "nelle sue memorie". What these *memorie* might be is unclear (*and the Theatre Montcavrel* [sic] *did not open until 1864*). It may be in Benoit's novel, *Le Commandeur*? Félicie de Montazon in his adulatory *Aventures de Cazeneuve prestidigitateur, suivies d'une notice biographique* (1864) says merely that Cazeneuve was Bosco's pupil and that he was deservedly named "le *Petit Bosco*".

[2] In Bordeaux — *La Gironde* 16 Oct.1859: "Demain Dimanche, 16 octobre, représentation extraordinaire donnée par M. B. Cazeneuve, professeur de magnétisme, physicien prestidigitateur, seul élève de Bosco, accompagné de la somnambule Ernestine Cazeneuve, surnommé la Sybille du XIXe siècle…".

[3] *L'Espérance* 4 Mar.1860: "…cet éminent artiste, dont M BOSCO, son professeur, s'enorgueillit à juste titre".

[4] "gendre de Bosco": *Le Phare de la Loire* 2, 9 Apr.1860. He makes the same claim in *L'Argus et le Vert-vert réunis* [Lyon] 7 Oct.1860: "…je suis l'élève et le gendre du célèbre Bosco…".

[5] "élève de Bosco": *Le Curieux: journal des théâtres* [Montpellier] 1 Dec.1867

[6] *L'Écho Saumurois* 4 July 1871.

[7] *Journal des Pyrénées Orientales* 17 Nov. (continued in 20 Nov.) 1868: this is the same story that has the officer turn out to be the son of Bosco's colonel in the Russian campaign (B1 n.5).

[8] "élève puis rival du célèbre Bosco", *La République française* 17 Apr.1913, and widely reprinted.

C14. Charlesco

In Chalon-sur-Saône and Dijon in 1894 is "Charlesco" who, among much else, is "a pupil of Bosco" — "le célèbre Charlesco, dit Mephisto, originaire de la Pologne russe, l'inimitable de l'Exposition de Lyon, où il a obtenu les plus grands succès au cirque Rancy et au Velodrôme [sic]... L'homme diable, nommé l'homme squelette, ventriloquiste, imitateur dans huit langues différentes, equilibriste des salons, physicien des salons, élève de Bosco... deux séances vraiment extraordinaires et uniques dans leur genre".
(*Courrier de Saône-et-Loire* 28 Oct.1894; *Le Progrès de la Côte d'Or* 1 Nov.1894)

C15. L.M. Cohn

The Dutch magician and ventriloquist L.M. Cohn called himself "a follower of Bosco" (*hij noemt zich den navolger van Bosco*). A review of his performance of "Egyptian Magic and ventriloquism" found that "[tr.] he performed tricks that are worthy of that great master and won the acclaim of the public" (*Drentsche courant* 26 Feb.1850).

C16. Professor Debraine

Advertised in Altona in 1858 is "Erste Vorstellung (als Bosco) des Herrn Professor Debraine aus Paris in der natürlichen Magie" — vaguely saying that he was performing "as Bosco" (*Altonaer Nachrichten* 13, 14 Mar.1858).

C17. Philippe Demeure

In Namur in 1852 is an otherwise unknown Philippe Demeure, announced to give "[tr.] an extraordinary performance which will leave far behind it everything ever given on this stage. Besides the dissolving views, the diorama, the scene of the fall of Rome, M. Philippe Demeure will show us new magic tricks into which he was initiated by the famous Bosco, whose pupil he was". (*Le Journal de Belgique* 12 Feb. 1852)

C18. Mdlle Élisabeth

In 1862 in Gaillac the local newspaper reported a performance by "Mdlle Élisabeth, élève de M. Bosco" ('pupil' clearly used in a very general sense), who "[tr.] amazed the audience with her magic tricks"; she may have been very young as "[tr.] we have never seen smaller hands perform such marvels" (*Le Mémorial de Gaillac* 6 Sep.1862).

C19. Faure-Nicolay

The well-known Faure-Nicolay (real name Nicolas Maurice Faure, born Chalabre, Languedoc, 1831; died Rio de Janeiro 1903) is said to have been taught by Bosco in an article published when Faure and his daughter were touring Poland in 1867 (*Dziennik Warszawski* 21 May 1867). Presumably using material supplied by Faure, this states:

"[tr.] … In southern France, he met the famous magician Bosco, who, seeing the unusual dexterity in him, initiated him with all honesty into all his art. Soon the student equalled the teacher and Bosco himself called him publicly his alter ego" (*W poludaiowej Francji poznal się z slawnym magikiem Bosco, który dostrzeglszy w nim niezwykla zręczość, wtajemniczyl go z cala szczer scia w wezystkie swe sztuki. Wkrótce uczén dorówral nauczyclelowi i sam Bosco nazywał go publicznie swoim alter ego*).

Faure does not make this claim later in his autobiography, *Memorias e confidencias*, published in Rio de Janeiro in 1901, saying only that as a child he saw Bosco perform —"[tr.] I have fun breaking eggs like the famous Bosco whom I had seen in my childhood at a fair in Montpelier".

C20. Emil Gottlieb (Georg Gottlieb; Georg Homes), 1851-1934

Gottlieb has an entry in the *Lexikon* (under Georg Gottlieb), and much has been written on his later anti-spiritist and cinema careers.

In his early days as a conjuror he regularly billed himself as a pupil of Bosco ("Emil Gottlieb, Schüler des bekannten Bosco": *Laibacher Tagblatt* 17 Apr.1878; "Schüler des berühmten Bosco": *Innsbrucker Nachrichten* 16 Sep.1878; "učenec mnogo imenovanega Bosco": *Slovenski narod* 21 Apr.1878).

C21. August Günther

Günther, found performing as a magician in Latvia and northern Germany 1848-1853, advertised himself as "brother-in-law of the famous Bosco" ("Schwager des berühmten Herrn Bosco").

He is first sighted in Riga in 1848, arrived from St Petersburg, "magisch-physikalischer Künstler aus Berlin", advertising a show of Egyptian Magic. He had previously performed in Dorpat (modern Tartu) for four weeks and had an even longer run in Riga, where his brilliant apparatus and hundred candles drew the crowds, and won him acclaim as holding a high place in his profession and "equal to his brother-in-law Bosco".
(*Rigasche Zeitung* 18, 25, 31 Aug.; 4, 18 Sep.1848)

The following year he was just as successful in Libau (Liepāja), or almost — rated among the best in his profession and *almost equal to his brother-in-law Bosco.*
(*Libausches Wochenblatt* 11 June 1849).

He is noted passing through Riga with his family in January 1850, and passing through Libau in August — possibly performing there or on his way to St Petersburg.
(*Rigasche Zeitung* 24 Jan.1850; *Libauische Wochenblatt* 2, 5 Aug.1850).

But back in Dorpat in May 1850 all has changed: "A famous magician intends to fill the house here using the name of his brother-in-law Bosco, but it no longer has any pulling power. It seems someone has already copied the trick. The poor man is now staying with a Jewish tailor and is said to be unwell. If his brother-in-law only knew...!". Then three months later we hear "Bosco's brother-in-law has gone to Polangen [modern Palanga], where seventy families are said to be bathing".
(*Das Inland* 8 May, 14 Aug.1850).

He is last heard of in 1853 in Magdeburg, still claiming to be "Schwager des berühmten Herrn Bosco" — Bosco's brother-in-law— advertising a show of Egyptian Magic at the Neustädter Bierhalle, followed by favourite operatic songs by Bertha and Gustav Günther.
(*Magdeburgische Zeitung* 4 Sep.1853)

C22. Heer Heijneman

A "Heer Heijneman" advertised a Soirée in the *Pax Intrantibus* Coffee-house in Middelburg in September 1868, claiming to be "first pupil of the world famous Bosco" ("eerste Leerling van den wereldberoemden Heer BOSCO": *Middelburgsche Courant* 1, 5 Sep.1868)

C23. K. Hofmann

A magician "K. Hofmann" (once as Hoffmann), said to be from Würzburg, is found performing in Germany in 1860 and 1866. He bills himself as "Artist der Magie" and in 1866 as "Artist der Magie und Schüler des berühmten Bosko" — *Nürnberger Beobachter* 14 Jan.1860 ("Vorstellung der neuen Magie oder der scheinbaren Zauberei ohne Apparat..."); *Fürther Tagblatt* 28 Jan.1860; *Schweinfurter Tagblatt* 19, 20 Mar.1866; *Fränkischer Kurier* 14 Dec.1866.

C24. Eduard Jentzsch

Jentzsch has an entry in the *Lexikon* noting his first appearance, at the Leipzig fair in 1861, and quoting his claim that "[tr.] he worked for a considerable time under the guidance of some of the most famous conjurors, Bosco, Becker, Frikell, etc., and picked up a lot from them".

The following year in Magdeburg he grandly claimed to have been "a great supporter of Bosco senior for many years" and that his own skills "had a precision and elegance that deserved the unreserved recognition of his now famous teacher Bosco senior" (*er steht in Betreff seiner Leistungen Bosco senior seit langen Jahren innerhalb seiner Sphäre in erster Linie zur Seite ... mit einer Präcision und Eleganz, welche ... seinem zur Zeit berühmten Lehrer Bosco senior die unumwundendste Anerkennung abgenöthigt haben...: Magdeburgische Zeitung* 5 Mar.1862)

C25. Franz (Franzisco, Francisco) Kehry

Franz Kehry is first sighted in March 1866, arriving in New York from Bremen, age 46, "artist", place of origin Kreuznach, with wife Elisabeth and sons Rudolph, 7, and Clemens, 4.[1]

By May he is in San Francisco and as "Francisco Kehry, the Circassian", is giving his "grand exhibition of Oriental Magic" at Platt's Hall, advertised as "the first entertainment of the kind ever given in America". A disappointed reviewer said that "his feats consisted almost exclusively of mechanical feats of substitution… cleverly done" but "not new", though he praised young Rudolph's "Terrific Crystal Act" in which he spun round on his head on a pyramid of fifteen decanters, then drank water from one "up instead of down". (*Daily Alta California* 7 to 12 May 1866)

They moved on to Sacramento (promising "Feats of Legerdemain of the Oriental Nations", but one paper called it "infernal 'bilk' … German charlatanism"), and they are last seen in America in Calaveras County in June.
(*Sacramento Daily Union* 18 May 1866; *Shasta Courier* 26 May 1866; *Calaveras Chronicle* 16 June 1866)

We next see him in Kaiserlautern and Zweibrücken in November 1871, still performing in his Circassian costume ("Franzisko Kehry aus Tscherkessien") and proclaiming himself a pupil of Bosco senior ("Er is ein Schüler von Bosco sen."). He claims performances before the Czar of Russia, the Sultan of Turkey, the Grand Vizier of Egypt, the Shah of Persia and, interestingly, the former Circassian leader Shamyl (possibly when he was in Constantinople).
(*Pfälzische Volkszeitung* 8 to 13 Nov.1871; *Zweibrücker Zeitung* 18 Nov.1871)

His full name is given as Franz Jakob Kehry in the marriage registration of his son Clemens in Lambrecht in 1887 and in the baptisms of his children.

[1] Passenger list transcription on *https://www.immigrantships.net*; image on *ancestry.com*.

C26. Sakarinie Kinsbergen (Isaac Roelof, *aka* Izak Rudolph, Kinsbergen), 1824-

Advertising himself as a pupil of Bosco in the Netherlands between 1862 and 1867 is magician "Sakarinie Kinsbergen", a member of the large Kinsbergen circus dynasty which included *artistes* of all sorts, musicians, actors, scene painters, equestrians, clowns, gymnasts, performers with dogs and birds, the "Gebroeder Kinsbergen" with their camera obscura, and a succession of magicians.

"Sakarinie" was Isaac Roelof (Izak Rudolph) Kinsbergen, born in Groningen on July 7th 1824, son of Roelof (Rudolph) Hermanus Kinsbergen and Clara b. Isaac van Praag.[1] His father, Roelof (Rudolph) Hermanus, 1790-1871, had a long performing career,[2] as did Isaac's older brothers Jacob, 1818-1900,[3] and Leendert, 1823-1907.[4]

Isaac was performing as a magician by 1850, then is first found using the stage name "Sakarinie", and claiming to be "a pupil of Bosco and others", in 1862 in den Helder.[5] The "and others" soon disappears and in 1863 in Leiden, now with his family in the show, he calls himself the "only pupil of Bosco", "Professor of Natural Magic, known as the Devil's Magician".[6]

In March 1864 we find him in Leeuwarden, and in April in Zwolle, still making much of being a pupil of Bosco — "[tr.] He is said to have a precious collection of apparatus with him, which he must have taken from his teacher, the great Bosco". [7] In June that year he was performing in Leiden ("Extraordinary Performance of Chinese Magic..."),[8] and the following year again in Zwolle, performing with his wife at a thanksgiving festival for the fiftieth anniversary of Waterloo, still advertising as Bosco's sole pupil.[9] And the same in Assen that year, in Zwolle the following year,[10] and in 1867 in Harderwijk, the last occasion he is found with the claim "eenig élève van BOSCO".[11]

In 1867 in Tiel he advertises "Groote Voorstelling in de Physische Magische Tooverijen, van FAUST in verband met BOSCO en DAVENPORT",[12] and is still invoking Bosco in Tilburg the following month — "Groote Voorstelling A LA BOSCO & DAVENPORT...".[13]

Then in late 1869 he took over the management of Ernst Basch's "Cagliostro's Theater", billing himself as "Sakarinie-Kinsbergen, known as Cagliostro II".[14] In 1870 we find in Steenwijk the "Cagliostro-Theater Basch under the management of Sakarinie-Kinsbergen, known as Cagliostro II",[15] and he continues this connexion with Basch as "Cagliostro II" until at least 1873.[16]

Isaac is last recorded in 1900; his death date is unknown.

NOTES
[1] An earlier child also named Isaac, born in 1821, died in 1822.

In official records Isaac ("Sakarinie") is variously listed as "Goochelaar" (1850), "Mechanicus" (1856), "Toneelspeler, Schouwburgdirecteur" (1884), "Mechanicus" (1887), "Goochelaar" (1888, 1900); he is named as "Sakarini van Kinsbergen" in the death registration of his daughter Helena. In 1850 he married performer Eva b. Levi de Jong; their children joined them in the show from the 1860s, and his son Lion (Leon), born 1860, took over the stage name "Sakarinie", performing until the 1930s; Lion died in 1940, he, his wife, and several of their children Holocaust victims.

[2] "Muzikant" (1814), "Koorddanser" (1817), "Kunstenaar" (1818), "Voltigeerder" (1821), "Vertoner" (1825), "Goochelaar" (1828), "Googchelaar" (1850), "Gochelaar" (1871).

[3] "Goochelaar" (1845), "Toneelspeler" (1849), "Mechanicus" (1850-1868), "Kermisreiziger" (1878), "Kunstenaar" (1881), "Verhuurder van Schouwburgtenten" (1885), "Goochelaar" (1897). He and his father performed as Jacques Kinsberger, Senior and Junior — "*Soirée Pariesiène,* Jacques Kinsberger, Senior, Professor de Tours d' Adresse et Physique ... Suspension Ethereénne, in eene horizontale rigting, ingevolge den beroemden Robin..." (*Dagblad van 's Gravenhage* 21 Jan.1850); "Soirée Mystérieuse, Jacques Kinsbergen, Junior, Professor in de Physica..." (*Dagblad van 's Gravenhage* 30 Jan.1850). Jacob married Rachel Boaz in 1844; their children included Levi-Ruben, "goochelaar".

[4] Leendert Lion (Leon; also occasionally given in records as Levie) was performing in Amsterdam from 1851 as Lion Kinsbergen, "Professeur en Physique in Tours d' Adresse en uitheemsche Touren" and in 1852 is offering soirées of "Egyptische Tooverkunst à la Bosco". He is recorded over the years as "Goochelaar" (1851), "Paardrijder" (1852, 1853), "Mechanicus" (1852, 1853, 1858), "Kunstpaardenrijder"

(1857), "Kermisreiziger" (1868), "Artist" (1875), "oneeldirecteur" (1875), "Verhuurder van Schouwburgtenten" (1885), "Goochelaar" (1877, 1887, 1888). He is probably the "L. Kinsbergen-Maju, Professor of Magic to the King of Holland", performing in London June to December 1863 (*Globe* 1 June 1863. at the Colosseum; *Uxbridge & W. Drayton Gazette* 15 Sep.1863: "…clever specimens of Legerdemain …a chaste solo on the lately-invented brass instrument, the Saxophon"). He married his cousin, circus rider Jeannette Blanus (Blanes), in 1851; their children performed with them from the 1860s and sons Mozes, Roelof, and Jacob are all later recorded as "Goochelaar".

[5] "Vorstelling van Toeren uit de Hooge Goochelkunst door den Heer Sakarinie Kinsbergen, Professor in de Naturlijke Magie … Groote Brillante Egyptische Voorstelling in die Magie, door den wereldberoemden Prestidigateur Sakarinie Kinsbergen, élève van den beroemden Bosco en anderen" (*Nieuwe Courant van Den Helder* 5 Nov.1862).

[6] "…den wel-beroemden Toovenaar en Kunstenaar der Zwarte Kunst SAKARINIE KINSBERGEN, eenig Elève van BOSCO Professor der Natuurlyke Magie bekend onder den naam van Duivelskunstenar…SAKARINIE KINSBERGEN en Familie…" (*Leidsch Dagblad* 6 June 1863; *Leydse Courant* 8, 19 June 1863).

[7] *Leeuwarder Courant* 15, 25 Mar.1864; *Provinciale Overijsselsche en Zwolsche Courant* 1, 5 Apr.1864.

[8] "Koffijhuis *De Pauw*. Buitenewone Voorstelling in de Chinesche Magie of de Tooverijen der Negentiende Eeuw…" (*Leydse Courant* 6 June 1864).

[9] "1815 WATERLOO 1865, Volksfeesten de Zwolle … 6° Voorstellingen door den Heer en Mad. SAKARINI KINSBERGEN, eeinig élève van BOSCO" (*Provinciale Overijsselsche en Zwolsche Courant* 16 June 1865).

[10] *Provinciale Drentsche en Asser Courant* 24 Oct.1865; *Provinciale Overijsselsche en Zwolsche courant* 15 June 1866.

[11] *Overveluwsch Weekblad* 9 Nov.1867.

[12] *Tielsche Courant* 8 Dec.1867.

[13] *Weeklblad van Tilburg* 11 Jan.1869.

[14] "Groote Vauxhall … te Haarlem … Cagliostro's Theater van Sakarinie-Kinsbergen, bijgenaamd Cagliostro II. Physica, Magie, Optica, en Hydrauliek à la Basch" (*Opregte Haarlemsche Courant* 29 Oct.1869; and a very similar advertisement in Nieuwediep soon after: *Heldersche en Nieuwedieper Courant* 21 Nov.1869.

[15] "Cagliostro-Theater Basch, onder leiding van Sakarinie-Kinsbergen, genaamd Cagliostro II" (*Opregte Steenwijker Courant* 19 Dec.1870).

[16] *Provinciale Drentsche en Asser courant* 4, 7 Feb.1873; *Leeuwarder courant* 21 Mar.1873.

C27. Johann Krämer

Johann Krämer, calling himself in his advertisements and visiting-cards "Professor of Magic and Phrenology", was prosecuted for fortune-telling in Gießen in 1871 in a case that was reported at length across Europe.[1]

He told police he was a conjuror and magician, a pupil of Bosco (*"er sei ein Taschenspieler und Zauberkünstler, ein Schüler Bosco's"*), born in 1833 in Nordheim in Bavaria and apprenticed as a tailor, now retired after touring for many years in England, America, Switzerland, France and Belgium, and an American citizen receiving a pension for wounds received fighting the Indians. He had met Maria Sophia Winzenburg in Bremen in 1858, they had a son in 1859, and married in London in 1864 (the last, at least, is correct). It was shown that in Germany he had served several prison sentences for charging the gullible for fortune telling and deception, promising health, husbands, and lottery winnings.

These required the purchase of a "lucky ticket", which was to be worn on the breast for 27 days. It contained the following magic words [*beware:* the versions in various papers differ, so I cannot guarantee that these will work]: "Indurbieda Schurseh-Rekua Barkua Markua Mulkablie, Die Immerwährende Liebe und Glück in mein Herz N. K. d M." At the two lower corners are the words: "Nomen Kokus Actus - Mutus fraute frase", and in the other corners instead of the last words: "Oplolumus Gabalu Copia."

During his two months in Gießen alone his victims were said to number hundreds. A Dutch paper reports that a shoemaker with haemorrhoids was charged 8 florins for two sorts of tea, one to drink, one to sit in; an English paper discreetly alters his complaint to rheumatism: "the shoemaker drank and sat, but in vain…".

[1] For example: *Neues Fremden-Blatt* 15 July 1871; *Feldkircher Zeitung* 19 July 1871; *De Locomotief* 21 Sep.1871 ("goochelaar en toovenaar, een leerling van Bosco"); *La Gazette de France* 19 July 1871 ("élève de Bosco"); *Pall Mall Gazette* 18 July 1871, a shorter account, which compares the case to the recent similar prosecution in London of "Professor Zendavesta" (John Dean Bryant) and others.

C28. Julius Laschott

Laschott, who had a very successful career with his combination of skilled conjuring and his (then novel) dissolving views, did not advertise himself as a pupil of Bosco, but an early reviewer in his native Carniola certainly thought he deserved that title. An article headed 'Ein neuer Magier als Schüler Bosco' (*A new magician as a pupil of Bosco*) in *Illyrisches Blatt* 13 Oct.1846 opens: "[tr.] When a pupil brings honour so decisively to his master in a short time, the decision is difficult whether the greater part of the merit is owed to the teacher or the pupil…"; he is several times referred to in the review as "a pupil of Bosco", and "…If this excellent pupil of Bosco intends to entertain us further with such performances, he can be assured of a good reception…".

C29. Signora Laurenzia

Touring in France (Dieppe in 1861, Valenciennes in 1863) is Saint Aubin Wampa, "prestidigitateur, physicien de Paris" accompanied by La signora Laurenzia, "physicienne italienne, élève du célèbre Bosco".

A review praised the "grand nombre de tours des plus variés qui ont fait grand plaisir" and a further show would follow with "les expériences les plus intéressantes de divination, et les tours les plus abracadabrants".
(*La Vigie de Dieppe* 3, 12 Nov.1861; *L'Écho de la Frontière* 5 May 1863; *Le Courrier du Nord* 6 May 1863).

Wampa (sometimes spelt Vampa) is earlier found without the signora in Nantes in 1852, Paris in 1854, Toulouse 1857, Pau 1860.

C30. Hermann Lindmüller

Hermann Lindmüller is found performing with his wife between 1853 and 1867, consistently advertising as a pupil of Bosco. In Magdeburg in 1853 with "einige Vorstellungen aus der Aegyptischen Zauberkunst" he bills himself as "magisch-physikal. Künstler Herr Lindmüller aus Danzig (Schüler des berühmten Bosco)".[1]

They are performing in Hamburg in August and September 1854, then advertised to appear in Leipzig in April 1857: "Grosses Concert und Zauber-Vorstellung des Herrn Lindmüller nebst Frau, Zögling von Bosco…",[2] but this did not go ahead. The reason was that in Naumburg earlier in the year he and his wife were charged with exhibiting obscene pictures ("unzüchtige Bilder"). They failed to appear for the hearing in Suhl and in their absence were fined 10 Thalers (plus costs), or a week's gaol, and the authorities were ordered to detain them when found. He made a payment in March 1858, and the charge was finally withdrawn in July 1858.[3] Thanks to the arrest warrant we learn that his full name was **Emil Friedrich Hermann Lindmüller** and his wife **Emma, née Leinung**.

They were performing again in Altona in early July 1858, "Hermann Lindmüller und Frau, Zögling von Bosco", and in Hamburg in August.[4] We next hear of him in Cologne in April 1859, where a widely reported "piquant incident" tells of him issuing a challenge to Bils, who was performing there at the same time. Bils had offered 1000 ducats to anyone who could imitate his tricks. During the show Lindmüller publicly told Bils he could replicate any of his tricks and took exception to certain allusions made to himself. The pair were compared to two Homeric heroes boasting of their prowess before battle, and "[tr.] the people of Cologne are now very excited about the outcome of the struggle, whether Lindmüller-Achilles or Bils-Hector will be the loser".[5]

The Lindmüllers are last sighted in 1865, performing in Magdeburg.[6]

[1] *Magdeburgische Zeitung* 17 to 29 Sep.1853.
[2] *Deutsche Allgemeine Zeitung* 26 Apr.1857.
[3] *Königlich Preußischer Staats-Anzeiger* 6 Feb.; 4 Mar.; 7 June 1857; 23 July 1858; *Eberhardt's allgemeiner Polizei-Anzeiger* 19 June 1857; 12 Mar.1858.
[4] *Altonaer Nachrichten* 26 June to 20 July 1858; *Hamburger Nachrichten* 3 to 7 Aug. 1858.
[5] *Fremden-Blatt* 3 Apr.1859; *Vereinigte Laibacher Zeitung* 6 Apr.1859.
[6] *Magdeburgische Zeitung* 12 to 22 June 1865.

C31. Manuel Lopez

Manuel Lopez, "the famous magician", is found advertising as a pupil of Bosco in France in 1871, in Brazil in 1874-5, and in Switzerland and France in 1877; he also claimed in 1874 that he had performed in Rome. He is usually accompanied by signora Alvina (also as Elvina and Albina), a dancer but later a magician.

In Marseille in September and October 1871 he is "le célèbre prestidigitateur Manuel Lopez, élève de Bosco", and indeed "M. Lopez surpasserait ce maître si habile"; with him is "signora Alvina, danseuse des meilleurs théâtres d'Italie" in "une soirée fantastique d'un genre nouveau".[1]

The following month they are in Saint-Étienne, where he is "élève de l'incomparable feu Bosco" and "senora Alvina" is "danseuse et prestidigitatrice de Théatre de Séville".[2]

In 1874-5 they toured Brazil, opening at the *Theatro Lyrico Fluminense* in Rio de Janeiro on July 7th 1874, Lopez billing himself as "Célebre Magico Hespanhol D. Lopez, Discipulo do cavalheiro e verdadeiro Bosco!" (*Pupil of the Chevalier and genuine Bosco*).[3]

The following month he and Albina are in Pernambuco: here he changes his billing from being a pupil of Bosco to being "discipulo e successor do finado Hermann" — *pupil and successor of the late Hermann.* This caused some amusement, the editor of the paper that featured his large ad pointing out in the same issue that Hermann was alive and well.[4]

In early 1875 they are back performing in Rio de Janeiro. His name is now spelt as D. Lopes; he is again "Discipulo do cavalheiro e verdadeiro Bosco", but he now adds not only a large picture of himself but the claim that he is identical to the famous one-legged dancer Donato — "Em unico com o famoso dançarino Mr. Donato" (a claim discussed below), and the show ends (as it did in Pernambuco) with dances by him and Albina.[5] When back in Europe he also claimed to have performed for Don Pedro II, Emperor of Brazil.

We next see them in 1877 in Switzerland. In Lausanne in July he is "D. Lopez, physicien de premier force, successeur de Bosco, dont la réputation est européenne" and she is now "la Signora Elvina, la charmante physicienne italienne"; in August in Vevey he is "le célèbre professeur Lopez".[6] He never mentions Donato in his advertising in Switzerland, probably as Donato never performed there.

In Dijon in September 1877 as "Professeur Lopez, physicien de première force, successeur de défunt Bosco" he repeats his claim that he was Donato, "le fameux danseur qui a fait courir tout Paris en dansant sur un pied"; she is "signora Elvina, la charmante physicienne et prestidigitatrice italienne".[7] Next was Chalon-sur-Saône,[8] then Romilly,[9] and Tours, where he opens his advertising with his Donato claim, "le fameux danseur sur une jambe, qui a fait courir tout Paris, et dont la presse parisienne a tant retenu…", only then calling himself "physicien de première force, le plus habile de cette époque…".[10]

The following year Alvina has the lead billing: in Saumur in January we have: "…la charmante physicienne et prestidigitatrice italienne, Signora Alvina, — accompagnée del [sic] professor Lopez, physicien de première force, le plus habile de cette époque…"[11] similarly in Bordeaux,[12] and in Toulouse, where they were joined by the Edwardo Brothers, acrobats.[13]

In April they arrived in Carcassonne, greeted with some fanfare by the newspapers,[14] which later in very similar reviews dismissed Lopez as a "saltimbanque", a mountebank or charlatan — "[tr.] he is incapable of anything whatsoever, not even the commonest trick..."; hissing brought the show to an early end — but a large audience had paid their money for tickets...[15] In May in Perpignan the review could not have been more different, warmly applauding his skill and the variety of his tricks ("all of a piquant originality");[16] it states that Lopez was Italian and did not speak French well, though the audience enjoyed a long account of his performance for Don Pedro II.

From there they left for Montpellier,[17] then Clermont,[18] and apparently Lodève, where the newspaper, after reporting an excellent play at the theatre, adds the cryptic comment: "Félicitons la direction qui a eu la main plus heureuse cette fois que le jour où elle a recruté le *fameux* Lopez qui a trop fait courir les Lodévois et pas du tout les Clermontais". (*a happier choice than the day they hired the "famous" Lopez...*).[19]

Lopez and Alvina then disappear out of sight.

The question of Lopez also being the famous one-legged dancer "Donato" is rather interesting. He was not the original Donato but a successful impostor.

Donato had burst into fame in Vienna in May 1864, though he had been performing for some time prior to that. The combination of graceful skill and grotesque novelty intrigued and astounded audiences, especially his 'Spanish cloak dance' in matador costume. He was said to be *Juliano Donato*, son of a Spanish colonel, and lost his leg in the war in Morocco, or more colourfully as a matador who had been gored in the thigh by a bull; also said to be Italian and originally in the San Carlo ballet.[20]

After Vienna came successes in Brno, Hamburg, Cologne and Berlin, then he was a sensation in the Covent Garden Christmas pantomime in London in 1864, despite legal tussles over his contract[21] and a host of imitators at London music halls,[22] including "Max Donati", "Don Pattos", comedian F. Robson *a la Donato*, and soon the Swimming Donatos, and the two other London Christmas pantomimes also featured their own one-legged dancer in the harlequinade, Her Majesty's Theatre had "Capello" (in fact Chapell, a London theatre clown, not a success) and Drury Lane had **"Signor Tescano"**, who became popular, but not the great sensation that Donato was, with a 'Donato waltz' and a dancing toy soon available. "Signor Tescano", who danced on one leg but never denied having two (his left leg folded back and tied), was our magician Manuel Lopez.[23]

This is the earliest sighting of him, though he claimed that two flags which he used in his dance 'Pas de Nations' were presented to him by Emperor Maximilian in Mexico soon before this, on September 5th.[24] He also claimed to have once been in the Barcelona ballet.

His reception at Drury Lane on opening night was not encouraging, the *London Star* reviewer, while saying of Donato that he "achieved a complete success ... incredible agility and natural grace", said of "Tescano": "the exhibition was dreary, mournful, and dispiriting ... hopped dismally about, until many of the audience intimated by cries and hisses that they had rather too much of the hospital-ward style of entertainment".[25]

Nevertheless he remained with the pantomime until its close and in March 1865 immediately opened at the Strand and South London Music Halls, followed by the Knightsbridge, showing great athleticism one night when his cloak touched the footlights and in saving it from catching fire he fell into the orchestra pit, leaping back on stage to finish his act.[26]

In December came the new pantomime season and "Tescano", now billed as "the Cousin and Rival of the late Donato", opened at the Canterbury Hall in 'Ri-Fum! Ti-Fum!', which ran successfully until the end of March 1866.[27]

He now headed to the Continent, opening in Prague in April under the name Donati, said to be born in Spain. A review stated that only twenty spectators attended and received a refund.[28] The real Donato had died in France from a lung infection on June 10th 1865 soon after leaving Covent Garden,[29] and Manuel no doubt felt safe in claiming to have been his teacher; but he then made the bold move of venturing to Vienna, where Donato had been so successful — and where his widow still lived.[30]

He was announced to open at the *Carltheater* in late June under the name "Donato" — not, said *Fremden Blatt,* "[tr.] the late Donato in a *Todtentanz*, though in the *saison morte* that is not so incredible", but Manuel Donato, "inventor of one-legged dancing and teacher of the original Donato". Manuel told a long story of how he had met Donato — Manuel was a dancer (he said) in the ballet corps of Barcelona theatre; after a performance they drank till morning, and he decided to walk off his hangover. In a field he saw something hopping around — was it a human or an animal? It proved to be an emaciated person moving with great dexterity on one leg, and judging by his clothes he was in desperate circumstances. The creature explained he had lost his leg to a bull and after that had sat on church steps begging but received more sympathy than donations; he then joined a band of travelling tightrope walkers, jumping round like a tree frog as a foil for the clown's jokes. He left them and now hung round the fields starving. Manuel gave him a home as his servant; Donato watched him dancing at the ballet and successfully copied his cloak dance. Manuel now dedicated an hour a day to teaching him until in 1862 Donato was good enough to open in London…[31]

Donato's widow was naturally incensed at this nonsense, especially on the anniversary of his death, and the following day published a detailed rebuttal (probably at least partly accurate), revealing for the first time Donato's real surname, Anguiz. He had no teacher, she said; his father was a Spanish colonel named D. Anguiz and his mother, still alive in Paris, was principal court dancer for Queen Amélie of France, and she had trained him before he became a matador; prior to his success in Vienna in 1864 he had already been performing for six years, in Spain, Portugal, part of Africa, and the south of France. He had never begged, and after losing his leg as a matador had received a pension from Queen Isabella; in 1862 Donato was not in London but in Marseille, and not in Barcelona when Manuel claimed he was. Manuel Donato, whom she identified as "Tescano" at Drury Lane, was not his teacher as he said, not a relative, and had offered her half the profits to support his story and travel with him to towns where the original Donato had never appeared.[32]

Manuel duly opened at the *Carl* on June 23rd, a series of guest performances accompanying a farce. Reviews were unanimous in their criticisms — *Die Debatte* said he had some similarity to the late Donato I, but lacked his grace and temperament and would do better if he tried it on two feet; *Fremden Blatt* thought he performed with reasonable sureness but had not the verve and speed of Donato I; *Morgen Post* called him a flop, a clumsy imitation of the original; *Wiener Zeitung* said he did what Donato did, but without his dexterity and sureness and winning charm; for *Neues Fremden Blatt* he was a complete failure, the audience not staying till the end; and *Blätter für Musik, Theater und Kunst* thought he possessed none of the fiery temperament, the spirit, the adroitness, the endurance, or the expressiveness of his predecessor; *Wiener Tagblatt* called it an unsuccessful performance of a poor copy of the late Donato.[33]

He closed on June 27th. At the *Thalia-Theater* a new "Donato" took the stage, "Herr Donato II", named as Herr J. Baum from Vienna,[34] but Manuel was off to France.

In July he performed in Mulhouse, in Alsace — he or the theatre manager contriving a marvellous advertisement beginning "[tr.] The art of dancing has many celebrities…".[35] He then performed briefly at the Hippodrome in Paris in early August, the announcements lauding him as "[tr.] having done marvels at the *Carl* in Vienna"![36] and he was then said to be leaving for London.[37] But the only sign of him in England is at a fête in Luton on August 13th as "Signor Tescano" (possibly an impostor)[38] and he was soon back in France.

In October 1866 a booklet was published in Paris, *Manuel Donato, danseur espagnol monopode*, by W. Fortunio, promoting Manuel, making no secret that he really had two legs. It states he was born *ca.*1837, son of a Madrid surgeon Don Lopez and got the idea of dancing on one foot from watching children play hopscotch. He trained as a dancer, then taught a one-legged beggar to dance — and the beggar [by implication Juliano Donato] made so much money that Manuel took this up himself.[39]

He is seen performing in Paris in November,[40] then in Rouen in January 1867, where his act was not appreciated — "[tr.] a flop, a deplorable exhibition worthy only of a village fair".[41] But he gained wide publicity by advertising for a wife, "[tr.] A European celebrity … choreographic artiste on one and two feet, aged twenty … send a photograph…".[42] In February he had some success in Bordeaux,[43] then was in Madrid, "el célebre artista, D. Manuel Donato, gran bailarín con una pierna sola",[44] and in March in Marseille.[45]

He performed at the 1867 Paris Exposition (*Exposition universelle*) and at the *Théatre Déjazet* in July, winning wild applause and encores, well deserving this ovation, said a reviewer, doing on one leg what many dancers cannot do on two.[46]

In November he is in Nice,[47] and it was probably now that he was in Italy (he later quotes reviews in Verona and Palermo papers). He spent several months of 1868 in England, though (despite soon claiming that he performed at the Alhambra in London — and for Queen Victoria) he is found only in the provinces (Stamford, Northampton, Chesterfield, Hull…). By November 1868 he was in France (St-Étienne, Valence), now billed as "Donato 1er".

In June 1869 he is in Montpellier and, interestingly, is accompanying a magician, Numa. Numa is billed as "le célèbre sorcier du midi … physicien du Pré Catelan à Paris". This is the first association of Donato / Manuel Lopez the dancer with magic and may well be where he learnt it, as he was performing as a magician himself by 1871.[48]

We next see Donato, still with Numa, at the *Arènes* in Nîmes. Donato is "Asmodée boiteux', the Devil on two Sticks, who has tossed away his crutch and his wooden leg...[49]

Then in June 1870 Donato is again performing in Madrid.[50] That is the last trace of Manuel Lopez the one-legged dancer: by September 1871 he was "le célèbre prestidigitateur Manuel Lopez, élève de Bosco" in Marseille — which is where we came in.

In 1876 a very successful hypnotist, M. Donato, first appeared in Paris, drawing crowds for several months, then elsewhere in Europe: this was not Lopez in yet another guise — Donato was still in France in 1877 doing his magnetism act when Lopez was doing his magic in Switzerland.

[1] *Le Petit Marseillais* 27 Sep. to 28 Oct.1871.
[2] *Mémorial de la Loire et de la Haute-Loire* 19 Nov.1871.
[3] *Jornal do Commercio* 6 July 1874; *A Vida Fluminense* 11 July 1874.
[4] *Diario de Pernambuco* 14 Aug.1874; the note on Hermann was reprinted in several other papers.
[5] *O Mercantil* 27 Feb.1875 (online at url:179).
[6] *La Revue* 13 July 1877; *Journal de Vevey* 2 Aug.1877.
[7] *Le Progrès de la Côte-d'Or* 31 Aug. to 3 Sep.1877
[8] *Courrier de Saône et Loire* 15 Sep.1877.
[9] *L'Avenir républicain* 27 Oct., 10 Nov.1877
[10]. *L'Union Libérale* 29 Dec.1877 to 5 Jan.1878.
[11] *L'Écho Saumurois* 11, 15 Jan.1878.
[12] *La Gironde* 29 Jan.1878.
[13] *La Dépêche* 15, 17, 25 Mar.1878.
[14] *Le Bon sens* 3, 6 Apr.1878; *La Fraternité* 11 Apr.1878.
[15] *Le Bon sens* 10 Apr.1878; *La Fraternité* 4, 7 Apr.1878.
[16] *Le Cri-cri* 5, 12 May 1878.
[17] *Le Petit Méridional* 22, 24 May 1878; *Le Messager du Midi* 23 May 1878.
[18] *Le Petit Méridional* 5 June 1878.
[19] *L'Indépendant de Lodève* 16 June 1878. Ten years later when Eugenio performed in Lodève he received a poor reception because the locals remembered being once deceived by a magician pompously calling himself "Lopez-Bosco" who had cut short his act and made an early departure with the takings (see B2 p.185).
[20] A wonderfully detailed account in *Berliner Gerichts-Zeitung* 25 Aug.1864 pictures him attending matador-school as a child, the accident (still dispatching the bull), staggering to the Queen's box before collapsing, and rewarded with a royal pension. There is no mention of this in Spanish papers and no mention of him as Donato in Spain at all until January 1865, reporting him (in fact an impostor) in France.

[21] An injunction was dismissed on a technicality: details of the case, in which he was formally named as *Ignace Fernand Donato*, are given in *London Evening Standard* 26, 27, 28 Dec.1864; 4 Jan.1865; *Era* 15 Jan.1865; the parties eventually came to a compromise, with Donato to perform at the Oxford and Cambridge Music Hall at the end of the Covent Garden pantomime, but he left England unwell at that date and died soon after.

[22] There was a similar rash of impostors (one as young as 14) in Germany and France. A warning notice about an impostor Corradini calling himself "Donato II" was published by Juliano's agent in July 1864; in September 1864 when Juliano was in Berlin there were said to be three impostors in Hamburg; a young impostor claiming to be "Donato" himself opened in Paris in January 1865 (at that time there were said to be six Donatos in the field), another in April, and one in Brussells in May 1866. The French papers vied with each other to find new expressions for *danseur à une jambe* — *unijambe, unipède, unijambiste, monojambe, monopode, solipède, solipatte*... America also had its share of Donato impostors.

[23] *Morning Advertiser* 23 Dec.1864; *Bell's Life in London* 24 Dec.1864. Performing with him was "the Infant Deteto, four years of age", perhaps a daughter, doing the dances of Senora Parea Nena.

[24] Quite possible, but no mention of him in Mexican papers — however we do not know what name he was using or what his act was. The Italian Opera was in Mexico City at the time and performed for Maximilian, so perhaps he was associated in some way with them.

[25] Quoted *Dundee Advertiser* 29 Dec.1864.

[26] *London Evening Standard* 1 Mar.1865; *Era* 5 Mar.; 4, 25 June 1865.

[27] *Sun* 20 Dec.1865; *Morning Herald* 28 Dec.1865 ("a la Donato"); *Morning Advertiser* 29 Mar.1866.

[28] *Fremden Blatt* 1 Apr.1866; *Neues Fremden Blatt* 6 Apr.1866.

[29] Newspapers copying each other all over the world (as far as New Zealand) reported that he died in *Cyragne*, said to be a French spa town near Avignon: it is actually *Eyragues*, the error resulting I suspect from an early report (such as *Era* 9 July 1865) being in a German paper printed in *Fraktur* in which capital E and C are very similar.

A final bizarre footnote on Donato surfaced in 1875 at the widely-publicised trial in Marseille of two impostors and fraudsters, Mme Saulnier, claiming to be the daughter of an Austrian archduchess, and her accomplice Dr Boissy. Saulnier was said to have fallen madly in love with Donato and when he died put on an elaborate funeral for him with paid mourners; another account claimed to give the inside story on Donato (Ruquis said to be his real surname) and on Julia (said to be his mistress not his wife): *Le Petit Marseillais* 8 Feb. 1875; *L'Avenir républicain* 10 Feb.1875.

[30] On June 13th 1864 Donato aged 24 married the popular Viennese actress Antonie (Antoniette) Julius (*"Fräulein Julius"*, age 19, daughter of famous actor *"Friedrich Julius"*, born Friedrich Julius von Kleist). The wedding filled the newspapers, and an entertaining fanciful account ("[tr.] A Three-Legged Couple") appeared in *Gemeinde-Zeitung* 18 June 1864. After his death she returned to the stage as "Frau Donato".

[31] *Fremden Blatt* 10 June 1866.

[32] *Fremden Blatt* 11 June 1866. Very similar accounts appeared in *Der Zwischen-Akt* 11 and 13 June 1866.

[33] *Die Debatte, Fremden Blatt, Morgen Post, Neues Fremden Blatt* 24 June 1866; *Wiener Zeitung* 25 June 1866; *Blätter für Musik, Theater und Kunst* 26 June 1866; *Wiener Tagblatt* 1 July 1866.

[34] Baum, who lost his leg as a soldier in 1849, had considerable success as a one-legged dancer: *Aussiger Anzeiger* 3 Aug.1867.

[35] *L'Industriel alsacien* 19 July 1866.

[36] *La Presse* 1 Aug.1866, etc. — the same text, "…*a fait merveille au grand Carl-Théâtre*", word for word in at least six papers, so clearly his own press release; he certainly wrote to several papers inviting their attendance at his shows: Timothée Trimm (for whom see B12 note 57) quotes in *Le Petit Journal* 28 Aug.1866 the letter dated August 10th he received from Manuel.

[37] *Le Constitutionnel* 12 Aug.1866.

[38] *Luton Times* 18 Aug.1866.

[39] Online at url:180. Reviewed in *L'Evènement* 5 Oct.1866. The pamphlet is largely a reprint of an article on Donato by A. Rigault in the Lyon paper *Le Salut publique* 12 Sep.1866,

[40] *Le Soleil* 9 Nov.1866.

[41] *La Comédie* 13 Jan.1867.

[42] *Le Figaro* 19 Jan.1867 — the marriage notice was reprinted in papers across France.

[43] *La Gironde* 2 Feb.1867.

[44] *El Lloyd español* 23 Feb.1867.

[45] *Le Soleil* 26 Mar.1866.

[46] *Le Figaro* 2 June 1867; *Le Soleil* 25, 31 July 1867.

[47] *La Situation* 9 Nov.1867.

[48] *La Liberté* 10, 13 June 1869; *L'Union nationale* 13 June 1869. Interesting article at url:181 with much on the 'Théâtre de magie' in the *Pré-Catelan* in the Bois de Boulogne.

[49] *Courrier du Gard* 25 June 1869; *L'Opinion du Midi* 27 June 1869; their performance is also listed in Jules Rostain, *Huit ans de direction aux arènes de Nîmes, de 1864 à 1871*, p.161.

[50] *Diario oficial de avisos de Madrid* and *La Época* 23 June 1870.

C32. Loramus

Loramus, real name **Alexandre-Charles Dabain**, 1834-1895, has an entry in the *Lexikon*. When performing in Valenciennes in 1874 a newspaper report described him as "[tr.] born in 1838 [*sic*], a printer at age sixteen, all his aspirations led him to magic; a regular at Bosco's shows, Bosco became his teacher, and Robert-Houdin also; he handed over his savings and in exchange they gave him lessons".
(*Le Courrier du Nord* 30 Sep.1874).

C33. Herr Lorch

The Stadtmuseum in Leipzig has a poster for a performance at the Fair *ca.*1860 by a group of athletes, wrestlers, boxers and fencers under Otto Wünsch. In addition there are some dancers and "[tr.] the Chinese magic palace in higher magic of Herr Lorch, pupil of Bosco" (*Der chinesische Zauberpalast in der höheren Magie von Herrn. Lorch, Schüler des Professor Bosco*).

The poster is online at url:182.

C34. Bartolomeo Marchelli, 1834-1903

Marchelli advertised himself as "Unico Allievo del celebre professore Bosco di Torino" (*Bosco's only pupil*) and Eugenio confirmed in 1892 that he had been a genuine pupil of Bartolomeo for two years from 1854. He is discussed by Rusconi (p.167) and Eugenio's letter is reproduced (and translated) at url:183 and in the biography by Emilio Costa, *Bartolomeo Marchelli, Capitano Garibaldino, 1834-1903* (Ovada 1961, p.13, online at url:097).

C35. Mares

A self-proclaimed "pupil of Bosco" is found in Spain in 1886. In Lugo in Galicia in July an ad announces that "Mr. Mares, discipulo del célebre Bosco, primer fisico y escamoteador de Europa" will be performing "una función de prestidigitación moderna" at the Circulo de las Artes. His acts include 'Cartomancía de Mr. Bosco'. (The ad appears in two Lugo papers, *Eco de Galicia, diario de la tarde* and *El Lucense, diario católico de la tarde* 24 July 1886)

C36. Jean (Joh.) Mesjetz

"Zauberer Herr Joh. Mesjetz" from Zelacofen (Zollikofen, near Bern) advertises a "Kunstvorstellung" in Magdeburg in January 1857 and again in December that year when he signs himself "Jean Mesjetz aus Zelacofen, (Schüler Bosco's)". (*Magdeburgische Zeitung* 1 Jan., 5 Dec.1857).

C37. Victor Mihoy

"Victor Mihoy, professeur de physique amusante, véritable élève de M. Bosco" performed in Luxemburg in 1860 — "Grande Représentation de Physique, Magie et Prestige…" (*Courrier du Grand-Duché de Luxembourg* 24, 27 Nov.1860).

C38. Charles Mirano

Charles Mirano, said to be from Malta, bills himself as a pupil of (the non-existent) *Carlo Bosco* (B5). He is advertised as a guest artist in the "Salon-Agoston", the travelling magic-theatre of Gustav Böhm, in Landshut in September 1868 and in St Gallen in October.

In Landshut we have "Gastspiel des Herrn Charles Mirano, dem einzigen noch lebenden Schüler des Carlo Bosco" (*last surviving pupil of Carlo Bosco*) together with a "Schülerin aus dem Gebiete der moderne Salon-Magie" (*Kurier für Niederbayern* 6, 7 Sep.1868), and in St Gallen "Gastvorstellung des Herrn Charles Mirano aus Malta, dem einzigen noch lebenden Schüler des verstorbenen Carlo Bosco, sowie 4tes Auftreten der Schülerin des Unterzeichneten" (*St. Galler Zeitung* 21 Oct.1868).

Two similarly-worded posters for such a performance, printed in Munich in 1868, are illustrated by Antiquariat Turszynski at url:184.

C39. G. Moreni

G. Moreni, described as Italian, probably Swiss-Italian, is found performing from 1865, largely in Switzerland, as "Herr Moreni" and "M. Moreni", advertising himself until 1867 as a pupil of Bosco. When first sighted, in Bern in September 1865, he makes much of working with little apparatus or machinery, and his masterpiece is the cups — "*Jeu de Gobelets à la Bosco*"; his "comic Italian-French-German speech" is said to add to the entertainment.[1]

The following month he is in Fribourg (im Üechtland)[2] and in Lausanne, accompanied by his wife doing a mentalist act,[3] then in Geneva, now "Bosco's sole pupil" and proclaiming that he has seen Robin, Hamilton, Hermann and [Joseph] Velle and only Velle, he says, can approach the skill and simplicity of his method of working; alas, he attracted a good review but a small audience.[4]

In 1866 he is again performing in Geneva in February ("professeur italien") and March, promising stunning effects with electricity and a clairvoyance and memory act from Mme Moreni, and then in Neuchâtel in April, where his show is free on the first night so the public "can judge his skill and dexterity".[5]

He was in Draguignan in April 1867, the last time he advertises as a pupil of Bosco. A large advertisement lists his act in detail, opening with "Jeu d'adresse absolue à bras nus, en costume du chevalier Bosco, satisfant [*sic*] l'œil le plus intelligent et le plus rusé. Une prestidigitation de cartes, jeu du célèbre Bosco…".[6] He ended that year back in Switzerland, performing in Geneva, his show closing with an exposure of the Davenports, and then in Fribourg.[7]

In Lausanne in October 1871 he announces that he has been made a member of the Academy of Occult Sciences in Florence, and has recently been touring Spain, where he made great progress in his art and the press honoured him with the title *Cagliostro* for his performances with the black mirror which showed images of dead people.[8]

He is in Bern in September 1873, and in Marseille, Nantes and Rennes in 1874 with the mirror the highlight of his act.[9] A long review of his show in Nantes is very critical, revealing how he did his trick of pouring bordeaux, marsala, absinthe and olive oil from a jug containing clear water (wiping the glasses first with "la serviette magique"), then mocking his failed attempts at picturing the dead — the cards selecting not the audience's requests for locals or family members but Joan of Arc, Bérenger and General Cambronne — but even then all goes astray as the wrong faces are shown, provoking angry boos, and advice from the reviewer to drop that part of his act.[10]

That is the last we hear of Moreni and his mirror, but in 1876 we find "Professor Volta-Moreni" in Paris and in 1877 in Bern, which seems to be him — no mention of Cagliostro's mirror so perhaps he took the reviewer's advice.[11]

[1] *Intelligenzblatt* [Bern] 29, 30 Sept.1865 ("Zauberkunstspiele mit physikalischen Experimenten, ausgeführt durch den Professor der Physik und Kunstspieler Moreni, Schüler des berühmten Bosco").
[2] "Grande soirée fantastique et physique amusante... élève du célèbre chevalier Bosco": *Le Confédéré de Fribourg* 8 Oct.1865.
[3] *Gazette de Lausanne* 24 Oct.1865 ("...jeux de prestidigitation, expériences physiques et mécaniques" by himself and "étude de forces mentales" by Mme Moreni').
[4] *Journal de Genève* 17, 22 Dec.1865 ("M. Moreni, professeur de physique et membre de l'Académie de Rome, seul élève du chevalier Bosco dans la prestidigitation...").
[5] *L'Express* 7 Apr.1866.
[6] *Le Var* 28 Apr.1867.
[7] *Journal de Genève* 15 Nov.1867; *Le Chroniqueur* 7 Dec.1867.
[8] *Gazette de Lausanne* 12 October 1871.
[9] "...unique soirée Cagliostro offerte par le célèbre thaumaturge G. Moreni — la soirée sera terminée par le *Miroir Noir* dans lequel apparaitront les images des trépassés...": *Le Petit Marseillais* 25 June 1874.
[10] *Le Phare de la Loire* 3 Sep.1874 ("...un fils de la Suisse italienne; il parle le français assez confusément, en y mêlant des locutions, empruntées à la langue de Bosco"). The events of the night were retold for years as examples of a showman caught out — *Le Phare de la Loire* 19 Mar.1882; *L'Indépendant rémois* [Reims] 2 May 1884.
[11] *Le Siècle* 3 Dec.1876 ("prestidigitateur italien"); *Intelligenzblatt* 13 Sep.1877 ("aus Florenz").

C40. Adolphe P***

Performing in Nîmes in 1837 is "M. Adolphe P.***, prestidigitateur", "[tr.] preceded by a brilliant reputation ... young pupil of the famous magician Bosco ... the most elegant and difficult tricks will be performed, and the name of Bosco, which is inevitably connected with that of his pupil, is recommendation enough to arouse the curiosity"
(*Courrier du Gard* 10, 13 Jan.1837).

C41. Henryk Rapelewski

Rapelewski, whose surname is diversely spelt (see below), is first sighted performing in 1864 in France and claiming to be a pupil of Bosco.

In Nice in March 1864 as "M. Rappelle, prestidigitateur polonais" he received a warm welcome as he donated the profits of his first show to charity,[1] and next in Draguignan he announced his arrival with a *tour de force* worthy of Eugenio, bamboozling a shopkeeper by asking for black silk and turning it into white linen, and back again.[2]

In August that year he is in Aix, "un physicien polonais de mérite", said to be age 25 and performing with "mademoiselle Robina". Here, and soon in Marseille he is "a pupil of Bosco", a claim he continues to make in France this and the following year, never in Germany or Poland, but revives in Holland in 1870.[3]

In Montpellier in 1865 a reviewer rated his claim to be Bosco's pupil in fact *too modest*, as he was far superior to Bosco, though, the reviewer concedes, the Bosco seen in Montpellier was in the decline of his career.[4]

In late 1865 he toured Spain, now as "señor Rappelleski", the Polish migrant, wounded twice in the uprising against the Russians, we are told, his property confiscated and his house razed.[5]

Back in France in 1866 in Bayonne and Biarritz he is now "M. Henri de Rappelleski", en route to Portugal, claiming appearances before the Emperor of Austria, the King of Prussia, the King of the Belgians, and the Queen of Spain, and quoting glowing reviews from Brussells, Madrid, Barcelona, Vichy and Bagnères-de-Bigorre.[6]

In 1867-8 he toured widely in France, sighted in Clermont-Ferrand, Saint-Étienne, Lyon, St-Chamond, and the Auvergne.[7]

He opened 1869 in Bavaria — Würzburg, Nürnberg, Bad Kissengen;[8] then the following year embarked on an extensive tour of Holland. In Venlo in October 1871 he is "Le Célèbre Professeur de Physique Sans Rival H. de Rappelleski, Prestidigitateur de LL.MM. l'Empereur d'Autriche, le Roi de Portugal, le Roi d'Italie et du Vice-Roi d'Egypte…"; in Gouda he is again billing himself "pupil of the famous Bosco — and has shown himself worthy of his master"; and in Schoonhoven we are told that "if we examine the foreign journals, we discover that, after the great Bosco, Mr. de Rappelleski is the only one who can equal him".[9]

In September and October 1871 he was back in Bavaria, magnetising an assistant, Fräulein Allesse (Allesi), then in November he travelled to Poland, performing with success in Kraków,[10] and remaining several months, sighted in Warsaw, Łódź and Kalisz. The following year he is in Teplice and Hesse, then back in Poland in 1874.

Early 1875 found him in Rome, where there were the familiar jokes that he would out-trick the Finance Minister;[11] 1876 in Hungary, and in 1877-78 on another tour of France, seen in Cannes and Marseille, now with a small theatrical company 'Salon Fantastique',[12] then in Saint-Étienne, and finally in 1878 in Dijon — the last sighting of him — performing "séances de thaumaturgie et d'anti-spiritisme" with Madame Rose.[13]

His name: Even in Polish newspapers he appears variously as *Rappelleski, Rappeleski, Rapelewski*, and *Rappellewski*. I have listed him as 'Henryk Rapelewski' because in Kraków in 1871 his name is given as "p. Henryk Rapelewski, który pisze się 'Rappelleski'" (*Czas* 5 Nov.1871). In 1876 he is referred to as "Rapelewski, żydek z Warszawy", "a Jew from Warsaw" (*Kronika Codzienna* 25 July 1876) but none of the variants of his surname appear in Jewish genealogical databases. The name may be a fabrication, especially if he was a political refugee, and possibly chosen to suggest a connexion with the Rappo family, but he never alludes to them directly. In France he is first "*M. Rappelle*" or "*M. Rapelle*", later "*Henri de Rappelleski*"; in Spain "*señor Rappelleski*"; in Germany usually "*Professor Rappelleski*" or "*von Rappelleski*"; in Holland "*H. de Rappeleski*"; in Italy "*Professore De Rappelleski*".

The Polish satirical journal *Kurjer Świąteczny* made sport of his protean nomenclature when he was there in 1872, saying he was *Rapelow* in St. Petersburg, *Rapelsztejn* in Berlin, *Signiore de Rappellini* in Rome, *Monsieur de Rapelle* in Paris, *sir Rapelgham* in London, and *beja Rapla* in Egypt. It makes a tantalising reference to him not succeeding in London (*bo u nas, zupełnie mu się to nie udało*) but I have not been able to find him in Britain under any name; he is "Rapla Bey" in Egypt because he advertised in the 1870s as 'Magician to the Viceroy of Egypt'.

[1] *Journal de Monaco* 20 Mar.1864.
[2] *Le Var* 29 May 1864.
[3] *Le Mémorial d'Aix* 14 Aug.1864; *Le Sémaphore de Marseille* 19 Aug.1864.
[4] *Le Messager du Midi* 7 Jan.1865; *Journal de Montpellier* 14 Jan.1865.
[5] *El Lloyd Español* 27 Nov.1865. But if he was a participant in the 1863 'January Uprising' as this implies, it is surprising that he was able to return and perform in Poland in 1871.
[6] *Courrier de Bayonne* 7 Sep.1866.
[7] *Le Moniteur du Puy-de-Dome* 26 Oct.1867; *Mémorial de la Loire et de la Haute-Loire* 3 Jan.1868 ("Un des rares élèves du célèbre Bosco..."!); *Le Courrier de la Drôme et de l'Ardèche* 5 Jan.1868.
[8] *Würzburger Stadt- und Landbote* 13 Jan.1869 ("Hr. Professor v. Rappelleski"); *Würzburger Journal* 15 Jan.1869 (where an appropriated anecdote of the tormented waiter calls him "Heinrich v. Rappelleski"); *Nürnberger Anzeiger* 5 Feb.1869 (stressing his expertise in "Indian, Chinese, and Japanese magic"); *Fränkischer Kurier* 14 Mar.1869 (the highlights of his act including 'The King of the Magicians', 'The New Chassepots', 'The Journey to Australia', and magnetising a lady from the audience).
[9] *Venloosch weekblad* 22 Oct.1870; *Goudsche Courant* 20 Nov.1870 ("Leerling van den beroemden Bosco, heeft hij bewezen zijn meester waardig te zijn"); *Schoonhovensche Courant* 1 Dec.1870.
[10] *Czas* 5 to 21 Nov.1871, with no reference of his former life there.
[11] *La Frusta* 25 Mar.; 1, 4 Apr.1875 ("...è in grado di sbancar Marco Minghetti").
[12] *Le Petit Marseillais* 1 Apr.; 5 June 1877.
[13] *Mémorial de la Loire et de la Haute-Loire* 1, 7 Nov.1877; *Le Progrès de la Côte-d'Or* 7 to 11 June 1878.

C42. Giovanni Rossi

Rossi is mentioned as performing in Alessandria in Piedmont in 1844, "un variato trattenimento di fisica, di prestigio, d'incantesimi, di inusitate apparizioni". He is said to be from Florence and "[tr.] a pupil and rival of the famous Bosco" (*Lo si dice allievo ed emulo del celebre Bosco*), with a range of tricks and ventriloquial scenes, received with "unanimous acclaim and universal satisfaction". Bosco himself, we are told, could not have amused us better (...*il quale però difficilmente avrebbe potuto meglio divertirci pei quali giuochi il sullodato Rossi eccitò la sorpresa, l'ammirazione ed il plauso in chicchessia.col guanto magico, palla furtiva, tesoro viaggiatore, pennacchio faggiasco e carte viventi...*).
(*Bazar di novita artistiche, letterarie e teatrali* 31 Aug.1844)

C43. Le sieur Royné

Royné is found performing in Bourges in 1833: "le sieur Royné, élève de M. Bosco, premier physicien d'Europe, donnera ... une soirée de Magie Egyptienne..."
(*Journal du Cher* 5 Oct.1833)

C44. Sarrade

The only reference found to the "prestidigitateur" M. Sarrade is in Aix in 1860, billing himself as a pupil of Bosco (with "pupil" in small letters and "BOSCO" writ large). He is praised for his skill and subtlety, but warned to moderate his language (*Le Mémorial d'Aix* 12 Feb.1860: "Un prestidigitateur qui s'intitule sur l'affiche élève (en petit caractères) de Bosco, (en gros lettres) M. Sarrade...").

C45. Professeur Sartini

"Le professeur Sartini, élève du célèbre Bosco" is found performing in Marseille, Toulouse and Paris in 1880 and 1882.

In Marseille he gave "une séance de thaumaturgie-physique, expérimentale", and he was "[tr.] preceded by such a reputation that we can guarantee his success in advance".

In Toulouse, where he is said to be well-known, he gave "une grande représentation de magnétisme et de thaumaturgie", his act including for the first time "Bosco mort et vivant, et l'Étoile noire de la Pensée".

And he was later in Paris: "une séance intime de magnétisme et de somnambulisme, offerte par la Société fermière".
(*Le Petit Provençal* 11 June 1880; *La Dépêche* 12 Sep.1880; *Figaro* 14 Feb.1882; *Le Temps* 20, 28 Mar.1882).

C46. Madame Schulz

The magician "Madame Schulz" is found performing in France from January to September 1868, consistently claiming to be Bartolomeo's daughter.

In January 1868 she and her husband are in Nice,[1] in April in Nîmes,[2] July in Toulouse,[3] August in Carcassonne,[4] and finally in September in Bagnères-de-Bigorre.[5]

Then in 1875 they turn up in India —"An entertainment is about to be given in the Banqueting Hall, Madras, by a Madame Schulz, 'Daughter of the World renowned Prestidiggiatore, the Cavalier Bartholomeus Bosco,' and her husband Mr. Albert Schulz. The lady 'will perform a variety of quite new and most astonishing feats of legerdemain wherein the most recent inventions of Physics, Mechanics, Sleight of hand, &c., will be brought into play'. She claims to have 'obtained the greatest success in the first Theatres of Europe and America, where the people were amazed at the novelty, and the precision, and exactitude, with which such plays were performed by Madame Schulz, having herself chosen the most surprising pieces from the wonderful cabinet of her late Father'".

"The 'tricks'", said a review, "were for the most part original, and the whole of them performed with admirable neatness and facility".[6]

[1] *Courrier du Gard* 17 Jan.1868 ("la fille de Bosco").
[2] *Courrier du Gard* 11 Apr.1868 ("fille du célèbre prestidigitateur Chev. Barthélemi Bosco ... une variété de tours extraordinaires de physique, de mécanisme, d'adresse, et d'autres jeux électro-magnétiques").
[3] *Journal de Toulouse* 29 July 1868 ("fille du célèbre chevalier Bosco").
[4] *Le Courrier de l'Aude* 13 Aug.1868.
[5] *La Petite Gazette* 5 Sep.1868 ("...séance extraordinaire de Mme Schulz").
[6] *Indian Statesman* 16 Feb., 4 Mar.1875.

C47. Ferdinand Stärff

Stärff, a successful conjuror and ventriloquist, has a brief entry in the *Lexikon*. I believe he is the person of that name born 27 Oct.1811, died Luisenstadt, Berlin 22 Apr.1862, who at his marriage in 1833 is listed as a magician.

He is described in 1834 as "a former associate of Bosco" (ein ehemaliger Compagnon des Herrn Bosko: *Sundine* 18 Apr.1834) and in 1845 as "a pupil of Bosco" (Schüler Bosco's: *Privilegirte Schlesische Zeitung* 2 Aug.1845); there is no evidence that he was either.

He is last found performing in Magdeburg in 1848 — "...außerordentliche Production des rühmlichst bekannten Escamoteurs und Bauchredners Stärff" (*Magdeburgische Zeitung* 20 Aug.1848)

C48. Bernhard Steffen

Performing in Germany and Austria (Munich, Salzburg, Znaim) in 1857-8, Steffen (Danish says the *Lexikon*) bills himself as a pupil of Bosco — "B. Steffen, Artist der Magie, Schüler des berühmten Bo. Bosko".
(*Neueste Nachrichten aus dem Gebiete der Politik*, 14 Dec.1857; *Neue Salzburger Zeitung* 2 Jan.1858; *Znaimer Wochenblatt* 25 Apr.1858).

C49. Professor St. Roman, *ca.*1830-1916

The magician Professor, or Herr, St. Roman, real name Samuel Thiersfeld, long advertised himself as Bartolomeo's nephew, and as born in Milan rather than Poland. In the 1860s, after Bosco's death, he made great play of this across Europe, from around 1864 to at least 1868.

His career is well-known with detailed articles in the *Lexikon* and elsewhere. Standard sources give his birth as Jaroław *ca.*1828, from Willmann's 1896 *Zauberwelt* article, but the well documented family tree at url:185 does not agree.

In Holland — "Heer St. Roman, neef van den wereld beroemden Bosco" (*Opregte Haarlemsche Courant* 1 July 1864); "De heer St. Roman mag sich te regt beroemen op verwantschap met den in Nederland nog niet vergeten Bosco…" ("Mr. St. Roman may rightly boast of his affinity with Bosco, not yet forgotten in the Netherlands…": *Rotterdamsche Courant* 16 Aug.1864).

In Germany and Austria, now also claiming he was born in Milan — "Professor St. Roman, Neffe des Bosco aus Mailand" (*Schweinfurter Tagblatt* 29 Aug.1865); "Herr Saint-Roman, ein geborner Mailänder, der Neffe Bosco's" (*Jörgel Briefe* 29 Sep.1866); "der große Neffe seines großen Oheims Bosco" (*Der Wiener Elegante* 10 Oct.1866); "Neffe Bosco's" (*Wiener Zeitung* 23 Oct.1866); he would have been pleased with reviews that pronounced his performance "worthy of his uncle", "did his uncle proud" — "…seines Oheims würdig": *Marburger Zeitung* 23 Nov.1866; "Der Künstler macht dem Namen seines Onkels Bosco alle Ehre" (*Grazer Volksblatt* 19 Oct.1868).

In Sweden — "Professor St, Roman. nevö af Bosco från Mailand" (*Dagens Nyheter* 30 Mar.1867).

In Poland — "Prof. St. Romana, (siostrzeńca znanego Bosco)": *Czas* 11 Feb. 1868.
He is the subject of the book:
Jedermann Zauberkünstler: Anleitung zur Vorführung der effektvollsten Kunststücke des berühmten Zauberers St. Roman, mit einem Anhang, die wichtigsten Kunstgriffe der Magie sowie mit einer Biographie des unerreicht dastehenden Künstlers, von H.F.C. Suhr. Stuttgart: Schwabacher'sche Verlagsbuchh [1898]. viii,153,[7]pp.

C50. Karl Töpfer

"Karl Töpfer, Mechanikus aus Magdeburg, wirklicher Schüler des berühmten Bosko", giving "eine Kunstvorstellung aus dem Reiche der natürlichen Zauberei" in Nürnberg in 1836 (*Allgemeine Zeitung von und für Bayern* 10 Sep.1836) is probably the well-known German writer, playwright, and theatre director Karl (Carl) Friedrich

Gustav Töpfer, 1792-1871. He has a brief entry in the *Lexikon*; the biographies in *Allgemeine Deutsche Biographie* and *Biographisches Lexikon des Kaiserthums Oesterreich* say little of his early days as a travelling performer.

C51. Unidentified "pupil"

An impostor claiming to be Bosco's pupil ("annoncé ... comme élève de l'*incomparable* Bosco") arrived in Oloron (Oloron-Sainte-Marie) in early 1845 and left after taking advance payments for a promised *brillante soirée* — "Les amateurs attendaient un tour d'escamotage: ils n'ont pas été tout-à-fait décus".
(*Journal des débats politiques et littéraires* 29 Jan.1845; quoting the *Mémorial de Pau*)

C52. Unidentified (Herr François?)

A series of ads in *Hamburger Nachrichten* in 1846 for magic shows by a "pupil of Bosco" at various venues may all relate to the same person (unnamed except in the last) or they may be rivals —

Mar.24 1846: "Heute, Dienstag, wird sich in meinem Local ein Schüler Bosco's in der natürlichen Magie und Ägyptischen Zauberei produziren...";

May 9 1846: "Große Kunst-Vorstellung in der natürlichen Magie und ägyptischen Zauberei, von einem Schüler Bosco's..." at Hildebrandt's Wein- u. Caffee-Halle;

June 13 1846: at Frascati in Bergedorf "...ein Schüler Bosco's (in altdeutscher Tracht) mit außerordentlichen Kunstücken";

July 6 1846: "Joachimsthal (neu decorirte Salon) ... Tanz-Musik... Auch wird diesen Mittewochen Herr François, ein Schüler Bosco's, eine große Kunst-Vorstellung in der natürlichen Magie und ägyptischen Zauberei in unserm Locale veranstalten",

C53. Herr Winter

There were several magicians performing under this name in Germany in the 19th century, one calling himself a pupil of Döbler, another of Linsky, and one "a very worthy pupil of Bosco" —"ein sehr würdiger Schüler Bosco's", performing "Natural magic" at the Odeonsaale in Munich in 1846 (*Münchener Tagblatt* 18 Dec. 1846)

C54. Carlo Zenetti

Carlo Zenetti, (probably pseudonymous) author of a collection of tricks with cards, numbers, dice and coins first published in 1860, *Das Zauber-Theater, oder, Das Ganze der Taschenspielerkunst: eine reichhaltige Sammlung der neuesten, interessantesten und leicht ausführbaren Kunststücke mit Karten, Zahlen, Würfeln,*

Münzen u. dergl., 1860 (LGe194), declares himself on the title-page: "pupil of the great Bosco" (*Schüler des großen Bosco*).

No record has been found of Zenetti performing, though he appears in a story published in *Leitmeritzer Wochenblatt* 18 June 1870, set in Paris, "...producirte der berühmte Zauberer Carlo Zenetti, Professor der höhern Magie, seine unglaublichen Künste in Paris und zog die *Crême* der seinem Gesellschaft unwiderstehlich an": perhaps the character in the story derives from the pseudonymous author of the book?

A few magicians adopted names similar enough to "Bosco" to suggest a deliberate attempt at deception.

Prof. Alexander Boskos is found in New Orleans in 1868 "in his unrivaled performance of Natural Magic and Pistol Duel, never executed in this country before" (*Times-Picayune* 20 Mar.1868).

In Britain in the late 1870s we have a magician **Boz** (real name Arthur William Weston, born 1848, claiming to be a pupil of "Herr Dobler") and using the term "Enchanted Palace of Illusions" (see *Appendix Z2: Bill Matter*), finally changing his stage name to **Signor Boz**. He was highly regarded and very successful ("Boz, the Great Sensational Conjuror...", *Western Mail* [Cardiff] 23 Dec.1876; "...extraordinary feats of Sleight of Hand, the Wonderful and Genuine Automaton Yorick...", *The Scotsman* 8 Jan.1878; "Without doubt one of the most accomplished conjurors of the present day...", *Sheffield Independent* 15 Feb.1879; "...undoubtedly the monarch of conjurors", *Derry Journal* 30 July 1879). He died in 1880, age 33, in Dumfermline committing suicide by suffocation (*Glasgow Evening Citizen* 1 Apr.1880).

Another technique was to advertise with Bosco's name in the ad in larger letters than one's own — a nice example is L.K.Maju (Levie Kinsbergen: see B1 note 545) in *Provinciale Overijsselsche en Zwolsche courant* 12 Feb.1850 who offers: "Voorstelling van Egyptische Tooverkunst **A LA B. BOSCO,** te geven door **L. K. MAJU**..."; and Sarrade (C44) in Aix in 1860 does the same.

The two books on magic by Romanoff (Giovanni Battista Romano) pictured at url:186 employ this technique.

Several magicians invoked Bosco's reputation by performing tricks they claimed to have learnt from him, or by naming one of their tricks after him.

Among many examples are

Adrien ("Adrien Delille", born Victor Bonaventure Antoine Goujon, 1800-1877) performing in Reims in 1842 ended his run with "Le Grand Vol, expérience digne d'admiration, et communiquée à M. Adrien par le célèbre Bosco. Tour Suprenant. M. Adrien escamotera sa dame, sous un gobelet de six pieds de haut, avec autant de facilité qu'une muscade" (*L'Industriel de la Champagne* 13 Apr.1842).

Ciotti's *Cirque Royal de Turin* in Nantes in 1864 included ***Les baguettes de Bosco*** (*Le Phare de la Loire* 9 Jan., 10 Feb.1864).

One of Nicolay's (C19 above) tricks was ***Le Grand Succès du père Bosco*** (*Vert-vert* 30 Dec.1869, in Paris; *Journal du Cher* 25 Aug.1870, in Bourges; *Courrier de Saône-et-Loire* 11 Sep.1873. in Chalon-sur-Saône); in Rio de Janeiro in 1872 (*Jornal da Tarde* 8 Jan.1872) he called it ***O triumpho do célebre Bosco***.

A trick with a similar name, ***Le Triomphe de Bosco et la Corbeille Japonaise*** was done in France by the Greek magician George Melides (not to be confused with Georges Méliès) fairly soon after Nicolay and often in the same towns (*Le Var* 4 Apr.1875, in Draguignan; *Courrier du Berry* 14 May 1875, in Bourges; *Le Progrès de la Côte-d'Or* 16 June 1875, in Dijon). Melides is not found performing this trick before or after this. Originally from Missolonghi, he travelled widely, performing in national dress in Greece, Beirut, Vienna, making several visits to Turkey and France; last sighted in Alexandria in Egypt in 1907 (*The Egyptian Gazette* 14 May 1907).

Presumably the same trick, now named ***Le triomphe de Bosco ou la Boîte Japonaise***, is being performed in Morlaix in 1884 by Professeur Laurent Bonnet and his daughter Mlle Joséphine Bonnet (*Ar Wirionez: journal politique de l'arrondissement de Morlaix* 28 May 1881).

M. Volta, "the celebrated illusionist" included ***Le Cuisinier de Bosco*** in his act in Reims in 1884 (*L'Indépendant rémois* 15 Jan.1884).

A magician named Stot-Taï, said to be Persian, is found in Holland between 1874 and 1886, Britain in 1879 and 1880, France and Spain in 1880, and quotes reviews from New York, Rome, and Berlin. In one performance only, in Château-Gontier in 1880, his act includes ***Une réminiscence de Bosco*** (*La Gazette de Château-Gontier* 19 Aug.1880).

In Toulouse in 1880 "Professeur Sartini, physicien" (C45) is giving "une grand représentation de magnétisme et de thaumaturgie" and will present for the first time the greatest success of the day ***Bosco mort et vivant, et l'Étoile noire de la Pensée***" (*La Dépêche* 12 Sep.1880).

Professor Erdely in Semarang in Java in 1883 made no apology for performing "[tr.] the wonderful tricks of old Bosko (*de wonderbare toeren van den ouden Bosko*). These tricks were performed with the greatest success by Bosko 25 years ago in St Petersburg, Vienna, Paris, Milan, Berlin and London. The tricks are old but still wonderful" (*De Locomotief* 4 Jan.1883).

Ventriloquist Ernst Schulz had a sketch ***Der alte Bosco*** when performing in Reval (Tallinn) in 1884 (*Revalsche Zeitung* 28 Jan.1884).
This was probably his account of talking to Bartolomeo shortly before his death, asking him what was his favourite trick (Reading the Czar's thoughts) and ending with Bosco's last trick… Schulz's account was published as 'Der große Zauberer' in

the periodical *Artist;* reprinted in *Düsseldorfer Sonntagsblatt* 2 Apr.1893 (online at url:187; it clearly owes something to 'Boscos Tod', by H. Truhn: see *Fiction F35*).

Herr Schöpl, a magician performing in Olmütz (Olomouc) in 1885, featured **Souvenier de Bosko** in a long list of tricks (*Mährisches Tagblatt* 11 Feb.1885).

A "First Great Brilliant Presentation" in Baden bei Wien in 1893 by various performers opened with 'Salon-Magie' by an unnamed artist featuring **Bosko's Lieblingspiel** (*Badener Bezirks-Blatt* 25 May 1893).

Edouard-Joseph Raynaly (1842-1918) in his *Séances* at Robert-Houdin (*Le Parisien* 20 June 1893) included **Un souvenir de Bosco**. In his book *Les propos d'un escamoteur* (1894; online at url:188) Raynaly says Bosco is immortalised for his cup and balls proficiency and well known for his superb trick (*tour sublime*) of finding money in eggs at the market — a trick everyone talks about but no one has actually seen…

Ironically, perhaps, the card trick "Bosko Biati kennt alles" is named for a mnemonic not for Bartolomeo.

"Bosco" as a Generic Term

Very early in Bartolomeo's career his surname had become a general term for 'magician'. Examples are legion but a few of interest are:

In France most famously of Thiers — "Le nom du célèbre prestidigitateur a passé dans la langue: entre nous soit dit, on s'en est même servi pour désigner des hommes politiques habiles à jeter de la poudre aux yeux. Et c'est en ce sens que Cormenin dit un jour: "M. Thiers est le Bosco de la tribune" (*Journal de Montélimar* 28 Feb.1885)

"Der Bosco der Deutschen Politik"
Kladderdatsch 11 Aug.1850

This was never common in England, but in 1857 we have
"But is the Premier to be allowed thus to cajole us all with our eyes open. Is he to be a political Bosco, and we the staring audience, sure of a trick, and yet only exclaiming, How clever."
Pembrokeshire Herald 27 Nov.1857

"…les escamotages des Bosco de notre ville…"
Le Messager du Midi 13 Oct.1885

"…l'égal de Robert Houdin, Philippe et autres Bosco"
Le Journal pour rire 10 July 1852

There was a **Club Bosco** in *Ketels Bier-Haus* in Altona in 1863 for those with an interest in Natural Magic
Altonaer Nachrichten 22 Jan.1863

"…Louis Barthélemy, appelé le *Bosco du billard"*
La Petite République 27 Nov.1883

Snakes

By the late 19th century a "Bosco Act" meant a snake-handling and usually a snake-eating act, much to the annoyance of Houdini who famously says in *The Unmasking of Robert-Houdin:* "…never has posterity put the name of a great performer to such ignoble uses. For who has not heard the cry of the modern Bosco, 'Eat-'em-alive'? Of the twentieth-century Boscos there are, alas, many. You will find them all over the world, in street carnivals, side-shows, fair-booths, and museums, and why the public supports such debasing exhibitions I have never yet been able to understand…".

These Bosco acts also annoyed the conjuring Boscos — in Buffalo in 1899 (*Buffalo Evening News* 2 Oct.1899) a notice stated: "Prof. Bosco, the well-known sleight-of-hand performer of this city, is in no way connected with Bosco, the snake eater, who has been giving exhibitions in this city. Many people have confused the two"; this is by either Louis Susser or David Hyam who both lived in Buffalo (B65, B66).

An ad in the *New York Clipper* 4 May 1891 reads: "Snakes. To Friends and Managers of Bosco Shows. [We] have opened a snake farm at Greely, Pa., and are now ready to furnish Bosco dens from $20.00 up … Get the black and yellow back rattlers. They last the longest…". Such ads were soon common —
"Wanted. Party to do Snake Eating Bosco Act";
"Wanted, Man or Woman for Bosco Act. All Snakes Fixed. Good Money";
"$10 to $25 each. Small snakes for Bosco act…".

The "All Snakes Fixed" note upset a subscriber to the Montana *Great Falls Tribune* (20 June 1900) complaining about "snake-eating fakirs".

Most of the many performers called themselves "Bosco" and such shows lasted at least until the 1920s, in U.S.A. and beyond (one, **Alan Bosco**, in England in the 1920s is also listed as a conjuror and has an entry above as a Bosco impostor: B88).

"Bosco the Wonder" was probably the best known in late 19th century U.S.A., said to have been from "a savage tribe inhabiting the lowlands of Australia… the name is derived from a settlement known as Bosco", captured by Captain Anderson and brought to America in 1871. He dressed as a woman in the act but "Bosco the Wonder is neither man nor woman, but is part human and snake…", and was usually referred to as *she* — "Even Bosco, the wonderful snake woman was here, in a den of over 140 horrible, wriggling, writhing and venomous reptiles. This freak of a so-called woman sits in this den, and eats, plays and sleeps with the horrible creatures…".

"Bosco the Wonder" was described as dead more than once ("died in terrible agony at Buckstown, Kentucky … a postmortem … revealed … his stomach was a veritable den of living serpents… hatched from eggs deposited by the snakes which Bosco swallowed at every performance").

Perhaps the same "performer" was "the Abyssinian phenomena, Bosco, the snake eater, part human, part snake … she neither walks nor talks but is immune to the bite of a snake …", on display to men only in Helena, Montana (*The Independent-Record* 3 June 1900).

We also hear of Richard Bailey of Canton, Ohio, of the Gaskill Midway company (a travelling carnival), known as Bosco, "died Thursday afternoon at the Allegheny Hospital, from the effects of a rattler's bite" (*Akron Daily Democrat* 1 Dec.1899).

Other reports said Bosco's "real name is Dalley and … hales from Canton, Ohio", or more often John H. West, known as "Bosco, the Australian Snake Eater", his ads announcing: "daily devours poisonous snakes. To this queer creature a rattlesnake is a meal, a half dozen adders a banquet … Have You Seen 'Bosco'? The Australian Wonder … the greatest curiosity of its kind ever brought to this city …. She lives on a diet of rattlesnakes …'Bosco' is an interesting sight and scientific study for men, women and children". West, also said to be born in New York City, wrote an article in 1900 on treating snakebite, saying he drifted into his profession when he met showman 'Arizona Bill' in California about 1896 — "I saw the money that was in it … to anyone that had the nerve and courage to handle the reptiles … I am known almost from the Atlantic to the Pacific as 'Bosco'. Of course, the reader will understand that a showman always adopts some name suitable".

There were serious discussions as to who was the *real* Bosco — "There is abundant evidence that the Bosco who was sat down upon in Scranton last week is not the one who appeared here at the Elks' fair last summer. The trouble is that every fellow who has anything to do with snakes now calls himself Bosco. The genuine Bosco, as we understand it, is a native of Indianapolis…".

Mechanical Boscos

There are a few references to mechanical figures performing Bosco's or Bosco-like tricks; whether the figures were made to resemble him is uncertain. Anton Watzek in Vienna in 1845 had an automata show which included "[tr.] the mechanical conjuror of wood, which, without any assistance on the table all of a sudden surprises you by copying Bosco's three transformation" (see B1 p.53).

And in Berlin in 1848-49 Sebhard advertised a "[tr.] mechanical tableau with humorous transformations and funny scenes" that he called 'Bosculos Zauberreich', later 'Boscos Zaubereien' and 'Bosculos Zaubereien' (see B1 p.64).

There was also the marionette Bosco: the *Marionnettes du Passe-Temps*, the puppet theatre at 12 Boulevard Montmartre (the Passage Jouffroy) in 1859 featured 'Séances de magie, par Bosko, l'un de nos plus habiles prestidigitateurs" (*Le messager de Paris* 6 Feb.1859; B1 p.153).

BOSCO IN FICTION

Bartolomeo anecdotes began to appear in newspapers very early in his career, extolling his expertise and usually making gentle fun of others, such as market-sellers, waiters, or Cossacks. These were no doubt originally his own invention for promotional purposes, though they soon took on a life of their own. But he also appeared early as a character, major or minor, in stories (and later in longer novels) not of his own creation and not necessarily complimentary to him.

This listing includes references to Bartolomeo, Eugenio, and to Bosco used generically.

F1. [Untitled humorous article] by Eduard Maria Oettinger in his satirical journal *Das Schwarze Gespenst* 26 Jan.1830. This was significantly in the 'Allgemeine Lügenzeitung' (*Fake News*) section and announced that Bosco was now in Madrid (he was in fact in Pomerania) and "[tr.] all the papers tell the following story as the *ne plus ultra* of his conjuring tricks…", a story clearly meant to make fun of playwright Carl Meisl, though the point of the story is now obscure: discussed in B1 p.25 and note 121. Oettinger printed several Bosco anecdotes in various journals over the years, but must have formed some strong personal association with the family *as after Bartolomeo's death he was appointed the legal guardian of his daughter Adelaide* (see *Excursus on Family*).

F2. *Oesterreichische Senfkörner: eine Sammlung nationaler Charakterzüge und belustigender Anekdoten*, by Hanns Normann [pseudonym of Anton Gross-Hoffinger]. Leipzig: Wigand'sche Verlags-Expedition, 1833.
['Austrian Mustard Seeds: a collection of national characteristics and hearty anecdotes']
This includes an anecdote of Bosco in a Viennese market in 1829 "finding" 20-kreuzer coins in bread: he livens up the story by quoting the reaction of the woman at the stall, one of the legendary *Fratschelweiber*, known (like "fish wives" in English) for their loud language and coarse wit. See B1 note 93. Online at url:189.

F3. An intriguing-sounding Bosco item, in verse but possibly with a plot and telling a story, may date from early 1835, a printed 8 page poem in German, a dialogue between Bosco, Faust and Mephistopheles. This was sold, together with an autograph signature by Bosco dated January 30th 1835, at a French auction in 1858; buyer and current whereabouts unknown (the catalogue is online at url:031). However the poem may be later than the autograph and could be a copy of F59 below.

F4. *Humoristische Kleinigkeiten*, by Leopold Schick.
Wien: In Commission bey Carl Gerold, 1835.
Prose, some verse and a farce, published for the author; pp.46-7 are 'Das neue Bosco' (Unterhält das Publikum mit Taschenspieler Stückchen.)' consisting of six short statements.
A very impressive list of subscribers is headed by 50 fl. from the Kaiser.
Online at url:190.

F5. 'Les Escamoteurs'.
L'Indépendance Belge 18 July 1841
A tongue-in-cheek discussion, signed "M.", of the various magicians of the day. The only reference to Bosco is bizarre: "Bosco seul, qui n'était pas bien merveilleux, avait au moins un tour qui lui était propre, il escamotait sa femme et la changeait en dinde, ce n'était peut-être pas très-galant, mais il y avait dans ce tour une certaine originalité" (*he had one original trick, he used to turn his wife into a turkey*)
Online at url:191.

F6. ['How Bosco Became Famous']
This very odd story of Bosco starting his career under various names (*Michalief, Lutzaris, Boghos, Wormser...*), changing his name to Bosco in London, and finding success only when patronised by an English aristocrat, is not terribly complimentary to him. It can hardly be his own creation and significantly was not included with other early anecdotes in *Satanas*. The story is found in French, German, Italian and Polish (never in English that I know of). The earliest version found is in French in *La Presse* 3 Oct.1843, with no title, part of the anonymous *Feuilleton* headed 'Sport. Anecdotes et Variétés'. The story is discussed further in B1 pp.45-6.

The *La Presse* version is online at url:193.

F7. 'Bosco's letztes Kunststück', by Dr. Carl Herloßsohn' *Der Wanderer* 24 Feb. 1846
[stated to be previously published in the *Komet* 26 Oct.1844; Carl Herloßsohn was the pen name of Borromäus Sebastian Georg Carl Reginald Herloß, 1804-49; the story may have been included in his *Kometenstralen. Eine Sammlung von Erzählungen, ernsten und humoristischen Aufsätzen.*]

('Bosco's Final Trick'). Bosco is approached by Death who wants a rest and to make some money; Death offers a deal: [*a footnote added by the editor of* Der Wanderer *jokes that Bosco certainly did the deal because of his escape from the exploding rockets in Vienna in January that year*] in return for the half the takings of Bosco's final show every audience member will not age and not die — this will draw a large crowd and the takings will be huge. Death insists on sitting in the box office but Bosco not trusting him changes him without his being aware of it into the form of an attractive young woman. The whole town streams in and Death, unaware of the trick played on him, was pleasantly surprised about how friendly people were to him. Afterwards he took his half share of the huge takings and re-entered private life for a period, heading off for a holiday in Bozen in the Tyrol because the climate was mild there even in winter; but there had been a strong draught in the box office and even though he was inured he caught a nasty head cold. Bosco, however, expressed his gratitude to the public in another way, conjuring up for each visitor as they left a bottle of champagne, *Creme de Bouzy* by Jacquesson; only the envious, the over-serious people who begrudged life to the rest, found in the bottle when they got home *Grüneberger 1844*. "This story is literally true", ends this version (url:193).

The significance of the vintage at the end is clear from two anecdotes then current in German papers: (1) A review of a terrible book of verse says: 'Plant two leaves of this book in the soil of Champagne and the following year the whole vintage will be the most appalling *Grüneberger*' (a sparkling wine from Grün(e)berg in Silesia); (2) 'From Grüneberg rings out the lament: 'We must almost give up hope that there will be a vintage here this season': Poor world which will have to do without an 1844 *Grüneberger*'!

The point of the joke was obscure enough at the time and the ending was changed altogether when the story was reprinted.

It was published in Polish in a Kraków paper when Bosco was there in 1847 (*Gazeta Krakowska* 29 Oct.1847): most of the story loosely follows the original but with some fresh touches — When Death (*Śmierć*) comes uninvited to introduce herself Bosco is at breakfast, drinking *Veuve Cliquot*, which Death helps herself to; Bosco, addressing her as *Ma chère madame Mort*, jokes that he is her priest and offers her absolution. But the same deal is done with both sides satisfied. "It is not known," ends this version "*whether this contract continues, but Bosco must certainly be on good terms with her, as last year in Vienna when his rockets exploded he escaped from her power, and the public say at his shows that he is looking younger not older*".

The version of the story in *Satanas* and in *Biographie und Anecdoten aus den Reisen des alten Bosco* (which has '*Bosco und der Tod*' on the rear cover) and in *Il Nuovo Bosco* ends very lamely, Death leaving after the show and Bosco waking to find it was all a dream.

F8. 'Bosco im Monde', humorous article in *Der Humorist* 5 Sep.1844 in its 'Bunterlei' section, which pretends to quote from issue No.274 of the *Allgemeiner **Monde**zeitung*, edited by *Count Saint-Germain*, that on August 23rd, Bartolomeo Bosco, great grandson of Merlin, had given, at prices increased five-fold, a performance of Egyptian magic on the moon, the first magician to do so, and will then perform for King Schahahahahaham LXXIV… (B1 p.47)

Prague 1845. During (and soon after) Bosco's time there the Prague papers were full of Bosco news, reviews and anecdotes, with an explosion of Bosco fiction and fantasy. These are discussed further in B1 pp.49*ff*.

F9. 'Ein Besuch bei Bosco', humorous story in *Ost und West* (and *Prag*) 8, 10 Mar.1845 (reprinted in *Der Wanderer* 19 Mar.1845);

F10. Moritz Saphir, who had been writing Bosco pieces since 1828 (see B1 pp.23, 49 and esp. note 91), published at this time 'Der ewige Bosco' ([tr.] 'Eternal Bosco') in *Wiener Bazar* no.12 (a weekly supplement to his *Der Humorist* of 15 Mar.1845). This has Bosco as 'the eternal magician' ("Ahasver, der ewige Jude, ist eine wahre Fabel gegen Bosco, den ewigen Zauberer!") putting black heads on Noah's white doves and performing Moses' magic before the Pharaoh, and much else.

F11. 'Der Dämon der Magie: Memoiren aus B. Bosco's Leben', by "Kleroth" (Prague writer Clemens von Wey(h)rother), published in the 25th annual volume of the miscellany *Erinnerungen an merkwürdige Gegenstände und Begebenheiten* (url:194).

These entertaining sketches are purely fiction, an epistolary novella (with no information in them not available from newspapers of the day): discussed in B1 pp.42, 49 and in *Excursus on the Family* p.211.

F12. 'Bartolomeo Bosco: Ein Capriccio in Callot-Hoffmann'scher Manier', by J. P. Lyser.
Published in *Bohemia* in seven instalments 14, 16, 18, 21, 23, 25, 28 Feb.1845 (url:195).

Lyser, actually Ludwig Peter August Burmeister, 1804-1870, born in Flensburg, was both a painter and a writer and here alludes to both E.T.A. Hoffmann and Jacques Callot. A Bosco fantasy which has Bosco arriving from Leipzig in an unnamed German town where he plays some tricks on the philosopher, editor and lawyer Staarpuntzel who disbelieves in magic, finally sending him as an ink blob (*Dintenklex*) on a letter to a Brahmin on the Ganges in Dschinnistan (Wieland's fairy land) where he is turned instead into a poet and humorist, which he hates. He is returned by the same method to Saphir in Vienna but he goes mad... (B1 p.49).

F13. *Reise-Bilder aus dem Leben Boscos in zwölf Sprachen...* by Felix Francesconi. "Zweite Auflage". Wien, Prag und Venedig, 1845. No copy survives of the first edition (of which this second was probably an unchanged reprint). The author was a Professor of Languages at the Karl-Ferdinands-Universität in Prague, and planned to publish the book in German in Vienna and Prague (with editions in Czech, English, French, Greek, Italian, Hungarian, Polish, Portuguese, Russian, Spanish and Turkish promised, to be translated by his pupils).

The book gives a colourful account of Bosco's time in Egypt.
Copy at the National Library of the Czech Republic available online at url:049.
(Discussed in more detail in B1 pp.49-50 and note 366.)

F14. A series of Bosco anecdotes and stories appeared in early 1845 in the journal *Passavia*, published in Passau (*Pasavia* in Italian, *Pasov* in Czech) in Bavaria.

The first, 'Die Champagner-Gäste' ([tr.] 'The Champagne Guests'), *Passavia* 13 Jan.1845, pp.1-2, is set in Hamburg; the second 'Bosco unter den Räubern' ([tr.] 'Bosco among the robbers', *Passavia* 15 Jan.1845 pp.1-3; 16 Jan.1845 pp.1-2; 17 Jan.1845 pp.1-2 is set in Italy.

The next story, 'Wer kann daraus klug werden?' ([tr.] 'Who can make sense of it?') is attributed to Oettinger, *Passavia* 21 Jan.1845, and is followed by a shorter story, 'Der Teufel im Gasthofe' ([tr.] 'The Devil in the inn').

The last two in this sequence are 'Die Sängerin und der kleine Sänger' ([tr.] 'The lady singer and the small songster', *Passavia* 26 Jan.1845 pp.1-2, and 'Bei der Königlichen *Soirée* in Versailles' ([tr.] 'At the Royal *Soirée* in Versailles'), *Passavia* 29 Jan.1845, pp.1-2; the latter is an extended anecdote about Bosco performing for Louis Philippe.

The author of 'Die Sängerin und der kleine Sänger' (here anonymous) was Hermann Kothe, 1822-1859, who made a career of lecturing and writing on the technique of memory, calling himself variously a *Mnemoniker*, *Gedächtnißlehrer*, or *Gedächtnißkünstler*. In his 1848 book *Lehrbuch der Mnemonik oder Gedächtnißkunst* he quotes passages from various books with the consonants turned into numbers for easy(?) memorising, including, pp.113-5, 'Die Sängerin und der kleine Sänger', which he states is taken from his *Teufeleien des neunzehnten Jahrhunderts.* He probably also wrote 'Bei der Königlichen Soirée in Versailles', and he certainly wrote 'Ein Visite des Teufels, Ein sehr harmlose Bagatelle', published anonymously in *Passavia* 13, 14 June 1845 (the second instalment ends with "continuation follows" but may be complete).

His book *Bosco, Teufeleien des neunzehnten Jahrhunderts,* appeared in two parts in 1844 and 1845, published on commission by Theodor Thomas in Leipzig (listed *Börsenblatt für den deutschen Buchhandel* 26 Nov.1844; Part 2 listed 6 May 1845).

The *Allgemeines Bücher-Lexikon* gives Part 1 as 'Bosco hier, Bosco da, Bosco dort' (with a portrait of Bosco), Part 2 as 'Krieg den Schnurrbärten. Ein Visite des Teufels'. Part 1 is listed in the November 1844 issue of the book trade monthly *Monatliches Verzeichnis der Neuigkeiten und Fortsetzungen des deutschen Buchhandels*, No.11, Monat November, 1844) and in newspapers as for sale in late December (earliest found: *Nürnberger Kurier* 29 Dec.1844). Some advertisements (e.g. *Wiener Zeitung* 5 Apr.1845) include a blurb: "[tr.] This piquant collection of Bosco anecdotes (by no means a description of his tricks) characterizes the great artist very aptly, and tells us of the many wonderful deliberate misunderstandings (*qui pro quo*) which he perpetrated on his world trips to the amusement and amazement of all".

The complete edition, Parts 1 and 2, was advertised in *Hamburger Nachrichten* 3 Dec.1845, when Kothe was in town delivering his lectures on mnemonics.

Unlike Francesconi's book there is never any mention of this being sold at Bosco's own shows. It would appear that there is only one surviving copy, in Universitätsbibliothek, Eberhard Karls Universität Tübingen (not digitised). Part 2 is catalogued as: Krieg den Schnurrbärten: Zauberposse in einem Aufzuge [with added work:] Die Visite des Teufels: eine sehr harmlose Bagatelle.

F15. 'O Bosco !', by Christinus Sieben. *Wiener Zeitschrift* 4 Apr.1845
Asking Bosco for the last twenty years again… (Online at url:196.)

F16. 'Drei Aesopische Fabeln', by B. Heidler. *Der Wanderer* 25 Nov.1845
Three stories about Bosco. The first is a twist on the anecdote of Bosco finding valuables in fruit; the second has Bosco in America, working wonders while strolling down "Kentuky-Street" in Philadelphia (it was at this time that Bosco was advertising regularly that he would soon travel to America and may never return to Europe: see B1 p.51); the third, set in Vienna, tells what happens when a friend, knowing Bosco's "Rivalisirungsbereitwilligkeit", gets him to copy a trick he had seen Döbler do… (Online at url:197).

F17. *Briefe des Hans Michel aus Obersteier an seinen Göd, den Sensenschmid in der Oed über Steiermark und Gratz,* by Jakob Franz Dirnböck. Graz: The Author, 1845.
Volume 4 of his ongoing whimsical *Briefe* ('Letters of Hans Michel from Obsteier to his godfather, the scythe-maker in Oed'), written in the local dialect. Includes two Bosco stories, both really variations on well-worn Bosco anecdotes. Discussed in B1 p.54. Online at url:050.

F18. *Der arme Geigenmacher und sein Kind*, by Gustav Nieritz.

A children's story, ([tr.] 'The Poor Fiddle-maker and his Child'), by a popular writer of the day, Karl Gustav Nieritz, 1795-1876. First published in the 1846 volume of his *Deutsches Volksbüchlein für Jung und Alt;* not published separately until 1907. Serialised in *Der Grenzbote* 13 July to 24 Aug. 1851.

Bosco makes only a brief appearance in the chapter 'Bosko, der Hexenmeister', conjuring money out of the audience's pockets into his own: "der große — nein, der kleine, dicke Magier Bosko ... seine Menschen beglückenden Künste zeigte. Außer der allbekannten Hexereien zauberte der schlaue Italiener in zwei Stunden seinen zweihundert Zuschauern eben so viele Speziethaler aus ihren Taschen in die seinige...".

This section (7 Aug.1851) is online at url:198.

F19. 'Ein Scherz', by Josef Seidner, *Passavia* 29 Apr.1846

A short humorous piece on Bosco, which has him doing wonders everywhere from England to China, telling us his first cry after his birth was an unarticulated '*spiriti miei*', soon afterwards telling the midwife 'I'm fine', then, when offered a wet-nurse, saying he would prefer a few glasses of champagne. Online at url:199.

F20. When Bartolomeo was in Preßburg (Bratislava) in late 1847 the journal *Pannonia* (really a literary supplement to the *Preßburger Zeitung*) published several humorous stories on him, opening with an anecdote (Bosco at breakfast) on November 16th, more anecdotes on November 20th (one ascribed to humorist Louis Weyl of Bosco in the Berlin stock exchange), a comic dialogue with Ahasuerus on November 27th by Josef Weyl (of the *Pannonia* staff), Bosco receiving new tricks and a new magic wand from Egypt, and having Bosco say (in Bosco-ese), on the subject of high prices: "Lieber ick macken weniger Einnahme ... Bosco reicker Mann, fort bien, Bosco armer Teufel, macken auch nicks! Ein Jahr man speisen Anananas, ander Jahr man essen Herdäpfel... (*one year tasting pineapple, next year only spuds to eat)*".

Early 1848 saw the publication of several pieces invoking Bosco to make political points. Even in reviews of his performances we find comments such as "...no better way of recovering from the current political troubles than in the house of King Bosco I, soon alas to cross the seas, whose subjects (*spiriti infernali*) will not so soon successfully revolt..."

F21. Oettinger in his *Charivari* (23 Mar.1848) joked that Bosco had recently been performing at the Austrian court and, placing a large pyramid over the head of the Emperor and tapping it with his magic wand, made the Emperor disappear: when Metternich asked where he'd gone, Bosco said: 'You've got His Majesty in your pocket'.

F22. *Leipziger Zeitung* 13 May 1848

This styles Bosco the "[tr.] Autocrat (*Selbstherrscher*) of All Magicians, the Russian Alexander in the Kingdom of the Magic Arts, he whose throne, of all the thrones in this world, remains unshaken and unshakable, because it is a throne of Art, which he did not usurp, but rose onto it by his own genius, his *spiriti miei*...", and wishing he would pull off the trick of uniting all Germany...; ending with a poem (F57 below) on the same theme of Bosco's unifying powers.

F23. *Leipziger Zeitung* 27 May 1848
   An extravagant lengthy effusion of Bosco *leaving for Dresden, then probably America, to make comparisons between German liberty and American liberty... all other magicians bow down before Bosco, and lose their lustre before his brilliance, just as in true Germanic times, when Germany was still an Empire, all generals and petty princes paid homage to the one Emperor... Bosco is the sole-ruler of all magicians, a Russian Nicholas ...one day he will descend from the throne of magic and lay down his wand of his own accord, and there will be no one who deserves to be his worthy successor ... and the empire of magic ... will become an elective empire with hundreds of pretenders; but then, because no one is worthy of ascending the throne of magic nor able to take it by force, the electoral empire will constitute a republic...*

F24. In July a reviewer (*Dresdner Journal* 3 July 1848) opened by saying that Bosco had gone to the school of the diplomatic magician ("trickster") Prince Metternich, but the student has surpassed the master. Metternich, too, knew very well how to transform a living bird into a dead one, but he used a double-headed eagle for this experiment ... while Bosco uses only a canary.

F25. The radical Vienna paper *Wiener Katzenmusik* (15 July; 12, 31 Aug.; 25 Oct. 1848) suggested several imaginary political shows and tricks for Bosco to perform and compared ministerial tergiversations and pretensions to his stage deceptions.

F26. In the satirical *Berliner Krakehler* the editors, principally Carl Otto Hoffmann and Ernst Litfaß, put into Bosco's mouth three macaronic French-German pieces announcing '[tr.] Great Extraordinary Exhibitions of Magic' of the 'The Goddess of Freedom' (22 July 1848 p.3; 21 Oct.1848 pp.1-2; 1 Nov.1848 p.1).

F27. 'Bosco's Traum', signed "Mephistopheles". *DAZ* 10 June 1848
   Despite the title ('Bosco's dream') — and the author — this "dream" had several serious points to make, both political and theatrical, complaining of "outdated privileges" both in society and in the theatre, the latter preventing foreign performers such as Bosco who arrived in Leipzig within a set time prior to the Fair from opening there until the Fair began: see B1 pp.60-1.

F28. 'Les Deux Escamoteurs', by "Asmodée". *Le Courrier Batave* 21 July 1850.
"Asmodée" was the pen name of the editor of this radical Amsterdam journal, Adriaan van Bevervoorde.
   Satirical story ([tr.] 'The Two Magicians') published when Bosco was opening in Rotterdam comprising an imaginary comic dialogue between him and the Minister of Finance, Pieter Van Bosse, who was then implementing unpopular currency reforms.

The story was reprinted as a booklet in Dutch, titled *Bosco en Van Bosse, of De Twee Gochelaars.*

Abridged versions of the satire in French, German and Italian, titled '[tr.] Bosco in Holland', wrongly dating it to *February* 1850, appear in *Satanas,* in *Biographie und Anecdoten,* and in *Il Nuovo Bosco*. These miss much of the contemporary political allusion — and some of the humour — of the original. Discussed in detail in B1 pp.69-71.

F29. 'Bosco au Manoir d'Ango', by "Roger de Beauvoir" (pen name of the novelist and playwright Eugène Augustin Nicolas Roger). *La Vigie de Dieppe* 24, 31 Aug. 1852; reprinted in the Paris papers *Le Nouvelliste* and *Vert-vert* 31 Aug.1852.

A story, perhaps embroidered from a real visit, which has Bosco while in Dieppe travelling in his carriage ("which he bought from the King") to the 15th century manor of Jehan Angot, amazing and alarming the locals with his turns and tricks.

F30. *Gilbert et Gilberte,* by Eugène Sue (serialised in *Le Siècle* 1852-3; as a book 1853).

Sue's long novel, described in a contemporary review as "une féerie, un rêve ... un aimable livre... où la fantaisie a pris toute ses aises..." (*Almanach de la littérature, du théâtre et des beaux-arts* 1854). has a character pretending to be Bosco. Online at url:200 (and elsewhere)

F31. 'A Night of Horrors in the Wizard's Workshop, Being the Confession of a Curious Man relative to Sig. Bosco'. *Portsmouth Times and Naval Gazette* 11 July 1857

The anonymous writer tells us he went to a Bosco show in Gosport (which would have been Epstein, though he did not know that); after the show he hides in a broom closet so he can examine the apparatus. This brings out the imps, whom he dismisses with the magic wand, then having already taken medication for a fever he starts drinking whisky from the inexhaustible bottle... he finally raps on the spirit-rapping table and goes through the stage trap-door, waking up in New Zealand. Online at url:201.

F32. 'Bosco Il Prestigiatore. Prima Rappresentazione', by "Ciliegia". *L'Arlecchino* 27 Apr.1860 (online at url:202)

A political piece published when Bosco was performing in Turin (B1 p.87) shortly after the signing of the Treaty which would see Napoleon III not oppose Garibaldi, Cavour and Vittorio Emanuele in the further unification of Italy. The commentator imagines Bosco at his 'First Performance', *which will start with laughter but whose end is unknown... by means of his cup and balls and his magic wand he will change the minds of the audience from no to yes...* and he then regales them with the story of *a sea horse — you see him there in a corner of the room, I tell you that he is a sad beast of burden. He has always deceived all the wretched knights who trusted in him, pretending to be a meek and noble steed, and he has a strong resemblance to the Dauphin. He also caused an irreparable fall to a relative of mine, who had the gullibility to get on his back to cross the sea, and he would like to deceive me too ...*

but I caught him in the same net that he set for me... I want and hope in a short time with my cups, my balls, and my wand, to make him so weak that he can no longer harm anyone. He would like to go wild, but in vain because I hold him by the hair and he will not escape me. To this effect, I first wanted to tame that colossal bear that you can see there in that very remote point of the room. I am glad I succeeded, and here's how. I first treated it as an enemy, I hit it with my magic wand; and then when it held out its right hand I gave it some sugar, I soothed it, I showed it the weak side and the perfidy of the screaming sea horse, and I believe I am close to reaching the goal. At this moment the sea-horse is heard neighing in a very sinister and frightening way, so that the spectators are very moved.... Bosco heard the neighing of the seahorse, smiled with compassion, and concluded with these words: Gentlemen, do not disturb the demeanour of that furious beast. I have reason to believe that I will be luckier than my relative in making him in a short time quite docile to my will. Meanwhile, the hour being very late, I put an end to the show, reserving for the future the explanation, of the method I have adopted to isolate the sea horse from the other animals, once his faithful companions, and to prepare him in spite of himself to be totally tamed. For this evening, therefore, thanking you courteously, I take my leave of you...

F33. [Imaginary letter by Bosco] *Kladderdatsch* 29 July 1860
    Denying he is General Bosco (B1 p.87).
    Online at url:203.

F34. 'Wie sich der 'rothe Hofmann' auf Bosco spielte', by M.A. Reitler.
    Story of a poor comic actor who performs a Bosco act. (Online at url:204)
First found in *Tetschner Anzeiger* 22 Dec.1860 (published in Tetschen, modern Děčín) where the author's name is given and it is said to be Part III of 'Historietten eines Sanguinikers'. Reprinted anon. in *Nürnberger Kurier* 19 Sep.1861; *Erzähler zum Fürther Tagblatt* 1861; and in *Wöchentlicher Anzeiger des Westens* (St. Louis, Missouri) 25 July 1861. The author was Marzellin Adalbert Reitler (who wrote as Emil Arter), 1839-1909, born in Prague; a railway official in Baden, who also wrote on railway management.

F35. 'Boscos Tod', by H. Truhn, *Der Bazar: Illustrirte Damen-Zeitung* 16 Jan.1871 (also in *Aussiger Anzeiger* 15 July 1871)
    Fictionalised account of Bosco's last days. Online at url:205

F36. 'Aus dem Leben Bosco's'
Extra-Felleisen: belletristische Beilage zum Würzburger Stadt- und Landboten, Ein Unterhaltungsblatt 30 May 1872
    Anonymous story of Bosco in Brno. Online at url:206.

F37. 'Sultan Abdul Aziz in der Comödie' by "W.S. and M.S."
Wiener Sonn- und Montags-Zeitung 24 July 1876 (online at url:207);
also in *Wiener Theater-Chronik* 28 July; 3 Aug.1876

An imaginary account of Eugenio's time in Turkey in 1864: discussed in B2 pp.167-8.

F38. Essentially an earlier version of the same story (see B2 pp.167-8): 'Sultan Abdul-Aziz im Theater, (Eine Reise-Erinnerung.)', signed "Z.", *Die Presse* 23 July 1867 (online at url:208).

F39. 'Der gordische Knoten, Humoreske aus dem Bühnenleben', by Max Besozzi. *Pettauer Wochenblatt* 8 Dec.1878 (online at url:209)
Story about "Dagobert Bosco, nephew of the great Bosco" arriving at a town in Westphalia to give magic shows. Besozzi, 1847-1914, was an Austrian journalist.

F40. *Jacques l'Honneur*, by Léon Sazie (1862-1939) and Georges Grison (1841-1928).
Sensation novel, published as a serial in *Le Petit Journal* from 26 June 1892 (first instalment at url:210); also in Dutch papers; play 1894; book 1895 (cover at url:211); filmed in 1913 (see F65).
One character is "Le Célèbre Professeur Bosco, dit Le Docteur Satan, et son élève Mlle Eugénie" — Bosco is here used generically for a magician and does not represent Bartolomeo as such.

F41. 'Bosco's Benefit'
A widely reprinted anonymous story about an imaginary circus performer "Signor Alfredo Bosco ...in private life... plain Alfred Green") forced by the circus owner to do a William Tell act on his son. This appeared in several English, American, New Zealand and other papers between 1894 and 1909, sometimes credited to London *Tit-Bits,* where it probably first appeared.
Online in a New Zealand paper at url:212.
A Norwegian version appeared in *Romsdals Amtstidende* 12 May 1897 (url:212).

F42. 'Bosco in Rußland. Erzählung nach Tatsachen', by A. Dolleczeck [*sic*]
serialised in *Die Ostschweiz* [St. Gallen] between 29 May and 13 June 1900.
A colourful account of Bartolomeo's experiences in the army in Russia, twice using a pistol to save his life, and ending with Eugenio injuring his hand: "...Es war dieselbe Pistole, die seinem Vater zweimal das Leben gerettet hatte" (*...it was the very same pistol that had twice saved his father's life*). Online (first instalment) at url:213
Written by Anton Dolleczek [Dolleček], a serving officer in the Austro-Hungarian Army who died in 1918, author of *Geschichte der österreichischen Artillerie von den frühesten Zeiten bis zur Gegenwart* and other military works and articles; under the pseudonym "A.D. Borum" he wrote the libretto for Viktor Parma's operetta 'Die Amazonen der Czarin' and under that name his historical stories were republished in Leipzig in 1932 as *Um einen Dukaten und andere geschichtlichen Erzählungen.*

F43. 'Der falsche Bosco. Eine lustige Diebsgeschichte', by Hermann Hirschfeld.
This is listed, described as "Alltägliches aus der Vogelperspektive. Mit 8 Illustrationen", in an advertisement in *Grazer Volksblatt* 8 Sep.1906 as published in *St.Josef-Kalender 1907* [no copy located]. Hirschfeld, 1842-1921, who also wrote as Walter Vogel, was a popular novelist of the day. Not seen.

F44. *Il Tre Paletti, Racconto storico, 1812,* by Luigi Gramegna. Torino: Lattes, 1933; new edition, Torino: Edilibri-A. Viglongo, 1971
I have not read this historical novel by the Piedmontese author Gramegna, 1846-1928, of the experiences of Bartolomeo's 111th Regiment in the Russian campaign.

F45. 'Een Banneling, die kon Gochelen. Hoe een jonge gevangene zijn strengen oppasser op de vlucht dreef'. *Alkmaarsche Courant* 13 May 1939
An anonymous illustrated account for children of Bosco's life and career, opening with the Cossack... (Online at url:214)

F46. *Il Mistero della Locanda Serny,* by Marco Fabio Apolloni. Milano: Ponte alle Grazie, 2003.
I have not read this novel which includes Bartolomeo, Stendhal, Gogol and Giuditta Grisi together in Rome in 1839. Is there a contemporary source that places Bartolomeo there? He is not mentioned in the detailed account in *Diario di Roma* of this "festa splendidissima" (see B1 p.40) and two days later, on Friday 11th, he was performing in Naples, more than 200 km away.

Plays

F47. *Vosculo [sic] von Barcelona und Greif von Kasan, oder die beiden Taschenspieler in Krähwinkel.* Berlin: Verlag von Cosmar und Krause, 1828. Online at url:017.
A one-act farce (*Quodlibet*) arising out of the controversy between Bartolomeo and Habitt in Berlin. Catalogued as *Vosculo...* by German libraries; referred to in some contemporary newspapers as *Bosculo...*, and one gets the impression that the publishers carefully chose a Fraktur fount with minimal difference between *V* and *B*.
Possibly written by the publisher Cosmar according to Goedeke *Grundriss zur Geschichte der deutschen Dichtung aus den Quellen* XI.1 (1951) p.603.

F48. 'Chieppe lo Smargiasso, ossia I ridicoli giuochi di Pulcinella e Pangrazio Biscegliese, sciocchi professori di Magia Egiziana', a comedy by Orazio Schiano, making fun of Bartolomeo ('I ridicoli giochi del Cavalier Bosco'), performed in Naples in 1838 (see B1 p.39 & note 264). Probably not printed or published.

F49. 'Bosco'. A one-act German farce of this title by the popular comic actor, director and producer William Büller, 1851-1923, was performed in Leipzig on January 28th 1888. Büller played the title role of the masterly magician and performed the tricks — he had previously done magic shows for charity at private houses (*Wiener Allgemeine Zeitung* 31 Jan.1888). Probably not printed or published.

Poems

F50. 'Spiriti miei obedite, oder Bosco's Zauberformel', by "Richard Roos" (Karl August Engelhardt).

Poem on Bosco finding money in bread rolls being sold by a baker (*"Wer kennt den Taschenspieler Bosco nicht?..."*). Published in the anthology *Huldigung den Frauen*, 1823; reprinted in *Hamburger Nachrichten* 9 June 1830 when Bartolomeo was in town; also in 1844 in the anthology *Declamatorium: Auswahl ernster und heiterer Dichtungen zum Vortrage in öffentlichen und Privat-Gesellschaften* (ed. Ernst Littfas), Heft 18; and in editions of Roos's *Gedichte*. See B1 note 129.

Online (*Huldigung* and *Declamatorium*) at url:215

F51. 'An Herrn Bartholomeo Bosco', signed 'Baum'.

An adulatory poem published in *Libausches Wochenblatt* 24 Dec.1824 when Bartolomeo was in Libau (Liepāja) (*"Ein selt'nes Spiel ergötzte uns're Augen, / Was Künstler du, so treu uns hier gezeigt ..."*). Online at url:216.

F52. Luigi Muzzi.

While in Bologna in 1836 Bosco was honoured with an adulatory verse inscription by Luigi Muzzi, "pubblico ripetitore d'eloquenza italiana e latina nell' Università di Bologna e professore di belle lettere", published in *La Fama* 20 June 1836 (and in *Delle iscrizioni di Luigi Muzzi accademico della Crusca,* Padova: Al Signo di Minerva, 1836; url:217).

He published a similar piece when Bosco was again in Italy in August 1845 (*Il Piccol Reno* 16 Aug.1845; url:218)

F53. [Untitled adulatory Latin poem on Bartolomeo, *Quas magicas adhibes artes dic...*] by Michelangelo Poggioli, published in *Diario di Roma* 21 June 1838, accompanied by an Italian paraphrase by Giuseppe Cocchi, di Todi.

Both texts were reprinted (with some minor spelling and punctuation changes) in *Giornale Scientifico-Agrario-Letterario-Artistico di Perugia ed Umbra Provincia. Dispensa Sesta dell'Anno 1863,* then as a booklet, *Intorno alcuni scritti inediti di Michelangelo Poggioli pubblicati per cura del figlio Avv. Giuseppe. Nota di Sebastiano Purgotti.* Perugia: Tipografia di Vincenzo Bartelli, 1864 (both the *Diario* and the booklet are on Google Books, and the latter also at url:040). See B1 p.40 and note 273.

F54. 'Bartolommeo Bosco soprannornato Turandò l'incantatore', by Giuseppe Gioachino Belli.

Written when Bartolomeo was in Rome in 1839; not printed (only recited) at the time, but included in Belli's *Versi inediti* of 1843 (on Google Books); also printed in Mario Verdone's article 'Bartolomeo Bosco in una poesia italiana del Belli' *Strenna dei Romanisti* 25 (1964) pp.511-6 (online at url:039), and in Rusconi pp.226-8. See B1 p.40 and note 272.

F55. 'Täuschung und Wahrheit. (An Barth. Bosco)', by A. Palme, *Der Wanderer* 9 Apr.1845

Poem addressed to Bartolomeo on leaving Vienna (*"Verzeihlich ist's in unsrer düstern Zeit, / Wenn man sich über Zauberkünste wundert..."*). Online at url:219

F56. 'Zum Abschied an B. Bosco', signed Mollner, *Der Wanderer* 2 Mar.1846
(*"Bosco, zweiter Prometheus ... Bosco, göttergleicher Zeus, Ruhmgekrönnter Prometheus..."*).

An adulatory poem to Bartolomeo on leaving Vienna. Comparing him to Prometheus, bringer of fire, suggests a humorous reference to his recent fireworks accident but apparently that was not intended. Online at url:220

F57. 'An B. Bosco in Leipzig'. *Leipziger Zeitung* 13 May 1848
(*"Um den Kessel schlingt den Reih'n, / Daß es braus' und siede, / Bosco wird uns jetzt zerstreun / Mit des Zaubers Blüthe..."*)

Poem on Bosco sorting out the political troubles of the time. Online at url:221

This also appeared as 'An Bosco in Potsdam' in *KPBZ* 29 Dec.1848, signed C.A.

F58. 'Spiriti miei infernali!' *Leipziger Zeitung* 28 May 1848
(*"Wer ist's wol, der die Zauberwelt / In seinen Kern zusammenhält..."*)

A poem in praise of Bosco's talents, printed following one of his advertisements (*"...Sein Zweck ist uns nur zu erfreun"* — His aim is only to give us enjoyment...)

Online at url:222.

F59. *Deutschlands Einheit hergestellt durch die Zauberei des B. Bosco: Ein Dialog zwischen Faust, Mephistopheles und Bosco*. This was published in Leipzig in 1848.

Poem on Bosco's solution for unifying Germany. Undated but listed in Hinrichs' *Verzeichniß* for July-Dec. 1848 and in *Börsenblatt für den deutschen Buchhandel* 11 July 1848 (under 'Joachim's Separat-Conto in Leipzig'). Printed by C. W. Vollrath for the publisher C. Dederich. There were two printings, one with the author given only as "Zanoni", the other naming the author as Dr. C. Zehmen (see B1 p.63; and note 504 for the author).

There are surviving copies in German libraries and in the British Library. It has not been digitised.

F60. 'Une Séance de Magie. A Mon Ami Bartolomeo Bosco', by Gaston D'Argy, *Revue des races latines* 30 June 1861.

A long poem on Bartolomeo, said to be published posthumously and edited by D. de R[ochefort]. Further "posthumous" poems by "Gaston Dargy" were published the following year and at least one reviewer suspected that the real author was the ostensible editor, Rochefort. In fact he too was probably a fabrication and Dargy was the pen name of Charles Dècle, a St Quentin distiller, who died March 1st 1888, age 61.

Music

F61. 'Bosco-Galopp', by Gustav Kunze. Op.53. Dresden: Paul, 1844.

A polka for piano, composed when Bartolomeo was in Dresden in 1844.
Allgemeine Musikalische Zeitung 18 Dec.1844; Hofmeister: *Musikalisch-literarischer Monatsbericht* 12, 1844. A copy is held in the Staatsbibliothek zu Berlin.

F62. 'The Necromancer's Polka', by T. Barbor Might. 1856

Written by Epstein's (B12) accompanist in Dublin and dedicated to him (*Dublin Evening Post* 27 Mar.1856); "extremely pretty" and "danceable", said the Irish papers, but *The Musical World* pronounced it "ungrammatical". No surviving copies are recorded.

F63. 'Bosko's Zauberkopf. Urkomisches Gesammtspiel für 1 Dame und 6 Herren', by Wilhelm Malek. Op.88. Leipzig: Glaser, 1899.

Malek was a composer of humorous songs. This is listed as published in *Börsenblatt für den deutschen Buchhandel* 21 Nov.1899, and in Hofmeister: *Verzeichniss der im Jahre 1899 erschienenen Musikalien, auch musikalischen Schriften und Abbildungen mit Anzeige der Verleger und Preise* (Hofmeister XIX <http://www.hofmeister.rhul.ac.uk>, Sep.1889, p.414); but I cannot trace any surviving copies.

Films

F64. *Der berühmte Zauberer Bosko*

A short film of this title is advertised as being shown in cinemas in Olmütz (Olomouc), Klagenfurt, Baden, and Linz in 1908-9 (*Mährisches Tagblatt* 4 May 1908 the earliest reference found). No mention of this in the periodical *Der Kinematograph* and nothing further is known of it.

F65. *Jacques l'Honneur*

A magician named Bosco was a character in the film based on the story and play *Jacques l'Honneur* (F40). Directed by Henri Andréani; Jean Toulout played Bosco, it also featured Jacques Normand, Berthe Bovy, and Georges Wague, all well-known stage actors of the day. The film had a trade release in Paris on March 31st 1914, and by April 14th twenty copies were on show round France (*Comoedia* 31 Mar., 14 Apr. 1914).

The Bibliothèque Nationale has material on the film — url:223.

Bosco here (in the book, the play and the film) was used generically as a name for a magician, and did not represent Bartolomeo as such.

F66. Chaplin.

The Chaplin films are discussed by David Robinson in 'Who was Professor Bosco?' (online at url:224), which includes some stills.

George Davis played magician Professor Bosco in Chaplin's 1928 film *The Circus,* and in 1919 Chaplin himself played a Professor Bosco, proprietor of a flea-circus, in scenes that were never used, though he thought about including them in *The Professor* in 1922, which was never released: see 'The Professor' at url:225.

Robinson suggests that if Chaplin had in mind a real magician it was Leotard Bosco (B77), whose moustache matched that of the film sharacter. (By a nice coincidence Charles Chaplin Senior was performing at Leotard Bosco's Empire Palace of Varieties on the date his son Charlie was born, 16 April 1889.)

F67. *Ain't He Grand*

Another cinematic magician named Professor Bosco appeared in the 1916 film *Ain't He Grand*, directed and written by Roy Clements, with Edward Sedgwick as The Professor.

A contemporary synopsis in *Moving Picture World* 25 Mar.1916 reads: "Prof. Bosco, 'The World's Famous Magician and Hypnotist,' and his 'Metropolitan Company', which consists of 'Grip' Hoaley, reach Centerville after a long walk from their last stand …Prof. Bosco bills the town and gives a performance at the opera house. [His] 'punch' trick is the standing of 'Grip' Hoaley, supposedly under hypnotism power, on his head. This trick made a great hit with the Centerville audience, but when Prof. Bosco attempted the stunt with the town belle the cowboys in the audience start to shoot up the show. 'Grip' Hoaley makes a get-away, but Prof. Bosco 'gets his'.

Motion Picture News 25 Mar.1916 said: "Roy Clements has extracted a good deal of fun from the incident of the bunk magician operating in a small town". From a note in *Motion Picture News* 19 Feb.1916 it appears the film was originally to be titled 'When Bosco Disappeared'.

F68. *The Evil Eye*

The 1914 American film *The Evil Eye* had a character named Bosco as the villain, a hypnotist who performed as "Dr. Satan" but the plot is not the same as that of *Jacques l'Honneur* (summary in *Moving Picture World* 15 Aug.1914).

F69. *Die erklärbaren Wunder*

A two part documentary on the history of magic; made in 1980 and shown on German television in 1981. According to a note which was formerly on http://magier-joro.de/english.html, Joro (Bruno Hennig) "lent his magical hands to the German actor Jürgen Schmidt who played the role of Bartolomeo Bosco".

"BOSCO BOOKS"

I have tried here to list the many books in many languages claiming to be by Bosco (or by Carl or Carlo Bosco), or naming him in the title, or claiming to include tricks by him.

(For Fiction about him and items humorously attributed to him see *Fiction* section.)

Bartolomeo himself published no book. We hear of poems he wrote to shower over his audiences on closing nights — we have the full text of a poem in Danish from 1830 (B1 note 146); poems in French in 1833 and 1834 (B1 notes 192 & 218); and in German in 1844 (B1 note 350). It is possible, though unlikely, that Bosco himself wrote the 8 page poem in German, a dialogue between Bosco, Faust and Mephistopheles, dating perhaps to 1835 (*Fiction* F3) but this may be the 1848 poem, F39. The Universitätsbibliothek Leipzig has a 2 leaf manuscript in French written by Bosco in Dresden on November 30th, titled 'Pour moi tous les pays' (B1 note 360).

He did write the "play", 'Die Bescheerung im Serail oder Bosco überall' (never printed) with himself not merely conjuring in it but playing a character role. He performed it as part of his act in 1848 in Leipzig, Dresden, and Berlin and subsequently elsewhere (B1 note 479). The title of the play is given in French as 'Le Cadeau du Sérail', so 'Bescheerung' refers to the distribution of presents, not "shearing".

Eugenio wrote a book, *La magia di viaggi e avventure di Eugenio Bosco: cenni biografici di Prrrr*. It is a pity no one has reprinted this: two surviving copies are recorded, both of the 3rd edition — see p.180.

Eugenio mentions another book, *La Prestidigitation de l'Avenir*, when in Laval in 1882 (*L'Avenir de la Mayenne* 20, 24 Feb.1882; *L'Ouest-Éclair* 24 Feb.1882). I can find no trace of this: he probably wrote it in Italian but again neither *La prestidigitazione del futuro* nor *La prestigiazione del futuro* are recorded. Perhaps he intended to write it but never published it? Or this may have been a later or revised edition of his earlier book.

Many of the books listed here were undated and where possible I have added references to book trade journals and to the earliest newspaper advertisement or review found.

Most of the entries are given as in library catalogues; occasional errors are pointed out not for mere pedantry but because a search, for example, for *Carl Bosco's Zauberkünste* in the LC online catalogue is unsuccessful as the title is misspelt there. Similarly the University of Frankfurt catalogues that book as *Carl Bosko's Zauberkünste* whereas their own online digitised copy clearly reads *Carl Bosco's Zauberkünste*.

Ideally here the exact wording of the title would of course be transcribed from the book itself: that not being possible, digitised copies or at least photographs of the title-page have been used where available and in those cases I have usually transcribed the text of the title-page in full with line endings indicated by vertical bars: this is to avoid the introduction of capitalisation, punctuation (and often abbreviation), which is inevitably done inconsistently, even arbitrarily, and obscures changes made to the wording of title-pages in successive editions (a typical example is *Carl Bosco's Zauberkünste; oder, Die Taschenspielerkunst* which will be found catalogued with and without the inserted semi-colon and/or comma, neither of which is on the original title-page).

Later editions with exactly the same title are indicated by ———
Titles with altered wording are indicated by [...]
Different titles are separated by ===

At least one holding library is given (where traced) for each edition: for abbreviations used see p.12.).

Czech

LCz1.
Bosco.
Boscovo umění kejklířské: Na zkušenosti založené navedení, jak provésti lze přemnohé kejkle obdivení vzbuzující bez velkých příprav a výloh: Ku poučení a zábavě kruhů veselých

Brno: Inter Magic, 1991. 103pp.; 21cm. ISBN 9788090079908. Afterword by Antonín Hančl.

Held National Library of the Czech Republic (digitised but apart from the cover and title-page accessible only in the library)

===

LCz2.
Jaroslav Černý

Malý Bosko: sbírka kouzelných kousků, žertů a rúzných zábavek počtářských. Pro zábavu ve společnostech sestavil a vzdělal Jaroslav Černý

Jilemnice: Al. Neubert [1898]. 48pp., 12cm.

Held National Library of the Czech Republic; listed *Oesterreichische Buchhändler-Correspondenz* 2 Nov.1898 (="Der kleine Bosko"); Jindřich: *Abecedni soupis vsech knih vsech nakldatelu ceskych vydanych za poslednich tri let (až do konce dubna 1900)*, p.14.

Online at url:226.

LCz3.
2nd ed., 1901

———

Jilemnice: Al. Neubert, 1901. 48pp., 12cm

Held National Library of the Czech Republic; listed *Abecedni soupis vsech knih vsech nakldatelu ceskych vydanych za poslednich tri let (až do konce dubna 1900)* p.96

===

LCz4.
F. Hočárek
Malý Bosko, čili, 100 kouzelných kouskú, které se dají velmi snadno vyváděti pro zábavu a obveselení ve spole čnostech: s přídavkem několika žertovných kouskuús kartami.../ dle vlastní zkušenosti a nejlepších spisů sestavil F. Hočárek.
    Prague: B. Stýblo [1865]. 110pp., 14cm.
    Held National Library of the Czech Republic; listed *Oesterreicische Buchhändler-Correspondenz* 1 May 1865 p.104.

LCz5.
[*2nd ed.?*]
Malý Bosko, čili, Dobré dvě kopy kouzelných kouskú, které se velmi snadno vyváděti dají pro zábavu a obveselení ve společnostech: s přídavkem rozmanitých žertovných kouskú
    Prague: B. Stýblo [1889?]. 150pp., 14cm
    Held National Library of the Czech Republic
    A copy for sale of the 2nd ed is at url:227.

LCz6.
[*7th ed.*]
———
    7. rozmnožené a obrázky ozdobené vyd.
    Prague: B. Stýblo [1889?]. 159pp., 14cm
    Held National Library of the Czech Republic

===

LCz7.
Bosco český, dokonalý umělec kouzelnický. Obsahuje vybrané umělecké kousky a produkce z oboru přirozené magie, fysiky a lučby, karetni kejkle a jiné zábavné i žertovné úkoly.
[*on cover:*] Malé Bosko. Ctvrté opravené a rozmnožené vydáni.
    127pp.
    Listed *Oesterreichische Buchhändler-Correspondenz* 27 May 1882

LCz8.
[*4th edition*]
Bosco český, dokonalý umělec kouzelnický. Obsal vybrané umělecké kousky a produkce z oboru přirozené ma fysiky, lučby, karetni kejkle a jiné zábavné i žertovné úkoly.
[*on cover:*] Malé Bosko. Ctvrté opravené a rozmnožené vydáni.
    Prague: Al. Hynek, 1899. 142pp., 8vo.
    Listed *Oesterreichische Buchhändler-Correspondenz* 23 Aug.1899.

===

LCz9.
František Krátký.
Dokonalý Bosko. Dle nejpřednějších escamoteurú ku společenské zábavé sestavil.
    Třebič: J.F. Kubeš [1876]
    Listed *Oesterreichische Buchhändler-Correspondenz* 22 Apr.; 30 Dec.1876 (with note: "Krátkú, F., *Vollständiger Bosko*). 224pp., 16mo. No surviving copy traced.

===

LCz10.
F.P. Trudný [*pseud. of* František Jaroslav Peřina, 1844-1902]
Bosko v kapse: četná sbírka vybraných, lehkých pokusú eskamotérských, zábavných kouskú s kartami a počty, s přídavkem návodu k dělání strojených ohňú a s předpisy k připravování sympatetických inkoustú.
    Jindřichův Hradec: Alois Jos. Landfras syn, 1865. 105pp., 13cm.
    Held National Library of the Czech Republic.

LCz11.
New edition
_____

    Jindřichův Hradec: A. Landfras syn, 1884, 105pp., 13cm.
    Held National Library of the Czech Republic; listed *Oesterreichische Buchhändler-Correspondenz* 29 Nov.1884.

LCz12.
5th revised edition
[...] k delání ohňostrojú a s předpisy k připravování sympatických inkoustú.
    "5. přeprac. rozmnožené vyd". Jindřichův Hradec: A. Landfras a syn, 1887. 98,[6]pp.
    Held National Library of the Czech Republic

===

LCz13.
X.Y.
Čaroděj Bosco: Rychlost nejsou žádné čáry / sepsal X.Y.
    Telč: Nákladem knihkupectví Emila Šolce [1900]
    110pp., 18cm.
    Held National Library of the Czech Republic; listed *Český katalog bibliografický ža Léta 1898 až 1903* p.58; *Oesterreichische Buchhändler-Correspondenz* 23 Aug. 1899; 17 Jan.1900.

LCz14,
New edition?
Čaroděj Bosco: Rychlost nejsou žádné čáry / sepsal Vilibald Praktický
    Praha-Karlín: Emil Šolc [between 1920 and 1940]
    112pp., 20cm.
    Held National Library of the Czech Republic.

LCz15.
Revised edition?
Hybš, Karel (*et al.*)
Čaroděj Bosco
　　Prague: Josef Kaiser, 2018. ISBN 9788027052905
　　According to url:228 an updated reprint.

Danish and Norwegian

LDaN1.
Blik i den naturlige Magies Enemærker, eller Bosco's aabnede Tryllekabinet: tilligemed nogle dermed forbundne Original-Anekdoter, til Morskab og Opinsning for Enhver, som ensker at gjennemskue eller anstille den nyere Tids vidunderlige Taskenspillerkunster.
　　Copenhagen: C. Steens Forlag, 1831. 40pp.
　　A very early Bosco book, published following his appearances in Copenhagen in Aug-Sep 1830. A translation of *Scharfblicke in das Gebieth der natürlichen Magie.* (LGe149); Royal Danish Library states "Translated by Hans Chr. Lund".
　　Held Royal Danish Library (2 copies, one catalogued as '...*nogle* clermed *forbundne*'); listed *Supplement 1831-1840 til Bibliotheca Danica* p.47; *Almindeligt dansk-norsk forlagscatalog*, 1841 p.26 (giving full title and publisher's name); adv. *Fyens Stifts Kongelig allene privilegerede Adresse-Avis og Avertissements-Tidende* 5 Apr. 1831; *Kiøbenhavns Kongelig alene priviligerede Adresse-Contoirs Efterretninger* 30 Apr.1831 ("Fra pressen er udkommen…")

===

LDaN2.
Hexemesteren: en Samling af letfattelige Taskenspillerkunster til Fornøielse i Selskaber. (Efter Carlo Bosco, das Ganze der Taschenspielerkunst.).
　　Christiania: Guldberg & Dzwonkowski, 1843. 58pp.; 14cm.
　　Held Norwegian National Library, Oslo; Hadeland Folkemuseum, Tingelstad. Stated to be a translation of Carlo Bosco, *Das Zauber-Kabinet, oder Das Ganze der Taschenspielerkunst.*
　　Online (one copy complete, another copy in part) at url:229

===

LDaN3
„Trolderi Altsammen!" Samling af mærkelige Taskenspiller-Konster, uddragen af Cagliostro's, Bosco's, Philadelphia, Comte Peterelli og mange Andre Værker.
　　Copenhagen: H. P. Møller, 1860. 15,[1]pp.
　　Held Royal Danish Library; adv. *Kjøbenhavns Adressecomptoirs Efterretninger* 29 Feb.1860
　　Online at url:230.

LDaN4
2nd ed.
———

    2. oplag., 1862. Kbh, 1862
    Held Royal Danish Library.

LDaN5
3rd ed.
———

    3. oplag., 1869.
    Held Royal Danish Library.

LDaN6
Carl Ferdinand Leischner
Den naturlige Magie, eller Tryllekunsten fra den æygptiske Alderdom, og det nittende Aarhundrede: indeholdende de opdagede Hemmeligheder af de ægyptiske Spaamænd og Orakler, Bugtalerier og Kortomanciet, i mangfoldige udvalgte skjønne, forlystende og belærende Kunststykker af Physik, Chemie, Optik, Mechanik, Mathematik, Arithmetik og Experimenteerkunsten efter Philadelphia, Bosco, Petorelli, Comte og Andre, af Carl Ferdinand Leischner; oversat af M. Christophersen
    Kbn., 1839. 219pp.
    Held Royal Danish Library; listed *Tidsskrift for litteratur og kritik* 1839, 'Bøger, udkomne fra 20. Juni til 20 Septbr. 1839'; *Fyens Stifts Kongelig ene privilegerede Adresse- og politiske Avis samt Avertissementstidende* 22 Aug.1839

Dutch

LDu1
Rhadamantus
Bosco, de Toovenaar in Holland, of De ontdekte Geheimen aller Toovenaars en Goochelaars, bevattende 200 der meest verrassende Kunststukken uit het gebied der Goochelarij, der Tooverij, van het Magnetismus, der Optica, der Physica, der Vuurwerkkunst en der Sympathie, Naar het Italiaansch in het Hoogduitsch en daar uit naar vier en twintigsten Druks in het Nederduitsch overgebragt door Rhadamantus.
    Amersfoort: W.J. van Bommel van Vloten [1845]. xiv,86pp.
    Held Royal Library of the Netherlands. Online at url:231
    States translated from Italian into German and from the 24th edition of that into Dutch by Rhadamantus: no German Bosco title had reached a 24th edition by this date.

LDu2
2nd ed.: not traced

LDu3
3rd ed., 1864
[...] bevattende 200 der meest verrassende Kunststukken uit het gebied van Goochelarij, Tooverij, Magnetismus, Optica, Physica, Vuurwerkkunst en Sympathie, Naar het Hoogduitsch.

Derde Druk. Amsterdam: G. Theod. Bom [1864]. xii,[13]-100pp.; 17cm. Preface is signed "D.". States translated from German.

Held Royal Library of the Netherlands; Bibliotheek Universiteit van Amsterdam; listed *Brinkmann's Catalogus 1850-1882*.

Online at url:232.

LDu4
4th ed. [1871?]
Advertised *Algemeen Handelsblad* 10 Nov.1871 ("...Vierde druk"; title and publisher as 3rd ed.)

LDu5
5th ed. [187-?]
———

"5. druk.". Kampen: Laurens van Hulst [187-?]. iv,91pp., 18cm.
"G.B. van Gorr Zonen, Gouda": cover.
Held LC (Houdini Coll.)

LDu6
6th ed. [1878]
———

"Zesde druk". Kampen: Laurens van Hulst [1878]. iv,91pp., 17cm.
Held ULSH; listed *Brinkmann's Catalogus 1850-1882*.

===

LDu7
Carlo Bosco's Toover-kabinet, of Kunstjes met de Kaart, waaronder de Kunst om uit de Kaarten de Toekomst te voorspellen, ... naar den tienden verbeterden Hoogduitschen druk van Professor Kerndörffer

Deventer: A. Tjaden [*ca.* 1858]. [2],96pp., 17cm.
Held Athenaeum Bibliotheek, Deventer; adv. *Algemeen Handelsblad* 18 Oct. 1858.

LDu8
2nd ed. [1859?]
Carlo Bosco's Toover-kabinet, of Kunstjes met de Kaart, waaronder ook de Kunst om uit de Kaarten de Toekomst te voorspellen, benevens een Antaal Optische, Geometrische en andere Kunststukken. Naar den tienden verbeterden Hoogduitschen druk van Professor Kerndörffer.

2de druk. Deventer: A. Tjaden [*ca.* 1859]. [2],96pp., 17cm.
Cover-title: Het Nieuw Toover Kabinet van Carlo Bosco. kunstjes met de kaart, alsmede de kunst om uit de kaarten de toekomst te voorspellen; benevens optische

chemische en andere kunststukken… (illustration of cover from 2017 auction at url:233).

Critical review in *Vaderlandsche Letteroefeningen 1859* (online at url:234): "[tr.] … The true lovers of the noble art of magic will no doubt be offended by the annoying abuse made in this title of the great Bosco's name…".

LDu9
New ed., 1866
Carlo Bosco's Toover-kabinet, of Kunstjes met de Kaart, waaronder ook de kunst om uit de kaarten de toekomst te voorspellen, benevens een antal optische, chemische en andere kunststukken. Naar den tienden verbeterden Hoogduitschen druk.
    Deventer: A. Tjaden, 1866. 112pp., 15cm.
    Cover-title: Nieuwe toover-kabinet van Carlo Bosco
    Held Royal Library of the Netherlands

===

LDu10
[1st ed., 1873]
Carlo Bosco's tooverkabinet. Onder anderen bevattende 154 verrassende kunststukken …
    Tiel: H.C.A. Campagne & Zoon, 1873.
    Listed *Brinkmann's Catalogus 1850-1882*: "Bosco's (C.) tooverkabinet; o.a. bevattende 154… Tiel, H.C.A. Campagne (& Zn) 1873". No surviving copy traced.

LDu11
2nd ed. [1884?]
Carlo Bosco's tooverkabinet. Onder anderen bevattende 154 verrassende kunststukken uit de natuurlijke tooverkunst, met kaarten, kogels, geldstukken, ringen, enz., benevens 46 kunststukken met speelkaarten, en 13 der onderhoudendste rekenkunstige raadsels. Met 24 afbeeldingen.
    Tweede druk. Tiel: H.C.A. Campagne & Zoon [1884]. xvi,203pp., 17cm.
    Held Royal Library of the Netherlands; NYPL; adv. *Java-Bode* 25 Mar.1885.
    Online at url:235

LDu12
3rd ed. [1890?]
———
    3e dr. Amsterdam: Campagne [*ca.* 1890]. xvi,203pp., 17cm.
    Held Bibliotheek Universiteit van Amsterdam; Tilburg University Library

===

LDu13
De Roode Duivel in den Gezelligen Kring, of Bosco voor iedereen verklaard en navolgbaar gemaakt.
Gouda: G.B. Van Goor Zonen, 1875. 176pp., 20cm.
Contents: 1. De kleine toverkunst. 2. De groote tooverkunst. 3. De kunst van het eskamoteeren. 4. Kunstjes met de kaart.
Held by Bibliotheek Universiteit van Amsterdam; Tilburg University Library; NYPL; listed *Brinkman's Catalogus* 1884; *Nederlandsche staatscourant* 18 Aug. 1875; adv. *De locomotief* 16 Sep.1875
Online at url:236.

LDu14
The book was reprinted in 1976 by Van Goor in Gouda, 176pp., 9789000023851, stating it was from an 1861 edition: if correct that has not been traced.

LDu15
Bosco. De roode duivel of volmaakte toovanaar en goochelaar, met 111 afbeeldingen.
A book of this title is advertised in several newspapers in 1904 (e.g. *Middelburgsche Courant* 26 Jan.1904) at a reduced price. This may have been a remainder issue of LDu14 with a new cover-title.

===

LDu16
Nieuw Goochelaars Handboek. Philippe Opré Robin Bosco Bamburg De Linsky Bekker.
[*this is the text on the engraved title-page and on the coloured cover; the half-title adds a sub-title:* of de Geheimen der tooverkunst ontsluierd].
Utrecht: Van der Post [1852]
also issued: Amsterdam: Diederichs [1852].
[4],vi,[2],182pp., 19cm.
Held Universiteitsbibliotheek Amsterdam [Van der Post imprint]; and Royal Library of the Netherlands; LC (Houdini Coll.) [both Diederichs imprint]; adv. *Handelsblad* 6 Jan.1853.
Online at url:237. Collection of tricks. Part 1 includes several attributed to Bosco. Personal introduction by the unnamed compiler who claims some of the tricks are his own. A detailed review in *Vaderlandsche letteroefeningen* 1853, pp.527-8 (online at url:238) gives some corrections and suggested improvements.

LDu17
New edition (same text, re-set; new title and title-page)
De Volmaakte Toovenaar: Korte Handleiding voor ieder, die op eene aangename wijze zich zoowel in het Tooveren als in Vlugheid met Kaarten wil oefenen en zich daardoor in den Gezilligen Kring zoowel Onderhoudend als Verrassend Voordoen. Goochelen is slechts handigheid.
Utrecht: Gebr. van der Post [1885]. vii,144pp., 8vo.

Held Leiden University Library.
Online at url:239.

===

LDu18
De Nieuwe Vrolijke Toovenaar en Droomuitlegger welkom in alle Gezelschappen, door Carl Bosco. Bevattende: Kunstjes met de kaart, waaronder ook de kunst om uit de kaarten de toekomst te voorspellen; optische, chemische, rekenkunstige en verschillende andere kunststukjes; alsmede een droomuitlegger en verschillende Voorschriften voor Eenvoudig Vuurwerk. Naar de Nieuwste Fransche en Engelsche Methode.
 Deventer: A. Tjaden [1880?]. Preface by 'Den Vertaler'.
 Held Athenaeum Bibliotheek, Deventer; adv. *Venloosch weekblad* 13 Apr.1881; listed *Brinkman's Alphabetische Lijst* 1885 p.163 with imprint "Gebr. E. & M. Cohen".
 Online at url:240

English

LEn1
The New Universal Conjuror: with the Lives and Adventures of Professor Anderson ... and ... Bosco.
 London: T. Duggan [*ca.*1850]. 32pp.
 Held ULSH. Date uncertain — not listed in *The English Catalogue of Books*.

LEn2
Hanky Panky, A Book of Conjuring Tricks.
 London: John Camden Hotten [undated but December 1872]: includes pp.47-8 (and the same text in the "new edition" dated 1875) a story about "the magician Bosco, of Milan" demonstrating the sandframe over tea at the Princess's Theatre in London to "the negro *prima donna*... 'the Black Malibran'". For details of this see *Appendix Z10: The Sandframe*.

LEn3
An English translation of *Satana raccolta Europea* [LIt52] by Lori Pieper, with introduction by Ricky Jay, appeared in *Gibecière* Vol. 3, no.1 (2008), published by The Conjuring Arts Research Center in New York.

Estonian

LEs1
Jakob Permann, ?-1881
Bosko kunstükid / Seltskondlikuks armsaks ajawiiteks ja õpetuseks kokkupannud J. Permann.
    Tartu: Schnakenburg, 1876 . 40pp., 14cm.
    Held: ESTER (https://www.ester.ee) lists 2 copies (states "digitised", but apparently not accessible; adv. *Eesti Postimees ehk Näddalaleht* 14 July 1876; 24 Nov. 1876; 19 Jan.1877; rev. *Eesti Postimehe lisaleht* 1 Aug.1878

LEs2
2nd ed.
———
    2., parand. tr. Tartu: Schnakenburg, 1879. 47pp., 14cm.
    Held: ESTER (https://www.ester.ee) lists 4 copies; adv. *Eesti Postimees ehk Näddalaleht* 14 Nov.1879; also (another edition?) adv. *Postimees* 7 June 1886

French

LFr1
Satanas, Recueil Européen. Aventures de B. Bosco de Turin, professeur de prestidigitation.
    Paris: D'Aubusson, printer, 1851. 40pp.; 8vo.
    The Preface is signed "L.C.", a pseudonymn used by theatrical and satirical writer Léon Guillemin, who also wrote as Léon Chaumont.
    Held BNF; Arsenal; ULSH; listed *Bibliographie de la France* 31 July 1852: 4449

LFr2
Aventures de Bosco. Sa vie et ses prodiges.
    Paris: Imp. de N. Chaix [1852]
    Held BNF; listed *Bibliographie de la France* 20 Mar.1852: 1684 ('in-4° d'une feuille"); *Norton's Literary Gazette and Publisher's Circular* (New York) 15 Apr.1852 under "French. Books Published during the Month of February".

LFr3
Satanas Recueil Européen. Aventures de B. Bosco de Turin, Professeur de Prestidigitation.
    Poitiers: A. Dupré, 1854. 40pp., 21cm.
    Cover illus. of Bisco by "Gigoux".
    Held Université Toulouse – Bibliothèque de l'Arsenal; ULSH
    Photo of cover online at url:241.

LFr4
Satanas. Recueil Universel, Biographique, Anecdotique des Aventures de Bosco de Turin, Professur de Prestidigitation, par Mr J.-M.-T.-M.-L..... Collaborateur de plusieurs revues et journaux artistiques et littéraires.
    Marseille: Imp. Gravière, 1859. 48pp.
    Held BNF; listed Bibliographie de la France 2 April 1859: 3057; adv. *Le Sémaphore de Marseille* 25 Mar.1859.
    'Bosco et la Mort' on back cover (see F7 above for the origin of this story).
    Cover illus. of Bosco by "Gigoux". This edition has slight textual differences.
    Cover online at url:242.

===

These are apparently all different editions of the same book, variously catalogued as *La Nouvelle Magie Blanche Dévoilée* and as *Nouveau Manuel de Physique et de Chimie Amusantes*. The copy digitised (1857) certainly has *La Nouvelle Magie Blanche Dévoilée* on both half-title and title: this may be true of all editions and they have on cover *Nouveau Manuel de Physique et de Chimie Amusantes* (as LFr5).

LFr5
La Nouvelle Magie Blanche Dévoilée, grande initiation à la vraie pratique des célèbres physiciens prestidigitateurs,... complètement démontrée pour la première fois et mise à la portée des curieux, par un amateur...
    Paris: Ruel aîné, 1852.
    Cover-title: Nouveau manuel de physique et chimie amusantes.
    Held BNF

LFr6
Nouveau Manuel de Physique et de Chimie Amusantes: grande initiation à la vraie pratique des célèbres physiciens-prestidigitateurs Comus, Pinetti, Jérôme Sharp, Decremps, Wals, Robertson, Olivier, Comte, Philippe, Robert Oudin, Bosco, etc. / complètement démontrée pour la première fois ... par un amateur ... Prestidigitation en tous genres, escamotage, prestige, illusion, jeux de gobelets, tours de cartes, de gibecière et de passe-passe; subtilités ingénieuses, combinaisons singulières, physique et chimie amusantes, curiosités de l'optique et de la mécanique, etc., etc., etc
    2e édition, revue, corrigée et augmentée. Paris: Ruel ainé 1853. 324pp., 16cm.
    Held ULSH

LFr7
La Nouvelle Magie Blanche Dévoilée: grande initiation à la vraie pratique des célèbres physiciens-prestidigitateurs Comus, Pinetti, Jérôme Sharp, Decremps, Wals, Robertson, Olivier, Comte, Philippe, Robert Houdin, Bosco, etc. / Complètement démontrée pour la première fois ... par un amateur ...
    3e édition, revue, corrigée et augmentée. Paris: Ruel ainé 1854. 324pp., 16cm.
    Held BNF

LFr8
La Nouvelle Magie Blanche Dévoilée ... initiation à la vraie pratique des célébres physiciens-prestidigitateurs Comus, Pinetti, Jerôme Sharp ... Bosco, etc. Complètement démontrée pour la première fois ... par un amateur.
    Paris, Ruel ainé, 1855. [2],324pp., 18cm.
    Held NYPL; LC (Houdini Coll.); BNF (as Nouveau manuel de physique et de chimie amusantes...)

LFr9
La Nouvelle Magie Blanche Dévoilée, Amusantes, Grande Initiation à la vraie pratique des célébres Physiciens-Prestidigitateurs Comus, Pinetti, Jérôme Sharp, Decremps, Wals, Robertson, Olivier, Comte, Philippe, Robert Oudin, Bosco, etc. Complètement démontrée pour la première fois et mise à la portée des curieux, par un Amateur. Prestidigitation en tous genres, escamotage, prestige, illusion, jeux de gobelets, tours de cartes, de gibecières, et de passe-passe; subtilités ingénieuses, combinaisons singulières, physique et chemie amusantes, curiosités de l'optique et de la mécanique, etc., etc., etc.
Paris: S. Renault et Cie, Libraires-Editeurs, 1857.
    Held BNF; ULSH.
    Online at url:243.

LFr10
La Nouvelle Magie Blanche Dévoilée, grande initiation à la vraie pratique des célébres physiciens prestidigitateurs ... complètement démontrée pour la première fois et mise à la portée des curieux, par un amateur...
    Paris: B. Renault, 1858. 324pp.
    Held LC; ULSH; BNF (as Le Nouveau manuel de physique et de chimie amusantes...)

LFr11
La Nouvelle Magie Blanche Dévoilée, grande initiation à la vraie pratique des célébres physiciens prestidigitateurs ... complètement démontrée pour la première fois et mise à la portée des curieux, par un amateur...
    Paris: Ruel aîné, 1860.
    Held BNF (also as Nouveau manuel de physique et de chimie amusantes...).

LFr12
La Nouvelle Magie Blanche Dévoilée...
    Paris: Ruel, 1862. 202pp., 15cm.
    Copy listed for sale by Librairie Livres 113.

German

Books in German naming Bosco as author or in the title far outnumber those in any other language. Many of the titles from different publishers are very similar in their wording both to each other and to numerous other books of magic tricks (here ignored) not mentioning Bosco.

They are listed here (each section alphabetical by title) in seven sequences —
those crediting **Bosco (or Bosko)** LGe1-47
those crediting **Carl Bosco (or Bosko)** LGe48-66
those crediting **Carlo Bosco (or Bosko)** LGe67-76, LGe78-97
those crediting **Carlo Bosco der Jünger** LGe77
those crediting **Bosco (or Bosko) der Zweite** LGe98-101
those crediting no author but **naming Bosco (or Bosko) in the title** LGe102-110
and books attributed to a **named author** (often imaginary) LGe111-195

Of the trade journals, the *Börsenblatt für den deutschen Buchhandel,* published weekly from 1834 (daily from 1867), now searchable online, is generally more useful than the *Gesamtverzeichnis,* as in its composite form now available the latter often blends the entries for successive editions together, giving the date of only the first and last ("1.—7. verm.Aufl. … Berlin: Mode's Verlag, 1869-77").

The name "Bosco" on a book, while it earned Bosco himself nothing except some publicity (though Francesconi's *Reise-Bilder aus dem Leben Boscos,* F13, was sold at his shows and he may have received a percentage), certainly served the German book trade well for over fifty years and there were a few fond references to him by the trade. An article talks of small publishers popping up and disappearing *wie unter Bosco's Zauberstab* (*Börsenblatt* 14 Jan.1851). A librarian (*Börsenblatt* 25 Sep.1849) quotes a subscriber complaining of two books from different publishers and allegedly by different authors but with exactly the same text, and wonders if one publisher is perhaps the natural son of the other, or perhaps his heir and successor, or perhaps not related at all but a *Bosco der Zweite,* who conjured one book into the other, the whole thing a *Bosco-Streich.* And in 1847 the Kreuznach bookseller L.C. Kehr (Ludwig Christian Kehr, 1775-1848) placed a humorous advertisement in the *Börsenblatt* (28 May 1847) requesting copies of an imaginary book, *Bosco: Die Kunst, Bücher in Kartoffeln zu verwandeln. Zum Nutzen und Frommen des lieben deutschen Buchhandels* (Bosco on how to turn books into potatoes for the use and profit of the trade).

BOSCO

LGe1
[*Fraktur*] Biographie und Anecdoten | aus | den Reisen | des alten | [*fancy roman fount*] BOSCO. | [*illus. of Bosco, signed 'Gigoux'*] | [*Fraktur*] Zusammengestellt | von einem | Freunde Bosco's. | [*fancy rule*] | Dresden, | Buchdruckerei von Julius Ernst.
[*cover-title:*] [*all inside fancy border*] [*Fraktur*] Der alte | [*roman*] BOSCO | [*Fraktur*] und | seine Kunst. | [*illus. of Bosco, signed 'Gigoux'*] | Dresden, | Buchdruckerei von Julius Ernst.
On rear cover "Bosco und der Tod" (see F7 above for the origin of this story).
    [1-3],4-40pp., 8vo [undated, but 1863]

Held SLUB (Sächsische Landesbibliothek - Staats- und Universitätsbibliothek), Dresden (dating "[circa 1850]"); BL (dating "1863"): listed *Börsenblatt für den deutschen Buchhandel* 29 May 1863 ("In Comm." = published at the author's expense); price 3 Ngr.

The book is a German version of *Satanas*.

Online at url:244.

===

Bosco als Kartenkünstler *see under* John Carter

===

LGe2
Bosco am Klavier. Picant komische, Staunen erregende, leicht ausführbare Kunststücke.
    Leipzig: J.J. Schmidt [1871?]
Tricks for the piano — "no piano should lack a copy".

No copy located. Advertised (sometimes as *Clavier*) in German newspapers 1871-72, the earliest found is in *Kladderadatsch Beiblatt* 22 Oct.1871 ("Liszt übertroffen").

===

LGe3
Bosco, der einzig ächte und wahre oder der perfecte Zauberkünstler.
    9 verb. Aufl. Harburg: Elkan, 1887. 130pp.
    Listed GV XIX p.35. No surviving copy of any edition traced.

===

LGe4
Bosko, der Hexenmeister.
    Berlin: A. Weichert, 1896. 80pp., 15cm.
    Held Brown UL; listed GV XIX p.33.

===

LGe5
Bosco der Kartenkünstler, oder höchst interessante Kunststücke, mit der deutschen Karte leicht ausführbar. Zur angenehmen Unterhaltung.
    Mügeln (Leipzig, Genf's Buchh.) 1865. 80pp., 32mo.
    Listed GV XIX p.34; *Börsenblatt für den deutschen Buchhandel* 7 June 1865.

LGe6
New ed.

Mügeln (Leipzig, Genf) 1872. 71pp., 16mo.
Listed GV XIX p.34; *Börsenblatt für den deutschen Buchhandel* 11 Mar.1872.
No surviving copies traced of either edition.

===

LGe7
Bosco, der kleine Hexenmeister: Eine Auswahl der neuesten, interessantesten und unterhaltendsten Kunststücke, welche ohne große Vorbereitungen leicht ausgeführt werden können. Zur Unterhaltung in geselligen Kreisen für Jung und Alt.
Reutlingen: Enßlin und Laiblin [1867] (Series: Neue Volksbücher 69). 64pp.
Held (probably this edition) SIKJM (Zürich); Württembergische Landesbibliothek; Union Catalogue of the Czech Republic (Národní muzeum - Knihovna Praha); listed GV XIX p.33; *Börsenblatt für den deutschen Buchhandel* 17 Sep.1868 (no edition stated).

LGe8

Reutlingen: Enßlin und Laiblin, 1868.
Listed GV XIX p.33 (this edition dated; the previous edition undated)

LGe9

Neue Ausg. Reutlingen: Enßlin und Laiblin, 1870. 64pp.
Listed GV XIX p.33 (this edition dated)

LGe10

2.—4. Aufl. Enßlin und Laiblin, 1869-75. 64pp.
Listed GV XIX p.33; 4th ed. listed *Börsenblatt für den deutschen Buchhandel* 4 Sep.1875.

LGe11

Stereotyp-Ausgabe. Reutlingen: Ensslin und Laiblin [1870]. 64pp., 17.5cm.
Held LC (Houdini Coll.); NYPL (microfilm).

LGe12

5. Aufl., 1877.
listed GV XIX p.33

An undated edition is listed for sale with photos of coloured cover, title-page and some text at url:245 — the title-page omits "für Jung und Alt":

[*Fraktur*] Bosco, | der kleine Hexenmeister. | Eine Auswahl | der neuesten, interessantesten und unterhaltendsten | Kunststücke, | welche ohne große Vorbereitungen leicht | ausgeführt werden können. | [*short rule*] | Zur Unterhaltung in geselligen Kreisen. | [*publisher's device*] | [*double rule*] | Enßlin & Laiblins Verlagsbuchhandlung. | Reutlingen.

LGe13
New edition with altered title
Bosco, der kleine Taschenkünstler oder Anleitung zur Erlernung von mehr als 200 der interessantesten Kunst- und Zauberstücke, welche ohne Instrumente auf leichte Art ausgeführt werden können und durch ihren schönen Erfolg allgemein überraschen. Zur angenehmen Unterhaltung für Jung und Alt.
 32. Aufl. Reutlingen: Bardtenschlager [1902?]. [1-4],5-64pp., 16.5×10.5cm.
 Listed (with full title) *Börsenblatt für den deutschen Buchhandel* 15 Aug.1902; held Württembergische Landesbibliothek (dated "[ca.1890]", stating this is a new edition of *Bosco der kleine Hexenmeister*).

LGe14
This may be a different book
Bosco, der kleine Hexenmeister, hrsg. von Erminio Ariosto.
 Stuttgart: Junginger [ca.1895] (Series: Stuttgarter Volksbücher 2a)
 Held Württembergische Landesbibliothek

===

Bosco der kleine Taschenkünstler, *see* LGe13

===

LGe15
Bosco, der kleine Taschenspieler und angenehme Gesellschafter: enthaltend ueberraschende Kunststücke, scherzhafte Räthsel und Rechnungs-Aufgaben, muntere Gesellschafts-Spiele, Toaste, Gesundheiten und Buntes zur fröhlichen Unterhaltung.
 Berlin: Druck und Verlag von Trowitzsch und Sohn [188-?]. 36 pages; 18 cm.
 Held LC (Houdini Collection).

===

LGe16
Bosco, der unübertreffliche Hexenmeister, oder die Kunst binnen 10 Minuten ein Zauberer zu werden.
 Bonn: Jenni, 1883. 12mo.
 Listed GV XIX p.33; adv. *Neue Freie Presse* 14 Feb.1886 etc. (secondhand?)

No copy located. This is probably a reprint of the old book *Der unübertreffliche Hexenmeister, oder Kunst binnen 10 Minuten ein Zauberer zu werden* (1846, 1847), with "Bosco" added to the title. The 1847 edition of that title (online at url:246) has no mention of Bosco in title or text.

===

LGe17
Bosco, der unübertreffliche Tausendkünstler. Eine reiche Sammlung der besten Kunst-Zauberstücke, welche mit geringen Kosten und ohne Instrumente leicht ausgeführt werden können.
    1. Aufl. Teschen: Feizinger, 1874. 64pp.
    Listed GV XIX p.35.

LGe18
———
    2. verb. u. verm.Aufl. Teschen: Felzinger, 1875. 71pp.
    Held NYPL (microform); listed GV XIX p.35; *Börsenblatt für den deutschen Buchhandel* 24 Sep.1875.

LGe19
Bosco, der unübertreffliche Tausendkünstler. Eine Sammlung der besten Kunst-Zauberstücke.
    2. Aufl. Neutitschein [now Nový Jičín]: L. V. Enders, 1881. 71pp.
    Listed GV XIX p.35.

LGe20
Bosco, der unübertreffliche Tausendkünstler. Eine reiche Sammlung der besten Kunst-Zauberstücke, welche mit geringen Kosten leicht ausgeführt werden können.
    3. Aufl. Wien; Leipzig: Herm. Winkler's Verlag. 89pp., 15cm.
    Held LC (Houdini Coll.) [dating 1884 "from GV"]; listed *Börsenblatt für den deutschen Buchhandel* 12 July 1884; *Oesterreichischer Katalog ... Juli bis Dez.*1884.

LGe21
Bosco, der unübertreffliche Tausendkünstler. Eine Sammlung der besten Kunstzauberstücke.
    5. Aufl. Brünn: C. Winkler's Buch. und Wien: Herm, Winkler, 1884. 89pp.
    Listed GV XIX p.35.

LGe22
Bosco, der unübertreffliche Tausendkünstler. Eine Sammlung der besten Kunst-Zauberstücke, welche mit geringen Kosten leicht ausgeführt werden können.
    3. Aufl. Wien: Daberkow, 1884. 93pp., 16mo.
    Listed GV XIX p.35.

LGe23
Bosco, der unübertreffliche Tausendkünstler. Eine Sammlung der besten Kunst-Zauberstücke, welche mit geringen Kosten und nur wenig einfachen Apparaten leicht ausgeführt werden können.
    4. verb. u. nochmals sehr verm. Aufl. Thorn: Ernst Lambert, 1886. ix,101pp.
    Formerly held Staatsbibliothek zu Berlin; listed GV XIX p.35

LGe24
Bosco, der unübertreffliche Tausendkünstler. Eine Sammlung der besten Kunst-Zauberstücke, welche mit geringen Kosten leicht ausgeführt werden können.
    4. Aufl. Wien: C. Daberkow, 1901. 93pp., 16mo.
    Listed GV XIX p.35.

===

LGe25
Bosco, der unübertroffene Zauberer und Hexenmeister. Eine Sammlung leicht ausführbarer überraschender Zaubereien und Hexereien, Kartenkunststücke, Scherze *ie*, sowie Bosco's berühmten Zauberkarten, mit denen man jede von einer anderen Person gedachte Zahl, jedes Alter *ie*. sofort errathen kann. herausgegeben von einem Schüler Bosco's.
    Hamburg: Kramer, 1877. 64pp.
    Listed GV XIX p.35; *Börsenblatt für den deutschen Buchhandel* 22 May 1877

===

LGe26
Bosko, der Zauberer. Eine reichhältige Sammlung Wunder erregender, leicht ausführbarer Kunststücke, nebst Scherzfragen und Räthseln zur heiteren Unterhaltung in gemütlichen Kreisen.
    Hainichen: G.C. Hoffmann [18-?]. 64pp. 16mo.
    No surviving copy or contemporary trade listing recorded. Listed in the *National Union Catalog* (NUC NB 0662689) as held by NYPL (catalogued in 1911) but not in their current catalogue and no copy located elsewhere.

===

LGe27
Bosco, der Zauberkünstler. Eine Sammlung der überraschendsten Taschenspielerkünste.
    2 Aufl. Leipzig: Verlag von Heinrich Matthes [1876]. 2 p.l., [9]-60pp., 11cm. (Series: Miniaturbibliothek. Neue Folge, 9. Bändchen).
    Held LC (Houdini Coll.); listed ("2. Aufl.") GV XCVI, p.275; *Börsenblatt für den deutschen Buchhandel* 14 Nov.1876, giving a list of the series 'Miniatur-Bibliothek'.

===

LGe28
Bosco. Handbuch der Taschenspielerei. Enthaltend die überraschendsten Kunst- und Zauberstücke, welche von Jedermann ohne Instrumente ausgeführt werden können.
    Chemnitz: Hager, 1871. 64pp.
    Listed GV XIX p.35; *Börsenblatt für den deutschen Buchhandel* 4 July 1871.

LGe29
———
    GV XIX p.35 lists "2.—4. Aufl." 1880, 1881; 4th ed. listed *Börsenblatt für den Deutschen Buchhandel* 23 Nov.1880

LGe30
[6th ed.]
———
    Chemnitz: Druck und Verlag von C.A. Hager [188-?]. 64pp., 15cm.
    Held LC (Houdini Coll.)

===

LGe31
Bosco in der Westentasche. Eine Sammlung von Karten- und Zauberkunststückchen, welche auch Kinder leicht ausführen können.
    Berlin: Gebr. Radetzki, 1891. 34pp.
    Listed GV XIX p.34

For works titled Bosco in der Westentasche *published Hamburg: Berendsohn see below under* J.A. Philadelph-nein (LGe164-192).

===

LGe32
Bosco, oder, Die 1001 Taschenspieler-Stückchen: Reichhaltigste Sammlung der überraschendsten und interessantesten Kunststücke aus der natürlichen Magie zur Unterhaltung in geselligen Kreisen.
    136pp, 16mo. Harburg: Elkan, 1873.
    GV XIX p.33 lists "1.— 8. verb. und verm. Aufl. 1873-76".

LGe33
———
    8. verb. und verm. Aufl. Harburg a. d. Elbe: Gustav Elkan's Verlag [1876] 136pp., 12 cm.
    Held LC (Houdini Coll.); 8 Aufl. listed *Börsenblatt für den deutschen Buchhandel* 23 Oct.1876; GV XIX p.33 lists "1.— 8. verb. und verm. Aufl. 1873-76".

LGe34
———
9. verm. Aufl. Harburg: Elkan, 1893. 136pp., 32mo.
Listed GV XIX p.33; *Börsenblatt für den deutschen Buchhandel* 13 May 1893.

LGe35
———
11. verb. und verm. Aufl. Stuttgart: S. Lutz-Steinweg Verlag [190-?]
136pp., 12cm.
Cover title: *1001 Taschenspieler-Stückchen*
"Publisher's label affixed to title-page; issued in brown paper wrappers".
Held Brown UL; listed GV XIX p.33.

===

LGe36
Bosco's enthüllte Geheimnisse der modernen Zauberei: ein untrüglicher Rathgeber, die überraschendsten Taschenspielerkünste mit Eleganz, Leichtigkeit und ohne Apparate von Dilettanten auszuführen / hrsg. von einem Schüler und ehemaligen Gehülfen Bosco's.
46. Aufl. Hamburg: Berendsohn, 1884. xv,120pp.; 3 ll. of plates (tables); 15cm.
Held LC (Houdini Coll.); listed GV XIX p.35.

LGe37
———
47. Aufl. Hamburg: Berendsohn [*ca.*1885]. xv,120pp.
Held Staatliche Museen zu Berlin.

It is uncertain if this is the same book
LGe38
Enthüllte Geheimnisse der modernen Zauberei: Ueber 200 Experimente / Bosco. Hrsg. von e. Schüler u. ehemal. Gehilfen Bosco's
Berlin & Weissensee: E. Bartels [no date]. 77pp., 2 plates.
Held DNB. A photo of the cover of this edition is online at url:247.
This may be the edition listed in *Börsenblatt für den deutschen Buchhandel* 14 Aug.1931 (80pp).

===

LGe39
Bosco's berühmte 7 Karten, mit welchen man jede von einer andern Person gedachte Zahl und jedes Alter sofort errathen kann. Zur Unterhaltung in heitern Gesellschaften.
Advertised by bookseller Voigt & Zieger in a list of "cheap books", this priced at 1 Ngr. (Neugroschen) in *Leipziger Zeitung* (and some other papers) between 8 Jan. 1862 and 11 Apr.1865.

===

LGe40
Bosco's Taschenspielerkunst, oder: der belustigende Tausenkünstler für Dilettanten, welcher auf eine leicht faßliche Weise ausführen lehrt: 102 lustige Kunststücke, 38 Kartenkunststücke, 57 verfängliche Rechenkunststücke, — und dann 154 belustigende Räthselfragen, und 79 Räthsel *ie* aufstellt und beantwortet.
    Ersfeld: Klein, 1857. 112pp.
    Listed GV XIX p.35. No surviving copy traced.

===

LGe41
Bosco's Zauber-Cabinet, Eine reichhaltige Sammlung von leicht ausführbaren, höchst interessanten und überraschenden Taschenspieler- und Kartenkunststücken und Scherzen zur heiteren Unterhaltung.
    Mülheim: J. Bagel, 1898. 62pp.
    Listed GV XIX p.36; *Hinrich's Verzeichniße* 1898 p.109.

===

LGe42
Bosco's Zauber-Cabinet: enthaltend die wunderbarsten Geheimnisse der natürlichen Magie, sowie Karten-Kunststücke und arithmetische Belustigungen.
    Neu-Ruppin: Druck und Verlag von Gustav Kühn [188-?]
    24pp., 14cm.
    Held LC (Houdini Coll.)

===

LGe43
BOSCO'S | Zauberkarten | oder die Kunst | jeder Person | zu sagen, wie alt sie | ist, wie viel Geld sie in | der Tasche hat, sowie | jede Zahl, jeden | Taufnamen und | jedes Sprichtwort | zu erraten. | ZUR UNTERHALTUNG in | geselligen Kreisen.
    Reutlingen: Ensslin & Laiblin [1874]
    Title from envelope which contains [8] cards (12.3 × 8cm) in an envelope; seven of the cards have tables and the eighth is 'Belehrung über den Gebrauch der 14 Tabellen'; 13 cm.
    Held: LC (Houdini Coll.)
    Title transcribed from copy with photo from Antiquariat Thomas Mertens on abe.com.
    GV XIX p.36 lists two editions with title as:
Zauber-Karten, ein untrüglicher Wahrsager, jede gedachte Zahl zu errathen, jeder Person zu sagen, wie viel Geld sie in der Tasche hat, wie alt sie ist u.s.w. Zur Unterhaltung in geselligen Kreisen. ("In Umschlag"). Reutlingen: Ensslin & Laiblin [1874]; and the same title. "In Futteral". Reutlingen: Ensslin & Laiblin [1876]

===

LGe44
Bosco's Zauber-Salon.
    3.Aufl. Leipzig: Voigt, 1864
    Held SLUB (Sächsische Landesbibliothek - Staats- und Universitätsbibliothek).

LGe45
Zauber-Salon für gesellschaftliche Zirkel: 85 sogleich ausführbare Zaubereien und wundererregende Kartenkunststücke.
    4.Aufl. Leipzig: Fr. Voigt, 1871. viii,56pp. 16mo.
    Listed GV XIX p.36; *Börsenblatt für den deutschen Buchhandel* 15 June; 22 July 1871.

The change in the title (Zwecke *for* Zirkel) *seems rather odd and may be an error*
LGe46
Bosco's Zauber-Salon für gesellschaftliche Zwecke: 85 sogleiche ausführbare Zaubereien und wundererregende Kartenkunststücke.
    6. Aufl. Leipzig: Friedrich Voigt's Buchhandlung [187-?]
    64pp.; 14 cm; (the NUC card NB0662925 has this as [1871?], viii,(1),10-64pp.
    Held LC (Houdini Coll.).

===

LGe47
Der kleine Bosco oder Der Zauberer im Salon. Leicht faßliche Anleitung um eine Reihe der neuesten staunenserregendsten Kunststücke in Gesellschaften zu produzieren.
    Wien: Hegenauer [no date]. 24pp.
    Held Austrian National Library.

===

CARL BOSCO

LGe48
Carl Bosco's Kartenkünste oder 112 der interessantesten Kartenkunststücke nebst arithmetischen und anderen Belustigungen zur Unterhaltung in heiteren Kreisen. Mit Abbildungen (Holzschn. im Text).
    Berlin: Mode, 1866. viii,119pp.
    Held BL; listed GV XIX p.36; *Börsenblatt für den deutschen Buchhandel* 11 Aug.1865

LGe49
Carl Bosco's Kartenkünste oder 184 der interessantesten Kartenkunststücke nebst arithmetischen und anderen Belustigungen zur Unterhaltung in heiteren Kreisen. Mit Abbildungen (Holzschn. im Text).
    9. verm. Aufl. Berlin: Mode, 1879. viii,120pp 8vo.
    GV XIX p.36 lists "1.—9. verm. Aufl. Berlin: Mode, 1869-79".

LGe50

    11. verm. Aufl. [188-?]
    Held Brown UL

LGe51
———

    13. verm. Aufl. Berlin: Mode, 1888. viii,120pp 8vo.
    Formerly held Staatsbibliothek zu Berlin; listed GV XIX p.36; *Börsenblatt für den deutschen Buchhandel* 18 Sep.1888

LGe52
———

    16. verm. Aufl. Berlin: Mode, 1892. viii,120pp 8vo.
    GV XIX p.36; *Börsenblatt für den deutschen Buchhandel* 8 Aug.1892.

LGe53
———

    18. verm. Aufl. Berlin: Mode, 1896. viii,120pp 8vo.
    Held NYPL (microform); listed GV XIX p.36; *Börsenblatt für den deutschen Buchhandel* 28 July 1896

LGe54
———

    20. verm. Aufl. Berlin: Mode, 1903. viii,120pp 8vo.
    Held Brown UL. A photo of this edition formerly online at https://www.buch-antiquariat.ch shows the title on the cover as hyphenated: *Carl Bosco's | Karten-Künste | oder* [etc.]; listed GV XIX p.36; *Börsenblatt für den deutschen Buchhandel* 24 Sep.1903.

LGe55
———

    22. verm. Aufl. Berlin: Mode, 1907. viii,120,[8]pp.; 19 cm.
    Held Brown UL; Harvard; ULSH; listed GV XIX p.36; *Börsenblatt für den deutschen Buchhandel* 6 Feb.1907.

===

LGe56
Carl Bosco's Zauber-Geheimnisse, oder, Enthüllungen der interessantesten Taschenspieler-Künste: enthaltend gegen 500 von den berühmtesten Künstlern ausgeführte Kunststücke der Magie. Nebst vielen Karten-Kunststücken, arithmetischen und andere Belustigungen, nach den neuesten Erfahrungen von Bosco, Bellachini, Döbler, Robin, Philadelphia, Prof. Herrmann, u. A.
    1.—4. Aufl. Berlin: S. Mode's Verlag, 1877-84. vi,160pp.
    Listed GV XIX p.35 (1st ed. 1877; 4th ed.1884)

LGe57
Carl Bosco's Zauber-Geheimnisse, oder, Enthüllungen der interessantesten Taschenspieler-Künste: enthaltend gegen 500 von den berühmtesten Künstlern ausgeführte Kunststücke der Magie: nebst vielen Karten-Kunststücken, arithmetischen und andere Belustigungen, nach den neuesten Erfahrungen von Bosco, Bellachini, Döbler, Robin, Philadelphia, Prof. Herrmann, u. A.
    6. Aufl. Berlin: S. Mode's Verlag, 1888. vi,160pp.
    Held LC (Houdini Coll.) stating *Zauber-Geheimnisse* is xvi,120pp and following that is *Die Magie oder Zauberkunst*, 160pp; listed GV XIX p.35; *Börsenblatt für den deutschen Buchhandel* 18 Sep.1888 ("xvi,280pp.").

LGe58
Carl Bosco's Zauber-Geheimnisse, oder, Enthüllungen der interessantesten Taschenspieler-Künste: enthaltend gegen 500 von den berühmtesten Künstlern ausgeführte Kunststücke der Magie. Nebst vielen Karten-Kunststücken, arithmetischen und andere Belustigungen, nach den neuesten Erfahrungen von Bosco, Bellachini, Döbler, Robin, Philadelphia, Prof. Herrmann, u. A.
    9. Aufl. Berlin: S. Mode's Verlag, 1900. vi,160pp.
    Listed GV XIX p.35; *Börsenblatt für den deutschen Buchhandel* 9 July 1900.

===

LGe59
[1st ed., 1865]
Carl Bosco's Zauberkünste oder die Taschenspielerkunst in ihrem ganzen Umfange: Eine Sammlung von 253 der interessantesten Kunststücke, aus der natürlichen Magie, nebst vielen Karten-Kunststücken, arithmetischen und anderen Belustigungen etc,., Mit 36 erläuternden Abbildungen.
    263pp., 8vo. Berlin: Mode's Verlag, 1865.
    Listed GV XIX p.36 ("1.—4.Aufl....1865-67"); *Börsenblatt für den deutschen Buchhandel* 5 July; 11 Aug.1865.

LGe60
[4th ed., 1867]
Carl Bosco's | Zauberkünste | oder | Die Taschenspielerkunst | in ihrem ganzen Umfange. | [*short wavy rule*] | Eine Sammlung | von | 253 der interessantesten Kunststücke. | aus der natürlichen Magie, | welche in Gesellschaften die überraschendsten | Wirkungen hervorbringen, | nebst vielen | Karten-Kunststücken, arithmetischen und anderen Belustigungen | zum | Nutzen und Vergnügen für Jedermann, | sowie | zur Unterhaltung in geselligen Kreisen. | [*short wavy rule*] | Mit 36 erläuternden Abbildungen. | [*short wavy rule*] | Vierte Auflage | [*fancy rule*] | Berlin. | S. Mode's Verlag.
    "Druck von Julius Pleßner in Berlin." — p.[204]
    4. Aufl. Berlin: S. Mode's Verlag [1867]. 203pp.

Held Universitaetsbibliothek Johann Christian Senckenberg (Frankfurt a.M.); (catalogued as *Carl Bosko's...*); listed *Börsenblatt für den deutschen Buchhandel* 5 Nov.1867.

Online at url:248.

LGe61
[7th ed., 1877]
Carl Bosco's Zauberkünste oder die Taschenspielerkunst in ihrem ganzen Umfange: Eine Sammlung von 370 der interessantesten Kunststücke, aus der natürlichen Magie, welche in Gesellschaften die überraschendsten Wirkungen hervorbringen, nebst vielen Karten-Kunststücken, arithmetischen und anderen Belustigungen zur Unterhaltung in geselligen Kreisen. Mit 36 erläuternden Abbildungen.

1.—7. verm.Aufl. 8vo. xix,220pp. Berlin: Mode's Verlag, 1869-77.

"7. Aufl." listed GV XIX p.36; *Börsenblatt für den deutschen Buchhandel* 3 Nov.1877.

LGe62, LGe63, LGe64,
[8th ed., 1880; 9th ed. ca.1882; 10th ed. 1884]
Carl Bosco's Zauberkünste oder die Taschenspielerkunst in ihrem ganzen Umfange: Eine Sammlung von 370 der interessantesten Kunststücke, aus der natürlichen Magie, welche in Gesellschaften die überraschendsten Wirkungen hervorbringen, nebst vielen Karten-Kunststücken, arithmetischen und anderen Belustigungen zur Unterhaltung in geselligen Kreisen. Mit 36 erläuternden Abbildungen.

8.—10. verm. und verb. Aufl. 8vo. xix,200pp. Berlin: Mode's Verlag, 1880-84.
Listed GV XIX p.36

LGe65
[12th ed., 1888]
Carl Bosco's Zauberkünste oder Die Taschenspielerkunst in ihrem ganzen Umfange: Eine Sammlung von 970 der interessantesten Kunststücke aus der natürlichen Magie, welche in Gesellschaften die überraschendsten Wirkungen hervorbringen, nebst vielen Karten-Kunststücken, arithmetischen und anderen Belustigungen zur Unterhaltung in geselligen Kreisen; Mit 36 erläuerenden Abbildungen.

Zwölfte vermehrte Auflage. Berlin: S. Mode [1888]. xii,200pp., 8vo.

Held LC (Houdini Coll.; catalogued as *Carl Bosco's Zauberkünst,* though correct on the old catalogue card reproduced in *NUC*); formerly held Staatsbibliothek zu Berlin; listed GV XIX p.36; *Börsenblatt für den deutschen Buchhandel* 18 Sep.1888

LGe66
[15th ed., 1893]
Carl Bosco's Zauberkünste; oder, Die Taschenspielerkunst in ihrem ganzen Umfange. Eine Sammlung von 370 der interessantesten Kunststücke aus der natürlichen Magie, welche in Gesellschaften die überraschendsten Wirkungen hervorbringen, nebst vielen Karten-Kunststücken, arithmetischen und anderen Belustigungen zur Unterhaltung in geselligen Kreisen. Mit 36 erläuternden Abbildungen.

15. verm. und verb. Aufl. Berlin, A. Mode [1893]. xii,200pp.; front., illus. 19 cm.

Held NYPL (catalogued with *mait* for *mit* in error; correct on the old catalogue card reproduced in *NUC*); listed GV XIX p.36; *Börsenblatt für den deutschen Buchhandel* 18 Nov.1893.

===

CARLO BOSCO

LGe67
Carlo Bosco's Zauber-Buch, Enthaltend: Die wunderbarsten Geheimnisse der natürlichen Magie, sowie Karten-Kunststücke und arithmetischen Belustigungen.
    Berlin: Berolina-Versand-Buchhandlung, 1899. 15pp.
    Listed GV XIX p.35; *Börsenblatt für den deutschen Buchhandel* 25 July 1899.
    No surviving copy traced.

===

LGe68
Carlo Bosco's Zauberkünste oder Wunder über Wunder Enthüllte Geheimnisse aller Zauberer, Magier und Hexenmeister nebst vielen Karten-Kunststücken.
    Landsberg an der Warthe: W. Volger & Klein [1887]. 64pp., 8vo.
    Formerly held Staatsbibliothek zu Berlin; listed GV XIX p.36

LGe69
[*2nd. ed.*, 1893]
Carlo Bosco's Zauberkünste oder Wunder über Wunder Enthüllte Geheimnisse aller Zauberer, Magier und Hexenmeister nebst vielen Karten-Kunststücken.
    2. Aufl. Landsberg an der Warthe: W. Volger & Klein, 1893.
    Listed GV XIX p.36; *Börsenblatt für den deutschen Buchhandel* 6 Sep.1893

===

LGe70
Carlo Bosko, Der weltberühmte Zauberkünstler und Taschenspieler. Leicht ausführbare, interessante Kunststücke mit Karten, Würfeln, Kugeln, Ringen, Geldstücken und anderen Gegenständen von verblüffender Wirkung zur Unterhaltung und Belustigung.
    21. verb. und verm. Aufl. Leipzig: Ernst [1909]. xii,[2],181pp.; 19 cm.
    Held by Hungarian NL; listed GV XIX p.35; *Börsenblatt für den deutschen Buchhandel* 23 Aug.1909

LGe71
    22. Aufl. Leipzig: Ernst [1919?]
    Held ULSH; listed *Börsenblatt für den deutschen Buchhandel* 4 Aug.1919.

LGe72
Carlo Bosko, Der weltberühmte | Zauberkünstler und | Taschenspieler | Leicht ausführbare, interessante Kunststücke | mit Karten, Würfeln, Kugeln, Ringen, | Geldstücken und anderen Gegenständen von | verblüffender Wirkung | zur Unterhaltung und Belustigung | [fancy rule] | 23. Auflage | Mit Abbildungen | [decoration] | ** Ernst'sche Verlagsbuchhandlung, Leipzig **
    23 Aufl. Leipzig: Ernst'sche Verlagsbuchhandlung [ca.1920]
    190pp.; 20 cm; issued in brown paper wrappers; publisher's ads on back wrapper.
    Held: Brown UL; ULSH; title-page transcribed from a copy (with photo of cover and title-page) at url:249

LGe73
———

    24. Aufl. Leipzig: Ernstsche Verlh. [1922]. 190pp.
    Held: DNB; Brown UL; ULSH; listed GV 1911-1965 v.17; *Börsenblatt für den deutschen Buchhandel* 7 Mar.1922
    'Inhalt' section only is online at url:250.

===

LGe74
Carlo Bosco, der unübertroffene Zauberer und Hexenmeister: 101 auserlesene und überraschende Taschenspielerkünst und Scherzaufgaben / herausgegeben von Carlo Bosko.
    Oberhausen; Leipzig: Verlag von Ad. Spaarmann [1882]. 64pp.; 16 cm.
    Held LC (Houdini Collection); listed GV XIX p.35; *Börsenblatt für den deutschen Buchhandel* 15 July 1882.

LGe75
———

    5 Aufl. Oberhausen: Spaarmann [1885]
    Formerly held by Staatsbibliothek zu Berlin; listed GV XIX p.35; *Börsenblatt für den deutschen Buchhandel* 8 June 1885

===

LGe76
Carlo Bosko, der weltberühmte | Zauberkünstler und | Taschenspieler | Leicht ausführbare, interessante Kunststücke | mit Karten, Würfeln, Kugeln, Ringen, | Geldstücken und anderen Gegenständen von | verblüffender Wirkung | zur Unterhaltung und Belustigung | [fancy rule] | 25. Auflage | Mit Abbildungen | [ornament] | ** Ernst'sche Verlagsbuchhandlung, Leipzig **
    "Druck von Dr. F. Poppe, Leipzig-R." — p.[190]
    25. Aufl. [1-3],4-190pp.
    Held: Universiteitsbibliotheek Amsterdam. Online at url:251.

===

Carlo Bosco des Jüngern is named as the author of *Das Zauber-Kabinet* only in the first edition, the rest have **Carlo Bosco**. The book was "edited" (and presumably written) by Heinrich August Kerndörffer (spelt 'Kerndörfer' on some title-pages), 1769-1846, a compiler of books intended for children. Amongst his many earlier books were *Comus oder neue Belustigungen in dem Gebiete der natürlichen Magie und Taschenspielerkunst* (by "Carlo Cosani"); *Leicht faßliche Anleitung zur Kryptographie;* and *Der Kleine Taschenspieler und Magier* (or *Magiker*), of which the 3rd ed. is online in two versions at url:252 (one has *Magier* in the title, the other *Magiker*).

Der Kleine Taschenspieler is a very different book from *Das Zauber-Kabinet*: it opens with a section on the cup and balls but makes no mention of Bosco — though when Bosco was in Hamburg in 1830 the enterprising publisher implied in his advertising that it did: "B. Bosco's Künste, größtentheils, so wie viele andere magische Täuschungen, werden deutlich beschrieben und gelehrt in *Der kleine Taschenspieler...*" (*Hamburger Nachrichten* 28 Sep.1830).

Kerndörffer also edited the 6th edition (1825) of *Carl der Tausendkünstler* by "J. Jak. Funke" (Ludwig August Wilhelm Martell), and I suspect this is where he got the idea of inventing the name "Carl Bosco", which soon took on a life of its own.

The first edition of Das Zauber-Kabinet *remains uncertain. Bibliographic records give three variant titles, all published in Quedlinburg by Ernst in 1838, possibly two or three different books, but that seems unlikely. Only* 1a *is known to exist (one library copy; a second copy apparently lost);* 1c *may be an early reissue.*
1a. Carlo Bosco des Jüngern, Das Ganze der Taschenspielerkunst, oder leicht faßliche Anleitung…;
1b. Carlo Bosco des Jüngern, Das Ganze der Taschenspielerkunst, oder der Zauber-Kabinet…;
1c. Carlo Bosco, Das Ganze der Taschenspielerkunst, oder 61 Wunder erregende Kunststücke…;
Börsenblatt für den deutschen Buchhandel 24 July 1838 lists 'Bosco, Das Ganze der Taschenspielerkunst, herausgeg. von Kerndörffer', which could be any of the above three.
From the 2nd edition, 1840, the title was
Carlo Bosco, Das Zauber-Kabinet, oder, Das Ganze der Taschenspielerkunst…

LGe77a
1a.
Carlo Bosco des Jüngern Das Ganze der Taschenspielerkunst, oder leicht faßliche Anleitung zur gesellschaftlichen Unterhaltung in den neuesten Taschenspieler- und Kartenkünsten, enthaltend: 10 Kunststücke durch Mitwirkung eines Gehülfen. 40 mechanische Künste und 11 mechanische Künste mit Geräthschaften. Herausgegeben von Professor Kerndörfer [*sic*].
  Quedlinburg: Ernst, 1838. vi,160pp.
  Listed under this title: *Repertorium der gesammten deutschen Literatur* No.29, 20 July 1838; adv. *Herzogl.-Sachsen-Coburgisches Regierungs- und Intelligenzblatt* 4 Aug.1838; *Wiener Zeitung* 20 Oct.1838.
  Held Libris; formerly NYPL (NUC NB0662691): both with 'Kerndörfer'.

LGe77b
1b.
Carlo Bosco des Jüngern, Das Ganze der Taschenspielerkunst, oder der Zauber-Kabinet, *ie*. Herausgegeben von Kerndörfer.
>Quedlingburg: Ernst, 1838
>Listed GV XIX p.35; also listed in *Vollständiges Bücher-Lexicon* (1841)

LGe77c
1c.
Carlo Bosco, das Ganze der Taschenspielerkunst, oder 61 Wunder erregende Kunststücke, durch die natürliche Zauberkunst, mit Karten, Würfeln, Ringen, Kugeln, Geldstücken u.s.w. Zur gesellschaftlichen Belustigung mit und ohne Gehülfen auszuführen. Herausgegeben vom Professor Kerndörfer.
>Leipzig: Quedlinburg, 1838. 169pp.
>Advertised under this title: *Münchener Tagblatt* 13 Oct.1838; *Bayerische Landbötin* 22 Nov.1838; *Allgemeiner Anzeiger und Nationalzeitung der Deutschen* 22 Dec.1838.

LGe78
2nd edition, 1840
[*Fraktur*] Carlo Bosco | Das Zauber-Kabinet, | oder, | Das Ganze | der | Taschenspielerkunst, | enthaltend | 69 Wunder erregende Kunststücke | durch die natürliche Magie, mit Karten, Würfeln, Ringen, | Kugeln, Geldstücken, u.s.w., | nebst 24 arithmetischen Belustigungen | Zur | gesellschaftlichen Unterhaltung | mit und ohne Gehülfen auszuführen | [*short rule*] | Herausgegeben | von | Professor Kerndörffer | [*rule*] | Zweite vermehrte und verbesserte Auflage. | [*bold rule*] | Quedlinburg und Leipzig, 1840 | Verlag der Ernst'schen Buchhandlung., 1840.
[*this is the text of the cover, inside fancy border with price printed at foot, transcribed from a poor quality photograph on* https://www.booklooker.de]
>viii,216,[4]pp.; 18 cm; "Mit 24 Abbildungen"; publisher's ads (4pp.) at end.
>Held Brown UL (*Kabinet*); Aargauer Bibliotheksnetz (*Cabinet*); listed (all as *Kabinet*) GV XIX p.35; *Börsenblatt für den deutschen Buchhandel* 18 Feb.1840; *Literarische Zeitung* 26 Feb.1840; adv. *Wiener Zeitung* 4 Apr.1840 (*Cabinet*)

LGe79
3rd edition, 1842
>Listed GV XIX p.35 (1842); *Börsenblatt für den deutschen Buchhandel* 23 Nov.1841.
>No copy located.

LGe80
4th edition, 1843
[*Fraktur*] Carlo Bosco, | das Zauber-Kabinet | oder | das Ganze | der | Taschenspielerkunst, | enthaltend: | Wunder erregende Kunststücke | durch die natürliche Magie, mit Karten, Würfeln, Ringen, Ku- | geln, Geldstücken u.s.w. | nebst | 21 arithmetischen Belustigungen. | Zur | gesellschaftlichen Unterhaltung | mit und ohne Gehülfen auszuführen. | [*short rule*] | Herausgegeben | vom | Professor

Kerndörffer | [*double rule*] | Vierte verbesserte Auflage. | [*fancy rule*] | Quedlinburg und Leipzig, | Verlag der Ernst'schen Buchhandlung. | [*short rule*] | (Preis: 20 Sgr, oder 1 Fl. 12 Kr.)

The above is the title-page; the cover is a different setting of the same text inside a fancy border, with slight differences in the rules and with *Kugeln* not hyphenated but all on the following line.

"Halle. gedruckt bei Hendel" — p.192. ix,192pp.

Held Nat. Lib. Austria. Online at url:253; listed GV XIX p.35 (dating 1842); GV LXXIV p.261 (dating 1843); *Börsenblatt für den deutschen Buchhandel* 28 Oct.1842 and 5 May 1843; *Allgemeines Repertorium der neuesten in- und ausländischen Litteratur* 18 Aug.1843; Kayser *Vollständiges Bücher-Lexicon 9.Theil (1841 to 1846)*: "4. ver. Aufl. 1842"; *Allgemeiner Anzeiger der Deutschen* 6 Jan.1843; adv. *Wochenblatt der Stadt Nördlingen* 28 Feb.1843

LGe81
5th edition, 1845
Carlo Bosco, das Zauber-Kabinet, oder, Das Ganze der Taschenspielerkunst: enthaltend: einhundert Wunder erregende Kunststücke aus der natürlichen Magie, mit Karten, Würfeln, Kugeln, Geldstücken, Ringen ec. nebst 98 der interessantesten arithmetischen Belustigungen, zur gesellschaftlichen Unterhaltung und Belehrung / herausgegeben vom Kerndörffer

5. völlig umgearbeitete und verm. Aufl. Leipzig; Quedlingburg: Verlag der Ernst'schen Buchhandlung. ix,184pp.

Held Research Library of South Bohemia (České Budějovice); listed GV LXXIV p.261 (dating 1845); *Leipziger Repertorium der deutschen und ausländischen Literatur* 26 Sep.1845.

LGe82
6th edition, 1848?
[*Fraktur*] Carlo Bosco's | Zauberkabinet, | oder: | Das Ganze der | Taschenspielerkunst, | enthaltend: | 110 Wunder erregende Kunststücke | aus der natürlichen Magie | mit Karten, Würfeln, Kugeln, Geldstücken, Ringen ec. | nebst | 19 Kunststücken mit Spielkarten | und 68 der interessantesten arithmetischen | Belustigungen. | [*rule*] | Zur gesellschaftlichen Unterhaltung und Belehrung | herausgegeben | vom Professor Kerndörffer. | Sechste verbesserte und sehr vermehrte Auflage. | Mit 28 Abbildungen. | [*swelled rule*] | Quedlinburg und Leipzig. | Verlag der Ernst'schen Buchhandlung.

xii,180pp.; 2 copper plates with 24 illustrations; *ca.*17 × 11 cm.
Title transcribed from copy with photo listed by Antiquariat Hilbert Kadgien.
Listed GV XIX p.35 (xii,177pp.; 1851); *Börsenblatt für den deutschen Buchhandel* 13 May 1845; 18 July 1851. The following advertisements (some with varying title) all state they are for the 5th ed.:
Wiener Zeitung 17 Jan.1848 ("enthaltend (110) Wunder… 6te Auflage"); *Bayerische Landbötin* 24 Feb.1848 ("enthaltend 100 Wunder…Sechste Auflage"); *Allgemeine Anzeiger* 25 Oct.1848 ("enthaltend (110) Wunder… Sechste Auflage"); *Leipziger Zeitung* 15 Nov.1855 states 12,000 copies sold.

LGe83
7th edition, 1853
[*Fraktur*] Carlo Bosco's | Zauberkabinet, | oder: | Das Ganze | der Taschenspielerkunst, | enthaltend: | 110 Wunder erregende Kunststücke | aus der natürlichen Magie | mit Karten, Würfeln, Kugeln, Geldstücken, Ringen ec. | nebst | 19 Kunststücken mit Spielkarten | und | 68 der interessantesten arithmetischen | Belustigungen. | [*double rule*] | Zur | gesellschaftlichen Unterhaltung und Belehrung | herausgegeben | vom Professor Kerndörffer. | [*rule*] | Siebente vermehrte Auflage. | Mit Abbildungen. | [*swelled rule*] Quedlinburg und Leipzig 1853. | Verlag der Ernst'schen Buchhandlung.

    180pp., ill.; 16 cm [but probably: xii,180pp.]

    Title transcribed from copy formerly on *abe.com*.

    Held Hungarian NL (giving the imprint as "[Quedlinburg]: [Ernst], [1853] (Nordhausen: Thiele)"); listed GV XIX p.36 (7.Aufl., 1853); *Börsenblatt für den deutschen Buchhandel* 21 Mar.1853; adv. *Morgen-Post* 7 Aug.1855.

LGe84
*8th edition,*1854

    Listed GV XIX p.36 (8. Aufl., 1854); *Börsenblatt für den deutschen Buchhandel* 4 Dec.1854; adv. *Würzburger Stadt- und Landbote* 2 Apr.1856 ("enthaltend 100 Wunder …, 8 Aufl.").

LGe85
9th edition, 1857?
Carlo Bosco's Zauber-Kabinet, oder: das Ganze der Taschenspielerkunst, enthaltend: 151 Wunder erregende Kunststücke aus der natürlichen Magie mit Karten, Würfeln, Kugeln, Geldstücken, Ringen etc. nebst 36 Kunststücken mit Spielkarten, ferner 48 der interessantesten arithmetischen Belustigungen: Zur gesellschaftlichen Unterhaltung und Belehrung / hrsg. vom Kerndörffer.

    9 verb. und verm. Aufl. Quedlinburg; Leipzig: Verlag der Ernst'schen Buchhandlung. xiv,[2],199pp., 18cm.

    Held Warsaw University Library; adv. *Figaro* 16 Aug.1857 ("…Enthaltend 110 Wunder… 9. Auflage…"); *Bamberger Tagblatt* 20 Aug.1861.

LGe86
10th edition, 1860
[*Fraktur*] Carlo Bosco's | Zauber-Cabinet, | oder: | Das Ganze | der Taschenspielerkunst, | enthaltend: | 154 Wunder erregende Kunststücke, | aus der natürlichen Magie | mit Karten, Würfeln, Kugeln, Geldstücken, Ringen e*c* , | nebst | 46 Kunststücken mit Spielkarten, | ferner | 13 der interessantesten arithmetischen | Belustigungen. | [*rule*] | Zur | gesellschaftlichen Unterhaltung und Belehrung | herausgegeben vom | Professor Kerndörffer. | [*rule*] | Zehnte verbesserte und vermehrte Auflage. | Mit 24 Abbildungen. | [*swelled rule*] | Quedlinburg & Leipzig 1860. | Verlag der Ernst'schen Buchhandlung in Quedlinburg.

    Title transcribed from photo of title-page in Rusconi p.211

212pp.: ill.; 18cm.

Held Bibliotheek Universiteit van Amsterdam; listed *Börsenblatt für den deutschen Buchhandel* 25 Mar.1857

LGe87
11th edition, 1863
[*Fraktur*] Carlo Bosko's | Zauber-Cabinet, | oder: | Das Ganze | der Taschenspielerkunst, | enthaltend: | 154 Wunder erregende Kunststücke, | aus der natürlichen Magie | mit Karten, Würfeln, Kugeln, Geldstücken, Ringen ec. | nebst | 46 Kunststücken mit Spielkarten, | ferner | 13 der interessantesten arithmetischen Belustigungen. | [*rule*] | Zur | gesellschaftlichen Unterhaltung und Belehrung | herausgegeben vom | Professor Kerndörfer. [*sic*] | [*rule*] | Elfte verbesserte und vermehrte Auflage. | Mit 24 Abbildungen. | [*swelled rule*] | Quedlinburg & Leipzig 1863. | Verlag der Ernst'schen Buchhandlung.

Title transcribed from photo of title-page by bookseller Antiquariat Turszynski.

"Mit 2 lithograph. Tafeln mit 24 Abb. XII, 196 S." Listed *Börsenblatt für den deutschen Buchhandel* 3 Apr.1863. No library holdings located.

LGe88
Published?
"12. Aufl." is listed in *Börsenblatt für den deutschen Buchhandel* 21 Apr.1865 and 8 Sep.1865.

LGe89
12th edition, 1870
[*Fraktur*] Carlo Bosco's | Zauber-Cabinet, | oder | Das Ganze | der Taschenspielerkunst, | enthaltend: | 154 Wunder erregende Kunststücke, | aus der natürlichen Magie | mit Karten, Würfeln, Kugeln, Geldstücken, Ringen ec. | nebst | 46 Kunststücken mit Spielkarten, | ferner | 13 der interessantesten arithmetischen Belustigungen. | Zur | gesellschaftlichen Unterhaltung und Belehrung | herausgegeben von | Professor Kerndörfer. | [*rule*] | Zwölfte verbesserte und vermehrte Auflage. | Mit 24 Abbildungen. | [*swelled rule*] | Quedlinburg & Leipzig 1870. | Verlag der Ernst'schen Buchhandlung.

"Halle. Druck von Otto Hendel" — p.196.

xii,196pp.,18 cm.

Held NYPL (their copy online at url:254); listed GV XIX p.36 (1870); *Börsenblatt für den deutschen Buchhandel* 26 July 1870

LGe90
13th edition, date? [between 1870 and 1874]
Advertised *Tagespost* [Graz] 13 July 1877; *Die Gartenlaube* 1877 ("Bosko's Zauberkabinet... Enthalt 140 wundererregende... Dreizehnte Auflage...")

No copy traced

LGe91
14th edition, 1874
[*Fraktur*] Carlo Bosco's | Zauber-Cabinet, | oder | Das Ganze | der | Taschenspielerkunst, | enthaltend: | 154 Wunder erregende Kunststücke, | aus der natürlichen Magie | mit Karten, Würfeln, Kugeln, Geldstücken, Ringen ec. | nebst | 46 Kunststücken mit Spielkarten, | ferner | 13 der interessantesten arithmetischen Belustigungen. | Zur | gesellschaftlichen Unterhaltung und Belehrung | herausgegeben von | Professor Kerndörfer. | [*rule*] | Vierzehnte verbesserte und vermehrte Auflage. | Mit 24 Abbildungen. | [*swelled rule*] | Quedlinburg & Leipzig 1874 | Verlag der Ernst'schen Buchhandlung.
 Title transcribed from copy formerly on ZVAB, Antiquarische Fundgrube.
 196pp. Listed GV XIX p.36 (1874 and 1876)

LGe92
15th edition, 1876
Carlo Bosco`s Zauber-Cabinet, Das Ganze der Taschenspielerkunst, enthaltend 154 [*etc.*]
 15. Aufl. xii,196pp.
 Listed GV XIX p.36 (1876).
 No copy located

LGe93
16th edition, 1878
Carlo Bosco's Zauber-Cabinet, oder Das Ganze der Taschenspielerkunst: enthaltend 154 Wunder erregende Kunststücke aus der natürlichen Magie mit Karten, Würfeln, Kugeln, Ringen etc., nebst 46 Kunststücken mit Spielkarten, ferner 13 der interessantesten arithmetischen Belustigungen / Zur gesellschaftlichen Unterhaltung und Belehrung herausgegeben von Prof. Kerndörffer
 16. verb. Aufl, Quedlinburg; Leipzig: Verlag der Ernst'schen Buchhandlung, 1878. 196pp.
 Held: National Library of Estonia; listed GV XIX p.36 (1878).

LGe94
17th edition, 1885
Carlo Bosco's Zauber-Cabinet, oder Das Ganze der Taschenspielerkunst: enthaltend 154 [etc.]
 Listed GV XIX p.36 (1885)
 No copy traced.

LGe95
18th edition, 1890
[*Fraktur: in double-ruled border with decorated corners*] Carlo Bosco's | Zauber-Cabinet, | oder | Das Ganze der | Taschenspielerkunst. | Enthaltend: | 154 Wunder erregende Kunststücke, | aus der natürlichen Magie, | mit Karten, Würfeln, Kugeln, Geldstücken, Ringen [et]c | und | 46 Kunststücke mit Spielkarten, | ferner | 13 der interessantesten arithmetischen Belustigungen. | Zur | gesellschaftlichen Unterhaltung und Belehrung | herausgegeben vom | Professor Kerndörffer | Achtzehnte verbesserte

und vermehrte Auflage. | Mit 24 Abbildungen. | [*swelled rule*] | Quedlinburg & Leipzig 1870. | Verlag der Ernst'schen Buchhandlung. | *rule*] | Preis 2 Mark.
Title transcribed from photo of copy from Quicker than the Eye on abe.com.
States original yellow wrappers; 2 engraved plates at front; pagination not stated.
Held St.Galler Bibliotheksnetz (194 S., Ill.) and probably at ULSH (1890, edition not stated; xii,194p ; 8vo); listed XIX p.36 (1890).

LGe96
19th edition [1896?]
Carlo Bosco's Zauber-Cabinet oder Das Ganze der Taschenspielerkunst: enthaltend 214 Kunststücke mit Karten, Würfeln, Kugeln, Ringen, Geldstücken und anderen Gegenständen: zur gesellschaftlichen Unterhaltung herausgegeben vom Professor Kerndörffer.
19. verb. und verm. Aufl. Halberstadt; Leipzig: Verlag der Ernst'schen Buchhandlung. xiii,192pp.
Held Universitätsbibliothek Leipzig, Bibliotheca Albertina; listed GV XIX p.36 (1896).

LGe97
20th edition, 1899
Das Zauber-Cabinet oder das Ganze der Taschenspielerkunst. Enthaltend: 216 Kunststücke mit Karten, Würfeln, Kugeln, Ringen, Geldstücken und anderen Gegenständen. Hrsg. von Kerndörffer.
[*cover, with illus. of a mustachioed magician*]: Preis [ ] Mark | Carlo Bosko's | Zauber-Cabinet | oder | das | Ganze | der | Taschen- | Spieler- | Kunst. | Zur | gesellschaftlichen Unterhaltung und Belehrung | Herausgegeben von | Professor Kerndörffer. | Mit Abbildungen. | 20 vermehrte u. verbesserte Auflage | Ernstsche Verlagsbuchhandlung Leipzig
Cover transcribed from photo from Antiquariat Klabund formerly on abe.com
20. verb. u. verm. Aufl. Leipzig: Ernst, 1899. xx,181pp.
Listed GV XIX p.36 (1899)

Carlo Bosco: see also LGe118-125

====

BOSCO DER ZWEITE

LGe98
Bosko der Zweite. Zauberbuch enthaltend eine Sammlung der schönsten und überraschendesten Kunststücke, welche größtentheils ohne Kostenaufwand und mit geringer Mühe ausgeführt werden können.
Weißenfels: Sueß, 1843
No surviving copy recorded. Listed GV XIX p.35 as *Bosco d. Zweiten Zauberbuch* [etc.]. 1.-4.Aufl., 1843-48; listed *Börsenblatt für den deutschen Buchhandel* 11 July 1843; Kayser, *Vollständiges Bücher-Lexicon 9.Theil* as *Bosco des Zweiten*

Zauberbuch [etc.] 1843, 2 Aufl. 1844, 4 Aufl.1846; *Hinrichs' Halbjahrs-Katalog* Jan.-June 1843 (p.30); adv. *Transilvania, Beiblatt zum Siebenbürger Boten* 10 Feb. 1843.

LGe99

    4.Aufl. [1848?]
    Listed (see preceding entry), also in *J. P. Thun's wissenschaftlich geordneter Weihnachts-Catalog für Kinder und Gewachsene* 1848.

===

LGe100
[*1st ed.*]
Bosco, der Zauberer & Hexenmeister. Eine Sammlung der neuesten, interessantesten, unterhaltendsten und überraschendsten Kunststücke, welche ohne Gehülfen und kostspielige Apparate leicht ausgeführt werden können. Zusammengestellt von Bosco dem Zweiten.
    Dresden: Breyer (Ad. Wolf), 1865. 128pp.
    Listed GV XIX p.34; *Börsenblatt für den deutschen Buchhandel* 7 July 1865; *Allgemeines Deutsches Bücher-lexikon, oder Vollständiges ...1862-7;* adv. ("soeben ist wieder eingetroffen") *Würzburger Stadt- und Landbote* 15 Aug.1865.

LGe101
[*4th ed.*]
[*Fraktur*] Bosko, | der Zauberer und Hexenmeister. | [*fancy rule*] | Eine Sammlung | der | neuesten, interessantesten, unterhaltesten und über- | raschendsten Kunststücke, welche ohne Gehilfen und kostspielige Apparate leicht ausgeführt werden können. | Zur Selbstbelehrung, | sowie | zur Unterhaltung in fröhlichen Kreisen | für | Jung und Alt | zusammengestellt | von | Bosko dem Zweiten. | 4. Aufl. | [*wavy rule*] | Dresden. | Druck und Verlag von Adolph Wolf.
    Title transcribed from photo of NYPL copy
    128pp., 16cm. Coloured cover ('BOSKO | DER ZAUBERER | [und] | HEXENMEISTER') with illus. of Bosco wearing blue outfit.
    Held NYPL; GV XIX p.35 lists "1.—4. Aufl., 1868-75"; listed *Börsenblatt für den deutschen Buchhandel* 6 July1875

    An undated edition with the imprint given as "Dresden: Tittel und Wolf, *ca.* 1870" and described as 128pp., 13.5 × 10cm, was formerly listed for sale by Antiquariat Turszynski.

Weller's *Lexicon pseudonymorum* lists Bosko der Zweite: Bosko der Zauberer und Hexenmeister. 1865, 4. Aufl. 1875 among "Nichtenthuellte Pseudonymen".

===

UNDER TITLE

LGe102
Enthülltes Geheimniß, der Kunst Karten zu schlagen und daraus wahrzusagen, nebst leicht ausführenden überraschenden Kartenkunststücken zur Unterhaltung in frohen Kreisen, nach Herrmann, Bosco, Döbler, Frikel, Becker, Kratky-Baschik u.m.A.

Erfurt: G. Wilhelm Körner, 1853. 28pp., 12mo.

Listed GV XLIV p.332; *Börsenblatt für den deutschen Buchhandel* 11 Nov.1853; Heinsius *Allgemeines Bücher-Lexikon* 1858 p.321 lists this as published by Jaquet's Verlag in Augsburg. No surviving copies traced.

===

LGe103
Der neue Döbler und Bosco, oder, der allerneueste und vollkommenste Zauberer. Enthaltend eine vollständige Sammlung von 198 der neuesten, auffallensten, leichtest zu erlernenden und wenigst kostspieligen Zauberkünste und Taschenspielereien. Nach Döbler, Bosco, Pinetti, Philadelphia, Poppe und den übrigen vorzüglichsten Schriftstellern in diesem Fache.

Wien: "Zu haben bei R. Sammer", 1846. 48pp.

Held: Jihočeská univerzita v Českých Budějovicích (University of South Bohemia in České Budějovice); listed GV XXIX p.318; *Leipziger Repertorium der deutschen und ausländischen Literatur* 26 Sep.1845; *Börsenblatt für den Deutschen Buchhandel* 29 Apr.1845: "…Im Schiller-Format auf Velinpapier mit Kupfer im farbigen Umschlag broch. für den äußerst geringen Preis von 18 kr. NB. 50 Exemplare baar mit 50%" (i.e. in a fairly large and expensive format; terms 50 copies at half retail price for cash with order); in *Börsenblatt* 12 Nov.1860 the publisher reduces the price from 12 Ngr to 2 Ngr (netto baar); adv. *Kais. Königl. Schlesische Troppauer-Zeitung* 5 May 1845; *Wiener Zeitung* 8 May 1845; reviewed in *ATZ* 14 May 1845: "…Die Anwesenheit Boscos hat wieder das Interesse für Zauberkünste und Taschenspielereien rege gemacht, und wer seinem Hange, auch so eine Art Hexenmeister zu sein, Genüge leisten will, der kaufe dieses Büchlein, und er wird Dinge zu Stande bringen, welche den verblüfften Zuschauern Augen und Ohren anfreißen, *nota bene*, wenn diese Zuschauer nicht zufälliger Weise schon im Besitze dieses verrätherischen Hexenbüchlein sind; denn dann — ja dann wirds mit dem Uiberraschen seine Umstände haben. — Im Interesse der Taschenspielerei ist so ein Büchlein übrigens wahrlich nicht verfaßt, weil dadurch alle Illusion vernichtet und ersichtlich wird, daß gerade die frappantesten Kunststücken auf Kleinigkeiten, oder gar auf — Einverständnisen beruhen, — Zur Unterhaltung aber in häuslichen Cirkeln, dürfte dieses 'Dobler und Bosco,' als ein recht pfiffiger Rathgeber zu empfehlen sein".

===

LGe104
Der rothe Teufel im Salon, oder, Bosco in allen Gesellschaften: eine Sammlung der neuesten und interessantesten Belustigungen aus dem Gebiete der natürlichen Magie, nebst einer vollständigen Anleitung zum Becherspiel, einer grossen Anzahl von Kartenkunststücken und einer reichen Auswahl der unterhaltendsten Gesellschaftspiele.
    Weimar: Verlag und Druck von Bernhard Friedrich Voigt, 1858.
    xvi,265pp.; ill.; 19cm
    Held LC (Houdini Coll.); Hungarian Nat Lib (lacking leaves); listed *Börsenblatt für den deutschen Buchhandel* 24 Sep.1858; adv. *Der Bayerische Landbote* 27 Sep. 1858 ("mit 144 in den Text eingedruckten Illustrationen, aus der rühmlich bekannten xylographischen Anstalt von Eduard Kretzschmar in Leipzig … Höchst elegant geheftet"); *Augsburger Anzeigeblatt* 20 Nov.1858 ("…elegant broschirt").

LGe105
    [2nd. ed., 1866]
    Listed as "1866" *Börsenblatt für den deutschen Buchhandel* 20, 27 Nov.1865.

LGe106
    [3rd. ed., 1871]
    Copy formerly listed for sale by Antiquariat Löcker, Wien ("Der rothe Teufel im Salon, oder, Bosco… 3. Aufl. Weimar, Voigt 1871. XVI, 265 S. 144 Fig. im Text"); listed *Börsenblatt für den deutschen Buchhandel* 28 Sep.; 3 Oct.; 22 Nov.1870.

LGe107
―――
    4. Aufl. Weimar: Bernhard Friedrich Voigt, 1874.
    [3],vi-xvi,241pp., ill.; 21cm.
    Held LC (Houdini Coll.); Regionální muzeum v Kolíně Knihovna (Kolín Regional Museum, Czech Republic)

LGe108
―――
    5. Auflage. Weimar: Voigt, 1882.
    xvi,241,[3]pp.; ill.; 19 cm., publisher's advertisements (3pp.) at end
    Held Universitätsbibliothek Leipzig, Bibliotheca Albertina; NYPL; Brown UL; LC (Houdini Coll.); Hungarian Nat Lib.; listed *Börsenblatt für den deutschen Buchhandel* 29 Dec.1881 ("Unter der Presse"); and 12, 28 Jan.; 19 May 1882
    Photo of cover at url:255.

    David Singmaster, 'Books on Recreational Mathematics….', in the 1992 version but *not in the 2004 version* (url:256) suggested this may be based on *Le Magicien des Salons ou le Diable Couleur de Rose* (1856; online at url:257), which seems unlikely.

====

LGe109
Der Zauberstab: Praktische Anleitung, binnen wenig Tagen Meister in der Taschenspieler-Kunst zu werden. Mit mehreren hundert Beispielen.

Graz: In Commission bei Eduard Ludewig [1838]. xvi,256pp., 1 folded leaf of plates; 17 cm.

Held ULSH; Universitätsbibliothek Basel; adv. *Intelligenzblatt zur Laibacher Zeitung* 20 Nov.1838: "Was Bosco, Eckartshausen, Funk, Guyot, Halle, Ozanane [*i.e.* Ozanam], Pinetti, Wiegleb u.A.m. an vorzüglich geheimnißvollen physikalischen, mathematischen, egyptischen, chemischen, öconomischen, arithmetischen und anderen leicht zu bewerkstelligenden Kunststücken zur Belustigung darbothen, ist hier in deutlicher Kürze dargestellt, und besondere Rücksicht auf jene höchst überraschenden Kunststücke genommen, wozu keine kostspieligen Apparate erfordert werden".

LGe110
─────
[New edition, 1839].

"Neue Ausgabe" listed *Allgemeine Bibliographie für Deutschland* Vol.4 No.38 20 Sep.1839 p.557; Graesse, *Bibliotheca magica et pneumatica* p.116.

=====

BOOKS WITH A NAMED AUTHOR

The names Carlo Bosko and Döbler were added to the title-page of later editions only
LGe111
Carl Friedrich Bahr

Louis le petit, der immer gern gesehene Gesellschafter, Taschenspieler und Lustigmacher. Eine Sammlung scherzhafter Aufgaben, Wortspiele ... leicht auszuführender Taschenspieler- und Kartenkunststücke [...]

Exact full title of this edition uncertain.

Quedlinburg & Leipzig: Ernst, 1856. xii,114pp.; 8vo.

Held: BL; adv. *Kurier für Niederbayern* 22 July 1856; *Augsburger Postzeitung* 13 Sep.1856; *Fremden Blatt* 30 Oct.1856 ("...Ferner 40 Taschenspielerkünste, 26 Kartenstücke und 28 Gesellschaftspiele. Zur angenehmen Unterhaltung, Mit 18 Zeichnungen.").

LGe112
[*2nd ed.*]
"Zweite Aufgabe" listed *Börsenblatt für den Deutschen Buchhandel* 4 Feb.1859; adv. (these stated to be 2. Aufl.) *Augsburger Postzeitung* 29 Aug.1857; *Neustadter Zeitung* 7 Sep.1858; *Bayreuther Zeitung* 22 Aug.1860.

LGe113
[*3rd ed.*]
Louis le petit, oder der immer gern gesehene Gesellachafter, Taschenspieler und Lustigmacher. Eine Sammlung scherzhafter Aufgaben, Wortspiele, arithmetischer,

Belustigungen [...] sowie auch eine Sammlung Gesellschafts-Spiele, Räthsel und Räthselfragen. Zur angenehmen Unterhaltung.

    3 verb. Aufl. Quedlinburg: Ernst, 1863. xii,126pp.

    Held Staats- und Stadtbibliothek Augsburg; listed Avenarius *Bibliographisches Jahrbuch 1858; Börsenblatt für den deutschen Buchhandel* 26 Nov.1860.

LGe114
[*4th ed.*]

    Listed *Börsenblatt für den deutschen Buchhandel* 18 Mar.1864; adv. *Regensburger Tagblatt* 26 Dec.1863.

LGe115
[*5th ed.*]
Louis le petit oder der immer gern gesehene Gesellschafter, Taschenspieler und Lustigmacher [...].

    Quedlinburg: Ernst [no date]. iv,149pp.

    Held Staats- und Stadtbibliothek Augsburg; Bayerische Staatsbibliothek; adv. *Deutsches Volksblatt für Mähren* 30 Nov.1872.

LGe116
[*6th ed.*]

    "6. verbesserte Aufg." adv. *Würzburger Anzeiger* 10 June 1868.

LGe117
[*7th ed.*]

    "7. Aufl." listed *Börsenblatt für den deutschen Buchhandel* 2 Aug.1871; adv. *Neues Wiener Tagblatt (Tages-Ausgabe)* 1 Feb.1874

The earliest edition known to add the reference to Carlo Bosko and Döbler
LGe118
[*8th ed.*]
Louis le petit, der immer gern gesehene Gesellschafter, Taschenspieler und Lustigmacher: eine Sammlung von 18 scherzhaften Aufgaben, 26 arithmethischen Belustigungen, 50 Taschenspielerkünsten, 34 Kartenkunststücken, 25 Gesellschafts-, Frag- u. Antwortspielen, Punktirkunst, poetische Scherze und Gedichte launigen Inhalt, 90 Räthsel und Räthsel-Fragen / nach Carlo Bosko und Döbeler [*sic*]; herausgegeben von Karl Friedrich Bahr.

    Achte verbesserte Auflage. Quedlinburg & Leipzig: Verlag der Ernst'schen Buchhandlung [1874?]. x,132pp.

    Held Staats- und Universitätsbibliothek Bremen; listed *Börsenblatt für den deutschen Buchhandel* 29 Sep.1874 and 10 Sep.1875; *Kladderdatsch* 8 Nov.1874.

LGe119
[*9th ed.*]

    Listed *Börsenblatt für den deutschen Buchhandel* 28 Aug.1876.

LGe120
[*10th ed.*]
Louis le petit, der immer gern gesehene Gesellschafter, Taschenspieler und Lustigmacher. Eine Sammlung von 18 scherzhaften Aufgaben, 27 arithmetischen Belustigungen, 50 Taschenspielerkünsten [etc], nach Carlo Bosko und Döbler. Hrsg. von Karl Friedrich Bahr.
    10 verb. Aufl. Quedlingburg: Ernst, 1881.
    Listed F W Christern, *Catalogue of Books ... Published in Germany from July to December 1880* [title and date taken from this; no copy located].

LGe121
[*11th.ed.*]
Louis le petit, der immer gern gesehene Gesellschafter, Taschenspieler und Lustigmacher. Eine Sammlung von 18 scherzhaften Aufgaben, 27 arithmetischen Belustigungen, 50 Taschenspielerkünsten [*etc.*], nach Carlo Bosko und Döbler. Hrsg. von Karl Friedrich Bahr
    11. verb. Aufl. Quedlinburg & Leipzig: Ernst, 1885. xii,136pp.
    Held: Staatsbibliothek zu Berlin.

LGe122
[*12th. ed.*]
Louis le petit: der immer gern gesehene Gesellschafter, Taschenspieler u. Lustigmacher: eine Sammlung von 18 scherzhaften Aufgaben, 27 arithmetischen Belustigungen, 50 Taschenspielerkünsten, 32 Kartenkunststücken, 21 Gesellschaftspielen, Frage- und Antwortspiel, Punktirkunst, poetischen Scherzen und Gedichten launigen Inhalts, 94 Rätseln und Rätselfragen: nach Carlo Bosko und Döbeler [*sic*].
    12. verb. Aufl. Quedlinburg & Leipzig: Verlag der Ernst'schen Buchhandlung, 1890.
    Held LC (Houdini Coll.)

LGe123
[*13th. ed.*]
The last edition with Louis le Petit *in title*
Louis le petit: der immer gern gesehene Gesellschafter, Taschenspieler und Lustigmacher: eine Sammlung von 18 scherzhaften Aufgaben, 27 arithmetischen Belustigungen, 50 Taschenspielerkünsten, 32 Kartenkunststücken, 21 Gesellschaftspielen, Frage- und Antwortspiel, Punktierkunst, poetischen Scherzen und Gedichten launigen Inhalts, 94 Rätseln und Rätselfragen: nach Carlo Bosko und Döbeler / herausgegeben von Carl Friedrich Bahr.
    13. verb. Aufl. Halberstadt & Leipzig: Verlag der Ernst'schen Buchhandlung, 1895. x,158pp., 18cm.
    Held: LC (Houdini Collection); NYPL; Staatsbibliothek zu Berlin

LGe124
[*15th. ed.*]
Der immer gern gesehene Tausend-Künstler, Taschenspieler und Wippchenmacher: eine Sammlung von scherzhaften Aufgaben, spasshaft-listigen Wetten, arithmetischen Belustigungen, Taschen-spielerkünsten, Kartenkunststücken, Gesellschaftsspielen, einem Frage- und Antwortspiel, einer Punktierkunst, einer Anleitung zum Kartenlegen, 118 Rätseln und Rätselfragen nach Carlo Bosko und Döbeler / herausgegeben von Carl Friedrich Bahr.

15. verb. Aufl. Leipzig: Ernst'sche Verlagsbuchh. [1910]. x,[vi],158,2pp., 19cm.

Held Brown UL; Staatsbibliothek zu Berlin; listed *Börsenblatt für den Deutschen Buchhandel* 29 July; 10 Aug.1910.

LGe125
[*19th. ed.*]
Der immer gern gesehene Tausendkünstler, Taschenspieler und Wippchenmacher: eine Sammlung von scherzhaften Aufgaben, spasshaft-listigen Wetten, arithmetischen Belustigungen, Taschen-spielerkünsten, Kartenkunststücken, Gesellschaftsspielen, einem Frage- und Antwortspiel, einer Punktierkunst, einer Anleitung zum Kartenlegen, 118 Rätseln und Rätselfragen nach Carlo Bosko und Döbeler.

Leipzig: Ernst'sche Verlagsbuchh. [1915?]

Held Brown UL and probably at ULSH (152pp., 19cm.); the Hungarian National Digital Archive has a photo of the cover of probably this edition online at url:258.

===

LGe126
Carlo Bellachino.
Der interessante, erheiternde und überraschende Taschenspieler, oder, Bosco's enthüllte Geheimnisse. Eine ausgewählte und reichhaltige Sammlung höchst wirkungsvoller und leicht ausführbarer Kunststücke aus dem Gebiete der natürlichen Magie und Experimentirkunst sowie des Magnetismus und der Sympathie. Herausgegeben von Carlo Bellachino.

Elberfeld; Leipzig: Verlag von Julius Püttmann [1873]. 88,[4]pp, x leaves of plates; 18 cm.

Held LC (Houdini Coll.); listed GV XI p.349; adv. *Straubinger Tagblatt* 19 Sep. 1873 ("Mit brillantem Farbenbruchtitle [*sic*], elegant brochiert"; editor as "Carlo Belachino" and title as "…oder, Bosco's entschleierte Geheimnisse…").

LGe127
[*2nd ed.*]
Listed under title (without any author named) as *Der interessante, erheiternde und überraschende Taschenspieler, oder Bosco's enthüllte Geheimnisse*. 2 Aufl. 75pp., 8vo, in *Börsenblatt für den deutschen Buchhandel* 23 June 1876.

The original "Bellachini" was the stage name of magician Ernst (Samuel) Berlach, 1827-1885. His name was appropriated by a host of other performers (the *Lexikon* says about ninety) and further mythical *Bellachini* (and close variants of the name) were invented by publishers as alleged authors or compilers of books on magic. This is the only one of the many titles attributed to "Carlo Bellachino", or variants of that name, that includes *Bosco* or *Bosko* in the title.

===

LGe128
John Carter [*pseud. of* Peter Friedrich Ludwig Hoffmann]
    An advertisement by the publisher Berendsohn quoted in the entry for *Der Zauberstab. Das Neueste der Tachenspielerkunst* (see LGe147) states that *Bosco als Kartenkünstler* was written by Hoffmann.

Bosco als Kartenkünstler: oder leichtfaßliche Anweisung, wie man ohne Apparate die überraschendsten Karten-Kunststücke machen kann. Mit 9 Tafeln (auf 2 Bl. in Holzschn. in gr. 4.) und 3 Anhängen. ent.: 1) die Cartomantie, oder Wahrsagerei aus Karten. 2) Frag.- und Antworth-Spiel mit Karten.
    Hamburg: Berendsohn, 1848. xvi,78pp.
    Held Bibliotheek Universiteit van Amsterdam; listed GV XXIII p.215; *Börsenblatt für den deutschen Buchhandel* 31 Oct.1848; adv. *Magdeburgische Zeitung* 15 Oct.1848.

LGe129
———
    2. Aufl. Hamburg: Berendsohn, 1849. xvi,78pp.
    Held Union Catalogue of the Czech Republic; listed GV XXIII p.215; *Börsenblatt für den deutschen Buchhandel* 29 Mar.; 7 June 1850; *Allgemeine Bibliographie für Deutschland* 11 Apr.1850; adv. *Augsburger Postzeitung* 11 Apr.1850; *Nürnberger Kurier* 13 Dec.1850 (stating 6000 copies of this edition).

LGe130
Bosco als Kartenkünstler: oder leichtfaßliche Anweisung, wie man ohne Apparate die überraschendsten Karten-Kunststücke machen kann.
    3. Aufl. Hamburg: Berendsohn, 1856. xvi,78pp.
    Listed GV XXIII p.215; *Börsenblatt für den deutschen Buchhandel* 10 Nov.1856

LGe131
[*4th ed.*] 1857?
———
    "Vierte Aufl.". Advertised (still with author as "John Carter") *Eestimaa Kubermangu Teataja* 21 Oct.1857; *Die Neue Zeit: Olmüzer politische Zeitung* 15 Dec.1859 ("...mit 166 Abbildungen auf 9 Tafeln und zwei Anhängen").

LGe132
[*5th ed.*] 1860
"John Carter" no longer given as author; title changed.
Bosco als Kartenkünstler. Leichfaßliche Anweisung, ohne alle Apparate die überraschendsten Karten-Kunststücke zu machen; nebst Mlle. Lenormand's

Wahrsagerei aus den Karten und einem humoristischen Frage- und Antwortspiel mit Karten. Mit zahlreichen Abbildungen.

    5. verm. Aufl. Hamburg: B.S. Berendsohn, 1860. xvi,128pp., 4 woodcuts.

    Listed GV XIX p.34; *Börsenblatt für den deutschen Buchhandel* 22 Oct.1860; adv. *Würzburger Anzeiger* 29 Jan.1861.

LGe133
ULSH records an edition dated 1862.

LGe134
[*6th ed.*]
———

    6. Aufl. Hamburg: B.S. Berendsohn, 1864. xvi,128pp., 4 woodcuts.
    Listed GV XIX p.34

LGe135
[*7th ed.*]
———

    7. verm. Aufl. Hamburg: B.S. Berendsohn, 1864. xvi,128pp., 4 woodcuts.
    Listed GV XIX p.34

LGe136
[*8th ed.*]
    "8te … Aufl." adv. *Würzburger Stadt- und Landbote* 18 Dec.1867. A photo of the cover and part of the title-page of this edition is online at url:259.

LGe137
[*9th ed.*]
———

    9. Aufl. Hamburg: B.S. Berendsohn, 1867. xvi,128pp., 4 woodcuts.
    Listed GV XIX p.34; *Börsenblatt für den Deutschen Buchhandel* 15 Oct.1867.

LGe138
[*new edition*]
Der vollkommne Kartenkünstler: leichtfassliche Anleitung zu den überraschendsten Kartenkunststücken, vom einfachsten, bis zu den schwierigsten, die überhaupt nur ausgeführt werden können.

    12. stark verm. Aufl. Hamburg: B.S. Berendsohn, 1875. 80pp., 13cm.

    Held by Brown UL which states that this edition names Hoffmann as the author and is a new edition of *Bosco als Kartenkünstler*.

===

LGe139
Comte
Bosko's und Döbler's Zauberkünste oder: Natürliche Magie und Taschenspielerkunst für Dilettanten und zur angenehmen Unterhaltung für Gesellschaftskreise. Von Comte nach dem Französischen bearbeitet.
   3. Aufl. Quedlinburg: Gottf. Basse, 1839. viii,192pp., ills.
   Held ULSH (186pp.); Universitätsbibliothek J. C. Senckenberg, Frankfurt/aM; listed (3rd ed., with Comte's *Kleines Handbuch der Taschenspielerkunst*, 2nd ed.) GV XXIV p.241; Kayser, *Vollständiges Bücher-Lexicon, 1833-1840*); adv. *Allgemeiner Anzeiger* 1 Feb.1840; *Wiener Zeitung* 5 Oct.1843.
   Attributed to Louis Christian Emmanuel Apollinaire Comte, 1788-1859, but it is uncertain which French work this is based on: there is no mention of Bosco in the 1834 or 1837 editions of his *Manuel complet des sorciers*.

===

LGe140
F. Gallien
Das Ganze der Zauberei mit der Hand. Eine theoretisch-praktische Anleitung zur Ausübung des Becherspiels und zur Kunst des Volteschlagens, als Vorstudien zu allen übrigen Taschenspieler-Künsten. Nebst vielen, nur durch die Hände und ohne Apparate auszuführenden Karten- und anderen Kunststücken. Nach den Vorträgen von Bosko, Döbler, Filippi *ie*.
   Wien: Hartleben's Verlag, 1865. 62pp. (mit erläut. Abbild. auf 1 Holzschntaf.)
This may be the first edition of the following titles.
   Listed GV XLIII p.229; *Börsenblatt für den deutschen Buchhandel* 8 Sep.1865.
   BL and ULSH have an edition dated "1866"; a "2., mit erläuternden Abb. verm. Aufl." published Wien: A. Hartleben, 75pp., dated as "[1900?]" is held by the Czech National Library (catalogued as *Das Grenze* [sic] *der Zauberei mit der Hand...*).

LGe141
2nd ed., 1870
Eine Stunde der Täuschung; oder, Das Ganze der Zauberei mit der Hand Anleitung zur Ausübung des Becherspiels und zur Kunst des Volteschlagens Nach den Vorträgen von Bosko, Döbler, Herrmann, Hofzinser und anderen bearbeitet.
   2. verm. Aufl. Wien A. Hartleben, 1870. 76pp., 13cm.
   Held NYPL (microform); listed GV XLIII p.229; *Oesterreichische Buchhändler-Correspondenz* 20 Feb.1870.

LGe142
3rd ed., 1883
Eine Stunde der Täuschung, oder, Das Ganze der Zauberei mit der Hand: theoretisch-praktische Anleitung zur Ausübung von vielen, ohne Apparate, nur durch die Hände auszuführenden Wunder erregenden Karten- und anderen Kunststücken, nach den Vorträgen von Bosko, Döbler, Herrmann, Hofzinser und anderen berühmten Eskamoteurs.

3. mit vielen neuen Beiträgen und erläuternden Abbildungen verm. Aufl. Wien; Pest; Leipzig: A. Hartleben's Verlag [1883]. 79,[1]pp., 13cm.

Held Staatsbibliothek zu Berlin; Brown UL; LC (Houdini Coll.); listed GV XLIII p.229.

===

Professor Hermanns [*pseud. of* Peter Friedrich Ludwig Hoffmann: *see below*]
LGe143
[*"3rd edition"*, 1856]
Der Zauberstab [oder?] Das Neueste der Taschenspielerkunst und natürlichen Magie: enthaltend: 55 neue, von den bedeutendsten Künstlern ausgeführte, bisher nicht veröffentlichte, Wunder erregende mechanische Kunststücke; 93 Kunststücke aus dem Gebiete der Physik, Chemie und Optik; 12 magnetische Künste; 67 Kartenkunststücke; 65 arithmetische Belustigungen; nach eigenen Experimenten und mündlichen Ueberlieferungen der bedeutendsten Künstler der Neuzeit, Bosco, Döbler, Philippe, Robin u. Anderen, zum ersten Male der Oeffentlichkeit übergeben und durch 88 Abbildungen erläutert von Professor Hermanns.

Dritte, verbesserte und vermehrte Auflage. Hamburg: B.S. Berendsohn, 1856.
viii,[9]-360pp., 12 leaves of plates; 18 cm.
Held ULSH. First and second editions not traced.

LGe144
[*"3rd edition"*, 1859]
[*Fraktur*] Der Zauberstab, | oder das Neueste | der Taschenspielerkunst | und natürlichen Magie. | Enthaltend: | 55 neue, von den bedeutendsten Künstlern ausgeführte, bisher | nicht veröffentlichte, Wunder erregende mechanische Kunststücke. | 93 Kunststücke aus dem Gebiete der Physik, Chemie und Optik. | 12 magnetische Künste. 67 Kartenkunststücke. | 65 arithmetische Belustigungen. | Nach | eigenen Experimenten und mündlichen Ueberlieferungen der | bedeutendsten Künstler der Neuzeit | Bosco, Döbler, Philippe, Robin u. Anderen | zum ersten Male der Oeffentlichkeit übergeben | und | durch 88 Abbildungen erläutert | von | Professor Hermanns. | Dritte, verbesserte und vermehrte Auflage. | [*rule*] | Hamburg. | B. S. Berendsohn. | 1859.

"Druck von Ackermann & Wulff." — p.272.

xvi,272pp., 12 leaves of plates. This edition, also as "3rd edition", has *oder* in the title and is completely re-set.

Held Bayerische Staatsbibliothek; Bibliotheek Universiteit van Amsterdam.
Online at url:260

LGe145
[*"4th edition"*, 1861]
Der Zauberstab, oder das Neueste der Taschenspielerkunst und natürlichen Magie. Enthaltend: 425 neue... [*etc.*].

4., verb. und verm. Aufl. Hamburg: B.S. Berendsohn, 1861.
Held LC; University of Illinois

LGe146
[*"5th edition"*, 1873]
Der Zauberstab. Das Neueste der Tachenspielerkunst und natürlichen Magie, Enthaltend: 425 neue... [*etc.*].
    5. verb. und verm. Aufl. Hamburg: B.S. Berendsohn, 1873.
    viii,[9]-360pp., [14] folded pp of plates; 18 cm
    Held LC; Brown UL

LGe147
[*"6th edition"*, 1875]
[*Fraktur*] Der Zauberstab. | Das Neueste | der Taschenspielerkunst | und | natürlichen Magie. | Enthaltend: | 425 neue, von den bedeutendsten Künstlern ausgeführte, Wunder | erregende mechanische Kunststücke. | Kunststücke aus dem Gebiet der Physik, Chemie und Optik, magnetische Künste. Karten- | kunststücke. | arithmetische Belustigungen ie. | Nach den neuesten Erfahrungen, eignen Experimenten | und mündlichen Überlieferungen der bedeutendsten Künstler | der Neuzeit | Bosco, Döbler, Philippe, Robin, Philadelphia | und Anderen | der Oeffentlichkeit übergeben von | Professor Hermanns. | und bearbeitet von | P. F. L. Hoffmann. | Erläutert durch 108 Abbildungen | Sechste verbesserte und vermehrte Auflage. [*rule*] | Hamburg. | B. S. Berendsohn. | 1875.
    'Vorwort' signed "Hamburg, im October 1872. | P. F. L. Hoffmann."
    "Druck von Ackermann & Wulff." — p.360.
    360pp.; 14 plates.
    Held ULSH; LC; NYPL; Jagiellonian Library, Kraków. Online at url:261.
    Der Zauberstab has only one trick attributed to Bartolomeo, 'Die gelehrte Katze oder die Zauberschrift'.
    Probably all editions of this were written by Hoffmann — Peter Friedrich Ludwig Hoffmann, who wrote mainly on German lexicography but also *Der Wahrsager oder die Kunst aus den Karten wahrzusagen* and *Die 12 Menschentypen, Praktische Haus-Astrologie für Anfänger*. The publisher Berendsohn has a large advertisement in *Illustrirte Zeitung* 2 Jan.1875 for "Hoffmann's Zauberapparate", consisting of 14 separate items, and this comes with "erläuternder Gebrauchsanweisung" — "Der be- kannte und bestens accreditirte Verfasser von 'Bosco in der Westentasche', 'Bosco als Kartenkünstler' und 'Prof. Hoffmann's Zauberstab' ist der Erfinder dieser reizenden, besonders für Kinder anziehenden und unterhaltenden Apparate". So Hoffmann also wrote those three books.

===

LGe148
Hilarius Pfiffikus [*pseud. of* Georg Carl Ludwig Schöpfer]
    Bosco's und Frickel's Wunder über Wunder, oder die enthülthen Geheimnisse aller Zauberer, Magier und Hexenmeister *ie*. Herausgegeben und allen Freunden der Heiterkeit gewidmet von Hilarius Pfiffikus.
    3. Aufl. Bautzen: Reichel, 1851. viii,76pp.

This edition. the first to add the names Bosco and Frickel, is listed GV XIX p.35 and *Allgemeines Deutsches Bücher-Lexikon 1847-51* IV, 1 p.127, which describe it as a *Titelausgabe* (a reissue of an old text with text unchanged but a new title and title-page) of H. Pfiffikus, *Wunder über Wunder* [etc.]; adv. *Leipziger Zeitung* 7 Sep.1850; *Bayerische Landbötin* 3 Jan.1851.

The first edition of the original book appeared in 1835 — advertised in *Basler Zeitung* 29 Oct.1835; no copy recorded in a library but a copy was sold at auction by Zisska & Schauer in 2013; the second edition, 1839, is listed in GV LXI p.215; Graesse, *Bibliotheca magica et pneumatica* p.116; and *Repertorium der gesammten deutschen Literatur* XIX (1839), which gives its full title:

Wunder über Wunder oder die enthüllten eleusinischen Geheimnisse. Eine deutliche Anweisung, wie man eine Menge überraschender, leicht auszuführender und größtentheils noch ganz unbekannter Kunststücke ausführen kann. Aus dem Nachlasse der berühmtesten Tausendkünstler herausgegeben und allen Freunden der Heiterkeit gewidmet von Hilarius Pfiffikus, reisendem Künstler. 2te. völlig umgearbeitete und mit fast hundert ganz neuen nach und noch nie beschriebenen Künsten vermehrten Auflage. viii,76pp. Nordhausen: Fürst, 1839.

Hilarius Pfiffikus (*Pfiffikus* = a crafty fellow, originally student slang) was one of (at least) 32 pseudonyms used by Georg Carl Ludwig Schöpfer, 1802-1876, who wrote the first edition; whether he worked on this later edition is unknown. He churned out dozens of works of fact and fiction (as did his wife Irene), much of it for Reichel in Nordhausen: this pen name of his is not listed in his entry in *wikipedia.de* or at *https://nordhausen-wiki.de/wiki/Georg_Carl_Ludwig_Sch%C3%B6pfer* but it is included in Schmidt *Gallerie deutscher pseudonymer Schriftsteller* and Weller *Lexicon pseudonymorum*.

===

Jukundus Hilarius Possenreich
An unidentified pseudonym which suggests a humorous prankster. This is the earliest book to claim a link with Bosco.

LGe149
Scharfblicke in das Gebieth der natürlichen Magie, oder, Bosco's aufgeschlossenes Zauberkabinet: nebst einigen damit verbundenen Original-Anekdoten: eine freundliche Gabe für alle jene, welchen es darum zu thun ist, die angestaunten Taschenspielerkünste der neueren Zeit ganz zu durchblicken, oder auch selbst darzustellen, von Jukundus Hilarius Possenreich.
Leipzig und Halberstadt: bei Carl Brüggemann, 1830 [but probably late 1829]
The only recorded copies of this edition are all in the Harry Price Collection, Senate House Library, University of London. Their catalogue lists three copies (url:262):
b2007806~S24: 35,[1]pp.; 14 cm (8vo)
b2002933~S24: 37,[3]pp.; 14 cm (8vo)
b1932804~S24: 37pp.; 8vo.

Advertised in *Preßburger Zeitung* 28 Aug.1829 and in *Kais. Königl. Schlesische Troppauer-Zeitung* 21 Sep.1829 (title as above: "Noch ist folgende neue interessante Schrift um 30 kr. C.M. zu haben. Scharfblicke [...] 12mo. Leipzig und Halberstadt 1830. broschirt."); advertised also in *Wiener Zeitung* from 28 Aug.1829, where the two elements of the title are given in reverse order as *Bosco's aufgeschlossenes Zauber-Cabinet, oder Scharfblicke...*; listed *Hinrichs Halbjahrsverzeichnis der Neuerscheinungen des deutschen Buchhandel* July-Dec. 1829 ("Scharfblicke ... 16 (3 B.) Halberst., Brüggemann. geb. u. verkl.").

The book was co-published with Otto Wigand in Pest: this is stated in *Allgemeine Zeitung* [Munich] 2 Feb. 1830, and it is listed under Otto Wigand in *Ungarns deutsche Bibliographie 1801-1860...* I: 1801-1830 p.361 ("[...] 16° Pesth, 1830. Otto Wigand") and in Petrik: *Bibliographia Hungariae / Magyarország Bibliographiája 1712-1860,* III, 1891, p.127 ("Scharfblicke... Pesth, 1830 Otto Wigand").

Blik i den naturlige Magies Enemærk (LDaN1), 1831, is a translation of this.

LGe150
A second edition was published in Kaschau (now Košice in Slowakia) in 1836 under the title
Bosco's enthülltes und aufgeschlossenes Zauberkabinet, oder Scharfblicke in das Gebiet der natürlichen Magie. Erklärung der geheimnissvollsten Kunststücke aller berühmten Taschenspieler und deutliche Anweisung, neue, höchst überraschende physikalische, mechanische und Kartenstücke auf eine leichte Art selbst auszuführen. Eine freundliche Gabe für alle Jene, welchen es darum zu thun ist die angestaunten Taschenspielerkünste der neueren Zeit zu durchblicken, oder auch zur Belustigung einer Gesellschaft darzustellen / Jukundus Hilarius Possenreich.

2. verb. und verm. Aufl. Kaschau: Verl.-Comptoir, 1836.
116pp.; 13cm. Druck v. Carl Werfer.

The one recorded surviving copy is held by the Hungarian Nat. Lib., Budapest (http://nektar.oszk.hu/en/manifestation/3044135); listed *Ungarns deutsche Bibliographie 1801-1860...* I: 1801-1830 p.390: adv. *Wiener Zeitung* 31 Oct.1835.

That this is a later edition of the same book is stated in Petrik: *Bibliographia Hungariae / Magyarország Bibliographiája 1712-1860,* III, 1891, p.127, which lists the 1830 Pest edition then this as "Ujabb kiadása ezen cím alatt" (*New edition under the following title* [*Bosco's enthülltes...*])

Both editions are listed in Weller: *Index Pseudonymorum* (*Maskirte Lit., 1*, 1856) p.230 under 'Nichtenthüllte Pseudonymen".

===

Hermann Kothe, 1822-1859
Bosco, Teufeleien des neunzehnten Jahrhunderts, 1844-45.
A collection of Bosco anecdotes, not tricks: discussed in *Fiction:* F14.

=====

LGe151

Carl Friedr. Leischner [*then* Carl Ferdinand Leischner in *3rd & later eds.*]
   Possibly Carl Friedrich Ferdinand Leischner, baptised Dresden 24 May 1789.
1st ed., 1831
[*Fraktur*] Die | Zauberkunst | aller Zeiten und Nationen, | namentlich des | ägyptischen Alterthums und des neun- | zehnten Jahrhunderts. | [*short rule*] | Enthaltend die enthüllten Geheimnisse der ägyptischen | Wahrsager, der Orakel, der Bauchrednerei, der Te- | legraphie, der Cartomancie in 280 ausgewählt schö- | nen, belustigenden und belehrenden Kunststücken aus | der Physik, Chemie, Optik, Mechanik, Mathematik, | Arithmetik und Experimentirkunst | nach | Philadelphia, Bosco, Petorelli, | Comte und Anderen | von Carl Friedr. Leischner. | [*publisher's device*] | Mit einem Titelkupfer und 88 Abbildungen. [*swelled rule*] | Ilmenau, 1831. | Druck, Verlag und Lithographie von B. F. Voigt.
   Frontis. [i-iv] v-viii [ix] x-xx [1] 2-...-266 [2 pp ads]; 15cm.
   Held by Ohio State University; Koninklijke Bibliotheek, Den Haag; Bayerische Staatsbibliothek
   Online at url:264.

LGe152
2nd ed., 1833
[*Fraktur*] Die | Zauberkunst | aller Zeiten und Nationen, | namentlich des | ägyptischen Alterthums und des neun- | zehnten Jahrhunderts. | [*swelled rule*] | Enthaltend die enthüllten Geheimnisse der ägyptischen | Wahrsager, der Orakel, der Bauchrednerei, der Te- | legraphie, der Cartomancie in 280 ausgewählt schö- | nen, belustigenden und belehrenden Kunststücken aus | der Physik, Chemie, Optik, Mechanik, Mathematik, | Arithmetik und Experimentirkunst | nach | Philadelphia, Bosco, Petorelli, | Comte und Anderen | von Carl Friedr. Leischner. | [*publisher's device*] | Zweite unveränderte Auflage. | [*rule*] | Mit einem Titelkupfer und 88 Abbildungen. [*swelled rule*] | Ilmenau, 1833. | Druck, Verlag und Lithographie von B. F. Voigt.
   Title transcribed from photo of copy online at https://www.ebay.de
   xx,266,[2]pp.,[1], 3 leaves of plates (3 folded); 16 cm (12mo).
   Held Brown UL

LGe153
3rd ed., 1834
[*Fraktur*] Die | Zauberkunst | aller Zeiten und Nationen, | namentlich des | ägyptischen Alterthums und des neun- | zehnten Jahrhunderts. | [*swelled rule*] | Enthaltend die enthüllten Geheimnisse der ägyptischen | Wahrsager, der Orakel, der Bauchrednerei, der Te- | legraphie, der Cartomancie in 280 ausgewählt schö- | nen, belustigenden und belehrenden Kunststücken aus | der Physik, Chemie, Optik, Mechanik, Mathematik, | Arithmetik und Experimentirkunst | nach | Philadelphia, Bosco, Petorelli, | Comte und Anderen | von Carl Ferdinand Leischner. | [*publisher's device*] | Dritte sehr verbesserte und mit Kunststücken | vemehrte Auflage | [*rule*] | Mit einem Titelkupfer und 111 Abbildungen. [*swelled rule*] | Ilmenau, 1834. | Druck, Verlag und Lithographie von B. F. Voigt.

xxiv,298pp.; 12mo.

Held Staatliche Museen zu Berlin; Bayerische Staatsbibliothek; Staats- und Stadtbibliothek Augsburg; Universitätsbibliothek Würzburg; Herzogin Anna Amalia Bibliothek (incomplete copy); adv. *Allgemeine Zeitung* 12 Dec.1834.

Online at url:264.

LGe154
4th ed., 1838

...Leischner. | [*publisher's device*] | Vierte sehr verbesserte und mit Kunststücken | vemehrte Auflage | [*rule*] | Mit einem Titelkupfer und 111 Abbildungen. | [*swelled rule*] | Weimar, 1838. | Druck, Verlag und Lithographie von B. F. Voigt.

Title transcribed from photo of copy for sale by Quicker than the Eye (Chicago)
[3], vi-xxiv,297pp., front., diagrs., 4 fold. pl. 15 cm.

Held NYPL; LC (Houdini Collection); adv. *Herzogl.-Sachsen-Coburgisches Regierungs- und Intelligenzblatt* 3 Feb.1838

LGe155
5th ed., 1840

[...] ägyptischen | Wahrsager, der Orakel, der Bauchrednerei, der Tele- | graphie, der Cartomancie in 280 ausgewählt schönen, | belustigenden und belehrenden Kunststücken aus der Phy- | sik, Chemie, Optik, Mechanik, Mathematik, Arith- | metik und Experimentirkunst | nach | Philadelphia, Bosco, Petorelli, Comte | und Anderen | von Carl Ferdinand Leischner. | [*short rule*] | Fünfte unveränderte Auflage. | [*rule*] | Mit einem Titelkupfer und 111 Abbildungen. | [*swelled rule*] | Weimar, 1840. | Druck, Verlag und Lithographie von B. F. Voigt.

Title transcribed from photo of copy on sale by Antiquariat J.J. Heckenhauer
xxiv,297pp., [5] leaves of plates (4 folded); 15cm.

Held LC (Houdini Coll.); adv. *Zeitung für die elegante Welt* 23 Nov.1839

LGe156
6th ed., 1843

C. F. Leischner's natürliche Zauberkunst aller Zeiten und Nationen in einer Vollständigen Sammlung der schönsten, ... Kunststücke aus der Physik, Chemie, Optik, Mechanik, Mathematik, Arithmetik und Experimentirkunst ... / auf's neue durchges. und verb. von Ign. Bernh. Montag.

6., sehr verm. und verb. Aufl. Weimar: Voigt, 1843. xxiv,264pp.

Held Stadtbibliothek Mainz (alas "Vermisst"); listed Hinrich's *Allgemeine Bibliographie für Deutschland* Aug.1843 p.238; adv. *Bayreuther Zeitung* 2 Dec.1843; *Münchener Tagblatt* 10 Dec.1843, stating that editions 1 to 5 comprised 10,000 copies.

LGe157
7th ed., 1851
C. F. Leischner's natürliche Zauberkunst aller Zeiten und Nationen in einer vollständigen Sammlung der überraschendsten, bewunderungswürdigsten und belehrendsten Kunststücke aus der Physik, Chemie, Optik, Mechanik, Mathematik und Experimentierkunst nach Philadelphia, Bosco, Petorelli, Comte, Döbler, Becker und anderen / auf's neue durchges. u. verb. von Ign. Bernh. Montag.

7., sehr verb. u. mit einer Rechnenmaschine verm. Aufl. Weimar: B. F. Voigt, 1851. 266pp.

Held Finnish National Library; adv. *Wiener Zeitung* 20 Dec.1850

LGe158
8th ed., 1851
[*Fraktur*] C. F. Leischner's | natürliche | Zauberkunst | aller Zeiten und Nationen; | in einer vollständigen | Sammlung | der schönsten, überraschendsten, bewunderungswürdigsten | und belehrendsten Kunststücke, aus der Physik, Ch- | emie, Optik, Mechanik, Mathematik, Arith- | metik und Experimentierkunst, | nach | Philadelphia, Bosco, Petorelli, Comte, | Döbler, Becker und Anderen. [*short rule*] | Auf's Neue durchgesehen und verbessert | von | Ign. Bernh. Montag. [*short rule*] | Achte, sehr verbesserte mit einer Rechnenmaschine ver- | mehrte Auflage, | [*rule*] | Mit einem Titelkupfer und vielen Abbildungen. | [*fancy swelled rule*] | Weimar, 1851. | Verlag, Druck und Lithographie von B. F. Voigt.

Title transcribed from photo of copy for sale by Antiquariat.Wien.
xxvi,266pp.

Held SLUB (Sächsische Landesbibliothek); Universiteit Maastricht; listed *Börsenblatt für den deutschen Buchhandel* Sep.1851; adv. *Fremden-Blatt* 31 Dec.1851, stating that the first seven editions comprised 14,000 copies.

LGe159
9th ed., 1861
Die natürliche Zauberkunst aller Zeiten und Nationen: ... Kunststücke aus der Physik, Chemie, Optik, Mechanik ... nach Philadelphia, Bosco, Petorelli und Anderen / von C. F. Leischner.

9., sehr verb. u. verm Aufl. Weimar: Voigt, 1861. xxx,271pp., frontispiece and 63 ills on 8 plates.

Held Universitätsbibliothek Johann Christian Senckenberg, Frankfurt a.M.; adv. *Neueste Nachrichten aus dem Gebiete der Politik* 29 Nov.1861.

LGe160
10th ed., 1872
Die natürliche Zauberkunst aller Zeiten und Nationen: in einer vollständigen Sammlung der überraschendsten, bewunderungswürdigsten und belehrendsten Kunststücke aus der Physik, Chemie, Optik, Mechanik, Mathematik, Arithmetik und Experimentirkunst, nach Philadelphia, Bosco, Petorelli, Comte, Döbler, Becker und Anderen.

Weimar: Bernhard Friedrich Voigt, 1872. xvi,219pp., 19cm.
xvi,219pp.; ill.; 19 cm.
Held Hungarian NL; LC (Houdini Coll.) stating: "A reorganized selection from Zauberkunst aller Zeiten und Nationen, omitting material on occult phenomena"; listed *Börsenblatt für den deutschen Buchhandel* 7 Dec.1871; 29 Apr.1872.

LGe161
11th ed., 1886
Die natürliche Zauberkunst aller Zeiten und Nationen; in einer vollständigen Sammlung der überraschendsten, bewunderungswürdigsten und belehrendsten Kunststücke, aus der Physik, Chemie, Optik, Mechanik, Mathematik und Experimentierkunst nach Philadelphia, Bosco, Petorelli, Comte, Döbler, Becker und Anderen.
11. Aufl. Weimar: B.F. Voigt, 1886. xvi,230,[2] pp; 19cm; "Mit 63 in den Text eingedruckten Abbildungen"; issued in blue illustrated wrappers.
Held Brown UL; LC (Houdini Coll.); NYPL; ULSH.

===

LGe162
Paulo Malachini
Boscos Zauberkünste: eine Auswahl seiner besten Kunststücke.
Dresden: M. Fischers Verlagsbuchh. [192-?]. 124,[4]pp.; 18 cm.
Held Brown UL.

===

LGe163
Paulo Malachini
Der kleine Bosco: allerlei Zaubereien / von Paulo Malachini.
Dresden: M. Fischers Verlagsbuchh. [192-?]. 29,[2]pp; 18cm.
Held Brown UL; ULSH
Both these titles are listed in *Börsenblatt für den deutschen Buchhandel* 3 Mar. 1920, the former in series 'Große Volksbücher' (Mk.2,50), the latter in 'Kleine Volksbücher' (75 Pf.); by 4 Jan.1921 inflation had driven the prices up to Mk.4 and Mk.1.

====

J.A. Philadelph-nein [*pseud. of* Peter Friedrich Ludwig Hoffmann]
An advertisement by the publisher Berendsohn (quoted in the entry for *Der Zauberstab. Das Neueste der Tachenspielerkunst* (see LGe147) states that *Bosco in der Westentasche* was written by Hoffmann. The pseudonym is of course a play on Jakob Philadelph*ja*.

LGe164
[1st ed.] 1845?
Bosco in der Westentasche. Hamburg: Berendsohn [1845?]

Listed [as *Bosco*...] *Börsenblatt für den deutschen Buchhandel* 5 Sep.1845; [as *Bosko*...] *Intelligenz-Blatt zur Allgemeine Literatur-Zeitung* Oct.1845; [as *Bosco*...] GV XIX p.34 ("1.—3. Aufl." 1846); *Allgemeine Bibliographie für Deutschland*: Nr.5, 29 Jan.1846 p.24; adv. [as *Bosco*...] *Neue Würzburger Zeitung* and *Augsburger Postzeitung* 7 Oct.1845.

LGe165
[2nd ed.] 1846
Bosco in der Westentasche. Herausgegeben von Philadelph-nein.
   2. Aufl. Hamburg: Berendsohn. 1846. xii,112pp.
   Listed *Leipziger Repertorium der deutschen und ausländischen Literatur* Vol.15, 1846

LGe166
[3rd ed.] 1846
Bosco in der Westentasche, oder die entdeckten Geheimnisse aller Magier, Zauberer und Hexenmeister/ Enthaltend 200 der überraschendsten Kunststücke, welche sämmtlich von Dilettanten ohne Instrumente ausgeführt werden können. Herausgegeben von J.A. Philadelph-nein.
   3e Aufl. Hamburg: Berendsohn, 1846. 128pp. [title probably has 'Dillettanten' as in later editions].
   Listed *Börsenblatt für den Deutschen Buchhandel* 8 Sep.; 27 Oct.1846; Hinrichsen's *Verzeichniß der Bücher... vom Juli bis December 1846...*;

LGe167
[4th ed.] 1848
[*Fraktur*] Bosco | in der | Westentasche | oder | die entdeckten Geheimnisse | aller | Magier, Zauberer u. Hexenmeister. | Enthaltend | 200 der überraschendsten Kunststücke | aus der Gebieten der | Taschenspielerei, der Magie, des | Magnetismus, der Optik, der Physik, | der Feuerwerkerei, Sympathie u.s.w. | welche | sämmtlich von Dillettanten | ohne Instrumente ausgeführt werden können. | Herausgegeben von | J. A. Philadelph-Nein. | 4te Auflage. | [*fancy rule*] | Hamburg, | B. S. Berendsohn. | 1848
   xii,112pp.
   Held BL; Universitätsbibliothek Mozarteum Salzburg; adv. *KPBZ* 12 Jan.1848; GV XIX p.34 lists "4.—8. Auflage" 1848-51.
   Online at url:265.

LGe168
[5th ed.]
   "5. Auflage" listed *Allgemeines Verzeichniß der Bücher ... Michaelis 1848 bis Ostern 1849* p.34; adv. *Nürnberger Kurier* 13 Dec.1850 (stating 6000 copies of this edition).

LGe169
[6th ed.] 1850
[*Fraktur*] Bosco | in der | Westentasche, | oder | die entdeckten Geheimnisse | aller | Magier, Zauberer und Hexenmeister. | Enthaltend | 200 der überraschendsten Kunststücke | aus dem Gebiete der | Taschenspielerei, der Magie, des | Magnetismus, der Optik, der Physik, | der Feuerwerkerei, Sympathie u.s.w. | welche | sämmtlich von Dillettanten | ohne Instrumente ausgeführt werden können. | Herausgegeben von | . A. Philadelph-nein. | Sechste Auflage. | [*double rule*] | Hamburg, | B. S. Berendsohn. | 1850
Title transcribed from photo of copy formerly for sale on ZVAB.
[4],xii,112pp.
Held Universitätsbibliothek Johann Christian Senckenberg, Frankfurt a.M; listed *Börsenblatt für den deutschen Buchhandel* 7 June 1850; adv. *Aschaffenburger Zeitung* 5 Mar.1850.

LGe170
[7th ed.] 1850?
"7te Aufl." adv. *Tag-Blatt der Stadt Bamberg* 30 Dec.1850.

LGe171
[8th ed.] 1851
Bosco in der Westentasche, oder, Die entdeckten Geheimnisse aller Magier, Zauberer u. Hexenmeister enthaltend 200 der überraschendsten Kunststucke aus den Gebieten der Taschenspielerei, der Magie, des Magnetismus, der Optik, der Physik, der Feuerwerkerei, Sympathie u.s.w., welche sämmtlich von Dillettanten ohne Instrumente ausgeführt werden können
8. Auflage. Hamburg: B.G. Berendsohn, 1851. 110pp.
Held Zentralbibliothek Zürich; GV XIX p.34 lists "4.—8. Auflage" 1848-51,

LGe172
[9th ed.] 1852
Listed GV XIX p.34 (xvi,112pp.), 1852; *Börsenblatt für den deutschen Buchhandel* 22 June 1852.

LGe173
[10th ed.] 1853
Listed *Börsenblatt für den deutschen Buchhandel* 15 Apr.1853; GV XIX p.34 ("9.—10. Aufl., 1852-53", and "10.—16. Aufl., 1853-58").

LGe174
[11th ed.] 1854?
"11. Aufl.", adv. *Regensburger Tagblatt* 13 Aug.1854.

LGe175
[12th ed.] 1855
Listed *Börsenblatt für den deutschen Buchhandel* 1 Dec.1854; GV XIX p.34.

LGe176
[13th ed.] 1856
Bosco in der Westentasche, oder Die entdeckten Geheimnisse aller Magier, Zauberer u. Hexenmeister ... / hrsg. J. A. Philadelphenein [*sic?*]
    13. Aufl. Hamburg: Berendsohn, 1856. xii,112pp.; 10cm.
    Held Hungarian NL; listed GV XIX p.34

LGe177
[14th ed.] 1857
Bosco in der Westentasche oder Die entdeckten Geheimnisse aller Magier, Zauberer u. Hexenmeister: enthaltend 200 der überraschendsten Kunststücke aus den Gebieten der Taschenspielerei, der Magie, des Magnetismus, der Optik, der Physik, der Feuerwerkerei, Sympathie u.s.w.; welche sämmtlich von Dillettanten ohne Instrumente ausgeführt werden können.
    14. Aufl. Hamburg: Berendsohn, 1857. xvi,112pp.; 8vo.
    Held Universitäts- und Landesbibliothek Düsseldorf; adv. *Bohemia* 12 May 1857; *Eestimaa Kubermangu Teataja* 21 Oct.1857.

LGe178
[15th ed.] 1858?
    "15. Aufl.", adv. *Magdeburgische Zeitung* 9 Dec.1858; *Der Liberale Alpenbote* 11 Nov.1859.

LGe179
[16th ed.] 1858
    Listed *Börsenblatt für den deutschen Buchhandel* 29 Oct.1858; GV XIX p.34 ("10.—16. Aufl.", 1853-58.

LGe180
[17th ed.] 1859
    Listed GV XIX p.34 ("17.—25. Aufl., 1859-64").

LGe181
[18th ed.] 1860
Bosco in der Westentasche oder die entdeckten Geheimnisse aller Magier, Zauberer u. Hexenmeister: enthaltend: 200 der überraschendsten Kunststücke aus den Gebieten der Taschenspielerei, der Magie, des Magnetismus ... welche sämmtlich von Dilettanten ohne Instrumente ausgeführt werden können / hrsg. von J. A. Philadelphnein
    18. Aufl. Hamburg: Berendsohn, 1860. xvi,91pp.; 8vo
    Held Staats- und Universitätsbibliothek Hamburg Carl von Ossietzky

LGe182
[21st ed.] 1862
    Listed GV XIX p.34 ("21.—31.Aufl." 1862-66).

LGe183
[29th ed.] 1866
  "29. Auflage" listed *Börsenblatt für den deutschen Buchhandel* 20 Nov.1865; GV XIX p.34 ("29.—35. Aufl., 1866-68"; adv. *Kurier für Niederbayern* 5 Nov.1865.

LGe184
[30th ed.] 1866
Bosco in der Westentasche oder die entdeckten Geheimnisse aller Magier, Zauberer u. Hexenmeister: enthaltend: 200 der überraschendsten Kunststücke aus den Gebieten der Taschenspielerei, der Magie, des Magnetismus ... welche sämmtlich von Dilettanten ohne Instrumente ausgeführt werden können / hrsg. von J. A. Philadelph-nein
  30. Aufl. Hamburg: Berendsohn, 1866. xvi,91pp.
  Held Herzogin Anna Amalia Bibliothek / Klassik Stiftung Weimar

LGe185
[31st ed.] 1866
  "31. Aufl." listed *Börsenblatt für den deutschen Buchhandel* 1 & 12 Oct.1866.

LGe186
[32nd ed.] 1867
  Listed GV XIX p.34 ("32.—40. Aufl. 1867-70").

LGe187
[34th ed.] 1868
Bosco in der Westentasche oder die entdeckten Geheimnisse aller Magier, Zauberer u. Hexenmeister: enthaltend: 200 der überraschendsten Kunststücke aus den Gebieten der Taschenspielerei, der Magie, des Magnetismus ... welche sämmtlich von Dilettanten ohne Instrumente ausgeführt werden können...
  34e Aufl, Hamburg: Berendsohn, 1868. xvi,91pp.; 11cm.
  Held Bibliotheek Universiteit van Amsterdam

LGe188
[35th ed.] 1868
  "35. Aufl." adv. *Neues bayerisches Volksblatt* 12 Nov.1868.

LGe189
[36th ed.] 1868?
  "36. Aufl." listed *Börsenblatt für den deutschen Buchhandel* 12 Oct.1868.

LGe190
[40th ed.] 1870
  "40. Aufl." listed *Börsenblatt für den deutschen Buchhandel* 20 Dec.1870.

LGe191
[41st ed.] 1871
  Listed GV XIX p.34 ("41.—45. Aufl., 1871-82").

LGe192
[45th ed.] 1882
　　　Listed GV XIX p.34 ("41.—45. Aufl., 1871-82").

　　The book's title became a favourite catchphrase for jokes.
　　Figaro 8 May 1858 announced "[tr.] a counterpiece to the old favourite *Bosco in der Westentasche,* a handbook of black magic to be called 'Hofzinser in der Geldtasche' with tricks for turning coin into paper notes and share certificates, etc., etc.

　　The Munich humorous paper *Miau* (20 Nov.1867) listed some new tricks in *Bosco in der Westentasche,* "ein unentbehrliches zeitgemäßes Handbuch für Taschenspieler": allusions to the contemporary theatre — such as
Die Kunst aus der Haut zu fahren—
Man höre Fräulein Bayer als Operettensänger
Die Kunst Jemandem der Sprache zu berauben—
Man lasse ihn im Aktientheater das Ausstattungsstück 'Der artesische Brunnen' sehen [*etc.*]

　　In 1873 in Troppau (now Opava) in Silesia the *Kaiserliche Königliche Schlesische Troppauer-Zeitung* complaining (7 Apr.1873) of a poor magic show by a visiting "Professor" doing worn-out tricks said: we could have learnt them ourselves from the little 30 kreuzer book *Bosco in der Westentasche.*

　　Wiener Allgemeine Zeitung 27 Feb.1886 quoted a skit from the *Berliner Vespen* on a new edition of *Bosco in der Westentasche* called 'How to Make Policemen Disappear' — best done in London in Trafalgar Square when a mob starts making trouble... To conjure the policemen back again simply disperse the crowd...

　　A novel by Leo Norberg, *Der Falsche Tod: Roman aus dem Wiener Leben,* serialised in *Neues Wiener Tagblatt* has (instalment in issue of 19 Sep.1889) two people hiding a man under a blanket, "ganz Bosco in der Westentasche, wenn er seine Verschwindungskünste spielen läßt".

===

LGe193
L. Schellenberg jun.
[*Fraktur*] Ein Blick | in | Döbler's und Bosko's | Zauberkabinet, | bestehend | in neuen Belustigungen aus dem Gebiete | der natürlichen Magie, | im gesellschaftlichen Leben anwendbar. | Herausgegeben | von | L. Schellenberg jun. | [*double rule*] | Wiesbaden, | bei L. Schellenberg, Hofbuchhändler und Hofbuchdrucker, | 1832.
　　　viii,200pp., 3 folding plates; 17cm
　　'Vorwort' signed by the editor, Wiesbaden, May 1832, hopes "... dem Leser Gelegenheit gegeben zu haben, seinen Freunden in langen Winterabenden einige vergnügte Stunden verschaffen zu können".
　　　Held BL; Brown UL; NYPL; Université de Strasbourg; listed Hinrichs' *Verzeichniss der Bücher* Jan-June 1832 p.200; Heinsius *Allgemeines Bücher-Lexikon* 1828-34;

adv. *Morgenblatt für gebildete Stände* 21 Oct.1833; reviewed *Ergänzungsblätter zur Jenaische Allgemeine Literatur-Zeitung* 48 (1833).
    Online (BL copy) at url:266.

The printer and publisher was Ernst Ludwig (Louis) Theodor Schellenberg, 1772-1834; the book is said to have been written by Döbler. I have not seen the 2001 reprint with afterword and commentary:
LGe193a
"Fotomechanischer Nachdr. eines Ex. der Sammlung Volker Huber, Schellenberg, 1832 / mit einem Nachw. von Volker Huber zur Entstehungsgeschichte des Buches und mit einem Kommentar von Reinhard Müller zu den darin beschriebenen Kartenkunststücken."
    Offenbach am Main: Ed. Huber, 2001. viii, 223pp., 17cm; 3921785839.

===

LGe194
Carlo Zenetti
    The book does not mention Bosco in the title or text but Zenetti (C54) declares himself on the title-page "pupil of the great Bosco" (Schüler des großen Bosco),

[2nd ed.] 1861
Das Zauber-Theater, oder, Das Ganze der Taschenspielerkunst: eine reichhaltige Sammlung der neuersten, interessantesten und leicht ausführbaren Kunststücke mit Karten, Zahlen, Würfeln, Münzen u. derg*l*.
    "2. Aufl." adv. *Würzburger Anzeiger* 9 Mar.1861. No copy traced of this or 1st ed.

LGe195
[6th ed.]
    6. Aufl. Mülheim an der Ruhr: Reymann [no date]. 112pp. ill. 18 cm.
    Held Biblioteca civica di Arco (dating "1800?"); listed *Bibliographisches Jahrbuch für den deutschen Buch-, Kunst- und Landkarten-Handel* Vol.8, 1860; rev. *Klagenfurter Zeitung* 30 July1860.

Hungarian

LHu1
Takarki
Varázslatok, vagy Bosco, Philadelphia, Petorelli, Comte és mások jelesebb szemfényvesztési darabjai / kiad.: Takarki
    Kassa: Literaturai Int., 1835. xii,79pp., 14cm.
    Held Hungarian NL; listed *Tudománytár, közre bocsátja a Magyar tudós társaság* X, 1836 p.204.

===

LHu2
Takarki
A bűbájos ezermester
First edition not traced.

LHu3
2nd ed.
Takarki
A bűbájos ezermester: varázslatok vagy Bosco, Philadelphia, Petorelli, Comte és mások jelesebb szemfényvesztési darabjai 143 mutatványban / kiadta Takarki
    2. bőv. kiad. Kassán: Werfer Ny.c1836. 119pp., 15cm.
    Held Hungarian NL.

===

LHu4
Mester Pál
Bosco a bűvész és ezermester: a legújabb, legérdekesebb, mulattató és meglepő, seged- , és drága műszerek nélkül, könnyen keresztülvihető mindenféle ezermesterségeknek gyűjteménye a családi kör, vidám társaságok számára és önmüvelésre a legjobb kútfők után összeállitotta mester Pál
    Budapest: Révai [1876] (Budapest: Pallas ny.)
    128pp., 15cm.
    Held Hungarian NL; LC (Houdini Coll.); listed *Oesterreichische Buchhändler-Correspondenz* 21 Oct.1876.

===

LHu5
Garbai Miklós
Bosko a bűvészmester / [összeálll. Garbai Miklós]
    Budapest: Bíró [ca.1890] (Budapest: Neuwald Ny.)
    [16]pp., 19cm.
    Held Hungarian NL.

===

LHu6
Garbai Miklós
Boskó a veres ördög
First edition not traced

LHu7
2nd ed.
Boskó a veres ördög: a legújabb ... bűvészeti darabok gyűjteménye: magánoktatásra, valamint társaskörök mulatatására...
    2. jav. és [bőv.] kiad. Kassa: Werfer, 1873. 162,xi pp., 14cm.

Held Hungarian NL; listed *Oesterreichische Buchhändler-Correspondenz* 3 July 1875.

Probably a translation of *Der rothe Teufel im Salon*.

===

LHu8
Bosko bűvészkönyve: meglepő bűvészmutatványok, melyek segédeszközök nélkül előadhatók
    Budapest: Magyar Kiadó [1919] (Budapest: Muskát [Ny.]). 64pp., 15cm.
    Held Hungarian NL.

===

LHu9
Ezermester: bűvészeti szemfényvesztési-. spiritistikai-, és physikai mutatványok vezérfonala / Bosco
    Budapest: Vass, 1898 (Budapest: Markovits és Garai Ny.). 65pp., 14cm.
    Held Hungarian NL.

Italian

LIt1
Curiose Avventure e Brevi Cenni sulla vita di Bartolomeo Bosco da Turino esimio prestigiatore ed inventore della magia egiziana, con un compendio nominativo di dilettevoli giochi di fisica e di meccanica da lui ritrovati.
    Napoli: Dalla Stamperia e Cartiera del Fibreno, 1837. 58,[2]pp., 21cm.
    Held OPAC SBN (5 copies); BL; listed *Bibliografia italiana* March 1838 p.67.
    Online at url:268
    Biographical anecdotes of the life of Bartolomeo by an anonymous compiler who must have had access to his album.

LIt2
Reprinted 2020 (9781716872983) with afterword ('L'importanza delle *Curiose avventure*') by Alex Rusconi.

===

LIt3
Il Cavalier Bosco Giuocatore di Magia ovvero, Manuale dei Giuochi di Carte, di Prestigio e di Destrezza.
    Firenze: A. Salani [1875?]. 111pp., 15cm
    Held OPAC SBN (2 copies).
    This is probably the edition dated 1875 in Ada Gigli Marchetti, *Libri buoni e a buon prezzo. Le edizioni Salani (1862-1986)* 286 ("112pp.").

LIt4
Il Cavalier Bosco Giuocatore di Magia ovvero Manuale dei Giuochi di Carte, di Prestigio e di Destrezza.
    Firenze: A. Salani , 1877. 160pp.
    Listed Marchetti, *Libri buoni e a buon prezzo* 501.

LIt5
"3rd edition"
Il Cavaliere Bosco Giuocator di Magia, ovvero Manuale di Giuochi di Prestigio e di Destrezza i più piacevoli ed i più sorprendenti messi alla portata di tutti, da eseguirsi nelle riunioni colla massima facilità.
    Cover-title: Cav. Bosco. Giuocatore di Magia. Manuale di giuochi di prestigio e di destrezza.
    "Terza edizione illustrata". Napoli: Gennaro Monte, 1913. [1-5],6-96pp.
    Held OPAC SBN (1 copy); Brown UL. Online at url:269.

LIt6
It is uncertain if these titles are related to the above and if they refer to Bosco at all
Il nuovo giuocatore di magia, ovvero, Manuale dei giuochi di prestigio e di destrezza: i più piacevoli ed i più sorprendenti, messi alla portata di tutti ...
    Milano: Barbini, 1870. 143pp., 16cm
    Held OPAC SBN (1 copy)

LIt7
Il Nuovo giuocatore di magia: ovvero, Manuale di giuochi di prestigio e di destrezza ...
    Milano: C. Cioffi, 1885.
    Held LC ("4th ed.")

LIt8
Il giuocatore di magia; ovvero, Manuale dei giuochi di prestigio e di destrezza i più piacevoli ... messi alla portata di tutti.
    Author given as "Illensub Oirelay".
    Napoli: G. Regina, 1880. 119pp., 17cm.
    Held NYPL

===

LIt9
Gabinetto magico ossia Il complesso dell'arte di prestigio: contenente 110 giuochi sorprendenti di magia naturale ... / del cavaliere Bartolomeo Bosco; prima traduzione italiana per cura del professor Franc. Ant. Rosental dietro la sesta edizione tedesca ...
    Milano: Tipografia e libreria di Gio. Silvestri, 1853. viii,318pp., 17cm.
    Held OPAC SBN: 1 copy). Photo of title-page, cover and frontis online at url:270.

LIt10
2nd ed., 1854
Gabinetto magico del cavaliere Bartolomeo Bosco, ossia Il complesso dell'arte di prestigio: contenente 110 giuochi sorprendenti di magia naturale ... / traduzione del professore Francesco Ant. Rosental dietro la sesta edizione tedesca, ...
   Seconda edizione. Milano: Tipografia e Libreria di Gio. Silvestri, 1854. viii, 336pp., 17cm.
   Held OPAC SBN (3 copies listed with above pagination; 2 copies listed as viii,348,[2]pp., 17cm.
   Photo of title-page and frontis online at url:271.

LIt11
3rd ed., 1857
Gabinetto Magico del Cavaliere Bartolomeo Bosco, ossia, Il complesso dell'arte di prestigio: contenente 110 giuochi sorprendenti di magia naturale, con carte, dadi, palle, monete, anelli ecc.: non che 19 altri giuochi di carte, e 68 interessantissimi giuochi aritmetici adattati per l'ameno ed istruttivo trattenimento delle brigate / traduzione del Prof. F.A. Rosental.
   Terza edizione. Milano: Ditta Giovanni Silvestri, 1857. (Series: Biblioteca di famiglia e di conversazione, ossia, Raccolta di opere utili e dilettevoli per ogni classe di persone v.5). viii,316pp., 18cm.
   "Traduzione del prof. F. A. Rosental dietro la 6. ed. tedesca, assai corretta, aumentata ed adorna di 24 figure e del ritratto dell'A."
   Held LC (Houdini Coll.); Biblioteca Vigilianum (Trento); Austrian National Library.
   Online at url:272.

LIt12
4th ed., 1862
Gabinetto magico ... ossia Il complesso dell'arte di prestigio ...
   Quarta edizione. Milano: G. Silvestri, 1862. [1],vi-viii,248pp., 17cm.
   Held BL; NYPL; Biblioteca Mago Sales
   Online at url:273.

LIt13
5th ed., 1864
Gabinetto magico ... ossia Il complesso dell'arte di prestigio ...
   Quinta edizione. Milano: Agenzia Giornalistica Savallo, 1864
   Photo of cover and title-page online at url:274

LIt14
6th ed., 1868
Gabinetto magico: ossia l'arte del prestigiatore contenente 110 giuochi…
   6. ed. Milano: Giovanni Gussoni, 1868. 248pp., 15cm.
   Held OPAC SBN (1 copy)

LIt15
7th ed., 1871
Gabinetto magico del cavaliere Bartolomeo Bosco: ossia l'arte del prestigiatore contenente 110 giuochi sorprendenti di magia naturale con carte, dadi, palle, monete, anelli, ecc: ... e 68 interessantissimi giuochi aritmetici d'amena istruzione nei trattenimenti e nelle brigate.

    7a ed. Milano: Giovanni Gussoni Editore, 1871. viii,248pp., 16cm.
    Held Sistema Bibliotecario Ticinese, Lugano, Switzerland

LIt16
11th ed., 1879
Gabinetto magico ossia L'arte del prestigiatore contenente 110 giuochi ... / del cavaliere Bartolomeo Bosco.

    11a. ed. Milano: Tip. G. Gussoni editore, 1879. iv,250pp., 16cm.
iv,250pp., [3] leaves of plates: ill.; 16 cm.
    LC quotes pp.i-ii: "I suoi sorprendenti giuochi furono prima raccolti e pubblicati in un libro tedesco dell'illustre professore Krendörffer [!] ... noi ci affrettiamo di cercarne una corrispondente versione italiana dietro l'ultima edizione".
    Held OPAC SBN (1 copy); LC

LIt17
[new ed., 1887?]
Gabinetto magico del cavaliere Bartolomeo Bosco, ossia, L'arte del prestigiatore contenente 110 giochi sorprendenti di magia naturale con carte, dadi, palle, monete, anelli ...

    Milano: Gussoni [1887?]. 254pp., 16cm.
254pp.; 16cm
    Held Biblioteca Civica di Rovereto.

LIt18
A reprint edited by Alex Rusconi (9780244884383) was published in 2020.

===

LIt19
Libretto magico del cavalier Bosco: per imparare giuochi di carte di prestigio e destrezza di mano da eseguirsi nelle conversazioni.

    Firenze: Adriano Salani, 1901. 110pp.
    No copy traced; listed Ada Gigli Marchetti, *Libri buoni e a buon prezzo. Le edizioni Salani (1862-1986)* 2468.

LIt20
Libretto magico per imparare giochi di carte di prestigio e destrezza di mano: da eseguirsi nelle conversazioni / del cavalier Boschi.

    "Autore: Bartolomeo Bosco".
    Firenze: Tip. Salani [1908]. 23pp., 14cm.

Held OPAC SBN (1 copy: Biblioteca Statale - Lucca); also Vatican Library; listed Ada Gigli Marchetti, *Libri buoni e a buon prezzo. Le edizioni Salani (1862-1986)* 3034 dating this to 1908.

LIt21
Libretto magico del cavalier Bosco: per imparare giuochi di carte di prestigio e destrezza di mano da eseguirsi nelle conversazioni.
"Bartolomeo Bosco" on front cover.
Firenze: Adriano Salani, 1914. 110pp.
Held LC; NYPL (microfilm, but NUC has this as a real book); ULSH.

===

LIt22
Manuale de' giuochi destro-fisici del cav. Bosco, spiegati ad intelligenza d'ogni persona.
Palermo 1854.
Listed Alessio Narbone *Bibliografia sicola sistematica, o apparato metodico alla storia letteraria della Sicilia* vol.4 (1855) p.302. No copy traced.

===

LIt23
Il nuovo Bosco o esercizi di magia bianca: raccolta di giuochi di prestigio, di cartomanzia, numerici matematici e di destrezza... scelti tra quelli di Alberti, Delion, Philippe, Finetti e Bartolomeo Bosco.
2. ed. con incisioni. Milano: Paolo Carrara, 1878. 208pp., 15cm. (Series: Manuali Carrara 2).
Held OPAC SBN (1 copy)

===

LIt24
[*1st ed., 1861?*]
Il Nuovo Bosco, ossia il Diavolo Color di Rosa. Tesoro di Giuochi di Prestigio, Cartomanzia, Magia Bianca, di Compagnia, Conversazioni, Indovinelli, ecc. ecc. Con figure intercalate nel testo.
Listed *Österreichische Buchhändler-Correspondenz* 10 Nov.1861 (in "Fertige Bücher. Neuigkeiten"); this may be the next item listed prior to publication.

LIt25
[*2nd ed.?*] 1862
Il Nuovo Bosco, ossia il Diavolo Color di Rosa. Tesoro di Nuovi e Straordinari Giuochi di Prestigio, Cartomanzia, Magia Bianca, di Compagnia ... Opera che comprende ogni sorta imaginabile di giuochi da eseguirsi colla massima facilità da se soli. Coll'aggiunta delle meraviglie magiche / di B. Bosco.
Trieste: Colombo-Coen tipografo editore, 1862, vii,247pp., 15c.
Held OPAC SBN (1 copy); listed GV XIX p.33

LIt26
[*3rd ed.?*] 1863
Il Nuovo Bosco, ossia il Diavolo Color di Rosa. Tesoro di Nuovi e Straordinari Giuochi di Prestigio, Cartomanzia, Magia Bianca, di Compagnia, Conversazione, Indovinelli, ecc. ecc. Con figure intercalate nel testo. Opera che comprende ogni sorta imaginabile di giuochi da eseguirsi colla massima facilità da sè soli. Coll' aggiunta delle Mervaglie Magiche di B. Bosco.

    Trieste: Stabilimento Lib. Tip. Music e Belle Arti di Colombo Coen Edit., 1863.

    Orange wrappers with cover-title: Il Nuovo Bosco, ossia il Diavolo Color di Rosa. Tesoro di Nuovi e Straordinari Giuochi di Prestigio, Cartomanzia, Magia Bianca, di Compagnia, Conversazione, Indovinelli, ecc. ecc. Con figure intercalate nel testo.

    vii,239pp., frontisp., ills in text, 12mo.

    Copy sold at auction with photos of cover and title-page online at url:275.

    The book is mainly tricks but includes a biography (pp.167-77 in 1873 ed.), Bosco anecdotes (pp.185ff.); p.222 Bosco and Death [for which see *Fiction* F7]. The "title trick" is *come mutar colore ad una rosa,* p.112.

LIt27
[*New ed.?, 1868?*]
Il nuovo Bosco, ossia Il diavolo color di rosa: tesoro di nuovi e straordinari giuchi di prestigio, cartomanzia…

    Trieste: Colombo Coen.

    No copy traced; listed (with 255pp as in the 1870 edition) *Österreichische Buchhändler-Correspondenz* 20 Aug.1868; GV XIX p.33

LIt28
[*New ed.*] 1870
Il nuovo Bosco, ossia Il diavolo color di rosa: tesoro di nuovi e straordinari giuchi di prestigio, cartomanzia ... / di B. Bosco.

    Venezia; Milano; Trieste: C. Coen, 1870. 255pp., 17cm.

    Held OPAC SBN (2 copies); ULSH

LIt29
[*New ed.*] 1873
Il nuovo Bosco, ossia Il diavolo color di rosa: tesoro di nuovi e straordinari giuochi di prestigio, cartomanzia, magia bianca, di compagnia, conversazione, indovinelli ...: opera che comprende ogni sorte imaginabile di giuochi da eseguirsi colla massima facilità da sè soli, coll'aggiunta delle meraviglie magiche di B. Bosco.

    Venezia; Trieste: C. Coen, 1873. [1],239pp., 16cm (pp.214-216 misnumbered 114-116).

    Held OPAC SBN (4 copies); Brown UL.

    Online at url:276,

LIt30
[New ed.] 1894
Il nuovo Bosco; ossia, il diavolo color di rosa, tesoro di nuovi e straordinari giuochi di prestigio ... opera que comprende egal sorte imaginabile di giuochi da eseguirsi cella massima facilità da sè soli coll'aggiunta della meraviglie magiche di B. Bosco.
    Milano: Guigoni, 1894. 234pp.
    Formerly held by NYPL (NUC NB0662682)

LIt31
[later editions published by Bietti]
Il nuovo Bosco ossia il diavolo color di rosa: tesoro di nuovi e straordinari giuochi di prestigio cartomanzia - magia bianca - di compagnia conversazione - indovinelli - ecc. Con figure intercalate nel testo: opera che comprende ogni sorte imaginabile di giuochi da eseguirsi colla massima facilità da sè soli: coll'aggiunta delle Meraviglie magiche di D. [*sic*] Bosco
    Milano: Casa Editrice Bietti [no date]. 224pp., 19cm.
    Held OPAC SBN (3 copies); ULSH; Brown UL

LIt32
[new edition] 1947
Il nuovo Bosco, ossia Il diavolo color di rosa: tesoro di nuovi e straordinari giuochi di prestigio, cartomanzia, magia bianca, di compagnia, conversazione, indovinelli ... : opera che comprende ogni sorte imaginabile di giuochi da eseguirsi colla massima facilità da sè soli, coll'aggiunta delle meraviglie magiche di D. [*sic*] Bosco.
    Milano: Bietti, 1947. 232pp., 19cm.
    Held OPAC SBN (1 copy)

LIt33-38
Biblioteca Mago Sales lists editions dated 1928, 1947, 1954, 1959, 1964, 1965

===

LIt39
Il Piccolo Bosco, o Esercizi di Magia Bianca – raccolta di giuochi di prestigio e di destrezza i più piacevoli e più sorprendenti.
    Livorno: Giovanni Battista Rossi, 1863.
    No copy traced, but according to 'Tracce di Storia dall'Archivio' (online at url:277) a copy is held at Archivio storico del Comune di Novellara.

LIt40
2nd ed., 1864?

    Milano: tip. Guigoni. 288pp., 32mo. (Series: Biblioteca Enciclopedica Populare).
    No copy listed OPAC SBN; held by Biblioteca Mago Sales; listed *Annuario bibliografico italiano* 1864 (Torino, 1865), p.134

===

LIt41

Il Saputello in Conversazione, ovvero Giuochi Onesti per la Gioventù ed Il Mago Senza Magia.

Earlier editions (1828 onwards) as *Giuochi Onesti per la Gioventù, ovvero Il saputello in conversazione* did not include the reference to Bosco.

Caveat lector: a note in *Allgemeine Zeitung* Beilage 20 Apr.1854 states that the 1837 edition was placed on the *Index Librorum Prohibitorum* on April 13th 1854.

LIt42
5th ed., 1852
Il Saputello in Conversazione, ovvero Giuochi Onesti per la Gioventù ed Il Mago Senza Magia.

Quinta Edizione. Livorno: Tip. Egisto Vignozzi e C.º, 1852.

Cover-title: Il Saputello in Conversazione e Il Mago senza Magia. Giuochi Onesti per la Giovenù. Quinta Edizione Arricchita dei Giuochi Destro-Fisici del Cav. Bosco. Livorno: Tip. Egisto Vignozzi e C.º, 1853.

[*title-page dated 1852; cover and 'Parte Seconda' dated 1853*]

Held Pontificia Universita Gregoriana (Rome); probably also Biblioteca Comunale di Mantova.

Photos of cover, title-page etc at url:278.

LIt43
6th ed., 1857
Il saputello in conversazione ovvero giuochi onesti per la gioventù ed il mago senza magia.

Sesta edizione. Livorno: tip. Egisto Vignozzi e co. 1857. 408pp, 4.5cm. Blue wrappers.

Information from copy formerly for sale on *www.ebay.it* (with photo of cover).

LIt44-47

A book titled *Il saputello in conversazione ovvero giuochi di sala e passatempi curiosi* was published in several editions by Adriano Salani:
1880 ("Edizione illustrata", 352pp.); 1883; 1889; 1898 (287pp.).
It is uncertain if this was related or has Bosco references.

===

LIt48
Satana. Raccolta Europea: Passatempo dell'intermezzo nelle sedute di magia egiziana / del Cavaliere Bartolomeo Bosco di Torino; libera versione dal francese per cura del Professore F.A. Rosental.

Milano: tipografia e libreria di Gio. Silvestri, 1853. 93,[1]pp., 17cm. Frontispiece of Bosco; advertisement for *Gabinetto Magico* on back cover.

Held OPAC SBN (4 copies); listed in NUC as held by NYPL but not in current catalogue.

LIt49
A copy of *Satana. Raccolta Europea* was auctioned in 2021, catalogued as 1855.
Photo of cover (undated) online at url:279.

LIt50
Satana. Raccolta Universale, Biografica, Aneddotica delle avventure di Bosco da Torino Professore di Prestidigitazione.
Torino: Tip. G. Favale e Comp., 1860. 48pp., 22cm.
Held OPAC SBN (2 copies). Photo of cover online at url:280.
Rusconi p.51 records a change made in the 2nd edition. This relates to Frikell's use of the title *Chevalier,* received from the King of Greece (*Le Courrier Batave* 16 Feb.1851).

LIt51
A new edition edited by Alex Rusconi (9781716871146) was published in 2020.

An English translation of *Satana raccolta Europea*, by Lori Pieper, with introduction by Ricky Jay, appeared in *Gibecière* Vol. 3, no.1 (2008), published by The Conjuring Arts Research Center in New York (LEn3).

===

LIt52
La Selva incantata, ossia Modo di fare varj giuochi inventati dal professore cavaliere Bosco.
Nizza: A. Gilletta, 1867. 8pp., 18mo.
Held BNF

===

LIt53
Rosmondo Alliegri
Nuovissimo album del buontempone: raccolta di spiritelli, aneddoti, poesie amene, epigrammi ... / per Rosmondo Alliegri
Milano: Romeo Mangoni Editore, 1883. 384pp., 13cm.
Held OPAC SBN (1 copy) and Biblioteca Mago Sales, which states that it includes "Giuochi di sala e di Prestigio del Cav. Bosco".

===

LIt54
Eugenio Furno
33 Giuochi Destro-Fisici imitati dal celebre cav. Bosco e spiegati ad intelligenza di ogni persona / dal piemontese Furno Eugenio.
Roma: [no publisher], 1846. 15pp., 15cm.
Held OPAC SBN (one copy)
Online at url:281. No references to Bosco in text

Latvian

LLat1
Bosko, jeb Kabatas burvības mākslinieks: 110 viegli izdarāmi burvības un citi gabali.
    Rīga: Druk. pie Jakobsona [1888]. 58pp.
    Held Latvian National Library

LLat2
[new edition]
___

    Rīga: Druk. pie Jakobsona, 1901. 58pp.
    Held Latvian National Library

===

LLat3
Bosko, mazais burvības mākslinieks: krājums visjaunāko un interesantāko burvības gabalu / latviski no Blankenburgu Kārļa.
    Liepāja: Ukstiņš, 1895. 32pp., 19cm. "Translated by Kārlis Blankenburg".
    Held Latvian National Library

===

LLat4
[3rd ed.]
Skunstneeks westes kabatā: bagatigs krahjums no weegli isdarameem, leeliski patihkameem un pahrsteigdameem kabatu spehļu un kahrschu skunstu gabaleem, eepreezinaschanas is ķehmijas un rehķinumeem, jokeem un mihklam dehļ usjautrinaschanas weesibās: no slawenakeem wahzu skunstneekeem, kā Bosko, Filadelfia un ziteem isņemti, sakrahti un latweeschu walodā pahrzelti: 2 daļas.
    3. druka. Jelgava: J. Schablowsky, 1880-1910. 2 vols., 10cm.
    Held Latvian National Library. Earlier editions not traced.

LLat5
[4th ed.]
[...] ...sakrahti un latweeschu walodā pahrzelti: pirmā daļa
    4. druka. Jelgava: J. Schablowsky, 1910. 62,[2],1pp.
    Held Latvian National Library

===

LLat6
Possibly relevant is this title to which the Library gives the subject heading 'Burvju triki' (magic tricks)
Jaunais skunstnieks vestes kabatā.
    Rīga: Ozols [1932]. 38pp., 12cm.
    Held Latvian National Library

Norwegian: *see under* **Danish**

Polish

LPol1
Bosko, nowy czarnoksiężnik bez aparatow uzupełniony i powiększony wraz zobjasnioniami o mówiącej głowie i otak zwanych Incomburendi czyli Salamandry łatwy do zastosowania w kólkach towarzyskic. 54pp. "Lwow, 1871".

This is known only from an advertisement by Lemburg (Lviv) booksller H. Bodek in *Börsenblatt für den deutschen Buchhandel* 21 Apr. and 11 Nov.1871.

===

LPol2
Bosko Odrodzony, czyli Zbiór Sztuk Kartowych, Magicznych, Chemicznych i Mechanicznych. Przekład z Niemieckiego.
   Wilno: A. Syrkin, 1863. [iv],76pp.; 18 cm.
   p.[iii]: "Za pozwoleniem Cenzury. 2 Kwietnia 1863 r. Wilno."
   No introduction or biographical material; 46 card tricks, 77 scientific (chemical and other), 6 miscellaneous; and 74 riddles with answers. "Translated from German", but the book also contains original material as several tricks are ascribed to the legendary Polish sorcerer Twardowski.
   Held National Library of Poland; also at National Library of Lithuania.
   Online at url:282

===

LPol3
Bosko czarnoksiężnik czyli Nauka odkrycia tajemnic czarodziejskich.
   Warszawa: Nakładem ksiegarza Jana Breslauera, 1886. 110,ix pp., 16cm.
   Held Panevėžio apskrities G. Petkevičaitės-Bitės VB (Lithuania)

LPol4
New edition, 1894
Bosko czarnoksiężnik czyli Nauka odkrycia tajemnic czarodziejskich, karcianych, fizycznych i rachunkowych i ciekawych wiadomości według sławnych sztukmistrzów.
   Warszawa: J. Breslauer, 1894. 100,xi pp., 18cm.
   Held National Library of Poland
   Online at url:283.

LPol5
New edition, 1902
Bosko czarnoksiężnik czyli Nauka odkrycia tajemnic czarodziejskich, karcianych, fizycznych i rachunkowych i ciekawych wiadomości według sławnych sztukmistrzów.

Warszawa: nakł. księgarni Jana Breslauera, 1902 (Warszawa: drukiem Władysława Szulca). 100,xi pp., 18cm.
Held University of Warsaw Libraries.

====

LPol6
Czarnoksiężnik Bosko, czyli Bogaty zbiór najciekawszych sztuk magicznych i kuglarskich do wykonywania łatwo i taniem kosztem. Z ilustracyami.
Cieszyn: Nakładem Edwarda Feitzingera [1897] (Series: Książeczki Ludowe; t. 506). 61,[1]pp., 18cm.
Held National Library of Poland
Online at url:284

===

LPol7
Karola Bosko zabawny sztukmistrz kartowy czyli Jasny wykład 114 po większej części nieznanych jeszcze, a bardzo łatwych i nader ciekawych sztuk w karty.
Warszawa: w Drukarnia S. Orgelbranda, 1844. [2],ii.133.[1],v pp.; 16cm.
Held WBP Lublin; University of Warsaw Libraries.
Online at url:285.

===

LPol8
Bosko czyli zbiór najciekawszych i najzabawniejszych sztuczek magicznych obejmujący 60 sztuczek chemicznych kartowych i rachunkowych dla rozrywki w kółku towarzyskiem.
Kraków: Fr. Ksaw. Pobudkiewicz, 1862. 31pp., 13cm.
This edition is known only from the publisher's adv. in *Oesterreichische Buchhändler-Correspondenz* 1 June 1862.

LPol9
Bosko czyli zbiór najciekawszych i najzabawniejszych sztuczek magicznych obejmujący 60 sztuczek chemicznych kartowych i rachunkowych dla rozrywki w kółku towarzyskiem.
Kraków: Fr. Ksaw. Pobudkiewicz, 1878. 31pp., 13cm.
Held [listings on NUKAT]

===

LPol10
Nowy Bosko Czarnoksiężnik: tajemnice kabalistyki, spirytyzmu, hypnotyzmu, magnetyzmu [*cover-title*].
Weissensee: Księgarnia Nakładowa E. Bartels [*ca.* 1914]. 63,[1]pp., 19cm.

Held National Library of Poland; and probably also this edition at Biblioteka Jagiellońska, Kraków [dating "between 1898 and 1901"]. Online at url:286.

p.47: "... Alfikcya czyli kilka kartek 'Czarnej Magii'. Co jest 'Alfikcya' i 'Czarna Magia'? ... Podobnie jak ziemia aczkolwiek przeważnie dokładnie jest znana i zbadana — posiada jednak pewne obszary, dokąd izlowiek dotrzeć nie mógi, — posiada zarówno na powierziani jak w wnętrzu swojem tajemnice i zagadki, któryc (*"...What is 'Alfikcya' and 'Black Magic'? ... Like the earth, although it is for the most part thoroughly known and explored, it has certain areas where humans cannot reach, it has secrets and riddles ..."*)

===

LPol11
Alfiktor (Magik)
Nowy Bosko Czarnoksiężnik: zbiór najciekawszych sztuk z zakresu mechaniki, elektryki, akustyki, optyki, pirotechniki, sztuk ze sztyletami, nożami i pistoletami, czarodziejskich znikań i aportów, najciekawszych sztuk rachunkowych, sztuk z kartami i sztuk zartobliwych, oraz Alfikcya, Tajemnice kabalistyki, spirytyzmu i hyponotyzmu. Z starych ksiąg i rękopisów zebrał i ułożył Stary doświadczony Alfiktor (Magik). Z rysunkami.

Warszawa: Nakladem księgarni N. Cytrna, 1907. [2],96pp., 20cm.

Held National Library of Poland; Biblioteka Śląska, Katowice (incomplete)

Online at url:287. The authorship is credited to "Old, experienced Alfiktor (Magician), collected and edited from old books and manuscripts".

LPol12
New ed., 1923

Warszawa: Wydawnictwo Księgarni Popularnej, 1923 (J. Wegmejster). (Series: Wydawnictwo Księgarni Popularnej, nr. 34). [2],51-96pp (text in this and later editions starts at p.51 with trick no.4); 20 cm. Photo of cover at url:288.

Held National Library of Poland; Biblioteka Jagiellońska, Kraków; ULSH

LPol13
New ed., 1930
Tajemnice czarnej magji: zbiór najciekawszych sztuk [...] oraz Alfikcyja, tajemnice kabalistyki, spirytyzmu i hypnotyzmu / Cz. 2, Nowy Bosko Czarnoksiężnik.

Warszawa: Księgarnia Popularna, 1932. (Series: Wydawnictwo Księgarni Popularnej, nr 33). [2],51-96pp; 20 cm.

Held National Library of Poland;

LPol14
New ed., 1934

Held National Library of Poland.

====

LPol15
Nowy Bosco w kólkutowarzyskiem, czyli zbiór najciekawszych i najzbawniejszych sztuczek magicznych, zebrane przez starego kuglarza.
Known only from advertisement in *Kurjer Codzienny* 14 Feb.1873, "price 22½ kop.; available at all bookstores here and in the provinces".
No surviving copy traced.

====

LPol16
Czarnoksiężnik Hokus-Pokus, czyli: nauka tajemnic najzabawniejszych sztuczek czarodziejskich, oraz innych pięknych wiadomości ala Bosko, Schwanenfeld, Twardowski, Faust, Theophrastus, Paracelsus, Döbler, Filadelfia i wielu innych.
Bochnia: Wawrzyniec Pisz, 1864. 178pp., 13cm.
Held Biblioteka Jagiellońska, Kraków; listed *Oesterreichische Buchhändler-Correspondenz* 20. Nov.1863; Engel, *Zusammenstellung der Faust-schriften vom 16. jahrhundert bis mitte 1884* (1885): 1535.

LPol17
New edition
Czarnoksiężnik Hokus-Pokus czyli nauka odkrycia tajemnic i niezawodny sposób czarowania: według sławnych sztukmistrzów jako to: Bosko, Schwanenfeld, Twardowski, Faust, Theophrastus, Paracelsus, Doebler, Filadelfia i wielu innych.
Chicago, Ill.: Polish American Publishing Company [191-], 191pp., 17cm.
Held Connecticut State Univ. (2 copies, one with imprint as Chicago, Ill.: Nakładem W. Dyniewicza); LC (same imprint)

LPol18
New edition:
———

Toledo, Ohio: A. A. Paryski, 1899 (Series: Biblioteka polska, no. 9). 98pp., 20cm.
Held LC (imperfect copy)

===

LPol19
Czarnoksieznik Bosko czyli Tajemncice Czarnej Magji.... podlug Pinettiego....
Warsaw: Nakladem ksiegarni Ch. I. Rosenweina, 1922. 64pp.
Held ULSH.

===

LPol20
Magia i czarnoksięstwo: wielki zbiór tajemnic magicznych, karcianych, fizycznych, chemicznych i rachunkowych, wykonywanych przez Bosko, Pinettiego i innych sławnych magików i kuglarzy.

Warszawa: Księgarnia Ch. I. Rosenweina, 1905. [2],94pp., 19cm.
Held National Library of Poland; listed *Spisok knig, vyshedshikh v Rossii ... 1885-1908,* p.38.

LPol21
New edition
Magia i czarnoksięstwo: wielki zbiór tajemnic magicznych, karcianych, fizycznych, chemicznych i rachunkowych wykonanych przez Bosko, Pinettiego i innych sławnych magików i kuglarzy.
Warszawa: Ch. I. Rosenwein, 1922. 68pp., 21cm.
Held National Library of Poland; ULSH

===

LPol22
Najnowsze tajemnice magii: Wielki zbiór czarodziejsko-magicznych sztuk oraz wolty z kartami i objaśnieniami tajemnic kuglarskich / przez C. Bosko, Pinetti, Bekker.
Warszawa: nakład księgarni J. Klepfisza , 1902 (Warszawa: W. Thiella S-orów). 96pp., 17cm.
Held Libraries of the University of Warsaw.

===

LPol23
Tajemnice magii dawniejszych i nowych czasów czyli sztuki czarodziejskie podług: Pinettego, Petronell'ego, Bosc'a, Comt'a, Enselin'a, Eckartshausen'a i innych, oraz rzadkie doświadczenia oparte na nauce Arytmetyki, Matematyki, Fizyki, Chemii, Optyki, Mechaniki z niemieckiego przełożone.
Warszawa, nakładem S. Orgelbranda Księgarza i Typografa, 1851. 260pp.
Listed *Bibliotheka Warszawska* 1850 p.573; *Bibliografia Polska* 1851 no.5 (1 Apr.1851); adv. *Kurjer Warszawski* 24 Feb.1850; 15 Dec.1852. No library holding recorded. Copy formerly for sale with photo of title-page at url:289.

Russian
Titles are given in Cyrillic, then in transliteration.

LRu1
Боско, Карло.
Волшебный кабинет: Полн. объясн. тайн магов и волшебников: Пер. с 20 улучш. и увелич. нем. изд. / Соч. Боско.
Москва: Тайны мира, 1912.
Bosko, Karlo.
Volshebnyy kabinet: Poln. ob"yasn. tayn magov i volshebnikov: Per. s 20 uluchsh. i uvelich. nem. izd. / Soch. Bosko.
Moskva: Tayny mira, 1912. 220pp.

States translated from the 20th revised edition of Carlo Bosco *Das Zauberkabinet*.

Held RSL. Online at url:290

====

LRu2

Волшебный кабинет Карла Боско или Чародей молодежи.
    Санкт-Петербург: тип. Э. Праца, 1849.
Volshebnyy kabinet Karla Bosko ili Charodey molodezhi.
    Sankt-Peterburg: tip. E. Pratsa, 1849. xx,124pp.
    Held RNL

=====

LRu3

Опыты натуральной магии и волшебный кабинет Карла Боско, или полное собрание удивительных фокусов, представленных им во время пребывания его в С.-Петербурге и в Москве... С 18 грав. фигурами: Пер. с нем.
    Москва: тип. Александра Семена, 1849.
Opyty natural'noy magii i volshebnyy kabinet Karla Bosko, ili polnoye sobraniye udivitel'nykh fokusov, predstavlennykh im vo vremya prebyvaniya yego v S.-Peterburge i v Moskve... : S 18 grav. figurami : Per. s nem..
    Moskva: tip. Aleksandra Semena, 1849. [4],144pp.
    Held RNL. Reviewed in *Sovremennik* 1849, pp.122-3 (which is online at url:291)
    Copies listed for sale and sold by auction (with photos) are online at url:126 & 127. Some interesting misinformation from the book is discussed under 'Karla Bosko' (B6).

LRu4
2nd. ed., 1852

    2-е изд. - Москва: тип. Александра Семена, 1852.
    2-ye izd. – Moskva; tip. Aleksandra Semena, 1852. [2],viii,143pp.
    Held RNL (2 copies). Online at url:292.

====

LRu5

Волшебник и фокусник в домашнем кругу: Представление самых любопытных фокусов, которые приводят зрителя в неожиданное изумление и не требуют никаких затруднительных приготовлений, по способам Германа, Филадельфа, Пинетти, Боско и Мартини, представлявших фокусы в Москве и С.-Петербурге
    Москва: тип. Александра Семена, 1856.

Volshebnik i fokusnik v domashnem krugu: Predstavleniye samykh lyubopytnykh fokusov, kotoryye privodyat zritelya v neozhidannoye izumleniye i ne trebuyut nikakikh zatrudnitel'nykh prigotovleniy, po sposobam Germana [=Hermann], Filadel'fa, Pinetti, Bosko i Martini, predstavlyavshikh fokusy v Moskve i S.-Peterburge.
    Moscow: typ. Alexandra Semen, 1856. 144pp., 2 plates at end; 17cm.
    Held RNL. Online at url:293.

LRu6
2nd ed., 1860 (reprinted from the 1856 edition)

    [Напеч. с изд. 1856 г.].
    Москва: тип. Александра Семена, 1860.
    Moscow: typ. Alexandra Semen, 1860. 144pp., 17 cm
    Held RNL and RSL

====

LRu7
Доктор магии или Книга чудесных действий, заключающая в себе до 500 фокусов, изобретенных профессорами: Филадельфия, Петорели, Пинетти, Боско, Жан Мартини, Галюгие, Бекера и др.
    Москва: Ф.И. Анский [1874].
Doktor magii ili Kniga chudesnykh deystviy, zaklyuchayushchaya v sebe do 500 fokusov, izobretennykh professorami: Filadel'fiya, Petoreli, Pinetti, Bosko, Zhan Martini, Galyugiye, Bekera i dr.
    Moskva: F.I. Anskiy [1874]. [2],ix,180pp.
    Held RNL and RSL.

LRu8
New edition, 1890

    Москва: Ф.И. Анский 1890.
    Moskva: F.I. Anskiy 1890. [2],x,180pp.
    Held RSL

LRu9
New edition, 1894

    Москва: Е.А. Губанов, 1894.
    Moskva: E.A. Gubanov, 1894. 224pp.
    Held RSL

===

LRu10
Карточный фокусник, или Собрание увеселительных фокусов, удобно исполняемых всеми и каждым в домашнем кругу, на балах, на семейных вечерах, в собраниях и на сценах домашних театров: Сост. по опытам Боско, Германа, братьев Давенпорт, Юма, Куртуа, Кони и других проф. натуральной магии.

Санкт-Петербург: тип. В.А. Александрова, 1872.

Kartochnyy fokusnik, ili Sobraniye uveselitel'nykh fokusov, udobno ispolnyayemykh vsemi i kazhdym v domashnem krugu, na balakh, na semeynykh vecherakh, v sobraniyakh i na stsenakh domashnikh teatrov: Sost. po opytam Bosko, Germana, brat'yev Davenport, Yuma, Kurtua, Koni i drugikh prof. natural'noy magii.

Sankt-Peterburg: tip. V.A. Aleksandrova, 1872. 191pp.

Held NLR

Later editions add Новый *at the start of the title (*"New Card Magician..."*)*

LRu11

New edition, 1874

Новый карточный фокусник, или Собрание увеселительных фокусов, удобоисполняемых всеми и каждым в домашнем кругу, на балах, на семейных вечерах, в собраниях и на сценах домашних театров: Сост. по опытам: Боско, Германа, братьев Давенпорт, Куртуа, Юма и др. профессоров натур. магии.

Санкт-Петербург: тип. Ретгера и Шнейдера, 1874.

Novyy kartochnyy fokusnik, ili Sobraniye uveselitel'nykh fokusov, udoboispolnyayemykh vsemi i kazhdym v domashnem krugu, na balakh, na semeynykh vecherakh, v sobraniyakh i na stsenakh domashnikh teatrov: Sost. po opytam: Bosko, Germana, brat'yev Davenport, Kurtua, Yuma i dr. professorov natur. magii.

Sankt-Peterburg: tip. Retgera i Shneydera, 1874. 100,vii pp.

Held RNL and RSL

LRu12

New edition, 1877

[...] Боско, Германа, Б-в Давенпорт, Куртуа, Юма и др. проф. натур. магии с прил. спирит. сеансов и объяснения спиритизма.

Санкт-Петербург: Рус. скоропечатня П. С. Нахимова, 1877.

[...] *Bosko, Germana, B-v Davenport, Kurtua, Yuma i dr. prof. natur. magii s pril. spirit. seansov i ob"yasneniya spiritizma.*

Sankt-Peterburg: Rus. skoropechatnya P. S. Nakhimova, 1877. 121,vi pp., 15cm.

Held RNL and RSL

LRu13

New edition, 1880

[...] Боско, Германа, братьев Давенпорт, Куртуа, Юма и др. профессоров натур. магии: С прил. спирит. сеансов и объяснениями спиритизма.

Санкт-Петербург: типо-лит. Шмидта, 1880.

[...] *Bosko, Germana, brat'yev Davenport, Kurtua, Yuma i dr. professorov natur. magii: S pril. spirit. seansov i ob"yasneniyami spiritizma.*

Sankt-Peterburg: tipo-lit. Shmidta, 1880. 121,vi pp.
Held RNL (lost?) and RSL

LRu14
New edition, 1883 ("2nd edition")
———

2- е изд. Санкт-Петербург: [тип. Ф. Михеева], 1883.
2- ye izd. Sankt-Peterburg: [tip. F. Mikheyeva], 1883. 121,vi pp.
Held RNL and RSL

LRu15
New edition, 1891

[...] Боско, Германа, братьев Давенпорт, Куртуа, Юма и др. профессоров натур. магии: С прил. спирит. сеансов и объяснениями спиритизма.
Санкт-Петербург: [тип. Ф. Михеева], 1891.
[...] *Bosko, Germana, brat'yev Davenport, Kurtua, Yuma i dr. professorov natur. magii: S pril. spirit. seansov i ob"yasneniyami spiritizma.*
Sankt-Peterburg: [tip. F. Mikheyeva], 1891. 121,vi pp., 14cm.
Held RNL; listed *Spisok knig, vyshedshikh v Rossii...* books pub. Oct.24-31 1890.

LRu16
New edition, 1900
Новый карточный фокусник: Собрание различ. чудес. и таинств. фокусов, разнообраз. и увеселит. действий и представлений с картами и др. различ. предметами: Сост. по опытам известных проф. натур. магии: Цетореги, Пинетти, Филадельфия…
Киев: Т.А. Губанов, 1900.
Novyy kartochnyy fokusnik: Sobraniye razlich. chudes. i tainstv. fokusov, raznoobraz. i uveselit. deystviy i predstavleniy s kartami i dr. razlich. predmetami: Sost. po opytam izvestnykh prof. natur. magii: Tsetoregi, Pinetti, Filadel'fiya...
Kyev: T.A. Gubanov, 1900. 104pp.
Held RNL

LRu17
New edition, 1902
———

Киев: Т.А. Губанов, 1902.
Kyev: T.A. Gubanov, 1902. 104pp.
Held RNL (lost?)

===

LRu18
Все фокусы тут!: Книжка с картинкою маленькая, но удаленькая для всех, кто хочет уметь делать фокусы нем., фр., кит., япон. и превзойти самых знаменитых фокусников: Пенети, Боско, Петорелли, Конта, Мартини и пр., настоящих, прошедших и будущих.

Москва: тип. Шюман и Глушк., 1869.
Vse fokusy tut!: Knizhka s kartinkoyu malen'kaya, no udalen'kaya dlya vsekh, kto khochet umet' delat' fokusy nem., fr., kit., yapon. i prevzoyti samykh znamenitykh fokusnikov: Peneti, Bosko, Petorelli, Konta, Martini i pr., nastoyashchikh, proshedshikh i budushchikh.

 Moskva: tip. Shyuman i Glushk., 1869. [2],45pp., 14cm.

 Held RNL.

===

LRu19
Новейший полный оракул, заключающий в себе: угадывание будущего и настоящего на задуманные вопросы с приложением лучших фокусов Боско, Пинетти и др., а также и различных карточн. фокусов, с прибавлением: святочных и подблюдных песен и разных способов гадания на святках и сонник.

 Москва: Н.П. Барков, 1887.

Noveyshiy polnyy orakul, zaklyuchayushchiy v sebe: ugadyvaniye budushchego i nastoyashchego na zadumannyye voprosy s prilozheniyem luchshikh fokusov Bosko, Pinetti i dr., a takzhe i razlichnykh kartochn. fokusov, s pribavleniyem: svyatochnykh i podblyudnykh pesen i raznykh sposobov gadaniya na svyatkakh i sonnik.

 Moskva: N.P. Barkov, 1887. 143pp.

 Held RNL

Swedish

LSw1
Bosco i vestfickan, eller alla Magiers, Trollkarlars och Häxmästares hemligheter samlade på ett ställe.

 Stockholm: Hörbergska Boktr. (Brudins frlag), 1846. 80pp.

 No surviving copy traced. Listed *Svensk bokhandels-katalog utgifven år 1845; Frey...* 1845 (*'Böcker utkomna från den 16 December 1845 till den 16 Februari 1846*); *Svenskt boklexikon. Åren 1830-1865* (as Bosco i västfickan...); adv. *Correspondenten* 28 Jan.1846; included in the bibliography, url:294.

=====

LSw2
Bosco's åttio kortkonster.
 Stockholm: S. Flodin, 1867. v,56pp
 Held Libris

LSw3
2nd ed., 1877

———

 2a uppl. Stockholm, 1877

Held Libris; listed in the advertisements to *Nyaste trollkonstbok...* 3e uppl., 1882, and in the bibliography, url:294.

===

LSw4
Hexmästaren eller sättet att på konstens väg inom kort tid kunna lära sig trolla.: En samling af de mest uppseendeväckande äldre och nyare konststycken efter Bosco m.fl. trollkonstnärer samt till slut magnetiska konststycken och om enkel fyrverkerikonst.
    Tomteboda: Svenska småskrift- och visförlag, 1912. 31pp.
    Held Libris

LSw5
new ed.., 1914
———
Tomteboda: Svenska småskrift- och visförlag, 1914. 31pp.
    Held Libris

LSw6
new ed., 1916
———
Tomteboda: Svenska småskrift- och visförlag, 1914. 31pp.
    Held Libris

===

LSw7
Hexmästarnes pappa: Samling af lättfattliga taskspelarekonster, till nöje sällskaper. Efter Tyska originalet: "Carlo Bosco, das Ganze der Taschenspielerkunst".
    Stockholm: tryckt hos L. J. Hjerta. 1842. 60pp.; 17cm; printed pink wrappers
    Held National Library of Wales; Brown UL; listed *Svensk bokhandels-katalog utgifven år 1845* p.125

LSw8
2nd ed., "revised and enlarged", 1842
    "2 uppl. Genomaedd och tillökad, 1842"
    No surviving copy traced. Listed in *Svenskt boklexikon. Åren 1830-1865 / Förra delen. A - L* p.612; and in the bibliography, url:294.

LSw9
3rd ed., "enlarged, with party games, etc.", 1844
    "3 uppl., tillökad med sällskapslekar, m.m., 1844"
    No surviving copy traced. Listed in *Svenskt boklexikon. Åren 1830-1865 / Förra delen. A - L* p.612; and in the bibliography, url:294; adv. *Aftonbladet* 18 Dec.1846.

LSw10
4th ed., 1857
Hexmästarnes pappa: Samling af lättfattliga taskspelarekonster, till nöje sällskaper. Efter Tyska originalet:«Carlo Bosco, Das Ganze de Taschenspielerkunst.»
    Stockholm: Tryckt hos Jos. Beckman, 1857. 72pp.; 17cm; printed blue wrappers.
    Held Brown UL; listed *Svenskt boklexikon. Åren 1830-1865.*

===

LSw11
Den nyaste hexmästare-boken: omfattande ett rikt urval af de intressantaste taskspeleri- och kortkonster, hvilka hos oss förevisats af herrar Bosco, Döbler, Le Tort, Philippe, m. fl., jemte anvisning för hvar och en att sjelf verkställa desamma.
    Stockholm: C.M. Thimgren, 1859. [i],109,[3]pp.; 16 cm.
    Held Libris; Brown UL; listed (as Den Nyaste Hexmästareboken… Med talrika illustrationer i träsmitt.) in *Svenskt boklexikon. Åren 1830-1865 / Förra delen. A - L* p.612.

===

LSw12
Nyaste trollkonstbok som snart sagdt inom en handvñdning kan af en vanlig menniska göra en fullñadad trollkarl: en sammanfattning af de mest förvånande äldre och nyare, lätt verkställbara konststycken ur taskspeleriets, magiens, magnetismens, optikens, fysikens och fyrwerkeriets områden, efter Bosco m.fl. lika utmärkta trollkonstnärer.
    Stockholm: Sigfrid Flodins boktryckeri, 1868. 76pp.
    Held Libris; Brown UL

LSw13
2nd ed., 1873
Nyaste trollkonstbok som... kan af en vanlig menniska göra en fulländad trollkarl: En samling af...
    2.uppl., 1873
    Held Libris

LSw14
3rd ed., 1882
Nyaste trollkonstbok som...kan af en vanlig menniska göra en fulländad trollkarl: En samling af...
    3e uppl., 1882.
    Held Libris. Copy listed for sale by Antikvariat Hundörat (with photo of cover and leaf of advertising) on https://www.antikvariat.net/sv gives pagination of this ed. as 115,[1]pp.

LSw15
4th ed., 1890
Nyaste trollkonstbok som snart sagdt inom en handvñdning kan af en vanlig menniska göra en fullñdad trollkarl: en samling af de mest förvånande äldre och nyare, lätt verkställbara konststycken ur taskspeleriets, magnetismens, optikens, fysikens och fyrverkeriets områden: efter Bosco m.fl. utmärkta trollkonstnärer

    4. uppl. Minneapolis, Minn.: J. Leachman & Son, förläggare, 1890. 70pp., 20cm. (Series: Svensk-amerikanska biblioteket. No 8. Okt. 1890)

    Held Libris

===

LSw16
Trollstafwen: nyaste handbok i taskspelarekonsten och den naturliga magien; innehållande 135 mekaniska, fysikaliska, kemiska, optiska och magnetiska konststycken; med 35 upplysande figurer. Efter egna experimenter och muntliga meddelanden af nutidens största konstmakare: Bosco, Döbler, Philippe, Robin m. fl. offentliggjorda af Professor Herrmanns.

    Stockholm: S. Flodins forlag [1857]. [vi],100pp., [1] folded leaf; 17 cm.

    Held Libris; Brown UL.

BOSCO GAMES AND TOYS

Bosco's name was attached to several games and sets of amateur magic apparatus. Examples include —

In 1869 a large store in Krems is advertising "[tr.] A Sale of Magical Apparatus, with which anyone can immediately perform the most amazing tricks, and so entertain family and friends", including "Bosco's Magic Dice which march invisibly through any hat, table or mirror" (*Bosko's Zauberwürfel. welcher unsichtbar durch jeden Hut, Tisch, oder Spiegel marschirt*): *Kremser Wochenblatt* 30 Oct.1869.

What seem the same dice are for sale in Großbetschkerek (modern Zrenjanin) in 1870 — "on command they walk through any hat, table or mirror … absolutely amazing" (*Bosko's Zauberwürfel, welcher auf Kommando durch jeden Hut, Tisch oder Spiegel durchspazirt… höchst überraschend*): *Gr.-Becskereker Wochenblatt* 12 Oct.1870

and in Innsbruck in 1877 — "on command they walk through any hat" (*Bosko-Zauberwürfel, welcher auf Kommando durch jeden Hut durchspaziert*): *Innsbrucker Nachrichten* 9 May 1877.

Bazar Friedman in Vienna in 1873-75 offers a huge list of "Toys and Party Games, for young and old, rich and poor…", including "Magic caskets … a very pretty casket with various highly elaborate pieces of Magical Apparatus. All with instructions, so that anyone can easily do the finest magic tricks (à la Professor

Bosko)…" (*Zauber-Kassetten … ein hübsche Kassette mit verschiedenen, äußerst komplizirten Zauber-Apparaten. Alles mit genauer Anleitung, so daß Jeder mit größter Leichtigkeit die schönsten Zauberstücke (à la Professor Bosko) machen kann…*"): *Neues Wiener Blatt; Meraner Zeitung; Innsbrucker Nachrichten* 20 Dec.1873 to 18 Dec. 1875

A big list of items made by Jean Kieling, "Maker of Magical Apparatus", in Vienna in 1869 ends "[tr.] …through my large stock of magical apparatus at relatively low prices everyone is able to become his own Bosco" (*sein eigener Bosko zu werden*): *Gemeinde-Zeitung* 21 Dec.1869

A Dutch dealer selling magical apparatus in Arnhem in 1869 makes an identical claim — "my extensive inventory of magical devices, whose prices are very cheap, gives everyone the opportunity to become his own Bosco" (*is iedereen in de gelegenheid gesteld zign eigene Bosco te worden*): *Arnhemsche courant* 27 Aug.1869

In 1875 a shop in Bucharest was selling various pieces of "Magical Apparatus", including "*Disculu magicu alu lui Bosco*": *Telegraphulŭ de Bucuresci* 29 Jan.1875, etc.

In 1879 a London dealer, J. Bland, Professor of Legerdemain, at his Magical Palace in Oxford Street, is advertising among his magical apparatus "The Mystic 'Little Bosco', a New and Marvellous Invention, an Evening's Amusement for the Juvenile and Adult…": *Era* 21, 28 Dec.1879

Advertised for many years, especially in the pre-Christmas period, was "A package for boys aged 5 to 10" (*Gruppe für Knaben von 5—10 Jahren*) from a shop in Vienna, 63 or so items sold together, differing every year; mainly toys; in 1886 no.1 is *Bosko, der große Zauberer* — possibly a mechanical figurine, though perhaps a booklet: *Salzburger Volksblatt* 4 Dec.1886; (*Neuigkeits*) *Welt-Blatt* 11 Dec.1886.

In 1906 a shop in Czernowitz (Chernivtsi) is offering "12 Amusing Party Games" (*12 amüsante Gesellschaftsspiele*) including *Boskos Zauberkarten,* plus Gänsedieb, Schwarzer Peter, Wahrsagekarten, and more: *Czernowitzer Tagblatt* 1 Oct.1906

"Bosco's Magic Cards" (*Bosco's Zauber-Karten*) were also marketed in U.S.A. — offered by a dealer in Cincinnati: *Wichita Herald* (Kansas) 29 Feb.1888

Magic Lantern — "The latest Globe Magic Lantern 'Bosco', 'Improved Climax System'" was being advertised in a 1902 English language Catalogue (*Special Catalogue and Price List of Instructive Mechanical, Optical and Electrical Toys*) by the German manufacturer Gebrüder Bing in Nuremberg. The page with splendid illustrations and a 1904 German ad by the company are online at url:295.

As late as 1914 in Vienna we have: "2000 Jokes" comprising a game "Bosco's Magic Cards" plus a book and lot's more (*2000 Witze … Dazu 1 Spiel Bosko's*

Zauberkarten, 1 Buch 'Der Kartenkünstler' und hochinteressante Beilagen): *Wiener Bilder* 29 Mar.1914

A shop named *Deutschen Bosko* ("Zauber-Salon") at the address *Kreuzstraße 1* in Munich advertised magical apparatus for many years (at least 1891 to 1914) in German and Austrian papers.

Appendix Z1
MATHILDE BANNHOLZER

Soon after Bosco's arrival in Vienna in March 1845 there was already talk of a rival in town — "[tr.] 'Two Conjurors for One'. The famous magician Bosco, who in a few days will open his cycle of performances at the Josephstädter Theater, finds a rival in a female juggler, the eight-year-old daughter of former theatre-director Bannholzer. It is said that this little magician will give her shows at the Leopoldstadt".[1]

Due to illness Mathilde had to delay her opening and instead succeeded Bosco at the Josephstädter on April 10th. She quickly proved not only a great novelty, but a very accomplished performer, remaining there several weeks, and still performing in nearby Hietzing at the end of May.

The crowds loved her and the reviews were enthusiastic —"[tr.] everything ... was perfectly performed, executed with great skill, and her accomplishments found lavish and well-deserved applause", said the *Wiener Zeitschrift*;[2] the *Allgemeine Theaterzeitung* spoke of her "[tr.] feminine grace and teasing charm"[3]; and when the following month the *Österreichische Blätter für Literatur und Kunst* surveyed the April theatrical scene in Vienna[4] she and Bosco were compared, not to his advantage, saying that Bosco's performances of natural magic did not entrance us much — lots of apparatus, lots of covers, containers and stands, all of which contained nothing but what had been done many times before. The increased prices did not increase the takings — or the enjoyment. The little Bannholzer also made magic, it was a formal lesson in magic. Besides, the child had good manners and for this reason the audience actually enjoyed a few repeats of the oft-repeated lid and box tricks.

Mathilde had been trained in Pest by her father, comic actor, manager, and conjuror Josef Ban(n)holzer. She was performing by early 1844,[5] her show billed as "Wunderspielen eines Zauberkindes". She originally gave her commentary in Hungarian, later adding German and French.

There is a Roman Catholic baptism on January 8th 1836 in Trnava (Turnau) of an *Anna Mathildis Banholczer* (father Josephus Banholczer, *actor*; mother Aloysia Nagy), which is probably her, meaning that she was a little older than she was advertised to be.

Josef (his surname variously spelt) and Aloysia Nagy were also the parents of

Gyula Baunholczer (male), bap. Hungary 1837
Thersia Antonia Baumholtzer, bap. Hungary 1838
Carolus Henricus Bamkolczer, bap. Hungary 1840.[6]

Mathilde was soon being hailed as "dieser liebenswürdige weibliche Mignon-Döbler",[7] a "weiblich Döbler, und zwar ein zaubernden Wunderkind",[8] "ein weiblichen Bosko en miniature",[9] and as performing "*à la* Bosco und Döbler".[10]

This reputation preceded her to Vienna, where as soon as she arrived the papers were full of her — "ein neues Wunderkind in Wien";[11] "...sie fast Alles macht, was Döbler, Bosco und Philippe bisher zur Anschauung gebracht hat".[12]

After Vienna we find her over the next few years performing in Bohemia, Germany, and Austria (her billing now stressing the novelty of her sex rather than her youth — *Escamoteurin, Eskamotrice*), touring with her father, then from 1851 as the "Familie Bannholzer aus Wien" with her brother Ludwig, age four; and later with brothers Louis (Ludwig) and Karl — *"Mysterien der Geschwindigkeit, verbunden mit Phantasmagorien und Chromatropen ... Zauberbildern, komischem Szenen-Gesang, nebst lebende Schattenpantomimie"*.

Joseph is still with them in 1856, then there is a gap for them in the early 1860s until in 1865[13] we find Mathilde on stage in Vienna with Sigmund Epstein ("der mitternächtliche Zauberer": B12). By March 1866 she is performing in Vienna on her own and last found in April that year at the Apollo-Sälle in Vienna. She then disappears, aged about thirty.

[1] *Österreichisches Morgenblatt* 26 Mar.1845.
[2] *Wiener Zeitschrift* 12 Apr.1845: "alles ... war vollkommen gelungen, mit großer Geschicklichkeit ausgeführt, und ihre Leistungen fanden rauschenden und wohlverdienten Beifall".
[3] *ATZ* 12 Apr.1845: "...weiblicher Anmuth, und neckischer Grazie".
[4] *Österreichische Blätter für Literatur und Kunst* 15 May 1845: "...die uns wenig bezaubert habe. Viel Maschinerie, viele Deckel, Büchsen und Basen, die alle zusammen nichts enthielten, als schon oftmal Dagewesenes. Die erhöhten Preise erhöhten den Ertrag nicht — auch nicht den Genuß. Die kleine Banholzer zauberte auch, es war ein förmlicher Unterricht in der Zauberei. Übrigens hatte das Kind gute Manieren und um dieser willen ließ sich das Publikum einige Wiederholungen der oft wiederholten Deckel- und Schachtelkünste gefallen".
[5] *Der Siebenbürger Bote* 26, 29 Mar.1844.
[6] The records are on *https://www.familysearch.org*. One of the two boys is probably the son who later performed as Karl; another, probably born elsewhere, performed as Louis or Ludwig, said to be age 4 in 1851.
[7] *Der Wanderer* 4 June 1844.
[8] *Regensburger Zeitung* 12 Aug.1844.
[9] *Der Ungar* 15 Oct.1844.
[10] *Der Sammler* 24 Oct. 1844.
[11] *ATZ* 7 Jan.1845.
[12] *Der Wanderer* 25 Jan.1845.
[13] *Fremden-Blatt* 21 Nov.1865; *Neues Fremden-Blatt* 24 Nov.1865.
[14] *Fremden Blatt* 24 Mar.; 8, 12 Apr.1866.

Appendix Z2
BILL MATTER AND THE BOSCOS IN BRITAIN: *WHO WAS WHERE WHEN?*

The Boscos active in Britain in the 1860s and 1870s (two, sometimes four, concurrently, or five if David Hyam (B66) was performing then, plus a few strays) are often maddeningly difficult to distinguish. Very rarely they used their real name, and at times it is possible to identify them by following their route. If not, some sanity can be derived from their advertisements (both in newspapers or, if we are lucky, on surviving posters), which can sometimes identify them by unique *tricks* they performed, or unique *catchphrases* they used, or their *claims* of notables they had appeared before.

However, most of their tricks were far from unique and not their own invention (though the name they gave them might be), and few of their catchphrases were original (though a combination of them could be); the claims they made are a minefield (due to misprints or just plain lying).

TRICKS.
Japanese Top Feat

Of the Boscos in Britain Louis alone advertised what he called the "Japanese Top Feat", the top spinning along an invisible thread. He first advertised it in early 1869 — "…he will introduce the great Japanese Top feat; and the instantaneous growth of flowers. Signor Bosco is the only European who can perform this marvellous and beautiful feat…".[1] He lists it regularly until his 1875 departure, sometimes with the wording "…instantaneous growth of flowers. Bosco is said be the only European who can perform the last named marvellous feat…" and the last occurrence of the phrase "Japanese Top Feat" in U.K. papers is in March 1875 in Louis's final ad before he headed overseas.

Japanese Butterfly trick

Briefly (only from Feb. to Mar. 1869) Louis's ads list not merely the "Top Feat" but the "Butterfly Trick" or "Butterfly Illusion",[2] butterflies of folded paper kept in the air by means of a fan and made to alight upon flowers. Whether this was a regular part of Louis's act is uncertain, but the Top and Butterfly "feats" were usually performed together — perhaps by now the butterfly was so common that it was refarded as hardly worth highlighting?

In 1872 Saul starts advertising a whole new bevy of tricks, with the "Japanese Butterfly trick" included for the first time.[3]

After performing it in America in 1863 "Dr Lynn"[4] (who had learnt it in Nagasaki that year) performed it in Ireland in 1865, but the real craze began in February 1867 when a genuine Japanese troupe arrived in London headed by Matsui Gensui, including a butterfly trick specialist, Asakichi-san. Soon several British magicians had added it to their repertoires, notably Professor Anderson's daughter Lizzie, all this two years before Louis began performing it.

The Rope Feat

Of the Boscos Louis alone advertised the "rope feat". This was first seen in Britain in 1862 when "Herr Tolmaque"[5] performed his "Great Indian Rope Feat" at the Cremorne Gardens on June 3rd that year. It was escapology, not levitation: he was tied up by a member of the audience, freed himself while concealed, then reappeared. It proved a very successful act for him (despite one embarrassing failure to escape in Edinburgh in July) and soon found imitators, Edmund Redmond, Captain Austin, Anderson, among others.

In October 1864 the American Davenport Brothers attracted great interest in Britain with their more elaborate rope act, which was claimed to involve supernatural forces. They were attacked as frauds, not least by Tolmaque. He now advertised as an "Exposer of the Davenports", as did many others. Louis added "the Rope feat" to his act in November 1864 ("Signor Bosco … will introduce, in addition to his marvellous performance, the Great Rope Feat, as pretended by the Davenport Brothers to be Spiritual").[6] One unimpressed reviewer called his '*exposé*' "a tame affair" compared with the elaborate Davenport act — Louis once tied-up stepped behind a screen and reappeared forty seconds later "unshackled".[7] Louis continued performing this as a headline act until late 1868.

While all the Bosco advertisements that mention the "rope trick" are by Louis, a review of one of Saul's performances shows he also demonstrated it on occasion: "…At the conclusion Warschawski explained to those who chose to remain, a clever rope trick by means of which, he alleges, it was that the celebrated Davenport brothers were enabled to produce the manifestations which they attributed to spiritualism".[8]

Beheading act.

Louis never did this as part of his act; Saul did so (discussed in his entry), but not until 1882, after Louis's departure from Britain, so of no use in telling them apart. Morton Bosco also did a beheading act.

The Blood Trick

Saul alone of the Boscos performed this, first as "Dr Lynn's Great Blood Trick".[9] Lynn, calling it "blood writing on the arm", had performed it in America and brought it to Britain in 1865, debunking the practice of American spiritist Charles Henry Foster in which alleged names of spirits of the dead would appear on his arm. Foster had sensational success with this, attracting large audiences (and converts to spiritism) — Conan Doyle compared "the gift of blood-red letters upon Foster's skin" to stigmata. It remained a feature of Lynn's act and was soon copied by Herr Dobler,[10] Anderson, and others. Saul performed it until at least October 1875, calling it variously "the wonderful blood trick", "the blood illusion", or "Bosco's great blood illusion".

Plate spinning

Of the Boscos this was performed regularly by Louis (and earlier by Epstein, B12) but was also (very rarely) done by Saul and Morton Bosco (all assumed to be spinning the plates vertically on their *edges* not flat on a stand, as discussed in *Appendix Z7*). Louis calls it "Terpsichorean Delf" in 1859 (B65 note 11) and in 1874 a review lists "The Chinese plate spinning" among Louis's "novelties, along with the "Great Japanese top feat", "The Empress Eugenie's pocket handkerchief trick", plus other tricks he shared with Saul ("the watch trick" and "the enchanted bottle"), his show ending with "The Marvel of Deception" with broken plates and torn handkerchiefs all restored whole.[11]

The Spanish Salad

A trick of this name was done by both Louis and Saul, and earlier by Herr Dobler.

CATCHPHRASES

Both Louis and Saul in their advertising used the term *"Natural Magic"* and both stressed performing with little or no apparatus and *"with bare arms"*, a term first used in Britain by Epstein[12] (who of course took the term, and the idea, from Bartolomeo), so these terms are of no use in distinguishing between Louis and Saul.

Only one of the many catchphrases used by the British Boscos seems to be original to them, Louis's *entirely on the Indian and Egyptian Principles*. This appears to be unique to him: I can find no example which is *not* definitely attributable to him,[13] and he apparently was the inventor of it as a magical catch-phrase. He used it regularly and consistently, and significantly it is last found in Britain in March 1875 when he left the country (and he then used it in America, as late as 1900).

He launched it in June 1866[14] in a new advertisement stating (with my emphasis added): "Signor Bosco, *the greatest wonder of his age*, will open his *Enchanted Palace of Illusion*s, and will introduce his New and Original *Entertainment, entitled Magic, combining* the greatest novelties... bare arms ... *entirely on the Indian and Egyptian Principles*".

"*Entertainment, entitled Magic, combining*", which may sound common enough, is also distinctly Louis's. Similar phrases had been used by Barnardo Eagle ("Entertainment, entitled Magic and Mystery, consisting of...", 1855), and by Anderson ("Entertainment, entitled Magic and Mystery", 1857), but the exact wording *Entertainment, entitled Magic, combining* is used only by Louis (consistently, and together with the three other phrases in this advertisement) in Britain,[15] and later in America; and, again, this phrasing is not found in Britain after the departure of Louis in 1875.

After Louis's departure Saul in 1876 used a similar phrase "Entertainment, entitled Magic!" (but without Louis's "combining...").

The two other phrases in this ad. are less distinctive in that they were more widely used (but only Louis used all four together in the same ad., which is very useful for tracing his career).[16] "*The greatest wonder of his age*" and "*Enchanted Palace of Illusions*" (as distinct from similar phrases such as *The wonder of the world,* etc., or simply *Enchanted Palace*) were first used together by "Herr Dobler" in 1859[17] and still being used by him in 1875. The pairing of the two phrases was appropriated by others, including Professor Devono ("... the greatest Wonder of the Age ...in his Enchanted Palace of Illusions", 1864), and before that by Saul,[18] then by Louis. In August 1865 Saul began using this same combination of "Enchanted Palace of Illusions" and "the greatest wonder of the age".[19] It was now that Louis, wanting a totally new distinctive set of catchphrases, introduced in 1866 "entirely on the Indian and Egyptian Principles", which (so it appears) no one else ever copied.[20]

In 1859 Herr Dobler had come up with the combination of "The Greatest Wonder of the Age" and "Enchanted Palace of Illusions" and continued to use this pairing after it had been appropriated by others. But in 1860 he added a new (rather odd) text: *transfer his assembly to the gold and silver regions, and will fill silver dishes to the brim with gold and silver coins of all nations, catching them in the air as they fly in all parts of the room.*

This he first used in March 1860[21] and then used it regularly and consistently. It remained unique to him until April 1863 when Saul on his tour of Scotland[22] began to reproduce Dobler's text word for word, starting in Arbroath[23] (he had not used this wording the previous month in Dundee). Saul used this "transfer his assembly" text until the end of his Scottish tour in Kelso in October 1863.

Dobler meanwhile had continued using it but abandoned it for a new advertising text also in October 1863; Saul, travelling south (still performing under his real name, not as Bosco), also abandoned the *transfer* text in the same month. In December 1863 both he and Dobler were performing in Brighton at the same time,[24] but their ads were quite different from each other, neither including the *transfer* text, and there was no mention of a clash between them. However, Saul resumed using *transfer his assembly* in 1864,[25] and then, perhaps just to annoy him, Louis also started using the phrase, notably when they came head to head in Leamington Spa in 1866.[26]

An Olio of Incomprehensible Wonders

This favourite phrase of Maskelyne and Cooke in the 1860s was adopted by Saul in the 1870s and still used by him in 1892.

The Royal Illusionist

This was always appealing and had been used by Eagle in the 1830s, Alexandre in the 1840s, and then by others including Stodare, Evanion, and Maskelyne and Cooke. In the 1870s when more than one 'Bosco' adopted it, it was already in use by Antoni Myerns, Prof. Roselle, Prof. Oliver and Heller: Louis Bosco never seems to have used it, but Leotard Bosco did so from June 1874, and Saul Bosco from 1875, and in 1876, not to be outdone, headed an ad with "The Royal Illusionist!!!", also using in the same ad "The Monarch of Legerdemain". Saul kept using it in the 1870s and 1880s (especially when also laying claim to the Balmoral Palace performance), and was still doing so in the 1890s when Arthur St. Vincent, Madame Rose, Adalbert Frikell, and Prof. Field all took a liking to it; Horace Goldin was still using it in 1911.

The Great Monarch of Legerdemain

All examples of this by a Bosco (sometimes as *The Monarch of Legerdemain*) appear to be Saul, who used it from 1871 to 1876.

The Great Necromancer

Used as a 'title" by Laponi from 1838 and notably by Professor Beaumont in the 1860s, the only 'Bosco' to adopt is was Morton Bosco (B69), who also liked "The Great Wonder-Worker and Necromancer".

The Original Bosco

In Britain this was a byline of Saul's from 1871 to 1892 but there is at least one example of Louis calling himself "The Only Original Bosco, The Wonder of the Age…", probably to needle him.[27] In America this "title" was used by both Louis and by Hyam.

Magic, Mirth and Mystery

This had been used by Philippe in the 1830s, and by Horman and Anderson in the 1850s. Saul adopted it in 1870 and used it with relish until at least 1886.

Temple of Magic

This had been used from the 1840s by Anderson, Eagle, Thiodon, Buck and others, and a few times by Epstein (perhaps a suggestion by Prof. Millar). Herr Dobler adopted it in 1861 then Louis used it when touring Ireland in 1862, and sporadically until 1872 (nice illustrated example in url:151). Saul took it up in 1863 but used it only rarely after that. So, it is not a useful term to distinguish one Bosco from another.

Mysteries of Wonderland

A handy diagnostic phrase as the only Signor Bosco to use it was Morton Bosco (B69).

Most recherché...

Used by Epstein ("...Selections from the most recherche of his Experiments") but rarely by later male magicians: *see* Appendix *Z11: Annie Vernone* note 12.

CLAIMS

Many of the claims made by Louis and Saul in their advertising of having performed before various royals and aristocrats are false, the references stolen either from each other or from someone else (both Louis and Saul claimed Epstein's 1855 Balmoral performance: *Appendix Z12*) — or simply made up. Two claims which are both genuine and which were not stolen are Louis before the Duchess of Beaufort in 1860 and Saul before The Imperial Princes of Russia at Torquay in 1864 and Princess Charlotte of Prussia at Sandown in 1874, and any of these references in an ad will identify the Bosco in question. There is no evidence, despite their grand claims, that either Saul or Louis (until he left England in 1875) ever performed on the Continent, let alone "before the crowned heads of Europe".

NOTES

[1] *Oxford Times* 13 Feb.1869.

[2] *Dover Express* 19 Feb.1869; *Surrey Comet* 3 Apr.1869.

[3] *Tadcaster Post, and General Advertiser for Grimstone* 11 Mar.1872.

[4] Born John Wesley Simmons: for accurate information on his life and career see Dean Arnold's fascinating *https://drhslynn.com* site.

[5] Tolmaque's real name is unknown, though in 1884 he gave his next-of-kin as a brother, David *Salomer*, in Hamburg. In 1885 he said "I am known as Herr Tolmaque, or Professor Martin Beaufort Tolmaque. I have borne this name since the commencement of my professional career, 23 years ago". By his own account he was born in 1834 or 1835 in Altona (in Denmark until 1864) and his native language was German. He had a long and colourful career as entertainer, writer, magician, actor, and much more, performing in Britain and France and (he said) in Belgium, Italy and Spain. He settled in Australia in 1875, becoming increasingly eccentric, and died in Tasmania in 1907, his age given as 72. He was buried in a pauper's grave in Cornelian Bay Cemetery, Hobart (not in Melbourne as sometimes stated).

[6] *Norfolk Chronicle* 26 Nov.1864.

[7] *Norfolk News* 3 Dec.1864.

[8] *Bedfordshire Mercury* 12 Dec.1874.

[9] *Cheltenham Examiner* 19 Nov.1873.

[10] For this Dobler see *Appendix Z5*.
[11] *Lancaster Gazette* 14 Mar.1874.
[12] *Aberdeen Herald* 15 Sep.1855. Bare arms were also made much of by Frikell from 1842 in Europe (in England in 1857), Stodare in England in 1864, Rubini (*Appendix Z9*) in 1867.
[13] For example, in periods when of the Boscos touring Britain Louis was the only one in Scotland or Ireland the phrase is found only in newspapers there.
[14] *Ulverston Mirror* 9 June 1866.
[15] A typical example, including all four phrases (and the Japanese top and butterfly tricks), in the *Glossopdale Chronicle and North Derbyshire Reporter* 4 Mar.1871 is unequivocally by Louis as he ends with a condemnation of Saul, calling him "a certain person whose name is S. Warszawski, and travelling under the name of 'Bosco'…".
[16] For example the poster in the Houdini collection for "Signor Bosco" performing in Buxton (url:296) can be confirmed as Louis. For other examples see url:157 to 159.
[17] *Oxford University and City Herald* 12 Feb.1859.
[18] *Beverley Guardian* 19 May 1860.
[19] *Hampshire Chronicle* 19 Aug.1865.
[20] He continued to use it in America and also "Enchanted Palace of Illusions", but the latter was also used there by David Hyam (B66), his brother-in-law, before Louis's arrival.
[21] *Loughborough Monitor* 15 Mar.1860.
[22] Not as "Signor Bosco" but using his real name, as he did for a period from June 1862.
[23] *Arbroath Guide* 11 Apr.1863.
[24] Ads by both in *Brighton Guardian* 23 Dec.1863.
[25] *Hampshire Telegraph* 9 Apr.1864, in Gosport.
[26] Louis's ad is in the *Leamington Advertiser* 18 Jan.1866.
[27] *Bath Chronicle and Weekly Gazette* 8 Jan.1874.

Appendix Z3
"EMIL FRANZISCO" — FRANCESCO CETTI

This note aims to cover Cetti's name, birth, and family background and his early career as a magician, not his later ballooning career. The detailed genealogical information given here (with references) is intended to redress misinformation in standard sources (such as his birth name and that he was illegitimate), and to show that his own accounts of his family background, with an Italian great-grandfather, a father lost at sea, and a painter step-father, were substantially true, and the variety of names he used derived from his grandfather and his mother's relationships.

"Emil Franzisco" was an early stage name of the protean character variously known as (among other variants) Frants Forsberg, Frantz Emil Cetti Forsberg, Frantz Emil Cetti, Franzisco Alexandro Cetti, Francesco Alexandro Cetti, Francesco Cetti,

Frans Cetti, Frans Frandsen, and Frans Pedersen, successively musician, actor, magician, spiritist, starvation artist, and (most famously) balloonist. He was in fact baptised as *Frantz Emil*, son of sailor *Frantzisco Setti Forsberg*.

Francesco, as it is convenient to call him, has biographies in the *Norsk biografisk leksikon* and in the Norwegian wikipedia as Francesco Cetti; in the Swedish wikipedia as Frans Frandsen[1] (all these *qua* balloonist); and in the *Lexikon der Zauberkünstler* as Franzisco Alexandro Cetti (parentage uncertain; not mentioning him as *Forsberg* or *Emil Franzisco,* and he was never a singer).

All agree that he was born in Bergen on April 15th 1860.

Francesco claimed, when asked why he used the names Cetti and Forsberg,[2] that his grandfather had been the Italian Consul General in Stockholm, F.A. Cetti, who had a glass shop there and whose nephew was a famous actor, so making himself a member of the well-known Cetti family who had settled in Scandinavia from Lombardy as glass-blowers and barometer makers. He further claimed that his father was a seaman who had died in the sinking of the ship *Orpheus* when Francesco was six and he had been adopted as a minor by a master painter in Bergen named Forsberg. All very implausible,[3] but it is all true, apart from the statement that he was adopted by Forsberg after his father's death. He was in fact born with that name and it was the name his father grew up with from age nine.

Antonio Cetti, *ca.*1762-1835, his great grandfather, settled in Copenhagen in 1797 as a glass-blower and barometer maker, and soon also a theatrical entrepreneur.[4]

He was the father of the well-known Copenhagen actor and singer Giovanni Battista Cetti, 1794-1858 (whose son Fredrik Adolph Christensen Cetti, 1838-1906, followed him in the profession: see below), and of Francesco Alessandro (Frans Alexander) Cetti, 1803-1879, who learnt glass-blowing from his father's brother Francois in Stockholm[5] and took over his business there in 1828. He became Consul General in Stockholm for the Papal States in 1846 and later for Sardinia and for Italy after its unification.

Frans Alexander Cetti, who remained a Catholic until his death, married Axelia [*sic*] Löwenadler in 1829[6] and had five children with her (two sons and three daughters; two died in infancy); she died in 1860. He also had at least two illegitimate children, one of whom was the father of the balloonist.

The children clearly knew their parentage — all of Bergen did, as we shall see. His father may have kept in touch with him but there is no evidence for that, unlike his other known illegitimate child, Emilia Fransiska (no surname on her birth registration, but later Scheele), born in Stockholm on October 9th 1848 to Emilia Preumeyer (of a musical family who lived near the Cettis). The child was known first as Emilia Rodin, so may have lived with the family of Elisabet Rodin, wife of Antonio Cetti; she was later fostered by a schoolteacher Johanna Källström. Emilia married musician Johann Salberg in 1873 and at the birth of their son Emil August Salberg in 1874 Francesco was sponsor, and he later left her a substantial amount in his will. She died in 1909.[7]

Francesco's father's baptism entry records him as *Francesco Cetti,* illegitimate, born in Bergen October 12th 1835 to *Married man Francesco Cetti, barometer maker,* and *single girl Malene Jacobsd^{tr}*.[8]

We know that Francisco Cetti was in Norway marketing his barometers in early 1835 when the child was conceived. He is reported as arriving via Swinesund from Stockholm in October 1834 heading for Larvik, then in *Bergen* on January 14th 1835 heading for Trondheim, where he arrived on February 18th.[9]

Among the witnesses at the baptism is Jacob A. Jacobsen, probably Malene's older brother. She was born January 2nd 1812 to Isach Jacobsen and his wife Engel Marie Møller, who married in 1809. In the 1815 census the family are living in Bergen, Malene has two older brothers, Jacob and Isach; their father is a "[tr.] fisherman or sailor".[10] In the first quarter of 1837 Malene and her child are receiving financial help from the local parish — announced very publicly in the quarterly reports in the Bergen newspaper: "[tr.] Unmarried girl Malene Jacobsdatter, age 24, with her illegitimate child Francesco Cetti, age 1½ ...";[11] but not in the following quarter. Interestingly that year Francesco donated a number of glass eyes and other glass objects to the Bergen museum for use with preserved birds, fish, and animals.[12] In the 4th quarter of 1842 she is back on the relief list.[13]

Then on August 31st 1845, when young Francesco was nine, 33 year old Malene married 26 year old house painter Andreas Olsen Forsberg in Bergen,[14] and her son Francesco Cetti was now known as Francesco *Forsberg* or *Cetti Forsberg*.

She and Andreas had a son, Anthon Theodor Forsberg, in 1848, but Andreas died in 1849, age 30,[15] and Malene died on January 10th 1853, age 42.[16]

Young Francesco went to sea, probably in 1854. He is listed as a *Jungmand*, usually a second year apprentice who has already had at least one year as a deckhand, among Bergen seamen receiving relief payments from June 5th 1855.[17] In November 1856 he was gaoled for theft, and he was gaoled again for eight months in 1860 ("[tr.] ...for the second time common theft").[18]

He was now a married man and father: on April 13th 1857 in Bergen he had married Engel Margrethe Ne(e)rgaard, age 20. The marriage registration records him as *Francisco Zetti Forsberg: Matros* (sailor), father *Franz Cette, Barometer maker*.[19]

Their first child, Marie Magdalene, was born on July 19th 1857, but died on October 20th 1860.[20] Their next child was the future Francesco, born April 15th 1860 and baptised on April 29th as *Frantz Emil,* the father recorded as *Matros Frantzisco Setti Forsberg*.[21] Three further children followed, baptised as: Maria Magdalene on August 27th 1862 (the father as *Matros Franzisco Sethi Forsberg*);[22] Petter Lauritz Neergaard on September 12th 1864 (father as *Matros Franzisco Cetti Forsberg*);[23] and Antonia Theodora on December 11th 1865 (father as *Matros Fransischo Zetlie Forsberg*).[24] All the children are recorded as legitimate; the *Norsk biografisk leksikon* is incorrect in stating that the parents were unmarried.

The father was at home with the family when the 1865 Bergen census was taken (dated December 1st 1865 but the exact date earlier that year when each household was visited is unknown). They are listed (with the surname wrongly recorded as *Selho*) as *Fransisco Selho* 31 (*husfader matros*), *Engel Margrete* 30, *Frants Emil* 6, *Marie Magdalene* 4, *Peter Lauritz* 2, and *Anthonia Theodora* 1.[25]

Anthonia died the following year and at her burial on June 15th 1866 Engel was listed in the register as a widow and the child as *her* daughter with no reference to the father.[26] The father's ship, *Orpheus,* was lost with all hands in late November 1865 or soon after, the exact date and place unknown.[27]

One year later a series of death notices by the mothers and widows appeared in the *Bergens Adressecontoirs Efterretninger*, the first by the Captain's widow on 24 Nov.1866, announcing that her "[tr.] husband Paul Theodor Hog, Captain of the barque 'Orpheus' found his grave in the waves in November the previous year on a voyage from Newcastle to Alexandria". A similar notice by Engel on December 5th stated that "[tr.] ...my dearly beloved husband Frantzisko Setth. Forsberg, 30 years old, travelling from England to Alexandria with Capt. Hoeg, has found his grave in the waves, leaving me 3 small children who do not know their father has been lost, only me, his deeply saddened wife."[28]

At the start of 1869 Engel is living in the house of schoolteacher Oljen, advertising to teach sewing to young girls,[29] then in August that year she had a daughter, Henrikke Augusta, in Bergen with a Henrik Meyer (a clerical worker about her own age; the child died on her first birthday and received a charity burial.[30] In 1879 she spent a year in Oslo looking after her surviving daughter Maria Magdalene, who died there in November.[31] Then in March 1880 in Oslo she remarried, to Bernhard Edmünd Theodor Schütz, a musician (drummer), born in Danzig in 1846.[32] They lived in Stockholm with Bernhard's relatives from 1890 to 1896,[33] but in the 1900 Norwegian census they are living in Vinkelgade (then a slum) in Oslo, where Bernard is a musician at the Eldorado Teater.[34] They both died in Stockholm, Engel on April 26th 1908 (*"Cancer abdominis"*), and Bernhard in 1910.[35]

By his own account,[36] Francesco took up music at age ten and at fourteen was a trumpeter in the Bergen military band, leaving five years later to study for the stage at the Bergen theatre *Den Nationale Scene*. We get a glimpse of him in 1880 — "the young Norwegian debutant, Mr. Forsberg...",[37] but he soon left and in 1882 performed with the *Neumann Gerbeska Konsert- och Variété Sällskapet,* a Concert and Variety Company run by H. Neumann Gerbes.[38] He was with them, he says, at the Kristiania Tivoli when his "uncle" Fredrik Adolph Cetti[39] arrived in the city with his theatre company. He joined the company, playing some minor roles, but remained with them only briefly. At this time "Stuart Cumberland" was a big success touring with his antispiritist mind-reading shows and Francesco took up a similar act.

By September 1883 he was performing in Fredrikstad in Norway as "Franzisco, Illusionist og Antispiritist", featuring "moderne Salon-Magie", with Memory and Mind-reading acts, the Spirit Cabinet (as "Det røde Hus"), a "Flyvemaskine" which whisked people from the stage to the gallery,[40] and the gun trick, billing himself as a *target*, "Skydeskive", and claiming to be a pupil of Prof. Epstein.[41]

At the end of the year he was in Agder, now as "Emil Franzisco",[42] and in January 1884 in Moss, where a review reported warmly that his "[tr.] presentation yesterday ... in modern Salon magic for a very small audience. The professor, who must be the first Norwegian to act as a magician, has, under the guidance of the famous now-deceased Professor Epstein, acquired a considerable skill, and he performs his tricks without apparatus with a rare dexterity and neatness. The wide range of his tricks won the undivided applause of the small audience".[43]

He continued touring this act in Norway until August 1884, claiming that no one had performed the gun trick since the death of Epstein.[44]

In September he was in Sweden, still as "Emil Franzisco", doing the gun trick and calling himself a former "pupil" (sometimes "companion") of Prof. Epstein, but principally as a Mind-reader, claiming secrets known only to Cumberland and to Bishop, and performing the Spirit Cabinet act (now "Gröna Huset"). In Linköping in October he announced that this would be his last performance of the gun trick.[45] That month he had his brief association with "Henry Adams" (Brøndum, B12a) as his manager, in Örebro, Nora, Arboga, ending in Eskiltuna, where "Emil Franzisco" was sued for their board and lodging, blaming it on the contract signed by "Mr Adams".[46] Both now were giving similar mind-reading shows, including the spirit-cabinet act.

Emil is last sighted as "Emil Franzisco" in Enköping in December 1884. In May 1885 we find him performing as a mind-reader in Stockholm, now under the name "Franzisco Cetti",[47] and in Norway the following year under this name, which he now used consistently. In 1887 he was doing his "Hungerkünstler" starvation act in Berlin and London, but back in Scandinavia as a mind-reader and illusionist in 1888.[48]

In the 1891 Bergen census he is recorded as (probably) "Franzisco Emilio Farsberg Cetti"[49] and in the 1900 Stockholm census as "Fransesco Emilio Cetti".[50]

By late 1889 he was becoming a professional balloonist, and the last references found to him performing as a magician are in early 1894.[51]

He died in an Oslo hospital on April 3rd 1925.

NOTES

[1] A note inserted in the Norwegian *wikipedia* article also states that he was known in Sweden as Frans Frandsen, but no source for this statement is given in either article. This name is not mentioned in the article discussing him in the *Svenskt biografiskt lexikon*, and not found in Swedish newspapers, which consistently refer to him as Cetti. In the 1900 Stockholm census he is listed as *Fransesco Emilio Cetti*. He has probably been confused with a Frans Frandsen who shares his dates, 1860-1925, but he was born 27 July 1860 in Copenhagen: see also note 50.

[2] Versions in several newspaper accounts, for example *Bergens Tidende* in Norway 2 Oct.1886 (reprinted from *Nutiden*), and *Kalmar* in Sweden 16 July 1887.

[3] And the *Svenskt biografiskt lexikon* in its 1929 article on the Cetti family (online at https://sok.riksarkivet.se/sbl/artikel/14776), banishes Francesco to an afternote, stating that he was from a Cetti family from Genoa, which "[tr.] has no known connection with the one above".

[4] He has entries in the *Lexikon* as both 'Cetti, Antonio [1]' and [3], the latter with the wrong wife.

[5] Francois is the 'Cetti, Francesco [1]' in the *Lexikon, ca.*1781-1828.

[6] Daughter of Captain Axel Löwenadler; her first name is sometimes given as Alexia, from the Latin form of her name, *Alexiæ Magdalenæ Marianæ Lowenadler*, in the Catholic parish records.

[7] I have not been able to see the images of the baptism or the will: this account is based largely on the interesting evolving discussion at url:297.

[8] Online at url:298. The column on the right indicates that the child's status was reported by the midwife.

[9] *Morgenbladet* 12 Oct.1834; *Bergens Adressecontoirs Efterretninger* 17 Jan.1835; *Trondhjems borgerlige Realskoles* 20 Feb.1835.

[10] Her baptism (Jan 10th 1812) is at url:299; her entry in the 1815 census at url:300.

[11] "Af- og Tilgangs-Liste over Almisselemmer i Bergen i 1st Qvartal 1837. Afgaaen i Domkirkens Sogn ... 464. Pigen Malene Jacobsdatter, 24 Aar, med sit uægte Barn, Francesco Cetti, 1½ Aar, 18 R. No. 138, 60 k. maandelig": *Bergens Adressecontoirs Efterretninge* 13 May 1837.

[12] *Bergens Adressecontoirs Efterretninger* 9 Dec.1837.

[13] *Bergens Adressecontoirs Efterretninger* 15 Mar.1843: "...Fransciscus Cetti".

[14] Marriage registration online at url:301. His surname is transcribed as 'Forberg' but is clearly 'Forsberg' on the image.

[15] In a death notice by Malene in *Bergens Adressecontoirs Efterretninger* 14 Mar. 1849 we hear of "[tr.] a protracted weakness and long illness ... a painful loss for me and our one year old son".

[16] Buried on July 14th, url:302.

[17] 'Extract af Regnskabet for Understøttelsescassen for uheldige Sømænd i Bergen for Aaret 1855': *Bergens Adressecontoirs Efterretninger* 9 Feb.1856.

[18] Records at url:303.

[19] Marriage registration at url:304. Engel was a sailor's daughter, born in Bergen on December 12th 1836 to Johan Peter Nergaard and Clerche Marie Lund Kille, who married in 1833.

[20] Her birth registration at url:305 (the father as *Matros Fransisco Setti Forsberg*); her death registration at url:306 (*Matros Francisco Forsbergs Datter;* cause of death is 'Krampe', convulsions).

[21] His birth registration, url:307.

[22] Her birth registration is at url:308; she died in Christiana in 1879 age 17 (url:309); death notice signed by Engel in *Aftenposten* 4 Nov.1879 ("[tr.] six days of severe suffering...") and one by Frantz in *Bergens Tidende* 10 Nov.1879)

[23] His birth registration at url:310.

[24] Birth registration at url: 311; she died June 11th 1866 (url: 312; again, 'Krampe').

[25] Francesco and his parents in 1865 Bergen census, url:313.

[26] Burial of Antonia at url:314 ("Enka Engel M. Forsbergs dattar").

[27] The *Orpheus* (not to be confused with many ships of the same name) was a barque of 451 tons which carried cargo wherever business offered. In August 1865 she arrived in Shields from Iquique via Valparaiso (120 days' passage from Valparaiso) with a load of Chile saltpetre; she sailed from there on September 8th to Bergen arriving on September 20th (the last time the crew would have seen their families); she returned to Shields on November 4th, then sailed for Alexandria (probably carrying coal and bricks) on November 23rd, and was never heard from again. Reports of her loss first appeared in U.K. papers at the end of April 1866.

[28] *Bergens Adressecontoirs Efterretninger* 5 Dec.1866: "...min inderlig elskede Mand Frantzisko Setth. Forsberg, 30 Aar gammel, paa Reise fra England til Alexandria med Capt. Hoeg, har fundet sin Grav in Bølgerne, efterladende mig 3 smaa Børn, som ikke kjende Savnet af Fader uden alene mig hans hjertelig bedrøvede Kone".

[29] *Bergens Tidende* 11 Jan.1869.

[30] Birth of daughter at url:315 (Enke Engel Margrethe Nergaard; wrongly transcribed as Nesgaard); death of daughter at url:316.

[31] See note 20.

[32] Marriage registration at url:317.

[33] The couple are listed *Folkräkning 1890* (url:318) in Hedvig Eleonora församling rote 10, Bernhard a "Trumslagare", and in the *Husförhörslängd* ('Household Examination Book'; url:319), which includes their deaths.

[34] Census at url:320.

[35] Images of the death registrations are on *ancestry.com* ('Sweden, Indexed Death Records, 1840-1947', the surname wrongly transcribed as "Scheitz").

[36] From the biographies, which are not entirely consistent, in *Bergens Tidende* 2 Oct. 1886 (from *Nutiden*) and in *Kalmar* 16 July 1887; and the article 'Francesco Cetti og hans Bedrifter' in *Morgenavisen* 4 May 1920.

[37] *Aftenposten* 16 Nov.1880 ("[tr.] Whether or not the young Norwegian debutant, Mr. Forsberg, who played Adolf Møller, possesses some dramatic talent, it is impossible to judge from such an insignificant role as the one he played yesterday").

[38] *Göteborgs Handels-Och Sjöfartstidning* 9, 11 Dec.1882.

[39] In fact his grandfather's brother's son, so his first cousin once removed.

[40] *Fredriksstad Tilskuer* 29 Sep.; 13 Oct.1883.

[41] *Fredriksstad Tilskuer* 16 Oct.1883 ("...Iaften udfører han til Slutning Prof. Epsteins bekjendte Bravurnummer: at lade sig skyde paa med skarpe Kugler, et Kunststykke, han har lærnt af Prof. Epstein").

[42] *Nedenæs Amtstidende* 5, 8 Dec.1883.

[43] *Moss Tilskuer* 10, 12, 15 Jan.1884.

[44] *Bergens tidende* 11 Aug.1884.

[45] *Östgöta Correspondenten* 4 Oct.1884.

[46] See B12a p.250 and notes 15-17.

[47] A nice note in *Östgöta Correspondenten* 7 May 1885, 'En gengånare', *a revenant*, comments on his reappearance under a new name.

[48] In Agder in 1888 he grandly advertises as "Hr. Francisco Cetti, Hofexperimenter hos D.M. Kong Oscar II af Norge-Sverige og Alexander III af Rusland med hans nyeste og sensationelleste Kunststykker" (*Agderposten* 11 May 1888): no record has been found of him performing for King Oscar, let alone for Czar Alexander.

[49] At url:321 (rather hard to decipher).

[50] At url:322. There is no evidence that he used the name Frans Frandsen in Sweden (see note 1), and he was not the person of that name who married writer Ingeborg Platou in 1887. Nor was his birth (baptismal) name Frans Pedersen ("Frans Pedersen var hans virkelige navn fra dåpen ...") as stated in articles in *Norges Handels og Sjøfartstidende* 3 Sept.1960 and *Aftenposten* 21 Oct.1961.

[51] For example *Kalmar* 27 Jan.1894, billing himself here as both "Luftseglaren" and "Tusenkonstnären", the latter including a variety of tricks and "experiments". Even 19th century Swedish dictionaries define *tusenkonstnär* only as 'cunning fellow' or its modern meaning of 'Jack-of-all-trades', but there is abundant evidence from contemporary newspapers that it was widely used, like *Tausendkünstler,* for 'conjuror', 'magician'. Among many unequivocal examples that could be cited are "Den nye Hexmästaren af vår bekante tusenkonstnär, Hr Höökenberg, innehåller icke mindre än 150 kurt och taskspelarekonster" (*Dagligt Allehanda* 14 Dec.1843) and "En tusenkonstnär af första slaget, en ny Bosco och äfwen systerson till den bekante trollkarten med detta namn, hr St. Roman..." (*Härnösandsposten* 6 Apr.1867).

Appendix Z4
EPHRAIM HAMBUJER

Little information, largely misinformation, has been available on Hambujer and his career. He has a brief mention in Frost's *Lives of the Conjurors,* saying he was Danish and performed in Dublin in 1859; Whaley adds that he was born in 1848 and also performed in Boston in 1860; no entry in the *Lexikon.* From information given by descendants it is clear that he was **Ephraim Hambujer** (also spelt Hamburg, Hamburger), born Frankfurt 1 Oct. 1824, died Chicago 31 May 1913. One family member has a scrapbook of his ("1850-60 testimonial book").[1]

He married at least four times and had eleven children, the eldest, born Morris Hamburgher in Birmingham, U.K., in 1854, became a popular comedian "Billy Robinson" in America; the last, Estella, was born in 1881.

He is said to have settled in England in 1850. The earliest definite sighting of him performing anywhere is at the Mermaid Hotel, Yeovil, June 1852 — "Mr. Hamburger … A New Series of his Astounding Wonders … Mr. Hamburger will allow any person present to fire a pistol at him and he will vanish out of room unobserved, and return again uninjured holding a lighted candle in each hand". He claims here to have performed for The Queen and Prince Albert, the Emperor of Russia, the Emperor of Austria, the King of Prussia, the Grand Sultan of Turkey, and the King of Hanover, and "has upwards of 200 testimonials in various languages". It would be interesting if *any* of these are in the scrapbook held by the descendant.[2]

He continued on through Somerset and Dorset, then is next sighted in Preston and Liverpool in 1854, now as "Monsieur Hamburger"; in Birmingham in 1856, he is "Mons. Hamburger, The Great French Magician", claiming to have performed "before the Court of Vienna, the Court of Berlin, and at the private Soirees of the Principal Nobility and Gentry, both in England and on the Continent".[3]

Later that year he is in the north of England and in Glasgow; early in 1857 in Dover and Portsmouth, later in Leicester, Leeds and Liverpool; 1858 Sheffield, Stroud, Cheltenham, Bristol, and Wales — with mixed success. In March in Stroud he declined to perform for the small audience and returned to his inn. The crowd demanded a refund but the money taken at the door went straight to pay for the hire of the hall. He was placed in a cell overnight but the Bench next morning declined to take action.[4] And in Pontypridd in December he left town with his bills unpaid — "Mon. Hamburger, who styled himself King of Wizards. after humbugging the audience … vanished in a cloud of smoke".[5]

He was billing himself as Hambujer from at least October 1858 and now used this name consistently, soon advertising himself as "the only legitimate Bare-Armed Performer and Sleight-of-hand Wizard in the World". Accompanied by "Madame Saluinani, the novel Italian pianist", his wife, he was in the south of England and in Wales until March 1859, then headed to Ireland, where he toured successfully from April 1859 until January 1860.

He then left for America, arriving in New York by February 1860 when his third child was born (to his second wife). He opened in Hope Chapel, 719 Broadway, on April 19th 1860 — "Wizard's Palace... The Great Hambujer, Royal Wizard, First Appearance in America in his Grand Drawing Room Entertainment, as presented before her Majesty Queen Victoria…".[6] This went off "with good success", said a reviewer: "He is distinguished from his predecessors rather by his superiority of manner than by novelty of invention. Many of his tricks are new, however, and his audience… were very liberal with their applause".[7] He then had a good run at the Palace Garden Music Hall, accompanied by "Mad. Saluinani, Italian pianist" and "Sig. Leopold, the Brilliant Violinist",[8] before moving on to Boston and upstate New York. In April he had a New York agent, Alfred Cately, but fell out with him a few weeks later, Cately stating that "a regard for his own character and reputation impelled him to dissolve all connection with the Wizard".[9]

Hambujer toured widely, sighted in Toronto, Cleveland and Cincinnati ("with his dwarf Sprightly") that year; Kentucky, Brooklyn, Philadelphia, Montreal, Vermont in 1861 — where his old financial problems followed him: "Hambujer (Humbugger) the Royal Wizard is a 'tuff kuss'. He don't pay the printers. He victimized the press here; likewise at Montpellier. Pass him around brother editors".[10]

He was soon in Illinois, in Springfield as "the Great East India Magician" with "Madame Hambujer the world-renowned pianist"[11], then in Chicago, promising "the thrilling and tragic feat of murdering a boy and restoring him to life, and the beautiful and extraordinary suspension of a boy sixteen years of age, by a single hair of the head",[12] and in Iowa and St Louis in 1862.

He had settled with his second wife, Rebecca, in Buffalo, where his third and fourth child were born, and in November 1862 he "retired from public life" and opened a restaurant in Buffalo. "Hambujer's Café and Restaurant, On the European Style" offered free entertainment for patrons in a room upstairs, but this all came to nothing when his wife died on December 25th. In January he announced: "I, Prof. Hambujer, call on the citizens of Buffalo for a benefit ! … the death of my beloved wife, which misfortune has left four helpless children on my hands to maintain … having had to abandon my Restaurant … I would respectfully solicit your patronage … being forced to resume my magical evenings".[13]

He was back on the road for many years — Ohio in 1863; Delaware, Connecticut, Virginia in 1864, making much of his trick of murdering a boy and restoring him to life[14]; still performing in 1879 in Pontiac, Michigan. He remarried about 1865 and again in 1910. He also went in for land speculation with a subdivision in Roscommon, Michigan, and was a successful inventor, with more than 33 patents in his name. In 1893 he published a book, *The Family Tree,* designed to record family births, deaths and marriages — and property investments.[15]

By 1866 he was living in Detroit ("patent agent" in 1870 and 1880 U.S. census) and from 1891 in Chicago. He died in Chicago on May 31st 1913 and was buried in Ridge Lawn Cemetery on June 3rd. A death notice in the *Chicago Tribune* gave his age as 88, but the following day a very colourful obituary said he was 97, born in 1815, and had joined the Prussian army at 18, serving as a drill master until "he was detailed in 1850 for three years' detached service in London". He fought (we are told) in the American Civil War for four years, and returned to Europe to fight in the Franco-Prussian War…[16] Equally untrue was the claim that he had served in the military in India and learnt his "Indian mysteries" there.

[1] See url:323 for sites with useful information. Family members state that he was a devout Jew and that his father's name was Moishe (Moses).
[2] *Sherborne Mercury* 29 June 1852.
[3] *Aris's Birmingham Gazette* 30 June; 7 July 1856.
[4] *Stroud Journal* 27 Mar.1858.
[5] *Star of Gwent* 18 Dec.1858.
[6] *NY Tribune* 17, 23, 25 Apr.1860.
[7] *NY Herald* 26 Apr.1860.
[8] *NY Evening Express* 16 May 1860.
[9] *New York Clipper* 28 Apr.; 7 July 1860.
[10] *Vermont Phoenix* [Brattleboro] 14 Nov.1861, from another Vermont paper, the *Burlington Times*.
[11] *Sangamo Journal* 9 Oct.1861.
[12] *Chicago Tribune* 21 July 1862.
[13] *Buffalo Daily Courier* 25 Nov.; 2, 15 Dec.1862; 19, 24 Jan.1863.
[14] A striking advertisement in 1863 reads: "$500 REWARD FOR THE MURDERER. HAMBUJER Kills and Restores to Life a Boy…" (*Albany Morning Express* 1 June 1863).
[15] *The Interocean* [Chicago] 1 Apr.1893.
[16] *Chicago Tribune* 1, 2 June 1913.

Appendix Z5
HERR DOBLER

Not, of course, Ludwig Leopold ("Louis") Döbler but the Englishman George William Smith Buck, born in Newark, Nottinghamshire, on July 6th 1837. Some obituaries (e.g. *Bristol Times* 23 Mar.1904) mistakenly stated that he was the son of magician "Professor Buck" and this has crept into modern accounts, however a letter from a family member in *Bristol Times* 24 Mar.1904 corrects this: "He was not the son of Professor Buck, but the son of Job Hart Buck of Newark-upon-Tyne (where he was born), who was by profession an accountant and geographical lecturer. Professor Buck, the conjurer, was no relation to our family".

He began using the stage-name "Professor Dobler" from July 1858, then "Herr Dobler" from February 1859 until the end of his career. In the 1901 Scottish census he is listed as "George Dobler", society entertainer. He died in Aberdeen on March 21st 1904; probate listed under "George Buck or Dobler". His daughter Mary became a professional palm reader, and his son George a conjuror, showman, circus agent, and theatre manager.

Appendix Z6
KRATKY-BASCHIK

There are several modern accounts of Kratky-Baschik's career, many with errors — his correct birth date, place and name are given in the article at url:324: born Antonin Kratky on January 11th 1810 in Kozlany (now in the Czech Republic; German Kozlan), son of Karl Kratky and his wife Barbara (née Baššika).

While the addition of *Baschik* may well have been to hint at an Arabic or Turkish connexion, it was in fact the German form of his mother's maiden name.

Little has been written on his interesting period in England. As noted in the *Magicpedia* article, he performed before Queen Victoria at Windsor Castle — this was on November 1st [not 8th] 1858 (see 'Court Circular' of Nov. 2nd printed in *Globe* and other London papers 3 Nov.1858; and Ottokar Fischer's article in *The Sphinx* 10 May 1937 includes a facsimile of the dated royal programme. For years afterwards in Germany and Austria Kratky billed himself as *Virtuoso and Magician* ('Virtuos und Physiker') *of her Majesty Queen Victoria* — as on the Leipzig poster online at url:325 (which must be 1885 as September 27th is a Sunday).

The *Magicpedia* article repeats Fischer's error that it was Bartolomeo, not Epstein, whom Kratky worked with in England in 1857: see B12 note 35). Fischer (who took over Kratky's *Zaubertheater* after his nephew Mathias Kratky) clearly actually sighted the contract signed between Kratky-Baschik and "Alfred Bosco" in June 1857, but he concluded from the similarity of Alfred Bosco's signature with that of Bartolomeo that this in fact *was* Bartolomeo touring England under that name. The contract gave Kratky £10 a week, plus free board and travel, to perform at all Alfred's public shows and half the profits from their private shows.

After his stint with Epstein, Kratky-Batschik performed in Brighton in September 1857 ("a decided hit", said the *Era*), then a good run at the Theatre Royal in Marylebone (billed as "Polish" and "the greatest Musical and Thaumaturgical Phenomenon that ever visited this country"), followed by Woolwich, Maidstone, Chatham, Gravesend, Portsmouth, the Isle of Wight, Brighton, for the Queen at Windsor, then for the public in Windsor... He was then taken up by P.T. Barnum who was in England lecturing on the 'Art of Money Making', and Kratky, billed as "the Sclavonian Hungarian Artist", now accompanied him for three months giving his musical entertainment as a ten-minute interval. Added to the show was the exhibition of the "Feejee Mermaid" on stage after the lecture. Kratky then toured his "Magical and Musical Illusions" round Britain, with a very long successful run in Ireland until June 1860 when he left for America.

An infant named Juan Franzisko Kratky Baschik died in London in 1859, almost certainly a child of his.

Interestingly an article (*Grazer Volksblatt* 21 Aug.1883) later referred to him as "Kratky-Baschik or Bosco LXXX" but I can find no trace of him ever billing himself under that name.

Appendix Z7
PLATE SPINNING

Plate spinning (plate dancing, plate waltzing), with the plate spun vertically on a flat surface (not horizontally on a stand, a stick, or a finger) was never common.

When Maskelyne and Cooke opened at St James's Hall in 1873 reviewers were as much taken with the novelty and skill of Maskelyne's "Chinese Plate Dancing" as with the levitation, decapitation, transformation, and spirit cabinet acts. Plate dancing was uncommon enough even for American papers[1] to reprint the English reviews — "…The neatest feat introduced by Mr Maskelyne is one introduced into this country forty years ago by a prestidigitator named Signor Blitz, and which is so difficult of attainment that only two persons, since that person, have ever performed it in public. By the swift movement of the fingers half a dozen china desert [*sic*] plates are made to execute a quadrille, and go singly and collectively through a variety of curious evolutions. The dexterity of manipulations displayed in this really elegant accomplishment shows the unexpected extent to which the fingers can be educated…".

In London the *Era* said "A most astonishing feat was then performed by Mr Maskelyne … half-a-dozen large dessert plates being kept in a series of graceful evolutions at one time by means of a simple twist of the finger. We do not remember to have seen anything so dexterous", and later "Perhaps the most pleasing feat exhibited by Mr Maskelyne is what is described on the programme as 'Chinese Plate Dancing'. This feat was introduced to this country some forty years ago by Signor Blitz. It requires amazing digital dexterity, and Mr Maskelyne assures us that years of practice have been necessary on his part in order to ensure that proficiency in the art which he now manifests … he makes one of them dance a hornpipe and keep time with wonderful exactitude to the music. Another he turns into a kind of earthenware Ethardo, causing it to make the ascent and descent of one of those spiral frames with which the gymnast we have named first made us acquainted".[2]

Other London papers were equally impressed —
"…a very uncommon performance. It must have taken him years to acquire so through a mastery…";[3] "The cleverest feature of the whole performance is, in our opinion, what is called the 'Chinese plate Dancing' … one of the neatest and most dexterous feats that … we have ever seen accomplished".[4]

And still in the 1880s — "the dexterity with which Mr. Maskelyne sets a whole dinner service of plates waltzing round the table…";[5] "…this adroit master of legerdemain has himself excited wonder and applause by setting a whole table of plates waltzing by skilful manipulation…".[6]

This had been part of Maskelyne's act for some years, added for variety (it was after all a juggler's act, sheer manual (*digital!*) skill with no illusion involved) in early 1867 when they opened in Bath on January 5th — "The Japanese Animated Plates, or Dance of Wonder (new)".[7] And it was well received in Brighton later in the month — "the dancing of the Japanese animated plates excites applause in the audience from the clever handling they receive from Mr. Maskelyne, who waltzes three of them at one time with the great possible ease".[8]

They soon began describing the act as "Chinese" rather than "Japanese" — "the fan and butterfly trick, Chinese plate dancing, and other feats of jugglery, all of which were cleverly executed by Mr. Maskelyne";[9] "…in our estimation, the most wonderful feature of the first part of the entertainment is the Chinese plate dancing trick. This is a feat of great manual dexterity, and must have taken the manipulator much time to accomplish successfully …".[10]

Maskelyne had learnt plate spinning, as E.A. Dawes says, from "a magician named Blitz Junior".[11] Blitz Junior was John Blitz, *ca.*1821-1895, younger brother of Antonio (actually Samuel, *Shmuel*) Blitz, 1810-1877, both of whom performed plate spinning, no doubt learnt from their father Abraham Blitz, *ca.*1762-1848. Abraham, born in Moldavia (as Antonio claimed he also was, though both he and his brother were born in Kent), was in England by 1810, working as a jeweller, then as a magician from 1814; by the late 1820s both Abraham and Antonio were touring Britain, both billing themselves as *Antonio Blitz* and as *Signor Blitz*, Abraham usually accompanied by young John.

Abraham, by now in his sixties, is never found spinning plates himself, but it is regularly performed by Antonio and, from the age of eight (and possibly from age six) by John.[11] Young John occasionally performed with his brother rather than his father, and in Oxford in 1833 we find them spinning plates together — "Signor Blitz's Pupil … who will, in concert with him, introduce the Dance of the Ten Dinner Plates at One Time, passing through all the evolutions of the Mazy Dance".[12]

Antonio left for America in 1835,[13] while John continued his career in Britain. In 1836 we see him and his father in Saffron Walden in Essex, Abraham still doing the gun trick, the newspaper review noting that a local crack shot fired three bullets only to have them caught in "the Signor's magic hands", and that "the performance of young Signor Blitz on the dinner plates met with unbounded applause".[14] John also became well-known for barrel-running, but plate spinning remained the centre-piece of his act — "… he stands unrivalled; the dexterity of the young Signor, at the close of the performance, keeping five dinner-plates dancing at once at the end of his finger is truly admirable, and cannot fail creating the highest admiration".[15]

He is first found performing on his own in 1844, but soon after was back on tour with his father who performed until the year before his death in 1848. John now took over the "Signor Blitz" title in England. A poster advertises a performance by him at the Cricket Ground, Leicester, on June 16th 1851 — "…Will Go through his Singular, Astonishing, and Novel Performance on a Revolving Cask!!!", including a Steeple Chase, ascending one Forty-Round Ladder and descending another – "a feat never performed by any other man in the country"—and concluding with The Dancing of the Dinner Plates.[16]

His later career (and Antonio's) are treated in detail in my forthcoming book on the Blitz Family (and their Impostors)[17] but a few later aspects of John's career are relevant here:

In 1862 he is touring England with Professor Millar (B62) and his second wife, John still spinning plates — "the difficult feat of the dancing of the dinner plates, during which he informed the company he is the only person in England who accomplishes that feat".[18] In 1866 he was still dancing the plates and still barrel-rolling ("his Great Puncheon Feat"). He retired in 1873 to manage a hotel — but still listed himself as a "Professor of Legerdemain" in the 1881 census; he died in Bristol in 1895.

John had married in January 1849,[19] and in the 1851 census he, his wife and their Abraham (note 19) are staying at the Salutation Inn in Cheltenham run by John N. Maskelyne and his wife Harriet. These are the parents of John, the future magician, who is here age 12 with his six sisters. Young John, soon apprenticed as a watchmaker, was a keen amateur conjuror and was performing in public only a few years later. It was likely now that John Blitz first gave him lessons in plate-spinning.

In 1855 Epstein (B12) came on the scene in Britain, with plate spinning a regular feature of his repertoire throughout his stay — "the dish and plate dance",[20] "the Chinese plate and dish dance",[21] and in 1857 he was rated as highly as Blitz — "…the dance of the dinner plates and the *pas-seul* of the wash-hand basin, that Signor Blitz introduced into this country a quarter of a century since, but which we have never since seen so well accomplished, displays a nimbleness of the present professor's fingers to very great advantage".[22]

When Epstein left Britain in 1857 it was him that his contending successors as "Signor Bosco" were vying to emulate — and then each other — and we find occasional references to Warszawski, Susser, and Morton Bosco (B63, B65, B69) all including plate dancing in their acts. Susser in 1859 is advertising "The Terpsichorean Delf" and in 1861 making "sundry dishes perform wonderful gyrations", and still doing it in America in 1879;[23] Warszawski in 1863 is "spinning heavy plates at a prodigious rate" — the "Chinese plate and dish dance";[24] and in 1869 in Dundee Morton Bosco "first introduced his dancing plates, which he made spin round a table and keep time to music … thunderous applause".[25]

Some other exponents of plate spinning, probably spinning it on a flat surface, in Britain and America[26] during the 19th century include the following —

Phineas Taylor Barnum in his autobiography, *The Life of P.T. Barnum*, describes launching his career by finding in Albany in 1835 "one Antonio, an Italian, performing feats of balancing, plate-spinning, stilt-walking and the like. These things were then new in America..". Barnum hired him and changed his name to Signor Vivalla. His act featured plates spinning on sticks and in the air and probably also on a flat surface. The range of his plate juggling and the sad story of his career are told in detail by David Cain at url:328.

In England in the 1820s and 1830s is Mons. De Cour, "known throughout Europe by the appellation of the French Hercules from Franconi's Olympic Circus", doing a strongman act, but "he will also exhibit Indian Juggling and the laughable Performance of Six Dinner Plates Dancing, &c." He was in England by 1825, sighted in Bath in 1832, and in January 1839 teamed up with the illusionist Felix Testot (senior) to exhibit "their extraordinary Magical Illusions, Cabalistic Mirror, Feats of Strength, Balancing, and the Dancing of the Dinner Plates".[27]

W.J. Cooke, "the celebrated Ventriloquist and Magician from the United States" is sighted in Kingston, Jamaica, in 1839, his tricks including "Plate Dancing and Equi-librium".[28]

A very varied performance of "Novel Entertainments" advertised in Baltimore in 1844 included a blind singer and violinist; an exhibition of "nitrous oxyde"; nine living rattle snakes; and "Mr. Henry in Plate Waltzing".[29]

A certain "Mons. Palterini" performing in Blackburn in 1845 showed great dexterity with the 'Egyptian' cups and balls — "the 'dancing plates', however, excited most applause ... It is almost inconceivable how five of these could be kept in motion at once...".[30]

An unequivocal example is "Mons. le Tort" (Joseph Bartley?) touring Ireland in 1849, who "caused a number of delf plates to dance to music, on a board ... another feat which has won for the magician great credit".[31]

In 1860 "Herr Dobler" (*Appendix Z5*) showed "amazing skill in the feats of the dancing plates and dish" in Jersey, and the same in 1878 in Derby, "...his skill in spinning plates, dishes. and a large pancheon, called forth much applause", so this was probably a regular feature of his act.[32]

Advertising in the *Era* in late 1868[33] is "Mons. Verone, Oriental and Demon Illusionist, Japanese Butterfly Illusion, Bowls of Fish, the Charmed Doves, Indian Pistol feat, Hat Spinning, Spinning Plates, Juggling Chinese. Mystery, Mystic Glass in the Air, &c." What is interesting is that we can follow Verone's career from 1867 until his death in 1892 in reviews and his detailed advertisements and this is the only period in which he mentions plate spinning in his act. Performing as Louis Verone, he later added ventriloquism and antispiritualism. An 1874 review tells us that "striking out on a different style of performance from Anderson, Bosco, and Lynn, Professor Verone centres the combined talents of these great masters".[34] He died in Guildford in 1892, his death registered as "Louis Veroni" [no relation to Annie Vernone / Veroni of *Appendix Z11*], age 42, but his real name was Arthur George Webb. His son Harold George Webb is listed in the 1911 census as a "Professional Conjuror".

Fritz Renhard, "facial artist, ventriloquist, Chinese equilibrist and oriental prestidigitateur" in Eastbourne in 1878 has five tumblers of water on the end of a stick balanced on his chin, toe or knee, "and simultaneously spins a plate on the table... well worth seeing".[35]

The Blitz family had many impostors but only one is known to have had plate spinning in his repertoire and he was, by all accounts, a master of it, setting as many as twenty plates spinning at the same time. "Herr Blitz", billing himself as "Plate Charmer and Equilibrist", "Plate Manipulator", and "Spiral Plate Pyramid Ascensionist" had a very successful career in Britain between 1874 and 1903, on his own and later with Poole's and Hamilton's Dioramas and Tudor's Circus.

Reviewers were very taken with his performances — "... with his fingers alone he spins them ... both hands are employed, and two plates are made to ascend and descend simultaneously. Nor is this all, for at the same time the foot of Blitz is engaged with a tambourine, also kept whirling...", and: "He takes his plates up and down a spiral column, similar to that used by the great Ethardo in his marvellous ascents... In this kind of performance we may safely say that Herr Blitz is not only unsurpassed but is altogether unapproachable".[36] In 1900 he claimed to be "the only living plate charmer".[37] He advertised himself as Australian for many years but was in fact Matthias Hayward, born in Alverstoke, Hampshire, in 1850, died in Runcorn in 1940.

Herbert J. Collings ("Col Ling Soo") did plate spinning for many years, said to have been taught by Maskelyne, though Collings's himself states in his recollections 'Smilestones' (url:329) that he met Maskelyne late in 1902 but had been practising plate-spinning since 1900, age 17, and by the following year could nearly spin one with his left hand as well, and by August 1902 could spin four plates and a bowl — which he seems to be doing in a photograph included in 'Smilestones' which is dated 1901. He was still doing plate-spinning in his act in 1929.

An article in *Magic Circular* vol.29 no.325, Dec.1934 includes a picture of him dressed as Antonio Blitz at a Magic Circle Banquet in November that year.

There is an interesting photograph of Maskelyne performing plate spinning (posed, with the plates held stationary) in Anne Goulden's article 'Maskelyne & Cooke: the early years' (url:330), and many more photos of him in C. Lang Neil's *The Modern Conjurer and Drawing-Room Entertainer* (url:331) but that wrongly states that Maskelyne learnt from Antonio Blitz (who was by then in America).

Further illustrations and films are given in the 'Plate Waltzing' section of 'The Art of Plate Spinning' (url:332); the 1896 French film *Le tourneur d'assiettes* with Félicien Trewey is online at url:333; and Erich Brenn at url:334 is seen on the Ed Sullivan show simultaneously spinning plates on sticks and eight on a table.

---

[1] Among many examples are *Memphis Daily Appeal* 28 Apr. 1873 and *Janesville Gazette* 6 May 1873.

[2] *Era* 9 Mar.1873 (at the Crystal Palace); 6 Apr.1873 (in St James's Hall).

[3] *Daily News* 4 Mar.1873.

[4] *London and Provincial Entr'acte* 12 Apr.1873.

[5] *Penny Illustrated Paper* 14 Aug.1886.

[6] *Illustrated London News* 10 Aug.1889.

[7] *Bath Chronicle and Weekly Gazette* 3 Jan.1867.

[8] *Brighton Gazette* 31 Jan.1867.

[9] *Cheltenham Looker-On* 20 Feb.1869.

[10] *Hull and Eastern Counties Herald* 4 May 1871. An early 1871 ad reads "Chinese and Japanese Plate Dancing": *Leeds Times* 28 Jan.1871.

[11] Introduction by Edwin A. Dawes to *Maskelyne's Book of Magic* by Jasper Maskelyne, John's grandson (new edition, New York: Dover, 2009, p.iii).

[11] John spinning the dinner-plates: "Master Blitz, a child only eight years of age", *Suffolk Chronicle* 29 Aug., 5 Sep.1829; and probably him, rather than Antonio, two years earlier: *Nottingham Review* 18, 25 May 1827.

[12] *Oxford Journal* 12, 19, 26 Oct.; 2 Nov.1833.

[13] Not 1834 as often stated, even in his autobiography. He is not mentioned as plate spinning after 1846. As he aged and his fingers grew less flexible he effectively replaced plate spinning in his act with ventriloquism and "learned canary birds". He visited England in 1869 to see his daughter, now a successful prima donna.

[14] *Essex Standard* 9 Sept.1836.

[15] *Hereford Times* 7 Aug.1841.

[16] A photograph of the poster is held by the State Library of Victoria (url:327).

[17] When Antonio revisited England in 1873 American newspapers said "Signor Blitz has sailed for Europe leaving the sleight-of-hand business to 32 gentlemen of the same name": *St. Albans Daily Messenger* (Saint Albans, Vermont) 10 May 1873 (etc.).

[18] *Lincolnshire Chronicle* 3 Oct.1862.

[19] His son Abraham, born in November that year, was to become a professional magician and inherited Antonio's "magic and trick apparatus" from his uncle.

[20] *Star of Gwent* 17 Feb.1855.

[21] *Liverpool Daily Post* 11 June 1856.

[22] *Era* 7 June 1857.

[23] B65 notes 11, 16, 48.

[24] B63 note 14.

[25] B69 note 13.

[26] I have been able to find very few references for such performances in Europe by searching for likely terms such as 'assiettes tournantes', 'girare i piatti', 'Tellerdrehen', 'Tellerjonglage'. In his advertising in Germany and Holland Epstein used terms unique to himself: "Die lustigen Geschirre", "Der chinesische Tanz, oder: Das lustige Geschirr" and "Chineesche Dans" (B12 notes 36, 38, 79).

[27] *Liverpool Mercury* 30 Dec.1825; *Bath Chronicle* 16 July 1832; *Huntingdon, Bedford & Peterborough Gazette* 19 Jan.1839; *Stamford Mercury* 24 May 1839...

[28] *Morning Journal* (Kingston) 6 June 1839. Exactly what sort of plate dancing is unknown.

[29] *American Republican and Baltimore Daily Clipper* 12 Nov.1844.

[30] *Blackburn Standard* 26 Nov.1845.

[31] *Drogheda Argus and Leinster Journal* 17 Nov.1849.

[32] *Jersey Independent and Daily Telegraph* 1 June 1860; *Derbyshire Courier* 2 Feb. 1878.

[33] *Era* 29 Nov., 22 Dec.1868.

[34] *Waterford Standard* 17 June 1874.

[35] *Eastbourne Chronicle* 22 June 1878.

[36] *Era* 5 Sep., 17 Oct. 1875.

[37] *Longford Journal* 12 May 1900.

Appendix Z8
PHYSICIAN — FISICO — PHYSICIEN

It is interesting that, while *Fisico* and *Physicien* were frequently used in the 19th century in the sense of 'Conjuror', 'Magician', in English 'Physician' was apparently never so used.

When Bartolomeo briefly visited England in January 1851 his 'Port of London Certificate of Arrival' was filled in by the Port Officer but signed by Bartolomeo himself with his name and profession as "*Bartolomeo Bosco (fisico)*"; the British official, presumably misunderstanding the meaning of the word, wrote down his profession as 'Physician' (B1 p.72).

In English I can find no examples of this meaning in newspapers or books and it is not given in the *Oxford English Dictionary.*

However, while the *OED* aims to be absolutely comprehensive and *Tesoro della Lingua Italiana delle Origini* and *Le Trésor de la Langue Française, dictionnaire de la langue du XIXe et du XXe siecle (1789-1960)* do not so claim, it seems surprising that neither of these includes *fisico* or *physicien* in this sense.

Nineteenth century Italian examples of 'fisico' specifically meaning 'magician' with no reference to the study of natural science or to the practice of medicine are easily found — C. Pirini, "fisico prestigiatore e ventriloque" (*Il Pirata* 10 Feb.1846); "Carlo Pianca poi col suo bel gabinetto fisico-meccanico... Il signor Robin, allievo di M. Comte, prestigiatore fisico di sua maestà il re del francesi" (*Il Vaglio* 13 July 1844); "Richiesta del teatro da parte del prof. di fisica Luigi Bergheer per un corso di giuochi fisici e di prestigio nel marzo 1854" (*Archivo Storico del Teatro Regio*); "Luigi Bergheer, fisico d'Annover ... esperimenti fisici e variati giuochi di prestigio" in Modena in 1854; and in 1856 "Monsieur Auboin-Brunet Professore Fisico e Prestigiatore del Palazzo reale di Parigi"; Philippe, in his travels through Italy, is repeatedly billed as "fisico prestigiatore"; and a portrait of Bosco's pupil Bartolomeo Marchelli is labelled "Il Fisico Prestigiatore"; and in 1837 in Naples Bosco in the birth registration of his son Matteo is recorded as 'Fisico Meccanico'... and *Curiose Avventure* refers to his "giochi Fisico-meccanici"...

Why then does the *Tesoro della Lingua Italiana delle Origini* not include this meaning among its definitions? Nor is it found in Florio's Italian/English Dictionaries of 1598 and 1611; Cardinelli's *Dizionario della lingua italiana* (1846); *Vocabolario universale della lingua italiana* (1846); any edition of the *Vocabolario degli accademici della Crusca*; Hoare (1915, etc.); or the *Cambridge Italian dictionary* (1962).

And it is the same in French, where, especially in the 19th century, examples are legion — "...M. Robertson, physicien, escamoteur, inventeur de la fantasmagorie, etc., donnait une soirée" (Stendhal, 1838); "...Qu'appelez-vous escamoteur? ... physicien, s'il vous plaît..." (Jules Henri de Saint-Georges, *Le Petit monstre et l'escamoteur*, 1826); "En un mot, je suis physicien, escamoteur, prestidigitateur... (J. N. Barba, *Paris malade*, 1833); frequent in newspapers ("L'illustre physicien Comte n'a point été escamonté à l'Odéon...", 1818); and there are book titles such as the often reprinted *Le petit physicien contenant les secrets et les recettes de toutes les magies*... The classic example is in Robert-Houdin's *Confidences et Révélations — Comment on Devient Sorcier* (1868) where he describes Jules de Rovère conjuring up the grandiose new term 'prestidigitateur' for himself precisely because the standard words, 'escamoteur' and 'physicien' had become trite and commonplace ("Le nom vulgaire d'escamoteur avait été repoussé bien loin par lui comme une triviale dénomination; celui de physicien était généralement porté par ses confrères et ne pouvait par cela même lui convenir"). As regards England, in Paul Feval's novel *Jean Diable* (1863) in a scene in London with people shouting for a doctor "...Un physicien! un physicien!", he explains to his French readers that "A Londres, en effet, les médecins portent ce nom, adopté par Bosco et par Robert Houdin".

Yet, besides the *Trésor*, this meaning is not found in the other major French dictionaries, *Dictionnaire de L'Académie française; L'Encyclopédie; Boiste; Littré; Harrap, Dictionnaire Electronique des Synonymes...*

However, it is given in at least two smaller French dictionaries — the long standard 19th century *Dictionnaire général français-anglais: nouvellement rédigé d'après les dictionnaires français de l'Académie, de Laveaux, de Boiste, de Bescherelle, etc., les dictionnaires anglais de Johnston, Webster, Richardson, etc.,* compiled by the very industrious Alexander Spiers (Paris: Baudry 1857; and in the 8th edition, 1865); it is also found in *A new dictionary of the French and English languages: compiled from the dictionaries of the French Academy, Bescherelle, Littré, Beaujean, Bourguignon, Worcester, Webster, Ogilvie, Johnson, Cooley, etc., etc., and from the most recent works on arts and sciences,* by E.-C. Clifton and Adrian Grimaux, dating from the 1870s with many later editions.

Appendix Z9
RUBINI

The Rubini (not in the *Lexikon*) with whom Leotard Bosco (B77) performed early in his career (p.317 above) was identified by Constance Pole Bayer in her biography of John Henry Anderson, *The Great Wizard of the North.*[1] This "Rubini" was "Professor" Philip Prentice Anderson, 1844-1920, illegitimate son of John Henry Anderson, whose title and mantle he inherited. He worked with his father from 1858 until 1867, then toured Europe and the United States on his own as "Signor Rubini" from 1867. He then worked with Heller but took over his father's character of "The Wizard of the North" shortly before his father's death in 1874.[2]

His later career is rather interesting. According to an article by Luke McKernan (url:335), Anderson the younger made films in India in the 1890s and retired to Australia as a dentist in 1900. In fact he made a final tour of Australia and New Zealand from 1899-1902, opening in Adelaide (*South Australian Advertiser* 29 July 1899) and ending, apparently, in Perth (*The West Australian* 31 May 1902). In 1907 he was reportedly running a chemist's shop in Camperdown in Sydney (*Referee* 4 Dec.1907).

[1] As noted by E.A. Dawes in his annotations to Clarke's *Annals of Conjuring*.
[2] A very interesting account of Anderson senior's significant visit to Honolulu in 1859 is given by William F. Wilson, 'Professor John Henry Anderson 'The Wizard of the North' at Honolulu in 1859' *Annual Report of the Hawaiian Historical Society* 47 (1938) pp.50-70 — url:336)

Appendix Z10
THE SANDFRAME

Several modern references attribute the invention of the "sand frame" to Eugenio, but no contemporary review or advertisement has been found mentioning him inventing, or even using, it. Nineteenth-century magic instruction books that name its inventor specifically attribute its invention to *Bartolomeo*.

Hanky Panky, A Book of Conjuring Tricks, published in London by John Camden Hotten (undated but December 1872) pp.47-8 (and the same text in the "new edition" dated 1875)[1] includes a story about "the magician Bosco, of Milan" demonstrating it over tea at the Princess's Theatre in London to "the negro *prima donna* ... 'the Black Malibran'". This was Ana María Loreto Martínez, and both she and Bartolomeo were performing at the Princess's Concert Rooms in London in 1851 (see B1 p.74).

An article 'Conjurors and Conjuring' by "A London Professor" in *Boy's Own Paper* 5 Feb.1881,[2] again says (p.310): "…Another conjuror of this era [*sc.* the age of Robert-Houdin and Philippe], a native of Lombardy, called Bosco, had a trick peculiar to himself…" and describes the sand box in some detail.

Similarly "Professor Hoffmann" in his *Drawing Room Conjuring* (London: Routledge, 1887,[3] and several reprints; also published in *Every Boy's Annual*) says: "The piece of apparatus … was used, and we believe invented, by the elder Bosco; but on his retirement was lost sight of until a few years since…".

"Hoffmann" repeats this with minor variations in his later books: —
in his *More Magic,* (London: Routledge, 1890)[4] he states p.102: "The Sand Frame. This ingenious little piece of apparatus was the invention of the elder Bosco…";
and in his *Card Tricks with Apparatus* (London: Warne, 1892, and several times reprinted) he says (p.36): "The Sand Frame — This is a pretty little appliance… it was used by the elder Bosco, who was, I believe, its inventor. For a long period it was completely lost sight of, but within the last few years it has been re-introduced…".

The sand frame is also mentioned by A. Roterberg, *New Era Card Tricks* (London: Hamley, 1897) but with no references to an inventor.

[1] The two editions are available online at url:337. The first edition is listed as published in Dec.1872 in *English Catalogue of Books*, and the earliest advertisement found is in 'Mr Camden Hotten's New Books', *London Daily News* 13 Dec.1872.

[2] Online at url:267. The *BOP* is full of useful information for British lads, from how to do the gun-trick to dealing with constipation in pigeons.

[3] *Drawing Room Conjuring* is always said to be "an English translation of *Recueil de tours de physique amusante* written by L. P. in 1886": that may be, but the 1877 first edition of that book, *Prestidigitation moderne: recueil de tours...* (Paris, De La Rue 1877; online at url:338) discussing the sand frame ("*cadre au sable*", p.173) makes no mention of who invented it.

[4] Online at url:339.

519

Appendix Z11
ANNIE VERNONE (*stage name* VERONI)

"Annie Veroni" performed in Britain as a magician 1856-1874. There is no evidence she ever performed overseas.

She was born Annie Kathleen[1] Vernone probably in 1841. She is listed in the U.K. censuses of 1851, 1861, 1871, 1901 and 1911 and all except the first give her birthplace as London (Westminster; St. James); in 1851 only she is listed as born "America (B.S.)" = 'British Subject'. Her parents are listed there as William and Ann Mount; she and her two sisters, Ellen (Helen) and Florence, have the surname Vernone, suggesting her mother had remarried.[2] The family are living in Erith, near London, and William is a market gardener. Nothing is known of her presumed birth father except that at their marriages Annie and her sister Helen name him as James Vernone, merchant (deceased).

In the 1861 census, now in Chelsea, the mother is widowed and with them is another older daughter, Fannie, born Hackney *ca.*1838. The mother and the three older daughters are all listed as "*Artiste - Magicienne*" (Florence only 13 is at school).

Annie is first found performing in early 1856, aged 15 or 16, in Marlborough, "the youthful professor of Natural Magic … a large audience was delighted with her successful performance", said the papers, "…there was a very full attendance, the various tricks were very cleverly performed, and elicited great applause".[3] She had similar success in Wallingford the following week — "the company was not large, but were well pleased with the truly astonishing feats performed"; but not in Swindon, where the audience was "wretchedly small, and for the most part juveniles", her tricks were well-known and the lecture by her mother "Madame Vernone" exposing spirit rapping fell flat.[4]

They were now advertising in the *Era,* and her repertoire includes the gun trick — "open to an engagement in Town, Country, or Abroad … elegant French, German, and American delusions, with the astonishing Gun Trick, never before attempted by a Lady…".[5] Her "gun trick" is described in a performance in 1862: "she allows any gentleman in the room to load an ordinary gun with ball and fire it at her, and then catching the bullet in her hand".[6] We then hear nothing of her for some months. It is possible she was overseas, but when her ads resume in the *Era* there is no reference to any recent triumphs abroad.[7]

There is then another long silence until her next *Era* ads, a year later in October 1857.[8] Following this in November she reports she has "just completed a Provincial Tour"; this is her last ad under her own name,[9] and she now adopts the stage name "Annie Veroni".[10]

She performed with success in Plymouth in 1857 (claiming in later ads a season of 100 nights and seen by 40,000 people) then in Cornwall in early 1858. However on stage in Devonport in February she accidentally fired a pistol shot through her left hand: "fortunately the bone was not injured: but she exhibited great fortitude, and went on with the performances".[11]

She continued her tour, with six successful nights in March of "Veroni's Magic Evenings" in Falmouth, "The Great Original and Only Female Magician", advertising "selections from the most Recherché of her experiments",[12] four nights in Truro,[13] then Redruth, Camborne, Helston,[14] and Penzance.[15]

We catch sight of her again in July, still nearby in Weston-super-Mare, then later that month in Plymouth where she had been so successful the previous year.[16] However, in Teignemouth she had a very poor audience, then in Plymouth was "tricked by her business manager of all the property she had by her honest industry acquired".[17] Exeter followed,[18] then in September Bridport did not go well — "the audience was small, and the performance, we hear, unsatisfactory. A complaint of another nature also reached us from Lyme regarding this performance".[19]

She is home in London in January, advertising for work,[20] performing in Durham in February ("the attendance was only moderate"),[21] and in June taking part in a gala in Leeds, now for the first time "with her sister".[22]

She had more problems later that year when a promoter in Norwich variously known as Dillon or Story, having agreed to her standard terms of £8.8s. per week plus all expenses let her down badly; Dillon owed money to the printer, who took the ticket money at the door and retained it. Annie took Dillon to court but received only a donation from locals to get herself and her sister back to London.[23]

She continued her ads in the *Era* and in March 1860 opened in Brighton,[24] followed by Portsea, reported as "performing to delighted audiences ... being exceedingly dexterous, and introducing many tricks of her own invention, besides being exceedingly pleasing and graceful in her manner".[25] In August she was in Hull, accompanied by a singer Miss Thompson, next in Bridlington Quay, and then Scarborough; there the *Era* correspondent applauded "her extraordinary performances of natural magic ... exceedingly clever in her experiments".[26] And in Sheffield she was equally well received — "...continue to attract numerous audiences. Her feats of legerdemain are executed in a pleasing manner ...".[27]

In November she performed in Oxford, December in Buckingham,[28] and then did well in Aberdeen ("astounding the audience here by her clever illusions"), accompanied by "her page Florence", and again in Edinburgh — "We have lady preachers, lady doctors, lady editors, lady platform orators — and why not lady magicians ... Certainly the witches of old must have been very different creatures from the fascinating, elegant, and good-humoured enchantress who last night threw her spells over a pretty numerous audience in the Music Hall".[29] She was prominent in a quality line-up at the City of London Theatre in March 1861, "...Magical Wonders by Mademoiselle Veroni, the acknowledged female enchantress",[30] but soon performing to small audiences in schools in Chislehurst in Kent.[31]

June saw her in Bath in her "Temple of Magic Wonders", now with "her Page Wellington",[32] then accompanying tight-rope exhibitions by Blondin in York, Dublin, Belfast, and Hanley.[33] The Blondin shows proved a disaster for the promoter, a Sheffield tobacconist and coal merchant: he had agreed to pay Blondin £500, with £220 paid in advance, and £11.17s. to Mlle Veroni. Wet weather in Dublin reduced the hoped for takings and he ended up insolvent.[34]

Annie then performed at a Gala in Sheffield on August 26th, but an announced run of 15 shows in Bristol, billing her as "The Great American and Only Female Magician in the World" did not proceed.[35]

She performed in Ipswich in Easter week 1862, "the World's Wonder, Mademoiselle Veroni ... with 100 astounding Illusions never performed by any other Artiste, including her Great Gun Trick", and in May in Framlingham ("a series of well executed and clever tricks ... she is a complete master of the art, and combines with it great grace and ease");[36] Halesworth followed,[37] then King's Lynn.[38]

These all seem to have gone well enough, but she then had a poor run in Cambridgeshire. A large ad in the *Wisbech Chronicle* announced a show in Wisbech on May 29th, but the following issue of the paper reported "...a very limited audience. The receipts were so small that the wherewithal was not forthcoming to pay the advertising charges. Our contemporaries in other towns may possibly profit by our experience". And indeed the nearby *Stamford Mercury* noting her Wisbech show said "her magical powers, however, could not conjure from the public money sufficient to pay the poor printers".[39] She performed next in Chatteris, and the *Wisbech Chronicle* printed a generous review ("...the clever tricks in legerdemain are truly astonishing..."),[40] but in the town of March "she received no patronage whatever" and left without earning anything.[41] Ramsey was next and another disaster: "Caution.—The celebrated Madame Veroni visited this place on Friday, June 20, and hired the Institution for the evening, but we are sorry to say left forgetting to pay for the same".[42] The following month in Bishop's Stortford she fared little better. She gave a show for school children at 5 p.m. but they paid a penny each, and her evening show attracted only 23 adults. The paper there was very sympathetic, saying the inhabitants were wary as they had been gulled in the past, but "this highly talented young lady" deserved better.[43]

She was clearly not earning a living from her performances and when we next see her, in Dover in December, much has changed. She is no longer performing alone but is accompanying Walter J. Morris who had been successfully touring since 1854 in his "Olla Podrida" of "Musical Rocks and Ophonic Crystal, the music of which are like the Delicious Tones of Angels' Harps". Morris has also ramped up her billing — her "Magical Illusions as performed *before most of the crowned heads of Europe*"; he also gave away a lot of gold and silver presents at the end of his shows.

A long review confirmed that the gifts were good quality and there was no collusion in their distribution, with a detailed list of recipients, and even found room to praise Morris's music and Annie's "marvellous feats of magic ... we have never seen 'the inexhaustible bottle' and 'hat trick' better executed...".[44]

Next was Brighton where they had an excellent long run, and Morris now has again as part of the show "the Aztec Lilliputians, as well as a Female of the Earthman Tribe".[45] After more than two months in Brighton they moved on to Southampton in April, then Reading in May.

In London on June 10th Annie and Morris married. In the register she names her father as "James Vernone, merchant", and her sister Helen is one of the witnesses.

They were soon back on their travels, Sittingbourne in July (still with the Aztecs), then Thanet, and the Isle of Wight in September. In October they opened in Brighton, no doubt hoping to repeat their successes of the previous year. But local shopkeepers, feeling that Morris's gift presentations were hurting their business, had a charge brought against him for running an illegal lottery. This is one of the most interesting of many such cases, as Morris's defence lawyer argued that the tickets sold were not for a prize but merely for a seat at the show. The magistrates found both Morris and the bookseller who sold the tickets guilty, sentencing them to seven days' gaol. Their lawyers applied for bail and the case was taken to appeal.[46] Morris soon reopened, now auctioning his "Gold and Silver Treasures" following each show.[47]

We then see them in Birmingham, Burton, Warrington, and in December 1864 in London. In May 1865 Annie had her first child, named Annie Sibella Morris, and for several months she was replaced in the show by "Miss Florence Linden", with her "startling magical illusions", very likely her sister, and a ventriloquist, Mr. Russell. "Florence Linden" is with Walter in Gravesend and Dover in April, Thanet and Tonbridge in May, and in Henley in June.[48]

By August Annie was back on stage, now billed as "Mademoiselle Veroni (Mrs W. J. Morris)".[49] She and Walter continued to perform round England, with occasional interruptions for further children; by 1878 there were six, two daughters and four sons. In 1868 they renamed their show "Magic, Music, and Mystery", still the same combination of her conjuring and his music on the ophonic crystal, with gifts at the end; and in 1870 the Aztecs were briefly back with them.[50] They are last sighted performing in Kew in March 1874, Walter charmingly performing on his "euphonic crystal ... to the delight of everyone present", and Annie with her "astounding illusions ... the crystal bowl of goldfish, the inexhaustible hat out of which was produced 100 goblets, balls, and fancy knick-knacks, the flying ring, the magic eggs, the flying watch, the sybil coins ... all these and many more mysteries were wonderful to see"... but "the most sensational performance" was the cutting off of a boy's nose with a knife and plenty of blood.[51]

Walter died in 1895, and in the 1901 and 1911 censuses Annie is living in London with some of her children. She died in 1916, her age given as an unlikely 71.

Of her three sisters, Fannie, Helen and Florence, she, Fannie and Helen are all listed as magicians in the 1861 census; Florence only 13 was still at school.

Helen in 1866 married Richard Turner, a commercial traveller, and is unlikely to have performed after that — by 1881 she had six children.

Florence certainly practised as a magician, first as "page" to Annie, then probably as "Florence Linden" in 1865, and she has a card in the *Era* of 1 April 1866: "Mademoiselle Florence Veroni, the Youthful *Magicienne,* just arrived from the Continent, is open to an Engagement, for Half an Hour's Gem performance, in New Delusions...".[52] In the 1881 census she is unmarried, no profession, living with her married sister Helen.

Fannie in the 1871 census is unmarried, age as 31, living with Walter and Annie, profession "book keeper". But I believe Fannie had a successful career as a ventriloquist under the name of "Floretta Cavalho".

"Cavalho" (often billed as "Mdlle Cavalho") is last found performing in Eastbourne, Sussex, in 1873, with Annie and Walter, the only time she is found on stage with them.[53] She is billed here as "the Only Lady Ventriloquist in Europe", as she had been throughout her career, which had a spectacular opening in 1863 with a very long run at the prestigious Royal Polytechnic in London: significantly her act is "Vocal, Organophonic, and Ventriloquial" — *organophonic* strongly suggesting a link with Walter Morris.[54] Her "rude little girl, and squalling child" imitations were hugely popular there, and in early 1864 she moved to the Oxford Music Hall with similar success, "the celebrated Comedienne and Mimic". In 1865 she was in Margate, in 1866 another good run at the Oxford Music Hall, and back at the Royal Polytechnic in 1867. She toured widely in England — not only a ventriloquist but "gifted with a sweet voice and a good pianist".[55]

[1] Her middle name is *Kathleen* in her marriage registration, in the baptism of her daughter Annie Sibella, in the 1911 census, and in her death registration.

[2] Of Annie and her three sisters the only birth registration located is for the youngest, "Florence", born in Gravesend according to the 1861 census, so she is Sibella Lawrence Vernone, reg. Gravesend, first quarter 1848; the mother's maiden name is given as Thorn (Sibella was the mother's middle name). A possible brother James Henry Vernone died in London in February 1843 age 1 year 11 months.

[3] *Berkshire Chronicle* 23 Feb.1856; *Salisbury and Winchester Journal* 23 Feb.1856.

[4] *Reading Mercury* 1 Mar.1856; *Wilts and Gloucestershire Standard* 1 Mar.1856.

[5] *Era* 16 Mar.1856.

[6] *Halesworth Times and East Suffolk Advertiser* 6 May 1862.

[7] *Era* 19 Oct.1856.

[8] *Era* 4 Oct.1857.

[9] *Era* 15 Nov.1857.

[10] "Italianised for professional purposes", she said when testifying in court in 1859. The only well-known theatrical Veronis in U.K. at the time were the dancers Signor and Selina Veroni.

[11] *Cornish Telegraph* 10 Feb.1858 (quoting the *Plymouth Journal*).

[12] *Lake's Falmouth Packet and Cornwall Advertiser* 6 Mar.1858. The term *"most recherché of"* is first used by Epstein, probably invented for him by Prof. Millar, then adopted by all three of the main U.K. female magicians of the day (BF1, BF2 and Veroni) but by very few male magicians.

[13] *Royal Cornwall Gazette* 12 Mar.1858.

[14] *Royal Cornwall Gazette* 19 Mar.1858 (where we are told "she also possesses the additional charms of good face and figure … and of agreeable, lively manner").

[15] *Cornish Telegraph* 24 Mar.1858.

[16] *Weston-super-Mare Gazette* 3 July 1858; *Era* 18 July 1858.

[17] *Lake's Falmouth Packet and Cornwall Advertiser* 24 July 1858.

[18] *Exeter Flying Post* 19 Aug.1858; *Era* 22 Aug.1858.

[19] *Dorset County Chronicle* 23 Sep.1858.

[20] *Era* 9 Jan.1859.

[21] *Durham County Advertiser* 25 Feb.1859.

[22] Probably not Florence, who was later with her, as she was only eleven. *Leeds Times* 4 June 1859.

[23] Lengthy account in *Norfolk Chronicle* 17 Dec.1859.

[24] *Brighton Guardian* 7 Mar.1866; *Brighton Gazette* 8 Mar.1860.

[25] *Hampshire Telegraph* 31 Mar.1860.

[26] *Hull Packet* 31 Aug.1860; *Yorkshire Gazette* 1 Sep.1860; *Era* 2 Sep.1860.

[27] *Sheffield Independent* 8 Sep.1860; *Sheffield Daily Telegraph* 11 Sep.1860.

[28] *Oxford Chronicle and Reading Gazette* 17 Nov.1860; *Buckingham Advertiser and Free Press* 1 Dec.1860.

[29] *Aberdeen Press* 12 Dec.1860; *Era* 16 Dec.1860; *The Scotsman* 3 Jan.1861.
[30] *Lloyd's Weekly Newspaper* 24 Mar.1861; *Era* 31 Mar.1861.
[31] *Maidstone Journal* 16 Apr.1861.
[32] *Bath Chronicle* 13 June 1861.
[33] *Yorkshire Gazette* 13 July 1861; *Freeman's Journal* 8 Aug.1861; *Belfast Morning News* 12 Aug.1861; *Staffordshire Advertiser* 24 Aug.1861. One of many fake Blondins.
[34] *Sheffield Daily Telegraph* 22 Oct.1861.
[35] *Sheffield Independent* 10 Aug.1861; *Western Daily Press* 10 Aug.1861.
[36] *Suffolk Chronicle* 19 Apr.1862; *Framlingham Weekly News* 3 May 1862.
[37] *The Halesworth Times and East Suffolk Advertiser* 6 May 1862.
[38] The King's Lynn Museum has a poster for her performance there on May 28th; it is not digitised on their site but is online at url:340.
[39] *Wisbech Chronicle* 24, 31 May 1862; *Stamford Mercury* 6 June 1862.
[40] *Wisbech Chronicle* 14 June 1862.
[41] *Cambridge Chronicle and Journal* and *Wisbech Chronicle* 21 June 1862.
[42] *Cambridge Independent Press* 28 June 1862.
[43] *Herts Guardian* 12 July 1862.
[44] *Dover Telegraph* 29 Nov., 6, 13 Dec.1862.
[45] A huge amount has been written on the so-called "Aztecs", microcephalic *Mestizos* (with both Spanish and Native American blood), first exhibited in the 1840s in Central America, then in New York, and from 1853 in England. They were with Walter periodically from 1854. Their guardian at this time was J.M. Morris: whether he was related to Walter is uncertain. On sale at the shows were an illustrated booklet with a fabricated account of their nature and history, and 'The Aztec Polka'.
[46] *Brighton Gazette* 22 Oct.1863 (a very detailed account); *Brighton Guardian* 24 Oct.1863. The bookseller was subsequently granted a free pardon by the Home Office (*Brighton Guardian* 10 Feb.1864). If the case was appealed one might expect it to appear in *The Exchequer Reports: Reports of Cases Argued and Determined in the Courts of Exchequer & Exchequer Chamber ... Easter Term, 25 Vict., to* [*Michaelmas Term, 30 Vict.*], but it is not there.
[47] *Brighton Gazette* 5 Nov.1863.
[48] *Gravesend Reporter* 1 Apr.1865; *Dover Telegraph* 15 Apr.1865; *Thanet Advertiser* 6, 13 May 1865; *Maidstone Journal* 22 May 1865; *South Bucks Free Press* 3 June 1865.
[49] *Baner ac Amserau Cymr* 26 Aug.1865, in Denbighshire.
[50] *Maidstone Journalr* 23 Mar.1868; *Newbury Weekly* 18 Aug. 1870.
[51] *Surrey Comet* 7 Mar.1874.
[52] To avoid confusion Annie now advertised in the *Era* as "Mademoiselle Veroni (Mrs W. J. Morris)": *Era* 29 Apr.1866.
[53] *Eastbourne Chronicle* 29 Mar.1873. Cavalho cannot be the same sister as "Florence Linden", as Cavalho was elsewhere when Linden was with Annie and Walter in 1865.
[54] *Beehive* and *Marylebone Mercury* 15 Aug.1863.
[55] *Preston Herald* 18 July 1868.

Appendix Z12
Who performed at Balmoral September 24th 1855 ?

At least four Boscos claimed to have performed for Queen Victoria at Balmoral Castle specifically on Monday September 24th 1855.

Saul Warschawski (B63) and Louis Susser (B65) made the claim in their advertising for many years, Louis finally openly accusing his long time rival of lying. Louis had first made the claim rather subtly, by implication, saying in 1859 that "Herr Bosco will perform his two astonishing tricks (as shown before the Royal Family at Balmoral.)…".[1] Saul was making the same claim explicitly by 1861,[2] then in 1871 (when denounced as an impostor by Susser) actually quoted the testimonial signed by C.B. Phipps, Privy Purse, dated September 25th 1855 which stated that "Signor Bosco performed by Her Majesty's command at Balmoral Castle, yesterday evening" as if it referred to him.[3] The letter had been published soon after in the *Aberdeen Herald* and displayed in the window of the *Rochdale Pilot* newspaper in 1858, so its text was public knowledge.[4] Reading Dawes's article on Saul[5] he clearly believed that Saul was the performer at Balmoral, no doubt because Saul's descendants believed it. There is no evidence that Saul or Louis were even performing by September 1855, and, even if they were, they certainly did not have a sufficient reputation to secure a Royal command performance.

The actual performer at Balmoral was "Alfred Bosco" (Epstein, B12) and a full account of how the royal engagement was secured was given by his then manager Professor Millar in 1892.[6] Epstein, not content with merely advertising his command performance, soon added the claim that at Balmoral "the title of the Great Wizard of the World was graciously bestowed upon him" by the Queen.

The first Bosco to claim this Balmoral performance was also the least likely — Madame Bosco (BF1), Millar's wife. In early 1859, by now well away in Wheeling, West Virginia, her ad stated that her entertainment was "presented by her before Queen Victoria and the Court, at Balmoral castle, Scotland, September 24, 1855".[6]

Leotard Bosco (fond of using the title "Royal Illusionist") also claimed to have performed for Queen Victoria, but wisely gave no exact date or place.[7]

One magician who of course never made the claim was Bartolomeo — but see url:343 for Epstein's Balmoral programme wrongly ascribed to Bartolomeo.

[1] *Tavistock Gazette* 19 Aug.1859.
[2] *Chester Chronicle* 24 Aug.1861.
[3] *Cambridge Independent Press* 25 Feb.1871; *North Wales Chronicle* 26 Aug.1871.
[4] *Rochdale Pilot* 20 Feb.1858 ("now exhibiting in the shop window of the publishers of this paper").
[5] E.A. Dawes, 'Signor Bosco and Son:…': see p.284..
[6] *Dundee Evening Telegraph* 8 Sep.1892. He also later published his account as a booklet which I have not seen, *How an American brought the great Italian wizard before H. M. Queen Victoria:* see B62 p.240 note 7.
[7] *Wheeling Daily Intelligencer* 19 Jan.1859 (and in her later advertisements).
[8] "The Great Bosco, the only Genuine Artist of that Name, who has had the great honour of Performing before the Queen": *Leicester Chronicle* 18 Mar.1882.

URLs

Listed here are urls referred to in the text. I will gladly email this section to any owner of the book to provide live links.
Some sites require a subscription or institutional access

001 *Brockhaus Konversationslexikon,* 14. Aufl.1894-6:
https://www.retrobibliothek.de/retrobib/seite.html?id=122671
Nordisk Familjebok Konversationslexikon och Realencyklopedi 2nd ed., 1905:
http://runeberg.org/nfbc/0665.html

002 Mariano Tomatis 'Blog of Wonders' 7 Feb.2018:
http://www.marianotomatis.it/blog.php?post=blog/2018020

003 *Kurjer Nowogródzki* 3 Jan.1935:
https://polona.pl/item/kurjer-nowogrodzki-r-5-nr-2-3-stycznia-1935,MTM0NTk4NzI/1

004 1821 Hamburg poster:
http://dfg-viewer.de/show/cache.off?tx_dlf%5Bpage%5D=5&tx_dlf%5Bid%5D=http%3A%2F%2Fdigitale-sammlungen.gwlb.de%2Fcontent%2F834209691%2F834209691.xml&tx_dlf%5Bdouble%5D=0&cHash=492b599aca4663b7623bd07c234181a8

005 Heinrich Heine on Bosco:
http://www.hhp.uni-trier.de/Projects/HHP/werke/baende/D01/getpage?pageid=D06S0032&mode=1
and annotations:
http://hhp.uni-trier.de/Projekte/HHP/Projekte/HHP/werke/gedliste/K/getpage?pageid=D06S0441&mode=%3Cdtml-var%20mode%3

006 Saphir's *Konversations-Lexikon,* Band I.
http://www.lexikus.de/bibliothek/Lexikon-B/Bosco-Bartolomeo

007 1823 Russian and French poster
https://ru.bidspirit.com/ui/lotPage/source/catalog/auction/173/lot/42584

008 1827 Breslau poster
https://www.liveauctioneers.com/item/76237559_bosco-conjuring-broadside

009 Chopin at the *Hotel de Pologne in Breslau*
https://en.chopin.nifc.pl/chopin/places/poland/id/578

010 1827 Leipzig posters
https://www.stadtmuseum.leipzig.de/media/wmZoom/ST000/ST000284.jpg
https://www.stadtmuseum.leipzig.de/media/wmZoom/ST000/ST000283.jpg

011 1828 Berlin poster
https://www.akg-images.de/Docs/AKG/Media/TR5/6/3/1/8/AKG826630.jpg

012 Saphir 'Alles wiederholt sich nur im Leben...' in *Ausgewählte Schriften*
https://babel.hathitrust.org/cgi/pt?id=uc1.$b612202

013 *Der getödtete und dennoch lebende M.G. Saphir*
https://books.google.com/books?id=XePAOwAACAAJ [now inaccessible]

014 *Der lebende und dennoch maustodte M. G. Saphir*
https://books.google.com/books?id=FlKWj5ayrWgC

015 *Habitt's aus Moskau ...*
https://www.google.com/books/edition/Habitt_s_aus_Moskau_Nothgedrungene_Erkl/f1-vU6bDZuwC?hl=en&gbpv=1

016 'M.G. Saphir und Berlin...'
https://babel.hathitrust.org/cgi/pt?id=chi.48326949

017 *Vosculo von Barcelona*
https://books.google.com/books?id=6F1_kKMVCdcC&dq

018 'Ueber Herrn Bosco in Wien' *Oesterreichischer Beobachter* 20 Nov.1828
[these 2 pages are not included in the version on *Anno*].
https://books.google.co.nz/books?id=tjRDAAAAcAAJ&pg=PA1380

019 Seyfried, *Rückschau in das Theaterleben Wiens*
https://archive.org/details/rckschauindasth01seyfgoog/page/n10

020 Pemmer, 'Wiener Taschenspieler im ausgehenden 18. Jahrhundert ...'
https://www.zobodat.at/pdf/Jb-Landeskde-Niederoesterreich_35_0106-0123.pdf

021 Plates: 'Staberl als Physiker' and 'Staberl der konfuse Zauberer'
www.theatermuseum.at/de/object/30cd217b16
www.theatermuseum.at/de/object/f965cbef71
www.theatermuseum.at/de/object/b5f619fa78

022 Hungarian *Der Spiegel* (and many other Hungarian titles) online
https://adt.arcanum.com/hu/view/MTA_DerSpiegel_1829_1
http://real-j.mtak.hu/9460
The first site requires payment; the second does not but one needs to download a large pdf file

023 Letter by Bosco, Hamburg 23 May 1830
https://kalliope-verbund.info/de/ead?ead.id=DE-611-HS-941292

024 Borcherdt, *Das lustige alte Hamburg*
https://babel.hathitrust.org/cgi/pt?id=inu.39000005792218

025 Maltitz, *Pfefferkörner*, vol.4
https://babel.hathitrust.org/cgi/pt?id=njp.32101068362068

026 Gerlach, 'Assoziationen - Anzeigen - Ausstellungen Kunst...'
https://www.jstor.org/stable/24661447

027 Maurizio Fancello
http://www.seicorde.it/convegno/Atti_Convegno_2012.pdf

028 *Courrier de la Sambre*
https://donum.uliege.be/expo/courrier_sambre

029 Bosco's contract at the Théâtre du Palais-Royal, 1832
https://gallica.bnf.fr/ark:/12148/btv1b53123733c/f2.image [and following pages]

030 Pierre Bernadau, *Tablettes manuscrites*
https://bernadau.wordpress.com/2016/04/03/annee-1834

031 Auction catalogue, Paris 1858
https://gallica.bnf.fr/ark:/12148/bpt6k9677851f (page 15, item 135)

032 Mariano Tomatis on the *Bussolotti di cristallo*
http://www.marianotomatis.it/blog.php?post=blog/20180517 and http://www.mesmer.it/?id=mesmerlab4

033 *Annali di medicina omiopatica per la Sicilia*, Vol. I, 1837
https://books.google.com/books?id=Wx84AAAAMAAJ

034 Costanza, 'Bartolomeo Bosco esimio prestigiator'
https://books.google.com/books?id=DJswAAAAYAAJ

035 Costanza, Mariano Tomatis *Mesmer Project* 2013
http://www.praestigiator.com/index.php?p=storia/2013/04/08/bartolomeo_bosco_esimio_prestigiatore

036 "La Fata Morgana" 1838-1844
http://www.comune.reggio-calabria.it/on-line/Home/articolo103917.html
http://www.comune.reggio-calabria.it/on-line/Home/documento103339.html

037 *Programmi Giornali degli Spettacoli dati ne' teatri di Napoli...*
http://digitale.bnnonline.it/atn/doc/prgiorna-38_39-OCR.pdf

038 Belli, *Le lettere*, a cura di Giacinto Spagnoletti. 2 vols. Milan, 1961 www.abruzzoinmostra.it

039 Verdone, 'Bartolomeo Bosco in una poesia italiana del Belli'
http://www.gruppodeiromanisti.it/wp-content/uploads/2014/12/1964-parte-2-pp.-252-541.pdf

040 *Intorno alcuni scritti inediti di Michelangelo Poggioli ...,* 1864.
https://opacplus.bsb-muenchen.de/title/BV020953520

041 *Real Segreteria di Stato presso il Luogotenente Generale in Sicilia.*
https://www.saassipa.beniculturali.it/wp-content/uploads/2020/05/REPERTORIO-Luogotenenziale-Polizia-1839.pdf

042 Araci, 'Naum Theatre: the lost opera house of Istanbul'
https://emrearaci.weebly.com/naum-theatre.html

043 National Library of Russia newspaper list
http://nlr.ru/res/inv/ukazat55/record_full.php?record_ID=131435

044 *Moskovskiye Vedomosti* 17 Jan.1842
https://commons.wikimedia.org/w/index.php?title=File:%D0%9C%D0%BE%D1%81%D0%BA%D0%BE%D0%B2%D1%81%D0%BA%D0%B8%D0%B5_%D0%92%D0%B5%D0%B4%D0%BE%D0%BC%D0%BE%D1%81%D1%82%D0%B8_1842-05_(17_%D1%8F%D0%BD%D0%B2%D0%B0%D1%80%D1%8F).pdf&page=23

045 1842 Bosco posters in Turku (Åbo)
https://www.doria.fi/handle/10024/151123
https://www.doria.fi/handle/10024/151124

046 1844 Bosco letter to Edinger (not digitised)
https://kalliope-verbund.info/de/ead?ead.id=DE-611-HS-1656739

047 Bosco's *Zaubertheater* in Leipzig 1844
https://www.stadtmuseum.leipzig.de/media/wmZoom/ST000/ST000275.jpg

048 Bosco manuscript 'Pour moi tous les pays' (not digitised)
http://kalliope-verbund.info/DE-611-HS-1873699

049 Francesconi, *Reise-Bilder aus dem Leben Boscos in zwölf Sprachen...*
http://www.digitalniknihovna.cz/mzk/view/uuid:1c85e0d0-d5aa-11e4-ae4e-5ef3fc9ae867

050 Dirnböck, *Briefe des Hans Michel aus Obersteier*
https://digital.onb.ac.at/OnbViewer/viewer.faces?doc=ABO_%2BZ161339409

051 Bosco letter to Bäuerle 1846 (not digitised)
http://kalliope-verbund.info/DE-611-HS-1691564

052 Bosco letter 1846 in Harry Ransom Center (not digitised) - Houdini Collection Container 21.17
https://norman.hrc.utexas.edu/fasearch/findingAid.cfm?eadid=01275

053 Bosco letter 1846 in the Austrian National Library. (not digitised)
http://data.onb.ac.at/rec/AC14025461

054 Szuper Károly, *Szuper Károly színészeti naplója 1830–1850*
https://mek.oszk.hu/19500/19571/19571.pdf

055a   Siklóssy László, *Gyorskocsin Erdélyben: Kutatások, rajzok, emlékezése*
https://mek.oszk.hu/08600/08645/08645.pdf

055b   Antal Váradi, *Az elzárt mennyország*
https://library.hungaricana.hu/en/view/ORSZ_PIMU_PetofiKonyvtar_19

056 Bosco letter 1847 in the Staatsbibliothek zu Berlin (not digitised)
http://kalliope-verbund.info/de/ead?ead.id=DE-611-HS-1757013

057 1847 Kraków poster in Polish and German
https://jbc.bj.uj.edu.pl/dlibra/publication/601705/edition/614810/content

058 Pemmer, 'Wiener Taschenspieler ...'
https://www.zobodat.at/pdf/Jb-Landeskde-Niederoesterreich_35_0106-0123.pdf

059 Painting of 'Bartolomeo Boscos Zaubertheater', Leipzig 1848
https://www.stadtmuseum.leipzig.de   (then search for: ST000254)
[there is a direct link but it is 21 lines long]

060 Handbill for Bosco's Leipzig farewell show on May 28th 1848
https://www.stadtmuseum.leipzig.de/media/wmZoom/Z0100/Z0100944.jpg

061 Bosco letter at Stadtmuseum Leipzig, dated Leipzig 6 May 1848
https://www.stadtmuseum.leipzig.de/media/wmZoom/Z0110/Z0110830.jpg

062 Bosco letter at Stabi, Hamburg, dated Leipzig 6 May 1848 (not digitised)
http://kalliope-verbund.info/DE-611-HS-491367

063 Bosco letter at Harry Ransom Center, Texas, dated Leipzig 6 May 1848: "Letter (German) to unidentified recipient, 6 May 1848", Container 21.17 (not digitised)
https://legacy.lib.utexas.edu/taro/uthrc/01275/hrc-01275.html

064 *Krakehler* at Deutsches Historisches Museum Berlin 'Bild Index'
https://www.bildindex.de/document/obj03691482

065 *Krakehler* facsimile reprint
https://hdl.handle.net/2027/mdp.39015039624708

066 Article on Bosco at www.jedinat-zauberschule.de
http://www.jedinat-zauberschule.de/lexikon/bartolomeo-bosco-1793----1863__224.htm [dead?]

067 Bosco 1848 posters in Bremen
http://brema.suub.uni-bremen.de/suubtheater/periodical/pageview/1772155
http://brema.suub.uni-bremen.de/suubtheater/periodical/pageview/1772156

068 Adolf Bils in 1845 Danish census
https://www.danishfamilysearch.dk/cid6121490

069 Bosco letter to H.J. Keizer, 1849 (not digitised)
https://pid.uba.uva.nl/ark:/88238/b1990029643410205131

070 Dulce da Rocha Gonçalves on L. K. Maju (1823–1886)'
https://doi.org/10.1177/0963662520965093

071 *Le Courrier Batave* 21 July 1850: 'Les Deux Escamoteurs'
https://books.google.com/books?id=Yw9VAAAAcAAJ [in 'Tablettes' section on 3rd & 4th pages]

072 Biographies of Adriaan Bevervoorde, 1819-1851:
Nieuw Nederlandsch Biografisch Woordenboek
http://resources.huygens.knaw.nl/retroboeken/nnbw/#source=1&page=170;
De Digitale *Bibliotheek voor de Nederlandse Letteren*
https://www.dbnl.org/tekst/_str005195501_01/_str005195501_01_0075.php;
Biografisch Woordenboek van het Socialisme en de Arbeidersbeweging in Nederland
https://socialhistory.org/bwsa/biografie/engelbert

073 Pamphlets by Alex. A. Crafford, publisher of *Bosco en Van Bosse*
https://books.google.com/books?id=fih_Vni3dPsC
https://books.google.com/books?id=ft5PfKaHpvsC

074 Bosco poster, Royal Princess's Concert-room, London, 1851
https://hrc.contentdm.oclc.org/digital/collection/p15878coll22/id/3509

075 Biographical articles on Ana María Loreto Martínez
http://www.kresgeartsindetroit.org/wp-content/uploads/2015/09/La-Malibran-Noire.pdf
http://elecodelamemoria.blogspot.com/2010/10/ya-alegre-ya-apasionado-ya-quejumbroso.html
https://cadaverparaiso.wordpress.com/2020/04/28/martinez-linfortunee-los-anos-oscuros-de-la-malibran-noire
https://cadaverparaiso.wordpress.com/2020/05/12/a-malibran-preta-maria-martinez-en-la-corte-de-luis-i-de-portugal

076 Bosco note offering complimentary ticket, Paris 1851
https://gallica.bnf.fr/ark:/12148/btv1b53123733c/f10.image

077 Texier, *Tableau de Paris,* vol.2
https://gallica.bnf.fr/ark:/12148/bpt6k2057032

078 Bosco note offering complimentary ticket, Paris 1853
https://gallica.bnf.fr/ark:/12148/btv1b53123733c/f11

079 Bosco letter to a theatre director dated Paris, April 2nd 1853 (not digitised)
https://kalliope-verbund.info/de/ead?ead.id=DE-611-HS-1514484

080 Bellemaire, 'Les Sociétés Secrètes Musulmanes de l'Algérie'
https://gallica.bnf.fr/ark:/12148/bpt6k405799v

081 Bosco poster, Madrid 1858
https://en.todocoleccion.net/poster-shows/cartel-teatro-frances-calle-magdalena-40-madrid-magia-egipcia-por-bosco-ano-1858~x107083015#sobre_el_lote

082 Bartolomeo burial registration
https://www.ancestry.co.uk/imageviewer/collections/5406/images/41683_213cxxi20%5E148%5E-00299

083 Friederike burial registration
https://www.ancestry.co.uk/imageviewer/collections/5406/images/41683_213cxxi20^150a-00263

084 Eugenio civil marriage registration
http://dl.antenati.san.beniculturali.it/v/Archivio+di+Stato+di+Napoli/Stato+civile+italiano_Quartieri/San+Ferdinando/Matrimoni/1865/004906706_00909.jpg.html

085 Lübeck births 1829-1830
https://www.ancestry.com/search/collections/157

086 *M.U.M.* March 1918, with a translation of Eugenio's contract with his father
https://babel.hathitrust.org/cgi/pt?id=nyp.33433019398191&view=image&seq=127

087 Harry Houdini papers, Container 21.17 "… Agreement (French) between Bosco and his son Eugene with several typed English translations, 20 May 1852":
https://norman.hrc.utexas.edu/fasearch/findingAid.cfm?eadid=01275

088 Eugenio posters in Leipzig, 1858
https://www.europeana.eu/portal/en/search?q=what%3A%22Bosco+jun.%22

089 Eugenio performing for the Prince Regent of Prussia, 1858
http://www.bildarchivaustria.at/Preview/8191734.jpg

090 *Journal de Constantinople* 1864
https://archives.saltresearch.org/handle/123456789/129110
    and page 169 from which the extract is quoted:
https://archives.saltresearch.org/bitstream/123456789/129110/169/PFJCO8640219003.jpg

531

091 'Teatro Sociale di Voghera 1800-1912'
www.comune.voghera.pv.it [not accessible online 3 June 2021]

092 Raggi. *Il Teatro comunale di Cesena…*
https://archive.org/details/ilteatrocomunale00ragg
http://www.marianotomatis.it/index.php?page=biblioteca&code=RAG1906

093 Archivio di Stato di Piacenza
www.archiviodistatopiacenza.beniculturali.it

094 *Fête de l'Opéra donnée … 7 juin 1879*
https://gallica.bnf.fr/ark:/12148/bpt6k6539674d/f25.item

095 Scrapbook of newspaper clippings compiled by Maurice Valet
http://catalogue.bnf.fr/ark:/12148/cb41214615t

096 Interview with Eugenio reprinted in *Il Prestigiatore Moderno* 1893
https://clublanternamagica.blogspot.com/2011

097 Costa, *Bartolomeo Marchelli, Capitano Garibaldino, 1834-1903*
www.archiviostorico.net/libripdf/Bartolomeo_Marchelli.pdf

098 Italo marriage 1906
http://dl.antenati.san.beniculturali.it/v/Archivio+di+Stato+di+Roma/Stato+civile+italiano/Roma/Matrimoni/1906/n+1788-2185+Vol+6+Parte+1+Serie+A/007659879_01645.jpg.html

099 Marriage of Marianna Mlynarska and Alexandre Conti [top entry]
https://geneteka.genealodzy.pl/index.php?op=gt&lang=pol&bdm=S&w=71wa&rid=S&search_lastname=conti&search_name=&search_lastname2=&search_name2=&from_date=&to_date=

100 Starkman, *Cukiernie warszawskie* (Warsaw, 1895) p.8
https://polona.pl/item/cukiernie-warszawskie,NzUxODg3MTg/6/

101 Death registration of Marianna Conti, née Mlynarska (entry no.579)
http://metryki.genealodzy.pl/metryka.php?ar=1&zs=0159d&sy=1847&kt=3&plik=579-582.jpg

102 Death registration of Alexandre Conti, 1871 (no.1, top right)
https://metryki.genealodzy.pl/metryka.php?ar=1&zs=1216d&sy=1871&kt=3&plik=001-003.jpg

103 Geneteka (Polish bdm)
http://www.geneteka.genealodzy.pl/index.php

104 Death registration of Eugenio (Eugeniusz Bosko di toryno), 1826-1827 (see entry 209).
https://metryki.genealodzy.pl/metryka.php?ar=1&zs=0161d&sy=1827&kt=3&plik=208-213.jpg#zoom=2.25&x=611&y=1600

105 Birth registration of Matteo Fortunato Bosco, Naples 1837
http://dl.antenati.san.beniculturali.it/v/Archivio+di+Stato+di+Napoli/Stato+civile+della+restaurazione_Quartieri/San+Giuseppe/Nati/02_01_1837-23_09_1837/004907391_00218.jpg
 (also transcription at https://www.familysearch.org/ark:/61903/1:1:KXSM-RYY)

106 Death registration of Alexandryna Bosco, 1853
https://metryki.genealodzy.pl/metryka.php?ar=1&zs=0159d&sy=1853&kt=3&plik=423-426.jpg

107 'Encyclopedia of the Polish Theatre'
http://www.encyklopediateatru.pl/osoby/77482/aleksander-jedrzejewski

108 Birth registration of Adelaide Bosco, 1828 (no.85, top right)
http://metryki.genealodzy.pl/metryka.php?ar=8&zs=9233d&sy=131&kt=3&skan=083-086.jpg

109 Oettinger, *Moniteur des dates…* (Bosco, Vol.1 p.111)
https://www.google.com/books/edition/Moniteur_des_Dates/9INZAAAAcAAJ?hl=en

110 Telemaco Signorini's painting 'La Sala delle Agitate a S. Bonifazio di Firenze'
https://it.wikipedia.org/wiki/La_sala_delle_agitate_nell%27ospizio_di_San_Bonifacio

111 *Annali della Giurisprudenza Italiana*, XXI, 1887 (first sequence of pages)
https://www.google.co.nz/books/edition/Annali_della_giurisprudenza_italiana/P6krAQAAMAAJ?hl=en&gbpv=1

112 Beatification of Dom Bosco: Pope Pius XI 'Mirabilis Deus':
http://www.vatican.va/content/pius-xi/it/briefs/documents/hf_p-xi_briefs_19290602_mirabilis-deus.html

113 Canonisation of Dom Bosco:
Pope Pius XI (1 April 1934), Lettera Decretale di Sua Santità Pio XI "Geminata Laetitia":
http://www.vatican.va/content/pius-xi/it/letters/documents/hf_p-xi_lett_19340401_geminata-laetitia.html

114 On Dom Bosco as patron saint of magicians
https://www.magosales.com/index.php/2013-04-20-09-40-50/varie/article/31-il-mago-imploro-don-giovanni-bosco-proteggimi-tu
https://www.magosales.com/index.php/2013-04-20-09-40-50/biografia/article/91-i-prestigiatori-in-cerca-in-patrono
https://www.magosales.com/index.php/2013-04-20-09-40-50/biografia/article/19-un-prestigiatore-al-cospetto-del-pontefice

115 Don Bosco, *Memorie dell'Oratorio di S. Francesco di Sales dal 1815 al 1855*,
https://www.donboscoland.it/it/page/fonti [and elsewhere]

116 Don Bosco, *Memoirs of the Oratory of Saint Francis de Sales from 1815 to 1855…*
http://www.salesianym.com/uploads/3/0/0/6/30065457/st._john_bosco_-_memoirs_of_the_oratory.pdf

117 Review by Arthur Lenti of preceding work
http://journal.salesianstudies.org/wp-content/uploads/2013/12/Lenti-Memoirs_of_the_Oratory-The_Autobiography_of_St_John_Bosco-Journal_Salesian_Studies-Vol01_No1-Spring1990.pdf

118 Fr G.B. Lemoyne (*et al.*) *Memorie Biografiche di Don Giovanni Bosco*…
https://www.donboscoland.it/it/page/fonti-spirituali

119 Lemoyne, English translation as *Biographical Memoirs of Saint John Bosco*
https://donboscosalesianportal.org/wp-content/uploads/BM_01_en.pdf [*etc.*]

120 Arthur Lenti 'Don Bosco's "Boswell": John Baptist Lemoyne…' http://journal.salesianstudies.org/wp-content/uploads/2013/12/Lenti-Don_Boscos_Boswell-John_Baptist_Lemoyne-The_Man_And_His_Work-Journal_Salesian_Studies-Vol01_No2-Fall1990.pdf

121 Aldo Giraudo & Giuseppe Biancardi, *Qui è vissuto don Bosco*
https://www.ibs.it/qui-vissuto-don-bosco-itinerari-libro-aldo-giraudo-giuseppe-biancardi/e/9788801029703

122 English version of preceding, *Don Bosco Lived Here*
http://archivio.sdb.org/images/documenti/Com_Soc/DBLHhtml/DBLH.html

123 Children's books on Don Bosco referring to his magic
https://stripinfo.be/reeks/strip/93509_Don_Bosco_1_De_kleine_goochelaar
https://www.amazon.com/Johns-magic-story-about-Bosco/dp/0030416655
https://archive.org/details/saintjohnboscoch00beeb

124 Statues of Dom Bosco performing
In Becchi —'Don Bosco Lived Here': 3.1.6
https://www.flickr.com/photos/roby_the_pres/2360815788

125 Statue in the Museo della Magia in Cherasco
https://www.prestigiazione.it/wp/il-museo-della-magia-ce-e-si-vede/#jp-carousel-2882

126 Egorov Auction House Moscow, Auction no.8, item 30
https://egorovs.art/auction8/lot30

127 Antikvariat, Moscow booksellers
https://antikvaria.ru/product/opyty-naturalnoy-magii-i-volshebnyy-kabinet-karla-bosko-1849-god/

128 Queen Victoria's Journal
http://www.queenvictoriasjournals.org (*U.K. access only*); http://qvj.chadwyck.com/marketing.do

129 Marriage of "Alfred Bosco"
https://www.ancestry.co.uk/interactive/4994/40458_316961-00135?pid=1053176255

130 Epstein in Riga: *Estländische Gouvernements-Zeitung* 8, 11 Aug.1860
https://dea.digar.ee/article/ekmteataja/1860/08/08/3.1
https://dea.digar.ee/cgi-bin/dea?a=d&d=ekmteataja18600811.2.7.1

131 Letter in Epstein's album from Vicomte de Laferrière, 1869
https://www.liveauctioneers.com/item/57019376_epstein-sigmund-collection-of-certificates
(click on "View details" then the bottom thumbnail on the left).

132 Epstein performing at the Tuilleries: *Le Monde illustré* 3 April 1869
https://www.retronews.fr/journal/le-monde-illustre/3-avril-1869/189/2905857/5

133 'The Last Hours of the Life of Nicholas I', ridiculously said to be by Epstein
https://www.prlib.ru/item/438214
https://dlib.rsl.ru/viewer/01003543340#?page=1
and another copy at
https://vivaldi.nlr.ru/bx000023820/view/?#page=2
https://dc.lib.unc.edu/cdm/item/collection/rbr/?id=22141

134 French edition, 1855
https://reader.digitale-sammlungen.de/de/fs1/object/display/bsb10691847_00001.html
https://books.google.co.nz/books?id=989oAAAAcAAJ&pg=PA1

135 *Les dernières heures de sa Majesté l'Empereur Nicolas* (by Elisabeth Bagreef-Speranski)
http://digital.onb.ac.at/OnbViewer/viewer.faces?doc=ABO_%2BZ225986201

136 Joshua Jay, 'Tragic Magic'
www.joshuajay.com/tragic-magic/tragic-magic.doc

137 Epstein illustration, Sweden 1876
http://magicpedia.ru/%D0%9D%D0%BE%D0%B2%D0%BE%D1%81%D1%82%D0%B8/tabid/491/articleType/ArticleView/articleId/544/----.aspx

138 Birth and baptism record of Adam Brøndum
https://www.familysearch.org/ark:/61903/1:1:QG3G-GB3L

139 Naturalization records in U.S.A. of Adam Brøndum
https://www.ancestry.co.uk/imageviewer/collections/2280/images/32955_2421406261_0321-00581
https://www.ancestry.co.uk/imageviewer/collections/1629/images/31194_120871-01306

140 "Brøndum, Hans Adam Julius" in Copenhagen Poor Relief Records
https://issuu.com/fattigv/docs/fhv1881-1887

141 Posters of "Henry Adams" (Brøndum) in Helsinki, 1889 (the first and last)
https://www.alvin-portal.org/alvin/attachment/document/alvin-record:186262/ATTACHMENT-0028.pdf

142 Brøndum and wife in Copenhagen Police Register, 1899
https://kbharkiv.dk/brug-samlingerne/soeg-i-indtastede-kilder/post/17-757233

143 Baptism of Faustinus Petersen, 1868
https://www.familysearch.org/ark:/61903/1:1:QG3Y-4K61

144 The Trachtenbergs on the 'Russian Association of Magicians' site
http://magicpedia.ru/magicians/tabid/435/articleType/ArticleView/articleId/61/---1873-1943.aspx

Professor Millar and the African twins
145 State Archives of North Carolina, finding list of Millar's scrapbooks
http://digital.ncdcr.gov/cdm/ref/collection/p16062coll15/id/772
146 Pamphlets sold at their exhibitions
https://docsouth.unc.edu/neh/carolinatwin/carolinatwin.html
https://docsouth.unc.edu/neh/millie-christine/menu.html

147 Gold, 'Millie-Christine McKoy and the American Freak Show...'
https://escholarship.org/uc/item/39g057p3

148 Booklet on Millar's Diorama of India
https://archive.org/details/gri_000033125008505741/mode/2up

149 William Pack on Madame Bosco in his blog 'ChicagoMagic':
http://chicagomagic.blogspot.com/2006/07/who-is-madame-bosco.htm

150 Poster for "Signor Bosco" performance, Dartford 1866
https://issuu.com/potterauctions/docs/catalog_041_issuu   (item 409)

151 Saul Warschawski's railway accident, 1876
http://www.railwaysarchive.co.uk/eventsummary.php?eventID=4334

152 Poster for Saul Warschawski, Broadstairs, 1888 or 1893 or 1900
https://hrc.contentdm.oclc.org/digital/collection/p15878coll5/id/68

153 Poster for Saul Warschawski with son and daughters (on right)
https://hrc.contentdm.oclc.org/digital/collection/p15878coll22/id/3515

154 Family of "Louis Susser"
https://www.ics.uci.edu/~dan/genealogy/Krakow/Families/Susser.html

155 Family tree of Leibel (Louis) Susser
https://www.ancestry.co.uk/family-tree/person/tree/155424783/person/152052601154/facts

156 Louis Susser performing at St. John's College, Hurstpierpoint, 1859
http://sbgas.org/wp-content/uploads/2018/01/SBGAS-Transactions-2008.pdf

157 Poster for Louis Susser performing in Cork on February 8th and 9th [1861]
https://hrc.contentdm.oclc.org/digital/collection/p15878coll22/id/3513   (page 93)

158 Posters for Louis Susser Nov.1864 (page 92, the two lower posters)
https://hrc.contentdm.oclc.org/digital/collection/p15878coll22/id/3512/rec/1

159 Poster and handbill for Louis Susser in Kent, August 1871
https://hrc.contentdm.oclc.org/digital/collection/p15878coll5/id/69

160 John William Blake ("Fegetter") referred to under Lawrence Bosco (B75)
https://www.findagrave.com/memorial/17510581/john-feggetter-blake]

161 Greathead family website: Leotard Bosco (B77)
http://www.greathead.org/greathead2-o/p497.htm#i12411
http://www.greathead.org/greathead2-o/p530.htm#i13247

162 Leotard Bosco letter
https://www.lotsearch.net/lot/l-bosco-autograph-letter-signed-48438896?searchID=3077633

163 Carl Bosco in Thomas Robinson, *Oregon Photographers*
http://historicphotoarchive.com/oregon-photographers-online-edition/bosco-carl-portland/

164 Carl Bosco: the Pixley Sisters
http://archiveswest.orbiscascade.org/ark:/80444/xv61224

165 Julio Bosco — thesis by Carlos Otoniel Pacheso da Cunha
https://docplayer.com.br/36013965-Universidade-federal-de-pelotas-programa-de-pos-graduacao-em-memoria-social-e-patrimonio-cultural-dissertacao.html

166 Julio Bosco — Carmen Luz Maturana, *La Comedia de Magia* ...
https://scielo.conicyt.cl/scielo.php?script=sci_arttext&pid=S0718-71812009000100006,

167 Julio Bosco — Antonio Lerma Garay, 'El Cagliostro Rioplatense Llega a Mazatlán'
http://pe.globedia.com/cagliostro-rioplatense-llega-mazatlan;
[from his book *Mazatlan Decimonónico*, of which this section (pp.41-2) is accessible on Google Books]

168 Julio Bosco: review in *El Monitor Republicano* 13 Mar.1874
http://www.hndm.unam.mx/consulta/resultados/visualizar/558a35957d1ed64f16b9d62c?resultado=13&tipo=pagina&intPagina=3.

169 Julio Bosco — Chester Urbina Gaitán, 'Nigromancia, prestidigitacion...'
https://revistas.ucr.ac.cr/index.php/sociales/article/download/17620/17114,

170 Julio Bosco — advertisements
http://silos.ville-chaumont.fr/flora/jsp/system/win_main.jsp?profile=anonymous3&success=jsp%2Fsystem%2Fwin_main.jsp&failure=jsp%2Ferror.jsp
http://silos.ville-chaumont.fr/flora/jsp/system/win_main.jsp?profile=anonymous3&success=jsp%2Fsystem%2Fwin_main.jsp&failure=jsp%2Ferror.jsp

171 Julio Bosco — poster in Antonina, 1884
http://urublues1.blogspot.com/2014

172 Julio Bosco — Víctor Ramés 'El ilusionista en Córdoba, 1886':
http://www.diarioalfil.com.ar/2014/04/28/el-ilusionista-en-cordoba-1886

173 Julio Bosco — in Uruguay 1891
https://teatroescayola.blogspot.com

174 Children of Professor Ruchwaldy
https://www.hkmemory.hk/collections/hong_kong_cemetery/about/index.html

175 Ruchwaldy in *Reseña Histórica del Teatro en México*,
http://cdigital.dgb.uanl.mx/la/1080019194_C/1080019197_T4/1080019197_94.pdf

176 Ruchwaldy death registration
https://www.familysearch.org/ark:/61903/1:1:2W9V-BWD.

177 Ruchwaldy burial record
https://www.familysearch.org/ark:/61903/1:1:QK1G-FYXJ

178 Poster for Ferdinand Becker (C3)
https://www.stadtmuseum.leipzig.de/media/wmZoom/ST000/ST000280.jpg

179 Manuel Lopez (C31) — illustrated ad in Rio de Janeiro 1875
http://memoria.bn.br/DocReader/DocReader.aspx?bib=376493&pesq=bosco&pasta=ano%20187&hf=memoria.bn.br&pagfis=63

180 Manuel Lopez (C31) – pamphlet on him as "Donato"
https://gallica.bnf.fr/ark:/12148/bpt6k62127927

181 Manuel Lopez (C31) — 'Théâtre de magie' in the Pré-Catelan
https://gallica.bnf.fr/blog/17062021/benita-anguinet-1819-1887-la-celebre-illusionniste-du-pre-catelan.

182 Herr Lorch (C33) — poster at Leipzig fair *ca.*1860
https://www.stadtmuseum.leipzig.de/media/wmZoom/ST000/ST000400.jpg

183 Bartolomeo Marcelli (C34) — letter by Eugenio
https://www.findacadabra.com/index.php?fn=home&f=show&opt=892

184 Charles Mirano (C38) — posters 1868
https://www.buchfreund.de/de/d/p/95231980/gastvorstellung-des-herrn-charles-mirano-aus

185 Professor St Roman (Samuel Thiersfeld)(C49) — family tree
https://www.geni.com/people/Samuel-Thiersfeld/6000000023273062921

186 Books on magic by Romanoff (Giovanni Battista Romano)
https://rivistasavej.it/bartolomeo-bosco-of-turin-842aa3c95773

187 Ernst Schulz, 'Der große Zauberer'
http://digital.ub.uni-duesseldorf.de/ulbdzd/periodical/zoom/10357538

188 Edouard-Joseph Raynaly, *Les propos d'un escamoteur* (1894)
https://gallica.bnf.fr/ark:/12148/bpt6k5510830c

189 *Oesterreichische Senfkörner...* by Hanns Normann (F2)
https://www.google.com/books/edition/Oesterreichische_Senfk%C3%B6rner/Re0yAQAAMAAJ

190 *Humoristische Kleinigkeiten*, by Leopold Schick (F4)
https://books.google.com/books?id=0tROAAAAcAAJ

191 'Les Escamoteurs', *L'Indépendance Belge* 18 July 1841 (F5)
https://uurl.kbr.be/1052060 (and following pages)

192 ['How Bosco Became Famous'] (F6)
https://www.retronews.fr/journal/la-presse/3-octobre-1843/126/386397/1

193 'Bosco's letztes Kunststück', by Dr. Carl Herloßsohn' (F7)
https://anno.onb.ac.at/cgi-content/anno?aid=wan&datum=18460224&seite=6&zoom=33

194 'Der Dämon der Magie: Memoiren aus B. Bosco's Leben', by "Kleroth" (F11)
https://www.google.com/books/edition/Erinnerungen_an_merkw%C3%BCrdige_Gegenst%C3%A4nd/OMdaAAAAcAAJ?hl=en&gbpv=1 [and following pages]

195 'Bartolomeo Bosco: Ein Capriccio in Callot-Hoffmann'scher Manier' (F12)
http://kramerius.nkp.cz/kramerius/handle/ABA001/22115939 [and later issues]

196 'O Bosco !', by Christinus Sieben (F15)
https://anno.onb.ac.at/cgi-content/anno?aid=wzz&datum=18450404&seite=2 and next page

197 'Drei Aesopische Fabeln', by B. Heidler (F16)
https://anno.onb.ac.at/cgi-content/anno?aid=wan&datum=18451125&seite=1 (and next page)

198 *Der arme Geigenmacher und sein Kind*, by Gustav Nieritz (F18)
https://api.digitale-sammlungen.de/iiif/image/v2/bsb10502460_00257/full/full/0/default.jpg

199 'Ein Scherz', by Josef Seidner (F19)
https://www.digitale-sammlungen.de/en/view/bsb10503306?q=%28seidner+AND+bosco%29&page=482,483

200 *Gilbert et Gilberte,* by Eugène Sue (F30)
https://gallica.bnf.fr/ark:/12148/bpt6k58127007

201 'A Night of Horrors in the Wizard's Workshop...' (F31)
https://www.britishnewspaperarchive.co.uk/viewer/bl/0001365/18570711/049/0004

202 'Bosco Il Prestigiatore. Prima Rappresentazione' (F32)
https://www.senato.it/teca/giornalistorici/d62d53a4-042e-4cbd-b501-9cd9a47c0b19.html

203 [Imaginary letter by Bosco] *Kladderdatsch* 29 July 1860 (F33)
https://digi.ub.uni-heidelberg.de/diglit/kla1860/0138

204 Wie sich der 'rothe Hofmann' auf Bosco spielte' (F34)
https://anno.onb.ac.at/cgi-content/anno?aid=tet&datum=18601222&seite=1

205 'Boscos Tod', by H. Truhn (F35)
http://digital.ub.uni-duesseldorf.de/ihd/periodical/zoom/2975501

206 'Aus dem Leben Bosco's' (F36)
https://api.digitale-sammlungen.de/iiif/image/v2/bsb11032136_00264/full/full/0/default.jpg

207 'Sultan Abdul Aziz in der Comödie' by "W.S. and M.S." (F37)
https://anno.onb.ac.at/cgi-content/anno?aid=wsz&datum=18760724&seite=1 (& next page)

208 'Sultan Abdul-Aziz im Theater, (Eine Reise-Erinnerung.)' (F38)
https://anno.onb.ac.at/cgi-content/anno?aid=apr&datum=18670723&seite=1 (& next page)

209 'Der gordische Knoten, Humoreske aus dem Bühnenleben' (F39)
https://anno.onb.ac.at/cgi-content/anno?aid=pew&datum=18781208 (& next page)

210 'Jacques l'Honneur', first instalment *Le Petit Journal* 26 June 1892
https://www.retronews.fr/journal/le-petit-journal/26-juin-1892/100/403279/3

211 *Jacques l'Honneur*: cover of book
https://postermuseum.com/products/jacques-lhonneur

212 'Bosco's Benefit' (F41)
https://paperspast.natlib.govt.nz/newspapers/EP18940224.2.70
and in Norwegian:
https://www.nb.no/items/f6f7381d5bfda39316afa2d8ab514a3e

213 'Bosco in Rußland. Erzählung nach Tatsachen' (F42)
https://www.e-newspaperarchives.ch/?a=d&d=OSZ19000529-01.2.38

214 'Een Banneling, die kon Gochelen...' (F45)
https://kranten.archiefalkmaar.nl/issue/ACO/1939-05-13/edition/null/page/15

215 'Spiriti miei obedite, oder Bosco's Zauberformel' (F46)
Huldigung: https://www.digitale-sammlungen.de/en/view/bsb11044866?page=272
Declam. https://www.google.com/books/edition/Declamatorium/Rr9CAAAAcAAJ pp.61*ff*

216 'An Herrn Bartholomeo Bosco' (F51)
http://www.periodika.lv/periodika2-viewer/?lang=fr#panel:pa|issue:107122|article:DIVL20

217 Luigi Muzzi [Verse inscription for Bartolomeo] 1836 (F52)
https://www.google.cm/books/edition/Delle_iscrizioni_di_Luigi_Muzzi_accademi/ugBCHrTXoXUC

218 Luigi Muzzi [Verse inscription for Bartolomeo] 1845
https://www.google.com/books/edition/Il_Piccol_Reno/Xn5PAQAAMAAJ?gbpv=1 (pp.61*ff*).

219 'Täuschung und Wahrheit. (An Barth. Bosco)' (F55)
https://anno.onb.ac.at/cgi-content/anno?aid=wan&datum=18450409&seite=4

220 'Zum Abschied an B. Bosco' (F56)
https://anno.onb.ac.at/cgi-content/anno?aid=wan&datum=18460302&seite=3&zoom=33

221 'An B. Bosco in Leipzig'. *Leipziger Zeitung* 13 May 1848 (F57)
https://www.google.com/books/edition/_/lw5kAAAAcAAJ?hl=en&gbpv=1
page 3148 (in *Zweite Beilage*)

222 'Spiriti miei infernali!' *Leipziger Zeitung* 28 May 1848 (F58)
https://www.google.com/books/edition/_/Iw5kAAAAcAAJ?hl=en&gbpv=1
on page 3497 (in *Beilage*)

223 Material on the film *Jacques l'Honneur* (F65) at the Bibliothèque Nationale
https://catalogue.bnf.fr/ark:/12148/cb38743097f

224 David Robinson 'Who was Professor Bosco?' (F66, Chaplin films)
https://www.charliechaplin.com/en/articles/310

225 Chaplin as Professor Bosco
https://www.charliechaplin.com/en/films/9-Limelight/articles/306-The-Professor

226 *Malý Bosko*, 1898 (LCz2)
http://kramerius.nkp.cz/kramerius/handle/ABA001/21343521

227 *Malý Bosko,* 1889? (LCz5)
https://www.aron-antik.cz/eshop/11550/maly-bosko.html

228 *Čaroděj Bosco,* 2018 (LCz15)
https://magickyklubpraha.webnode.cz/aktualni-deni

229 *Hexemesteren: en Samling…* (LDaN2)
https://www.nb.no/items/URN:NBN:no-nb_digibok_2019040826002
https://www.nb.no/items/84ce2ca31808adfc395268167b053f17?page=1

230 „*Trolderi Altsammen!"* (LDaN3)
https://soeg.kb.dk/view/action/uresolver.do?operation=resolveService&package_service_id=19437628980005763&institutionId=5763&customerId=5760

231 *Bosco, de Toovenaar in Holland*, 1845 (LDu1)
https://www.google.com/books/edition/Bosco_de_toovenaar_in_Holland_of_De_ontd/JeFWAAAAcAAJ

232 *Bosco, de Toovenaar in Holland*. 3rd ed., 1864 (LDu3)
https://www.google.com/books/edition/Bosco_de_toovenaar_in_Holland_of_De_ontd/3Pi3xwEACAAJ

233 *Carlo Bosco's Toover-kabinet, of Kunstjes…* 2nd ed. (LDu8), cover
https://www.catawiki.com/en/l/11356871-magie-nieuw-toover-kabinet-by-carlo-bosco-modern-magic-by-professor-hoffman-1858-1904#&gid=1&pid=1 [scroll down]

234 *Carlo Bosco's Toover-kabinet, of Kunstjes…* 2nd ed. (LDu8), review
https://www.dbnl.org/tekst/_vad003185901_01/_vad003185901_01_0018.php

235 *Carlo Bosco's tooverkabinet, Onder anderen…* (LDu11)
https://babel.hathitrust.org/cgi/pt?id=nyp.33433017992813

236 *De Roode Duivel in den Gezelligen Kring* (LDu13)
https://books.google.com/books?vid=KBNL:UBA000146020

237 *Nieuw Goochelaars Handboek* (LDu16)
https://www.delpher.nl/nl/boeken/view?coll=boeken&identifier=MMUBA09:000000217:00005

238 Nieuw Goochelaars Handboek (LDu16), review
https://www.dbnl.org/tekst/_vad003185301_01/_vad003185301_01_0171.php

239 *Nieuw Goochelaars Handboek* (LDu17)
https://books.google.co.nz/books?id=8zL5DVeFuEQC

240 *De Nieuwe Vrolijke Toovenaar en Droomuitlegger…* (LDu18)
https://play.google.com/books/reader?id=QDNvXeOJNtgC

241 *Satanas Recueil Européen* (LFr3)
https://auctions.potterauctions.com/Satanas__Recueil_Universel__Biographique__Anecdoti-LOT22702.aspx

242 *Satanas. Recueil Universel...* (LFr4)
http://www.marianotomatis.it/?page=biblioteca&code=BOS1859#

243 *La Nouvelle Magie Blanche Dévoilée...*, 1857 (LFr9)
http://ark.bnf.fr/ark:/12148/bpt6k14151113

244 *Biographie und Anecdoten aus den Reisen des alten Bosco* (LGe1)
https://digital.slub-dresden.de/werkansicht/dlf/149646/1/

245 *Bosco, der kleine Hexenmeister*
https://articulo.mercadolibre.com.ar/MLA-604696159-bosco-derkleine-hexenmeister-magia-en-aleman-_JM

246 *Der unübertreffliche Hexenmeister*, 1847
https://www.google.com/books/edition/Der_unübertreffliche_Hexenmeister_oder/KRxbAAAAcAAJ

247 *Enthüllte Geheimnisse der modernen Zauberei* (LGe38)
https://www.booklooker.de/B%C3%BCcher/Carlo-BOSCO+Bosco-s-enth%C3%BCllte-Geheimnisse-der-modernen-Zauberei-Herausgegeben-von-einem-Sch%C3%BCler-und/id/A02o9HnB01ZZ9

248 *Carl Bosco's Zauberkünste*, 1867 (LGe60)
https://sammlungen.ub.uni-frankfurt.de/urn/urn:nbn:de:hebis:30:2-226470

249 *Carlo Bosko, Der weltberühmte Zauberkünstler und Taschenspieler* (LGe72)
https://www.ebay.de/itm/143560536799?hash=item216cdff2df:g:9I8AAOSwq89hA9W1

250 *Carlo Bosko, Der weltberühmte Zauberkünstler und Taschenspieler* (LGe73)
http://d-nb.info/572768354/04.

251 *Carlo Bosko, der weltberühmte Zauberkünstler und Taschenspieler* (LGe76)
https://www.delpher.nl/nl/boeken/view?coll=boeken&identifier=MMUBA09:000000224

252 Kerndörffer, *Der Kleine Taschenspieler und Magier* (or ...Magiker)
https://catalog.hathitrust.org/Record/00856006 (with *Magier* in title)
https://digital.staatsbibliothek-berlin.de/werkansicht/?PPN=PPN76673188X (with *Magiker* in title)

253 *Carlo Bosco, das Zauber-Kabinet*, 1843 (LGe80)
https://www.google.com/books/edition/Carlo_Bosco_das_Zauber_Kabinet_oder_das/8NMnnCdFN4EC

254 *Carlo Bosco`s Zauber-Cabinet*, 1870 (LGe89)
https://books.google.com/books?id=l1hNAAAAYAAJ

255 *Der rothe Teufel im Salon,* 1882 (LGe107)
https://mandadb.hu/tetel/70841/Der_rothe_Teufel_im_Salon_oder_Bosco_in_allen_Geselltschaften

256 (*Der rothe Teufel im Salon*). - Singmaster 'Books on Recreational Mathematics' 1992; 2004
http://docs.exdat.com/docs/index-45394.html?page=15 (1992; this version gone?)
https://www.puzzlemuseum.com/singma/singma6/SOURCES/singma-sources-edn8-2004-03-19.htm

257 *Le Magicien des Salons ou le Diable Couleur de Rose* (1856)
http://www.marianotomatis.it/?page=biblioteca&code=RIC1873&lang=ES

258 *Der immer gern gesehene Tausendkünstler* (LGe125)
https://en.mandadb.hu/tetel/65721/Der_immer_gern_gesehene_Tausend__Kunstler_Taschenspieler_und_Wippchenmacher

259 *Bosco als Kartenkünstler* (LGe136)
https://www.worthpoint.com/worthopedia/bosco-als-kartenkunstler-scarce-buch-1757358033

260 *Der Zauberstab*, 1859 (LGe144)
https://opacplus.bsb-muenchen.de/title/BV014165721

261 *Der Zauberstab*, 1875 (LGe147)
https://babel.hathitrust.org/cgi/pt?id=nyp.33433017993746

262 ULSH catalogue entries for Jukundus Hilarius Possenreich: *Scharfblicke...* (LGe149)
http://catalogue.libraries.london.ac.uk/record=b2007806~S24
http://catalogue.libraries.london.ac.uk/record=b2002933~S24
http://catalogue.libraries.london.ac.uk/record=b1932804~S24

263 Leischner: *Die Zauberkunst aller Zeiten und Nationen*, 1831 (LGe151)
https://catalog.hathitrust.org/Record/100595047

264 Leischner: *Die Zauberkunst aller Zeiten und Nationen*, 1834 (LGe153)
https://opacplus.bsb-muenchen.de/title/1046600/ft/bsb1013276

265 *Bosco in der Westentasche*, 1848 (LGe167)
https://books.google.com/books?id=V3YomxjXfcEC

266 L. Schellenberg jun.: *Ein Blick in Döbler's und Bosko's Zauberkabinet* (LGe193)
https://books.google.com/books?id=4BtkAAAAcAAJ

267 'Conjurors and Conjuring', *Boy's Own Paper* 5 Feb.1881
https://babel.hathitrust.org/cgi/pt?id=uc1.c2723972&view=1up&seq=347

268 *Curiose Avventure e Brevi Cenni sulla vita di Bartolomeo Bosco* (LIt1)
https://www.google.com/books/edition/Curiose_avventure_e_brevi_cenni_sulla_vi/eP1iAAAAcAAJ

269 *Il Cavaliere Bosco Giuocator di Magia*, 1913 (LIt5)
https://archive.org/details/BOS1913/page/n3

270 *Gabinetto magico ossia Il complesso dell'arte di prestigio* (LIt9)
https://auctions.potterauctions.com/_BOSCO__Giovanni_Bartolomeo__Italian__1793_1863___-LOT47485.aspx

271 *Gabinetto magico ossia Il complesso dell'arte di prestigio* (LIt10)
https://auctions.potterauctions.com/Gabinetto_Magico_ossia_il_Complesso_dell_Arte_di_P-LOT22700.aspx

272 *Gabinetto magico ossia Il complesso dell'arte di prestigio* (LIt11)
http://digital.onb.ac.at/OnbViewer/viewer.faces?doc=ABO_%2BZ202203104

273 *Gabinetto magico ossia Il complesso dell'arte di prestigio* (LIt12)
https://books.google.com.books?id=6p5gAAAAcAAJ

274 *Gabinetto magico ossia Il complesso dell'arte di prestigio* (LIt13)
https://auctions.potterauctions.com/_BOSCO__Giovanni_Bartolomeo__Italian__1793_1863___-LOT47486.aspx

275 *Il Nuovo Bosco, ossia il Diavolo Color di Rosa* (LIt26)
https://auctions.potterauctions.com/catalog.aspx?auctionid=92

276 *Il Nuovo Bosco, ossia il Diavolo Color di Rosa* (LIt29)
https://archive.org/details/nuovobosco

277 *Il Piccolo Bosco*, 1863 (LIt39) at Archivio storico del Comune di Novellara
http://www.comunedinovellara.gov.it/upload/novellara_ecm8/gestionedocumentale/ARCHIVIOSTORICO-aprile2016_784_19239.pdf

278 *Il Saputello in Conversazione* (LIt42)
https://auctions.potterauctions.com/_Bosco__Bartolomeo__Il_Saputello_in_Conversazione_-LOT22705.aspx

279 *Satana. Raccolta Europea...* catalogued as 1855 (LIt49)
https://auctions.potterauctions.com/_bosco__giovanni_bartolomeo__italian__1793_1863___-lot47487.aspx

280 *Satana. Raccolta Universale...* (LIt50)
https://www.lotsearch.net/lot/satana-raccolta-universale-biografica-aneddotica-delle-avventure-di-48438701?searchID=3077633

281 Furno: *33 Giuochi Destro-Fisici...* (LIt54)
https://books.google.com/books?id=XEMMKk1IBnQC

282 *Bosko Odrodzony, czyli Zbiór Sztuk...* (LPol2)
https://polona.pl/item/bosko-odrodzony-czyli-zbior-sztuk-kartowych-magicznych-chemicznych-i-mechanicznych,MzIxNzc1MzA/6

283 *Bosko czarnoksiężnik czyli...* (LPol4)
https://www.sbc.org.pl/dlibra/show-content/publication/edition/79593?id=79593

284 *Czarnoksiężnik Bosko, czyli Bogaty* (LPol6)
https://polona.pl/item/czarnoksieznik-bosko-czyli-bogaty-zbior-najciekawszych-sztuk-magicznych-i-kuglarskich-do,MzIxNzc1MjU/6

285 *Karola Bosko zabawny sztukmistrz...* (LPol7)
http://bc.wbp.lublin.pl/dlibra/doccontent?id=12683

286 *Nowy Bosko Czarnoksiężnik...* (LPol10)
https://polona.pl/item/nowy-bosko-czarnoksieznik-tajemnice-kabalistyki-spirytyzmu-hypnotyzmu-magnetyzmu,MjAzNDQ5OTk

287 *Nowy Bosko Czarnoksiężnik: zbiór najciekawszych sztuk ...* (LPol11)
https://www.sbc.org.pl/dlibra/publication/80410/edition/75868/content

288 *Nowy Bosko Czarnoksiężnik: zbiór najciekawszych sztuk ...* (LPol12)
https://www.vice.com/pl/article/jmwpmy/co-tracisz-nie-czytajac-zobacz-niesamowite-ksiazki-ze-zbiorw-biblioteki-narodowej [at foot of page]

289 *Tajemnice magii dawniejszy...* (LPol23)
https://www.antykwariat.waw.pl/ksiazka,1026136/praca_zbiorowa_tajemnice_magii_czyli_sztuki_czarodziejskie_1851_r,128598.html

290 *Bosko, Karlo: Volshebnyy kabinet...* (LRu1)
https://dlib.rsl.ru/viewer/01003788544#?page=1

291 *Opyty natural'noy magii i volshebnyy kabinet Karla Bosko* (LRu3)
https://books.google.com/books?id=rPQIAQAAIAAJ

292 *Opyty natural'noy magii i volshebnyy kabinet Karla Bosko* (LRu4)
https://books.google.com/books?id=OWtpAAAAcAAJ

293 *Volshebnik i fokusnik v domashnem krugu...* (LRu5)
https://play.google.com/books/reader?id=gNhTh-zzNK8C

294 'Bibliografi över svensk trollerilitteratur'
https://magiarkivet.se/bibliografi-over-svensk-trollerilitteratur/anonyma

295 "The latest Globe Magic Lantern 'Bosco'..."
https://lantern.mediahist.org/catalog/BingCatalog1902Images_0009
https://lantern.mediahist.org/catalog/BingOptischeSpielwaaren1902Images_0005

296 Poster in the Houdini collection for "Signor Bosco" (=Louis) performing in Buxton
https://hrc.contentdm.oclc.org/digital/collection/p15878coll22/id/3515/rec/1 (page 95, left).

297 (Francesco Cetti) Emilia Fransiska Scheele
https://proveniens.ifokus.se/discussions/4d715f89b9cb46222706dfc8-emilia-fransiska-scheele

298 (Francesco Cetti) Birth registration of his father
https://urn.digitalarkivet.no/URN:NBN:no-a1450-kb20070321640462.jpg

299 (Francesco Cetti) His mother Malene Jacobsdatter – her baptism
https://www.digitalarkivet.no/view/255/pd00000009211088;
bap Jan 10th 1812 birth date is from ancestry

300 (Francesco Cetti) His mother Malene Jacobsdatter – in 1815 census
https://www.digitalarkivet.no/census/person/pf01051079016916

301 (Francesco Cetti) Marriage of his mother to Andreas Olsen Forsberg.
https://www.digitalarkivet.no/view/327/pv00000001293265

302 (Francesco Cetti) Burial of his mother
https://www.familysearch.org/ark:/61903/3:1:3QHK-93P5-SLZS?cc=4237104&personaUrl=%2Fark%3A%2F61903%2F1%3A1%3A687Z-V434

303 (Francesco Cetti) Father's prison sentences 1856, 1860
https://www.digitalarkivet.no/en/view/84/pc00000000361021
https://www.digitalarkivet.no/en/view/84/pc00000000371534

304 (Francesco Cetti) Parents' marriage
https://media.digitalarkivet.no/view/8362/150 (entry no.13 at foot of page)

305 (Francesco Cetti) Birth registration of elder sister
https://www.digitalarkivet.no/view/255/pd00000007387713

306 (Francesco Cetti) Death registration of elder sister
https://media.digitalarkivet.no/view/8364/152

307 (Francesco Cetti) His birth registration
https://media.digitalarkivet.no/view/8358/27 (first entry)

308 (Francesco Cetti) Birth of sister Maria Magdalene
https://media.digitalarkivet.no/view/8358/195;

309 (Francesco Cetti) Death of sister Maria Magdalene
https://www.familysearch.org/ark:/61903/1:1:NWFH-HJ4

310 (Francesco Cetti) Birth of his brother Petter Lauritz Neergaard
https://media.digitalarkivet.no/view/8358/81

311 (Francesco Cetti) Birth of sister Antonia Theodora
https://media.digitalarkivet.no/view/8358/235

312 (Francesco Cetti) Burial of sister Antonia Theodora
https://media.digitalarkivet.no/view/8364/185

313 (Francesco Cetti) Family in 1865 Bergen census
https://media.digitalarkivet.no/view/38249/469 (last family on the page)

314 (Francesco Cetti) Burial of sister showing his mother a widow
https://media.digitalarkivet.no/view/8364/185

315 (Francesco Cetti) Birth of half sister
https://media.digitalarkivet.no/view/7144/183

316 (Francesco Cetti) Death of half sister
https://www.digitalarkivet.no/en/view/267/pg00000000912966

317 (Francesco Cetti) Mother's remarriage
https://www.familysearch.org/ark:/61903/1:1:NW7S-7DP

318 (Francesco Cetti) Mother remarried living in Stockholm
https://sok.riksarkivet.se/bildvisning/Folk_901010-525#?c

319 (Francesco Cetti) Mother remarried living in Stockholm
https://www.familysearch.org/ark:/61903/3:1:3Q9M-CSGH-MSDH-F?cc=2790465

320 (Francesco Cetti) Mother in 1900 Norwegian census
https://media.digitalarkivet.no/view/37045/113356/indv2

321 (Francesco Cetti) In the 1891 Bergen census
https://www.digitalarkivet.no/nn/census/person/pf01052994021483

322 (Francesco Cetti) In the 1900 Stockholm census
https://sok.riksarkivet.se/bildvisning/Folk_001007-123

323 Sites with information on Ephraim Hambujer and his family
http://chicagomagic.blogspot.com/2006/07/who-is-hambujer.html
http://graysonfamily.org/FamilyTree/aqwg99.htm#2214
http://doctorgrayson.com/genealogy/Hambujer/Hambujer%20Magic%20Show.pdf
http://doctorgrayson.com/genealogy/Hambujer/Ephraim%20Children%20Photo%20Album.pdf.

324 Kratky-Baschik biography
https://www.geschichtewiki.wien.gv.at/Anton_Kratky-Baschik

325 Kratky-Baschik poster
https://upload.wikimedia.org/wikipedia/commons/9/97/Kratky-Baschik_Theaterzettel_Leipzig.jpg

326 Kratky-Baschik programme (35pp) for 1881 Vienna performance.
https://www.digital.wienbibliothek.at/wbrobv/content/titleinfo/1935600

327 Poster for John Blitz, Leicester, 1851
http://www.slv.vic.gov.au/miscpics/gid/slv-pic-aab13394

328 'The Sad Tale of Signor Vivalla: P.T. Barnum's Juggler'
https://www.juggle.org/the-sad-tale-of-signor-vivalla-p-t-barnums-juggler

329 Herbert J. Collings ("Col Ling Soo"), 'Smilestones'
http://www.davenportcollection.co.uk/wp-content/uploads/2017/11/Smilestones-v2.pdf

330 Anne Goulden, 'Maskelyne & Cooke: the early years'
http://www.davenportcollection.co.uk/wp-content/uploads/2017/06/Goulden-Anne-2013-Hamburg.pdf

331 C. Lang Neil, *The Modern Conjurer and Drawing-Room Entertainer*
https://www.loc.gov/resource/dcmsiabooks.modernconjurerdr00neil/?st=gallery

332 'The Art of Plate Spinning'
https://www.juggle.org/the-art-of-plate-spinning

333 Louis Lumière - Félicien Trewey, Le tourneur d'assiettes
https://commons.wikimedia.org/wiki/File:Assiettes_tournantes_(1896)_-_Louis_Lumi%C3%A8re.webm

334 Ed Sullivan Show — 'Artists - Erich Brenn – Plate Spinner'
https://www.edsullivan.com/artists/erich-brenn-plate-spinner

335 (Rubini) Luke McKernan, 'Who's Who of Victorian Cinema'
http://www.victorian-cinema.net/anderson

336 William F. Wilson, 'Professor John Henry Anderson … at Honolulu in 1859'
http://evols.library.manoa.hawaii.edu/handle/10524/38

337 *Hanky Panky, A Book of Conjuring Tricks,* 1872 and 1875 editions
https://babel.hathitrust.org/cgi/pt?id=nyp.33433017993316
https://hdl.handle.net/2027/nyp.33433017993308

338 *Prestidigitation moderne: recueil de tours…* (Paris, De La Rue 1877
https://catalog.hathitrust.org/Record/008559737

339 "Professor Hoffmann", *More Magic* (London: Routledge, 1890)
https://archive.org/details/moremagic00hoffgoog/page/n7

340 Annie Veroni in King's Lynn
https://cs-cz.facebook.com/LynnMuseumNorfolk/photos/a.358876044235184/3514249962031094/?type=3

341 Variant photos of Houdini at Bartolomeo's original gravestone
https://digitalcollections.nypl.org/items/510d47de-f73e-a3d9-e040-e00a18064a99, and
https://www.alamy.com/harry-houdini-at-magician-boscos-grave-in-harry-houdinis-book-the-unmasking-of-robert-houdin-1908-image186060630.html

342 Playbill for Steinl's Kunsttheater, *The Ricky Jay Collection* Sotheby's 27 October 2021, lot 255
https://www.sothebys.com/en/buy/auction/2021/the-ricky-jay-collection [see lot 255]

343 Epstein's Balmoral programme, Aberdeen 1855, wrongly ascribed to Bartolomeo
Perhaps printed in a rush, explaining the misprint in the last line
https://www.sothebys.com/en/buy/auction/2021/the-ricky-jay-collection [see lot 89]

344 Poster for Bartolomeo in Breslau in 1827
https://www.sothebys.com/en/buy/auction/2021/the-ricky-jay-collection/bosco-bartolomeo-the-bullet-catch

INDEX

The Index is very selective, especially as regards the careers of Bartolomeo and Eugenio, and it does not include every impostor and "pupil" in the B and C sections. References are to pages unless preceded by B, C, F, L or Z (see *Abbreviations* p.12).

Agioscope 183, 203
Alfikcya, Alfiktor 481
Alliegri, Rosmondo LIt53
Anderlini, Antonio 210, 211, 216
Apolloni, Marco Fabio F46
Arènes de Nîmes 81, 379
Ariosto, Erminio LGe14
Arizona Bill 393
Asachi, Gheorghe 58, 131
Astley's Theatre 24, 103
Aztec Lilliputians 522-3, 525
Babaja, Domenico 114
Bahr, Carl Friedrich LGe111-25
Barbarossa, Frederick 62, 135
Baretta-Dorst, Mej. 270-1
Baring-Gould, Sabine 295, 303
Bäuerle, Adolf 54, 98, 100, 127
Béatrix, Mdlle 168, 183, 195-6, 203
Beckmann, Friedrich ("Fritz"), actor 46-7, 123
Bellachino, Carlo (books by) 450-1
Bellemaire, Alex. 82, 149
Belli, Giuseppe Gioachino 40, 115-6, F54
Bernadau, Pierre 32
Besozzi, Max F39
Bishop, Washington Irving 250-1, 257, 504
Bland, J. 492
Blanus (Blanes), Jeannette 370
Blitz, Emilio 206
Boernstein, Henry 326
Börne, Ludwig 22, 97
Böttiger, Karl August 21, 24, 97, 102, 105
Bosco, Alfredo (fictional character) F41
Bosco, Bartolomeo (B1)
    Algeria 40, 74-5, 82-3, 90, 134, 150, 364
    Chiora (his 'homme d'affaires') 32
    daughter Adelaide 22, 52, 65, 95, 126, 132, 191, 207-217
    daughter Alexandryna 77, 95, 207-217
    falling off the stage 29, 46, 68, 71, 84, 108, 123
    guitar 20, 23, 26, 96
    'How Bosco Became Famous' 45-6, F6
    Leipzig Fair 15, 20, 47-8, 60-1, F27
    marriages 17, 63, 94, 207-217
    miracle of San Gennaro 38
    Rouen disaster 30, 109
    Sicily 37-9, 41, 114, 117
    son Eugeniusz Bosko di toryno 19, 95, 208-9
    son Eugenio 26, 30, 72, 75, 81, 89, 104, B2
    son Matteo 38, 209
    tent 24, 25, 48, 98
    writings 409
Bosco, Carl (books by) 431-5
Bosco, Carlo (books by) 435-43, LRu1

Bosco, Carlo, der Jünger (book by) 437-8
Bosco, Dagobert (fictional character) F39
Bosco, Doctor ('The Guiding Star') 334
Bosco, Eugenio (B2)
    birth of first daughter 170
    birth of son Italo 172
    birth of daughter Juliet 176
    contract with father 75, 158, 165, 187
    decapitation act 185, 205
    his book(s) 180, 409
    hook in sleeve 183
    hypnotism of animals 184, 185, 204
    miracle of San Gennaro 168, 194
    stroke 184, 204
Bosco, Italo (B3)
    birth 168, 172
    performing 176, 179, 201, 202, (265)
Bosco, Ferdinando Beneventano del, *Generale* 87-8, 154, 213, F33
Bosco, Harry *see* Susser, Harry
Bosco, James 352, BF2 *passim*
Bosco, Józefina Muntzel 164, 191, 212, 213
Bosco and Megler 329
Bosco the Wonder 392
Bosko, Karla B6, LRu3-4
Bosko der Zweite (books by) 443-4
Buchtel, Joseph 328, 329
Buckingham, Professor 294
Büller, William F49
Capello (one-legged dancer) 374
Carl (Karl Andreas von Bernbrunn) 23, 101-2
Carter, John (books by) *see* Peter F.L. Hoffmann
Cascabel, M. 178
Casino des Arts, boulevard Montmartre 75, 144
Cately, Alfred 508
Cazzaniga, Carlo 72
Celli, Giovanni (Jan) 210-11
Černý, Jaroslav LCz2-3
Chaplin, Charlie F66
Chési Fenza, Mme 270
Christínn, Miss 176, 198
Chrystoworkeny, Miss 176, 198
"Ciliegia" F32
Ciotti, Achille (Cirque Royal) 390
Congar, Dr 330
Conti family 133, 173, *Excursus* 207ff
Corvi, Jacques 157
Costanza, Salvatore 38, 114
Crafford, Alex 140
Crola, Pierre Andres 72
Crowe, Joseph Archer 131
Cumberland, Stuart 251. 257, 503-4
D'Argy, Gaston F59

Day, Harry 333
De Beauvoir, Roger 76, F29
De Blassis, Antoninio 38
De Laferrière, Viconte 235
De Lonn, Miss (Harriet Watkins) 320
De Matharel de Fiennes, Charles 75
De Salle, Comte Eusèbe 41, 117
Decapitation act (by Boscos in Britain) 496
Delaune, Adele 44
delf 303
désenguignoné 202
Dirnböck, Franz 54, 127, 398
Dolleczek, Anton F42
Donato (one-legged dancer) C31
Donato II (J. Baum) 376, 379
Donato, M. (hypnotist) 377
Donizetti, Giuseppe 42, 167
Edinger, Burchard 47
Edwardo Brothers 373
"Eclectic Wizard" 329
"Electric Wizard, The" 329
"Enchanted Palace of Illusions" 285, 287, 290, 294, 297-8, 300-2, 307, 309, 311, 317-8, 389, Z2
"Entertainment, entitled Magic, combining" 497
"entirely on the Indian and Egyptian Principles" 497
Eton, Orazio 186
Eugenia, Señora (Eugénie Labat) 340, 342
Extase hors centre (estasi eccentrica) 177, 178, 179
Feggetter, John 317
Filhon, Augusto 341
Flebus, Herr (hat maker) 192
Folies-Mayer 145
Folies Toulousaines 178
Fox, C. 305, 307, 311
Francesconi, Felix 49-50, 118, 125, F13
Funke, J. Jak. (Ludwig August Martell) 437
Furno, Eugenio LIt54
Fusier, Léon 177, 266
Gallaher, Mr (ventriloquist) 228
Gallien, F. LGe140-2
Gazofski, Martini 70-1
Gentile, Charles 331
George IV, *King* 15, 92, 93
"German Wizard, The" 294-6
Gigliotti, Bernard 335
Gigoux, Jean François LFr1-4, LGe1
Gleave, Professor 323
Gleich, Friedrich 95
Gramegna, Luigi F44
Grandemange, Charles 144
"Great East India Magician, The" Z7
"Great Necromancer, The" 498
"Greatest wonder of his age, The" 497
Griffith, Professor 329
Guillemin, Léon LFr1
Hančl, Antonin LCz1
Hechner, Karl, actor 26, 102, 105
Heidler, B. F16
Heine, Heinrich 16, 93
Herberts, Dr Alfred 285
Herloßsohn, Carl F7
Hermanns, Professor (books by) *see* Peter F.L.Hoffmann

Hillyard, Professor 309
Hillyer, Prof. 306
Hillyer, Selden 307, 311
Hirschfeld, Hermann F43
Hočárek, F. LCz4-6
Hoffmann, Peter F.L. LGe128-38, LGe143-7, LGe164-92
Hofschwarzkünstler 266
Hyam, Annie 296, 298, 306
Inaudi, Giacomo 181, 201, 207
Isaacs, Sarah 282
J.-M.-T.-M.-L LFr4
Japanese Butterfly trick 495
Japanese Top Feat 495
Joann, M. 180, 266
Joliet, Ada 330, 332
Julius (von Kleist), Antonie 378
Kasj-Kalli, M. 178
Kehr, Ludwig Christian 422
Kemble, Annie B62 *passim*
Kerndörffer, Heinrich August 220, LDu7, 437*ff*
Kieling, Jean 492
Kleroth (Clemens von Weyrother) 42, 49, 126, 211, F11
Kothe, Hermann 50, 397-8
Krakehler 62-3
Krátký, František LCz9
Kunsttheater 13, 91
Kunze, Gustav F61
Lanari, Alessandro 40
The Last Hours of ... Nicholas I 236, 244-5
Leischner, Carl LDaN6, LGe151-61
Leon, Victor 302
Letizia, Miss 176-7
Lewin, Misses 27, 106
Longmore, Thomas William Trew 321
Loewenthal, Jacob 116
Łubieński, Tomasz 122
Lund, Hans Chr. LDaN1
Lyser. P. 49, F12
"Magic, Mirth and Mystery" 498-9
Malachini, Paulo LGe162-3
Malek, Wilhelm F63
Maltitz, Gotthilf August von 26
Margaretha, Ms. 273
Marin, Scipion 42, 43-4, 118-20,
Martínez, Ana María Loreto 74, 143, 519
May, Dr 177, 183, 195-6, 199
May, Jessie 321
Mayer, Yda 177, 199
Mechanikus 13-14, 90
Meers, Hubert 352
Meisl, Carl 25, 104, F1
Melino family 158, 187
Metternich, Klemens von 62, 135, F24
Might, T. Barbor 228, 240, F62
Millar, Kennedy B62 *passim*
Millie-Christine ("The African Twins") B62 *passim*, 319
Młynarski family *Excursus* 207*ff*
Mondeux, Henri 181, 201, 207
"Most recherché" 499, Z1 note 12
Mueller, Frau 213, 217
Muzzi, Luigi 113, 126, F52

Naum Theatre 43, 119, 142, 167
Nicolet, Jean-Baptiste 147
Nieritz, Karl Gustav F18
Norberg, Leo 466
Normann, Hanns 100, F2
Norton, Sarah Ann 356
Oettinger, Eduard Maria 25, 50, 62, 104, 212, 216, F1, 397, F21
"Olio of Incomprehensible Wonders" 498
Orlande, Annie 345
Paganini 28, 30, 35, 105, 106
Palme, A. F55
Pantoscope 203
Payne, Thomas (Strand Theatre) 231
Permann, Jakob LEs1-2
Petronio 178
Pfeiffer, Alexander, actor 326
Pfeiffer, Friederike Auguste (née Luther, later Bosco) 89, 213, 217
Pfiffikus, Hilarius *see* Georg Carl Ludwig Schöpfer
Philadelph-nein, J.A. *see* Hoffmann, Peter F..L.
Physician, Fisico, Physicien 141, Z8
Pixley sisters 329, 331
Plate spinning 224, 229-30, 234, 237, 243, 286, 302, 314, 496, Z7
Poggioli, Michelangelo 40, 115, F53
"Polish Necromancer, The" 303
"Polish Wizard, The" 241, 286-7, 294-5, 303
Pommereux, Charles 145
Possenreich, Jukundus Hilarius LGe149-50
Potts, W.E. 319
Prestidigitation 101, 519
Quitzmann, Ernst Anton 130
Reimers, Dr 238
Reitler, Marzellin F34
Rideli, Mr. 174, 197
Rhadamantus LDu1
Rhodes, James 315
Robina, Mlle 383
Robinson, Billy 507
Rodriguez, Lena Modesto 334
Roma, Ida 199
Roos, Richard 104, F50
The Rope Feat 495-6
Rose, Mme 383
Rosental, Franc. Ant. *Professore* LIt9*ff*, LIt48*ff*
Rossini 78, 211-2
"Royal Illusionist, The" 293
Rubini (Philip Prentice Anderson) 317, 500, Z9
Saluinani,, Madame Z7
San Agustín, Julián de 95
Sandframe 74, LEn2, Z10
Saphir, Moritz Gottlieb 23, 49, 93, 99, 116, F10
Saulnier, Madame 378
Sazie, Léon F40, F65
Schellenberg jun., Ludwig LGe193
Schiano, Orazio 39, F48
Schick, Leopold 394
Schmieder, Robert 48
Schöpfer, Georg Carl Ludwig LGe148
Sebhard, Herr 64, 393
Sedgwick, Edward F67
Seidner, Josef F19

Sieben, Christinus F15
Signorini, Telemaco 217
Siklóssy, László 130
silforama B108, B118
Simmonds, Mr. 294
Simmons, Joe 300, 305, 309
Singmaster, David 446
Società di incoraggiamento 180
Sourouth 75-6
Souville, Eugène 83, 150
Spanish Salad, The 497
Staberl als Tausendkünstler 23, 26, 27, 101-2
Sue, Eugène F30
Susser, Harry (son of B63) 296, 301, 303, 310
Sybilsky, General 136
Szuper, Károly 56, 130
Tavini, G.B. 171, 196
Teja, Casamiro 87
"Temple of Magic" 230-1, 329, 500
Tescano, Signor 374
Texier, Edmond 75
Théâtre des fluides animés 75, 144
Thiers, Adolphe 391
Tovini *see* Tavini
"transfer his assembly to the gold and silver regions" 497-8
Trimm, Timothée 236, 245, 379
Trudný, F.P. (František Jaroslav Peřin) LCz10-12
Truhn, H. F35
tusenkonstnär 506
Unione Illusionisti Herrmann 186, 206
Valet, Maurice 200
Van Bevervoorde, Adriaan 69-71, 140, F28
Van Bosse, Pieter 69-71, F28
Váradi, Antal 130
Verbeck, Eugene 182
Vesque, Charles-Théodore 109, 146
Virgo, Madge 285
Wagner, Clara (née Rossiter) 280
Waite, W.C. 309
Warren, Colonel 336
Watzek, Anton, Mechaniker 53, 393
West, John H. 393
Weston, Kate 326
Weyl, Louis 58, F20
Weyl, Joseph 59, F20
Wieniawski, Henryk 161-2
Wilpert, Johann 20
Wilson, Kitty 334
Winzenburg, Maria Sophia 371
Wlach, Louis 46, 122-3
Wünsch, Otto 380
Zanardelli, Antonio 168, 170, 195-6
Zanardelli, Dante 171-2, 195-6, 207
Zanardelli, Domenico 195-6
Zanardelli, Elisabetta (Elisa) 168-9, 186, 195-6
Zanardelli, Emma 183, 195-6
Zanardelli, Teresa 168
Zahradnik, Clara 360
Zanfretta family 271, BF8
Zehmen (Zehme), C. 63, 124, 134, 136, F59
Zendavesta, Professor (John Dean Bryant) 371
Zoni 154

OTHER MAGICIANS

Adams, Henry (=Brøndum) B12a
Adrien 389
Alexander, Max 258
Alvina (Elvina, Albina) Signora C31
Anderson, John Henry 307, 311. Z9
Ball, Marian BF2
Bamberg, D.L. 66-7, 68-9, 263
Bamberg. Tobias 68, 138
Bancroft, Frederick 346
Bannholzer, Mathilde (and family) 52, 135, Z1
Baron 60, 133
Basch, E. 270, 272, 370, 371
Basco = Bosco 13-16, 93
Becker, Ferdinand 367, C3
Bellachini (Ernst Berlach) 450
Bernhardt, Karoline 127, 402, C7
Bils, Adolf 64, 65, 137, 165, 372
Blitz family 10, 92, Z7 passim
"Blitz, Herr" (Matthias Hayward) 514-5
Böhm, Gustav 381
Bonnet, Laurent 390
Bork, J. 272
Bosco II C3
Bosco, A.H.J. 291
Bosco, Bernardo 214, B113
Bosco, Billy 324
Bosco, Carl (U.S.A.) B97, B98
Bosco, Charles 329
Bosco, Don (1) B4
Bosco, Don (2) B44
Bosco, Don Giovanni 355
Bosco, Fräulein BF4
Bosco, Hermann 214, B8
Bosco, "Herr" 214, B18
Bosco, J.R. Borkini 355, B37
Bosco, Julio 201, B118
Bosco, Lena 324
Bosco, Leonardo 214, 270, B35
Bosco, Leotard 214, 281, B77
Bosco, Lopez 185, C31
Bosco, Louise B111
Bosco, Madame(1) 229, 232, 233, B62, BF1
Bosco, Morton 214, 286, 291, 296, 298, B69
Bosco, Nellie B106
Bosco, Frau Nina 214, BF7
Bosco, Signor D. 308
Bosco, Signor L. 308, B65
Bosco, Signora 313
Bosco LXXX 510
Bosco-Buzinski C10
Bosco américain, Le 340
Bosco Millar B62
Boskos, Alexander 389
Boz, Signor 389
Brenn, Erich 515
Brignall, John 264
Broeta, Franz 361
Brøndum, Adam B12a
Buck, Professor 509
Cagliostro das Antilhas 341
Cagliostro del Río de la Plata 338
Cagliostro do Rio da Prata 338
Cagliostro II C26
Callet 186, 206, C11

Cavalho, Floretta Z11
Cazaneuve see Cazeneuve
Cazeneuve, Marius 145, 214, C13
Cetti, Francisco see Emil Franzisco
Collings, Herbert J. 515
Comte 29, 31, 32, 358, 413, LGe139
Comus 78, 356, 359
Conte 223, 358
Conus 35, 109-10
Cooke, W.J. 514
Crémy 168, 180, 265-6, B21
Dabain, Alexandre-Charles C32
D'Avila, José Curvello B115
De Cour, Mons. 513
De Lonno, Madame 320, B77 passim, BF3
Dent (Dinte), Philip 349
di Rhona, Albina BF4
Döbler, Ludwig 23,46, 48, 51, 53, 58, 101, 126, 127, 133, 162, 359, 363, 388, 398, 448, 467, 494
Dobler (Herr) 294, 304, Z2 passim, Z5, 515
Duval, Émile Alphonse 267
Engländer, Salomon see B12
Epstein, Adam Salomon 239, 255
Epstein, Dr. A. 290, B12c
Epstein, Sigismund see B12
Erdely, Professor 390
Faustinus 254, 256, 259, 274
Faucoult, L. 69, 140
Fedick, Professeur 268
Fischer, Ottokar 242, 511
Fisher, Daniel 322
Franzisco, Emil (Francisco Cetti) 256, 257, Z3
Frizzo, Henry 177, 199
Giordano, Professor 214, 355
Great Herman, The (Blumenfeld) 264
Greathead, James Frederick B77
Günther, August 214, C21
Habitt, Joseph 22, 98-9, 404
Hambujer 325, Z4
Heksch, Johann Jacob 237, 247, B12d
Hofmann, C. 196
Hofmann, K. 196, C23
Hofzinser 55, 60, 466
Homes, Georg C20
Houdmon, Victor B10
Hyam, David 10, 296, 299, 300, B66
Isaac, Charles 330
Ismail, Muhamed 234, 243
Jacobs, Joseph 142, 294
Joro (Bruno Hennig) F69
Kapper, M. 183
Kauffert, Carl 18
Kinsbergen family C26, 389
Kratky-Baschik, Anton 231, 241, 446, Z6
Le Tort, Mons. 514
Linden, Florence Z11
Linski, Chrétien-Jean-Baptiste 341
Lischke, Richard 275
Lopes, D. = Lopez C31
Lynn, Dr. 289, 495, 496, 499, 500, 514
MacAllister, Andrew 83, 84, 150
Maju, L.K. 138
Malini, Marco 94
Marchelli, Bartolomeo 186, C34

549

Marian, Miss BF2
Maschek, Johann 165
Maskelyne, John Nevil 177, 499, Z7 *passim*
Melé, R. 131
Melides, George 390
Méliès, Georges 351
Mephisto C14
"Midnight Magician, The" B12, 495
Millar, Bosco B62
Millar, Professor William B12, B62, BF1, 512, Z12
Molduano, Moritz 25
Moreni 194, C39
Morris, Walter J. 522
Nicolay, Faure 337, 390, C19
Numa 376-7
Olivier 14, 31, 92
Palterini, Mons. 514
Pasco = Bosco 13-14, 91
Pinetti 14, 20, 26, 35, 91, 92, 106, 132, 359, 362
Racskay-Bosko, Josef 268-9
Rappelle, Henri C41
Rappo, François 60, 133
Raynaly, Edouard-Joseph 391
Renhard, Fritz 514
Rosenfeld, Orginski 241, 303
"Rignoldi" (Thomas Rignold) 241, 282
Robert-Houdin 40, 82, 116, 282, 363, 379
Robin, Henri 60, 67, 70, 133, 143
Rössner, Max 355
Rodolphe 41, 42, 117
Rubini 317, Z9
Sakarinie-Kinsbergen C26
Sarrade, M. 389, C44
Sartini,, Professeur 390, C45
Schöpl, Herr 391
Schpinesky, Philip 349
Schumann, Carl 16

Schulz, Ernst 390-1
Schulz, Madame 214, C46
Shaw, George 316
Sinclair, Professor 323
St. Roman, Professor 214, C49
Steinl, Johann 14, 91
Stirling, Oscar 264
Stot-Taï 390
Stuller, Joe 275
Susser, Louis 263, B63 *passim*, B64 *passim*, B65, 313
Swales, Arthur Harper 323
Testot, Felix (senior) 513
Thiersfeld, Samuel C39
Tolmaque, Professor 499
Trachtenberg family 274
Trewey, Félicien 515
Twardowski LPol2
Uferini, Alfredo 266
Vanek, Joseph 343, 347, 348
Velle, Joseph 381
Vernone, Annie (stage name Veroni) 351, Z11
Verone, Louis (Arthur Webb) 514
Viarizio, Antoine 267
Vivalla, Antonio 513
Volta, M. 390
Volta-Moreni, Professor 382
Wampa (Vampa), Saint Aubin 371-2
Warszawski, Alfred 324, B64
Warszawski, Saul 233, 261, 282, B63, B63a, B65 *passim*, 313, Z2
Webb, Harold George 514
Weiß (mechanikus) 90, 91
Weiß, Rudolf 360
Wessely, John 343
Whautkins, Pio 320
Zenetti, Carlo C54, LGe194-5